SIXTH EDITION

Read, Reason, Write

Dorothy U. Seyler

Boston   Burr Ridge, IL   Dubuque, IA   Madison, WI   New York   San Francisco   St. Louis
Bangkok   Bogotá   Caracas   Kuala Lumpur   Lisbon   London   Madrid   Mexico City
Milan   Montreal   New Delhi   Santiago   Seoul   Singapore   Sydney   Taipei   Toronto

The McGraw·Hill Companies

Mc Graw Hill **Higher Education**

READ, REASON, WRITE: AN ARGUMENT TEXT AND READER

2 3 4 5 6 7 8 9 0 DOC/DOC 0 9 8 7 6 5 4 3

ISBN 0-07-285818-4

President of McGraw-Hill Humanities/Social Sciences: *Steve Debow*
Executive editor: *Lisa Moore*
Editorial assistant: *Jennifer Reilly*
Senior marketing manager: *David S. Patterson*
Senior media producer: *Todd Vaccaro*
Project manager: *Laura Ward Majersky/ctvillagomez*
Production supervisor: *Carol Bielski*
Coordinator of freelance design: *Mary E. Kazak*
Lead supplement producer: *Marc Mattson*
Cover and interior design: *Kay Fulton*
Cover image: *Copyright Phoenix Art Group, Sarah Tanner,* Intersection I, *published by Grand Image Ltd., Seattle, Washington.*
Typeface: *10/12 Goudy*
Compositor: *Carlisle Communications, Ltd.*
Printer: *R. R. Donnelley*

Library of Congress Cataloging-in-Publication Data

Seyler, Dorothy U.
    Read, reason, write / Dorothy U. Seyler.--6th ed. [updated]
      p. cm.
    Includes bibliographical references and index.
    ISBN 0-07-285818-4 (acid-free paper)
    1. English language—Rhetoric. 2. Persuasion (Rhetoric) 3. College readers. 4. Report
writing. I. Title.
PE1408 .S464 2003
808'.0427--dc21
                                     2002034338

Dorothy U. Seyler is Professor of English at Northern Virginia Community College. A Phi Beta Kappa graduate of the College of William and Mary, Dr. Seyler holds advanced degrees from Columbia University and the State University of New York at Albany. She taught at Ohio State University, the University of Kentucky, and Nassau Community College before moving with her family to Northern Virginia.

She has co-authored *Introduction to Literature* and *Language Power*, both in second editions. She is the author of *Understanding Argument*, *The Reading Context*, *Steps to College Reading*, and *Doing Research*, the last three in second editions, and *Patterns of Reflection*, now in its fourth edition. In addition, Professor Seyler has published articles in professional journals and popular magazines. She enjoys tennis and golf, traveling, and writing about both sports and travel.

Preface   xvii

SECTION I

Critical Reading and Analysis   1

CHAPTER 1

Writers and Their Sources   3

CHAPTER 2

SECTION II

The World of Argument   71

SECTION III

The Research Process   181

CHAPTER 6

Getting Started and Locating Sources (in the Library, Online, in the Field)   183

CHAPTER 7

Understanding Sources, Selecting Information, and Documenting (Using MLA)   215

CHAPTER 8

Completing the Research Project   249

CHAPTER 9

Other Styles of Documentation   281

SECTION IV

A Collection of Readings 303

CHAPTER 10

The Media: Image and Reality 305

CHAPTER 11

Euthanasia 331

CHAPTER 12

Guns and Society 351

CHAPTER 13

Capital Punishment 365

CHAPTER 14

Censorship, Pornography, and the Arts   389

CHAPTER 15

Internet Issues: Privacy, Ownership, Entrapment   405

CHAPTER 16

The Animal Rights Debate   423

CHAPTER 17

Immigration and Immigrants   447

CHAPTER 18

Issues in Education   469

CHAPTER 19

Race, Gender, and Identity   485

CHAPTER 20

Examining Marriage and Family   511

CHAPTER 21

Global Issues: The Environment, Poverty, and the New Global Economy   549

CHAPTER 22

Twenty-first-Century Living: Where Are We Headed? Where Do We Want to Go?   567

CHAPTER 23

Some Classic Arguments   585

APPENDIX

Understanding Literature   621

I have written in previous prefaces to *Read, Reason, Write* that being asked to prepare a new edition is much like being asked back to a friend's house: although you count on it, you are still delighted when the invitation comes. Well, the fifth edition maintained old friendships and made new ones as well—and even won an award in a "longevity" classification, a category in which the textbooks must be at least 15 years old. Of course, neither this text nor I am getting older, only better, as the sixth edition demonstrates!

Although some important new material adds strength to the sixth edition, the essential character of *Read, Reason, Write* remains the same. The text still combines instruction in critical reading and analysis, argument, and research strategies with a rich collection of readings providing practice for these skills and new ideas and insights for readers. A key purpose of *Read, Reason, Write* remains to help students develop into better writers of the kinds of papers they are most often required to write, in both college and the world of work: summaries, analyses, reports, arguments, and documented papers. To fulfill its mission, this text should do more than provide instruction and opportunities for practice; this text needs to demonstrate to student writers that these seemingly disparate skills connect in important ways. *Read, Reason, Write* remains a new kind of text because it shows students the interrelatedness of reading, analytic, argumentative, and research skills and seeks, in connecting these skills, always to extend each student's critical thinking ability.

Except for some assignments that ask students to draw exclusively on their personal experiences to develop essays, academic and professional writing requires summaries, analyses, or evaluations, or the use and synthesis of one or more sources, or some combination of these writing strategies. All of these assignments test a student's critical reading and thinking skills. Therefore, Section I of this text begins by emphasizing good reading skills for effective writing. The section provides instruction in reading for understanding, summary techniques, analyzing elements of style, understanding context, and preparing the book review.

Section II, "The World of Argument," begins with the concept of context: arguments are written to an audience, and they generate counterarguments. This section provides strategies for anticipating and coping with opposing views, focuses on recognizing various types of arguments, and bridges the gap between logical structures and the arguments we actually write. Both professional and student arguments are included as models of typical kinds of argumentative essays.

This text presents the research process, in Section III, as a complex intellectual and writing task that calls on all the previously developed skills of critical reading, analysis, synthesis, and sound argument. Students are guided through the writing process, not just the documentation patterns, and they are given direction in selecting and evaluating sources.

Exercises and writing assignments support the text's instruction throughout the first three sections. Then, the readings in Section IV provide varied examples of the uses of language and strategies for argument as authors debate many of today's issues and problems.

A closer look at each of the four sections reveals what is new in the sixth edition of *Read, Reason, Write*. Section I contains just two chapters now, as the material on analyzing literature has been moved to an appendix. This change is in response to users of the text whose departments discourage the use of literature in their argument/research courses. For those who still want some guidelines for reading and analyzing literature, the appendix is available. New to Chapter 2 is a sample student review of a book and two movie reviews for comparison.

Section II, on argument, has been reconfigured to more readily highlight the section's instruction in the Aristotelian and Toulmin models of argument. These are now presented in a fairly brief but important first chapter (Chapter 3). Chapter 4 then examines classical patterns of induction, deduction, and analogy, followed by causal arguments, the conciliatory argument, the uses of statistics, and logical fallacies. The chapter also has an expanded section on cartoons and advertising—two important types of visual arguments. Finally, Chapter 5, on writing arguments, contains much new material that guides writers through the process of planning, organizing, drafting, and revising an argument. Both professional and student arguments illustrate various types of arguments we commonly write.

The material on research, in Section III, has been further updated from the fifth edition to keep students and instructors current on the new electronic libraries. Much more space and guidance are now given to online databases and the use of the Internet rather than to paper indexes. This emphasis carries through the entire section, with guidelines for evaluating Internet sources, for documenting such sources, and for using a PC for notetaking and writing.

Section IV, an anthology of readings, has also been given a facelift. Instead of using three large subsections, the readings are now grouped into 14 chapters around more narrowly defined topics. The section has been expanded to include 70 articles, 50 of which are new to the sixth edition. The articles are not only new; they are (mostly) current works debating both current and enduring issues, issues as old as capital punishment and censorship and as new as Internet privacy and the global economy. Included in each chapter's introduction are some useful websites for the chapter's topic.

Our times demand that we understand what we read, that we think critically about others' ideas and argue effectively in support of our own, and that we can sort through the wealth of available information and ideas, rejecting what is unreliable and synthesizing the useful with what we already know and understand. We live in an information society, a society in which many people make their living by collecting, sorting, transmitting, and reacting to a constant flow of pictures, numbers, and words. In this new century, those who learn to read, reason, and write effectively will be successful in their work. Those who enjoy exercising these skills will be happy in that work.

No book of value is written alone. I am pleased to acknowledge the contributions of others in shaping this text. My thanks are due—as always—to the library staff at the Annandale Campus of Northern Virginia Community College, especially to Marian Delmore, Ruth Stanton, Ellen Westman, and Carol Simwell, who have helped me locate needed information and have kept me current with the new technology. They have reviewed the chapter on locating sources, made suggestions for updating, and then reviewed the revised version. Of course, any problems that remain are entirely my responsibility. Mary Atkins, our department secretary, has my gratitude for her patient help with technology issues. I would also like to thank students Ian Habel, Monica Becker, Chris Brown, J. Tupper Cole, Alan Peterson, and Connie Childress, whose essays grace this text; they should be proud of the skill and effort they put into their writing. I appreciate as well the many good suggestions of the following reviewers of the fifth edition and parts of the new sixth edition: Peter Vandenberg, DePaul University; Susan Romano, University of Texas at Austin; Todd Travaille, Buena Vista University; Chris Grooms, Collin County Community College; David Fabish, Cerritos College; L. Bensel-Meyers, University of Tennessee; Deborah Murray, Kansas State University; Kathy Walsh, Central Oregon Community College; P. Douglas McKittrick, DeVry Institute of Technology; Pat Medeiros, Scottsdale Community College; Allison York, Kirkwood Community College; David Hawes, Owens Community College; William Provost, University of Georgia; Stuart Barbier, Delta College; Phyllis Elmore, North Lake College; Michael Hricik, Westmoreland Community College; Jennifer Lehman, University of Texas at Austin; Peggy Richards, University of Akron; Patricia Brooke, Fontbonne College; Cathryn Amdahl, Harrisburg Area Community College; Donna Winchell, Clemson University; Patricia Lonchar, University of the Incarnate Word; Michael E. Cooley, Berry College; Lynee L. Gaillet, Georgia State University; Michael O'Rourke, Tennessee Technical University; Sonya Lancaster, University of Kansas; Timothy McGee, The College of New Jersey; Debora Coxwell Teague, Florida State University.

My former editor Steve Pensinger needs to be remembered for steering me, with good sense and good humor, through four editions of this book. I am also grateful to Tim Julet and Alexis Walker for guidance through the fifth edition and to Lisa Moore, Senior Editor, and Chris Narozny, Developmental Editor, for their direction in preparing the sixth edition.

I'll close by once again dedicating this book to my daughter Ruth who, in spite of a demanding career and busy social life, still found time to read drafts and help me select new essays for this edition. It is my wish that my students each year will come to understand what she now understands—that it is the liberal education that makes continued growth of the human spirit both possible and pleasurable.

Dorothy U. Seyler

Critical Reading and Analysis

CHAPTER 1

Writers and Their Sources

The Writer in a Writing Course

As you open this text, you may have a mix of feelings: both excitement over a new term and some anxiety about your composition course. Recognize that many students share your anxiety about writing courses but also understand that some nervousness, when you face a challenging task, is appropriate. Writing courses are challenging because writing well is not easy. But, with practice you can become a more confident writer. Let's consider some realities of the writing process:

- Writing is a skill like dancing or playing tennis. To be a competent writer you must develop your skills in the same way tennis players develop a spin serve: good instruction, a strong desire to succeed, and practice, practice, practice.

- Some writers are more talented than others, just as Tiger Woods is a more talented golfer than most. But Woods's golf skills did not come from a genie in a bottle, and neither did the great writers' skills with language. The exceptional in any field make their skills look "like magic." However, they also spent years of studying and practicing to achieve their excellence. Although most of us may never match Shakespeare's "magic," we can, with study and practice, become competent writers.

- Learning to write well is not easy because no clear set of instructions or rules exists. Composition texts and instructors can offer strategies for effective writing, but they cannot present, complete with pictures, "Ten Easy Steps to a Good Essay." Although thousands of writing texts are in print to help students improve, students need to see that guidelines for writing cannot be found in a slim technical manual. There are a fixed number of keys on a keyboard, but topics to write about, audiences to write for, and reasons for writing can never be completely cataloged, and the options for combining words into English sentences are infinite in their variety.

Two other realities create difficulties for students of writing. First, good writing comes from many revisions. Even if we are willing to devote the time to revising several drafts, we often lack skill in judging our own writing. As a result, beyond trying to catch any errors in punctuation or spelling, we don't know what to revise. One important skill you want to develop in this course is your ability to edit drafts: to know what to look for and how to gain enough distance to read with a critic's eye. Second, we have trouble accepting editing advice from others. We feel hurt or angry when a classmate or an instructor complains that a paragraph lacks coherence or a passage is awkward. Remember, though, that group reports, whether prepared in the classroom or the office, require cooperation both in their drafting and editing. Even though egos may become bruised because writing is so personal, we need to go beyond the hurt, learn from others' suggestions, and become good critics of our own writing.

If learning to write well is so difficult, why work on these skills? Here are some good answers to this question:

- Ask any student over 25 why he or she is now in college. While some are training for a second career, many are back to learn basic skills so that they can advance in their current jobs. They will tell you that one essential skill is writing ability.
- The more you develop your awareness of the writing process, the better reader you will become of the many books you will read before completing college.
- The more confident a writer you become, the more efficiently and successfully you will handle written assignments in all of your courses.
- Since writing is an act of discovery, the more you write, the more you will learn about who you are and what matters to you.

A composition course creates an artificial writing environment. In a composition course the subject is writing itself, the purpose is to demonstrate writing skills, and the audience is a "supercritic," your instructor. No wonder you feel anxious. You will cope better by "picturing" a somewhat kinder environment. Develop a less threatening sense of audience by picturing your readers as members of the class, not just the instructor. (In fact, in many classes, just as in the workplace, your audience will be your peers.) Understand the purpose of each assignment. (Your instructor will give you different kinds of assignments, to practice types of essays.) Finally, consider each assignment as a chance for increased self-awareness. After all, how do you know what you really think about stiffer penalties for drunk drivers until you have to write on the subject?

The Student Writer's Roles

Writers frequently wear many hats. Edgar Allan Poe did not write short stories and poems only. As a magazine editor, he also wrote reviews of other authors' works and essays on poetic theory. The anthropologist Margaret Mead published scholarly reports of her studies of primitive cultures—and short articles on contemporary issues for readers of the popular *Redbook* magazine. Both Poe and Mead wrote to different kinds of audiences to fulfill different purposes. Each time, they wrote differently: in a different format with a different style.

Both in this writing course and throughout your college and work experiences, you will need to shift writing roles, to wear many hats. At times you will be asked to write essay exams or prepare summaries of articles. Your audience will be the instructor, your purpose to demonstrate knowledge gained through reading and instruction. However, when your history instructor requests a review of a book from the reading list, he may be expecting you to write that review as if you were preparing it for a larger audience. He wants you to forget that you are completing an assignment for class and to use the format and style of published reviews. When you prepare the results of a survey of student attitudes for your sociology class, your instructor may be as interested in your demonstrating the correct format, style, and tone of reports in the social sciences as she is in what you actually have to report from your survey. She wants you to learn the *conventions* of a particular type of writing. *Conventions* are the etiquette of writing; they establish the relationship between writer and reader and smooth the way to clear communication.

To help you learn the expected format of different types of writing for different audiences, this book includes a variety of articles: informative essays, editorials, articles from scholarly journals, book reviews. Study assigned readings not just for their content but also as examples of various writing purposes, styles, and conventions. Pay close attention to each assignment so that you will know what hat you are wearing: a student demonstrating knowledge, a citizen arguing for tougher drunk-driving laws, a scholar presenting the results of research.

Responses to Sources

Having looked through the table of contents, you have observed that this text is not just "about writing"; it also contains many readings. There are good reasons for this:

1. As an adult reader in college and on the job, you will be expected to learn more complex information and understand more complicated ideas than you may have experienced before. In addition, the information and ideas may be presented in more complex writing than you are used to reading. This text will give you practice in reading more challenging texts.

2. You may need to read differently. You will be reading to learn, not just for pleasure. You cannot choose to skip some chapters in your psychology text because you are not "interested" in learning how memory works any more than you can skip reading a memo from your boss because you "don't feel like it." To be successful in either situation, you will need to read works given to you by others and to know those works thoroughly.

3. You will use your reading as a basis for writing. In other writing classes, you may have been asked to write about your interests, pet peeves, or career goals. That is, you were expected to draw on the information and ideas you already possessed. Now you will be writing papers based in some way on a source or sources you have been assigned or have selected in response to a particular assignment. You will be expected to draw on your reading to develop your papers, at times a challenging writing task. In such writing the focus of attention shifts from you to your subject, and format and style are usually somewhat more formal than in personal essays.

To explore a writer's possible use of or responses to sources, let's begin by reading "The Gettysburg Address," Lincoln's famous speech dedicating the Civil War battlefield. Because the speech is brief, well known, exquisitely written, and historically significant, it will help clarify the various ways writers respond—in writing—to the writing of others.

The Gettysburg Address

Abraham Lincoln

Fourscore and seven years ago our fathers brought forth on this continent a new nation, conceived in liberty and dedicated to the proposition that all men are created equal. Now we are engaged in a great civil war, testing whether that nation, or any nation so conceived and so dedicated, can long endure. We are met on a great battlefield of that war. We have come to dedicate a portion of that field as a final resting place for those who here gave their lives that that nation might live. It is altogether fitting and proper that we should do this. But, in a larger sense, we cannot dedicate—we cannot consecrate—we cannot hallow—this ground. The brave men, living and dead, who struggled here have consecrated it far above our poor power to add or to detract. The world will little note nor long remember what we say here, but it can never forget what they did here. It is for us, the living, rather to be dedicated here to the unfinished work which they who fought here have thus far so nobly advanced. It is rather for us to be here dedicated to the great task remaining before us—that from these honored dead we take increased devotion to that cause for which they gave the last full measure of devotion; that we here highly resolve that these dead shall not have died in vain; that this nation, under God, shall have a new birth of freedom; and that government of the people, by the people, for the people shall not perish from the earth.

DO YOU LIKE IT?
WHAT DID YOU GAIN FROM IT? **>** **THE PERSONAL RESPONSE**

The English instructor teaching a collection of famous speeches might ask her class to write a paragraph in response to one of these questions. Both questions ask students to express their personal values, tastes, and interests. Here, for example, is one young student's response to Lincoln's speech:

> I liked it. "The Gettysburg Address" helped me to understand what it's like to care about something and fight for it. I wonder, though, how many people today care enough about their country or some principle to go to war to protect it.

Because of the subjective nature of reader-response writing, instructors can, in fairness, evaluate only the clarity and force of the writing, not the student's preferences. Personal response writing should not be offered when the assignment calls for analysis or argument. When other responses are required, then you can expect to be judged on content: on your ability to reason, to analyze, and to support judgments. And on your ability to deliver the kind of writing demanded by the assignment.

WHAT DOES IT SAY? **>** **THE SIMPLEST RESPONSE**
TO CONTENT

Instructors often ask students to summarize or paraphrase their reading of a complex chapter, a supplementary text, a difficult poem, or a series of journal articles on library reserve. Frequently, book-report assignments specify that summary and evaluation be combined. Your purpose in writing a summary is to show your understanding of the work's main ideas and of the relationships among those ideas. If you can put what you have read into your own words and focus on the text's chief points, then you have command of that material. Can you state the main ideas in Lincoln's "Address" in your own words? Here is a sample restatement:

> Our nation was initially built on a belief in liberty and equality, but its future is now being tested by civil war. It is appropriate for us to dedicate this battlefield, but those who fought here have dedicated it better than we. We should dedicate ourselves to continue the fight to maintain this nation and its principles of government.

Sometimes it is easier to recite or quote famous or difficult works than to state, more simply and in your own words, what has been written. The ability to summarize or paraphrase reflects both reading and writing skills.

HOW IS IT WRITTEN?
HOW DOES IT COMPARE TO ANOTHER WORK? **>** *THE ANALYTIC RESPONSE*

You will find that summary requirements are often combined with analysis or evaluation, as in a book report, or used as a brief homework or classroom exercise. Most of the time you will be expected to *do something* with what you have read, and to summarize or paraphrase will be insufficient. Frequently you will be asked to analyze a work—that is, to explain the elements of structure and style that a writer has chosen. You will want to examine sentence patterns, organization, metaphors, and other techniques selected by the writer to convey attitude and give force to ideas. The ability to see how a writer has worked to create his or her text will make you a better reader, more alert to the writer's attitudes and the relative weight given to various ideas. Analytic skills will also make you a better writer as you become more sensitive to the power of words and more alert to the options you have as a writer.

Many writers have examined Lincoln's word choice, sentence structure, and choice of metaphors to make clear the sources of power in this speech.* If you were to analyze Lincoln's style, you would want to emphasize, among other elements, his effective use of tricolon: the threefold repetition of a grammatical structure, with the three points placed in ascending order of significance.

> Lincoln uses two effective tricolons in his brief address. The first focuses on the occasion for his speech, the dedication of the battlefield: "we cannot dedicate—we cannot consecrate—we cannot hallow. . . ." The best that the living can do is formally dedicate; only those who died there for the principle of liberty are capable of making the battlefield "hallow." The second tricolon presents Lincoln's concept of democratic government, a government "of the people, by the people, for the people." The purpose of government—"for the people"—resides in the position of greatest significance.

---

*   See, for example, Gilbert Highet's essay, "The Gettysburg Address," in *The Clerk of Oxenford: Essays on Literature and Life* (New York: Oxford UP, 1954), to which I am indebted in the following analysis.

A second type of analysis, a comparison of styles of two writers, is a frequent variation of the analytic assignment. By focusing on similarities and differences in writing styles, you can see more clearly the role of choice in writing and may also examine the issue of the degree to which differences in purpose affect style. One student, for example, produced a thoughtful and interesting study of Lincoln's style in contrast to that of Martin Luther King, Jr., as revealed in his speech "I Have a Dream"(see page 616):

> Although Lincoln's sentence structure is tighter than King's and King likes the rhythms created by repetition, both men reflect their familiarity with the King James Bible in their use of its cadences and expressions. Instead of saying eighty-seven years ago, Lincoln, seeking solemnity, selects the Biblical expression "Fourscore and seven years ago." Similarly, King borrows from the Bible and echoes Lincoln when he writes "Five score years ago."

IS IT LOGICAL? IS IT ADEQUATELY DEVELOPED? DOES IT ACHIEVE ITS PURPOSE? > *THE JUDGMENT OR EVALUATION RESPONSE*

Usually analytic responses to the writings of others lead to some evaluation of those writings. Often, even when the stated purpose of an essay is pure analysis, the analysis implies a judgment. We analyze Lincoln's style because we recognize that "The Gettysburg Address" is a great piece of writing and we want to see how it achieves its power. On other occasions, close reading and analysis serve as a basis for the stated purpose of judgment. The columnist who challenges a previously published editorial has analyzed the editorial and has found it flawed. The columnist may fault the editor's logic and want to explain how the editorial develops a weak argument. The columnist may object to the editor's lack of adequate or relevant support for the editorial's thesis or main idea. The columnist may choose to demonstrate that the editor gets sidetracked, that the editorial does not in fact develop the issue that it presumably sets out to develop. In each case the columnist makes a negative judgment about the editorial, but that judgment is an informed one based on the columnist's knowledge of language, of the principles of good argument, and of the concepts of unity and direction in writing.

Part of the ability to judge wisely the writing of others lies in recognizing each writer's purpose. It is unfair to judge a 200-word editorial as insufficiently developed when the purpose of an editorial is to express an opinion with force, to arouse reader interest in a current issue. Similarly, it would be inappropriate to assert that Lincoln's "Address" is weakened by its lack of facts about the battle. The historian's purpose is to record the number killed, to analyze the generals' military tactics, to judge the battle's significance in the war's outcome. Lincoln's purpose was different.

> As Lincoln reflected upon this young country's being torn apart by civil strife, he saw the dedication of the Gettysburg battlefield as an opportunity to challenge the country to fight for its survival and the principles upon which it was founded. The result was a brief but moving speech that appropriately examines the connection between the life and death of soldiers and the birth and survival of a nation.

These sentences establish a basis for an analysis of Lincoln's train of thought and use of metaphors, but this analysis, and positive judgment, is grounded in an understanding of Lincoln's purpose and the context in which he spoke.

How Does It Help Me to Understand Other Works, Ideas, Events? > *The Research Response*

Frequently you will read not to analyze or evaluate but rather to use the source as part of learning about a particular subject. You may examine the work in relationship to other sources relating to your study or perhaps develop an essay related to the topic based on just one source. Lincoln's "Address" is significant for the Civil War historian both as an event of that war and as an influence on our thinking about that war. "The Gettysburg Address" is also vital to the biographer's study of Lincoln's life or to the literary critic's study either of famous speeches or of the Bible's influence on English writing styles. Thus, Lincoln's brief speech is a valuable source for students in a variety of disciplines who are exploring different topics; it becomes part of their research process. As a single source it can be used to reflect on current national discussions. Able researchers study it carefully, analyze it thoroughly, place it in its proper historical, literary, and personal contexts, and make an informed judgment about its usefulness to their research.

To begin practice in reading and responding to sources, study the following article by Bruce Sterling. The exercises that follow will check your reading skills and your understanding of the various responses to reading just discussed.

Learning to Love Obsolescence

Bruce Sterling

Bruce Sterling (b. 1959) has written a number of science-fiction novels and stories in addition to nonfiction books and articles, usually on modern technology and its impact on us. He is editor and contributor to *Mirrorshades: The Cyberpunk Anthology* (1986), a collection of 12 science-fiction short stories celebrating the new electronic technology. The following article was published in *Newsweek* magazine on January 1, 2000.

1   Obsolescence is the future in reverse. Everything we design, make, covet and buy moves in a natural arc from the drawing board to the garbage.

2   Junk happens. Junk happens fastest in the areas of life where we are most intent, most engaged and most creative. In 1950s America, junk was about cars and planned obsolescence. In the '90s it was computers and Moore's Law, which decrees that computer chips get twice as zippy every 18 months. What we're really describing is the rate at which "state of the art" becomes garbage. Every time the digital season changes, vast herds of machines with nerd-macho names like SuperBrain and PowerBook are hauled ingloriously out to the dumps. And we go buy more. And that's good. Our machines are increasingly temporary, while we humans are increasingly permanent.

3   Imagine if it were otherwise. Imagine that you bought a computer that was the last computer you would ever own. You would be mortgaged to that machine like a medieval serf. It would still be indispensable, but irreplaceable as well, so you'd live in

terror of its various whims and illnesses. Instead, its place in your life is fleeting: that's what separates our world from Orwell's 1984, and the Internet from Big Brother.

4   Today all of our most vital technologies are racing to become junk. They're poorly regulated, but they don't last long enough to become tyrannical. Junk makes us free. The threats to our happiness aren't in our tidal wave of new, candy-colored gizmos. The real trouble lies in not sending our bad habits to their proper graveyards. Everything with moving parts, everything with electric plugs, everything that buzzes, rings, clicks, clacks, pings, cooks, chops, slices and dices, every *thing*, is a larval form of junk. It briefly passes through our hands and wallets into the long, sickening darkness of our mindless neglect. But since history goes in only one direction, the evidence of our denial can only mount up. We can only have more and more junk.

5   So we need to see junk very differently: as an integral part of the basic business of living. Handled sensibly, junk is a resource, a useful property that happens to be in the wrong place. It can be folded into the production stream, and brought to serve our desires again and again. But as sure as the sun's rising, repressed junk—dismissed or ignored—will return to hassle us, poison our grandchildren, render our world a little uglier. This means showing some adult respect for the trash.

6   We should never again feel all mind-boggled at anything that human beings create. No matter how amazing some machine may seem, the odds are very high that we'll outlive it. There is no technology around today or in the foreseeable future that won't swiftly become obsolete. Emerson once said that "Things are in the saddle and ride mankind," but he lived with big creaky telegraphs and steamships. We live with chips and bar codes, and we're in a position now to get a serious upper hand on our things.

7   We face a challenge to understand obsolescence, to learn to see its dynamics and to surf it. There is a genuine melancholic beauty in a well-designed mechanism that no longer serves any purpose. Like Duchamp's bottle-rack, it becomes a found objet d'art. A metallic fossil of some lost human desire. A kind of involuntary poem.

8   Things are too much with us because we have too much of the wrong kind of respect for things. Wonder is an emotion we need to reserve for phenomena like the size of galaxies and the spans of geological time. A human effort like technology is best regarded with pity. A weird, temporary gizmo like a nuclear missile is a merely material thing: its fuel goes bad, its space-age gyroscopes are hopelessly old-fashioned, even the oh-so-mighty warhead has a ticking half-life. We wouldn't have nuclear power plants if we'd asked real questions about their garbage. Coal power plants are even worse, smoldering all over the planet like half-crushed cigarette butts.

9   Tomorrow's garbage is very easy to predict: it's everything that we love today. Industrial designers are visibly itching to stuff smart chips into any object that can bear the stuffing: shoes that charge up your cell phone, coffeepots that talk. Inevitable? Probably. Amazing? No, not at all. It just means that tomorrow's junk is smart junk. We'll have intelligent garbage. We'll have tons of useless stuff busily computing all the way to its grave.

10   The things of earth return to Earth, and, properly handled, so will our technologies. The only things we've built that the Earth can't touch? Dead 20th-century machines, lying beautiful and obsolete in that timeless lunar dust.

Questions for Analysis and Response

1. Sterling writes that we make junk the fastest in those parts of our lives in which we are "most intent, most engaged and most creative." Why is this so?

2. How does Sterling think that we tend to look at junk? How does he think we should look at it?

3. How do we know what tomorrow's junk will be? Why?

4. Sterling's essay, for the most part, is a series of connected ideas, but he does include some examples. Study the specifics in paragraphs 2 and 3 and then write a short paragraph in which you explain how Sterling uses details to develop his point effectively.

5. Which one of the different responses to reading is illustrated by your paragraph?

6. The chapter noted that "The Gettysburg Address" is a valuable document for several kinds of research projects. For what kinds of projects would Sterling's essay be useful? List several possibilities and then be prepared to discuss your list with classmates.

Guidelines for Active Reading

Responses to written works vary, depending on our purpose in reading and writing. Most of us skim more of the daily paper than we read. When you first examine an article or book, you are wise to start with a "flip and skim" approach to see what the work contains, how it is organized, and how it may be useful to you. But once you become engaged in a particular text that you must know thoroughly, understanding rather than a quick overview is your goal. Reading actively means attending carefully to the text, reflecting on the work's information and ideas, and connecting your new knowledge to other texts and to what you already know about the topic. You can be an active reader by following these guidelines:

- *Become part of the writer's audience.* Not all writers have us in mind when they write. Writers from the past did not write for any of us today. Dale Russell, writing on the dinosaur's extinction for *Scientific American*, expects readers to know the geologic periods of earth's history. As an active reader, you need to prepare to join a writer's audience by learning about the writer, about the time in which the piece was written, and about the writer's expected audience. For works reprinted in this text, you will be aided by introductory notes. These notes will give you a useful *context* for reading; be sure to study them.

- *Think about your purpose and ask questions to guide your reading.* Don't just start turning pages to complete an assignment. Think first about your purpose in reading. Are you reading for knowledge that you will be tested on in some way? Are you reading to prepare for a group discussion? Focus on your purpose as you read, asking yourself, "What do I need to learn from this work?" As you read, turn titles and section headings into questions for which you seek answers. As you read this section, for example, ask, "What are the guidelines for active reading?"

- *Concentrate.* Slow down and give your full attention to the text. Pay attention to transition and connecting words that will show you how the parts connect. Read an entire article or chapter at one time. Do not let yourself get distracted halfway through; you will have to reread from the beginning to understand the material.

- *Read with an open mind.* Critical thinkers seek new knowledge and ideas. They withhold judgment until they have read attentively and give each writer a fair chance to develop ideas.

- *Consider the title before reading further.* Titles are the first words writers give us about their work. Take time to look for clues in a title that may reveal both the work's subject and perhaps the writer's approach or attitude as well. Henry Fairlie's title, "The Idiocy of Urban Life," for example, tells you both Fairlie's subject (urban or city living) and his position (urban living is idiotic).

- *Predict what is coming.* Look for a writer's thesis or some purpose statement. Observe the work's structure or organization. Then use this information to anticipate what is coming. When Bruce Catton writes, "Yet it was not all contrast, after all. Different as they [Grant and Lee] were—in background, in personality, in underlying aspiration—these two great soldiers had much in common," active readers understand that Catton will now explain how Grant and Lee were alike.

- *Annotate as you read.* The more senses you use, the more active your involvement. With reading, that means marking the text as you read (or taking notes if the material is not yours). Underline key sentences, such as the writer's thesis. Then, in the margin, indicate that it is the thesis. With a series of examples (or reasons), label them as examples (or reasons) and then number them. When you look up a word's definition, write the definition in the margin next to the word. Draw diagrams to illustrate concepts; draw arrows to connect example to idea. Studies have shown that students who annotate their texts get higher grades. Do what the successful students do.

- *Keep a reading journal.* In addition to annotating what you read, you may want to develop the habit of writing regularly in a journal. A reading journal is a place to record your responses to reading assignments. It gives you a place to note impressions and reflections, initial reactions to assignments, and ideas that you may use in your next writing. Purchase a notebook with sections; use one section for class notes and another for your reading journal.

Exercise: Active Reading

Read the following selection, noting the annotations that have been started for you. As you read, add your own annotations to help you understand the excerpt. Then write a journal entry (four to five sentences at least) to express your reactions to the excerpt.

Child Sexual Abuse

Rebecca J. Donatelle and Lorraine G. Davis

Rebecca J. Donatelle teaches at Oregon State University, and Lorraine G. Davis teaches at the University of Oregon. The following excerpt comes from the fifth edition of their textbook *Access to Health*, published in 1998.

1   Sexual abuse of children by adults or older children includes sexually suggestive conversations; inappropriate kissing; touching; petting; oral, anal, or vaginal intercourse; and other kinds of sexual interaction. The most frequent abusers are a child's parents or companions or spouses of the child's parents. Next most frequent are grandfathers and siblings. Girls are more commonly abused than boys, although young boys are also frequent victims, usually of male family members. Between 20 and 30 percent of all adult women report having had an unwanted childhood sexual encounter with an adult male, usually a father, uncle, brother, or grandfather. It is a myth that male deviance or mental illness accounts for most incidents of sexual abuse of children: "Stories of retrospective incest patients typically involved perpetrators who are 'Everyman'—attorneys, mental health practitioners, businessmen, farmers, teachers, doctors, and clergy."

def—abuse includes more than just intercourse

Who abuses

2   Most sexual abuse occurs in the child's home. Risky situations include:

1. When the child lives without one of his or her biological parents.
2. When the mother is unavailable to the child either because she is working outside the home or because she is disabled or ill.
3. When the parents' marriage is unhappy or rife with conflict.
4. When the child has a poor relationship with his or her parents or is subjected to extremely punitive discipline.
5. When the child lives with a stepfather.

3   Two points are worth making about the impact of child abuse in later life: 99 percent of the inmates in the maximum security prison at San Quentin were either abused or raised in abusive households; and 300,000 children between the ages of 8 and 15 are living on the nation's streets, willing to prostitute themselves to survive rather than to return to abusive households they ran away from.

4   Most people who were abused as children, of course, do not end up as convicts or prostitutes. But most do bear spiritual, psychological, and/or physical scars. Clinical psychologist Marjorie Whittaker has found that "of all forms of violence, incest and childhood sexual abuse are considered among the most 'toxic' because of their violations of trust,

the confusion of affection and coercion, the splitting of family align-
ments, and serious psychological and physical consequences."

Understanding Your Sources

Readers will always expect an accurate, fair, and sensitive use of sources. An inaccurate summary does not serve its purpose; a passage that is misquoted or quoted out of context makes readers wonder about your credibility. So, follow the guidelines for active reading, plan to read a complex work more than once, and think about a work's purpose, thesis, and strategies for supporting the thesis before responding to it in some way. After reading and annotating, develop your understanding more fully by conducting a preliminary analysis that seeks to answer the following questions:

1. *What is the work's primary purpose? Does it combine purposes?* Texts can be classified as primarily expressive (evoking feelings), expository (imparting information), or persuasive (arguing for a position on an issue). We can also distinguish between a serious purpose and a humorous one. But of course these purposes shade into one another. Arguments can appeal to emotions, and passionate fiction can teach us about human life and experience. Because the excerpt "Child Sexual Abuse" comes from a textbook, you can conclude that its primary purpose is to give information; note, though, that the authors express concern about the consequences of such abuse.

2. *What is the thesis, the main idea of the work?* At times the best way to get to an understanding of a thesis is to ask, first, "What is the author's subject?" Then ask, "What does the author assert about that subject, or want me to understand about that subject?" Stating the thesis as a complete sentence will help you move from subject to assertion. As you read, or when you reread, look for one or two sentences that may state the work's main idea. Often writers state a thesis near the beginning or at the end of their works, but keep in mind that writers do not have to state a thesis. Sometimes a writer's thesis is implied, so you will have to reflect on the whole text and then write your own thesis statement for it.

3. *How is the thesis developed and supported?* Consider: Does the writer present a series of examples to illustrate the main idea? Or a blend of reasons and evidence to develop an argument? Does the writer organize chronologically? Set up a contrast pattern or make an analogy? Explain causes? Observing both the type of support and its organization will help you read with understanding as you recognize how the parts fit together. When you "know what it says," you can write a summary or paraphrase or present passages in direct quotation.

Writing Summaries

Although summary may appear to be the simplest response to a source, preparing a good summary is not as easy as it sounds. *A summary briefly restates, in your own words, the main points of a work in a way that does not misrepresent or distort the original.* A good summary shows your grasp of main ideas and your ability to express them clearly. You need to condense the original while giving all key ideas their appropriate attention. As a student, you will be asked to write summaries in at least one of the following situations:

1. To show that you have read and understood assigned works ("Prepare a summary for each article on the reading list").

2. To complete a test question ("Who is at risk for child sexual abuse, and what are three 'risky' situations for children?").

3. To have a record of what you have read for future study or to prepare for class discussion.

4. To explain the main ideas in a work that you will also examine in some other way, such as in a book review or refutation.

If you are writing summaries in your reading journal, be sure to separate them from any personal responses that you may also want to include. If your instructor assigns a summary, not an evaluation, pay careful attention to your word choice as you restate an author's ideas. Avoid judgment words, such as: "Jones then proceeds to develop the *silly* idea that . . . " Follow these guidelines for writing good summaries:

Guidelines for Writing Summaries

1. Write in a direct, objective style, using your own words. Use few, if any, direct quotations, probably none in a one-paragraph summary.

2. Begin with a reference to the writer (full name) and the title of the work and then state the writer's thesis. (You may also want to include where and when the work was published.)

3. Complete the summary by providing other key ideas. Show the reader how the main ideas connect and relate to one another.

4. Do not include specific examples, illustrations, or background sections.

5. Combine main ideas into fewer sentences than were used in the original.

6. Keep the parts of your summary in the same balance as you find in the original. If the author devotes about 30 percent of the essay to one idea, that idea should get about 30 percent of the space in your summary.

7. Select precise, accurate verbs to show the author's relationship to ideas. Write Jones *argues*, Jones *asserts*, Jones *believes*. Do not use vague verbs that provide only a list of disconnected ideas. Do *not* write Jones *talks about*, Jones *goes on to say*.

8. Do *not* make any judgments about the writer's style or ideas. Do *not* include your personal reaction to the work.

With these guidelines in mind, read the following two summaries of Bruce Sterling's "Learning to Love Obsolescence" (see pages 9–10). Then answer the question: What is flawed or weak about each summary? To aid your analysis of flaws, (1) underline or highlight all words or phrases that are inappropriate in the summary and (2) put the number of the guideline next to any passage that does not follow that guideline.

Summary 1

I really thought that Bruce Sterling's "Learning to Love Obsolescence" (*Newsweek*, January 1, 2000) contained some interesting ideas about garbage. Sterling explains that today's favorite gadgets are tomorrow's junk and that we love things too much. I don't think that's always true. If we didn't love our computers, we wouldn't work so hard to make them better. Sterling says that in the 1950s cars were what we turned into junk; in the 90s it's computers. Tomorrow's junk will be smart junk, such as talking coffeepots.

Summary 2

In Bruce Sterling's "Learning to Love Obsolescence," published January 1, 2000, in *Newsweek*, Sterling talks about garbage or junk. He says that junk happens a lot, but mostly with our most creative gadgets. He says these things get old fast and that we should not love things so much, but we should respect our garbage. He goes on to say that we should wonder only at big things such as galaxies, not nuclear missiles. Tomorrow we will have smart but useless junk.

Although we can agree that the writers of these summaries have read and basically understood most of Sterling's essay, we can also find weaknesses in each summary. The second summary can be greatly improved by some eliminating, combining, and rewriting. Here is a much-improved version of summary 2:

Revised Summary 2

In "Learning to Love Obsolescence," published January 1, 2000, in *Newsweek*, Bruce Sterling asserts that since everything that humans make will inevitably become part of our garbage, we ought not be too impressed by the things we have made. He argues that we need to change our attitudes toward "things" and to keep our wonderment for the grand elements of the universe. He reminds us that no matter how clever our gadgets are, we are in control of them, not they of us, and we are likely to outlive them. We make the most garbage in those areas that most interest us; thus, today's junk comes from the computers of the 1990s and tomorrow's junk will be the computer-chip-driven gadgets we will be making in the near future.

At times you may need to write a summary of a page or two rather than one paragraph. Frequently, long reports are preceded by a one- or two-page summary. A longer summary may become part of an article-length review of an important new book. Or, instructors may want a longer summary of a lengthy or complicated article or text chapter. The following is an example from *Psychology Today* (January–February 2000) of a summary, written for the nonspecialist, of a recent study in the social sciences.

The Ties That Unbind

Aaron Dalton

1   Our cultural vocabulary indicates that marriages move one way—downhill. The "honeymoon period" implies post-honeymoon strife; the "seven-year itch" suggests that we tire of our mate at year seven.

2   Now, Wright State University psychology professor Lawrence Kurdek, Ph. D., confirms that our lexicon is accurate. His surveys of over 500 couples have revealed that most married couples experience a gradual but steady decline in marital quality over the four-year period after they tie the knot. Newlyweds tend to wear rose-colored glasses at first, says Kurdek, but reality kicks in after they see their partner drink from the milk carton or forget to take out the trash one too many times. Though happiness stabilizes after four years, it declines again around year seven. This dip is harder to explain, Kurdek says, but may stem from the tendency to reexamine life as time goes on.

3   Having kids is another factor: Pairs with biological children had lower marital quality than childless couples or those living with stepchildren, reports Kurdek in a recent issue of *Developmental Psychology*. "Caring for children may result in time taken away from the marriage," he says.

4   Not all spouses are destined for dissatisfaction, says Kurdek. To prevent disappointment down the road, new couples should temper high expectations with a dose of reality; like any relationship, wedlock has its ups and downs.

Observe the differences between the longer summary of Lawrence Kurdek's work and the paragraph summary of Bruce Sterling's essay:

- Some key terms or ideas may be presented in direct quotation (see paragraph 3).
- When summarizing a report of research, explain the methods used by the researchers and the results of the study in some detail.
- Use appropriate transitional and connecting words ("Having kids is another factor") to show how the parts of the summary connect.
- Repeat the author's name ("says Kurdek") to keep the reader's attention on the work you are summarizing, not on you, the writer of the summary.

Writing Paraphrases

Although the words *summary* and *paraphrase* are sometimes used interchangeably, they are not exact synonyms. Summary and paraphrase are alike in that they are both written responses to sources. They differ in *how* they respond and *why. Like a summary, a paraphrase is an objective restatement of someone's writing, but the purpose of a paraphrase is to clarify a complex passage or to include material from a source in your own writing.*

When using sources for research, you will incorporate some of their information and ideas in your own paper, in your own words, and with proper documentation. Usually each paraphrased passage is fairly brief and is blended in with your own thinking on the topic. (You will find this purpose of paraphrase discussed and illustrated in more detail in this text's section on research, p. 181.) When your purpose is to clarify a poem, a complex philosophical passage, or prose filled with figurative language, your paraphrase will be longer, maybe longer than the original. Your goal is to show that you understand what you have read. Here is an example, first a passage from British philosopher Bertrand Russell's "A Free Man's Worship," followed by a paraphrase. As you read Russell's passage, underline words or phrases you find confusing. Then, as you read the paraphrase, look back to the original to see how the writer has restated Russell's ideas.

From "A Free Man's Worship"

Bertrand Russell

[F]or Man, condemned to-day to lose his dearest, tomorrow himself to pass through the gate of darkness, it remains only to cherish, ere yet the blow falls, the lofty thoughts that ennoble his little day; disdaining the coward terrors of the slave to Fate, to worship at the shrine that his own hands have built; undismayed by the empire of chance, to preserve a mind free from the wanton tyranny that rules his outward life; proudly defiant of the irresistible forces that tolerate, for a moment, his knowledge and his condemnation, to sustain alone, a weary but unyielding Atlas [someone bearing a heavy load, as Atlas did, holding up the sky on his shoulders], the world that his own ideals have fashioned despite the trampling march of unconscious power.

Paraphrase of the Passage by Russell

All that we can do, before we lose our loved ones and then face our own death, is to place value on the important ideas that mark humans as special creatures and give meaning to our lives. We must reject any fear of dying that would make us slaves to Fate and instead be proud of what we have accomplished. We must not be distressed by the powers of chance or blind luck. We must not let their control over much that happens to us keep us from maintaining a mind that is free, a mind that we use to think for ourselves. Keeping our minds free and embracing knowledge are ways to defy the powers of the universe over which we have no control. And so, even though we may at times grow weary of battling the blind forces of the universe, we continue to find strength in the interior world that we have shaped by our ideals.

Note, first, that the paraphrase is longer than the original. The goal is to clarify a complex philosophical statement, not to highlight main ideas only, as in a summary. Second, the paraphrase clarifies the passage by turning Russell's one long sentence into several sentences and using simpler language. When you can state a writer's ideas in your own words, you have really understood the writer's ideas.

When you are asked the question "What does it say?" think about whether you need a summary or a paraphrase. When an instructor asks you to state, in your own words, the meaning of Lincoln's long concluding sentence in "The Gettysburg Address," the instructor wants a paraphrase. To restate and clarify all of the ideas woven into that long sentence, you will need to write several sentences of your own. When an instructor asks you what an assigned essay is about, the instructor wants a summary, a brief statement that presents the main ideas clearly and objectively.

Now read the following article by Robert Samuelson. Annotate as you read, anticipate what is coming, raise questions. Then analyze Samuelson's thesis, support, and organization. Complete this process by responding to the questions that follow Samuelson's essay.

Century of Freedom

Robert J. Samuelson

A graduate of Harvard University, Robert Samuelson (b. 1945) began his career as a reporter and is now a columnist whose articles are syndicated in many newspapers each week and biweekly in *Newsweek* magazine. Although he often writes about economics, Samuelson also examines political and cultural issues, especially those that have a connection to economic issues, as he does in the following column published December 22, 1999.

1   What 20th-century development most altered the human condition? There is no shortage of candidates: the automobile, antibiotics, the airplane, computers, contraceptives, radio and television, to name a few. But surely the largest advance in human well-being involves the explosion of freedom. In a century scarred by gulags, concentration camps and secret-police terror, freedom is now spreading to an expanding swath of humanity. It is not only growing but also changing—becoming more ambitious and ambiguous—in ways that might, perversely, spawn disappointment and disorder in the new century.

2   In 1900 this was unimaginable. "Freedom in the modern sense [then] existed only for the upper crust," says political sociologist Seymour Martin Lipset of George Mason University. There were exceptions—America certainly, but even its freedom was curtailed. In 1900 women could vote in only four western states. Not until the ratification of the 19th Amendment in 1920 could all women vote. In the South, a web of laws prevented black Americans from voting. It took the Voting Rights Act of 1965 to change that.

3   Elsewhere the picture was bleaker. In 1900 empires dotted the world. The British Empire contained roughly 400 million people, about a quarter of the world's population. Lesser empires were still enormous: the Austro-Hungarian, the Ottoman, the French and others. Human subjugation was the rule, not the exception.

4   Consider the situation now. In 1999 Freedom House—a watchdog group based in Washington—classified as "free" 88 of the world's 191 countries, with 2.4 billion people or about 40 percent of the total. These nations enjoyed free elections and traditional civil rights of speech, religion and assembly. Of course, there are shades of gray. In this twilight zone Freedom House placed 53 countries with 1.6 billion people, because either elections or civil liberties were compromised. Russia was "partially free"; China was "not free."

5   Still, the world's frame of reference has fundamentally altered. Even in societies where freedoms are abused, their absence usually becomes an issue. But freedom has not simply spread. It's also evolved, especially in the United States. The freedom that Americans expect as they enter the 21st century is not the same as the freedom they expected as they entered the 20th.

6   Traditional freedom historically meant liberation from oppression. But now freedom increasingly involves "self-realization." People need, it's argued, to be freed from whatever prevents them from becoming whoever they want to be. There's a drift toward "positive liberty" that emphasizes "the things that government ought to do for us," says sociologist Alan Wolfe of Boston College. This newer freedom blends into individual "rights" (for women, minorities, the disabled) and "entitlements" (for health care, education and income support) deemed essential for self-realization.

7   The broader freedom is not just American. In a new book, *Development as Freedom*, the Nobel-Prize-winning economist Amartya Sen argues that "the expansion of freedom is both the primary end and . . . principal means of development" in poorer countries. But Sen's freedom eclipses the classic political and economic freedoms. It includes "social opportunities" (expanded education and health care) "transparency guarantees" (a lack of corruption) and more "entitlements" (to ensure basic decency and prevent "abject misery"). Indeed, it seems to include almost anything that might advance human well-being.

8   In some ways, freedom's explosion connects the century's two great constants: war and economic progress. Deaths in World War I and World War II are crudely reckoned at 10 million and as many as 60 million, respectively. But these vast tragedies ultimately paid some dividends for common people, because they doomed colonial empires. Also, the nature of the wars emphasized freedom. They were too destructive to be mere contests of nations. They had to be about ideals. The Cold War—an ideological conflict—conveyed the same message.

9   If war expanded freedom, prosperity embellished it. Since 1900 the world's population has roughly quadrupled, from almost 1.6 billion to 6 billion. Meanwhile, the global production of goods and services—from food and steel to air travel and health care—has risen 14 to 15 times, estimates economist Angus Maddison for the Organization for Economic Cooperation and Development in Paris. As nations grew wealthier, traditional freedom wasn't enough. People ascended what psychologist Abraham Maslow called the human hierarchy of needs—from food and shelter to self-esteem and spiritual needs, such as justice and beauty. People could not (it was said) be "free" without realizing these larger yearnings.

10   Freedom's fate in the next century is fragile, in part because the very notion is now so ill-defined. Classic freedom—coupling the opportunity for success with the danger of failure—hardly ensures personal fulfillment or social order. "On the one hand, you're told you're free," says Lipset. "But on the other, you're a potential loser. And if you lose, you don't feel free." The traditional freedoms of belief and lifestyle also require, if they are not to foster anarchy, tolerance and self-restraint.

11   But at least traditional freedom is universal. Everyone can, in theory, enjoy the freedoms of speech, religion, assembly and property. This sort of freedom promises the absence of coercion. By contrast, the new freedoms of individual "rights" and "entitle-

ments" are increasingly exclusive, can involve social competition for benefits and may mean the subtle (or not so subtle) coercion of one group by another—all tending to weaken a sense of community. The "rights" of women, gays and the disabled cannot be directly enjoyed by men, straights or the nondisabled. Financing entitlements means taxes—a form of collective coercion—by which taxpayers subsidize beneficiaries.

12   Freedom, always a combustible concept, promises to become more so, because in a world of television and the Internet, ideas glide almost spontaneously across cultural and political boundaries. The eagerness of the West to export its ideals may increasingly collide with the willingness and capacity of others to abandon or modify their own. What we value, they may fear or mishandle. Freedom is a great blessing. But it has never been easy—and never will be.

Questions for Analysis

1. What is Samuelson's subject? What is his thesis? State his thesis in one sentence. Is there a sentence in the essay that resembles your statement? If so, underline Samuelson's sentence.

2. Look again at paragraph 1. There is more than one sentence in that paragraph that could be a thesis statement. Which one is the better choice for Samuelson's thesis? Why?

3. What kind of support does Samuelson provide for the idea of the "century of freedom"? What general plan or organization does the author use?

4. What was the traditional idea of freedom? What is the newer concept of freedom all about? Be prepared to explain these concepts. (To be prepared, you may want to paraphrase paragraphs 5, 6, and 7.)

5. How did the century's wars contribute to freedom?

6. Why, according to Samuelson, is the fate of freedom in this century "fragile"? What are some of the problems governments or people may face in trying to maintain new ideas of freedom?

Questions for Discussion and Response

1. Which of the problems mentioned in paragraphs 10, 11, and 12 most threaten freedom, in your view? Why? Be prepared to discuss the strains on freedom in the 21st century.

2. Do you agree with Samuelson that freedom is the most significant development in the 20th century? If so, why? If not, what development would you argue for instead? Be prepared to defend your views.

3. Samuelson refers to the organization Freedom House. Check out its website (www.freedomhouse.org). For what kinds of projects might material at the Freedom House website be useful? Select either an essay or a chart, read it, and then write a brief summary.

Acknowledging Sources Informally

Regardless of the way you are responding to sources, you need to identify the work (or works) you are using and make clear to readers how you are using the work. Remember that the sample summaries above refer to both the author and the work. Always identify each source by author and title and make clear your relationship to each source. What follows are some of the conventions of writing you need to use when writing about sources.

REFERRING TO PEOPLE AND SOURCES

Readers in academic, professional, and other serious contexts expect writers to follow specific conventions of style when referring to authors and to various kinds of sources. Study the following guidelines and examples and then mark the next few pages for easy reference—perhaps by turning down a corner of the first and last pages.

References to People

- In a first reference, give the person's full name (both the given name and the surname): *Bruce Sterling, Robert J. Samuelson*. In second and subsequent references, use only the last name (surname): *Sterling, Samuelson*.

- Do not use Mr., Mrs., or Ms. Special titles such as President, Chief Justice, or Doctor may be used in the first reference with the person's full name.

- Never refer to an author by her or his first name. Write *Dickinson*, not *Emily*; *Whitman*, not *Walt*.

References to Titles of Works

Titles of works must *always* be written as titles. Titles are indicated by capitalization and by either quotation marks or underlining. (In handwritten or typed papers, italic type is represented by underlining. Even with the ease of shifting type fonts when using a computer, nonpublished works, such as your essays for courses, should contain underlining, not italic type.)

Guidelines for Capitalizing Titles

- The first and last words are capitalized.

- The first word of a subtitle is capitalized.

- All other words in titles are capitalized except

  —Articles (*a, an, the*).
  —Coordinating conjunctions (*and, or, but, for, nor, yet, so*).
  —Prepositions of five or fewer letters (e.g., *in, for, about*); prepositions of more than five letters are capitalized (e.g., *Between, Through, Before*).

Titles Requiring Quotation Marks

Titles of works published within other works—within a book, magazine, or newspaper—are indicated by quotation marks.

Essays	"The Real Pregnancy Problem"
Short stories	"The Story of an Hour"

Poems	"To Daffodils"
Articles	"Choose Your Utopia"
Chapters	"Writers and Their Sources"
Lectures	"Crazy Mixed-Up Families"
TV episode	"Resolved: Drug Prohibition Has Failed" (one debate on the television show *Firing Line*)

Titles Requiring Underlining (*Italics* in Print)
Titles of works that are separate publications and, by extension, titles of items such as works of art and films are underlined.

Plays	<u>A Raisin in the Sun</u>
Novels	<u>War and Peace</u>
Nonfiction books	<u>Read, Reason, Write</u>
Book-length poems	<u>The Odyssey</u>
Magazines	<u>U.S. News & World Report</u>
Journals	<u>The New England Journal of Medicine</u>
Newspapers	<u>New York Times</u>
Films	<u>The Wizard of Oz</u>
Paintings	<u>The Birth of Venus</u>
Recordings	<u>Eine Kleine Nachtmusik</u>
TV programs	<u>Nightline</u>

Read the following article (published October 1, 1999, in the *Washington Post*) and respond by answering the questions that follow. Observe, as you read, how the author refers to the writer and source he uses to develop the article and how he presents material from the source. We will use this article as a guide to handling quotations.

The Real Pregnancy Problem

William Raspberry

William Raspberry writes both local and syndicated columns each week, usually focusing on urban or race problems or issues regarding the poor.

1   America has been fulminating for years about the problem of teen pregnancy. Me too. A quick computer search turns up 37 columns in which I mention the phrase. Maggie Gallagher wishes we'd give it a rest.

2   She didn't say it quite so directly; she's not that rude. What she did say, in an intriguing new "report to the nation" from the Institute for American Values, is that the problems we lump under the rubric of "teen pregnancy" often are about something quite different.

3   Listen: "The teen birth rate is, and has been for many years, much lower today than it was in the 1950s and early 1960s, when many teens married and began their families young. It is the unwed birthrate that has grown rapidly enough to earn the label 'epidemic.'"

4   In other words, while we've been harping on "teen pregnancy," what really has been happening is a striking decline in the importance we place on marriage.

5   But isn't the problem "children having children"? Surely Gallagher wouldn't want us to encourage child marriages. Listen again to what Gallagher, also a syndicated columnist in addition to being on the institute staff, and her research team have to say in "The Age of Unwed Mothers: Is Teen Pregnancy the Problem?":

> 6   The bulk of today's teen pregnancy problem is less 'children having children' than increasing numbers of young adult women having babies outside of marriage. . . . Unwed teen moms younger than 18 account for only 13 percent of babies born out of wedlock.

> 7   As a society, we aim a fair amount of public money and many strong words at the problem of 'teen pregnancy,' that is, at the 376,000 births in one recent year to single mothers under the age of 20. Yet we pay comparatively little attention—indeed it often seems that as a society we are stone-cold silent—regarding the 439,000 births that same year to single mothers in their early twenties.

> 8   Are we against the former but indifferent to the latter? If so, what is our reasoning? Consider the prospects for a typical 20- or 22-year-old single mother and her baby. Are they really that much different, or better, than those facing an 18- or 19-year-old single mother?

9   Gallagher, like the Manhattan-based Institute for American Values for which she led this investigation, is unabashedly pro-marriage. But that in no way diminishes the validity of her insight: We have, in some important respects, stopped being a marriage culture.

10   The trend may have begun with feminist (and other) reaction against the teen marriages of the 1950s as "traps." Increases in the divorce rate sparked talk about marriage for the "wrong" reasons. And then, perhaps along with increased career opportunities for women, marriage was spoken of increasingly as a "bad deal" for women. Teen mothers contend, with great earnestness, that they are terrific mothers but too young for marriage; that will come later, they say (though it frequently does not).

11   Not only has the stigma against single parenthood been greatly reduced (with what unintended consequences?) but, according to Gallagher, professional counselors today frequently advise pregnant young women quite specifically against marrying the fathers of their babies—against falling into the "trap."

12   The advice turns out to be somewhat less liberating than it sounds. As the report notes,

> A young man who gets his girlfriend pregnant, but declines to marry on the grounds that he is too young, will typically enjoy ample opportunities in the coming years, as he 'grows up,' to enter into a lower-risk marriage with another woman.

13   The same cannot be said for the girlfriend. Entering into single motherhood, as against marriage, is likely permanently to compromise her future prospects for marriage.

14   Gallagher's contribution is not to recount the well-documented economic arguments against single motherhood but to drive home the degree to which young people's separation of parenthood from marriage reflects an attitude shift in the larger society.

15   She ends the 50-page report with 16 public policy proposals, of which these two top the list:

[16] "Put an emphasis on marriage, not just age, at the center of all of our efforts and programs in the area of teen sexuality and teen pregnancy," and

[17] "Retire the term 'teen pregnancy' from our public discourse. As a popular name for a serious social problem, the term has outlived its usefulness and now obscures more than it reveals. . . . How about 'unwed parenthood' as a substitute?"

Questions for Analysis and Discussion

1. Who is Maggie Gallagher? What did she write?
2. What is the "real" pregnancy problem, according to Gallagher and Raspberry?
3. How big a problem is it, in Gallagher's view?
4. What may be, according to Raspberry, some of the causes of the problem?
5. What, for women, may be a result of having a child outside of marriage?
6. What are two of Gallagher's proposals for addressing the problem?
7. Does Raspberry agree with Gallagher's ideas? How do you know?
8. How does Raspberry first refer to the writer whose work he uses? How does he refer to her after paragraph 1? What other information does he give about the writer?
9. How does Raspberry refer to the source?

Presenting Direct Quotations: A Guide to Form and Style

Although most of your papers will be written in your own words and style, you will have occasion, when responding to sources, to use direct quotations. Just as there is a correct form for references to people and to works, there is a correct form for presenting borrowed material in direct quotation. Study the guidelines and examples and then mark these pages, as you did the others, for easy reference.

REASONS FOR USING QUOTATION MARKS

We use quotation marks in four ways:

- To indicate dialogue in works of fiction or drama.
- To indicate the titles of some kinds of works.
- To indicate the words that others have spoken or written.
- To separate ourselves from or call into question particular uses of words.

When Raspberry writes: "Listen: 'The teen birth rate is, and has been for many years, much lower today . . .'" we recognize that he is presenting Gallagher's ideas to us in her own words. That is the third use of quotation marks listed above. However, when Raspberry writes: "Increases in the divorce rate sparked talk about marriage for the 'wrong' reasons," Raspberry is not quoting Gallagher. Instead he is questioning the use of the word *wrong*. He also puts the word "traps" in quotation marks for the same reason. Having children without being married may turn out to be the bigger "trap." This is the fourth use of quotation marks. The following guidelines apply to all four uses of quotation marks.

GUIDELINES FOR QUOTING

1. Quote accurately. Do not misrepresent what someone has written. Take time to compare what you have copied with the original, paying particular attention to spelling and punctuation. Decide whether the following passage is quoted accurately from Raspberry's article: "The trend may have begun with feminist reaction against teens of the 1950s." Compare it with the original and make any necessary corrections.

2. Put *all* words taken from a source in quotation marks. (To lift words from a source without making it clear that they are not your words is to plagiarize, an action viewed as stealing in academic and professional communities.) Never change words. Never delete words without so indicating with spaced dots (. . .). If you need to add words to make the meaning of a passage clear, place the added words in square brackets ([ ]), not parentheses.

   Original: "In other words, while we've been harping on 'teen pregnancy,' what really has been happening is a striking decline in the importance we place on marriage."

   Incorrect: "While Raspberry and other writers have been harping on 'teen pregnancy,' what really has been happening is a striking decline in the importance society places on marriage."

   Correct: Raspberry explains that "while we've [columnists and other writers] been harping on 'teen pregnancy,' what really has been happening is a striking decline in the importance we place on marriage." (See 9 below for the use of single quotation marks within quotations.)

3. *Always* make the source of quoted words clear. If you do not indicate the author of quoted words, readers will have to assume that you are calling those words into question. Note that Raspberry introduces the author, on whose report he draws, in paragraph 1 and then repeats her name *five* times so that we are reassured that direct quotations continue to come from Gallagher's report. If Raspberry were drawing on two or more sources, he would need to include the appropriate author's name with each quoted passage so that readers will always know who said what.

4. If you want to quote words from an author (for example, Gallagher) quoted by another author (Raspberry), you must make clear that you are getting Gallagher's words from Raspberry's article, not directly from Gallagher's report.

   Original Quotation by Raspberry: "Put an emphasis on marriage, not just age, at the center of all of our efforts and programs in the area of teen sexuality and teen pregnancy."

   Incorrect: Gallagher says that we should "put an emphasis on marriage, not just age, at the center of all of our efforts and programs in the area of teen pregnancy."

   Correct: One of Gallagher's proposals, quoted by Raspberry, is to "put an emphasis on marriage, not just age, at the center of all of our efforts and programs in the area of teen pregnancy."

5. Place commas and periods *inside* the closing quotation mark—even when only one word is quoted:

> Raspberry explains that we have encouraged parenting outside of marriage by describing marriage as a "bad deal," a "trap."

6. Place colons and semicolons *outside* the closing quotation mark:

> Raspberry presents information from Gallagher's report "The Age of Unwed Mothers: Is Teen Pregnancy the Problem?": There were "376,000 births in one recent year to single mothers under the age of 20"; however, there were "439,000 births that same year to single mothers in their early twenties."

7. Do not quote unnecessary punctuation. When you place quoted material at the end of a sentence you have made, use only the punctuation needed to complete the sentence.

Original:	"[A]ccording to Gallagher, professional counselors today frequently advise pregnant young women quite specifically against marrying the fathers of their babies—against falling into the 'trap.' "
Incorrect:	Raspberry quotes Gallagher as observing that "professional counselors today frequently advise pregnant young women quite specifically against marrying the fathers of their babies—."
Correct:	Raspberry quotes Gallagher as observing that "professional counselors today frequently advise pregnant young women quite specifically against marrying the fathers of their babies."

8. When the words you quote make up only part of your sentence, do not capitalize the first quoted word, even if it was capitalized in the original source. *Exception:* The passage you quote follows an introduction that ends in a colon.

Incorrect:	Raspberry points out that "Not only has the stigma against single parenthood been greatly reduced . . . but, according to Gallagher, professional counselors today frequently advise pregnant young women . . . against marrying the fathers of their babies."
Correct:	Raspberry points out that "not only has the stigma against single parenthood been greatly reduced . . . but, according to Gallagher, professional counselors today frequently advise pregnant young women . . . against marrying the fathers of their babies."
Also correct:	Raspberry examines the impact of the idea that early marriage is a trap: "Not only has the stigma against single parenthood been greatly reduced . . . but, according to Gallagher, professional counselors today frequently advise pregnant young women . . . against marrying the fathers of their babies."

9. Use single quotation marks (the apostrophe key on your keyboard) to identify quoted material within quoted material:

   Raspberry observes that there has been a feminist "reaction against the teen marriages of the 1950s as 'traps.'"

10. Depending on the structure of your sentence, use a colon, a comma, or no punctuation before a quoted passage. A colon provides a formal introduction to quotes. Use it sparingly for emphasis or to introduce a long quotation. Use a comma *only* when your sentence structure requires it. Quoted words presented in a "that" clause are *not* preceded by a comma.

Original:	"Increases in the divorce rate sparked talk about marriage for the 'wrong' reasons."
Correct:	Raspberry offers this cause for increased parenting outside of marriage: "Increases in the divorce rate sparked talk about marriage for the 'wrong' reasons."
Correct:	"Increases in the divorce rate," Raspberry asserts, "sparked talk about marriage for the 'wrong' reasons."
Correct:	Raspberry observes that "increases in the divorce rate sparked talk about marriage for the 'wrong' reasons."

11. To keep direct quotations as brief as possible, omit irrelevant portions. Indicate that you have left out words by putting in ellipsis points (three spaced dots: . . .): Raspberry asserts that "Gallagher . . . is unabashedly pro-marriage."

12. Think about your reader. When you quote, give enough context to make the quoted material clear. Do not put so many quoted passages into a sentence that your reader gets tired trying to follow the ideas. Also, make certain that your sentences are both complete and correctly constructed. Quoting is not an excuse to write fragments or badly constructed sentences.

Awkward construction:	Raspberry notes causes for the decline in a marriage culture: "increased career opportunities for women" and "counselors . . . advise pregnant young women against . . . marrying the fathers of their babies."

    First, running the two ideas together in one sentence can be confusing to readers. Second, the two quoted passages are not in parallel structure. The first is a noun ("opportunities"); the second is a complete sentence ("counselors . . . advise . . . against . . . marrying").

Not enough context:	Raspberry talks about "marriage for the 'wrong' reasons."
Better:	Raspberry observes that "increases in the divorce rate sparked talk about marriage for the 'wrong' reasons."
Misleading:	Raspberry notes that columnists have written many columns on "teen pregnancy," and Maggie Gallagher "wishes we'd give it a rest."

Better: Raspberry notes that columnists have written many columns on "teen pregnancy," but Maggie Gallagher thinks that the "term has outlived its usefulness and now obscures more than it reveals."

Gallagher does not argue that we should stop focusing on the problem of teen pregnancy. She argues that the label "teen pregnancy" takes the public's attention away from the larger issue of women having children without being married.

✔ NOTE: All examples of quoting given above are in the present tense. We write that "Raspberry notes," "Raspberry believes," "Raspberry asserts." Even though his article was written in the past, we use the present tense to describe his ongoing ideas. (See p. 281 in "Other Styles of Documentation" for a variation of this convention.)

As you read the following article, practice active reading, including annotating the essay. Concentrate first on what the author has to say but also observe the structure or organization of the essay and the author's use of quotations and references to books and articles.

Beyond Gutenberg

Bill Gates

Bill Gates is the chairman of Microsoft and one of the world's most successful "techies." His essay on e-books appeared in January 2000 in a special publication of *The Economist* titled *The World in 2000.*

1   Reading on paper is so much a part of our lives that it is hard to imagine anything could ever replace inky marks on shredded trees. Since Johannes Gutenberg invented an economical way to make movable metal type in the 15th century, making it possible to produce reading matter quickly, comparatively cheaply and in large quantities, the printed word has proved amazingly resilient. So how could anyone believe that sales of electronic books will equal those of paper books within a decade or so?

2   First, it is worth remembering that paper is only the latest in a long line of reading "technologies" that were made obsolete each time an improved solution emerged. Pictures drawn on rock gave way to clay tablets with cuneiform characters pressed into the clay before it dried. Clay gave way to animal skin scrolls marked with text, and then to papyrus scrolls. By 100 AD the codex had arrived, but it was not until the ninth century that the first real paper book was produced. In Europe, paper was rare until after Gutenberg's breakthrough.

3   It took a few more centuries for e-books to emerge. They were first envisioned in 1945 by Vannevar Bush, director of the United States Office of Scientific Research and Development. In his classic essay, "As We May Think," Bush described a gadget he called a "memex"—"a device in which an individual stores all his books, records, and communications. . . . Most of the memex contents are purchased on microfilm ready for insertion. Books of all sorts, pictures, current periodicals, newspapers, are thus obtained and dropped into place. . . . Wholly new forms of encyclopedias will appear, ready-made with a mesh of associative trails running through them. . . ."

4   Although science-fiction writers eagerly adopted Bush's ideas—notably on the television show *Star Trek*, where portable electronic books featured regularly—the real world has remained loyal to paper. Only in the encyclopedia market, which was transformed by CD-ROMs in the mid-1980s, has the e-book made real progress. Far more encyclopedias, from Microsoft's *Encarta* to *Encyclopedia Britannica*, are sold on CD-ROM than were ever sold on paper, because they cost a fraction of the price and are easier to search. But attempts to broaden the appeal of e-book technology to "ludic" (or pleasure) readers have been unsuccessful. Since the late 1980s the electronic publishing world has seen several failed e-book ventures.

5   Why? Most of them used devices that were either too bulky to carry around, or forced users to "stock up" their electronic library in inconvenient ways. (One required visits to a "book bank," an ATM-like machine that was to be located in bookstores.) Before widespread adoption of the Internet, there was no universal way to download new reading material. But the most fundamental problem was the lack of a display technology that could compete with paper when it came to ludic reading.

6   For paper books, readability depends on many factors: typeface and size, line length and spacing, page and margin size, and the colour of print and paper. But for e-books there are even more factors, including resolution, flicker, luminance, contrast and glare. Most typefaces were not designed for screens and, thanks to a limited number of pixels, are just fuzzy reproductions of the originals. The result is that reading on-screen is hard on the eyes and takes a lot more effort. People do it only for short documents. The longer the read, the more irritating and distracting are all the faults in display, layout and rendering.

7   Most of these problems are now being solved. The World Wide Web offers an amazingly flexible way to deliver books in bits—and as investments in broadband infrastructure increase, it will get even easier to stock an e-library. And dozens of companies—including e-book pioneers and established publishing firms such as R. R. Donnelly, Penguin Putnam, Nokia, Barnes & Noble and Microsoft—have joined to create an open e-book standard, so that book-lovers will be able to read any title on any e-book.

8   There have also been some incredible technological breakthroughs that will make it much easier to read long texts on a screen. Microsoft has developed a font display technology called ClearType that, by manipulating the red, green and blue sub-pixels that make up the pixels on an LCD screen, improves resolution by up to a factor of three. Coupled with the latest e-book reading software and hardware, this provides an on-screen reading experience that begins to rival paper.

9   But why would anyone prefer an e-book to a p-book, regardless of improved readability? Because e-books have many other advantages. You will get instant delivery from your web bookshop to your e-book, and be able to store hundreds of novels on a device

the size of a paperback. E-book technology enables you to have an entire library in your pocket. Or you can keep it on your PC—a modern laptop can hold more than 30,000 books. You won't have to wait for out-of-stock books to be ordered, and books will never go out of "print." Your children will be able to listen to unfamiliar words pronounced for them as they read. You will have unabridged audio synchronized to the text, so you can continue the story in situations where you are unable to read—for example, while driving.

10   In addition, e-books promise to revolutionise the way the world reads. Whereas paper books are stand-alone entities, e-books can include hypertext links to additional content, whether it is in other books, databases or web sites. So e-books will not be restricted to a linear structure that is the same for everyone—every reader will be free to make use of the links, images and sounds differently. You will also be able to customise e-books by adding your own notes, links and images. In a paper book, content is fixed; with e-book technology it is flexible. Finally, you will be able to get sound and moving images to support the text, creating an entirely new multimedium.

11   The e-book will also revolutionise the economics of the industry. The cost of publishing books will fall dramatically, the result of savings on materials, labour, manufacturing and distribution. In the process, a lot of trees will also be saved and even the most obscure author will be able to self-publish, which means more choice for readers. The retail price of books will fall; sales will explode.

12   It is hard to imagine today, but one of the greatest contributions of e-books may eventually be in improving literacy and education in less-developed countries. Today people in poor countries cannot afford to buy books and rarely have access to a library. But in a few years, as the cost of hardware continues to decline, it will be possible to set up "virtual" public libraries which will have access to the same content as the Library of Congress.

Questions for Analysis

1. What is Gates's subject? What is his thesis?
2. How does Gates announce his subject in his title?
3. How does Gates organize his essay? What does he do first, after his introduction? Then what issues does he examine? How does he conclude? What is useful about his organizational strategy?
4. Gates refers to an essay, a TV series, and several encyclopedias. How does he handle these references?
5. What are the problems with e-books? How are these problems being solved?
6. What are the advantages of e-books, according to Gates?

Questions for Discussion and Response

1. Gates sees many advantages in e-books. Are you surprised? Do his promises for the advantages of e-books seem realistic to you?
2. Can you imagine preferring an e-book to a paper book? Why or why not?
3. Prepare a one-paragraph summary of Gates's essay. Analyze your summary to see if it meets the guidelines for writing summaries given in this chapter.

Writing Assignments

1. Write a one-paragraph summary of either Robert Samuelson's essay "Century of Freedom" or Bill Gates's essay "Beyond Gutenberg." Be sure that your summary clearly states the author's main idea or thesis. Take your time and polish your word choice.

2. Read actively and then prepare a one-and-a-half-page summary of either Brandon Centerwall's "Television and Violent Crime" (pages 306–16) or Linda J. Waite's "Social Science Finds: 'Marriage Matters'" (pages 532–39). Your readers are those who want an accurate and balanced but much shorter version of the original because they will not be reading the original article. Explain not only what the writer's main ideas are but also how the writer develops his or her essay. That is, what kind of research supports the article's thesis? Pay close attention to your word choice.

3. Robert Samuelson, in "Century of Freedom," reminds us that freedom is fragile and will, in his view, face threats in the 21st century. Which of the problems mentioned by Samuelson, or which problem not mentioned by him but chosen by you, will most threaten our freedom? In an essay explain and support your views on this topic. Refer correctly to the author and title, and present any quotations from Samuelson in correct form.

4. Suppose that you prefer paper books to e-books. How would you defend the paper book in response to Bill Gates's argument for e-books in "Beyond Gutenberg"? Think of several advantages of paper books and how you can defend them as advantages, as characteristics not found in e-books. Refer correctly to Gates and to his essay and present any quotations from Gates in correct form.

CHAPTER 2

Responding Critically to Sources

In some contexts, the word *critical* carries the idea of harsh judgment: "The manager was critical of her secretary's long phone conversations." In other words, the manager disapproved of the secretary's behavior. In other contexts, however, the term means to evaluate carefully, a positive attribute. When we speak of the critical reader or critical thinker, we have in mind someone who reads actively, who thinks about issues, and who makes informed judgments. Here is a more detailed list of attributes:

Traits of the Critical Reader/Thinker

- **Focused on the facts.**

    (Give me the facts and show me that they are relevant to the issue.)

- **Analytic.**

    (What strategies has the writer/speaker used to develop the argument?)

- **Open-minded.**

    (Prepared to listen to different points of view, to learn from others.)

- **Questioning/skeptical.**

    (What other conclusions could be supported by the evidence presented?
    How thorough has the writer/speaker been?
    What persuasive strategies are being used?)

- **Creative.**

    (What are some entirely different ways of looking at the issue or problem?)

- **Intellectually active, not passive.**

    (Willing to analyze logic and evidence.
    Willing to consider many possibilities.
    Willing, after careful evaluation, to reach a judgment, to take a stand on issues.)

Examining the Context

Reading critically requires preparation. We don't want to just start reading words on a page. Instead, we need to start by asking ourselves about the work's total context: Who is the author? Who is the expected audience for this work? What is the writer's purpose? We need to be able to answer these questions before analyzing and evaluating what we read.

WHO IS THE AUTHOR?

Does the writer have a reputation for honesty, thoroughness, and fairness? How is this author regarded by colleagues in his or her area of expertise? Is the work on a subject within the author's area of specialization? Is the author identified with a particular group or ideology?

The answers to these questions will help you judge the credibility of the author. If you do not recognize the name of a particular writer, or know anything about his or her reputation, some possible sources of information include biographical dictionaries and the *Book Review Digest* for reviews of the author's publications. These are available in the reference section of your library or online.

Another important consideration is whether the author is writing in his or her field of expertise. Advertisements often ask us to value a celebrity's opinion of a product about which the celebrity has no special knowledge. As consumers we need to become immune to the pleas of a famous actress to purchase a luxury automobile. As critical readers we need to remember that people cannot transfer expertise from one area of specialization to another. So when a well-known football player speaks in favor of a political candidate, he speaks only as a private citizen, not as an expert.

Besides examining the work for clues, how do you find out about an author's beliefs? It might help if you know the author's occupation or can identify the person as a participant in a particular institution or organization. For example, a member of a Republican administration may be expected to favor a Republican president's policies. A priest in the Catholic church may be expected to argue against abortion. But these clues give you only hints. Do not decide what the writer's bias will be before you have examined the work. Be alert to reasonable expectations, but avoid stereotyping the author.

WHAT KIND OF AUDIENCE IS BEING ADDRESSED?

Remember that you are not necessarily part of a writer's intended audience. Does the writer anticipate a popular or mass audience, a general but educated audience, or a specialized audience that will share professional expertise or cultural, political, or religious preferences?

Often you can judge the audience by noting in which kind of publication the work appears. For example, a popular magazine such as *Reader's Digest* is written to appeal to a mass audience. Other popular magazines such as *Psychology Today*, *Science*, and *Time* aim toward a general but more knowledgeable reader. You can expect their articles to provide competent introductions or overviews but not fully researched and thoroughly documented analyses. In contrast, articles appearing in a specialized journal such as the *New England Journal of Medicine* are written by medical doctors and research scientists for an audience with specialized knowledge.

Frequently, thinking about an author's expected audience will alert you to a particular bias. Some newspapers and magazines are fairly consistently liberal (for example, *Newsweek* and the *Washington Post*), while others are usually politically conservative (for instance, the *National Review* and *U.S. News & World Report*). The particular interests of magazines such as *Playboy* and *Ms.* should be taken into account if you are analyzing their articles. Since no writer is completely neutral, you need not distrust works with a bias; rather, be aware of writers' biases and judge their credibility in the light of their special interests.

WHAT IS THE AUTHOR'S PURPOSE IN WRITING?

Is the primary intention to report information or to persuade readers to accept a thesis? Is the work designed to entertain or to inspire? The title of a book or article or the preface or table of contents of a book may clarify the writer's purpose (for example, "Let's Save Our Lakes!"), but you will probably have to read the article or the first chapter to be certain of the author's intention. If the writer's purpose is to persuade, then you will have to pay particular attention to the handling of evidence. A writer intent on convincing readers of the validity of a thesis may, either willfully or unintentionally, distort or leave out some relevant information.

WHAT ARE THE WRITER'S SOURCES OF INFORMATION?

Has the writer made clear the sources of evidence? Is the information still valid? Where was it obtained? Be suspicious of writers who do not explain where they obtained their evidence or of those who urge readers to believe that their unnamed "sources" are "reliable." Pay close attention to dates to judge if the information is current. A biography of King George III published in 1940 may still be the best source; an article urging the curtailing of county growth based on population statistics from the 1980s would no longer be reliable.

Exercises: Examining the Context

1. What can you judge about the reliability or bias of the following? Consider author, audience, and purpose.
   a. An article on the Republican administration, written by a former campaign worker for a Democratic presidential candidate.
   b. A discussion, published in the *Boston Globe*, of the Patriots' hope for the next Super Bowl.
   c. A letter to the editor about conservation, written by a member of the Sierra Club. (What is the Sierra Club? Study some of its publications or check out its website to respond to this topic.)
   d. A column in *Newsweek* on economics. (Look at the business section of *Newsweek*. Your library has the magazine.)
   e. A 1948 article in *Nutrition Today* on food additives.
   f. A three-volume biography of Benjamin Franklin published by Oxford University Press.

g. A *Family Circle* article about a special vegetarian diet written by a doctor. (Who is the audience for this magazine? Where is it sold?)
h. A pamphlet by Jerry Lewis urging you to contribute to a fund to combat muscular dystrophy.
i. A discussion of abortion in *Ms.* magazine.
j. An editorial in your local newspaper entitled "Stop the Highway Killing."

2. Analyze an issue of your favorite magazine. Look first at the editorial pages and articles written by the staff, then at articles contributed by other writers. Answer these questions for both staff writers and contributors:
   a. Who is their audience?
   b. What is the purpose of the articles and of the entire magazine?
   c. What type of article dominates the issue?
   d. Describe their style and tone. How appropriate are the style and tone?

3. Select one environmental website and study what is offered. The EnviroLink Network (www.envirolink.org) will lead you to many sites. Another possibility is the Nature Conservancy. (www.tnc.org). Write down the name of the site you chose and its uniform resource locator (URL). Then answer these questions:
   a. Who is the intended audience?
   b. What seems to be the primary purpose or goal of the site?
   c. What type of material seems to dominate the site?
   d. For what kinds of writing assignments might you use material from the site?

Understanding Attitude

Critical readers read for implication and are alert to tone or nuance, the subtle emotional impact of a work. They read to understand each writer's attitude, thinking about not just *what* is said but *how* it is said. Consider the following excerpt:

> What happened to the War on Drugs? Did Bush—the old man, not the son—think that we actually *won* that war? Or did he confuse the War on Drugs with the stupid Gulf War he's so proud of winning? Well, he never did understand "the vision thing."

First, we recognize that the writer's subject is the War on Drugs, an expression used in the past, during the Bush administration, to emphasize the government's programs to reduce drug use in the United States. Second, we understand that the writer does not believe that the war has been won; rather, we still have a drug problem that we need to address. We know this from the second sentence, the rhetorical question that we answer by thinking that maybe Bush thought the drug problem had been solved but the writer—and we—know better. What else do you observe in this passage? What is the writer's attitude toward George Bush? Note the writer's language. The former president is "the old man." He is proud of winning a "stupid" war. He, by implication, is stupid to think that he helped win the War on Drugs. And, finally, we are reminded of Bush's own words that he didn't have a vision of what he wanted to do as president.

How would you rewrite the passage to make it more favorable to Bush? Here is one version that students wrote to give the passage a positive attitude toward Bush:

What has happened to the War on Drugs? Did some members of President George Bush's administration think that government policies had been successful in reducing drug use? Or did the administration change its focus to concentrate on winning the Gulf War? Perhaps, in retrospect, President Bush should have put more emphasis on the war against drugs.

The writers have not changed the information—the position that the War on Drugs has not been won—yet they have greatly altered our outlook on the subject. This version suggests that the failure to win the drug war was the fault of Bush's administration, not of Bush himself, and that perhaps the failure is understandable given the need to focus attention on the Gulf War. In addition, references to the former president treat him with dignity. What is the difference in the two passages? Only the word choice.

DENOTATIVE AND CONNOTATIVE WORD CHOICE

The students' ability to rewrite the passage on Bush and the War on Drugs to give the passage a positive attitude tells us that, although some words may have similar meanings, they cannot always be substituted for one another without changing the message. Words with similar meanings have similar *denotations*. Often, though, words with similar denotations do not have the same connotations. A word's *connotation* is what the word suggests, what we associate the word with, that goes beyond its formal definitions. The words *house* and *home*, for example, both refer to a building or structure in which people live. These words, then, have the same denotation. But the word *home*, for most people, suggests ideas—and feelings—of family and security. Thus the word *home* has a strong positive connotation. The word *house*, by contrast, has little connotative meaning. *House* brings to mind a picture of a physical structure but little else because *house* doesn't carry any "emotional baggage."

We learn the connotative significance of most words the same way we learn their denotative meanings: in context. Most of us, living in the same culture, share the same connotative associations of words. Most of us respond to the positive feelings associated with the word *home*. Even those who have personally experienced an unpleasant home environment will know, from observing how others use and respond to the word, that the culturally shared response is positive, not negative.

At times the *context* in which a word is used will affect the word's connotation. For example, the word *sister* usually has positive connotations. We may think of a kid sister or college sorority sister or the sisterhood of those who identify with feminist values. But when an unfriendly person who thinks a woman may have pushed in front of him to get on the bus says, "Better watch it, *sister*," the word has a negative connotation. Particular social, physical, and language contexts will at times control the connotative significance of words.

Because the associations we make with common words are as familiar to us as the denotation of those words, we can read past loaded words without becoming conscious of a writer's use of language to affect our feelings. One author writes "Bush—the old man"; another writes "President George Bush." We are moved by the connotative power of these words even if we are unaware of their presence in the work we are reading. The best way to become more alert to connotation is to keep asking what words the writer could have used instead.

> ✓ Writers make choices; their choices reflect and convey their attitudes. *Studying the context in which a writer uses emotionally charged words is the only way to be sure that we understand the writer's attitude.*

Exercises: Connotation

1. For each of the following words or phrases, list at least two synonyms that have a more negative connotation than the given word:

   a. child
   b. persistent
   c. willowy
   d. a large group
   e. scholarly
   f. trusting
   g. underachiever
   h. quiet

2. For each of the following words, list at least two synonyms that have a more positive connotation than the given word:

   a. notorious
   b. fat
   c. politician
   d. old (people)
   e. fanatic
   f. reckless
   g. sot
   h. cheap

3. Read the following paragraph and decide how the writer feels about the activity described. Note the choice of details and the connotative language that make you aware of the writer's attitude.

   Needing to complete a missed assignment for my physical education class, I dragged myself down to the tennis courts on a gloomy afternoon. My task was to serve five balls in a row into the service box. Although I thought I had learned the correct service movements, I couldn't seem to translate that knowledge into a decent serve. I tossed up the first ball, jerked back my racket, swung up on the ball—clunk—I hit the ball on the frame. I threw up the second ball, brought back my racket, swung up on the ball—ping—I made contact with the strings, but the ball dribbled down on my side of the net. I trudged around the court, collecting my tennis balls; I had only two of them.

4. Write a paragraph describing an activity that you liked or disliked without saying how you felt. From your choice of details and use of connotative language, convey your attitude toward the activity. (The paragraph in exercise 3 is your model.)

5. Select one of the words listed below and explain, in a paragraph, what the word connotes to you personally. Be precise; illustrate your thoughts with details and examples.

   a. nature
   b. mother
   c. romantic
   d. nerd
   e. playboy
   f. artist

Group Exercises on Connotation

1. List all of the words you know for *human female* and for *human male*. Then classify them by connotation (positive, negative, neutral) and by level of usage (formal, informal, slang). Is there any connection between type of connotation and level of usage? Why are some words more appropriate in some social contexts than in others? Can you easily list more negative words used for one sex than for the other? Why?

2. Although many words have culturally shared connotations, these same words can be given a different connotation in some contexts. First, for each of the following words, label its connotation as positive, negative, or neutral. Then, for each word with a positive connotation, write a sentence in which the word would convey a more negative connotation. For each word with a negative connotation, write a sentence in which the word would suggest a more positive connotation.
   a. natural   **d.** free
   b. old   **e.** chemical
   c. committed   **f.** lazy

3. Each of the following groups of words might appear together in a thesaurus, but the words actually vary in connotation. After looking up any words whose connotation you are unsure of, write a sentence in which each word is used correctly. Briefly explain why one of the other words in the group should not be substituted.
   a. brittle, hard, fragile   **d.** strange, remarkable, bizarre
   b. quiet, withdrawn, glum   **e.** thrifty, miserly, economical
   c. shrewd, clever, cunning

RECOGNIZING TONE

Closely related to a writer's attitude is the writer's tone. We can describe a writer's attitude toward the subject as positive, negative, or (rarely) neutral. Attitude, then, is the writer's position on, or feelings about, his or her subject. The way that attitude is expressed—the voice we hear and the feelings conveyed through that voice—is the writer's *tone*. Writers can choose to express attitude through a wide variety of tones. We may express and reinforce a negative attitude through an angry, somber, sad, mocking, peevish, sarcastic, or scornful tone. A positive attitude may be revealed through an enthusiastic, serious, sympathetic, jovial, light, or admiring tone. But we cannot be sure that just because a writer selects a light tone, for example, the attitude must be positive. Humor columnists such as Dave Barry often choose a light tone to examine various social and political issues. Given their subjects, we recognize that the light and amusing tone actually conveys a negative attitude toward the topic.

Group Exercise on Tone

With your class partner or in small groups, examine the following three paragraphs, which are different responses to the same event. First, decide on each writer's attitude. Then describe, as precisely as possible, the tone of each paragraph.

1. It is tragically inexcusable that this young athlete was not examined fully before he was allowed to join the varsity team. The physical examinations given were unbelievably sloppy. What were the coach and trainer thinking of not to insist that each youngster be examined while undergoing physical stress? Apparently they were not thinking about our boys at all. We can no longer trust our sons and our daughters to this inhumane system so bent on victory that it ignores the health—indeed the very lives—of our children.

2. It was learned last night, following the death of varsity fullback Jim Bresnick, that none of the players was given a stress test as part of his physical examination. The oversight was attributed to laxness by the coach and trainer, who are described today as being "distraught." It is the judgment of many that the entire physical education program must be reexamined with an eye to the safety and health of all students.

3. How can I express the loss I feel over the death of my son? I want to blame someone, but who is to blame? The coaches, for not administering more rigorous physical checkups? Why should they have done more than other coaches have done before or than other coaches are doing at other schools? My son, for not telling me that he felt funny after practice? His teammates, for not telling the coaches that my son said he did not feel well? Myself, for not knowing that something was wrong with my only child? Who is to blame? All of us and none of us. But placing blame will not return my son to me; I can only pray that other parents will not have to suffer so. Jimmy, we loved you.

Analyzing Style

We have begun the process of understanding attitude by becoming more aware of context and connotation and more alert to tone. Tone is created and attitude conveyed primarily through word choice and sentence structure but also through several other techniques.

WORD CHOICE

In addition to responding to a writer's choice of connotative language, observe the kinds of words that are chosen, the *level of diction* used. Are the writer's words primarily typical of conversational language, or of a more formal style? Does the writer use slang words or technical words? Is the word choice concrete and vivid or abstract and intellectual? These differences help to shape tone and affect our response to what we read. For example, Bruce Sterling's informal style (see p. 9) is created in large part by his word choice. He writes that "no matter how amazing some machine may seem, the odds are very high that we'll outlive it." He could have written, if he had wanted to sound more formal, that "no matter how startling some machine may appear, the percentages are considerable that we will outlive that machine." The second option isn't technical or scholarly, but it is more formal than what Sterling chose to write. Lincoln's word choice in "The Gettysburg Address" (see p. 6) is even more formal and abstract than Sterling's. Lincoln writes: "on this continent" rather than "in this land," "we take increased devotion" rather than "we become more committed." Another style, the technical, will be found in some of the articles in this text's collection of readings. The social scientist may write that "the child . . . is subjected to extremely punitive discipline," whereas a nonspecialist, writing more informally, would write that "the child is controlled by beatings or other forms of punishment."

One way to produce an informal style is to choose simple words: "land" instead of "continent." To create greater informality, a writer can use contractions: "we'll" for "we will." Bruce Sterling uses 14 contractions in his short essay on obsolescence. There are no contractions in either "The Gettysburg Address" or Rebecca Donatelle and Lorraine Davis's "Child Sexual Abuse" (p. 13). Contractions are one of the chief marks of a highly informal style. In your academic and professional writing, you should aim for a style informal enough to be inviting to readers but one that, in most cases, avoids contractions or slang words.

SENTENCE STRUCTURE

The eighteenth-century satirist Jonathan Swift once said that writing well was a simple matter of putting "proper words in proper places." Choosing the words is only part of the task; writers also think carefully about the arrangement of words into sentence patterns. Examining a writer's choice of sentence structures will reveal how these patterns affect style and tone. Are the writer's sentences generally long or short, or varied in length? Are the structures primarily:

- *Simple* (one independent clause)
  Obsolescence is the future in reverse.

- *Compound* (two or more independent clauses)
  The things of earth return to Earth, and, properly handled, so will our technologies.

- *Complex* (at least one independent and one dependent clause)
  Our machines are increasingly temporary, while we humans are increasingly permanent.

The longer the sentence and more complex the structure, the more formal the style. Long compound sentences joined by *and* do not increase formality much because these sentences are really two or more short, simple sentences hooked together. However, long simple sentences, those with one independent clause that have been expanded by many modifiers, will create a formal style. The following simple sentence, from an essay on leadership by Michael Korda, is more complicated than the sample compound sentence above:

- *Expanded simple sentence*
  [A] leader is like a mirror, reflecting back to us our own sense of purpose, putting into words our own dreams and hopes, transforming our needs and fears into coherent policies and programs.

In "The Gettysburg Address" three sentences range from 10 to 16 words, six sentences from 21 to 29 words, and the final sentence is an incredible 82 words. All but two of Lincoln's sentences are either complex or compound-complex sentences. Sterling's typical sentence lengths and structures contrast with Lincoln's and reflect the important role sentences play in creating style. Sterling has some sentences of over 20 words, but most range between 10 and 18 words, and some are 4 words or less. In paragraph 2, for example, the nine sentences are composed of 2, 18, 10, 21, 15, 24, 5, 3 and 11 words each.

Other elements of sentence structure shape a writer's style. Although many teachers work hard to rid student writing of *sentence fragments* (incomplete sentences), professional writers know that the occasional fragment can be used effectively for emphasis. Sterling writes, about the "melancholic beauty" of a gadget no longer serving any purpose:

> Like Duchamp's bottle-rack, it becomes a found objet d'art. A metallic fossil
> of some lost human desire. A kind of involuntary poem.

The second and third sentences are, technically, fragments, but because they build on the structure of the first sentence, we tend to add the missing words: "It becomes." The brevity, repetition of structure, and involvement of the reader who "completes" each fragment, all contribute to an emphatic conclusion to the paragraph.

An overly simplistic sentence structure, just like an overly simplistic vocabulary, can be used to show that the writer thinks the subject is silly or childish or insulting. In one of her columns, journalist Ellen Goodman objects to society's oversimplifying of addictions and need to believe in quick and lasting cures. To emphasize her point, she presents several well-known examples, but notice her technique:

> Hi, my name is Jane and I was once a bulimic but now I am an exercise
> guru . . .

> Hi, my name is Oprah and I was a food addict but now I am a size 10.

Parallelism (coordination of elements) and *antithesis* (contrast) are two more techniques of structuring sentences that writers can use to convey attitude. When two or more items (phrases, clauses) are parallel in structure, this signals readers that the items are equally important. Look back at the expanded simple sentence. Korda, coordinating three verbal phrases, asserts that a leader is like a mirror in three ways; a leader:

1. Reflects back our purpose
2. Puts into words our dreams
3. Transforms our needs and fear

Antithesis creates tension; the sentence using a contrast structure says "not this" but "that." Lincoln delights in this kind of structure. A good example is the following:

> The world will little note nor long remember
> <u>what</u> we say here,
> but
> it [the world] can never forget
> <u>what</u> they did here.

Notice that this sentence combines parallel structure *and* antithesis. The two main parts of the sentence have the same pattern, each part ending with a *what* clause, but the shift of key words in the second part creates the contrast of ideas.

METAPHORS

When Korda writes that a leader is like a mirror, he is using a *simile*. When Lincoln says that the world will not remember, he is using a *metaphor*. Similes and metaphors are more alike than different. Both draw a comparison between two things that are not really alike but seem, in the writer's mind, to be alike in some significant way. The difference between metaphors and similes is only one of expression. Metaphors state directly, or imply, the comparison; similes express the comparison by using a connecting word such as *like* or *as*. We can see the difference between metaphors and similes by using Korda's idea:

Simile: A leader is like a mirror.

Metaphor: A leader mirrors the desires of his or her followers.

What is most important is not the correct label for the expression. What is most important is that we:

- Recognize the use of figurative language.
- Observe the two items being compared.
- Understand the point of the comparison.
- Grasp the emotional impact of the figurative comparison.

Some writers use many figurative expressions; others do not. After noting a writer's tendency to figure of speech, you want to focus on the impact of the chosen metaphors. The comparisons that writers make reveal much about their perceptions of and attitudes toward their subjects. Korda's simile of a leader as a mirror captures his perception that a leader is successful only in reflecting the desires of his or her followers. When Bruce Sterling writes that, if you thought that the computer you bought was the last one you would ever buy, "you would be mortgaged to that machine like a medieval serf," he is expressing a negative feeling about the situation. To be a serf to your computer is to lose your freedom and power over the machine, to let the machine have control over you.

Metaphors, like connotative words, are so powerful, so emotionally compelling, that we respond to them even if we are not conscious of their use. But to be fully aware of a writer's attitude, we need to recognize metaphors and then take time to "open up" each one. During World War II, E. B. White, the essayist and writer of children's books, defined the word *democracy* in one of his *New Yorker* columns. His definition contains a series of metaphors, including the statement that democracy "is the hole in the stuffed shirt through which the sawdust slowly trickles." This clever and complex metaphor, when examined, makes an important statement about democracy. We can explain, or "open up" (a metaphor, too), the metaphor thus:

Just as one can punch a hole in a scarecrow's shirt and discover that there is only sawdust inside, nothing to be frightened of, so the idea of equality in a democracy "punches" a hole in the notion of an aristocratic ruling class and reveals that aristocrats, underneath, are ordinary people, just like you and me.

Note that one source of power in a metaphor lies in its compression. Here are two more of White's metaphors on democracy. Open up each one in a few sentences.

Democracy is "the dent in the high hat."

Democracy is "the score at the beginning of the ninth."

ORGANIZATION AND EXAMPLES

As you study a writer's word choice and sentence structure, do not neglect the work's organization and choice of examples, for both reveal attitude and shape the reader's response. When analyzing organization, consider both volume and placement. What parts of the discussion are developed at length? What points are treated only briefly? The amount of development can tell us something about a writer's attitude. Placement is also significant. Ideas introduced at the beginning or end of a paragraph or essay gain, by that placement, more weight than the ideas placed in the middle.

Examples chosen to illustrate points also merit attention. Can we agree that the examples are representative, or has the writer distorted the realities of the issue to support the thesis? Was the junk of the 1950s, as Sterling indicates, mostly about cars? And the junk of the 1990s mostly about computers? If these examples ring true, we read on in concert with the author. If they don't sound "right" to us, then we need to think about why the picture doesn't seem right, and we may begin to question the author's credibility.

REPETITION

Some repetition of key words and phrases will occur in well-written and unified essays. Some writers, though, go beyond this technique of unified writing and use repetition to produce an effective cadence, like a drum beating in the background, keeping time with the speaker's fist pounding the lectern for emphasis. In his repetition of the now-famous phrase "I have a dream," Martin Luther King, Jr., gives emphasis to his vision of an ideal America (see p. 618). In the following paragraph a student tried her hand at repetition to give emphasis to her definition of liberty:

> Liberty is having the right to vote and not having other laws which restrict that right; it is having the right to apply to the university of our choice without being rejected because of race. Liberty exists when a gay person has the right to a teaching job and is not released from the position when the news is disclosed. Liberty exists when a woman who has been offered a job in the labor force does not have to decline for lack of access to day care for her children, or when a 16-year-old boy from a ghetto has the right to get an education and is not instead compelled to go to work to support his needy mother and sisters.

These examples suggest that repetition generally gives weight and seriousness to a work and thus is appropriate when serious issues are being discussed in a forceful manner.

HYPERBOLE, UNDERSTATEMENT, AND IRONY

Three other techniques for shaping tone and expressing attitude include hyperbole (overstatement), understatement, and verbal irony. The three are similar in that all function by creating a discrepancy between what the writer says and what the writer actually means for the reader to understand. *Hyperbole* is the easiest of the three to recognize, for the writer so overstates the case that we spot the joking or satiric intent. When an exasperated parent says to a five-year-old, "I've told you a million times to brush your teeth," we recognize that humor, created by exaggeration, is being used to get the youngster into the bathroom. Although hyperbole can be used to satirize, usually the tone is light, because of the humorous quality in overstatement.

Understatement and irony can also be used with a light hand but often create a more serious or biting tone. To play down what is important is to give emphasis to the issue's seriousness. Recall Goodman's sentences from her column on addiction (see p. 42). They can also be noted as examples of understatement, for the sentences play down the complex causes for addiction and the difficulties of becoming—and staying—cured.

Hyperbole expresses more than is meant and understatement expresses less; *verbal irony* can be defined as expressing the opposite of what is meant. Recognizing verbal irony in writing takes skilled reading and some practice. When the once-again exasperated parent says to the scruffy-jeans-and-sweatshirt-dressed teenager, "Dressed for dinner, I see," the teenager can tell from the tone of voice and body language, as well as the social context, that the parent really wants the outfit changed before the family goes to dinner. In writing, the body language is missing and the tone somewhat harder to "hear," so we have to rely on the context of the passage, and indeed the subject and purpose of the entire piece, to determine if irony is present. Consider, for example, the title journalist Grace Lichtenstein chose for her examination of college sports: "Playing for Money." In one sense the statement is without irony, for the athletes do play a game. In another sense, though, the title is ironic, for Lichtenstein makes clear in her article that college sports are not "play," that they are serious business for the athletes, the coaches, and the schools. The bringing together of presumably disparate items, "play" and "money," ironically underscores the problem in college athletics.

QUOTATION MARKS, ITALICS, AND CAPITAL LETTERS

Finally, several visual techniques signal the reader to give special attention to certain words. A writer can place a word or phrase in quotation marks and thus question its validity or its meaning in that context. Ellen Goodman writes, for example:

> I wonder about this when I hear the word "family" added to some politician's speech. . . .

Goodman does not agree with the politician's meaning of the word *family*, as she reveals in her essay, but we know this immediately from her use of quotation marks. The expression *so-called* has the same effect:

> There has been a crackdown on the Chinese people's *so-called* liberty.

Italicizing (or underscoring when typing) a key word or phrase gives it added emphasis. Sterling uses italics in his essay:

> Everything with moving parts, . . . every *thing* is a larval form of junk.

Capitalizing words not normally capitalized has the same effect as italicizing; the words are highlighted. As with exclamation points, a writer needs to use italics or capitalization sparingly, or the emphasis sought through contrast will be lost.

Exercises: Recognizing Elements of Style

1. Name the technique or techniques used in each of the following passages. Then briefly explain the idea of each passage.

    a. We are becoming the tools of our tools. (Henry David Thoreau)

    b. The bias and therefore the business of television is to *move* information, not collect it.

    c. If guns are outlawed, only the government will have guns. Only the police, the secret police, the military. The hired servants of our rulers. Only the government—and a few outlaws. (Edward Abbey)

    d. Having read all the advice on how to live 900 years, what I think is that eating a tasty meal once again will surely doom me long before I reach 900 while not eating that same meal could very well kill me. It's enough to make you reach for a cigarette! (Russell Baker)

    e. If you are desperate for a quick fix, either legalize drugs or repress the user. If you want a civilized approach, mount a propaganda campaign against drugs. (Charles Krauthammer)

2. Read the following essay by Dave Barry. Use the questions that follow the essay to help you determine Barry's attitude toward his subject and to characterize his style.

Remote Control

Dave Barry

A humor columnist for the *Miami Herald* since 1983, Dave Barry (b. 1947) is now syndicated in more than 150 newspapers. A Pulitzer Prize winner in 1988 for commentary, Barry has written several books, including *Dave Barry Slept Here* (1989). The following piece appeared in March 2000.

1   Recently the *Washington Post* printed an article explaining how the appliance manufacturers plan to drive consumers insane.

2   Of course they don't *say* they want to drive us insane. What they *say* they want to do is have us live in homes where "all appliances are on the Internet, sharing information" and appliances will be "smarter than most of their owners." For example, the article states, you could have a home where the dishwasher "can be turned on from the office" and the refrigerator "knows when it's out of milk" and the bathroom scale "transmits your weight to the gym."

3   I frankly wonder whether the appliance manufacturers, with all due respect, have been smoking crack. I mean, did they ever stop to ask themselves *why* a consumer, after loading a dishwasher, would go to the office to start it? Would there be some kind of career benefit?

4   YOUR BOSS: What are you doing?

5   YOU (tapping computer keyboard): I'm starting my dishwasher!

6   YOUR BOSS: That's the kind of productivity we need around here!

7   YOU: Now I'm flushing the upstairs toilet!

8   Listen, appliance manufacturers: We don't *need* a dishwasher that we can communicate with from afar. If you want to improve our dishwashers, give us one that senses when people leave dirty dishes on the kitchen counter, and shouts at them: *"Put those dishes in the dishwasher right now or I'll leak all over your shoes!"*

9   Likewise, we don't need a refrigerator that knows when it's out of milk. We already have a foolproof system for determining if we're out of milk: We ask our wife. What we could use is a refrigerator that refuses to let us open its door when it senses that we are about to consume our fourth Jell-O Pudding Snack in two hours.

10   As for a scale that transmits our weight to the gym: Are they *nuts?* We don't want our weight transmitted to our own *eyeballs!* What if the gym decided to transmit our weight to all these other appliances on the Internet? What if, God forbid, our refrigerator found out what our weight was? We'd never get the door open again!

11   But here is what really concerns me about these new "smart" appliances: Even if we like the features, we won't be able to use them. We can't use the appliance features we have *now*. I have a feature-packed telephone with 43 buttons, at least 20 of which I am afraid to touch. This phone probably can communicate with the dead, but I don't know how to operate it, just as I don't know how to operate my TV, which has features out the wazooty and requires *three* remote controls. One control (44 buttons) came with the TV; a second (39 buttons) came with the VCR; the third (37 buttons) was brought here by the cable man, who apparently felt that I did not have enough buttons.

12   So when I want to watch TV, I'm confronted with a total of 120 buttons, identified by such helpful labels as PIP, MTS, DBS, F2, JUMP and BLANK. There are three buttons labeled POWER, but there are times—especially if my son and his friends, who are not afraid of features, have changed the settings—when I honestly cannot figure out how to turn the TV on. I stand there, holding three remote controls, pressing buttons at random, until eventually I give up and go turn on the dishwasher. It has been, literally, years since I have successfully recorded a TV show. That is how "smart" my appliances have become.

13   And now the appliance manufacturers want to give us even *more* features. Do you know what this means? It means that some night you'll open the door of your "smart" refrigerator, looking for a beer, and you'll hear a pleasant, cheerful voice—recorded by the same woman who informs you that Your Call Is Important when you call a business that does not wish to speak with you personally—telling you: "Your celery is limp." You will not know how your refrigerator knows this, and, what is worse, you will not know who else your refrigerator is telling about it ("Hey, Bob! I hear your celery is limp!"). And if you want to try to make the refrigerator *stop,* you'll have to decipher Owner's Manual instructions written by and for nuclear physicists ("To disable the Produce Crispness Monitoring feature, enter the Command Mode, then select the Edit function, then select Change Vegetable Defaults, then assume that Train A leaves Chicago traveling westbound at 47 mph, while Train B . . .").

14   Is this the kind of future you want, consumers? Do you want appliances that are smarter than you? Of course not. Your appliances should be *dumber* than you, just like your furniture, your pets and your representatives in Congress. So I am urging you to let the appliance industry know, by phone, letter, fax and e-mail, that when it comes to "smart" appliances, you vote NO. You need to act quickly. Because while you're reading this, your microwave oven is voting YES.

Questions for Analysis and Discussion

1. What is Barry's subject? What is his purpose in writing? That is, what does he want to accomplish in this column?

2. After thinking about Barry's subject and purpose, what do you conclude to be his thesis? Does he have more than one main idea?

3. How would you describe the essay's tone? Serious? Humorous? Ironic? Angry? Something else? Does a nonserious tone exclude the possibility of a degree of serious purpose? Explain your answer.

4. What strategies does Barry use to create tone and convey attitude? List, with examples, as many as you can.

5. What passages in the article do you find funniest? Why?

Writing about Style

PURPOSE AND AUDIENCE

Analyzing a writer's style requires answering the question "How is it written?" (see p. 7). This means examining the writer's choice and arrangement of language. You do not want to get sidetracked into either summarizing the writer's ideas or challenging those ideas, because neither summary nor evaluation is appropriate when the assignment is style analysis. Summary is inappropriate because the audience for a style analysis is assumed to be one that has read the work. To judge a writer's ideas leads to a counterargument, an altogether different kind of paper. You need to separate your response to a writer's views from your analysis of the techniques used to present those views. You do not have to agree with a writer to appreciate the writer's skill.

Some readers have difficulty at first with the need to restrain judgment, especially if they disagree with a writer, but the discipline required is worth achieving because without it readers never get past the content to understand style. Understanding how other writers put words and sentences together effectively will help you become a better writer, and that, remember, is the primary purpose of the course you are taking. A style analysis may imply, or even briefly express, a positive evaluation of the author's writing ability, but that is not the same as applauding or disagreeing with the author's ideas. (Of course, in a book review, a combination of summary, analysis, and evaluation, the analysis of style can be negative, but in English classes students are usually assigned skilled writers to read and analyze.)

ORGANIZATION AND CONTENT

An analysis of style should be organized according to elements of style, not according to the organization of the work being examined. Trying to comment on a work paragraph by paragraph increases the risk of summarizing rather than illustrating characteristics of the writer's style. Think of an essay as being like the pie of Figure 2–1. We could divide the pie according to its main ideas, as we would if we were summarizing. But we can also, as the diagram shows, carve the pie according to elements of style, the techniques we have

FIGURE 2–1 **Analyzing Style**

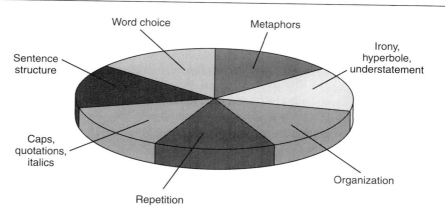

discussed in this chapter. An organization that reinforces your purpose aids your reader; it also helps you stay on target.

In writing an essay on style, your task is to select those stylistic techniques that are most important in conveying a writer's attitude and to discuss them, one at a time. If you were asked to write a style analysis you could devote one paragraph to Barry's use of parody, another to his use of irony, and a final one to his use of hyperbole. In your paragraph on hyperbole, you will need three elements:

1. A topic sentence that announces the coming analysis of hyperbole.
2. Three or more examples of hyperbole from throughout the essay.
3. An explanation of how each example connects to the author's thesis—that is, how each example works, through idea and emotion, to convey Barry's attitude.

The third element *is* the analysis. Remember that if all you do is quote examples of each technique, paragraph by paragraph, you will not have written an *analysis*.

MANUSCRIPT FORM

When writing about style, include in your introduction the author, the title, the date of the work being analyzed, and, if it's an article, the periodical in which it was published. Remember that titles of articles and essays are placed in quotation marks, and titles of magazines, books, and newspapers are underlined. Also, when you illustrate word choice and metaphors, place the author's words in quotation marks. These points and other requirements of manuscript form are discussed and illustrated in Chapter 1 and are illustrated in this chapter's student paper.

To test your understanding of style, read the following essay by Ellen Goodman, answer the questions that follow, and then study the student essay that analyzes Goodman's style.

Choosing Families

Ellen Goodman

Author of *Close to Home* (1979), *At Large* (1981), and *Keeping Touch* (1985), collections of her essays, Ellen Goodman (b. 1941) has been a feature writer for the *Boston Globe* since 1967 and a syndicated columnist since 1976. She has won a Pulitzer Prize for distinguished commentary. In addition to appearing in the *Globe*, the following column was printed in many newspapers across the country, including the *Washington Post*, on November 24, 1988.

1   BOSTON—They will celebrate Thanksgiving the way they always do, in the Oral Tradition. Equal parts of food and conversation. A cornucopia of family.

2   These are not restrained people who choose their words and pick at their stuffing. These are people who have most of their meals in small chicken-sized households. But when they come together, they feast on the sounds as well as tastes of a turkey-sized family.

3   Indeed, their Thanksgiving celebrations are as crowded with stories as their tables are with chairs. Arms reach indelicately across each other for second helpings, voices interrupt to add relish to a story. And there are always leftovers too enormous to complete, that have to be wrapped up and preserved.

4   But what is it that makes this collection of people a family? How do we make a family these days? With blood? With marriage? With affection? I wonder about this when I hear the word "family" added to some politician's speech like gravy poured over the entire plate. The meaning is supposed to be obvious, self-evident. It is assumed that when we talk about family we are all talking about the same thing. That families are the same. But it's not that simple.

5   For the past eight years, the chief defender of the American family has lived in the White House. But Reagan's own family has always looked more like our contemporary reality than his traditional image. There has been marriage and divorce among the Reagans, adoption and blending, and more than one estrangement. There is a mother, this holiday season, who hasn't talked to her daughter for more than a year.

6   The man who will take his place as head of this family ideology has wrapped himself in a grandfatherly image. Yet Bush's family is also extended in ways that are common but not always comforting to other Americans.

7   As young people, George and Barbara Bush left home again and again, setting up temporary quarters in 17 cities. Now they have five children scattered in an equal number of states: Texas and Florida, Colorado, Virginia and Connecticut. Theirs, like many of ours, do not live at home, but come home, for the holidays.

8   We hold onto a particular primal image of families—human beings created from the same genetic code, living in the same area code. We hold onto an image of *the* family as something rooted and stable. But that has always been rare in a country where freedom is another word for mobility, both emotional and physical.

9   In America, families are spliced and recombined in as many ways as DNA. Every year our Thanksgiving tables expand and contract, place settings are removed and added. A guest last year is a member this year. A member last year may be an awkward outsider this year. How many of our children travel between alienated halves of their heritage, between two sets of people who share custody of their holidays?

10   Even among those families we call stable or intact, the ride to the airport has become a holiday ritual as common as pumpkin pie. Many parents come from retirement homes, many children from college, many cousins from jobs in other Zip Codes. We retrieve these people, as if from a memory hole, for reunions.

11   What then makes a family, in the face of all this "freedom"? It is said that people don't choose their parents. Or their aunts and uncles. But in a sense Americans do choose to *make* a family out of these people. We make room for them in our lives, choose to be with them and preserve that choice through a ritual as simple as passing seconds at a table.

12   All real families are made over time and through tradition. The Oral Tradition. We create a shared treasure trove of history, memories, conversation. Equal parts of food and conversation. And a generous serving of pleasure in each other's company.

Questions for Analysis and Discussion

1. What is Goodman's subject? Why is it incorrect to say that her subject is Thanksgiving?

2. What is Goodman's attitude toward families; that is, what does she assert about families in this column? Is there one sentence that states her thesis? If so, which one? If not, write a thesis for the essay.

3. Characterize Goodman's style. Analyze her word choice, metaphors, sentence structure, organization, and use of the Reagan and Bush families as examples. How does each contribute to our understanding of her point?

4. Why are Goodman's metaphors especially notable? Open up—or explain—three of her metaphors.

Student Essay

GOODMAN'S FEAST OF STYLE

Alan Peterson

Thanksgiving is a time for "families" to come together, eat a big meal, share their experiences and each other's company. In her November 24, 1988, article "Choosing Families," which appeared on Thanksgiving Day in the <u>Washington Post,</u> Ellen Goodman asks the question: "Who makes up these families?" By her definition, a family does not consist of just "blood" relatives; a family contains

Introduction includes author, title, and date of article.

acquaintances, friends, relatives, people who are "chosen" to be in this year's "family." An examination of Goodman's essay reveals some of the elements of style she uses to effectively ask and answer her question.

Goodman's clever organization compels the reader to read on. She begins by focusing on a Thanksgiving dinner scene, referring to families and households in terms of food. After setting the table by evoking the reader's memories of Thanksgivings

past, Goodman asks the central question of her essay: "What is it that makes this collection of people a family?" Goodman argues that the modern meaning of family has evolved so much that the traditional definition of family is no longer the standard. To clarify modern definitions, she provides examples of famous families: First Families. After suggesting that the Reagans have been the "chief defenders of the American family" for the last eight years, she points out that the Reagans, with their divorces, their adoptions, their estrangements, are anything but the traditional family they wish to portray. Rather, the Reagans represent the human traits that define the "contemporary reality" of today's families. Next, President Bush's family is examined. Goodman points out that the Bushes' five children live in five different states, and that Barbara and George Bush, as young people, set up "temporary quarters in 17 cities." She develops an answer to her question in the ensuing paragraphs. She observes that families, "these days," are disjointed, nontraditional, different from one another. She refers to families that are considered "stable or intact" and shows how even those families can be spread out all over the country. In her closing paragraphs she repeats the question "What makes a family?" Then, after another reference to Thanksgiving dinner, she concludes the article by stating her main point: "All real families are made over time and through tradition." Goodman's organization—a question, some examples, several answers, and strong confirmation—powerfully frames her thesis.

In an essay written about a theme as homespun as family and Thanksgiving celebrations, a reader would not expect the language to be too formal. Choosing her words carefully, Goodman cultivates a familiar and descriptive, yet not overly informal style. Early in the essay, Goodman uses simple language to portray the Thanksgiving meal. She refers to voices interrupting, arms reaching, leftovers that have to be wrapped up. Another effective technique of diction Goodman employs is the repetition of words and sounds. She points out that the Bushes, as young people, "left home again and again." She defines the image we have of families as that of people created from the same "genetic code, living in the same area code," and of cousins in "other Zip Codes." Then, characterizing the reality of the configuration of today's American families, Goodman states: "A guest last year is a member this year," while a "member last year may be an awkward outsider this year." An additional example of repetition appears in the first and last paragraphs. Goodman repeats the sentence fragment "Equal parts of food and conversation." This informal choice of words opens and closes her essay, cleverly setting the tone in the beginning and reiterating the theme at the end.

Analysis of Goodman's word choice and repetition

Perhaps the most prevalent element of style present in Goodman's piece, and a dominant characteristic of her essay style, is her use of metaphors. From the opening sentences all the way through to the end, this article is full of metaphors. Keeping with the general focus of the piece (the essay appeared on Thanksgiving Day), many of the metaphors liken food to family. Her references include "a cornucopia of family," "chicken-sized households" and a "turkey-sized family," people who "feast on the sounds as well as the tastes," and voices that "add relish to a story." She imparts that a politician can use the word "family" like "gravy poured over the entire plate." Going to the airport to pick up family members of these disjointed American families has become "a holiday ritual as common as pumpkin pie." Goodman draws parallels between the process of "choosing" people to be with and the simple ritual of passing seconds at the table. Indeed, the essay's mood emphasizes the comparison of and inextricable bond between food and family.

Analysis of Goodman's metaphors

Ellen Goodman's "Choosing Families" is a thought-provoking essay on the American family. She organizes the article so that readers are reminded of their own Thanksgiving experiences and consider who is included in their "families." After asking "What is it that makes this collection of people a family?" Goodman provides election-year examples of prominent American families, then an explanation of "family" that furnishes her with an answer. Her word choice and particularly the repetition of words and sounds make reading her essay a pleasure. The metaphors

Conclusion restates Goodman's position and student's thesis

> Goodman uses link in readers' minds the images of Thanksgiving food and the people with whom they spend the holiday. Her metaphors underscore the importance she places on having meals with the family, which is the one truly enduring tradition for all people. Perhaps the most important food-and-family metaphor comes in the last sentence: "a generous serving of pleasure in each other's company."

Recognizing Language Abuses

JARGON

Some of the materials you will read as a college student may not be immediately clear because the ideas are complex. You may have to study these materials, reading them more than once and using the reading guidelines discussed in Chapter 1. Other works may not be clear because, unfortunately, they are not written in plain English. To evaluate the reliability and significance of some sources—even at times just to understand them—you must learn to see through the smoke screen of gobbledygook or jargon. *Jargon*, in its pejorative meaning, refers to a mix of writing techniques that includes abstract, pretentious words and phrases from the sciences, social sciences, and technical fields. Jargon also means the specialized language of a particular field, and in this sense the term is not negative. The spy novelist John le Carré has introduced many American readers to the jargon of British intelligence; we know that "moles" are double agents and that "Cousins" are the (usually) friendly U.S. intelligence gatherers. Intelligence specialists have their shorthand way of speaking to one another, as do other professional groups.

Jargon becomes objectionable when professionals use their special language with nonspecialists to sound important or to confuse, and when people outside a specialized field try to copy the professionals to show off. Although jargon is the language we often associate with bureaucratic memos and reports, many other places—literary criticism, the speech of sportscasters, student papers—harbor it as well. Some writers produce gobbledygook, believing that they have said something clear and intelligent, perhaps profound. But school administrators who write about *evaluative instruments* instead of *tests* have not really been more intelligent. They have tried to "dress up" the language of education in the hope, perhaps, that someone will take their research or recommendations seriously.

DOUBLESPEAK

Some writers, especially those in powerful positions, appear to write jargon out of viciousness rather than foolishness. Their desire is to hide the fact that they have nothing to say or to hide what they are really saying behind vague, polite terms called *euphemisms*. George Orwell, author of *Animal Farm* and *1984*, has called the deliberate kind of political jargon writing *doublespeak*. In his essay "Politics and the English Language," Orwell asserts that doublespeak is language used as a "defense of the indefensible"; it is language we use to gloss over behavior that is too brutal for us to think about. Doublespeak is the language that speaks of "police action" instead of "war," of "economic slowdown" instead of "depression," of "covert operations" instead of "spying."

CHARACTERISTICS OF JARGON

Knowing what elements of style result in jargon will help you both to figure out what a writer of jargon is trying to say and to avoid these pitfalls in your own writing. Most pieces of jargon or doublespeak combine some, but not necessarily all, of the following characteristics:

1. *Wordiness* (produced by repetition, by vague modifiers, and by unnecessary qualifying phrases)

   The quarterback, Ferragamo, has audibilized a new play at the line.   *[repetition]*
   TRANSLATION: Ferragamo has called a new play.

   [long qualifier]   In the not unlikely event that a great number of persons plan to take considerable advantage of our sales, we must lengthen our weekend hours.   *[vague modifiers]*
   TRANSLATION: Because many are likely to come to the sale, we will stay open longer this weekend.

2. *Pretentious diction* (produced by abstract nouns, by "-tion" words, by technical, pseudoscientific terms, by inflated expressions)

   [abstract nouns]   After examination of the numerous factors operating within the parameters of the situation we came to the realization   *["-tion" word]*
   [inflated expression]   that a move [at this point in time] would be counterproductive.
   TRANSLATION: After examining the costs of moving and the problems of our children changing schools, we have decided not to move.   *[technical terms]*

3. Excessive and unnecessary use of *the passive voice*

   A decision has been made regarding the current tardiness rule.
   (Notice that no actor is mentioned and the kind of decision made is not clear.)
   TRANSLATION: The principal *decided* to revise the tardiness rule.
   (Now a speaker is named, and the action taken is clear.)

4. Use of *euphemisms* (choice of words with positive connotations—e.g., *powder room* for *toilet*)

   [passive voice]   It has been decided that the public areas and facilities will   *[inflated language]*
   have an improved appearance if the night-time staff devotes
   more of its work effort to debris collection.   *[euphemisms]*
   TRANSLATION: Night-time janitors will spend more time collecting trash in the hallways and bathrooms.

Doublespeak, the kind of jargon that especially concerned Orwell, frequently combines the passive voice and euphemisms, or "weasel words." Indeed, Orwell felt that jargon's inflated word choice and sentence structure is a kind of extended euphemism, because this style hides the truth rather than helping readers to understand reality. Haig Bosmajian, in his essay "The Language of War," emphasizes that words used to downplay or cover up the evils of war lose their original meaning. They can't be used later without continuing to connote what they stood for in the doublespeak use. He gives as an example *pacification*, a word used extensively during the Vietnam War to describe the total destruction of villages by killing the people and animals and burning the dwellings.

✓   You will not be able to escape jargon in scholarly and technical sources you will be reading. You can, though, as you learn the specialized vocabulary of your field, learn to recognize when jargon is just bad writing and not imitate it. Orwell gives good advice when he writes: "Never use a foreign phrase, a scientific word or jargon word if you can think of an everyday English equivalent." And we can all do something about the weasel words of advertising and the doublespeak of political leaders: We can refuse to be manipulated by tricks of language.

Group Exercise on Jargon and Doublespeak

With your class partner or in small groups, revise each of the following examples of jargon into plain English. Revision is easiest if you can first separate the particular characteristics of jargon used in each passage and then rewrite the passage segment by segment. Then consider: Which passages go beyond the bounds of jargon and use the deceptiveness of doublespeak? (If you have trouble making sense of some examples, remember that that may have been the writer's intention.)

1. Congresswoman Smith, whose track record is highly exceptional, must be considered a very real candidate for the office of U.S. senator.

2. This school is open and available to everyone regardless of age, sex, race, creed, or national origin.

3. In this modern world in which we live today, we cannot fail to locate a rather significant variety of TV sitcoms in different time slots during both the daytime and evening hours.

4. To participate fully in your total self, you must get your head together, understand where you're at, and not let others press in on your needed space.

5. In making a determination of which testing instruments to utilize, of the highest order of prioritization should be criterion reference instruments rather than tests which are normative on a national scale.

6. Because the exceptional student does not utilize all potential conceptual tools automatically and without hesitation, a specialized environment that will allow for dynamic interaction between student and all resources in the learning situation is essential.

7. The socialization of adolescent offspring of urban adults experiencing a disadvantaged lifestyle occurs predominately in nonstructured environments or in environments in which the structuralization is peer-induced.

8. At this present moment my memory can form no recollection of that incident.

Combining Summary, Analysis, and Evaluation: The Review

Writing a review calls for all the skills you have been polishing: critical reading; accurate summary; analysis of style; and evaluation of the work in the context of the author's subject, purpose, intended audience, and success in comparison to other works on the subject. That's a tall order that you can best approach by looking first at the review's parts and then at how they can fit together.

Students sometimes think—or hope—that because they have been asked to evaluate as well as analyze they can write whatever they please. But remember that your reader—probably your instructor—will also be evaluating your review, and your instructor will have read the book or seen the movie you are reviewing. So study your subject carefully and think about the purpose of your review.

Balance is important. You do not want most of your review to be summary, with just a few sentences of evaluation added at the end. You also do not want a detailed summary of the book's or film's beginning followed by little treatment of the rest of the work. (Lack of balance may suggest to your instructor that you have not read or seen the entire work!) Professional reviewers may focus their attention on a section of a book or movie that they especially admire—or object to—but they also make sure that their readers have an accurate picture of the work's total contents. Exception: When reviewing a novel or movie, do not explain the entire plot; you do not want to give away the ending.

The analysis part of your review should include two elements: comment on the work's structure and special features and discussion of the writer's (or director's) style. How is the work put together? For a nonfiction book, how many chapters or sections does it have, and what does each cover? Does the book contain photographs? Maps or charts? An index? For a film, how does the story unfold? What is the story about? What actors are in the lead roles? These are the kinds of questions a reader expects a reviewer to answer.

Your analysis of style should be connected to the writer's intended audience. Is, for example, the biography informally written, designed for a nonspecialist, or is it heavily documented with notes and filled with undefined specialist terms? Be sure to include information about the author's style, not just an assertion that you found the work easy or hard to follow.

A good summary of content and analysis of features and style can point the way to a fair and sensible evaluation. If, for example, you have many problems understanding a book aimed at a general audience, then it is fair to say that the author has not successfully reached the intended audience. If, on the other hand, you selected a book to review that was written for specialists, then your struggle to read is not relevant to a fair evaluation. A reviewer's job is to judge if the book can reach its intended audience.

Your evaluation should include an assessment of content and format. Did the book or film fulfill its apparent purpose? Was it as thorough as you expected in the light of other works on the same or similar subject? For instance, a study of American literature in the 1920s that fails to mention Ernest Hemingway would surely be viewed as incomplete and thus flawed.

There is no simple formula for synthesizing summary, analysis, and evaluation in a review. Some instructors simplify the task by requiring a two-part review: summary first and then analysis and evaluation. If you are not encouraged to make this separation, then some blending is probably expected, but you still may want to begin with some summary. Often reviewers begin with a sentence that is both an attention-getter and a broad statement of the work's subject. An evaluation, in general terms, follows in sentence two, and then the reviewer uses a "summary–analysis–evaluation" pattern.

Study the following annotated review by John Tallmadge for the *New York Times Book Review* to see how he blends summary, analysis, and evaluation. Note how much information he provides in just one long paragraph.

Rediscovering America: John Muir in His Time and Ours

By Frederick Turner (Viking, $25)

Attention-getting opening sentence that includes author, subject of biography, and intriguing quotation.

Statement of the book's subject

Information about the author

Summary

With implied evaluation; biography would have been better with this material included.

Content evaluation—negative

Details from the book

Evaluation of style

Analysis: subjects not included in study

Style evaluation—positive

According to Frederick Turner, when John Muir and Theodore Roosevelt spent three nights camping out in the Yosemite region, "two major figures in American history enacted in microcosm one of the culture's persistent dreams: creative truancy in the wild heart of the New World." How Muir (1838–1914), first president of the Sierra club, chose that dream and made it his own is the subject of this imaginative, beautifully written biography. Mr. Turner, a historian who has traveled to many of the places Muir knew, vividly evokes the ancient Scottish town where Muir was born, the Wisconsin farm where he grew up under a brutal fundamentalist father, his thousand-mile walk from Indiana to the Gulf of Mexico and the ecstatic first summer in the Sierra Nevada where he realized his calling as a naturalist-prophet. Mr. Turner shows Muir's major concepts maturing against the background of contemporary cultural history. Experienced readers will long for more detailed treatments of Muir's literary development, his complex personal relationships, his life as a fruit rancher and businessman, his impact on rich and powerful contemporaries like E. H. Harriman, and his Alaskan journeys, which Muir himself saw as the climax of a lifetime of studying glaciers. This book, written in masterly and loving style, still leaves a good many questions unanswered and many good stories untold.

Exercise: Analyzing a Review

Read the following book review by student Ian Habel and annotate it thoroughly, indicating passages of summary, analysis, and evaluation. Remember that one sentence can combine these elements. After reading and annotating, answer these questions:

1. Has the student provided enough summary to give readers a good idea of the book's subject matter?

2. Is the student's evaluation clear and forceful?

3. Based on reading this review, would you be inclined to read the book? Why or why not?

Student Review

WINCHESTER'S ALCHEMY: TWO MEN AND A BOOK

Ian Habel

One can hardly imagine a tale promising less excitement for a general audience than that of the making of the *Oxford English Dictionary*. The sensationalism of murder and insanity would have to labor intensely against the burden of lexicography in crafting a genuine page-turner on the subject. Much to my surprise, Simon Winchester, in writing *The Professor and the Madman: A Tale of Murder, Insanity, and the Making of* The Oxford English Dictionary, has succeeded in producing so compelling a story that I was forced to devour it completely in a single afternoon, an unprecedented personal feat.

The *Professor and the Madman* is the story of the lives of two apparently very different men and the work that brought them together. Winchester begins by recounting the circumstances that led to the incarceration of Dr. W. C. Minor, a well-born, well-educated, and quite insane American ex-Army surgeon. Minor, in a fit of delusion, had murdered a man whom he believed to have crept into his Lambeth hotel room to torment him in his sleep. The doctor is tried and whisked off to the Asylum for the Criminally Insane, Broadmoor.

The author then introduces readers to the other two main characters: the *OED* itself and its editor James Murray, a low-born, self-educated Scottish philologist. The shift in narrative focus is used to dramatic effect. The natural assumption on the part of the reader that these two seemingly unrelated plots must eventually meet urges us to read on in anticipation of that connection. As each chapter switches focus from one man to the other, it is introduced by a citation from the *OED*, reminding us that the story is ultimately about the dictionary. The citations also serve to foreshadow and provide a theme for the chapter. For example, the *OED* definition of *murder* heads the first chapter, relating to the details of Minor's crime.

Winchester acquaints us with the shortcomings of seventeenth- and eighteenth-century attempts at compiling a comprehensive dictionary of the English language. He takes us inside the meetings of the Philological Society, whose members proposed the compilation of the dictionary to end all dictionaries. The *OED* was to include examples of usage illustrating every shade of meaning for every word in the English language. Such a mammoth feat would require enlisting thousands of volunteer readers to comb the corpus of English literature in search of illustrative quotations to be submitted on myriad slips of paper. These slips of paper on each word would in turn be studied by a small army of editors preparing the definitions.

It is not surprising that our Dr. Minor, comfortably tucked away at Broadmoor, possessing both a large library and seemingly infinite free time, should become one of those volunteer readers. After all, we are still rightfully assuming some connection of the book's two plot lines. Yet what sets Dr. Minor apart from his fellow volunteers (aside from the details of his incarceration) is the remarkable efficiency with which he approached his task. Not content merely to fill out slips of paper for submission, Minor methodically indexed every possibly useful mention of any word appearing in his personal library. He then asked to be kept informed of the progress of the work, submitting quotations that would be immediately useful to editors. In this way he managed to "escape" his cell and plunge himself into the work of contemporaries, to become a part of a major event of his time.

Minor's work proved invaluable to the *OED*'s staff of editors, led by James Murray. With the two plot lines now intertwined, readers face such questions as "Will they find out that Minor is insane?" "Will Minor and Murray ever meet?" and "How long will they take to complete the dictionary?" The author builds suspense regarding a meeting of Minor and Murray by providing a false account of their first encounter, as reported by the American press, only to shatter us with the fact that this romantic version did not happen. I'll let Winchester give you the answers to these questions, while working his magic on you, drawing you into this fascinating tale of the making of the world's most famous dictionary.

Analyzing Two or More Sources

Newswriters and analysts, influenced by their particular ways of seeing the world, view events differently. Scientists examining the same set of facts do not always draw the same conclusions; neither do historians and biographers agree on the significance of the same documents. How do we recognize and cope with these disparities? As critical readers we analyze what we read, pose questions, and refuse to believe everything we find in print or hear on television. To develop your skills in recognizing differences, instructors frequently ask students to contrast the views of two or more writers. In psychology class, for example, you may be asked to contrast the views of Sigmund Freud and John B. Watson on childhood. In a communications course, you may be asked to contrast the moderator styles of two talk-show hosts. We can examine differences in content or presentation, or both. Here are guidelines for preparing a contrast of sources.

Guidelines for Preparing a Contrast of Sources

1. Work with sources that have something in common. Think about the context for each, that is, each source's subject and purpose. (It would not make much sense to contrast a textbook chapter on abusive parents, for example, with a TV talk show on the same subject because their contexts are so obviously different.)

2. Read actively to understand the content of written sources. Tape films, radio, or TV shows so that you can listen/view them several times, just as you would read a written source more than once.

3. Analyze for differences, focusing on your purpose in contrasting. If you are contrasting the ideas of two writers, for example, then your analysis will focus on ideas, not on writing style. To explore differences in two news accounts, you may want to consider all of the following: the impact of placement in the newspaper/magazine, accompanying photographs or graphics, length of each article, what is covered in each article, and writing styles. Prepare a list of specific differences.

4. Organize your contrast. It is usually best to organize by points of difference. If you write first about one source and then about the other, the ways that the sources differ may not be clear for readers. It is better to take the time to plan an organization that clearly reveals your contrast purpose in writing. To illustrate, a paper contrasting the writing styles of two authors can be organized according to the following pattern:

    Introduction: Introduce your topic and make clear your purpose to contrast styles of writer A and writer B.

    A1
    B1   > Sentence structures of writer A and writer B

    A2
    B2   > Word choice of writer A and writer B

    A3
    B3   > Metaphors used by writer A and writer B

    Conclusion: Explain the effect of the differences in style of the writers.

5. Be sure to illustrate and discuss each of the points of difference for each of the sources. Provide examples of word choice, for example, and then explain the differences in level of formality or connotation.

6. Always write for an audience who may be familiar with your general topic but not with the specific sources you are discussing. Be sure to provide adequate context (names, titles of works, etc.).

Exercise: Analyzing Two Sources

Read and annotate each of the following reviews. Think about differences in content, analysis, and evaluation. Prepare a list of points of difference you would include in a paper. Examine lists with your class partner or in small groups. Discuss differences and decide on one list. Organize your selected points of difference and list the details you would include to develop each point. Be prepared to explain and defend your choice of outline with other groups in the class.

Dinosaur

Sean O'Connell

An editor at City Search, Sean O'Connell wrote this review on May 19, 2000, for MSN.com Entertainment.

1   The first 15 minutes of Disney's *Dinosaur*, a blend of digital animation and lush scenic photography that chronicles a dinosaur egg's majestic journey over sea and sky, form the finest clip of modern animation audiences have ever seen. That is, until they watch the next 15 minutes. Disney's instant classic, which speculates on the events surrounding the meteor crash that may have wiped out the Earth's dinosaur population, manages to consistently one-up itself, at least visually, with groundbreaking assertiveness and ease.

2   The dinosaur in the egg is named Aladar (D. B. Sweeney), an Iguanodon raised by a clan of monkey-like creatures on an isolated but fertile island. When their world is unpredictably decimated by a fiery meteor storm in one of the film's many breathtaking sequences, Aladar and his friends join a band of surviving dinos who are searching for an undisturbed Eden dubbed the Nesting Grounds. Along the way, Aladar must face physical and moral challenges as he comes to lead the tribe and rescue his species from extinction.

3   Utilizing footage shot in such tropical locales as Kauai and Western Samoa, the animators have created a remarkable vision of Earth's Mesozoic Age. You can almost sense the filmmakers' pride and confidence as they pull the camera's eye back at regular intervals to show the magnitude of the world they've created. The simplistic plot, recycled from bits and pieces of recent Disney fare, might be the film's only flaw. *Dinosaur* labors at meticulous visual details adults will marvel over and then presents them with a story only a child could appreciate.

Disney's Digital *Dinosaur:* A Cretaceous Bambi

Stephen Hunter

This review of the movie *Dinosaur,* by *Washington Post* staff writer Stephen Hunter, was published in the *Post* on May 19, 2000.

1   See, I like it better when they come out of the sea and attack cities and eat people and stuff.

2   I don't like it when they're all cuddly and have eyes so moist and gooey with feeling that you could be looking into the young Michael J. Fox's baby blues.

3   So I didn't really like the Disney spoonful of sugar called *Dinosaur,* which appears to have more to do with the human potential movement than with life in the Cretaceous. In fact, it seems to be set in a new geological epoch: the Sensitivaceous.

4   That was an era when nature was less red in tooth and claw than pretty in pink. Aside from a few nasty predators, it was one big happy family, a big tent, a rainbow coalition, a multi-species hoedown.

5   The movie also reveals this astonishing fact, heretofore unsuspected in the annals of paleobiology: Dinosaurs were actually American teenagers of the '50s! That conceit—chipper, lovesick, spunky iguanodons with the character complexity of David and Ricky Nelson—all but destroys the film. When, after a few minutes of ravishingly pure visual storytelling, one of the creatures opens his yap and gives out with something like "Aw, Mom, we were just havin' fun!" the movie dies as if a giant meteorite had struck it and suffocated all the life forms in the Burbank digitalization lab.

6   Really. Who wants to see dinosaurs flirt? Who wants to see them spat? Who wants to see them bicker, whine and fib? Who wants dinosaur high jinks and zaniness? These are the largest and most splendid creatures that ever walked the Earth. With their lumbering grace and pure, shivering aggression, they have stalked our collective unconscious for generations, notably invading many a small child's mind and freeing him to see the pleasures of imagination.

7   They deserve so much better.

8   Is *Dinosaur* spectacular? And how. But maybe spectacle is overrated. Disney spent 10 years and millions of dollars on it, and the results are eerie: digitally created creatures so brilliantly engineered that their heavy flesh wobbles on their bones when they move, whose sense of weightiness, of skeletal structure, of power and palpable presence is astonishing. For at least 7, and possibly as many as 11, seconds.

9   In fact, some of the work may be *too* brilliant. Untold millions have been spent especially on faces, which have all the expressiveness of renowned actors: eyes that swell with pride or shrink with fear, throats that tighten, lips that dry, tongues that flick, subtle shifts in subcutaneous facial muscle that alter the structure, and therefore the emotional meaning, of the physiognomy.

10   But do animals really look this expressive? Contemplate one of the dino's closest living relatives, the 300-pound lizard called the Komodo dragon of the South China Sea. With depthless eyes and placid musculature hidden behind droopy swaths of greenish leather, his face is a study in impassivity. It looks like a sack hanging on a fence post until he strikes and devours dog or feral pig or child or photographer, and even then the only emotion is the con-

tortion of energy. Afterward, he returns to passivity, his eyes flat and black as opals. Although quite real, he's not nearly enough of an actor for the Mouse Factory.

11   Plot? The usual feel-good piffle played against a musical score that sounds like a collaboration among Nietzsche, Wagner and the chorus of the 13th Mechanized Panzer Infantry. Aladar (read by the less than illustrious ex-star D. B. Sweeney) is smarter than your usual dinosaur because he's been raised by lemurs.

12   Mixed at birth? Yes, it happened even then. In any event, under the impression that he is a 25-ton warmblooded arboreal proto-primate, he lives his life in the trees of some pretty off-shore island, happy but slightly miffed that he can't get a date.

13   One night, fire streaks across the night sky and a meteorite crashes into the sea—probably the movie's most spectacular moment. On the island, life is wiped out; Aladar and his immediate lemur circle escape to the mainland, where all the other dinosaurs have gathered for a trip.

14   One interesting note: I thought from the previews that this meteorite was the big one that ended the age of the dinosaurs, and so the movie, like Disney's many-generations-previous foray into dino life (the "Rite of Spring" sequence in 1940's *Fantasia*) would turn on the resonance of world's end. But no: It's just a plot device to get the dinosaurs from Point A to Point B.

15   So it's basically the story of a dinosaur wagon train with upstart Aladar, the sensitive, lemur-educated one, fighting the nasty Kron (voiced by Samuel E. Wright), a Marine lieutenant-colonel type, for command of the herd and its philosophy: go-getting militaristic seriousness or a more humane, less disciplined ethos of listening to the heart. If you can't figure out which way this one is going to tip, you haven't been to a movie in years.

16   Also at stake: the hand of Kron's sister, Neera (read by Julianna Margulies). Can an iguanodon look sexy? Well, depends on your taste, but this much is fact: The animators, with that unbelievable expressiveness of image, have given this big babe of a thunderliz a delicate, almost poetic look and a sense of wisdom and gentleness in her warm eyes. No question about it: I'd date her!

17   Meanwhile, carnotaurs—evidently the state-of-the-art term for *T. Rex*—and what look to be Disney's rip-off of Steven Spielberg's far more frightening velociraptors—nasty little speed merchants, with beaks and too many teeth, who travel in packs—stalk the big dinosaur herd as it wanders across the blasted zone in search of the promised land. Holy Moses! Many trivial adventures are encountered.

18   The occasional big moments are stunning, and kids from the ages of, say, 6 years to 6 years and 3 days will love it. Anyone younger will be scared; anyone older, bored.

Now read, analyze, and be prepared to discuss the following two essays. Consider: How is each essay related to the material covered in this chapter?

Word Games We Play

John Leo

Formerly an editor of *Commonweal*, a reporter for the *New York Times*, and an associate editor at *Time*, John Leo (b. 1935) writes a regular column for *U.S. News & World Report*. His essay on labeling appeared in that newsmagazine December 6, 1999.

1   Several columns ago, when I wrote that "students, disability activists, and pro-lifers" were demonstrating at Princeton, the copy desk here at *U.S. News* wanted to change "pro-lifers" to "abortion opponents." The proposed change was by the book. Like most news organizations, this magazine uses "abortion-rights activists" and "abortion opponents," not "pro-choice" and "pro-life." But in this case "abortion opponents" was clearly not an adequate term. The issue at Princeton wasn't abortion. It was infanticide. The university had appointed a professor who believes parents should be allowed to kill their severely disabled babies.

2   Here's the verbal issue, debated for years in newsrooms: Pro-lifers don't like the word "pro-choice" because it eliminates the noun that faces up to the violent act involved (abortion) and replaces it with a warm and toasty abstract word that always scores well in focus groups (choice). And pro-choicers don't like "pro-life" because it implies that supporters of the abortion option are pro-death.

3   But pro-lifers aren't one-issue activists. They strongly oppose euthanasia, doctor-assisted suicide, ordinary suicide, infanticide, and (often, but not always) capital punishment. Terms such as "antiabortion advocates" and "abortion opponents" fail to reflect this broad commitment to the "life" side of so many life-or-death issues. Out of fairness (and accuracy), the media should restore the "pro-life" tag or come up with something similar. Given the ideological makeup of the newsroom today, this change is unlikely. In fact, in editorial columns at least, there is a small but growing trend toward using the sneering term "anti-choice" to describe pro-life beliefs. The general newsroom tendency to let every group call itself whatever it wants to (gays, Native Americans, African-Americans) is suspended for right-to-life activists.

4   **Hot button.** A lot of word games are in play in the continuing dispute over "partial-birth abortion." The *U.S. News* stylebook warns that this term is "arguably inflammatory, so if you must use it, put 'partial-birth' in quotation marks." This seems like a fair way to handle it. The term points clearly to the procedure under discussion (as the journalistic catch-phrase "certain late-term abortions" does not), while the quote marks signal that the term is a contested one.

5   Again, the *U.S. News* stylebook makes sense: "Alternative terms, which have problems of their own, include 'a form of late-term abortion,' (which is so broad that it is obfuscating) and 'intact dilation and extraction' (which is obfuscatingly clinical)."

6   Skirmishes over language are everywhere these days, often driven by the culture war. The left strongly favors the term "affirmative action," which draws a warm response in polls, and strongly resents the term "race and gender preferences," which always draws heavy poll opposition. So when opponents of affirmative action gathered petitions to get a ban on race and gender preferences on the ballot in the City of Houston, the mayor and City Council undermined the effort by changing the ballot wording at the last minute. The original antipreference text, derived from the 1964 Civil Rights Act, said "the City of Houston shall not discriminate against or grant preferential treatment to any individual or group on the basis of race, sex, ethnicity, or national origin. . . ." This wording was changed to "Shall the Charter of the City of Houston be amended to end the use of affirmative action for women and minorities . . . ?" Because of the positive aura around the term "affirmative action," voters said no. (Versions of the original wording passed handily in California and Washington State.) A Texas judge threw out the results of the vote. An appeals court is considering

the language issue, which has been legally contested for two years now, with months or perhaps another year still to go.

7   Support for affirmative action is now regarded as so sensitive to language that the left is busy looking for words to substitute for "preferences." The White House has discussed "race-based" proposals, several scholars favor "race-sensitive" college admissions and Jesse Jackson talks of "race-caring" policies. Success is presumed to be in the wording, not the plans themselves.

8   Wording, in fact, is often crucial. For instance, the euthanasia/assisted suicide issue has widely become known as the "right-to-die" issue. Committing suicide with the help of a doctor, in fact, is not broadly recognized as a right, but the "right-to-die" language has created the opinion that it already is.

9   As the word "euthanasia" gives way to the term "assisted suicide," issues of consent are beginning to blur. Some forms of nonconsensual "assistance" to the extremely ill are discussed under the heading of "suicide," just as the first wave of serious proposals for medical killing are being positioned as "assistance."

10   This intellectual and moral blurring is helped along by terms like "aid in dying," which can cover everything from holding a dying person's hand to employing doctors to dispatch sick people who have never requested death. Doctors in the Netherlands have indeed slid down this slippery slope, which is made all the more slippery by slick language. The obvious is true: Words matter.

Questions for Reading and Analysis

1. What are *U.S. News*'s acceptable terms for those supporting and those opposing abortion?

2. What are the objections to the terms *pro-life* and *pro-choice*?

3. Why did the author want to use *pro-life* in his column on Princeton demonstrations?

4. Why does Leo doubt that *pro-life* will ever be acceptable in newsrooms? What are we invited to infer about those who work in newsrooms?

5. What is the issue over the procedure known as "partial-birth" abortion?

6. What is the connotation of *affirmative action*? What is the connotation of *race and gender preferences*?

7. What terms are now being substituted for *euthanasia*?

8. What is Leo's thesis?

Questions for Discussion and Response

1. Explain why the term *affirmative action* is considered more positive than *race and gender preferences*.

2. Explain how the new terms for euthanasia lead, in Leo's view, to "intellectual and moral blurring." Do you agree with Leo's judgment here? Why or why not?

3. Leo refers, in paragraph 3, to the idea that each group has a right to name itself. A corollary to this idea is that groups can refer to themselves with words that

outsiders cannot use without fear of retaliation. Do these ideas make sense to you? (For example, is it appropriate to call your friend Charles "Chuck" when he does not want to use that nickname?) Explain your position.

4. Leo gives three examples of acceptable group labels. Can you think of other groups for whom there are acceptable and unacceptable names? What are the differences in connotation that make the unacceptable name unacceptable?

Let the Going Get Tough—We Have Our SUVs

Ronald R. Fraser

A former transportation specialist, Ronald Fraser holds a Ph.D. in public policy from George Mason University and is president and senior editor of the Cheshire Company, an organization that provides research, writing, and editorial services to business and government.

1   At first glance, America's SUV craze seems illogical. Only when it is viewed as part of an emerging grass-roots highway policy does it make sense. After all, why would millions of Americans trade in comfortable two-wheel-drive vehicles for rugged, four-wheel-drive Broncos, Pathfinders and Cherokees—vehicles capable of handling adverse road conditions seldom found anywhere in the United States? The only explanation that makes any sense is that Americans dearly want a more challenging driving experience.

2   Starting in the 1950s, U.S. highway policies focused on constructing the 41,000-mile Interstate system, a smooth, high-speed network designed for two-wheel-drive vehicles. Perhaps the grandest public works project in history, the Interstate, completed in 1991 at a cost of $129 billion, is a symbol of the auto's golden age.

3   Much of this aging roadway system needs a face lift, though, and we are looking at skyrocketing maintenance costs over the coming decades. But is that what American motorists really want?

4   Because so many people now are eager to spend their own money to equip their vehicles for a roadless environment, perhaps it makes little sense for the federal government to continue overspending on our highway infrastructure.

5   If Americans want the frontier experience promised by their Broncos and Durangos, why should out-of-date highway policies stand in their way? Why should taxpayers who drive conventional cars spend billions to maintain smooth roads when millions of American drivers are ready for the off-road experience?

6   Here's a highway plan for the new century.

7   First, Interstate maintenance spending should reflect the growing number of SUVs. As their numbers go up, Interstate maintenance spending should go down. Once four-wheel drive SUVs top 50 percent, we can cease maintaining half of all Interstate lanes and allow them to revert to the mud-and-rut conditions of the 19th century trails from which they are descended.

8   Next, because the SUV people will drive readily in the more challenging unmaintained Interstate lanes, they will be spared paying federal gas taxes at the pump. Conventional automobiles, on the other hand, will continue to enjoy the smooth ride found in the lanes that are well maintained and will continue to pay the federal gas taxes.

9   Finally, while the gas-sucking SUV set might boost our national fuel consumption, this cost will be offset by the huge savings associated with lower road repair costs. On balance, the environment will benefit from a new policy that no longer attempts to pave America. The new policy promises to return thousands of miles of highway to their earlier condition. SUV drivers, accused of fouling the environment through their wasteful use of fossil fuels, can represent themselves as dedicated conservationists.

10   With the passage of time, the Interstate system will take on a frontier look and feel, but Americans are ready for it. A rugged John Wayne frontier spirit already rules on most city and suburban roadways. All we need is a national highway policy to match it.

Questions for Reading and Analysis

1. What is Fraser's subject?

2. What are the details of Fraser's "highway plan"? Are we to embrace this highway plan?

3. What is the author's primary strategy? What is Fraser's attitude toward SUVs? What word choice helps you answer this question?

4. What, then, is Fraser's thesis? What key points does he want us to understand?

Questions for Discussion and Response

1. Do you enjoy and appreciate the strategy that Fraser uses, or are you bothered by it in some way? If you appreciate it, what makes it clever? If you are bothered, why?

2. Can you explain the current appeal of SUVs?

3. Should SUVs be held to the same emissions standards as cars? Should the Federal government require more fuel-efficient cars and other vehicles? Why or why not?

Writing Assignments

1. Analyze the style of one of the essays from Section IV. ("The Idiocy of Urban Life," p. 574, and "I Have a Dream," p. 616, are good choices.) Rather than trying to comment on every element of style, select several elements that seem to characterize the writer's style and examine them in detail. Remember that style analyses are written for an audience familiar with the work. Thus, summary is not necessary or appropriate.

2. Many of the authors included in this text have written books that you will find in your library. Select one that interests you, read it, and prepare a review of it that synthesizes summary, analysis, and evaluation. Prepare a review of about 300 words; assume that the book has just been published.

3. Choose two newspaper and/or magazine articles that differ in their discussion of the same person, event, or product. You may select two different articles on a person in the news, two different accounts of a news event, an advertisement and

a *Consumer Reports* analysis of the same product, or two reviews of a book or movie. Analyze differences in both content and presentation and then consider why the two accounts differ. Organize by points of difference and write to an audience not necessarily familiar with the articles.

4. Choose a recently scheduled public event (the Super Bowl, the Olympics, a presidential election, the Academy Award presentations, the premiere of a new television series) and find several articles written before and several after the event. First compare articles written after the event to see if they agree factually. If not, decide which article appears to be more accurate and why. Then examine the earlier material and decide which was the most and which the least accurate. Write an essay in which you explain the differences in speculation before the event and why you think these differences exist. Your audience will be aware of the event but not necessarily aware of the articles you are studying.

The World of Argument

CHAPTER 3

The Basics of Argument

In this section we will explore the processes of thinking logically and analyzing issues to reach informed judgments. Why should you be able to present sound arguments and understand the arguments of others? Recognizing good evidence and making good sense are powerful tools on the job, in our personal lives, and in our roles as citizens. Your ability to shape an intelligent, effective argument will win the respect of thoughtful people. Mature people do not need to agree on all issues to respect one another's good sense, but they do have little patience with uninformed or illogical statements masquerading as argument.

Characteristics of Argument

ARGUMENT IS CONVERSATION WITH A GOAL

When you enter into an argument (as speaker, writer, or reader), you become a participant in an ongoing debate about an issue. Since you are probably not the first to address the issue, you need to be aware of the ways that the issue has been debated by others and then seek to advance the conversation, just as you would if you were having a more casual conversation with friends. If the time of the movie is set, the discussion now turns to whose car to take or where to meet. If you were to just repeat the time of the movie, you would add nothing useful to the conversation. Also, if you were to change the subject to a movie you saw last week, you would annoy your friends by not offering useful information or showing that you valued the current conversation. Just as with your conversation about the movie, you want your argument to stay focused on the issue, to respect what others have already contributed, and to make a useful addition to our understanding of the issue.

ARGUMENT TAKES A STAND ON AN ARGUABLE ISSUE

A meaningful argument concentrates on a debatable issue. We usually do not argue about facts. "Professor Jones's American literature class meets at 10:00 on Mondays" is not arguable. It is either true or false. We can check the schedule of classes to find out. (Sometimes the facts change; new facts replace old ones.) We also do not debate personal preferences for the simple reason that they are just that—personal. If the debate is about the appropriateness of boxing as a sport, for you to declare that you would rather play tennis is to fail to advance the conversation. You have expressed a personal preference, interesting perhaps, but not relevant to the debate.

ARGUMENT USES REASONS AND EVIDENCE

Some arguments merely "look right." That is, conclusions are drawn from facts, but the facts are not those that actually support the assertion, or the conclusion is not the only or the best explanation of those facts. To shape convincing arguments, we need more than an array of facts. We need to think critically, to analyze the issue, to see relationships, to weigh evidence. We need to avoid the temptation to "argue" from emotion only, or to believe that just stating our opinion is the same thing as building a sound argument.

ARGUMENT INCORPORATES VALUES

Arguments are based not just on reason and evidence but also on the beliefs and values we hold and think that our audience may hold as well. In a reasoned debate, you want to make clear the values that you consider relevant to the argument. In an editorial defending the sport of boxing, one editor wrote that boxing "is a sport because the world has not yet become a place in which the qualities that go into excellence in boxing [endurance, agility, courage] have no value" (*Washington Post*, February 5, 1983). But James J. Kilpatrick also appeals to values when he argues, in an editorial critical of boxing, that we should not want to live in a society "in which deliberate brutality is legally authorized and publicly applauded" (*Washington Post*, December 7, 1982). Observe, however, the high level of seriousness in the appeal to values. Neither writer settles for a simplistic personal preference: "boxing is exciting" or "boxing is too violent."

ARGUMENT RECOGNIZES THE TOPIC'S COMPLEXITY

Much false reasoning (the logical fallacies discussed in Chapter 4) results from a writer's oversimplifying an issue. A sound argument builds on careful analysis that begins with an understanding that most issues are terribly complicated. The wise person approaches such ethical concerns as abortion or euthanasia or such public policy issues as tax cuts or trade agreements with the understanding that there are many philosophical, moral, and political issues that complicate discussions of these topics. Recognizing an argument's complexity may also lead us to an understanding that there can be more than one "right" position. The thoughtful arguer respects the views of others and avoids ridiculing opposing points of view.

The Shape of Argument: The Aristotelian Model

Still one of the best ways to understand the basics of argument is to reflect on what the Greek philosopher Aristotle describes as the three "players" in any argument: the *writer (or speaker)*, the *argument itself*, and the *reader (or audience)*. Aristotle calls the argument itself the *logos*—the assertion and support for that assertion. A successful argument needs a logical and convincing *logos*. An argument also implies an audience, those whose views on our topic we want to influence. Aristotle calls this part of argument *pathos*. Good arguers need to be alert to the values and attitudes of their audience and to appeal effectively to the emotions of that audience. However, Aristotle also explains that part of our appeal to an audience rests in the *logos*, our logic and evidence. An "argument" that is all emotional appeal will not move thoughtful audiences.

FIGURE 3–1   Aristotelian Structure of Argument

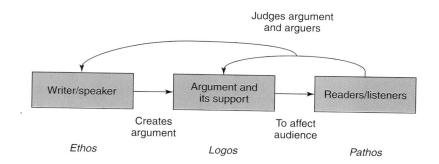

Finally (and for Aristotle the most important of the three players) is the writer/speaker, or *ethos*. No argument, Aristotle asserts, no matter how logical seeming, no matter how appealing emotionally, will succeed if the audience rejects the arguer's credibility, the writer's "ethical" qualities. As members of the audience we need to believe that the arguer is a person of knowledge, honesty, and goodwill or we will not respond favorably.

As Figure 3–1 illustrates, we argue, always, in a specific context of three interrelated parts. We present support for a concrete assertion, thesis, or claim to a specific audience whose demands and expectations and character we have given thought to when shaping our argument. And we present ourselves as informed, competent, and reliable so that our audience will give serious attention to our argument. Remember: your audience evaluates *you* as a part of their evaluation of your argument. Lose your credibility and you lose your argument.

The Shape of Argument: The Toulmin Model

British philosopher Stephen Toulmin adds to what we have learned from Aristotle by focusing our attention on the basics of the argument itself. First, consider this definition of argument: *An argument consists of evidence and/or reasons presented in support of an assertion or claim that is either stated or implied.* For example:

1. Claim: We should not go skiing today
   Evidence: because it is too cold.

2. Evidence: Because some laws are unjust,
   Claim: civil disobedience is sometimes justified.

3. Evidence: All human life is sacred.
   Claim: Therefore abortion is wrong.

The basics of a complete argument, Toulmin asserts, are actually a bit more complex than these examples suggest. Each argument has a third part that is not stated in the

FIGURE 3-2   The Toulmin Structure of Argument

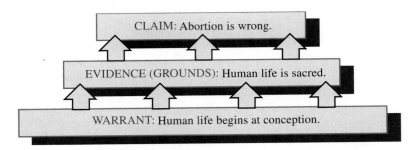

above examples. This third part is the "glue" that connects the support—the evidence and reasons—to the argument's claim and thus fulfills the logic of the argument. This glue, what Toulmin calls the argument's *warrants*, are the principles or assumptions that allow us to assert that our evidence or reasons—what Toulmin calls the *grounds*—do indeed support our claim. (Figure 3–2 illustrates the basics of the Toulmin model of argument.)

Look again at the sample arguments to see what principles or assumptions must be accepted to make each one work:

1. Claim: We should not go skiing today.
   Evidence: It is too cold.
   Underlying assumptions   When it is too cold, skiing is not fun; the
   (warrants):   activity is not sufficient to keep one from
                                     becoming uncomfortable.

2. Claim: Civil disobedience is sometimes justified.
   Evidence: Some laws are unjust.
   Underlying assumptions   To get unjust laws changed, people need to
   (warrants):   be made aware of the injustice. Acts of civil
                                     disobedience will get people's attention and make
                                     them aware that the laws need changing.

3. Claim: Abortion is wrong.
   Evidence: Human life is sacred.
   Underlying assumptions   Human life begins at conception.
   (warrants):

Assumptions play an important role in shaping an argument, so you need to be sure to clarify those assumptions on which your argument rests. Note, for instance, another assumption operating in the first argument, namely, that the temperature considered "uncomfortable" for the speaker will also be uncomfortable for her companions, an uncertain assumption. In the second example, the assumption is less debatable, for acts of civil disobedience usually get media coverage and serve to dramatize the participants' views. (Not everyone may agree that the laws are unjust, but that is another argument.)

The underlying assumption in the third example underscores the importance of becoming aware of each argument's glue, for often the warrants themselves need to be defended or supported in some way. The debate over when human life begins is at the center of the debate over abortion rights.

Group Exercise: Building Arguments

With your class partner or in small groups, examine each of the following claims. Select two claims, think of one statement that could serve as evidence for each claim, and then think of one or more underlying assumptions (warrants) that complete each of the arguments.

1. Professor White is not a good teacher.
2. Colleges should admit students only on the basis of academic merit.
3. Americans need to reduce the fat in their diets.
4. Tiger Woods is a great golfer.
5. Physical education classes should be graded pass/fail.

The Language of Claims and Support

To build sound arguments, you need to recognize the kinds of statements that function as claims and as support. An argument's claim makes an assertion that can be debated. Arguments are not about questions that ask for information (Are you going to dinner?), personal preferences (My favorite dessert is pecan pie), or obvious facts (This is Chapter 3). These are not arguable assertions; they do not need support from reasons and evidence. The statement "I liked President Reagan" states a personal preference, but the statement "President Reagan was a great president" is open to debate and thus becomes a claim needing support.

> ☑ NOTE: Sometimes we present arguable assertions in statements that are qualified to sound like personal preferences. If you were to write, "I believe that high school students should be required to do more homework," you would have a claim that should be supported with reasons. Placing such qualifiers as "I believe," "I think," or "I feel" in an assertion does not free you from the need to support your claim. The statement "I believe that President Reagan was a great president" calls for an argument based on evidence and reasons.

Claims to arguments are usually either inferences or judgments, for these are debatable assertions. And the support provided for claims will be composed of facts, opinions based on facts (inferences), or opinions based on values, beliefs, or ideas (judgments)—

or some combination of the three. Let's consider what kinds of statements each of these terms describes.

FACTS

Facts are statements that are readily verifiable. Factual statements refer to what can be counted or measured or confirmed by reasonable observers or trusted experts.

> There are 26 desks in Room 110.
>
> In the United States about 400,000 people die each year as a result of smoking.

These are factual statements. We can verify the first by observation, by counting. The second fact comes from medical records: We rely on trusted record-keeping sources and medical experts for verification. By definition, we do not argue about the facts. In a dispute over "facts," one person has the facts and the other does not. Usually. Sometimes "facts" change, as we learn more about the universe we live in. For example, only in the last 30 years has convincing evidence been gathered to demonstrate the relationship between smoking and various illnesses of the heart and lungs. Further, except for the trivia buff, facts are useful only when we understand what they mean. How many desks there are in Room 110 really does not matter unless more students arrive for class than there are desks for them to use.

INFERENCES

Inferences are opinions based on facts. They are the conclusions we draw from an analysis of facts.

> There will not be enough desks in Room 110 for upcoming fall-semester classes.
>
> Smoking is a serious health hazard.

Predictions of an increase in student enrollment for the coming fall semester lead to the inference that most English classes scheduled in Room 110 will run with several more students per class than last year. The dean should order new desks. Similarly, we infer from the number of deaths that smoking is a health problem; statistics show more people dying from tobacco than from AIDS, or murder, or car accidents, causes of death that get media coverage but do not produce nearly as many deaths.

Inferences vary in their closeness to the facts supporting them. That the sun will "rise" tomorrow is an inference, but we count on its happening, acting as if it is a fact. However, the first inference stated above is based not just on the fact of 26 desks but on another inference—a projected increase in student enrollment—and two assumptions. The argument looks like this:

Fact:	There are 26 desks in Room 110.
Inference:	There will be more first-year students next year.
Assumptions:	1. English will remain a required course.
	2. No additional classrooms are available for English classes.
Claim:	There will not be enough desks in Room 110 for upcoming fall-semester classes.

This inference could be challenged by a different analysis of the facts supporting enrollment projections. Or, if additional rooms can be found, the dean will not need to order new desks. Inferences can be part of the support of an argument, or they can be the claim of an argument.

JUDGMENTS

Judgments are opinions based on values, beliefs, or philosophical concepts. (Judgments also include opinions based on personal preferences, but we have already excluded these from argument.) Judgments concern right and wrong, good and bad, better or worse, should and should not. When support other than purely personal preferences can be presented, judgments are arguable:

> No more than 26 students should be enrolled in any English class.

> Cigarette advertising should be eliminated, and the federal government should develop an antismoking campaign.

To support the first judgment, we need to explain what constitutes overcrowding, or what constitutes the best class size for effective teaching. If we can support our views on effective teaching, we may be able to convince the college president that ordering more desks for Room 110 is not the best solution to an increasing enrollment in English classes. The second judgment also offers a solution to a problem, in this case a national health problem. To reduce the number of deaths, we need to reduce the number of smokers, either by encouraging smokers to quit or not to start. The underlying assumption: Advertising does affect behavior.

Exercise: Facts, Inferences, and Judgments

Compile a list of three statements of fact, three inferences, and three judgments. Try to organize them into three related sets, as illustrated here:

- Smoking is prohibited on flights within the United States.
- Secondhand smoke is a health hazard.
- Smoking should be prohibited on all flights, national and international.

We can classify judgments to see better what kind of assertion we are making and, therefore, what kind of support we need to argue effectively.

FUNCTIONAL JUDGMENTS (guidelines for judging how something or someone works or could work):

> Jack Nicklaus is the best golfer to play the game.

> Antismoking advertising will reduce the number of smokers.

AESTHETIC JUDGMENTS (guidelines for judging art, literature, music, or natural scenes):

> The sunrise was beautiful.

> *The Great Gatsby*'s structure, characters, and symbols are perfectly wedded to create the novel's vision of the American dream.

ETHICAL JUDGMENTS (guidelines for group or social behavior):

> Lawyers should not advertise.

> It is discourteous to talk during a film or lecture.

MORAL JUDGMENTS (guidelines of right and wrong for judging individuals and for establishing legal principles):

> Taking another person's life is wrong.

> Equal rights under the law should not be denied on the basis of race or sex.

Functional and aesthetic judgments generally require defining key terms and establishing criteria for the judging or ranking made by the assertion. How, for example, do we compare golfers? On the amount of money won? The number of tournaments won? Or the consistency of winning throughout one's career? What about the golfer's quality and range of shots? Ethical and moral judgments may be more difficult to support because they depend not just on how terms are defined and criteria established but on values and beliefs as well. If taking another person's life is wrong, why isn't it wrong in war? Or is it? These are difficult questions that require thoughtful responses.

Exercises: Understanding Assumptions, Facts, False Facts, Inferences, and Judgments

1. Categorize the judgments you wrote for the previous exercise (p. 79) as either aesthetic, moral, ethical, or functional. Alternatively, compile a list of three judgments that you then categorize.

2. For each judgment listed for exercise 1, generate one statement of support, either a fact or inference or another judgment. Then state the warrant (underlying assumption) required to complete each argument.

3. Read the following article and then complete the exercise that follows. This exercise tests both careful reading and your understanding of the differences among facts, inferences, and judgments.

Paradise Lost

Richard Morin

Richard Morin, a journalist with the *Washington Post*, writes a regular Sunday column titled "Unconventional Wisdom," a column presenting interesting new information from the social sciences. The following article was Morin's column for July 9, 2000.

1   Here's my fantasy vacation: Travel back in time to the 1700s, to some languid South Pacific island paradise where ripe fruit hangs heavy on the trees and the native islanders live in peace with nature and with each other.

2   Or at least that was my fantasy vacation until I talked to anthropologist Patrick Kirch, one of the country's leading authorities on the South Pacific and director of the Phoebe Hearst Museum of Anthropology at the University of California at Berkeley.

3   The South Seas islands painted by Paul Gauguin and celebrated by Robert Louis Stevenson were no Gardens of Eden, Kirch writes in his riveting new history of the South Pacific, *On the Road of the Winds*. Many of these islands witnessed episodes of environmental depredation, endemic warfare and bloody ritual long before seafaring Europeans first visited. "Most islands of the Pacific were densely populated by the time of European contact, and the human impact on the natural ecosystem was often disastrous—with wholesale decimation of species and loss of vast tracts of land," he said.

4   Kirch says we can blame the French for all the loose talk about a tropical nirvana. "French philosophers of the Enlightenment saw these islands, especially Tahiti, as the original natural society where people lived in a state of innocence and food fell from the trees," he said. "How wrong they were."

5   French explorer Louis Antoine de Bougainville visited Tahiti for two weeks in 1769 and thought he discovered a paradise awash in social tolerance and carefree sex. Bougainville's breathless description of Tahiti became the basis for Jean Jacques Rousseau's concept of *l'homme naturel*—the noble savage.

6   Savage, indeed. Even as Bougainville poked around their craggy volcanic island, Rousseau's "noble savages" were busy savaging each other. The Tahitians were in the midst of a bitter civil war, complete with ritual sacrifice to their bloodthirsty war god, Oro. On Mangaia in the Cook Islands, Kirch discovered ovens and pits filled with the charred bones of men, women, and even children.

7   And forget that free-love nonsense. Dating, mating and reproduction were tricky business throughout the South Seas several hundred years ago. To keep the population in check, the residents of tiny Tikopia in the Santa Cruz Islands practiced infanticide. Abortion also was common. And to "concentrate" their bloodlines, Kirch said, members of the royal class in Hawaii married their brothers and sisters. If they only knew . . .

8   Not all South Seas islands were little cesspools. On some of the smaller islands, early Polynesians avoided cultural collapse by adopting strict population control measures, including enforced suicide. "Some young men were encouraged to go to sea and not return," he said.

9   Perhaps the best example of the havoc wrought by the indigenous peoples of the South Pacific is found on desolate Easter Island, home of the monolithic stone heads that have gazed out from the front of a thousand travel brochures. Until recently, researchers believed that Easter Island's open, grassy plains and barren knife-point volcanic ridges had always been, well, grassy plains and barren ridges.

10   Not true, says Kirch. The island was once covered with dense palm and hardwood forests. But by the 1700s, when the first Europeans arrived, these forests had been burned by the islanders to clear land for agriculture, transforming lush groves into semitropical tundra. "On Easter Island, the ultimate extinction of the palm and other woody plants had a further consequence: the inability to move or erect the large stone statues" because there were no logs to use as rollers to move the giant heads from the quarries, Kirch writes.

11   The stone carvers' society collapsed, as did Easter Island culture. By the time Dutch explorer Jacob Roggeveen arrived on Easter Sunday in 1722, residents had taken to living in underground caves for protection from the social chaos that had enveloped their island home.

12   When viewed today, Kirch says, the monoliths remain an "imposing stone text that suggests a thousand human sagas." They also carry a lesson to our age, he argues—warning us "to achieve a sustainable relationship with our planet"—or else.

Label each of the following sentences as F (fact), FF (false fact), I (inference), or J (judgment).

_____   **1.** In the 1700s native South Pacific islanders lived in peace and harmony.

_____   **2.** It is foolish to romanticize life on South Sea islands.

_____   **3.** French philosopher Rousseau based his idea of the noble savage on the Tahitians.

_____   **4.** The stone statues on Easter Island suggest many stories.

_____   **5.** In the past, noble Hawaiians married within their families.

_____   **6.** Tahitians were savage people.

_____   **7.** Some South Pacific islanders used to practice abortion and infanticide.

_____   **8.** Easter Island has always had grassy plains and barren ridges.

_____   **9.** We must find and use "sustainable" strategies, or we will destroy our environment.

_____   **10.** Marrying family members is not a smart idea.

More on Toulmin's Analysis of Argument

Philosopher Stephen Toulmin was particularly interested in stressing the great range in the strength or probability of various arguments. Some kinds of arguments are stronger than others because of the language or logic they use. Other arguments must, necessarily, be heavily qualified for the claim to be supportable. Toulmin developed his language for the structure of arguments to provide a strategy for analyzing the degree of probability in a given argument and to remind us of the need to qualify some kinds of claims. You have already seen how the idea of warrants, or assumptions, helps us think about the "glue" that presumably makes a given argument work. Additional Toulmin terms and concepts can help us analyze the arguments of others and prepare more convincing arguments of our own.

CLAIMS

A claim is what the argument asserts or seeks to prove. It answers the question "What is your point?" In an argumentative speech or essay, the claim is the speaker or writer's main idea or thesis. Although an argument's claim "follows" from reasons and evidence, we often present an argument—whether written or spoken—with the claim stated near the beginning of the presentation. We can be aided in recognizing an argument's claim by recognizing that we can have claims of fact, claims of value, and claims of policy.

Claims of Fact

Although facts usually support claims, we do argue over some facts. Historians and biographers may argue over what happened in the past, although they are more likely to argue over the significance of what happened. Scientists also argue over the facts, over how to classify an unearthed fossil, for example, or whether the fossil indicates that the animal had feathers. For example:

> Claim: The small, predatory dinosaur *Deinonychus* hunted its prey in packs.

This claim is supported by the discovery of several fossils of *Deinonychus* close together and with the fossil bones of a much larger dinosaur. Their teeth have also been found in or near the bones of dinosaurs that have died in a struggle.

Assertions about what will happen are sometimes classified as claims of fact, but they can also be labeled as inferences supported by facts. Predictions about a future event may be classified as claims of fact:

> Claim: The United States will win the most gold medals at the 2004 Olympics.

> Claim: I will get an A on tomorrow's psychology test.

What evidence would you use today to support each of these claims? (And, did the first one turn out to be correct?)

Claims of Value

These include moral, ethical, and aesthetic judgments. Assertions that use such words as *good* or *bad*, *better* or *worse*, and *right* or *wrong* will be claims of value. The following are all claims of value:

> Claim: Pete Sampras is a better tennis player than Andre Agassi.

> Claim: *Adventures of Huckleberry Finn* is one of the most significant American novels.

> Claim: Cheating hurts others and the cheater too.

> Claim: Abortion is wrong.

Arguments in support of judgments demand relevant evidence, careful reasoning, and an awareness of the assumptions one is making. Support for claims of value often include other value statements. For example, to support the claim that censorship is bad, arguers often assert that the free exchange of ideas is good and necessary in a democracy. The support assertion is itself a value statement. The arguer may believe, probably correctly, that most people will more readily agree to the support value (the free exchange of ideas is good) than to the claim (censorship is bad).

Claims of Policy

Finally, claims of policy are assertions about what should or should not happen, what the government ought or ought not to do, how to best solve social problems. Claims of policy debate, for example, college rules, state gun laws, or federal aid to Africans suffering from AIDS. The following are claims of policy:

Claim: College newspapers should not be controlled in any way by college authorities.

Claim: States should not have laws allowing people to carry concealed weapons.

Claim: The United States must provide more aid to African countries where 25 percent or more of the citizens have tested positive for HIV.

Claims of policy are often closely tied to judgments of morality or political philosophy, but they also need to be grounded in feasibility. That is, your claim needs to be doable, to be based on a thoughtful consideration of the real world and the complexities of public policy issues.

GROUNDS (OR DATA OR EVIDENCE)

The term *grounds* refers to the reasons and evidence provided in support of a claim. Although the words *data* and *evidence* can also be used, note that *grounds* is the more general term because it clearly can include reasons or logic as well as more concrete evidence such as examples or statistics. We determine the grounds of an argument by asking the question "Why do you think that?" or "How do you know that?" When writing your own arguments, you can ask yourself these questions and answer by using a *because* clause:

Claim: Abortion is wrong

           because

Grounds: human life is sacred.

Claim: Pete Sampras is a better tennis player than Andre Agassi

           because

Grounds: 1. he has been ranked number one longer than Agassi,

           2. he has won more tournaments than Agassi, and

           3. he has won more major tournaments than Agassi.

WARRANTS

Why should we believe that your grounds do indeed support your claim? Your argument's warrants answer this question. They explain why your evidence really is evidence. Sometimes warrants reside in language itself, in the meanings of the words we are using. If I am *younger* than my brother, then my brother must be *older* than I am. In a court case attempting to prove that Jones murdered Smith, the relation of evidence to claim is less assured. If the police investigation has been properly managed and the physical evidence is substantial, then Smith may be Jones's murderer. The prosecution has—presumably beyond a reasonable doubt—established motive, means, and opportunity for Smith to commit the murder. In many arguments based on statistical data, the argument's warrant rests on complex analyses of the statistics—and on the conviction that the statistics have been developed without error. In some philosophical arguments, the warrants are the logical structures (often shown mathematically) connecting a sequence of reasons. Still, without taking courses in statistics and logic, you can develop an alertness to the "good sense" of some arguments and the "dubious sense" of others. You know, for example, that good SAT scores are a predictor of success in college. Can you argue that you will do well in college because you have good SATs? No. We can determine only a statistical probability. We cannot turn probabilities about a group of people into a warrant about one person in the group. (In addition, SAT scores are only one predictor, one variable. Another key variable is motivation that translates into the time and energy a particular student will give to course work.)

In the anti-abortion argument we have begun as an example, the warrant is an assumption, a belief: *Human life begins at conception.* If human life does not begin until a baby is born, then, even if we agree that human life is sacred, we are not obligated to agree that abortion is wrong. Thus, the warrant is essential to make this argument work. What is the warrant for the Sampras claim?

Claim:	Pete Sampras is a better tennis player than Andre Agassi,
Grounds:	The three facts listed above.
Warrant:	It is appropriate to judge and rank tennis players on these kinds of statistics. That is, the better player is one who has held the number one ranking for the longest time, has won the most tournaments, and also has won the most major tournaments.

BACKING

Standing behind an argument's warrant may be additional *backing*. Backing answers the question "How do we know that your evidence is good evidence?" You may answer this question by providing authoritative sources for the data used (for example, the Census Bureau or the U.S. Tennis Association). Or, you may explain in detail the methodology of the experiments performed or the surveys taken. When scientists and social scientists present the results of their research, they anticipate the question of backing and automatically provide a detailed explanation of the process by which they acquired their evidence. In the O. J. Simpson trial, defense attorneys challenged the backing of the prosecution's argument. They questioned the handling of blood samples sent to labs for DNA testing. The defense attorneys wanted jury members to doubt the *quality* of the evidence, perhaps even to doubt the reliability of DNA testing altogether.

In the anti-abortion argument, what backing can be offered in defense of the grounds and warrant of the argument? Most who make this argument assume that we would all agree that human life is sacred (even if we might not use this religious terminology) and therefore should be protected by U.S. laws. It is the warrant that may be harder to provide backing for. One form of backing comes from religion: *Each human, including the fetus, contains a soul valued by God.* But of course many people do not share this religious belief and would, therefore, challenge this backing. Some have sought a scientific explanation of the beginning of human life, but with this approach there is also no agreed-upon answer, just the views of particular scientists who want to participate in this debate.

This discussion of backing returns us to the point that one part of any argument is the audience, those whom we want to convince. To create an effective argument, you need to assess the potential for acceptance of your warrants and backing. Is your audience likely to share your values, your religious beliefs, or your scientific approach to issues? If you are speaking to a group at your church, then backing based on the religious beliefs of that church may be effective. If, however, you are preparing an argument for a general audience (what your instructor is likely to tell you to prepare for most of the time), then using specific religious beliefs as warrants or backing probably will not produce an effective argument.

QUALIFIERS

Remember that Toulmin was especially interested in assessing the degree of probability in each argument. Some arguments are absolute; they can be stated without qualification: *If I am younger than my brother, then he must be older than I am.* Most arguments need some qualification; many need precise limitations. If, when playing bridge, I am dealt 8 spades, then my opponents and partner together *must* have 5 spade cards—because there are 13 cards of each suit in a deck of cards. My partner *probably* has one spade, but *could be* void of spades. My partner *possibly* has two or more spades, but I would be foolish to count on it.

To turn again to the anti-abortion argument, consider the absolute quality of the claim and the support for it. Suppose that a pregnant woman's life is in danger, and carrying the baby will kill her. If *all* human life is sacred—the grounds for the claim in our example—then presumably the mother's life is as sacred at the baby's. Perhaps the claim we have been using needs to be qualified: *Abortion is wrong except when the mother's life is in danger.*

Sweeping generalizations often come to us in the heat of a debate or when we first start to think about an issue. For example, *Gun control is wrong because it restricts individuals' rights.* But surely you do not mean all forms of gun control. (Remember: an unqualified assertion is understood by your audience to be absolute.) Would you sell guns to felons in prison or to children on the way to school? Obviously not. So let's try the claim again, this time with some qualifiers:

> Qualified claim: Adults without a criminal record should not be restricted in
> the purchase of guns.

Others may want the claim further qualified to eliminate certain types of guns or to control the number purchased or the process for purchasing. The gun-control debate is always about how the assertions should be qualified. In sum, think about the degree of probability of your claims or how much of an absolute can reasonably be defended.

REBUTTALS

Most arguments can be challenged. Smart debaters assume that there are people who will disagree with them and seek to anticipate the ways that opponents can counter their arguments. When preparing an argument, think about including rebuttals to the challenges you anticipate. Think of yourself as an attorney in a court case preparing *both* your argument *and* a defense of the other attorney's challenges to your argument. If you ignore the important role of counterarguments, you may not win the jury to your side.

Here is a simple argument broken down into its parts using Toulmin's terms:

Grounds:	Because Dr. Bradshaw has an attendance policy,
Claim:	students who miss more than seven classes will
Qualifier:	most likely (last year, Dr. Bradshaw did allow one student, in unusual circumstances, to continue in the class)

Claim (con't):   be dropped from the course.

Warrant: Dr. Bradshaw's syllabus explains her attendance policy, a

Backing: policy consistent with the concept of a discussion class that depends on student participation and consistent with the attendance policies of most of her colleagues.

Rebuttal: Although some students complain about an attendance policy of any kind, Dr. Bradshaw does explain her policy and her reasons for it. She also reminds students that the syllabus serves as a contract between them; if they choose to stay, they agree to abide by the guidelines explained on the syllabus.

Exercises: Applying Toulmin's Approach to Argument

1. You have seen Toulmin's terms of argument structure applied to the anti-abortion argument. Now, with your class partner or in small groups, develop an argument for abortion rights. Set up your argument on a page with each of Toulmin's terms listed down the left margin and your parts of the argument opposite the terms, as in the sample argument about class attendance given above.

2. In groups or on your own, build an argument for the claim "It is foolish to romanticize life on South Sea islands." Use information from Richard Morin's article "Paradise Lost" (pp. 80–82) for some of your grounds. Set up your argument on a page (or more) with each of Toulmin's terms listed down the left margin and your parts of the argument opposite the terms. (This exercise will give you some practice in incorporating information from your reading into the development of your argument.)

3. Select one of the following claims, or one of your own if your instructor approves, and build an argument, listing as many grounds as you would include if you were to develop this into an argumentative essay and paying careful attention to possible rebuttals of counterarguments. Use the same format as described in the previous exercises. Expect your outline to be more than one page.

   a. Professor White is (or is not) a good teacher.
   b. Colleges should (or should not) admit students only on the basis of academic merit.
   c. Americans need (or do not need) to reduce the fat in their diets.
   d. Physical education classes should (or should not) be graded pass/fail.
   e. Public schools should (or should not) have dress codes.
   f. Helmets for bicyclists should (or should not) be mandatory.
   g. Sales taxes on cigarettes should (or should not) be increased.
   h. All cigarette advertising should (or should not) be prohibited.

The Language of Argument

Because argument is more complex than we might first think, we have given some time to examining the basics of argument. But you know, of course, that arguments are not written in the bare-bones shapes we have been working with in this chapter. So, let's also think about the language we use to present an argument.

FIGURE 3–3   A Continuum of Argumentative Language

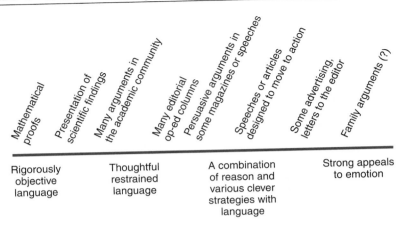

| Mathematical proofs | Presentation of scientific findings | Many arguments in the academic community | Many editorial op-ed columns | Persuasive arguments in some magazines or speeches | Speeches or articles designed to move to action | Some advertising, letters to the editor | Family arguments (?) |

Rigorously objective language

Thoughtful restrained language

A combination of reason and various clever strategies with language

Strong appeals to emotion

ARGUMENT OR PERSUASION?

We have looked at argument as a reasonable conversation with a goal; a claim is put forward and then defended with logic and evidence. Ideally underlying assumptions are understood and also defended when necessary. However, the heated debate at yesterday's lunch does not resemble this definition of argument. Often the term *persuasion* is used as a label for the heated debate and to separate such debates from the carefully reasoned argument. Unfortunately, this neat distinction between argument and persuasion does not describe the real world of debate. The thoughtful arguer also wants to be persuasive, to win over the audience. And highly emotional presentations of one's views can also contain relevant facts and sound claims. Instead of thinking of two separate categories—argument on the one hand and persuasion on the other—we are wiser to think in terms of a continuum from the most rigorous logic at one end to extreme flights of fantasy in some advertisements at the other end. Figure 3–3 suggests this continuum with some kinds of arguments placed along it.

IRONY OR SARCASM?

As you learned in Chapter 2, irony is a rhetorical strategy for giving one's words greater emphasis by actually saying (or writing) the opposite of what one means. Many writers use irony effectively to give punch to their arguments. Irony catches our attention, makes us think, and engages us with the text. Molly Ivins, in her characteristically dramatic style, writes, in an article titled "Ban the Things. Ban Them All":

> Let me start this discussion by pointing out that I am not anti-gun. I'm pro-knife. Consider the merits of the knife.
> In the first place, you have to catch up with someone to stab him. A general substitution of knives for guns would promote physical fitness. We'd turn into a whole nation of great runners. Plus, knives don't ricochet. And people are seldom killed while cleaning their knives.

Now, do we really think that Ivins is "pro-knife"? That doesn't make much sense. And there are better ways to encourage physical fitness than to have all of us running after people trying to stab them. Ivins uses irony not to encourage knifing but to dramatize the absurdity, in her view, of any defense of the ownership of guns.

Sarcasm is not quite the same as irony. Irony can cleverly focus our attention on life's complexities. Sarcasm is heavy-handed irony, more often vicious than insightful, relying on harsh, negative word choice. Probably in most of your academic work, you will want to avoid all sarcasm, and you will want to think carefully about the effect of a use of irony or of any strongly worded appeal on your audience. Better to persuade your audience with the force of your reasons and evidence and with the clarity of your language than to lose them—or have them lose sight of your reasons—because of the static of nasty language. The key, as always, is to know your audience and to understand how you should present your argument to that audience to be most effective. Think about the continuum model in Figure 3–3 and place yourself appropriately along that continuum based on the type of argument you are preparing.

Exercises: Reading for Analysis

Analyze the following argument by Marie Winn, using Toulmin's terms. Be careful about the wording of your statement of Winn's claim, paying attention to the ways in which she qualifies her claim. Then answer the following questions:

1. Is Winn's argument convincing?

2. Do her reasons effectively support her claim?

3. How does her important qualification add to the argument's effectiveness?

4. If you disagree with Winn, how would you challenge her argument?

A Commitment to Language

Marie Winn

A graduate of Radcliffe College and Columbia University, Marie Winn is author of books for parents and children, including *Children Without Childhood*, 1983. The following excerpt is the concluding section from a chapter on verbal and nonverbal thought in Winn's best-known book, *The Plug-In Drug*, first published in 1977.

1   Given the evidence that environmental experience affects brain development in definable, measurable ways, and that early experience is more influential than later experience, it seems inevitable that the television experience, which takes up so many hours of a child's waking day, must have some effect upon his brain development. And yet children's brains cannot be dissected and examined to satisfy a scientist's curiosity. Nor can animal experiments cast reliable light on questions dealing with mental functions peculiar to the human species, such as thinking or verbalizing.

2   Nevertheless, the fact that the brain of a young child is different in important ways from an adult brain may help us to localize the areas of neurological impact of the television experience. For it will be in those *changing* areas that any neurological change will presumably occur.

3   Such an area of difference between the child's and the adult's brain is precisely that of brain-hemisphere specialization, and the balance that exists between verbal and non-verbal forms of mental organization. It is here that the television experience may prove to have its greatest impact.

4   This is not to suggest that television viewing will prevent a normal child from learning to speak. Only in cases of gross deprivation where children are almost totally isolated from human sounds will they not proceed according to a fairly universal language-learning schedule and fail to acquire the rudiments of speech.

5   It is not the child's actual acquisition of language but his *commitment* to language as a means of expression and to the verbal mode as the ultimate source of fulfillment that is at stake, a commitment that may have a physiological basis in the balance of right- and left-hemisphere development.

6   For a young child in the process of developing those basic mental structures, concepts, and understandings required to achieve his highest potential as a rational human being, a child who has only recently made the transition from nonverbal to verbal thought, much depends upon his opportunities to exercise his growing verbal skills. The greater the child's verbal opportunities, the greater the likelihood that his language will grow in complexity and his rational, verbal thinking abilities will sharpen. The fewer his opportunities, the greater the likelihood that certain linguistic areas will remain undeveloped or underdeveloped as critical time periods come and go.

7   To a grown-up, nonverbal mental activities carry connotations of relaxation from the ardors of normal logical thinking and promise to a much-sought-after achievement of peace and serenity. But to a young child in his formative, language-learning years, any extended regression into nonverbal mental functioning such as the television experience offers must be seen as a potential setback. As the child takes in television words and images hour after hour, day after day, with little of the mental effort that forming his own thoughts and feelings and molding them into words would require, as he *relaxes* year after year, a pattern emphasizing nonverbal cognition becomes established.

8   For unlike the tired businessman or professional woman or harried housewife who turns on the televison set to "unwind," the young child has a built-in need for mental activity. He is a learning machine, an "absorbent mind," a glutton for experience. In a culture that depends upon a precise and effective use of spoken and written language, his optimal development requires not merely adequate, but abundant opportunities to manipulate, to learn, to synthesize experience. It is his parents, fatigued by his incessant demands for learning in the broadest sense of the word (learning that may involve whining, screaming, throwing things, pestering), who require the "relaxation" afforded by setting him before the television screen and causing him to become, once again, the passive captive of his own sensations he was when nonverbal thought was his only means of learning.

Analyze the following argument by Richard Leakey, using Toulmin's terms. Then answer the following questions:

1. What does Leakey seek to accomplish in his opening four paragraphs? How does his opening help to remind readers of his credentials? What part of the Aristotelian model of argument does this opening help to underscore?

2. Why is Leakey uneasy encouraging wildlife conservation?

3. How does talking about the costs of conservation and about who needs to help meet those costs aid his argument? What part of the Toulmin model does this discussion come under?

4. When the author speaks of the complexities of the task and of making mistakes, what does he want to accomplish?

5. Is Leakey's argument effective? If you disagree, how would you counter him?

Extinctions Past and Present

Richard Leakey

A well-known paleontologist and conservationist who has been in charge of the Kenya Wildlife Service, Richard Leakey is currently overseeing Kenya's civil service. The following article appeared in the April/May 2000 issue of *Time* magazine.

1   I spent some of the most exciting days of my life working on the eastern shores of Kenya's Lake Turkana, searching for the fossilized remains of our early ancestors. We did not always find what we wanted, but every day there was much more to discover than the traces of our own predecessors. The fossils, some quite complete, others mere fragments, spoke of another world in which the ancestors of many of today's African mammals roamed the rich grasslands and forest fringes between 1.5 million and 2 million years ago. The environment was not too different from the wetter grasslands of Africa today, but it was full of amazing animals that are now long extinct.

2   One in particular I would have loved to see alive was a short-necked giraffe relative that had huge "antlers," some with a span across the horns of close to 8 ft. (almost 3 m). There were buffalo-size antelopes with massive curving horns, carnivores that must have looked like saber-toothed lions, two distinct species of hippo and at least two types of elephant, one of which had tusks that protruded downward from the lower jaw. We may never know the full extent of this incredible mammalian diversity, but there were probably more than twice as many species a million years ago as there are today.

3   That was true not just for Africa. The fossil record tells the same story everywhere. Most of life's experiments have ended in extinction. It is estimated that more than 95% of the species that have existed over the past 600 million years are gone.

4   So, should we be concerned about the current spasm of extinction, which has been accelerated by the inexorable expansion of agriculture and industry? Is it necessary to try to slow down a process that has been going on forever?

5   I believe it is. We know that the well-being of the human race is tied to the well-being of many other species, and we can't be sure which species are most important to our own survival.

6   But dealing with the extinction crisis is no simple matter, since much of the world's biodiversity resides in its poorest nations, especially in Asia, Africa and Latin America. Can such countries justify setting aside national parks and nature reserves where human encroachment and even access is forbidden? Is it legitimate to spend large sums of money to save some species—be it an elephant or an orchid—in a nation in which a sizable percentage of the people are living below the poverty line?

7   Such questions make me uneasy about promoting wildlife conservation in impoverished nations. Nonetheless, I believe that we can—and should—do a great deal. It's a matter of changing priorities. Plenty of money is available for scientific field studies and conferences on endangered species. But what about boots and vehicles for park personnel who protect wildlife from poachers? What about development aid to give local people economic alternatives to cutting forests and plowing over the land? That kind of funding is difficult to come by.

8   People in poor countries should not be asked to choose between their own short-term survival and longer-term environmental needs. If their governments are willing to protect the environment, the money needed should come from international sources. To me, the choice is clear. Either the more affluent world helps now or the world as a whole will lose out.

9   Of course, we must be careful not to allow the establishment of slush funds or rely on short-term, haphazard handouts that would probably go to waste. We need a permanent global endowment devoted to wildlife protection, funded primarily by the governments of the industrial nations and international aid agencies. The principal could remain invested in the donor nations as the interest flowed steadily into conservation efforts.

10   How to use those funds would be a matter of endless debate. Should local communities be entitled to set the agenda, or should outside experts take control? Should limited hunting be allowed in parks, or should they be put off limits? Mistakes will be made, the landscape will keep changing, and species will still be lost, but the difficulty of the task should not lead us to abandon hope. Many of the planet's natural habitats are gone forever, but many others can be saved and in time restored.

11   A major challenge for the 21st century is to preserve as much of our natural estate as possible. Let us resist with all our efforts any moves to reduce the amount of wild land available for wild species. And let us call upon the world's richest nations to provide the money to make that possible. That would not be a contribution to charity; it would be an investment in the future of humanity—and all life on Earth.

CHAPTER 4

Types of Arguments: Classical Patterns and Current Approaches

You can build on your knowledge of the basics of argument, examined in Chapter 3, by understanding some traditional forms of argument: induction, deduction, analogy, definition, and causal arguments. It is also important to be familiar with such modern approaches as the Rogerian or conciliatory argument, the use of statistics, and the visual arguments of cartoons and advertisements.

Induction

Induction is the process by which we reach inferences—opinions based on facts, or on a combination of facts and less debatable inferences. The inductive process moves from particular to general, from support to assertion. We base our inferences on the facts we have gathered and studied. In general, the more evidence, the more convincing the argument. No one wants to debate tomorrow's sunrise; the evidence for counting on it is too convincing. Most inferences, though, are drawn from less evidence, so we need to examine inductive arguments closely to judge their reasonableness.

The pattern of induction looks like this:

Evidence: There is the dead body of Smith. Smith was shot in his bedroom between the hours of 11:00 P.M. and 2:00 A.M., according to the coroner. Smith was shot by a .32-caliber pistol. The pistol left in the bedroom contains Jones's fingerprints. Jones was seen, by a neighbor, entering the Smith home at around 11:00 the night of Smith's death. A coworker heard Smith and Jones arguing in Smith's office the morning of the day Smith died.

Claim: Jones killed Smith.

The facts are presented. The jury infers that Jones is a murderer. Unless there is a confession or a trustworthy eyewitness, the conclusion is an inference, not a fact. This is the most logical explanation; that is, the conclusion meets the standards of simplicity and frequency while accounting for all of the known evidence.

The following paragraph illustrates the process of induction, in this case of generalizing from facts about a social condition:

American society has become increasingly violent in the last 25 years, in that people of many ages and backgrounds seem more ready to use violence to solve problems. According to figures quoted in a 1986 article by Adam Smith, each year in America now about 10,000 people die from gun deaths, in contrast to 3 in Great Britain and 17 in West Germany. An increasing number of victims are children and teenagers who are settling quarrels over drug territories or girlfriends by shooting. Sometimes the victims are parents, the murderers their children who are ending arguments over money or the use of the car. And sometimes the victims are children. In the first three months of 1989 in Washington, DC, over 100 people were murdered, many teenagers, many deaths drug-related. A youngster in a Maryland community shot both parents in a quarrel over money. A Virginia teenager shot his stepmother and left her body in a truck by the roadside. The trial of a Manhattan man who beat his adopted daughter to death is only one recent celebrated case of child beating. Further, we have children killing children in a number of mass shootings at schools. Added to that are the Los Angeles freeway shootings and road rage everywhere. The causes for this increase in violence are certainly numerous and complex, but the conclusion that "average" citizens, not crooks, are increasingly resorting to violence seems inescapable.

Observe that the writer organizes evidence by type of violence. Notice also that all facts relate to the issue of increasing violence among ordinary people. The writer does not get sidetracked into statistics for armed robberies or gang killings. A good inductive argument is based on a sufficient volume of *relevant* evidence. The basic shape of this inductive argument is illustrated in Figure 4–1.

In the following paragraph from their book *Discovering Dinosaurs*, authors Mark Norell, Eugene Gaffney, and Lowell Dingus answer the question "Did dinosaurs really rule the world?"

For almost 170 million years, from the Late Triassic to the end of the Cretaceous, there existed dinosaurs of almost every body form imaginable: small carnivores, such as *Compsognathus* and *Ornitholestes*, ecologically equivalent to today's foxes and coyotes; medium-sized carnivores, such as

FIGURE 4–1   The Shape of an Inductive Argument

Claim:	American society has become increasingly violent.
Grounds:	The facts presented in the paragraph.
Assumption: (Warrant)	The facts are representative, not isolated incidents, and thus reveal a trend, justifying the conclusion drawn.

Velociraptor and the troodontids, analogous to lions and tigers; and the monstrous carnivores with no living analogs, such as *Tyrannosaurus* and *Allosaurus*. Included among the ornithischians and the elephantine sauropods are terrestrial herbivores of diverse body form. By the end of the Jurassic, dinosaurs had even taken to the skies. The only habitats that dinosaurs did not dominate during the Mesozoic were aquatic. Yet, there were marine representatives, such as the primitive toothed bird *Hesperornis*. Like penguins, these birds were flightless, specialized for diving, and probably had to return to land to reproduce. In light of this broad morphologic diversity [number of body forms], dinosaurs did "rule the planet" as the dominant life form on Earth during most of the Mesozoic [era that includes the Triassic, Jurassic, and Cretaceous Periods, 248 to 65 million years ago].

Group Exercise: Induction

With your class partner or in small groups, make a list of facts that could be used to support each of the following inferences:

1. Whole-wheat bread is nutritious.
2. Fido must have escaped under the fence during the night.
3. Sue must be planning to go away for the weekend.
4. Students who do not hand in all essay assignments fail Dr. Bradshaw's English class.
5. The price of Florida oranges will go up in grocery stores next year.

Deduction

Although induction can be described as an argument that moves from particular to general, from facts to inference, deduction cannot accurately be described as the reverse. Deductive arguments are more complex than suggested by such a description. *Deduction is the reasoning process that draws a conclusion from the logical relationship of two assertions, usually one broad judgment or definition and one more specific assertion, often an inference.* Suppose on the way out of American history class, you say, "Abraham Lincoln certainly was a great leader." Someone responds with the expected question "Why do you think so?" You explain: "He was great because he performed with courage and a clear purpose in a time of crisis." Your explanation contains a conclusion and an assertion about Lincoln (an inference) in support. But behind your explanation rests an idea about leadership, in the terms of deduction, a *premise*. The argument's basic shape is illustrated in Figure 4–2.

FIGURE 4–2 **The Shape of a Deductive Argument**

<u>Claim:</u>	Lincoln was a great leader.
<u>Grounds:</u>	1. People who perform with courage and clear purpose in a crisis are great leaders.
	2. Lincoln was a person who performed with courage and a clear purpose in a crisis.
<u>Assumption:</u> (Warrant)	The relationship of the two reasons leads, logically, to the conclusion.

Traditionally, the deductive argument is arranged somewhat differently from these sentences about Lincoln. The two reasons are called *premises*; the broader one, called the *major premise*, is written first and the more specific one, the *minor premise*, comes next. The premises and conclusion are expressed to make clear that assertions are being made about categories or classes. To illustrate:

Major premise: All people who perform with courage and a clear purpose in a crisis are great leaders.

Minor premise: Lincoln was a person who performed with courage and a clear purpose in a crisis.

Conclusion: Lincoln was a great leader.

If these two premises are correctly, that is, logically, constructed, then the conclusion follows logically, and the deductive argument is *valid*. This does not mean that the conclusion is necessarily *true*. It does mean that if you accept the truth of the premises, then you must accept the truth of the conclusion, because in a valid argument the conclusion follows logically, necessarily. How do we know that the conclusion must follow if the argument is logically constructed? Let's think about what each premise is saying and then diagram each premise to represent each assertion visually. The first premise says that all people who act a particular way are people who fit into the category called "great leaders":

The second premise says that Lincoln, a category of one, belongs in the category of people who act in the same particular way that the first premise describes:

If we put the two diagrams together, we have the following set of circles, demonstrating that what the conclusion asserts follows from the premises:

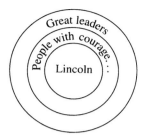

We can also make negative and qualified assertions in a deductive argument. For example:

> Premise: No cowards can be great leaders.
> Premise: Falstaff was a coward.
> Conclusion: Falstaff was not a great leader.

Or, to reword the conclusion to make the deductive pattern clearer: No Falstaff (no member of this class) is a great leader. Diagramming to test for validity, we find that the first premise says no A's are B's:

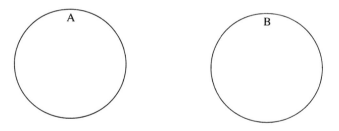

The second premise asserts all C's are A's:

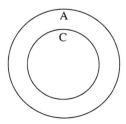

Put together, we see that the conclusion follows necessarily from the premises: No C's can possibly be members of class B.

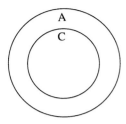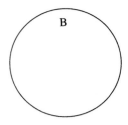

We can, in addition, shape a deductive argument with a qualified premise and conclusion.

Premise: All boys in my class are seniors.
Premise: Some boys in my class are football players.
Conclusion: Some seniors are football players

or

Some football players are seniors.

Diagramming to test the argument's validity, we observe that, indeed, the conclusion follows from the premises:

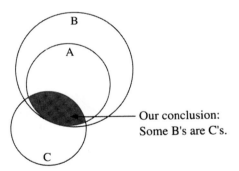

Some deductive arguments merely look right, but the two premises do not lead logically to the conclusion that is asserted. We must read each argument carefully or diagram each one to make certain that the conclusion follows from the premises. Consider the following argument: *Unions must be communistic because they want to control wages.* The sentence contains a conclusion and one reason, or premise. From these two parts of a deductive argument we can also determine the unstated premise, just as we could with the Lincoln argument: *Communists want to control wages.* If we use circles to represent the three categories of people in the argument and diagram the argument, we see a different result from the Lincoln argument:

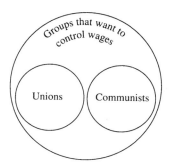

Diagramming the argument reveals that it is invalid; that is, it is not logically constructed because the statements do not require that the union circle be placed inside the communist circle. We cannot draw the conclusion we want from just any two premises, only from those that provide a logical basis from which a conclusion can be reached.

We must first make certain that deductive arguments are properly constructed or valid. But suppose the logic works and yet you do not agree with the claim? Your complaint, then, must be with one of the premises, a judgment or inference that you do not accept as true. Consider, as an example, the following argument:

Major premise: (All) dogs make good pets.

Minor premise: Fido is a dog.

Conclusion: Fido will make a good pet.

This argument is valid. (Diagram it; your circles will fit into one another just as with the Lincoln argument.) However, you are not prepared to agree, necessarily, that Fido will make a good pet. The problem is with the major premise. For the argument to work, the assertion must be about *all* dogs, but we know that not all dogs will be good pets.

When composing a deductive argument, your task will be to defend the truth of your premises. Then, if your argument is valid (logically constructed), readers will have no alternative but to agree with your conclusion. If you disagree with someone else's logically constructed argument, then you must show why one of the premises is not true. Your counterargument will seek to discredit one (or both) of the premises. The Fido argument can be discredited by your producing examples of dogs that have not made good pets.

A deductive argument can serve as the core of an entire essay, an essay that supports the argument's claim by developing support for each of the premises. Since the major premise is either a broad judgment or a definition, it will need to be defended on the basis of an appeal to values or beliefs that the writer expects the reader to share. The minor premise, usually an inference about a particular situation (or person), would be supported by relevant evidence, as with any inductive argument. You can see this process at work in the Declaration of Independence. Questions follow the Declaration to guide your analysis of this famous example of the deductive process.

The Declaration of Independence

In Congress, July 4, 1776
The unanimous declaration of the thirteen
United States of America

1   When in the course of human events, it becomes necessary for one people to dissolve the political bands which have connected them with another, and to assume among the powers of the earth, the separate and equal station to which the Laws of Nature and of Nature's God entitle them, a decent respect to the opinions of mankind requires that they should declare the causes which impel them to the separation.

2   We hold these truths to be self-evident, that all men are created equal, that they are endowed by their Creator with certain unalienable rights, that among these are life, liberty and the pursuit of happiness. That to secure these rights, governments are instituted among men, deriving their just powers from the consent of the governed. That whenever any form of government becomes destructive of these ends, it is the right of the people to alter or to abolish it, and to institute new government, laying its foundation on such principles and organizing its powers in such form, as to them shall seem most likely to effect their safety and happiness. Prudence, indeed, will dictate that governments long established should not be changed for light and transient causes; and accordingly all experience hath shown, that mankind are more disposed to suffer, while evils are sufferable, than to right themselves by abolishing the forms to which they are accustomed. But when a long train of abuses and usurpations, pursuing invariably the same object evinces a design to reduce them under absolute despotism, it is their right, it is their duty, to throw off such government, and to provide new guards for their future security. Such has been the patient sufferance of these Colonies; and such is now the necessity which constrains them to alter their former systems of government. The history of the present King of Great Britain is a history of repeated injuries and usurpations, all having in direct object the establishment of an absolute tyranny over these States. To prove this, let facts be submitted to a candid world.

3   He has refused his assent to laws, the most wholesome and necessary for the public good.

4   He has forbidden his Governors to pass laws of immediate and pressing importance, unless suspended in their operation till his assent should be obtained; and when so suspended, he has utterly neglected to attend to them.

5   He has refused to pass other laws for the accommodation of large districts of people, unless those people would relinquish the right of representation in the Legislature, a right inestimable to them and formidable to tyrants only.

6   He has called together legislative bodies at places unusual, uncomfortable, and distant from the depository of their public records, for the sole purpose of fatiguing them into compliance with his measures.

7   He has dissolved representative houses repeatedly, for opposing with manly firmness his invasions on the rights of the people.

8   He has refused for a long time, after such dissolutions, to cause others to be elected; whereby the legislative powers, incapable of annihilation, have returned to the people

at large for their exercise; the State remaining in the meantime exposed to all the dangers of invasion from without and convulsions within.

9   He has endeavoured to prevent the population of these States; for that purpose obstructing the laws of naturalization of foreigners; refusing to pass others to encourage their migration hither, and raising the conditions of new appropriations of lands.

10   He has obstructed the administration of justice, by refusing his assent to laws for establishing judiciary powers.

11   He has made judges dependent on his will alone, for the tenure of their offices, and the amount and payment of their salaries.

12   He has erected a multitude of new offices, and sent hither swarms of officers to harass our people, and eat out their substance.

13   He has kept among us, in times of peace, standing armies without the consent of our legislatures.

14   He has affected to render the military independent of and superior to the civil power.

15   He has combined with others to subject us to a jurisdiction foreign to our constitution, and unacknowledged by our laws; giving his assent to their acts of pretended legislation:

16   For quartering large bodies of armed troops among us:

17   For protecting them, by a mock trial, from punishment for any murders which they should commit on the inhabitants of these States:

18   For cutting off our trade with all parts of the world:

19   For imposing taxes on us without our consent:

20   For depriving us, in many cases, of the benefits of trial by jury:

21   For transporting us beyond seas to be tried for pretended offences:

22   For abolishing the free system of English laws in a neighbouring Province, establishing therein an arbitrary government, and enlarging its boundaries so as to render it at once an example and fit instrument for introducing the same absolute rule into these Colonies:

23   For taking away our Charters, abolishing our most valuable laws, and altering fundamentally the forms of our governments:

24   For suspending our own Legislatures, and declaring themselves invested with power to legislate for us in all cases whatsoever.

25   He has abdicated government here, by declaring us out of his protection and waging war against us.

26   He has plundered our seas, ravaged our coasts, burnt our towns, and destroyed the lives of our people.

27   He is at this time transporting large armies of foreign mercenaries to complete the works of death, desolation and tyranny, already begun with circumstances of cruelty and perfidy scarcely paralleled in the most barbarous ages, and totally unworthy the head of a civilized nation.

28   He has constrained our fellow citizens taken captive on the high seas to bear arms against their country, to become the executioners of their friends and brethren, or to fall themselves by their hands.

29   He has excited domestic insurrections amongst us, and has endeavoured to bring on the inhabitants of our frontiers, the merciless Indian savages, whose known rule of warfare, is an undistinguished destruction of all ages, sexes, and conditions.

30   In every stage of these oppressions we have petitioned for redress in the most humble terms; our repeated petitions have been answered only by repeated injury. A prince whose character is thus marked by every act which may define a tyrant is unfit to be the ruler of a free people.

31   Nor have we been wanting in attention to our British brethren. We have warned them from time to time of attempts by their legislature to extend an unwarrantable jurisdiction over us. We have reminded them of the circumstances of our emigration and settlement here. We have appealed to their native justice and magnanimity, and we have conjured them by the ties of our common kindred to disavow these usurpations, which would inevitably interrupt our connections and correspondence. They too have been deaf to the voice of justice and of consanguinity. We must, therefore, acquiesce in the necessity, which denounces our separation, and hold them, as we hold the rest of mankind, enemies in war, in peace friends.

32   We, therefore, the Representatives of the United States of America, in General Congress assembled, appealing to the Supreme Judge of the world for the rectitude of our intentions, do, in the name, and by the authority of the good people of these Colonies, solemnly publish and declare, That these United Colonies are, and of right ought to be Free and Independent States; that they are absolved from all allegiance to the British Crown, and that all political connection between them and the State of Great Britain, is and ought to be totally dissolved; and that as Free and Independent States, they have full power to levy war, conclude peace, contract alliances, establish commerce, and to do all other acts and things which Independent States may of right do. And for the support of this declaration, with a firm reliance on the protection of Divine Providence, we mutually pledge to each other our lives, our fortunes, and our sacred honor.

Questions for Analysis

1. What is the Declaration's central deductive argument? State the argument in the shape illustrated above: major premise, minor premise, conclusion. Construct a valid argument. If necessary, draw circles representing each of the three terms in the argument to check for validity. (*Hint:* Start with the claim "George III's government should be overthrown.")

2. Which paragraphs are devoted to supporting the major premise? What kind of support has been given?

3. Which paragraphs are devoted to supporting the minor premise? What kind of support has been given?

4. Why has more support been given for one premise than the other?

Exercises: Completing and Evaluating Deductive Arguments

Turn each of the following statements into valid deductive arguments. (You have the conclusion and one premise, so you will have to determine the missing premise that would complete the argument. Draw circles if necessary to test for validity.) Then decide which arguments have premises that could be supported by noting the kind of support that might be provided. Explain why you think some arguments have insupportable premises. Here is an example:

Premise:	All Jesuits are priests.
Premise:	No women are priests.
Conclusion:	No women are Jesuits.

Since the circle for women must be placed outside the circle for priests, it must also be outside the circle for Jesuits. Hence the argument is valid. The first premise is true by definition; the term *Jesuit* refers to an order of Roman Catholic priests. The second premise is true for the Roman Catholic Church, so if the term priest is used only to refer to people with a religious vocation in the Roman Catholic Church, then the second premise is also true by definition.

1. Mrs. Ferguson is a good teacher because she can explain the subject matter clearly.

2. Segregated schools are unconstitutional because they are unequal.

3. Michael must be a good driver because he drives fast.

4. The media clearly have a liberal bias because they make fun of religious fundamentalists.

Analogy

The argument from analogy is an argument based on comparison. Analogies assert that since A and B are alike in several ways, they must be alike in another way as well. The argument from analogy concludes with an inference, an assertion of a significant similarity in the two items being compared. The other similarities serve as evidence in support of the inference. The shape of an argument by analogy is illustrated in Figure 4–3.

Although analogy is sometimes an effective approach to an issue because clever, imaginative comparisons are often moving, analogy is not as rigorously logical as either induction or deduction. Frequently an analogy is based on only two or three points of comparison, whereas a sound inductive argument presents many examples to support its conclusion. Further, to be convincing, the points of comparison must be fundamental

FIGURE 4–3   The Shape of an Argument by Analogy

Grounds:	A has characteristics 1, 2, 3, and 4.
	B has characteristics 1, 2, and 3.
Claim:	B has characteristic 4 (as well).
Assumption: (Warrant)	If B has three characteristics in common with A, it must have the key fourth characteristic as well.

to the two items being compared. An argument for a county leash law for cats developed by analogy with dogs may cite the following similarities:

- Cats are pets, just like dogs.
- Cats live in residential communities, just like dogs.
- Cats can mess up other people's yards, just like dogs.
- Cats, if allowed to run free, can disturb the peace (fighting, howling at night), just like dogs.

Does it follow that cats should be required to walk on a leash, just like dogs? If such a county ordiance were passed, would it be enforceable? Have you ever tried to walk a cat on a leash? In spite of legitimate similarities brought out by the analogy, the conclusion does not logically follow because the arguer is overlooking a fundamental difference in the two animals' personalities. Dogs can be trained to a leash; most cats (Siamese are one exception) cannot be so trained. Such thinking will produce sulking cats and scratched owners. But the analogy, delivered passionately to the right audience, could lead community activists to lobby for a new law.

Observe that the problem with the cat-leash-law analogy is not in the similarities asserted about the items being compared but rather in the underlying assumption that the similarities logically support the argument's conclusion. A good analogy asserts many points of comparison and finds likenesses that are essential parts of the nature or purpose of the two items being compared. The best way to challenge another's analogy is to point out a fundamental difference in the nature or purpose of the compared items. For all of their similarities, when it comes to walking on a leash, cats are *not* like dogs.

Exercises: Analogy

1. Analyze the following analogies. List the stated and/or implied points of comparison and the conclusion in the pattern illustrated on p. 103. Then judge each argument's logic and effectiveness as a persuasive technique. If the argument is not logical, state the fundamental difference in the two compared items. If the argument could be persuasive, describe the kind of audience that might be moved by it.

    a. College newspapers should not be under the supervision or control of a faculty sponsor. Fortunately, no governmental sponsor controls the *New York Times*, or we would no longer have a free press in this country. We need a free college press, too, one that can attack college policies when they are wrong.

    b. Let's recognize that college athletes are really professional and start paying them properly. College athletes get a free education, and spending money from boosters. They are required to attend practices and games, and—if they play football or basketball—they bring in huge revenues for their "organization." College coaches are also paid enormous salaries, just like professional coaches, and often college coaches are tapped to coach professional teams. The only difference: the poor college athletes don't get those big salaries and huge signing bonuses.

    c. Just like any business, the federal government must be made to balance its budget. No company could continue to operate in the red as the government does and expect to be successful. A constitutional amendment requiring a balanced federal budget is long overdue.

2. Read and analyze the following analogy by Zbigniew Brzezinski. The questions that follow his article will aid your analysis.

War and Football

Zbigniew Brzezinski

Former national security advisor to President Jimmy Carter, Dr. Brzezinski (b. 1928) is an expert on politics and foreign affairs. He has published many books and articles, including *The Grand Chessboard: American Primacy and Its Geostrategic Imperative* (1997), and currently works at the Center for Strategic and International Studies. His article on football was published in the *Washington Post* on January 7, 2000.

1   I discovered American football late in life. Initially, I thought the game was a bore. When I saw my first football match after coming to America as a child reared on soccer, I was even appalled. Why are all these men, helmeted and wearing protective gear, bending over and then piling on top of one another? I was mystified by their conspiratorial huddling. And when I first heard the referee announce "penalty declined," I remember turning to my American guide and naively noting that it was chivalrous of the rewarded team to have done so.

2   After my appointment to the White House in the mid-'70s, I was favored by invitations to sit in the Redskins' owner's box—and the Washington thing to do, of course, was to go. Before long it dawned on me: The game is unique in the manner it translates into sport all the main ingredients of real warfare. Henceforth I was hooked.

3   Consider the following parallels:

4   • The owners of the teams are like heads of state. Some are nasty dictators, some merely preside like monarchs. Some posture and are loudmouths, but all are treated with a deference worthy of kings. The senior Cooke—my occasional and very regal host—both reigned and ruled; his son merely reigned. The new, post-Cooke owner conveys an intelligent passion for football, reminiscent of President Nixon, that will probably benefit the team.

5   • The coaches are the CinCs, to use Washington jargon. They set the overall strategy and supervise its tactical implementation in the course of combat. In constant wireless contact with their forces as well as with their scouting experts (a k a intelligence), examining instant play photos (a k a overhead imagery) and consulting their deputies for offensive and defensive operations, they are clearly the commanders in chief. Some are like Gen. Eisenhower; others remind you of Gen. MacArthur. The truly victorious ones (e.g., Gibbs or Parcells) reflect the needed ability to simultaneously inspire, intimidate and innovate.

6   • The quarterbacks, as is often noted, are the field commanders. They make last-minute tactical decisions on the basis of direct observation of hostile deployments, and they're expected, when necessary, to improvise tactically, though in the context of their CinCs' overall strategy. Some hustle and take risks; some stay put and just grind away. Again, shades of Gen. Patton or of Gen. Westmoreland.

7 • The teams engage in offensive and defensive maneuvers, as in real war. They rely either on a concentration of power (especially in ground attacks), on flanking attacks or on sudden deployment behind enemy lines (passing). Deception, speed and force are the required ingredients for success. Skill, precision and iron discipline are instilled by intense training.

8 • Good intelligence is also essential. Hence much effort is spent on the constant monitoring of the enemy's tactics, with specialists (high in the stands, equipped with long-distance observation equipment) seeking to spot potential weaknesses while identifying also the special strengths of the opponent. Timely strategic as well as tactical adjustments (especially during halftime) are often a key to the successful completion of the campaign (a k a game).

9 • As in real combat, teams suffer casualties, and these can cripple even a strong team. It is especially important to protect the field commander-quarterbacks; they are a key target of enemy action since their loss can be especially disruptive.

10 • Last but not least, the home front also plays a role. Systematic motivation of the morale of civilians (the spectators) can play an important role in stirring the combatants into greater passion while demoralizing the enemy. The home-field advantage is thus the equivalent to fighting in the defense of your own homeland.

11 Once I understood the above, the mindless piles of bodies, the strange posturing of grown men and the armored uniforms all came to make sense to me. A great game. Like a war.

Questions for Analysis and Discussion

1. What were Brzezinski's initial views of American football?

2. What are the points of comparison between football and war? State these in summary form in your own words.

3. The author's subject is clear, as is his use of analogy as a strategy. But, what is his purpose in writing? What does he want readers to conclude from his analogy? (Consider: How do you read the last two sentences? What are most people's attitudes toward war?)

4. What, then, is Brzezinski's thesis, the claim of his argument?

5. What elements of style add to the analogy's effectiveness? How would you describe the essay's tone?

6. What kinds of readers are least likely to be moved by the author's analogy? Why?

7. If you do not accept Brzezinski's analogy, how would you counter it?

Arguments about Cause

Because we want to know *why* things happen, arguments about cause abound. We want to understand past events (Why was Kennedy assassinated?), to explain current situations (Why do teens start to do drugs?), and to predict the future (Will the economy improve if there is a tax cut?). All three questions ask for a causal explanation, including the last. To answer the last question with a yes (or no) is to assert that a tax cut is (or is not) a cause of economic improvement.

Causal arguments are similar in their purpose rather than in their structure. Causal arguments explain either why a particular situation or phenomenon occurred (or will occur) or what produced (or will produce) a general state of affairs. Napoleon's loss at Waterloo is a particular situation, although it certainly developed from more than one cause. Teen drug use is a general social problem, for which there is also more than one cause. One consideration in any causal argument is how broad a generalization one can support. For example, teen drug use may be a national problem, but a particular researcher may choose to examine causes in only one city or area of the country. The results of research would lead to an understanding in only that area studied—although the results may offer suggestions to other parts of the country.

When looking for the cause of A, we are looking for an *agent:* a person, a situation, another event that brought A into existence. To discover that a lit cigarette dropped in a bed caused a particular house fire is, presumably, to have found the fire's cause. But if we continue to probe the situation, we uncover a more complicated sequence of causes. Why did the person in bed drop the cigarette? Because he fell asleep, we learn. Why did he fall asleep, unaware of his cigarette? Because, old and ill, he had taken a sleeping pill to help induce sleep. Did the sleeping pill cause the fire? Did his illness or age cause the fire? Where do we stop in the chain of causes?

The answer to the last question is that it depends, finally, on the purpose of the argument. Further, distinguishing among types of causes, or complex causal relationships, reveals that events do not occur in a vacuum. There are *conditions* surrounding an event, making the assigning of only one cause difficult at best. In the example above, the man's age and illness are existing conditions that contributed to, although they did not directly cause, the fire. We also speak of *influences* when discussing cause. The sleeping pill certainly influenced the man's behavior that led to the fire. To change the example, you might say that a particular teacher influenced your decision to attend the college you chose. The teacher is not the cause of your attending the college but rather an influence on your decision. Some conditions and influences may qualify as *remote causes*, for example, the man's age and illness. *Proximate causes* are more immediate, usually closer in time to the event or situation. The man's dozing off with a lighted cigarette is a proximate cause of the fire. Moving to the final step in the process, we come to the *precipitating cause*, the triggering event—in this example, the cigarette's igniting the combustible mattress fabric. Isolating a precipitating cause is usually necessary to prevent events from recurring, but often we need to go further back to determine remoter causes or conditions, especially if we are interested in assigning responsibility for what has occurred.

Consider Craig's situation, for example. Last week he had a rear-end collision with the car in front of him. The precipitating cause was his car's closeness to the car in front, too close to make stopping without a collision possible. If Craig wants to avoid another accident of this kind, he should not get too close to the car ahead of him. However, the car is not responsible for the accident because it was too close; Craig must accept responsibility for tailgating. Craig may prefer to believe that his car developed a will of its own or was suddenly possessed by the devil, but neither the state trooper nor Craig's insurance company will accept that explanation of cause.

Good causal arguments can be evaluated according to the following criteria:

- The arguer recognizes the complexity of causation and does not rush in to assert only one cause for a complex event or situation.

- The arguer distinguishes carefully among types of causes. Word choice is crucial here. Do you want to argue that (1) A, and A alone, caused B; (2) A was one of several contributing causes; or (3) A was an influence?

- The argument demonstrates more than just a *time relationship* or *correlation* between A and B. The argument proves *agency*. March precedes April, but March does not cause April to arrive. Good SAT scores do not cause good college grades. There is a correlation between good scores and good grades, but that is not the same as cause. (It is wise to infer, however, that whatever knowledge or skill produces good scores also contributes to good grades.)

- The argument presents believable causal agents, agents consistent with our knowledge of human behavior and scientific laws. Most people do not believe that personalities are shaped by astrological signs or that scientific laws, as we understand them at present, are suspended in the Bermuda Triangle, allowing planes and ships to vanish or enter a fourth dimension.

John Stuart Mill, a nineteenth-century British philosopher, explained in detail some important ways of investigating and demonstrating causal relationships: commonality, difference, and process of elimination. We can benefit in our study of causes by using his methods.

1. *Commonality.* One way to isolate cause is to demonstrate that one agent is *common* to similar outcomes. For instance, 25 employees attend a company luncheon. Later in the day, 10 report to area hospitals and another 4 complain the next day of having experienced vomiting the night before. Public health officials will soon want to know what these people ate for lunch. Different people during the same 12-hour period had similar physical symptoms of food poisoning. The common factor may well have been the tuna salad they ate for lunch.

2. *Difference.* Another way to isolate cause is to recognize one key *difference.* If two situations are alike in every way but one, and the situations result in different outcomes, then the one way they differ must have caused the different outcome. Studies in the social sciences are often based on the single-difference method. To test for the best teaching methods for math, an educator could set up an experiment with two classrooms similar in every way except that one class devotes 15 minutes three days a week to instruction by drill. If the class receiving the drill scores much higher on a standard test given to both groups of students, the educator could argue that math drills make a measurable difference in learning math. But the educator should be prepared for skeptics to challenge the assertion of only one difference between the two classes. Could the teacher's attitude toward the drills also make a difference in student learning? If the differences in student scores are significant, the educator probably has a good argument, even though a teacher's attitude cannot be controlled in the experiment.

3. *Process of elimination.* One can develop a causal argument around a technique we all use for problem solving: *the process of elimination.* When something happens, we examine all possible causes and eliminate them, one by one, until we are satisfied that we have isolated the actual cause (or causes). When the Federal Aviation Administration has to investigate a plane crash, it uses this process, exploring possible causes such as mechanical failure, weather, human error, or terrorism. Sometimes the process isolates more than one cause, or points to a likely cause without providing absolute proof. You will see how Lester Thurow uses the process-of-elimination method in his article at the end of this chapter (p. 136).

Exercises: Causal Arguments

1. From the following event or situations, select the one you know best, and list as many conditions, influences, and causes—remote, proximate, precipitating—as you can think of. (You may also want to do this exercise with your class partner or in small groups.)
   a. Teen suicide.
   b. Global warming.
   c. Increase in numbers of women elected to public office.
   d. High salaries of professional athletes.
   e. Increased interest in soccer in the United States.
   f. Comparatively low scores by U.S. students on international tests in math and science.

2. Read the following article and examine it as a causal argument by answering the questions that follow.

Pumps and Pocketbooks

Pietro Nivola

A graduate of Harvard University, Pietro Nivola, Ph.D., is a senior fellow in the Governmental Studies Program at the Brookings Institution. He is the author of numerous articles and books in his areas of research, including trade and energy policies and urban problems. His latest book is *Law of the Landscape: How Policies Shape Cities in Europe and America* (1999). The following article appeared in the *Washington Post*, April 24, 2000.

1   One good way to reduce this country's emissions of carbon dioxide as well as our dependence on foreign oil, suggests an April 17 editorial ["Saving Gas, and the Planet"], is to set tougher standards for the fuel efficiency of motor vehicles.

2   Sorry, but Congress has entertained this notion for almost a quarter-century with disappointing results. Since 1978 the United States has been attempting to do what no other industrial country has tried: reduce the consumption of oil just by imposing regulations—fuel-economy requirements—on new fleets of automobiles. At least two difficulties bedevil this command-and-control approach to energy conservation.

3   For one, the policy reaches only new vehicles. This means that it takes decades, not just a year or two, to raise the efficiency of the on-road fleet. If, tomorrow morning, federal regulators were to ratchet up the standards for SUVs, minivans and light trucks, most of the existing ones would remain in use, guzzling fuel and spewing greenhouse gases for years to come.

4   Worse, though the vehicular fleet gradually can be forced to record better gas mileage, doing so scarcely dissuades motorists from driving the "improved" vehicles more than ever. The unrelenting increase in vehicle miles traveled vitiates the fuel savings from improvements in mileage per gallon. Indeed, during periods of stable or declining gasoline prices, greater fuel economy of vehicles lowers the marginal cost of driving, actually encouraging motorists to log more miles.

5   The recent surge in nominal gasoline prices has slowed this boomerang, though not for long. Prices will begin to sag in the months ahead. Moreover, adjusting for inflation, even the current price of self-service regular is barely above where it stood in 1996 and well below its peak 18 years ago.

6   By 1997 Americans were motoring some 2.6 trillion miles a year—the equivalent of 10,715,511 trips to the moon. The federal government's fuel-efficiency rules did nothing to moderate this astronomical amount of motion, at least some of which is extravagant and wasteful.

7   Naturally, this failure has implications for the nation's thirst for oil and its environmental side effects. Transportation in the United States burns most of the petroleum we buy. It accounts for most of our rising volume of imported oil (which is now up to half our consumption), and for more than half of the damaging chemicals we emit into the atmosphere. While the use of oil dropped in virtually every other sector of the economy between 1973 and 1998, transportation's was up 36 percent. If the aim of government policy is to reverse this trend, reduce the level of oil imports and improve air quality, something other than automotive fuel-economy mandates is necessary.

8   Like it or not, that something is a higher price at the pump. In an election year, politicians wince at the thought, but if the current spike were permanent, it would likely conserve energy more efficiently over the long haul than does the flawed fuel-economy law. A few years ago, a joint study by the Century Foundation and the Brookings Institution estimated that a 25-cent increase in the federal gasoline tax would have saved more oil than the fuel-economy scheme did from its inception. The reason: economics. Steeper fuel costs affect driving habits, not just the vehicle design, and have an effect on the use of all vehicles, not just new models.

9   Rather than waste time tweaking the anachronistic 1978 regulatory regime, policymakers might consider these facts: Each year Americans chalk up approximately twice as many vehicle miles per capita as Germans and more than three times as many as the Japanese. This is not because Japanese and German consumers cannot afford cars. Nor is it because Germany and Japan regulate their automobile industries more stringently. Instead, much of the explanation for why people in those countries drive less, ride public transit, walk more and consume far less oil per person is simply that gasoline costs a lot more than it does here.

Questions for Analysis and Discussion

1. What is the occasion for Nivola's writing; that is, what has led him to write this article?

2. What is Congress's approach to reducing U.S. oil consumption?

3. What two reasons does Nivola offer for rejecting Congress's approach? That is, why does this approach fail to cause a reduction in oil consumption?

4. What activity uses the most petroleum and produces the greatest volume of environmentally damaging chemicals? Given that answer, what should be the best way to reduce oil consumption and help the environment?

5. What, then, is Nivola's claim? What action will cause the desired result?

6. How does the author support his claim?

7. In his final paragraph, Nivola compares U.S. driving miles to Japanese and German driving miles. What is the point of his comparison? Which one of Mill's strategies for finding cause does he use in this paragraph?

8. Has the author found a solution to the U.S. oil consumption problem? Judge the effectiveness of his argument—regardless of how you feel about his recommendation.

The Rogerian or Conciliatory Argument

There's an old saying: You can catch more flies with honey than with vinegar. The saying contains good advice for arguers. When you move beyond seeing argument as a chance to express your views in the strongest possible language and see it instead as an opportunity to move an audience, you will be ready to embrace the conciliatory argument. And you will probably be rewarded with "more flies."

You will find that many good writers go out of their way to establish common ground with readers who may disagree with them or who otherwise may feel threatened or become defensive. Recognizing that readers who feel the need to defend their position (or lifestyle) will not be open to new information or different ideas, good writers often seek a conciliatory tone and approach. In his book *On Becoming a Person*, psychologist Carl R. Rogers recommends developing conciliatory arguments. He describes such arguments as:

- Using nonthreatening language.

- Expressing opposing views fairly.

- Stressing the common ground that opposing sides may share.

Consider, for example, the opening of an article on city life by C. R. Creekmore. He begins "Cities Won't Drive You Crazy," by writing:

> Trapped in one of the Olympian traffic jams on the Garden State Parkway in New Jersey, I waited to pay my toll for the Newark exit. Horns, insults, and exhaust fumes had settled in a noisy, dark-tempered cloud. As I finally reached the end of the exact-change line, I faced a sudden dilemma. There was the automatic toll collector side-by-side with a human toll taker standing in his little booth. I stared into the impersonal mouth of the collection machine, then at the person, and chose him. The man looked

shocked. He regarded the quarter I thrust at him as if it were a bug. "Grow up!" he screamed at me with a sense of indignation that I assumed was generated by a life dedicated to the parkway system. "Grow up and use the machine!"

To me, the incident has always summed up the essence of what cities are: hotbeds of small embarrassments, dehumanizing confrontations, momentary setbacks, angry people and festering acts of God.

Many Americans agree with this stereotype and believe firmly that the dirty, crowded, dangerous city must gradually destroy an urbanite's psyche. . . . A large body of research conducted in the past 15 years by a diverse group of social scientists challenges these heartfelt prejudices.

Creekmore begins by relating a personal experience that can explain the negative view many hold of cities, a view that he describes as "heartfelt," though mistaken. Essentially, his opening says to readers: "I understand how you feel about cities, but let's look at some facts that may lead to a different view." Using a conciliatory approach may give unpopular or new ideas a chance to be heard.

OCCASIONS FOR SELECTING A CONCILIATORY ARGUMENT

Here are four situations that invite the use of a conciliatory approach, if you want to have an impact on your audience:

- *When you know that your views will be unpopular with at least some, perhaps many, members of your audience.* Try to show them how much you do have in common or how much you can understand their views and feelings. Examples include a pitch for higher gas prices, more complex recycling procedures, or school uniforms.

- *When an issue, perhaps a highly emotional one, has been debated for some time.* The arguments of each side are clear and well established and no one has any new arguments to add to the conversation. It may be time to try to find some common ground. Examples includes the emotional debates over abortion and gun control.

- *When both sides are entrenched so that no progress can be made on public-policy issues that need to be addressed.* Those who are ready to settle for some movement toward a desired goal can start some action with a conciliatory argument. Examples include not only the Middle East peace talks but also campaign finance reform.

- *When you need to continue to interact with members of your audience.* When the context in which you are debating is ongoing—as with coworkers, neighbors, or members of the PTA, for example—you need to consider the value of presenting yourself as a person of goodwill with the goals of the group in mind. Using a conciliatory approach can strengthen your credibility, your *ethos*.

Read and analyze the following article by Abigail Trafford, focusing on her conciliatory strategies. The questions that follow will aid your analysis.

On the Streets of Philadelphia, Prescriptions for Progress

Abigail Trafford

Abigail Trafford has a syndicated weekly column, "Second Opinion," and is health editor for the *Washington Post*. She is also the author of *Crazy Time: Surviving Divorce and Building a New Life* (1992). The following column was published on August 8, 2000.

1   "Do you have to be Republican?" the young woman asks.

2   "Oh, no," replies Carolyn Aldige of the Cancer Research Foundation of America as she stands outside the free health screening van at the Republican National Convention. "You can be Republican, Democrat, Libertarian, Reform, anything!"

3   This oasis of bipartisanship is a $400,000, 40-by-12-foot, high-tech mobile medical van tucked away under an arched overpass by the convention center. It was open to the public, and throughout the convention people came to get their blood pressure taken and their cholesterol levels checked. Men received PSA tests for prostate cancer; women got mammograms. These procedures would normally cost hundreds of dollars.

4   A similar van will be set up at the Democratic National Convention in Los Angeles next week. Both parties agreed to find a place for the booth at the conventions.

5   The health van symbolizes the kind of nonpartisan approach to health issues that's needed in Washington.

6   Congress has a poor record on passing health legislation. The Clinton administration hasn't got much to brag about, either. Major initiatives on patients' rights, drugs for older Americans and safeguards for consumers in health plans have all bogged down in bitter partisan battles. Meanwhile, the ranks of the uninsured have swelled to 44 million people.

7   The bipartisan health van highlights the disconnect between the political leaders who are looking for hot issues to fight over on the campaign trail and ordinary people who are looking for some relief from the problems of high costs and lack of coverage for needed services.

8   Away from the partisan rhetoric inside the convention halls, there was amazing consensus on health issues among those who came to the mobile van for free screenings.

9   Philadelphia cop Joe Bannon, 38, with a family history of heart disease and strokes, despairs of Congress. His blood pressure is a terrific 110/80—"and I smoke two packs of cigarettes a day," he announces—and he's got good health coverage with the police department. But he thinks everyone should have coverage. With the politicians in this Congress, "I would expect nothing," says Bannon, a registered Democrat. "They forgot where they came from."

10   Deborah Conrad 48, a self-employed artist from Madison, Wis., agrees. She has no health insurance. When she gets sick, she barters with her doctor. Once she gave her gynecologist a jacket she'd made—worth $500 in the high-end craft market. She describes herself as an independent and a feminist. She supports universal coverage and prescription drug benefits for her elderly parents. "I have no faith in this Congress," she says. And it's not just the Republicans. "I'm not impressed with the Democrats, either."

11   Hilda Bielecki, 47, with the police department parking detail, remembers when she went on welfare for a couple of years after her marriage fell apart. It was the only way to get health coverage, she says. "Health care should be for everybody." She describes herself as a law-and-order Republican. "I can't find anybody in politics—Republican or Democrat—who is worried about us, because they're not living like us. Give them health care like I had, and they'll change their policy."

12   Members of Congress, of course, and workers in the federal government enjoy excellent health benefits But for many people, coverage is too expensive and costs of uncovered drugs and services too high.

13   Shellie Cooke, 51, who is in a state training program for hotel management, gets health coverage through the program. She's a Democrat, and she knows she's lucky. "There are a lot of people who can't afford it—my daughter, for example," she says.

14   Gloria Scott, 56, the wife of a convention delegate from Washington State, has no health coverage. Her husband, 62, a longtime Republican party activist, has enough money to pay for the family's routine medical care. They also have a catastrophic insurance policy to protect them from major expenses.

15   But what about people who are hit with a major chronic illness and have to sell their home to pay the medical bills? "I don't think that should happen," says Scott, a conservative Republican. And what about prescription drugs for senior citizens? "I think the price of medication is way out of line," she says. "We have to take a hard look at making sure health care is available to everybody for a responsible amount. I don't want Canadian [government-run] health care, but everybody should have affordable health care."

16   Annette Hammie, 41, who just started as a banquet cook at the Ritz-Carlton Hotel, comes to the van for free screening tests because her insurance hasn't kicked in yet.

17   "I was able to get a mammogram without worrying about the cost," says Hammie, a Democrat. She doesn't see why her party can't work with Republicans to pass legislation. "Republicans are down-to-earth people, too. They have the same concerns, the same problems."

18   If only the politicians could see that!

19   But party rivalry is so intense these days there seems to be little chance of a bipartisan approach to major health care issues.

20   The mobile medical van is one thing on the health agenda that the two parties have in common at their respective conventions. Organized by the Cancer Research Foundation, it is administered by the Hutchinson Clinic of Kansas in partnership with the Fox Chase Cancer Center in Philadelphia and with UCLA and the Watts Neighborhood Health Foundation in Los Angeles.

21   The screening program is but a small step toward bipartisanship. Still, it's a start. If George W. Bush and Al Gore were to step outside for a blood pressure check, they might learn something. At the very least, they'd be reminded that the need for health services crosses party lines.

Questions for Analysis and Discussion

1. What is the occasion for this column? That is, what is the situation and the particular event that is a part of the situation to which Trafford refers?

2. How does Trafford open her article? What is effective about her opening paragraphs relative to her purpose in writing?

3. What is Trafford's claim? Where does she state it?

4. How many Americans are without health insurance?

5. What is the primary strategy by which Trafford develops her essay? That is, what grounds or evidence does she provide to support her claim?

6. Which of the strategies for developing a conciliatory argument does Trafford use? How does her evidence support a conciliatory approach?

7. Which of the four situations calling for a conciliatory approach might apply to Trafford and her topic?

8. How has Trafford's argument affected you? Be prepared to discuss your response to and your evaluation of her appeal.

The Uses of Authority and Statistics

Because many arguments provide statistical information and the views of authorities as support for claims, a study of argument is incomplete without examining how we use and evaluate such evidence.

JUDGING AUTHORITIES

We all know that movie stars and sports figures are not authorities on cereals and soft drinks. But what about *real* authorities? When we present the opinions or research findings of authorities as support for a claim, we are saying to our audience that the authority is trustworthy and the opinions valuable. But, what we are asserting is actually an assumption, part of the glue connecting evidence to claim, and as such it can be challenged. If our "authority" can be shown to lack authority, then the logic of our argument is invalid. Therefore, we must make careful judgments about the quality of the authorities used by others and those we use in our own arguments. Here is a checklist of questions to use to evaluate authorities:

- ✔ Is the authority actually an authority on the topic under discussion? When a famous scientist supports a candidate for office, he or she speaks as a citizen, not as an authority.

- ✔ Is the work of the authority still current? Times change; expertise does not always endure. Galileo would be lost in the universe of today's astrophysicists.

- ✔ Does the authority actually have legitimate credentials? Are the person's publications in respected journals; is he or she respected by others in the same field?

✔ Do experts in the field generally agree on the issue? If there is widespread disagreement, then quoting one authority does not prove much. Remember that disagreement abounds in the social sciences; in many cases, the experts just do not agree on what the evidence means.

Expect challengers to take a close look at the uses of authority in any argument.

UNDERSTANDING AND EVALUATING STATISTICS

Keep in mind the cliché "Statistics don't lie, but people lie with statistics." Numbers— statistical information and the results of polls—are facts, but when they are presented in an argument, they are being used by a person interested in supporting a claim. This is not to say that no one using statistical information can be trusted. Some writers use numbers without being aware that they are incomplete or not representative. Some present only part of the relevant information. Some may not mean to distort, but they do choose to present the information in a language that helps their cause. There are many ways, some more innocent than others, to distort reality with statistics. Therefore, we need to be alert to ways that numbers can be misleading in the arguments we read and also in the arguments we write.

Here is a checklist to use to evaluate the presentation of statistical information:

✔ Is the information current and therefore still relevant? Crime rates in your city that are based on 1991 data probably are no longer relevant, certainly not current enough to serve as a basis for police-department spending.

✔ If a sample was used, was it randomly selected and large enough to be significant? Sometimes in medical research, the results of a small study are publicized to guide researchers to important new areas of study. When these results are reported in the popular press or on TV, however, the size of the study is not always made clear.

✔ What information, exactly, has been provided? When you read "Two out of three chose the Merit combination of low tar and good taste," you must ask "Two-thirds of how many altogether?"

✔ Note carefully how the numbers have been worded, and then evaluate the effect of that wording. Numbers can be presented as fractions, whole numbers, or percentages. Writers who want to emphasize budget increases present whole numbers, billions of dollars; writers who want to de-emphasize those increases use percentages. Writers who want their readers to respond to the numbers in a certain way add words to direct their thinking: "a *mere* 3 percent increase" or "the *enormous* $5 billion increase." When you read that the number of women earning more than $25,000 a year has *doubled* in the last 10 years, instead of automatically thinking that women are finally catching up, ask yourself how many women actually earn more than $25,000. Also ask what percentage of the total workers with that salary or more they represent.

READING AND PREPARING GRAPHICS

Statistical information is frequently presented in some graphic format. Graphics include tables, pie charts, bar charts, and line graphs. Tables present numerical information in columns, summarizing and focusing that information. Pie charts show the relative size of sections of a whole category, all students at your school divided by gender, or by age, for exmple. Bar charts, popular in textbooks and periodicals, reveal relative proportions or variations in a visually effective way. Different colors or shadings can be used to represent different groups, such as the numbers of males (one color) and females (another color) participating in unhealthy behaviors, such as smoking or drinking Line graphs show a changing relationship between the item represented on the vertical line and the item represented on the horizontal line. Line graphs are good for showing trends over time.

Graphics can present a great deal of information in a condensed—but also visually engaging—format. Do not be fooled by the visual format; graphics contain writing, too. Read graphics by following these steps—and keep these steps in mind when you choose to include graphics within your written materials. We will use Figure 4–4 as our example.

1. *Study the graphic at the point at which it is referred to in the text.* Graphics may not be placed on the same page as the text reference. Stop your reading to find and study the graphic; that's what the writer wants you to do. For example, the line graph (Fig. 4-4) appearing on page 344 in the textbook from which it was borrowed, is referred to on page 343: "Figure 10.3 (on p. 344) shows the percentage of married women in the U.S. labor force according to the age of their youngest child."

2. *Read the title or label of the graphic and any source information at the bottom.* Every table, chart, or diagram is given a title. Figure 4-4's title is "Percentage of the U.S. Labor Force Made Up of Married Women with Children." Many graphics also include a source line; the data on which Figure 4-4 is based came from the U.S. Bureau of the Census in 1997. Ask yourself, "What is this graph showing me? Is this coming from a reliable source? Is it current?"

3. *Study the labels—or other words—that appear as a part of the graphic.* For a line graph, study the labels that appear on both the vertical and horizontal axes. Figure 4-4 shows the percentage of different groups of women in the workplace

FIGURE 4–4 Percentage of the U.S. Labor Force Made Up of Married Women with Children

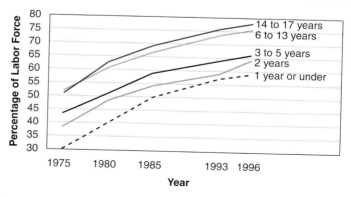

Source: Data from the U.S. Bureau of the Census, 1997.

from 1975 to 1996, categorized (by the colored lines) according to the age of their youngest child. You cannot draw useful conclusions unless you understand exactly what is being shown.

4. *Study the information, making certain that you understand what the numbers represent.* Are the numerals whole numbers, numbers in hundreds or thousands, or percentages? In Figure 4-4 we are looking at a relationship between percentages and the passing of time.

5. *Draw conclusions.* Think about the information in different ways. Ask, "Why are these numbers significant?" Or, "How are they significant?" How would you answer these questions for the line graph we have been studying?

Exercises: Using Statistics and Reading Tables and Charts

1. Figure 4–5, a table from the *Statistical Abstract of the United States, 1999*, shows U.S. family income data. Percentages and median income are given for all families and then, in turn, for white, black, and Hispanic families. Study the data and then complete the exercises that follow.

    a. In a paper assessing the advantages of a growing economy, you want to include a paragraph showing growth in family income as one way to show that a booming economy helps everyone, that "a rising tide lifts all boats." Select data from the table that best support your claim. Write a paragraph beginning with a topic sentence and including your data as support. Think about how to present the numbers in the most persuasive form.

    b. Write a second paragraph with the following topic sentence: "Not all Americans have benefited from the boom years," or "a rising tide does not lift all boats." Select data from the table that best support this topic sentence and present them in the most persuasive form.

    c. Exchange paragraphs with a classmate and evaluate each other's selection and presentation of evidence.

2. Study Figure 4–6, a bar chart from a college psychology textbook. Study and reflect on the information. Then consider: What conclusions can be drawn from the evidence? What are the implications of those conclusions?

Responding to Visual Arguments

Many arguments bombard us today in visual forms, or, as we have seen with statistics presented in graphic form, in a combination of images and words. Two such visual arguments are political cartoons and advertising. Most major newspapers have a political cartoonist whose drawings appear regularly on the editorial page. (Some comic strips are also political in nature, at least some of the time.) These cartoons are designed to make a political point in a visually clever and amusing way. (That is why they are both "cartoons" and "political" at the same time.) Their uses of irony and caricatures of known politicians make them among the most emotionally powerful, indeed stinging, of arguments.

FIGURE 4–5   Money Income of Households—Percent Distribution, by Income Level, Race, and Hispanic Origin, in Constant (1997) Dollars: 1970 to 1997

[Constant dollars based on CPI-U-X1 deflator. Households as of **March** of **following year.** Based on Current Population Survey; see text, Section 1, Population, and text this section, and Appendix III. For definition of median, see Guide to Tabular Presentation]

Year	Number of House-holds (1,000)	Percent Distribution							Median Income (dollars)
		Under $10,000	$10,000–$14,999	$15,000–$24,999	$25,000–$34,999	$35,000–$49,999	$50,000–$74,999	$75,000 and over	
All Households[1]									
1970	64,778	13.4	7.5	15.1	16.1	21.1	17.7	9.0	33,942
1975	72,867	12.6	8.7	15.9	15.3	19.4	18.3	9.9	33,699
1980	82,368	12.4	8.2	15.8	14.0	19.2	18.4	12.0	34,538
1985	88,458	12.3	8.2	15.1	14.1	17.9	17.9	14.4	35,229
1990	94,312	11.6	7.9	14.8	13.8	17.7	18.2	16.0	36,770
1995	99,627	11.4	8.4	15.3	14.0	16.7	17.7	16.5	35,887
1996	101,018	11.5	8.4	15.1	13.6	16.1	18.2	17.1	36,306
1997	102,528	11.0	8.1	14.9	13.3	16.3	18.1	18.4	37,005
White									
1970	57,575	12.2	7.0	14.5	16.1	21.8	18.6	9.7	35,353
1975	64,392	11.2	8.2	15.6	15.2	20.0	19.3	10.6	35,241
1980	71,872	10.8	7.7	15.4	14.1	19.7	19.4	12.8	36,437
1985	76,576	10.7	7.8	14.8	14.1	18.4	18.8	15.5	37,154
1990	80,968	9.8	7.5	14.6	14.0	18.1	19.1	17.0	38,352
1995	84,511	9.8	8.0	15.1	14.0	17.0	18.5	17.7	37,667
1996	85,059	9.8	8.0	14.9	13.7	16.4	19.0	18.1	38,014
1997	86,106	9.5	7.8	14.6	13.2	16.5	18.8	19.7	38,972
Black									
1970	6,180	24.3	12.2	20.9	15.8	14.5	9.2	3.0	21,518
1975	7,489	24.6	13.5	18.8	15.9	14.3	9.8	3.2	21,156
1980	8,847	25.3	12.8	19.2	13.3	14.7	10.5	4.2	20,992
1985	9,797	25.2	11.9	18.3	13.6	14.1	11.1	5.6	22,105
1990	10,671	25.8	11.3	16.5	13.0	15.0	11.5	6.9	22,934
1995	11,577	22.8	11.3	18.0	14.3	14.6	11.9	7.2	23,583
1996	12,109	22.6	11.5	17.6	13.9	14.1	12.6	7.8	24,021
1997	12,474	21.4	10.5	17.9	14.2	14.9	13.1	7.9	25,050
Hispanic[2]									
1975	2,948	16.5	11.2	21.8	17.2	18.7	10.8	3.8	25,317
1980	3,906	16.1	10.5	20.2	16.5	17.1	13.6	6.0	25,317
1985	5,213	17.3	12.1	18.6	15.3	16.9	12.7	7.1	26,622
1990	6,220	16.2	11.5	18.5	15.7	17.1	12.9	8.1	26,051
1995	7,939	18.8	11.9	21.0	15.2	14.1	12.1	6.9	27,421
1996	8,225	16.7	12.0	20.8	14.9	15.0	12.5	8.1	24,075
1997	8,590	16.8	10.7	19.7	15.0	16.6	12.2	9.1	25,477

[1]Includes other races not shown separately. [2]Persons of Hispanic origin may be of any race. Income data for Hispanic origin households are not available prior to 1972.

Source: Statistical Abstract of the United States, 1999.

FIGURE 4–6   Differences in Suicide Rate According to Race, Gender, and Age

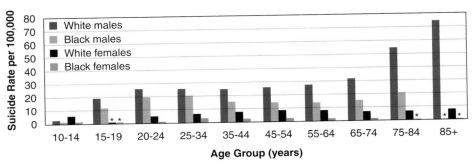

Source: Data from the U.S. Bureau of the Census, 1994.

Advertisements are among the most creative and powerful forms of argument today. Remember that ads are designed to take your time (for shopping) and your money. Their messages need to be powerful to motivate you to action. With some products (what most of us consider necessities), ads are designed to influence product choice, to get us to buy Brand A instead of Brand B. With other products, ones we really do not need or which may actually be harmful to us, ads need to be especially clever. Some ads do provide some information (car X gets better gas mileage than car Y). Other ads (perfume ads, for example) take us into a fantasy land so that we will spend $50 on a small but pretty bottle. Another type of ad is the "image advertisement," an ad that assures us that a particular company is top-notch. If we admire the company, we will buy its goods or services.

We want to be able to "read" visual arguments with as much skill as we read written arguments. Here are some guidelines for reading visual arguments with insight. You can practice these steps with the exercises that follow.

Guidelines for Reading Political Cartoons

1. What scene is depicted? Identify the situation.
2. Identify each of the figures in the cartoon. Are they current politicians, figures from history or literature, the "person in the street," or symbolic representations?
3. Who speaks the lines in the cartoon?
4. What is the cartoon's general subject? What is the point of the cartoon, the claim of the cartoonist?

Guidelines for Reading Advertisements

1. What product or service is being advertised?
2. Who seems to be the targeted audience?

3. What is the ad's primary strategy? To provide information? To reinforce the product's or company's image? To appeal to particular needs or desires? (For example, if an ad shows a group of young people having fun and drinking a particular beer, to what needs/desires is the ad appealing?)

4. Does the ad use specific rhetorical strategies such as humor, understatement, or irony?

5. What is the relation between the visual part of the ad (photo, drawing, typeface, etc.) to the print part (the text, or copy)? Does the ad use a slogan or catchy phrase? Is there a company logo? Is the slogan or logo clever? Is it well known as a marker of the company? What may be the effect of these strategies on readers?

6. What is the ad's overall visual impression? (Consider both images and colors used.)

Exercises: Analyzing Cartoons and Ads

1. Analyze each of the following cartoons, using the guidelines listed on the previous page. You may want to jot down your answers to the questions to be well prepared for class discussion.

2. Analyze each of the following ads, again using the guidelines listed on the previous page. After answering the questions listed there, consider these as well: Will the ad appeal effectively to its intended audience? If so, why? If not, why not?

Visionary.

The richest coffee in the world.*

Courtesy of The National Federation of Coffee Growers of Colombia

THEY'D RATHER BE IN COLORADO.

Taking the same dull vacation can start eating away at you after a while. So why not try Colorado?
The mountains. The magic. The plains. The people. The history. The culture. The fun. The sheer
exhilaration of something new. Something you can't experience anywhere else.
Call us or give our Web site a nibble.

COLORADO
1-800-COLORADO · WWW.COLORADO.COM

We've been North America's growth company for 100 years.

It's not all that unusual for a company to anticipate growth over a period of quarters, or even years. But what about decades? Or centuries?

At Weyerhaeuser, that kind of long-term thinking has been second nature since our founding in 1900. We started North America's first tree farm to make timber an endlessly renewable resource. We developed High Yield Forestry to increase wood yields for decades to come. Now we're finding innovative ways to produce our products more efficiently and profitably.

And this year, like every year, we're planting over 100 million seedlings. Trees that will be ready for harvest later this century. Because when you've been growing as long as we have, you like to think ahead a hundred years or so.

Weyerhaeuser
The future is growing™

www.weyerhaeuser.com

125

Arguments That Do Not Work: Logical Fallacies

A thorough study of argument needs to include a study of logical fallacies because so many "arguments" fail to meet standards of sound logic and good sense. Before examining specific types of arguments that do not work, let's consider briefly why people offer arguments that aren't sensible.

CAUSES OF ILLOGIC

Ignorance

One frequent cause for illogical debate is simply a lack of knowledge of the subject. Some people have more information than others, either from formal study or from wide-ranging experiences. The younger you are, the less you can be expected to know about or understand complex issues. On the other hand, if you want to debate a complex or technical issue, then you cannot use ignorance as an excuse for producing a weak argument. To illustrate: Following the 1992 riots in Los Angeles, then press secretary Marlin Fitzwater asserted that welfare programs of the 1960s and 1970s caused the riots. When reporters asked which programs, Fitzwater responded that he did not have a list with him! Instead of ducking the need for evidence, you want to read as much as you can, listen carefully to discussions, ask questions, and, when called on to write, select topics about which you have knowledge or which you are willing to study before writing.

Egos

Ego problems are another cause of weak arguments. Those with low self-esteem often have difficulty in debates because they attach themselves to their ideas and then feel personally attacked when someone disagrees with them. Usually the next step is a defense of their views with even greater emotion and irrationality, even though self-esteem is enhanced when others applaud our knowledge and thoughtfulness, not our irrationality.

Prejudices

A third cause of irrationality is the collection of prejudices and biases that we carry around, having absorbed them "ages ago" from family and community. Prejudices range from the worst ethnic, religious, or sexist stereotypes to political views we have adopted uncritically (Democrats are all bleeding hearts; Republicans are all rich snobs), to perhaps less serious but equally insupportable notions (if it's in print, it must be right; if it's not meat and potatoes, it is not really dinner). People who see the world through distorted lenses cannot possibly assess facts intelligently and reason logically from them.

A Need for Answers

Finally, many bad arguments stem from a human need for answers—any answers—to the questions that deeply concern us. We want to control our world because that makes us feel secure, and having answers makes us feel in control. This need can lead to illogic from oversimplifying problems, from refusing to settle for qualified answers to questions.

The causes of illogic lead us to a twofold classification of bad arguments: logical fallacies that result from (1) oversimplifying the issue or from (2) ignoring the issue by substituting emotion for reason.

FALLACIES THAT RESULT FROM OVERSIMPLIFYING

Errors in Generalizing

Errors in generalizing include overstatement and hasty or faulty generalization. All have in common an error in the inductive pattern of argument. In each fallacy, the inference drawn from the evidence is unwarranted, either because too broad a generalization is made or because the generalization is drawn from incomplete or incorrect evidence. *Overstatement* occurs when the argument's assertion is an unqualified generalization—that is, it refers to all members of a category or class, although the evidence justifies an assertion about only some of the class. Overstatements often result from stereotyping, giving the same traits to everyone in a group. Overstatements are frequently signaled by words such as *all, every, always, never,* and *none*. But remember that assertions such as "children love clowns" are understood to refer to "all children," even though the word *all* does not appear in the sentence. It is the writer's task to qualify statements appropriately, using words such as *some, many,* or *frequently,* as appropriate. Overstatements are discredited by finding only one exception to disprove the assertion. One frightened child who starts to cry when the clown approaches will destroy the argument. Here is another example:

- Lawyers are only interested in making money.
  (What about Ralph Nader, who works to protect consumers, or public defenders, who take care of those unable to pay for a lawyer?)

Hasty or faulty generalizations may be qualified assertions, but they still oversimplify by arguing from insufficient evidence or from ignoring some relevant evidence. For example:

- Political life must lead many to excessive drinking. In the last six months the paper has written about five members of Congress who have either confessed to alcoholism or have been arrested on DUI charges.

(Five is not a large enough sample from which to generalize about *many* politicians. Also, the five in the newspaper are not a representative sample; they have made the news because of their drinking.)

Forced Hypothesis

The *forced hypothesis* is also an error in inductive reasoning. The explanation (hypothesis) offered to account for a particular situation is "forced," or illogical, because either (1) sufficient evidence does not exist to draw any conclusion or (2) the evidence can be explained more simply or more sensibly by a different hypothesis. This logical fallacy often results from failure to consider other possible explanations. You discredit a forced hypothesis by providing alternative conclusions that are more sensible or just as sensible as the one offered. Consider the following example:

- Professor Redding's students received either A's or B's last semester. He must be an excellent teacher.

(The grades alone cannot support the conclusion. Professor Redding could be an excellent teacher; he could have started with excellent students; he could be an easy grader.)

Non Sequitur

The term *non sequitur,* meaning literally "it does not follow," could apply to all arguments that do not work, but the term is usually reserved for those arguments in which the conclusions are not logically connected to the reasons, those arguments with the "glue" missing. In a hasty generalization, for example, there is a connection between support (five politicians in the news) and conclusion (many politicians with drinking problems), just not a convincing connection. With the *non sequitur* there is no recognizable connection, either because (1) whatever connection the arguer sees is not made clear to others or because (2) the evidence or reasons offered are irrelevant to the conclusion. For example:

- Donna will surely get a good grade in physics; she earned an A in her biology class.

(Doing well in one course, even one science course, does not support the conclusion that the student will get a good grade in another course. If Donna is not good at math, she definitely will not do well in physics.)

Slippery Slope

The *slippery slope* argument asserts that we should not proceed with or permit A because, if we do, the terrible consequences X, Y, and Z will occur. This type of argument oversimplifies by assuming, without evidence and usually by ignoring historical examples, existing laws, or any reasonableness in people, that X, Y, and Z will follow inevitably from A. This kind of argument rests on the belief that most people will not want the final, awful Z to occur. The belief, however accurate, does not provide a sufficiently good reason for avoiding A. One of the best-known examples of slippery slope reasoning can be found in the gun-control debate:

- If we allow the government to register handguns, next it will register hunting rifles; then it will prohibit all citizen ownership of guns, thereby creating a police state or a world in which only outlaws have guns.

(Surely no one wants the final dire consequences predicted in this argument. However, handgun registration does not mean that these consequences will follow. The United States has never been a police state, and its system of free elections guards against such a future. Also, citizens have registered cars, boats, and planes for years without any threat of these belongings being confiscated.)

False Dilemma

The *false dilemma* oversimplifies an issue by asserting only two alternatives when there are more than two. The either–or thinking of this kind of argument can be an effective tactic if undetected. If the arguer gives us only two choices and one of those is clearly unacceptable, then the arguer can push us toward the preferred choice. For example:

- The Federal Reserve System must lower interest rates, or we will never pull out of the recession.

(Clearly, staying in a recession is not much of a choice, but the alternative may not be the only or the best course of action to achieve a healthy economy. If interest rates go too low, inflation can be triggered. Other options include the government's creating new jobs and patiently letting market forces play themselves out.)

False Analogy

When examining the shape of analogy, we also considered the problems with this type of argument.(See p. 103.) Remember that you challenge a false analogy by noting many differences in the two items being compared or by noting a significant difference that has been ignored.

Post Hoc Fallacy

The term *post hoc,* from the Latin *post hoc, ergo propter hoc* (literally, "after this, therefore because of it") refers to a common error in arguments about cause. One over-simplifies causation by confusing a time relationship with cause. Reveal the illogic of *post hoc* arguments by pointing to other possible causes:

- We should throw out the entire city council. Since the members were elected, the city has gone into deficit spending.

   (Assuming that deficit spending in this situation is bad, was it caused by the current city council? Or did the current council inherit debts? Or is the entire region suffering from a recession?)

Exercises: Fallacies That Result from Oversimplifying

1. Here is a list of the fallacies we have examined so far. Make up or collect from your reading at least one example of each fallacy.
   - **a.** Overstatement
   - **b.** Stereotyping
   - **c.** Hasty generalization
   - **d.** Forced hypothesis
   - **e.** *Non sequitur*
   - **f.** Slippery slope
   - **g.** False dilemma
   - **h.** False analogy
   - **i.** *Post hoc* fallacy

2. Explain what is illogical about each of the following arguments. Then name the fallacy represented. (Sometimes an argument will fit into more than one category. In that case name all appropriate terms.)
   - **a.** Everybody agrees that we need stronger drunk-driving laws.
   - **b.** The upsurge in crime on Sundays is the result of the reduced rate of church attendance in recent years.
   - **c.** The government must create new jobs. A factory in Illinois has laid off half its workers.
   - **d.** Steve has joined the country club. Golf must be one of his favorite sports.
   - **e.** Blondes have more fun.
   - **f.** You'll enjoy your Volvo; foreign cars never break down.
   - **g.** Gary loves jokes. He would make a great comedian.
   - **h.** The economy is in bad shape because of the Federal Reserve Board. Ever since they expanded the money supply, the stock market has been declining.

 i. Either we improve the city's street lighting, or we will fail to reduce crime.

 j. DNA research today is just like the study of nuclear fission. It seems important, but it's just another bomb that will one day explode on us. When will we learn that government must control research?

 k. To prohibit prayer in public schools is to limit religious practice solely to internal belief. The result is that an American is religiously "free" only in his own mind.

 l. Professor Johnson teaches in the political science department. I'll bet she's another socialist.

 m. Coming to the aid of any country engaged in civil war is a bad idea. Next we'll be sending American troops, and soon we'll be involved in another Vietnam.

 n. We must reject affirmative action in hiring or we'll have to settle for incompetent employees.

3. Examine the logic in this famous passage from Lewis Carroll's *Alice in Wonderland*. What logical fallacy does the King commit?

The King turned pale, and shut his note-book hastily. "Consider your verdict," he said to the jury, in a low trembling voice.

"There's more evidence to come yet, please your Majesty," said the White Rabbit, jumping up in a great hurry: "this paper has just been picked up."

"What's in it?" said the Queen.

"I haven't opened it yet," said the White Rabbit; "but it seems to be a letter, written by the prisoner to—to somebody."

"It must have been that," said the King, "unless it was written to nobody, which isn't usual, you know."

"Who is it directed to?" said one of the jurymen.

"It isn't directed at all," said the White Rabbit; "in fact, there's nothing written on the *outside*." He unfolded the paper as he spoke, and added, "It isn't a letter, after all: it's a set of verses."

"Are they in the prisoner's handwriting?" asked another of the jurymen.

"No, they're not," said the White Rabbit, "and that's the queerest thing about it." (The jury all looked puzzled.)

"He must have imitated somebody else's hand," said the King. (The jury all brightened up again.)

"Please, your Majesty," said the Knave, "I didn't write it, and they can't prove that I did: there's no name signed at the end."

"If you didn't sign it," said the King, "that only makes the matter worse. You *must* have meant some mischief, or else you'd have signed your name like an honest man."

There was a general clapping of hands at this: it was the first really clever thing the King had said that day.

"That *proves* his guilt, of course," said the Queen, "so, off with—"

"It doesn't prove anything of the sort!" said Alice. "Why, you don't even know what they're about!"

FALLACIES THAT RESULT FROM IGNORING THE ISSUE

There are many arguments that divert attention from the issue under debate. Of the six discussed here, the first three try to divert attention by introducing a separate issue or "sliding by" the actual issue; the following three seek diversion by appealing to the audience's emotions or prejudices. In the first three the arguer tries to give the impression of presenting an argument; in the last four the arguer charges forward on emotional manipulation alone.

Begging the Question

To assume that part of your argument is true without supporting it is to *beg the question.* Arguments seeking to pass off as proof statements that must themselves be supported are often introduced with such phrases as "the fact is" (to introduce opinion), "obviously," and "as we can see." For example:

- Clearly, lowering grading standards would be bad for students, so a pass/fail system should not be adopted.

(Does a pass/fail system lower standards? No evidence has been given. If so, is that necessarily bad for students?)

Red Herring

The *red herring* is a foul-smelling argument indeed. The debater introduces a side issue, some point that is not relevant to the debate:

- The senator is an honest woman; she loves her children and gives to charities.

(The children and charities are side issues; they do not demonstrate honesty.)

Straw Man

The *straw man* argument attributes to opponents erroneous and usually ridiculous views that they do not hold so that their position can be easily attacked. We can challenge this illogic by demonstrating that the arguer's opponents do not hold those views or by demanding that the arguer provide some evidence that they do:

- Those who favor gun control just want to take all guns away from responsible citizens and put them in the hands of criminals.

(The position attributed to proponents of gun control is not only inaccurate but actually the opposite of what is sought by gun-control proponents.)

Ad Hominem

One of the most frequent of all appeals to emotion masquerading as argument is the *ad hominem* argument (literally, argument "to the man"). Sometimes the debate turns to an attack of a supporter of the issue; other times, the illogic is found in name calling. When someone says that "those crazy liberals at the ACLU just want all criminals to go free," or a pro-choice demonstrator screams at those "self-righteous fascists" on the other side, the best retort may be silence, or the calm assertion that such statements do not contribute to meaningful debate.

Common Practice or Bandwagon

To argue that an action should be taken or a position accepted because "everyone is doing it" is illogical. The majority is not always right. Frequently when someone is defending an action as ethical on the ground that everyone does it, the action isn't ethical and the defender knows it isn't. The bandwagon argument is a desperate one. For example:

- There's nothing wrong with fudging a bit on your income taxes. After all, the superrich don't pay any taxes and the government expects everyone to cheat a little.

(First, not everyone cheats on taxes; many pay to have their taxes done correctly. And if it is wrong, it is wrong regardless of the number who do it.)

Ad Populum

Another technique for arousing an audience's emotions and ignoring the issue is to appeal *ad populum*, "to the people," to the audience's presumed shared values and beliefs. Every Fourth of July, politicians employ this tactic, appealing to God, mother, apple pie, and "traditional family values." As with all emotional gimmicks, we need to reject the argument as illogical.

- Good, law-abiding Americans must be sick of the violent crimes occurring in our once godly society. But we won't tolerate it anymore; put the criminals in jail and throw away the key.

(This does not contribute to a thoughtful debate on criminal justice issues.)

Exercises: Fallacies That Result from Ignoring the Issue

1. Here is a list of fallacies that result from ignoring the issue. Make up or collect from your reading at least one example of each fallacy.
   - a. Begging the question
   - b. Red herring
   - c. Straw man
   - d. *Ad hominem*
   - e. Common practice or bandwagon
   - f. *Ad populum*

2. Explain what is illogical about each of the following arguments. Then name the fallacy represented.
   - a. Gold's book doesn't deserve a Pulitzer Prize. She has been married four times.
   - b. I wouldn't vote for him; many of his programs are basically socialist.
   - c. Eight out of 10 headache sufferers use Bayer to relieve headache pain. It will work for you, too.
   - d. We shouldn't listen to Colman McCarthy's argument against liquor ads in college newspapers because he obviously thinks young people are ignorant and need guidance in everything.
   - e. My roommate Joe does the craziest things; he must be neurotic.
   - f. Since so many people obviously cheat the welfare system, it should be abolished.
   - g. She isn't pretty enough to win the contest, and besides she had her nose "fixed" two years ago.

   h. Professors should chill out; everybody cheats on exams from time to time.

   i. The fact is that bilingual education is a mistake because it encourages students to use only their native language and that gives them an advantage over other students.

   j. Don't join those crazy liberals in support of the American Civil Liberties Union. They want all criminals to go free.

   k. Real Americans understand that free trade agreements are evil. Let your representatives know that we want American goods protected.

3. Examine the following letter to the editor by Christian Brahmstedt that appeared in the *Washington Post* on January 2, 1989. If you think it contains logical fallacies, identify the passages and explain the fallacies.

Help Those Who Help, Not Hurt, Themselves

1   In the past year, and repeatedly throughout the holiday season, the *Post* has devoted an abnormally large share of newsprint to the "plight" of the vagrants who wander throughout the city in search of free handouts: i.e., the "homeless."

2   As certain as taxes, the poor shall remain with civilization forever. Yet these "homeless" are certainly not in the same category as the poor. The poor of civilization, of which we have all been a part at one time in our lives, are proud and work hard until a financial independence frees them from the category. The "homeless" do not seek work or pride. They are satisfied to beg and survive on others' generosity.

3   The best correlation to the "homeless" I have witnessed are the gray squirrels on Capitol Hill. After feeding several a heavy dose of nuts one afternoon, I returned the next day to see the same squirrels patiently waiting for a return feeding. In the same fashion, the "homeless" are trained by Washington's guilt-ridden society to continue begging a sustenance rather than learning independence.

4   The *Post* has preached that these vagrants be supported from the personal and federal coffers—in the same manner as the squirrels on Capitol Hill. This support is not helping the homeless; it is only teaching them to rely on it. All of our parents struggled through the depression as homeless of a sort, to arise and build financial independence through hard work.

5   The "homeless" problem will go away when, and only when, Washingtonians refuse to feed them. They will learn to support themselves and learn that society demands honest work for an honest dollar.

6   It would be better for Washington citizens to field their guilt donations to the poor, those folks who are holding down two or more jobs just to make ends meet, rather than throwing their tribute to the vagrants on the sewer grates. The phrase "help those who help themselves" has no more certain relevance than to the "homeless" issue.

Exercises: Analyzing Arguments

1. Analyze the following letter to the editor titled "Beer Commercials Do No Harm," published on January 28, 1989, and written by James C. Sanders, president of the

Beer Institute. How effectively does Sanders make his case? How convincing is the evidence that he presents? Do you accept his warrant that his evidence is authoritative? If not, what do you think he should have included in the letter? Try to answer these questions in detail to be prepared for class discussion.

1   With respect to the letter to the editor of Jan. 13 concerning the banning of beer commercials, we believe it is appropriate to respond. While the tragedy of drunk driving and other abuses of alcohol beverages is of concern to us all, there are much broader problems and solutions that must be addressed.

2   First, we must consider the empirical evidence on the effect or lack of effect of alcohol beverage advertising and its impact on abuse. There exists a substantial body of evidence that suggests that the only impact of alcohol beverage advertising is that of brand preference, shifting those who choose to drink to a particular beverage or brand name.

3   There exists no sound evidence that alcohol beverage advertising has an adverse impact on abuse. Alcohol beverage advertising does not promote excessive consumption, influence nondrinkers to become drinkers or induce young people to drink.

4   In fact, studies show that parents and peers, respectively, are the major contributors to a young person's decision to consume or not to consume. Furthermore, studies have shown that "the best controlled studies show no overall effect of alcohol advertising on consumption."

5   Another related issue is the right to commercial free speech. The alcohol beverage industry—specifically, the beer and wine industries—advertises on television legal products whose responsible, moderate consumption is enjoyed by the majority of our population. This is not to disregard a certain percentage of citizens who should not consume our products—specifically, underage persons and alcoholics.

6   The alcohol beverage industry is concerned and involved in programs that educate, inform and support positive, realistic solutions to alcohol abuse. We are working with many organizations whose goals are to reduce the problems associated with the misuse of our products. Radical or empirically unsound approaches to alcohol problems serve only to divert us from sound, positive solutions.

2. Analyze the logical fallacies in the following student essay. Make notes of specific problems to be prepared for class discussion.

DEATH

In the editorial section of the *Washington Post* I came across an article titled "New York on the Brink." The article is about New York thinking and trying to impose the death penalty. The editors are against the death sentence, and I disagree with them.

The death sentence is obviously a moral and political issue. But is it right to let killers just serve time and be released back into society after taking someone's life? The death penalty has been around as long as man. It is needed to get rid of the murderers and keep the innocent safe and secure.

The article says that President George Bush's speech in New York urging a mandatory federal death penalty for the killing of law enforcement officers is unfair. Why is that unfair? The police are out to protect the innocent. It is unfair not to serve justice on those individuals. If a criminal goes around killing the protectors of law and peace, who knows what they can and will do to the common citizens.

Another thing to think about is the overcrowding of prisons. There is very little room for prisoners these days. The author didn't even think of that. By ridding society of the killers, it will make room for other criminals to serve time. I wonder if the author is willing to pay extra taxes to build new prisons.

The author also argues that the death penalty doesn't prevent murders from happening. There have always been murderers throughout history, and there will always be murders. But I think that I would think twice about killing someone if I knew that I would die as well. But there will always be people who take the chance. The death penalty would just get rid of those who do them.

The author's final argument is that sanctioned killing is as abhorrent as murder. I think the author would have a change of heart if someone close to him or her was murdered. It is only fair that the murderer pay the same price as the victim.

It is time that people start to open their eyes and realize that it is a life and death world out there. And the only way to change the suffering of the law abiders is to get rid of the law breakers. The death penalty is the price a free society pays to stay free.

Writing Assignments

1. **a.** Develop one of the following analogies, listing as many similarities as you can, and thinking as you write about a conclusion your analogy reasonably leads to.

Life is like a ride on the starship *Enterprise*.
Students are like the early explorers to the North Pole.
Humans are like spiders in a web.
The mind is like a vast ocean.
Modern science is like magic.

b. Exchange analogies with a classmate and check your classmate's analogy to see if there is a fundamental difference that negates the argument. If a classmate discovers a flaw in your argument, revise either some of your comparisons or the conclusion if necessary.

c. Develop your analogy into a short essay. The conclusion of your analogy is your essay's thesis; the points of comparison, developed and explained, are the support of your thesis. Since your analogy will probably rest in part on metaphorical language, remember that your support may be based more on verbal cleverness than on strict logic. You should, therefore, qualify your thesis.

2. Think of your own analogy to develop an argument regarding student needs, student rights, or student responsibilities. Follow the guidelines for the first assignment.

3. Select an event from your life and trace the conditions, influences, and various causes that brought it about. Develop your causal analysis into a biographical essay. Possible topics include the causes behind your choice of college or career or your selection of a summer or part-time job.

4. Analyze the following argument by Lester Thurow by answering the questions that follow the article. Then write on one of the topics following the questions.

Why Women Are Paid Less Than Men

Lester C. Thurow

A professor at the MIT Sloan School of Management and consultant to both government and private corporations, Lester C. Thurow (b. 1938) has written extensively on economic and public-policy issues. His books include *Poverty and Discrimination* (1969), *The Political Economy of Income Redistribution Policies* (1977), and *Dangerous Currents* (1983).

"Why Women Are Paid Less Than Men," published in the *New York Times* (March 8, 1981), offers an explanation for the discrepancy between the incomes of men and women.

1   In the 40 years from 1939 to 1979 white women who work full time have with monotonous regularity made slightly less than 60 percent as much as white men. Why?

2   Over the same time period, minorities have made substantial progress in catching up with whites, with minority women making even more progress than minority men.

3   Black men now earn 72 percent as much as white men (up 16 percentage points since the mid-1950s) but black women earn 92 percent as much as white women. Hispanic men make 71 percent of what their white counterparts do, but Hispanic women make 82 percent as much as white women. As a result of their faster progress, fully employed black women make 75 percent as much as fully employed black men while Hispanic women earn 68 percent as much as Hispanic men.

4   This faster progress may, however, end when minority women finally catch up with white women. In the bible of the New Right, George Gilder's "Wealth and Poverty," the 60 percent is just one of Mother Nature's constants like the speed of light or the force of gravity.

5   Men are programmed to provide for their families economically while women are programmed to take care of their families emotionally and physically. As a result men put more effort into their jobs than women. The net result is a difference in work intensity that leads to that 40 percent gap in earnings. But there is no discrimination against women—only the biological facts of life.

6   The problem with this assertion is just that. It is an assertion with no evidence for it other than the fact that white women have made 60 percent as much as men for a long period of time.

7   "Discrimination against women" is an easy answer but it also has its problems as an adequate explanation. Why is discrimination against women not declining under the same social forces that are leading to a lessening of discrimination against minorities? In recent years women have made more use of the enforcement provisions of the Equal Employment Opportunities Commission and the courts than minorities. Why do the laws that prohibit discrimination against women and minorities work for minorities but not for women?

8   When men discriminate against women, they run into a problem. To discriminate against women is to discriminate against your own wife and to lower your own family income. To prevent women from working is to force men to work more.

9   When whites discriminate against blacks, they can at least think that they are raising their own incomes. When men discriminate against women they have to know that they are lowering their own family income and increasing their own work effort.

10   While discrimination undoubtedly explains part of the male-female earnings differential, one has to believe that men are monumentally stupid or irrational to explain all of the earnings gap in terms of discrimination. There must be something else going on.

11   Back in 1939 it was possible to attribute the earnings gap to large differences in educational attainments. But the educational gap between men and women has been eliminated since World War II. It is no longer possible to use education as an explanation for the lower earnings of women.

12   Some observers have argued that women earn less money since they are less reliable workers who are more apt to leave the labor force. But it is difficult to maintain this position since women are less apt to quit one job to take another and as a result they tend to work as long, or longer, for any one employer. From any employer's perspective they are more reliable, not less reliable, than men.

13   Part of the answer is visible if you look at the lifetime earnings profile of men. Suppose that you are asked to predict which men in a group of 25-year-olds would become economically successful. At age 25 it is difficult to tell who will be economically successful and your predictions are apt to be highly inaccurate.

14   But suppose that you were asked to predict which men in a group of 35-year-olds would become economically successful. If you are successful at age 35 you are very likely to remain successful for the rest of your life. If you have not become economically successful by age 35, you are very unlikely to do so later.

15   The decade between 25 and 35 is when men either succeed or fail. It is the decade when lawyers become partners in the good firms, when business managers make it onto the "fast track," when academics get tenure at good universities, and when blue-collar

workers find the job opportunities that will lead to training opportunities and the skills that will generate high earnings.

16   If there is any one decade when it pays to work hard and to be consistently in the labor force, it is the decade between 25 and 35. For those who succeed, earnings will rise rapidly. For those who fail, earnings will remain flat for the rest of their lives.

17   But the decade between 25 and 35 is precisely the decade when women are most apt to leave the labor force or become part-time workers to have children. When they do, the current system of promotion and skill acquisition will extract an enormous life-time price.

18   This leaves essentially two avenues for equalizing male and female earnings.

19   Families where women who wish to have successful careers, compete with men, and achieve the same earnings should alter their family plans and have their children either before 25 or after 35. Or society can attempt to alter the existing promotion and skill acquisition system so that there is a longer time period in which both men and women can attempt to successfully enter the labor force.

20   Without some combination of these two factors, a substantial fraction of the male-female earnings differentials are apt to persist for the next 40 years, even if discrimination against women is eliminated.

Questions for Analysis and Discussion

1. What situation is the subject of Thurow's analysis?

2. What question should you ask about Thurow's numbers? Do you know the answer to the question?

3. When he asks "Why?" at the end of paragraph 1, what kind of analysis or argument does Thurow signal he will develop?

4. Briefly explain why Thurow rejects each of the possible explanations that he covers.

5. What is Thurow's explanation for the discrepancy between the earnings of white women and white men, for the apparent single difference that accounts for the lower earnings?

6. Thurow's conclusion about women's lower earnings can be expressed as a partial deductive argument: Women fail to achieve big earnings because they are not working and advancing between the ages of 25 and 35. What, then, is the major premise? How does Thurow support the minor premise?

7. Thurow's support for the major premise is a series of assertions in paragraph 15. Are these facts or assumptions? Is it true that most people who are going to be successful are so by age 35? Can you think of people who did not become successful until after 35? Is this the kind of assumption that can create its own reality—that is, if people believe it to be so, will it become so?

Essay Topics

1. Evaluate the two solutions Thurow offers in the light of other solutions you can think of that he has not presented. Make clear which solution or solutions you think is (or are) best and defend your judgment.

2. Thurow's figures are based on the total earnings of all full-time workers; they are not comparisons by job category. What are other facts about jobs that men and women hold that may account for some of the discrepancy in pay? Develop your ideas into an essay that can be viewed as adding to Thurow's discussion. (Be certain to cite Thurow for all quoted or paraphrased ideas from his article.)

CHAPTER 5

Preparing Good Arguments

The basics of good writing remain much the same even for works as seemingly different as the personal essay, the argument, and the research paper. Good writing is focused, organized, and concrete. Essays are focused and unified when all material included effectively develops and supports a clear main idea, the claim of your argument. A clear organization supports unity, and specifics develop the main idea and engage readers. Sound principles, all well known to you. But how, exactly, can you achieve them when writing argument? This chapter will establish both general guidelines for developing arguments and specific guidelines for writing the most typical kinds of arguments.

The stages in the writing process—inventing, drafting, and revising—can guide our thinking. For many writers, invention is the most complex and demanding stage. As you develop a topic, keep in mind that your thinking needs to be directed by your total writing context, a context that includes your audience and purpose as well as your topic.

Knowing Your Audience

Too often students plunge into writing without thinking much about their audience, for, after all, their "audience" is only the instructor who has given the assignment, just as their purpose in writing is to complete the assignment and get a grade. These views of audience and purpose are likely to lead to badly written arguments. First, if you are not envisioning readers who may disagree with your views, you may not develop the best defense of your claim, which should include a challenge to potential counterarguments. Second, you may ignore your essay's needed introductory material on the assumption that the instructor, knowing the assignment, has a context for understanding your writing. Here are important questions to ask yourself about audience.

WHO IS MY AUDIENCE?

If you are preparing an essay for the student newspaper, your audience consists—primarily—of fellow students. But do not forget that faculty and administrators also read the student newspaper. If you are preparing a letter-to-the-editor refutation of a recent column in your town's newspaper, your audience will be the readers of that newspaper—adults in your town or city. Often instructors give argument assignments that create an audience such as those just described so that you will practice writing with a specific audience in mind. If you are not assigned such a concrete writing context, imagine your classmates as well as your instructor as part of your audience so that you are writing to many readers of varied beliefs. Imagine readers who are intelligent and thoughtful but who are looking for sound reasoning and convincing evidence.

WHAT WILL MY AUDIENCE KNOW ABOUT MY TOPIC?

What can you expect a group of diverse readers to know? Whether you are writing on a current problem or a centuries-old philosophical debate, you must expect most readers to have some knowledge of the issues. Their knowledge does not free you from the responsibility of developing your argument fully, however. In fact, their knowledge imposes additional demands on you. For example, most readers will know the main arguments on both sides of the abortion issue. For you to write as if they do not, and thus to ignore the arguments of your opposition, is to produce an essay that probably does not advance the conversation on this topic in any meaningful way. On the other hand, what some of your readers "know" may be little more than an overview of the issues obtained from television news—or the emotional outbursts of a family member. Other readers may be misinformed or prejudiced, but they hold their views enthusiastically nonetheless. As you plan, you will have to assess your audience's degree of knowledge and sophistication on your topic. This assessment will help you decide how much background information to provide or what false facts may need to be addressed.

WHERE DOES MY AUDIENCE STAND ON THE ISSUE?

You are wise to imagine readers holding a range of views. This may be true even if you are writing specifically to students on your campus, or if you are addressing an organization of which you are a member. Students at the same college and members of the same organization do not think alike on most issues. It is not true that all students want pass/fail grading or more reading days before exams. Besides, if everyone already agrees with you, you have no purpose in writing; an argument has to be about a topic that is open to debate.

So assume that some of your audience will probably never agree with you but will offer you grudging respect if you prepare a good argument. Assume that some do not hold strong views on your topic and may be open to convincing, if you prepare a good argument. Also assume that those who share your views will still want to hear a strong argument for their position. With some specific topics, you may be able to guess that most of your audience will disagree with you. You know, that is, that you hold unpopular views on your subject. In this writing context, you are wise to take a conciliatory approach, as discussed in Chapter 4.

HOW SHOULD I SPEAK TO MY AUDIENCE?

You need to imagine your audience as a guide to planning your argument. Remember that your audience will also form an image of you, based on how you write and how you reason. Sometimes writers create a special "voice," a *persona*, someone not like themselves, as part of their persuasive strategy. (Jonathan Swift creates a persona different from himself in his famous essay, "A Modest Proposal," on pages 585–91.) You may want to try this strategy sometime; it is a writing challenge but also fun. Most of the time, though, your persona will closely resemble you. Still, you have different roles in your life, and you use different voices as appropriate to each role. You speak (presumably) with courtesy and intelligence to teachers and employers, but you use slang with friends, or speak condescendingly (surely not often!) to a younger brother or sister. What persona is best for most of your arguments? Unless you create an unusual persona to achieve a special effect, you should select the serious voice you normally use for serious discussions with other adults. This is the persona that will help to establish your credibility, your *ethos*.

Understanding Your Writing Purpose

There are many kinds of arguments. As you consider possible topics for a paper, you need to think about what you actually want to do with each topic—beyond wanting to write convincingly in defense of your claim. Different types of arguments demand different approaches, or different kinds of evidence. It helps to be able to recognize what kind of argument your topic is.

If you are given the assignment of collecting evidence in an organized fashion to support a claim about advertising strategies or the amount of violence in children's television programming, you need to recognize that you have the task of an inductive argument or an investigative paper similar to those in the social sciences. If you are given the assignment to argue for your position on euthanasia, capital punishment, or abortion, you need to recognize that this assignment calls for a claim of values. You will be writing a position paper, a rather philosophical argument presenting reasons in support of a complex and controversial issue. If you are asked to consider the qualities or traits that we should look for in a president or a Supreme Court judge, you are being asked to define "the good president" or the "good Supreme Court judge." If you are given the broad subject "What should we do about _____?" and you have to fill in the blank, you have the task of a problem/solution argument, a claim of policy. If you are not given any directions beyond "Write an argument," then you may want to consider choosing among the topics given at the end of this chapter (p. 178). But notice that they are grouped according to these different kinds of claims. It helps, when choosing a subject to write about, to think about the kind of argument you would need to write. You will keep your focus and argue more convincingly if you understand from the outset what will be required to shape a successful argument. Most of the rest of this chapter provides specific guidelines for, and models of, different kinds of arguments, but first let's continue through the writing process, identifying additional tasks in the inventing stage and then turning to drafting and revising.

Moving from Topic to Claim to Support

When you write a letter to the editor of a newspaper, you have chosen to respond to a particular issue, to someone else's argument that has distressed you. In this writing context, you already know your topic and, probably, your claim. You also know that your purpose will be to refute the article you have read. In composition classes, though, the invention process is not always so clear. Still, you will usually be given some context, some guidelines that will get you started.

SELECTING A TOPIC

Suppose that you are assigned to write an argument that is in some way connected to First Amendment rights. Your instructor has limited topic choices and focused your purpose. Start thinking about possible topics that relate to freedom-of-speech and censorship issues. To aid your topic search and selection, use one or more invention strategies:

- Brainstorm (make a list).
- Freewrite (write without stopping for 10 minutes).
- Map or cluster (connect ideas to the general topic in various spokes; a kind of visual brainstorming).
- Read (in this case, look through appropriate chapters in this text for ideas).

Your invention strategies lead, let us suppose, to the following list of possible topics:

Administrative restrictions on the college newspaper

Hate speech restrictions or codes

Deleting certain books from high school reading lists

Controls on alcohol and cigarette advertising

Restrictions on Internet "smut"

Restrictions on violent television programming

Dress codes/uniforms

Looking over your list, you realize that the last item, dress codes/uniforms, may be about freedom but not freedom of speech, so you drop it from consideration. All of the other topics have promise. Which one do you select? Two considerations should guide you: interest and knowledge. First, your argument is likely to be more thoughtful and lively if you choose an issue that matters to you. But, you can also appreciate the usefulness of information and ideas on a topic. Unless you are selecting a research topic and will have the time to read and become informed, you are wise to choose a topic to which you have given some thought and feel comfortable exploring. To continue our example, let's suppose that you decide to write about television violence because you are concerned about violence in American society and you have given this issue some thought. It is time to phrase your concern as a thesis or claim.

DRAFTING A CLAIM

Good claim statements will keep you focused in your writing (in addition to establishing your main idea for readers), so give thought both to your position on an issue and to the wording of your claim. Here are some problem claim statements to avoid:

- Claims using vague words such as *good* or *bad*.
  Vague: TV violence is bad for us.
  Better: We need more restrictions on violent TV programming.

- Claims in loosely worded, "two-part" sentences.

    Unfocused: Campus rape is a serious problem, and we need to do something about it.

    Better: College administrators and students need to work together to reduce both the number of campus rapes and the fear of rape.

- Claims that are not appropriately qualified.

    Overstated: Violence on television is making us a violent society.

    Better: TV violence is contributing to viewers' increased fear of violence and insensitivity to violence.

- Claims that do not help you focus on your purpose.

    Unclear purpose: Not everyone agrees on what is meant by violent programming.

    (Perhaps this is true, but more important, the claim suggests that you will seek to define violent programming. Such an approach would not keep you focused on a First Amendment issue.)

    Better: Restrictions on violent TV programs can be justified.

    (Now your claim directs you to the debate over restrictions of content.)

PLANNING YOUR SUPPORT

As you learned in Chapter 3, you can develop grounds to support a claim by adding a "because" clause after a claim statement. We can start a list for the topic we have been using as illustration in this way:

We need more restrictions on violent television programming *because*

- many people, including children and teens, watch many hours of TV

- logic tells us that people are shaped by dominant activities in their lives

- evidence supports a connection between violent programming and desensitizing and fear of violence, and possibly more aggressive behavior, in heavy viewers

- classic arguments in support of free speech always make exceptions for children; society needs to protect young people and that protection will require some restrictions

Some of the items you list may be reasons, a sequence of logically connected statements. Other items may be inferences drawn from evidence. You may want to do some reading or Internet searching for evidence to support what you believe to be sensible inferences—what you may have read or heard some time ago.

Just as you can develop the core of an argument by using Toulmin's terms *claim* and *grounds*, you can also be guided in your planning by using all of Toulmin's terms. As a part of your planning process, you may want to review the discussion of Toulmin argument in Chapter 3 so that you can work through all of the parts of the Toulmin structure of argument. If you examine warrants and ask yourself about backing for your argument and check to be sure that you have qualified statements appropriately and then think about rebuttals to your developing argument, you are likely to develop a thoughtful and thorough argument. Use the Toulmin terms not as ends in themselves but as guides to shaping a good outline from which you can draft a sound argument.

Drafting Your Argument

While it is certainly true that some writers are highly intuitive, discovering what they want to say only as they actually write, many of us can benefit from the careful, step-by-step process of invention. In addition, the more detailed your planning, the more notes you have from working through the Toulmin structure, the easier it will be to get started on your draft. Many students report that they can control their writing anxiety when they generate good notes through various invention strategies. A page or two of notes that also suggest an organizational plan can remove that awful feeling of staring at a blank page (whether that "blank page" is your notebook or computer screen).

You will find some specific suggestions for organization in the guidelines for each kind of argument covered in the rest of the chapter. In your planning and drafting stages, you can always rely on either of two basic organizations for argument; keep these in mind as you draft:

Plan 1: Organizing an Argument

Attention-getting opening (why the issue is important, or current, etc.)

Claim statement

Reasons and evidence in order from least important to most important

Challenge to potential rebuttals or counterarguments

Conclusion that reemphasizes claim

Plan 2: Organizing an Argument

Attention-getting opening

Claim statement (or possibly leave to the conclusion)

Order by main arguments of opposing position, with your challenge to each one

Conclusion that reemphasizes (or possibly states for the first time) your claim

Here are a few words of advice on the drafting stage: Remember that you will revise, so what you write first does not need to be perfect. Try to get a complete draft of an essay in one sitting, so that you can "see" the whole piece. If you can't think of a clever opening, state your claim and move on to the body of your essay. After you draft your reasons and evidence, a good opening may occur to you. If you find that you need something more in some parts of your essay, leave space there as a reminder that you will need to return to that paragraph later. Try to avoid using either a dictionary or the-saurus while drafting. Your goal is to get the ideas down. You will polish later. Learn to draft at your computer. Revising is so much easier that you will be more willing to make significant changes if you work at your PC. If you are handwriting your draft, leave plenty of margin space for additions or for directions to shift parts around.

Revising Your Draft

If you have drafted at the computer, begin revising by making a print copy of your draft. Most of us cannot do an adequate job of revision by looking at a computer screen. Then remind yourself that revision is a three-step process: rewriting, editing, and proofreading.

REWRITING

You are not ready to polish the writing until you are satisfied with the argument. Look first at the total piece. Do you have all the necessary parts: a claim, support, some response to possible counterarguments? Examine the order of your reasons and evidence. Do some of your points belong, logically, in a different place? Does the order make the most powerful defense of your claim? Be willing to move whole paragraphs around to test the best organization. Also reflect on the argument itself. Have you avoided logical fallacies? Have you qualified statements when appropriate? Do you have enough support? The best support for your argument?

Consider development: Is your essay long enough to meet assignment requirements? Are points fully developed to satisfy the demands of readers? One key to development is the length of your paragraphs. If most of your paragraphs are only two or three sentences, you have not developed the point of each paragraph satisfactorily. It is possible that some paragraphs need to be combined because they are really on the same subtopic. More typically, short paragraphs need further explanation of ideas or examples to illustrate ideas. Compare the following paragraphs for effectiveness through development:

First Draft of a Paragraph from an Essay on Gun Control

One popular argument used against the regulation of gun ownership is the need of citizens, especially in urban areas where the crime rate is higher, to possess a handgun for personal protection, either carried or kept in the home. Some citizens may not be aware of the dangers to themselves or their families when they purchase a gun. Others, more aware, may embrace the myth that "bad things only happen to other people."

Revised Version of the Paragraph with Statistics Added

One popular argument used against the regulation of gun ownership is the need of citizens, especially in urban areas where the crime rate is higher, to possess a handgun for personal protection, whether it is carried or kept in the home. Although some citizens may not be aware of the dangers to themselves or their families when they purchase a gun, they should be. According to the Center to Prevent Handgun Violence, from their Web page "Firearm Facts," "guns that are kept in the home for self-protection are 22 times more likely to kill a family member or friend than to kill in self-defense." The Center also reports that guns in the home make homicide three times more likely and suicide five times more likely. We are not thinking straight if we believe that these dangers only apply to others.

A quick trip to the Internet has provided this student with some facts to support his argument. Observe how he has referred informally but fully to the source of his information.

EDITING

When you have added to or deleted from your draft, or moved parts of the draft around to shape a more effective argument, make your changes, print another copy, and begin the second phase of revision: editing. As you read through this time, pay close attention to unity and coherence, to sentence patterns, and to word choice. Read each paragraph as a separate unit to be certain that everything is on the same subtopic. Then look at your use of transition and connecting words, both within and between paragraphs. Ask yourself: Have you guided the reader through the argument? Have you shown how the parts connect by using appropriate transitions, connectors such as *therefore, in addition, as a consequence, also,* and so forth?

Read again, focusing on each sentence, checking to see that you have varied sentence patterns and length. Read sentences aloud to let your ear help you find awkward constructions or unfinished thoughts. Strive as well for word choice that is concrete and specific, avoiding wordiness, clichés, trite expressions, or incorrect use of specialized terms. Observe how Samantha edited one paragraph in her essay "Balancing Work and Family":

Draft Version of Paragraph

vague reference

wordy

short sentences

vague reference

Women have come a long way in equalizing themselves, but inequality within marriages do exist. One reason for this can be found in the media. Just last week America turned on their televisions to watch a grotesque dramatization of skewed priorities. On *Who Wants to Marry a Millionaire*, a panel of women vied for the affections of a millionaire who would choose one of them to be his wife. This show said that women can be purchased. Also that men must provide and that money is worth the sacrifice of one's individuality. The show also suggests that physical attraction is more important than the building of a complete relationship. Finally, the show says that women's true value lies in their appearance. This is a dangerous message to send to both men and women viewers.

Edited Version of Paragraph

Although women have come a long way toward equality in the workplace, inequality within marriages can still be found. The media may be partly to blame for this continued inequality. Just last week Americans watched a grotesque dramatization of skewed priorities. On *Who Wants to Marry a Millionaire*, a panel of women vied for the affections of a millionaire who would choose one of them to be his wife. Such displays teach us that women can be purchased, that men must be the providers, that the desire for money is worth the sacrifice of one's individuality, that physical attraction is more important than a complete relationship, and that women's true value lies in their appearance. These messages discourage marriages based on equality and mutual support.

Samantha's editing has eliminated wordiness and vague references and has combined ideas into one forceful sentence. If you have a good argument, you do not want to lose readers because you have not taken the time to polish your writing.

PROOFREADING

You also do not want to lose readers because you submit a paper filled with "little" errors, errors in punctuation, mechanics, and incorrect word choice. Most readers will forgive one or two little errors but will become annoyed if they begin to pile up. So, after you are finished rewriting and editing, print a copy of your paper and read it slowly, looking specifically at punctuation, at the handling of quotations and references to writers and to titles, and at those pesky words that come in two or more "versions": *to, too,* and *two; here* and *hear, their, there,* and *they're;* and so forth. If instructors have found any of these kinds of errors in your papers over the years, then focus your attention on the kinds of errors you have been known to make. Refer to Chapter 1 for handling references to authors and titles and for handling direct quotations. Use a glossary of usage in a handbook for homonyms (the words that sound alike but have different meanings), and check a handbook for punctuation rules. Take pride in your work and present a paper that will be treated with respect. What follows is a checklist of the key points for writing good arguments that we have just examined.

A Checklist for Revision

✔ Have I selected an issue and purpose consistent with assignment guidelines?

✔ Have I stated a claim that is focused, appropriately qualified, and precise?

✔ Have I developed sound reasons and evidence in support of my claim?

✔ Have I used Toulmin terms to help me study the parts of my argument, including rebuttals to counterarguments?

✔ Have I found a clear and effective organization for presenting my argument?

✔ Have I edited my draft thoughtfully, concentrating on producing unified and coherent paragraphs and polished sentences?

✔ Have I eliminated wordiness, clichés, jargon?

✔ Have I selected an appropriate tone for my purpose and audience?

✔ Have I considered a conciliatory approach and emphasized common ground with those who might disagree with me?

✔ Have I used my word processor's spell check and proofread a printed copy with great care?

Guidelines for Preparing Specific Kinds of Arguments

In the section "Understanding Your Writing Purpose" you were asked to think about the kind of argument you are planning to write. Classifying arguments helps writers think about what they need to include in the essay and what kind of organization may be suited to accomplish the writing purpose. What follows are guidelines for and examples of five different kinds of arguments. Although certainly some complex arguments combine the types presented here, most of the time you will be wise to try to place your proposed argument into one of the categories and see how that helps you to write a more effective argument.

THE INVESTIGATIVE ARGUMENT: GATHERING AND ANALYZING EVIDENCE

The first step in writing an investigative argument is, of course, to select a topic, a subject to explore. Composition students, even if not highly skilled in research in the social sciences, can write successful investigative papers on media and campus issues or on various local concerns. Although you will not begin with a claim, since you have to gather your evidence first, you probably should review possible topics and select one that you are both interested in and have some ideas about. For example, you may have noticed with interest some clever ads for jeans or beer, or perhaps you are concerned about a proposal to build another shopping area along a major street near your home. Either one of these topics could lead to a good investigative argument.

Next, think about what strategies you will need to use to gather evidence. If you want to study magazine advertising for one kind of product, you will need to collect many ads for that product. In addition, think about your procedure for obtaining these ads. You will want to select a time frame and a number of representative magazines. Then, to be thorough, you must collect and study all the ads for that product that appear in those magazines during that time period. If you have a notion that your area does not need another strip mall, how can you gather evidence to support such a claim? You could locate all existing shopping malls within a 10-mile radius of the proposed new mall site, visit them, and count the number and types of stores already available. For various campus issues, you may want to prepare and distribute a questionnaire to obtain student opinions. In short, instead of reading to find some statistics relevant to a topic, you are making the statistics. Just remember to devise objective procedures for collecting evidence so as not to bias your results.

Finally, you need to study the evidence you have obtained and think about the inference or inferences that evidence allows you to draw. The inference becomes the claim of your argument. When you have completed your investigation and reached a claim, think carefully about how to present your evidence to readers. Readers are turned off by disorganized lists of facts from which they are supposed to draw the same conclusion as the writer. Instead, you want to guide your readers through the evidence and explain to them how that evidence supports your claim. Here are some guidelines for writing your paper:

Guidelines for Preparing an Investigative Argument

1. *Begin with an opening paragraph that introduces your topic in an interesting way.* Possibilities include beginning with a startling statistic or explaining how the essay's facts will impact on readers.

2. *Devote space early in your paper to explaining your methods or procedures,* if you have conducted your own investigation to generate facts. For example, if you have obtained information through questionnaires or

interviews, recount the process: the questions, the number of people involved, the basis for selecting those people, and so on.

3. *Classify the evidence that you present.* Devising a meaningful organization is part of the originality of your study and will make your argument more forceful. It is the way you see the issue and want readers to see it. If you are contrasting incomes, for example, organize by points of contrast. To present all the statistics from the 1980s first and then the 1990s dilutes the purpose of contrast and challenges readers to remember which numbers from the first part of the paper are to be compared to those in the second half.

4. *Consider presenting evidence in several ways, including charts and tables as well as within paragraphs.* Readers are used to visuals, especially in technical reports and works containing statistical data.

5. *Analyze evidence.* Do not ask your reader to do the thinking that is your job. Explain how your evidence *is* evidence by discussing the connection between facts and the inference they are supporting.

In a study of selling techniques used in computer ads in business magazines, a student finds four major selling techniques, one of which he classifies as "corporate emphasis." Brian begins his paragraph on corporate emphasis thus:

In the technique of corporate emphasis, the advertiser discusses the whole range of products and services that the corporation offers, instead of specific elements. This method relies on the public's positive perception of the company, the company's accomplishments, and its reputation.

Brian then provides several examples of ads in this category, including an IBM ad:

In one of its eight advertisements in the study, IBM points to the scientists on its staff who have recently won the Nobel Prize in physics.

But Brian does not stop there. He explains the point of this ad, connecting the ad to the assertion that this technique emphasizes the company's accomplishments:

The inference we are to draw is that IBM scientists are hard at work right now in their laboratories developing tomorrow's technology to make the world a better place in which to live.

Study the following student essay as a good model of an investigative paper. The student discusses a large number of ads, classifies evidence in a logical pattern, summarizes evidence in a helpful table, and analyzes examples to show how they support her conclusion.

MAGAZINE ADVERTISING FOR COMPUTER PRODUCTS

Monica Becker

Introduction

Subheadings are used to show parts of the study.

The tactics used for advertising computer technology products in popular magazines include the usual strategies of advertising such as the inclusion, placement, and design of ads, as well as more specific tactics intended to target consumers based upon their demographics and psychological profiles. The increasing use of computer technology in all contexts—home, family, education, and business—results in a larger and increasingly diverse target audience for product promotion. Ad specialization, targeting different types of computer users, is becoming a requirement for effective marketing. These realities are reflected in the ads sampled for this study.

Methodology

Student explains process of selecting ads for the study

The 13 magazines listed in Figure 1 were selected for this study based upon their collective ability to represent a diverse sampling of target audiences. To qualify for inclusion in the study, an advertisement must be for a computer hardware or software product. If an advertisement combined a computer technology product with another product—for instance, a shared ad for Canon printers and photocopiers—the advertisement was excluded from the sample. Only full-page and multiple full-page display ads were included; half-page, quarter-page, and sidebar-styled ads were omitted from this evaluation. Advertising supplements designed to look like articles, booklet-style, perforated tear-out formats and any ads not included in a magazine's continuous paging were disregarded. Of the selected publications that are released monthly, all are from the month of October 1997. Those publications included in the sample that are published on a weekly basis were selected from a date as close to the middle of October 1997 as possible.

FIGURE 1   PUBLICATIONS INCLUDED IN SAMPLE

Publication	Publication Date
Atlantic Monthly	October 1997
Business Week	October 13, 1997
Forbes	October 6, 1997
GQ	October 1997
Harper's Magazine	October 1997
Mother Jones	October 1997
Newsweek	October 13, 1997
Out	October 1997
Parents	October 1997
Self	October 1997
Time	October 13, 1997
Vanity Fair	October 1997
Working Woman	October 1997

The Strategies

Inclusion within Publications

The most obvious strategy for advertising computer technology products is the decision to place an ad within a publication at all. In *Harper's* and *Mother Jones* one finds no ads for hardware or software. These highly intellectual publications, with their socially focused content, do not provide an obvious forum for targeting consumers of computer products. On the other end of the spectrum, businesspeople are likely candidates for purchasing these products; the computer advertising in Business Week, Working Woman, Time, Forbes, and Newsweek comprises between 10 and 25 percent of their total advertising content. (See Figure 2.) The increasing popularity of the Internet as an entertainment medium, new user-friendly operating systems such as Microsoft's Windows95, and the emergence of a younger, more computer-savvy generation to a position of purchasing power have increased the incidence of computer-related

Student presents information visually as well as in words.

advertising in non-business publications. <u>Vanity Fair</u> and <u>Gentlemen's Quarterly</u>, the advertising content of which are typically almost exclusively in fashion merchandise, are beginning to run computer ads. <u>Parents</u>, <u>Out</u>, and <u>Self</u>, which target the parents of young children, the gay community, and young athletic females, respectively, all contain some computer advertising.

Layout

Most advertisements in the sample used conventional full-page bleed and two-page spread formats. Each format has its advantages: the full-page bleed is more affordable and allows the ad to be featured next to articles or other content of interest to the reader, whereas a two-page spread dominates the open-magazine landscape, providing significant impact upon the consumer. The main disadvantage of the two-page spread is the tendency of readers to flip past the ad while in search of reading material; the spread format also isolates the ad from the content of the publication. In response to this "flipping

FIGURE 2   PERCENTAGE OF ADVERTISEMENTS FOR COMPUTER TECHNOLOGY PRODUCTS IN SAMPLED PUBLICATIONS

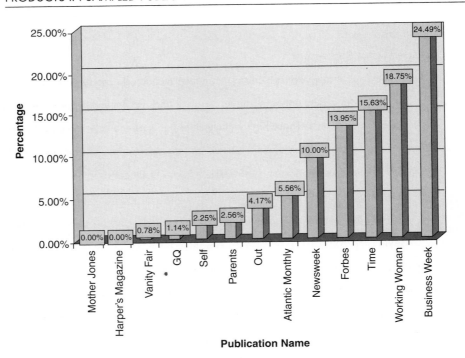

by" tendency, Microsoft has used a novel layout strategy in <u>Time</u>. On pages 55 and 57, an ad for Internet Explorer is staggered in the midst of an article. Page 55, featuring only a picture of a computer and the word "Internet," reveals little about the nature of the product, but its striking graphics are likely to command the reader's attention. Page 57 offers closure to this curiosity by adding copy to clarify the ad's purpose. In <u>Business Week</u> a similar tactic is used for IBM's RS/6000 Supercomputer, except that each of these staggered pages could conceivably stand alone as single-page ads.

Placement within Publication

Two companies took advantage of outside back-cover placement for their advertisements. Intel placed their Pentium II Processor ads on the back covers of <u>Self</u> and <u>Vanity Fair</u>, and Apple Computer was featured on the back of <u>Business Week</u>. Back-cover placement is costly but effective in that it forces product exposure on the reader, even when the magazine is closed. Intel's purchase of back-cover space in <u>Self</u> and <u>Vanity Fair</u> was likely based on the assumption that a young, computer-smart readership is beginning to purchase these magazines. Technology advertising in health and fashion publications was previously rare or non-existent; the inclusion of these ads for a central processing unit—a rather technical component—is testament to the changing profile of today's computer consumer.

Microsoft, IBM, and Compaq all took advantage of a similar strategy—inside-cover placement. These two-page spreads impact the reader immediately after opening the front cover of October's <u>Time</u>, <u>Business Week</u>, and <u>Newsweek</u>, respectively. This costly strategy tends to engage the reader more effectively than two-page placements embedded within a publication; most readers begin their magazine browsing by opening the front cover.

Ad placement within a magazine in close proximity to related features or columns is an effective arrangement designed to capture the attention of readers with prior interest in the product. Several ads within the sample appeared in locations rich with related content. <u>Newsweek</u> published an article on Esther Dyson, chairwoman of the Electronic Frontier Foundation and a computer expert, activist, writer, and speaker. The article's layout was interrupted by a two-page advertisement for Sony's VAIO line of computers and peripherals. At the closing of the Dyson feature, an ad for Micron Electronics' PC systems appears on the facing page. The regular "Technology" component in <u>Forbes</u>, featuring an article on collaborative software, was appropriately followed by a two-page ad for Silicon Graphics. Also embedded in the <u>Forbes</u> "Technology" section was a two-page spread for Compaq products. Even <u>Parents</u> magazine placed their ad for Gateway2000 following their "Learning" section that contained an article entitled "Essential Software." In <u>The Atlantic Monthly</u>, between pages of the "Near Myth of Our Failing Schools" piece, IBM purchased advertising space for their CD-ROM release of the <u>1998 World Book Encyclopedia</u>. The ad features photographs of teenagers and the caption "At least now they have a reason to think they know everything." This is a strategic placement that relates to the educational theme of the surrounding article.

Demographics and Psychological Profiles

One realizes that Bill Gates's vision of a "computer on every desk and in every home" is coming true when <u>Parents</u> has determined that computers have become like any other appliance we have in our homes and that the time is right for developing and promoting an Internet site to complement their magazine. <u>Self</u>, Conde Nast's fashion and fitness magazine, targeted at young career women, is also promoting a World Wide Web site, "Phys.com," which complements all of their women's magazines.

Gender-specific tactics in computer advertising are clearly displayed in <u>Working Woman</u>, a magazine devoted to the office experiences of career women. In the October issue, four out of five computer ads featured female models using the products. IBM ran an ad for their Thinkpad line of notebook computers featuring a profile of a successful business woman. The copy begins: "You're a woman. Hispanic. In L.A. And you want to start your own business. Not just any business. A construction business." This strategy is engineered to appeal to women who may still feel outnumbered or disenfranchised in the business world.

Despite—or perhaps because of—changing family roles, companies like Microcom are running copy like that seen in <u>Working Woman</u>: "Finally, a way to spend more time with what's-his-name and the kids." This ad shows family photographs—a husband, children, and family pets—displayed in frames on a desk. The other sampled business magazines did not have a male equivalent to this family-oriented approach. The approach used in <u>Time</u> for Microsoft Office is similar: a businessman is exiting an elevator next to the words, "You could work a twelve-hour day. Why not just do it in eight?" This tactic plays on the motivation to leave work early, but unlike the Microcom ad, it does not introduce family into the theme.

IBM displays a photograph of a baby with the words, "Protects coastlines, ozone levels, blood cells and future generations," in their campaign for the RS/6000 Supercomputer. Their promotion for the "Reinventing Education" program warms us with a photograph of a school teacher "putting names to faces." An NEC ad from <u>Business Week</u> displays the caption, "Perhaps the first instance where computers are being replaced by people." And Compaq tells us that "Something incredible happens when you give people the power to succeed. They succeed." These ads are designed to humanize computers and the companies that manufacture them by taking the focus away from business and placing it on social issues, or by emphasizing people rather than machines.

As with all products, humor is a particularly effective sales tool. Micron uses humor in their ClientPro MRE ad by showing a depressed looking executive begging for change on a park bench. He *didn't* use their products. Sony, showing a baby suspended atop a man's muscular arm, tells us to "Send a crying baby 3,000 miles in under 2 minutes." When shock of this statement wears off, we realize that we can transmit images over long distances by using their VAIO notebooks and peripherals.

The desire to be different is exploited in Lotus's ad for Domino web server software with its rebellious twist on a familiar quotation, "The great invisible guiding hand of capitalism has just smacked the Internet upside the head—now what?" Apple Computer is even more forceful with this tactic in <u>Business Week</u>, accompanying their photograph of Thomas Edison with two words: "Think different."

Conclusion

Student concludes with a reminder of the ever expanding role of technology in our lives.

The strategies used to promote computer technology in popular magazines are as diverse as the uses we find for this technology in our lives. The advent of digital cameras, computerized entertainment equipment, increasingly affordable home office equipment, improved multimedia and the popularization of the Internet will continue to enrich our computing experiences at home, on the job, and in education. As computer products become more affordable and easy to operate, the base of technology consumers will grow and diversify. Ultimately this will result in more innovative and diverse advertising, and perhaps new and exciting promotional strategies that will demand our future study and analysis.

THE POSITION PAPER: EXAMINING CLAIMS OF VALUE

The position paper is more philosophical, more abstract, than the investigative paper. It makes a claim about what is right or wrong, good or bad, for us as individuals or as a society. Topics can vary from capital punishment to pornography to endangered species. The writer supports a claim of value in large part by a logical sequencing of reasons. However, arguments in support of a principle also rely on relevant facts. (Remember that most of the Declaration of Independence (pp. 100–102), for example, is a list of specific abuses experienced by the colonists.) The position paper may be the most difficult of argument assignments because it may be perceived as the easiest. To argue effectively for a principle requires more than a forceful statement of one's personal values and beliefs. Remember (from Chapter 3) all the parts of an argument as outlined by Toulmin! Sound reasoning, care with word choice, and a sensitivity to your audience are especially important with a position paper.

Your first step in preparing a position paper should be to explore the grounds for your claim. You may want to list the reasons and evidence you would consider using to defend your claim. Also think about your assumptions (warrants) and the backing for your grounds. Then make a list of the grounds most often used by those holding opposing views. The second list will eventually help you prepare counterarguments, but first it will help test your commitment to your position. If you find the opposition's arguments persuasive and cannot think how you would challenge them, you may need to rethink your position. Ideally, your two lists will confirm your views but also increase your respect for opposing views. You may decide to embrace a conciliatory approach to your argument.

Armed with a reconfirmed position and a list of grounds (reasons and evidence) for your claim, you can now plan your paper. You need to decide which reasons and evidence to include and how you will develop each one. You also need to plan your challenge of opposing arguments and then how you will weave all of this into a unified essay. Studying the following guidelines and the sample student essay should help you with this task.

Guidelines for Preparing a Position Paper

1. *Begin with an opening section (a paragraph or two) that introduces your topic in an interesting way.* Possibilities include a statement of the issue's seriousness or reasons why the issue is currently being debated—or why we should go back to reexamine it. Some writers are spurred by a recent event that receives media coverage because it dramatizes the issue. Recounting such an event can produce an effective opening. You can also briefly summarize points of the opposition that you will challenge in supporting your claim.

2. *Decide where to place your thesis statement.* Your best choices are either early in your essay (paragraph 1 or 2) or at the end of your essay, after you have made your case. The second approach can be an effective alternative to the more common pattern of stating the thesis early.

3. *Organize reasons in a meaningful way.* One good plan is to move from the least important to the most important reasons, followed by rebuttals to potential counterarguments. Another choice is to organize by the arguments of the opposition, explaining why each of their reasons fails to hold up. (Doctors Singer and Siegler use this second pattern in "Euthanasia: A Critique"; see p. 332.)

4. *Provide a logical defense of or specifics in support of each reason.* You have not finished your task by simply asserting three or four or five reasons for your claim. You also need to present facts or examples for, or a logical explanation of, each reason. For example, you have not defended your views on capital punishment by asserting that it is right or just to take the life of a murderer. Why is it right or just? Executing the murderer will not bring the victim back to life. Do two wrongs make a right, or a further wrong? These are some of the thoughts your skeptical reader will have unless you explain your reasoning. Similarly, you cannot convincingly assert that the death penalty acts as a deterrent to subsequent murders unless you have evidence that it does act as a deterrent. If you want to use this reason, you need to do some research on the issue of deterrence. Remember: quoting another writer's opinion on your topic does not provide proof for your reasons. It merely demonstrates that someone else agrees with you.

5. *Maintain an appropriate level of seriousness for an argument of principle.* Of course, word choice must be appropriate to a serious discussion, but in addition be sure to present reasons that are also appropriately serious. If, for example, you are defending the claim that music CDs and tapes should not be subject to content labeling because such censorship is inconsistent with First Amendment rights, do not trivialize your argument by including the point that young people are tired of adults controlling their lives.

It may be true that teens are tired of control, but that is another issue for another paper; it is inappropriate in a paper debating First Amendment issues. Similarly, it would be demeaning to argue for capital punishment on the grounds of the cost of life imprisonment. To put a price on a human life is offensive to most readers.

6. *Examine your reasons and support them carefully to avoid logical fallacies.* Think logically. Qualify your statements and control your language. In the heat of debate over cherished ideas, we are prone to sweeping generalizations and verbal attacks on opponents, but these strategies rarely win converts. Hold on to your credibility.

EXAMINING THE ISSUE OF GUN CONTROL

Chris Brown

The United States has a long history of compromise. Issues such as representation in government have been resolved because of compromise, forming some of the bases of American life. Americans, however, like to feel that they are uncompromising, never willing to surrender an argument. This attitude has led to a number of issues in modern America that are unresolved, including the issue of gun control. Bickering over the issue has slowed progress toward legislation that will solve the serious problem of gun violence in America, while keeping recreational use of firearms available to responsible people. To resolve the conflict over guns, the arguments of both sides must be examined, with an eye to finding the flaws in both. Then perhaps we can reach some meaningful compromises.

Introduction connects ambivalence in American character to conflict over gun control.

Gun advocates have used many arguments for the continued availability of firearms to the public. The strongest of these defenses points to the many legitimate uses for guns. One use is protection against violence, a concern of some people in today's society. There are many problems with the use of guns for protection, however, and these problems make the continued use of firearms for protection dangerous. One such problem is that gun owners are not always able to use guns responsibly. When placed in a situation in which personal injury or loss is imminent, people often do not

Student organizes by arguments for no gun control.

think intelligently. Adrenaline surges through the body, and fear takes over much of the

1. Guns for protection

thinking process. This causes gun owners to use their weapons, firing at whatever threatens them. Injuries and deaths of innocent people, including family members of the gun owner, result. Removing guns from the house seems to be the only solution to these sad consequences.

Responding to this argument, gun advocates ask how they are to defend themselves without guns. But guns are needed for protection from other guns. If there are no guns, people need only to protect themselves from criminals using knives, baseball bats, and other weapons. Obviously the odds of surviving a knife attack are greater than the odds of surviving a gun attack. One reason is that a gun is an impersonal weapon. Firing at someone from 50 feet away requires much less commitment than charging someone with a knife and stabbing repeatedly. Also, bullet wounds are, generally, more severe than knife wounds. Guns are also more likely to be misused when a dark figure is in one's house. To kill with the gun requires only to point and shoot; no recognition of the figure is needed. To kill with a knife, by contrast, requires getting within arm's reach of the figure.

2. Recreational uses

There are other uses of guns, including recreation. Hunting and target shooting are valid, responsible uses of guns. How do we keep guns available for recreation? The answer is in the form of gun clubs and hunting clubs. Many are already established; more can be constructed. These clubs can provide recreational use of guns for responsible people while keeping guns off the streets and out of the house.

3. Second Amendment rights

The last argument widely used by gun advocates is the constitutional right to bear arms. The fallacies in this argument are that the Constitution was written in a vastly different time. This different time had different uses for guns, and a different type of gun. Firearms were defended in the Constitution because of their many valid uses and fewer problems. Guns were mostly muskets, guns that were not very accurate beyond close range. Also, guns took more than 30 seconds to load in the eighteenth century and could fire only one shot before reloading. These differences with today's guns affect the relative safety of guns then and now. In addition, those who did not live in the city at the time used hunting for food as well as for recreation; hunting was a necessary component of life. That is not true today. Another use of guns in the eighteenth century was as protection from animals. Wild animals such as bears and cougars were much more common. Settlers, explorers, and hunters needed protection from these animals in ways not comparable with modern life.

Finally, Revolutionary America had no standing army. Defense of the nation and of one's home from other nations relied on local militia. The right to bear arms granted in the Constitution was inspired by the need for national protection as well as by the other outdated needs previously discussed. Today America has a standing army with enough weaponry to adequately defend itself from outside aggressors. There is no need for every citizen to carry a musket, or an AK-47, for the protection of the nation. It would seem, then, that the Second Amendment does not apply to modern society.

Student establishes a compromise position.

To reach a compromise, we also have to examine the other side of the issue. Some gun-control advocates argue that all guns are unnecessary and should be outlawed. The problem with this argument is that guns will still be available to those who do not mind breaking the law. Until an economically sound and feasible way of controlling illegal guns in America is found, guns cannot be totally removed, no matter how much legislation is passed. This means that if guns are to be outlawed for uses other than recreational uses, a way must be found to combat the illegal gun trade that will evolve. Tough criminal laws and a large security force are all that can be offered to stop illegal uses of guns until better technology is available. This means that, perhaps, a good resolution would involve gradual restrictions on guns, until eventually guns were restricted only to recreational uses in a controlled setting for citizens not in the police or military.

Conclusion restates student's claim.

Both sides on this issue have valid points. Any middle ground needs to offer something to each side. It must address the reasons people feel that they need guns for protection, allow for valid recreational use, and keep guns out of the hands of the public, except for properly trained police officers. Time and money will be needed to move toward the removal of America's huge handgun arsenal. But, sooner or later a compromise on the issue of gun control must be made to make America a safer, better place to live.

The Definition Argument: Debating the Meanings of Words

"Define your terms" is good advice for all writers, but especially for writers of argument. People disagree more than we sometimes think over the meanings of terms such as *leader* or *patriot* or *good teacher*. The deductive argument about Lincoln's leadership, illustrated in Chapter 4 (see p. 95), turns on a definition of leadership. To support that argument successfully, you need to explain and defend a definition of leadership as well as demonstrate that Lincoln meets the specifics of your definition.

Sometimes we turn to definition because we believe that two words are being used incorrectly as synonyms. Columnist George Will has argued in a recent article that we should forget *values* and use instead the word *virtues*—and that we should seek and admire virtues, not values. Some writers bemoan the current loss of *community*, but David Gergen argues that America is developing a new sense of the word (see p. 582). Much of his argument depends on our agreeing with him that the signs to which he points are in fact indicators of community. What do we mean by *virtue*? Or *community*? The argument that depends on defining terms has become the definition argument.

The following guidelines and sample student essay will help you prepare a definition essay:

Guidelines for Preparing a Definition Argument

1. *Begin with an opening section (a paragraph or two) that introduces your subject in an interesting way.* Possibilities include the occasion— an event in the news or something you read, for example—that has led to your writing. Or, explain a misunderstanding about a term's meaning that you want to correct.

2. *Do not begin by quoting or paraphrasing a dictionary definition of the term.* "According to Webster . . ." is a tired approach lacking reader interest. If the dictionary definition were sufficient, you would have no reason to write an entire essay to define the term.

3. *State your thesis—your definition of the term—early in your essay, if you can do so in a sentence or two.* If you do not state a brief thesis, then be certain to establish your purpose in writing early in your essay. (You may find that there are too many parts to your definition to combine into one or two sentences.)

4. *Use several specific strategies for developing your definition.* Consider using some of the following means of development:

   - *Word origin or history of usage.* The word's original meaning can be instructive. If the word has changed meanings over time, explore those changes as clues to how the word should be used, especially if you are going to object to the word's current use.

   - *Descriptive details.* Be specific. For example, list traits of a leader or patriot or courageous person; explain the behaviors that make a wise or courteous person; describe the situations that demonstrate the existence of liberty. Use negative traits as well as positive ones; that is, what is *not* contained in the word.

- *Comparison and contrast.* Clarify and limit your definition by contrasting it with words of similar meaning. For example, what are the subtle but important differences between *freedom* and *liberty?* Between *courtesy* and *manners?* Between *knowledge* and *wisdom?*
- *Metaphors.* Consider the use of figurative comparisons. Whether expressed as metaphors or similes, they are effective because they are concrete and vivid.
- *Examples.* Illustrate your definition with actual or hypothetical examples. Winston Churchill, Abraham Lincoln, and Franklin D. Roosevelt could all be used as examples of leaders.
- *Function or use.* A frequent strategy for defining is explaining the item's use or function: a pencil is a writing instrument. A similar approach can give insight into general or abstract terms as well. For example, what is accomplished by courteous or patriotic behavior? What do we gain by seeking virtues rather than values?

WISDOM

J. Tupper Cole

Student introduces topic with reference to a famous wise person.

In Plato's "Apology of Socrates," Socrates tells the judges how Chaerephon consulted the oracle at Delphi. He asked who, if anyone, was wiser than Socrates; the oracle answered that there was none. Upon learning this, Socrates set out to learn why no one was wiser than he. He learned that he was wiser only because he knew he was not wise, while others thought that they were. Socrates was concerned with the wisdom of how best to live one's life, but there is another wisdom, practical and useful in human matters, that people can surely acquire.

Student distinguishes between wisdom and knowledge.

Wisdom is a matter of perspective and judgment, married to knowledge. Wisdom is a matter of ends, knowledge of means. Wisdom follows knowledge's question of "How can I?" with "What if I do?" Knowledge is the motor, wisdom the steering wheel. Common sense is the lowest form of wisdom. Common sense is the reason one wears a coat when it is cold, carries an umbrella when it is raining. Common sense is accumulated knowledge that eventually requires little thought.

Wisdom is different from intuition. Intuition is a feeling, based on gut instinct, without thought. Wisdom considers, sees facts, weighs evidence. Wisdom acquits a suspect because there is reasonable doubt; intuition convicts because it has a *feeling*. Wisdom looks at the reasons behind policies. Wisdom knows that alcohol and tobacco are more dangerous than marijuana, knows that the first two are legal only because they have more money. Wisdom sees the absurdity of the stealth bomber, a plane requiring 124 hours of maintenance for every hour of flight, a plane with no stated reason for existence, but providing billions of dollars for its manufacturer. Wisdom sees that some politicians make decisions based on campaign contributions rather than wisdom.

Student illustrates the use of wisdom.

Wisdom also sees all the possibilities, judges them, then acts accordingly. Wisdom was lacking in Detroit in the 1970s. The auto manufacturers refused to change, despite the evidence that Americans wanted more efficient cars, losing millions of dollars, costing tens of thousands of jobs for Americans. Wisdom also saw the safety of the airbag, knowing that Americans would pay for this safety. Wisdom had to drag Detroit kicking and screaming until it realized that American buyers were right.

Wisdom is often prudent, but not always. It may be wise to wait and see if the stock market returns after a large drop, but then again the wise sold their stock before the big crash of 1929. Practical wisdom applies to daily life. Wisdom doesn't gamble, doesn't drink and drive, doesn't smoke. Wisdom eats well and doesn't watch much television. Wisdom finishes early, never starts late. Wisdom doesn't act in anger.

Student gives examples of famous people.

Ghandi was wise. So were Roosevelt and Churchill. The framers of the U.S. Constitution were wise for the most part; they did fail to foresee political parties and the fund-raising problems that would follow. Nixon was not wise when he became involved with the Watergate scandal, wise when he resigned before impeachment proceedings started. Very few people are always wise. Socrates was profoundly wise, but that got him executed; I suppose that he found the wisest way to die.

Student concludes by reinforcing wisdom's general characteristics.

Wisdom is judgment more than anything else. It does not judge what it does not know, or rather judges not to judge. It sees the proper course; it advises. Many know wisdom and ignore it. Many are too concerned with fun and profit to listen to it, myself included.

THE PROBLEM-SOLUTION ARGUMENT: EXPLORING PUBLIC-POLICY ISSUES

Many of the arguments over public policy can usefully be understood as arguments over solutions to problems. Consider the following policy claims.

1. Drunk drivers should receive mandatory six-month suspension of their license.
2. We need a balanced-budget amendment.
3. We need to spend whatever is necessary to stop the flow of drugs into this country.
4. The school year in the United States should be extended by at least 30 days.

Each one of these policy claims offers an answer to a problem.

1. Fewer people will drink and drive, causing accidents, if they know they will lose their licenses.
2. A required balanced budget would stop the spiraling national debt.
3. The way to address the drug problem in this country is to eliminate the drugs.
4. For America to compete in the world, new generations will have to be better educated; the solution is a longer academic year.

When arguing about public-policy issues, you want to think first about what situation you are addressing and why you think the situation is a problem in need of change.

Many arguments for solutions concentrate on the nature of the problem, for how we define a problem has much to do with what kinds of solutions become appropriate. For example, some people are concerned about our ability to feed a growing population, especially given weather changes and other agricultural problems. But many will argue that the problem is not an agricultural one (how much food can we grow) but a political one (to whom will the food be distributed and at what cost). If the problem is agricultural, we need to worry about available farmland, water supply, and farming technology. If the problem is political, we need to worry about price supports, distribution to poor countries, and grain embargoes used for political leverage. To support a policy claim, you may first need to define the problem.

The argument for solutions can take many forms, depending on your primary purpose in writing. Possibly as many as six steps may be needed to support a proposed solution. When preparing such an argument, consider each of the six steps outlined in the following guidelines and decide which ones are relevant to your problem and your purpose in writing. Then organize your paper according to the steps you have selected as appropriate. Do not jump back and forth among the various steps; instead, discuss each step in turn.

Guidelines for Preparing a Problem-Solution Paper

1. *Demonstrate that a problem exists.* In many cases you can count on an audience who knows the world well enough to be aware of a situation that is considered a problem. Sometimes, though, people have to be warned of a problem before they are prepared to consider solutions to

it. For example, studies reveal that many parents and students are satisfied with what students are learning in high school in spite of comparative testing that shows American students ranking far behind their counterparts in other countries. Some people still need to be convinced that American education has some serious problems to be addressed. If you want to argue for increasing requirements in math and science, you may have to begin by reminding readers that we have a problem.

2. *Explain the cause or causes of the problem.* If your proposed solution is tied to removing the cause(s) of the problem, then you need to establish cause and prove it early in your essay. Remember, though, that some problems are created from many causes over a period of time; it may now be fruitless to try to pinpoint causes. Republicans and Democrats spend considerable energy blaming one another for inflation or crime. Sometimes one suspects that their fussing is a smoke screen for their lack of solutions. If cause is important, argue for it; if it is irrelevant, move to your solution.

3. *Explain your solution.* If television violence contributes to violence in society, then your proposal is simple: Eliminate violence from television programs. Ways to implement the solution may be open to debate, but the solution itself is clear-cut. Solutions to the problems of drunk driving or drugs in our society are far less obvious. Problems resulting from multiple causes will produce many proposed solutions. Before you seek to defend your solution against others, consider including the next two steps in your argument.

4. *Explain the process for achieving your solution.* Sometimes we have good proposals to offer but must defer to others for ways to achieve those proposals. If you have not examined the political or legal steps necessary to implement your solution, then this step cannot be part of your purpose in writing. However, anticipating a skeptical audience that says "How are we going to do that?" you would be wise to think about precise steps for achieving your solution. When proposing to eliminate violent TV programs, you might suggest, for example, that an appropriate government agency be commissioned to establish standards or guidelines for the TV industry and create a review board to rule when controversy arises. Showing your readers that you have thought ahead to the next step in the process can be an effective method of persuasion.

5. *Support the feasibility of your solution.* Offering a method for implementing your solution is a plus for your argument; demonstrating the feasibility of your method is even more convincing. Consider Prohibition, for instance. The method for eliminating alcohol was simple: make it illegal. But the method did not work; it wasn't feasible, in this case because it wasn't acceptable to the majority of Americans. When supporting the feasibility of your proposal, consider the cost of implementing your solution, the relative complexity of your proposal, and its acceptability to the majority of persons affected by the proposed solution.

6. *Demonstrate that your proposed solution is better than others.* Anticipate challenges to your solution by comparing it with others that have been or might be suggested and by showing how yours is better. One measure of a solution's worth is its feasibility; if it won't work, then it is a lousy idea. Another measure must be the proposal's potential effectiveness. Can you show how your solution will avoid the limited effectiveness of other solutions that have been tried? Of course another defense is that it is the right thing to do. Values also belong in public-policy debates, not just issues of cost and political acceptability.

Read and analyze the follow problem/solution argument. The questions that follow the essay will aid your analysis.

A New Strategy for the War on Drugs

James Q. Wilson

Author of *The Moral Sense*, James Q. Wilson is a professor of public policy at Pepperdine University. His solution to America's drug problem was published on April 13, 2000, in the *Wall Street Journal*.

1   The current Senate deliberation over aid to Colombia aimed at fighting narcotics reminds us that there are two debates over how the government ought to deal with dangerous drugs. The first is about their illegality and the second is about their control. People who wish to legalize drugs and those who wish to curtail their supply believe that their methods will reduce crime. Both these views are mistaken, but there is a third way.

2   Advocates of legalization think that both buyers and sellers would benefit. People who can buy drugs freely and at something like free-market prices would no longer have to steal to afford cocaine or heroin; dealers would no longer have to use violence and corruption to maintain their market share. Though drugs may harm people, reducing this harm would be a medical problem not a criminal-justice one. Crime would drop sharply.

Prices Would Fall

3   But there is an error in this calculation. Legalizing drugs means letting the price fall to its competitive rate (plus taxes and advertising costs). That market price would probably be somewhere between one-third and 1/20th of the illegal price. And more than the market price would fall. As Harvard's Mark Moore has pointed out, the "risk price"—that is, all the hazards associated with buying drugs, from being arrested to being ripped off—would also fall, and this decline might be more important than the lower purchase price.

4   Under a legal regime, the consumption of low-priced, low-risk drugs would increase dramatically. We do not know by how much, but the little evidence we have suggests a sharp rise. Until 1968 Britain allowed doctors to prescribe heroin. Some doctors cheated,

and their medically unnecessary prescriptions helped increase the number of known heroin addicts by a factor of 40. As a result, the government abandoned the prescription policy in favor of administering heroin in clinics and later replacing heroin with methadone.

5   When the Netherlands ceased enforcing laws against the purchase or possession of marijuana, the result was a sharp increase in its use. Cocaine and heroin create much greater dependency, and so the increase in their use would probably be even greater.

6   The average user would probably commit fewer crimes if these drugs were sold legally. But the total number of users would increase sharply. A large fraction of these new users would be unable to keep a steady job. Unless we were prepared to support them with welfare payments, crime would be one of their main sources of income. That is, the number of drug-related crimes *per user* might fall even as the total number of drug-related crimes increased. Add to the list of harms more deaths from overdose, more babies born to addicted mothers, more accidents by drug-influenced automobile drivers and fewer people able to hold jobs or act as competent parents.

7   Treating such people would become far more difficult. As psychiatrist Sally Satel has written on this page, many drug users will not enter and stay in treatment unless they are compelled to do so. Phoenix House, the largest national residential drug treatment program, rarely admits patients who admit they have a problem and need help. The great majority are coerced by somebody—a judge, probation officer or school official—into attending. Phoenix House CEO Mitchell Rosenthal opposes legalization, and for good reason. Legalization means less coercion, and that means more addicts and addicts who are harder to treat.

8   Douglas Anglin, drawing on experiences in California and elsewhere, has shown that people compelled to stay in treatment do at least as well as those who volunteer for it, and they tend (of necessity) to stay in the program longer. If we legalize drugs, the chances of treatment making a difference are greatly reduced. And as for drug-use prevention, forget it. Try telling your children not to use a legal substance.

9   But people who want to keep drugs illegal have problems of their own. The major thrust of government spending has been to reduce the supply of drugs by cutting their production overseas, intercepting their transfer into the U.S. and arresting dealers. Because of severe criminal penalties, especially on handlers of crack cocaine, our prisons have experienced a huge increase in persons sentenced on drug charges. In the early 1980s, about 1/12th of all prison inmates were in for drug convictions; now well over one-third are.

10   No one can be certain how imprisoning drug suppliers affects drug use, but we do know that an arrested drug dealer is easily replaced. Moreover, the government can never seize more than a small fraction of the drugs entering the country, a fraction that is easily replaced.

11   Emphasizing supply over treatment is dangerous. Not only do we spend huge sums on it; not only do we drag a reluctant U.S. military into the campaign; we also heighten corruption and violence in countries such as Colombia and Mexico. The essential fact is this: Demand will produce supply.

12   We can do much more to reduce demand. Some four million Americans are currently on probation or parole. From tests done on them when they are jailed, we know that half or more had a drug problem when arrested. Though a lot of drug users otherwise obey the law (or at least avoid getting arrested), probationers and parolees constitute the hard core of dangerous addicts. Reducing their demand for drugs ought to be our highest priority.

13   Mark Kleiman of UCLA has suggested a program of "testing and control": Probationers and parolees would be required to take frequent drug tests—say, twice weekly—as a condition of remaining on the street. If you failed the test, you would spend more time in jail; if you passed it, you would remain free. This approach would be an inducement for people to enter and stay in treatment.

14   This would require some big changes in how we handle offenders. Police, probation and parole officers would be responsible for conducting these tests, and more officers would have to be hired. Probation and parole authorities would have to be willing to sanction a test failure by immediate incarceration, initially for a short period (possibly a weekend), and then for longer periods if the initial failure were repeated. Treatment programs at little or no cost to the user would have to be available not only in every prison, but for every drug-dependent probationer and parolee.

15   These things are not easily done. Almost every state claims to have an intensive community supervision program, but few offenders are involved in them, the frequency with which they are contacted is low, and most were released from supervision without undergoing any punishment for violating its conditions.

16   But there is some hope. Our experience with drug courts suggests that the procedural problems can be overcome. In such courts, several hundred of which now exist, special judges oversee drug-dependent offenders, insisting that they work to overcome their habits. While under drug-court supervision, offenders reduce drug consumption and, at least for a while after leaving the court, offenders are less likely to be arrested.

17   Our goal ought to be to extend meaningful community supervision to all probationers and parolees, especially those who have a serious drug or alcohol problem. Efforts to test Mr. Kleiman's proposals are under way in Connecticut and Maryland.

18   If this demand-reduction strategy works, it can be expanded. Drug tests can be given to people who apply for government benefits, such as welfare and public housing. Some critics will think this is an objectionable intrusion. But giving benefits without conditions weakens the character-building responsibility of society.

Prevent Harm to Others

19   John Stuart Mill, the great libertarian thinker, argued that the only justifiable reason for restricting human liberty is to prevent harm to others. Serious drug abuse does harm others. We could, of course, limit government action to remedying those harms without addressing their causes, but that is an uphill struggle, especially when the harms fall on unborn children. Fetal drug syndrome imposes large costs on infants who have had no voice in choosing their fate.

20   Even Mill was clear that full liberty cannot be given to children or barbarians. By "barbarians" he meant people who are incapable of being improved by free and equal discussion. The life of a serious drug addict—the life of someone driven by drug dependency to prostitution and crime—is the life of a barbarian.

Questions for Reading and Analysis

1. What are the two solutions to the drug problem presented by others?

2. Why, according to Wilson, will legalizing drugs not be a good solution? What are the specific negative consequences of legalization?

3. Government strategies for controlling illegal drugs have included what activities?

4. What percentage of prisoners are now in prison on drug charges?

5. What are the problems we face trying to reduce the supply of drugs? What, according to Wilson, drives supply?

6. What is Wilson's proposed solution? Explain the details of his solution.

7. What are some of the difficulties with Wilson's solution? What does Wilson gain by bringing up possible difficulties?

8. How would the author expand the idea of his solution?

9. What does Wilson seek to accomplish in his concluding two paragraphs? What potential counterargument does he seek to rebut in his conclusion?

Questions for Discussion and Response

1. The primary argument for legalizing drugs is that legalization will eliminate the crimes generated by illegal drug use. Has Wilson convinced you that legalization will not reduce crime? Why or why not?

2. Is his argument against the supply-reduction approach convincing? Why or why not?

3. Has Wilson's defense of his solution convinced you that it is workable?

4. On what argument might one agree that Wilson's solution is workable and still object to it? (Think about his concluding comments.)

5. Do you have a solution to the drug problem?

THE REFUTATION ESSAY: EVALUATING THE ARGUMENTS OF OTHERS

When your primary purpose in writing is to challenge someone's argument rather than to present your own argument, you are writing a refutation. A good refutation does not merely point an accusing finger at another's argument. Rather, it demonstrates, in an orderly and logical way, the weaknesses of logic or evidence in the argument, or it both analyzes weaknesses and builds a counterargument. Refutations can challenge a specific, written argument, but they can also challenge a prevailing attitude or belief that is, in the writer's view, contrary to the evidence. The refutation that follows shows the first purpose. But first, study the following guidelines to prepare a good refutation essay:

Guidelines for Preparing a Refutation Essay

1. *Read accurately.* Make certain that you have understood your opponent's argument. If you assume views not expressed by the writer and accuse the writer of holding those illogical views, you are guilty of the straw man fallacy, of attributing and then attacking a position that the person does not hold. Take time, therefore, to understand the writer's

thesis. Look up terms and references you do not know and examine the logic and evidence thoroughly.

2. *Pinpoint the weaknesses in the original argument.* Analyze the argument to determine, specifically, what flaws the argument contains. If the argument contains logical fallacies, make a list of the ones you plan to discredit. Examine the evidence presented. Is it insufficient, unreliable, or irrelevant? Has the writer oversimplified the issues or presented an unworkable solution? Are the assumptions joining claim and evidence faulty? Decide, before drafting your refutation, exactly what elements of the argument you intend to challenge.

3. *Write your thesis.* After analyzing the argument and deciding on the weaknesses to be challenged, write a thesis which establishes that your disagreement is with the writer's logic, assumptions, or evidence, or a combination of these.

4. *Draft your essay, using the following three-part organization:*

   a. *The opponent's argument.* Usually you should not assume that your reader has read or remembered the argument you are refuting. Thus at the beginning of your essay, you need to state, accurately and fairly, the main points of the argument to be refuted.

   b. *Your thesis.* Next make clear the nature of your disagreement with the argument you are refuting. Your thesis might assert, for example, that a writer has not proved his assertion because he has provided evidence that is outdated, or that the argument is not sound because it rests on an unacceptable definition, or that the argument is filled with logical fallacies that discredit the piece.

   c. *Your refutation.* The specifics of your counterargument will depend upon the nature of your disagreement. If you are challenging the writer's evidence, then you must present the more recent evidence to explain why the evidence used is unreliable or misleading. If you are challenging assumptions, then you must explain why they do not hold up. If your thesis is that the piece is filled with logical fallacies, then you must present and explain each fallacy.

Gender Games

David Sadker

A professor of education at American University, David Sadker has written extensively on educational issues, especially on the treatment of girls in the classroom. He is the author of *Failing at Fairness: How Our Schools Cheat Girls* (1995). "Gender Games" appeared in the *Washington Post* on July 31, 2000.

1   Remember when your elementary school teacher would announce the teams for the weekly spelling bee? "Boys against the girls!" There was nothing like a gender show-down to liven things up. Apparently, some writers never left this elementary level of in-trigue. A spate of recent books and articles takes us back to the "boys versus girls" fray but this time, with much higher stakes.

2   May's *Atlantic Monthly* cover story, "Girls Rule," is a case in point. The magazine pub-lished an excerpt from *The War Against Boys* by Christina Hoff Sommers, a book advanc-ing the notion that boys are the real victims of gender bias while girls are soaring in school.

3   Sommers and her supporters are correct in saying that girls and women have made significant educational progress in the past two decades. Females today make up more than 40 percent of medical and law school students, and more than half of college stu-dents. Girls continue to read sooner and write better than boys. And for as long as any-one can remember, girls have received higher grades than boys.

4   But there is more to these selected statistics than meets the eye. Although girls continue to receive higher report card grades than boys, their grades do not translate into higher test scores. The same girls who beat boys in the spelling bees score below boys on the tests that matter: the PSATs crucial for scholarships, the SATs and the ACTs needed for college acceptances, the GREs for graduate school and even the ad-mission tests for law, business and medical schools.

5   Many believe that girls' higher grades may be more a reflection of their manageable classroom behavior than their intellectual accomplishment. Test scores are not influ-enced by quieter classroom behavior. Girls may in fact be trading their initiative and independence for peer approval and good grades, a trade-off that can have costly per-sonal and economic consequences.

6   The increase in female college enrollment catches headlines because it heralds the first time that females have outnumbered males on college campuses. But even these enrollment figures are misleading. The female presence increases as the status of the college decreases. Female students are more likely to dominate two-year schools than the Ivy League. And wherever they are, they find themselves segregated and channeled into the least prestigious and least costly majors.

7   In today's world of e-success, more than 60 percent of computer science and busi-ness majors are male, about 70 percent of physics majors are male, and more than 80 percent of engineering students are male. But peek into language, psychology, nurs-ing and humanities classrooms, and you will find a sea of female faces.

8   Higher female enrollment figures mask the "glass walls" that separate the sexes and channel females and males into very different careers, with very different paychecks. Today, despite all the progress, the five leading occupations of employed women are secretary, receptionist, bookkeeper, registered nurse and hairdresser/cosmetologist.

9   Add this to the "glass ceiling" (about 3 percent of Fortune 500 top managers are women) and the persistence of a gender wage gap (women with advanced degrees still lag well behind their less-educated male counterparts) and the crippling impact of workplace and college stereotyping becomes evident.

10   Even within schools, where female teachers greatly outnumber male teachers, school management figures remind us that if there is a war on boys, women are not the generals. More than 85 percent of junior and senior high school principals are male, while 88 percent of school superintendents are male.

11   Despite sparkling advances of females on the athletic fields, two-thirds of athletic scholarships still go to males. In some areas, women have actually lost ground. When Title IX was enacted in 1972, women coached more than 90 percent of intercollegiate women's teams. Today women coach only 48 percent of women's teams and only 1 percent of men's teams.

12   If some adults are persuaded by the rhetoric in such books as *The War Against Boys*, be assured that children know the score. When more than 1,000 Michigan elementary school students were asked to describe what life would be like if they were born a member of the opposite sex, more than 40 percent of the girls saw positive advantages to being a boy: better jobs, more money and definitely more respect. Ninety-five percent of the boys saw no advantage to being a female.

13   *The War Against Boys* attempts to persuade the public to abandon support for educational initiatives designed to help girls and boys avoid crippling stereotypes. I hope the public and Congress will not be taken in by the book's misrepresentations. We have no time to wage a war on either our boys or our girls.

Questions for Reading and Analysis

1. What work, specifically, is Sadker refuting? What is the claim advanced by this work?
2. What facts about girls' school records does Sadker grant to Sommers?
3. What facts about girls create a different story, according to Sadker?
4. What is Sadker's claim? What is he asserting about girls?
5. What does the author think about the whole idea of books such as Sommers'?
6. Where does he use strategies of the conciliatory argument?

Questions for Discussion and Response

1. What statistic is most startling to you? Why?
2. Has Sadker provided a sound refutation of Sommers? That is, do you agree that his statistics are more significant in telling us how women are doing in school, sports, and work? If you disagree with Sadker, explain why.
3. Think about your high school experiences. Do you think that teachers are waging a war against boys? What evidence do you have to support your views?
4. What can be done to encourage more girls to study math, science, computers, and engineering?

Exercise: Analyzing an Argument

Read the following article by Robert Bork and analyze his evidence and logic. As a part of your analysis, answer these questions:

1. What kind of argument is this?
2. What is Bork's claim?
3. What kinds of grounds does he present?
4. What is the tone of his argument? (Do you think that he expects readers to agree with him?)
5. Has he supported his claim to your satisfaction or not?
6. Do you find any logical fallacies in his argument? If so, how would you challenge them?

Addicted to Health

Robert H. Bork

A conservative legal scholar currently at the American Enterprise Institute for Policy Research, Robert Bork (b. 1927) has been acting attorney general and solicitor general of the U.S. Court of Appeals. His appointment to the Supreme Court, rejected by the Congress, has led to a book by Bork on the whole affair and to other books and articles on legal and public-policy issues. The following appeared in the *National Review* on July 28, 1997.

1   Government efforts to deal with tobacco companies betray an ultimate ambition to control Americans' lives.

2   When moral self-righteousness, greed for money, and political ambition work hand in hand they produce irrational, but almost irresistible, policies. The latest example is the war on cigarettes and cigarette smokers. A proposed settlement has been negotiated among politicians, plaintiffs' lawyers, and the tobacco industry. The only interests left out of the negotiations were smokers, who will be ordered to pay enormous sums with no return other than the deprivation of their own choices and pleasures.

3   It is a myth that today's Americans are a sturdy, self-reliant folk who will fight any officious interference with their liberties. That has not been true at least since the New Deal. If you doubt that, walk the streets of any American city and see the forlorn men and women cupping their hands against the wind to light cigarettes so that they can get through a few more smokeless hours in their offices. Twenty-five percent of Americans smoke. Why can't they demand and get a compromise rather than accepting docilely the exile that employers and building managers impose upon them?

4   The answer is that they have been made to feel guilty by self-righteous non-smokers. A few years back, hardly anyone claimed to be seriously troubled by tobacco smoke. Now, an entire class of the morally superior claim to be able to detect, and be offended by, tobacco smoke several offices away from their own. These people must possess the sense of smell of a deer or an Indian guide. Yet they will happily walk through suffocating exhaust smoke from buses rather than wait a minute or two to cross the street.

5   No one should assume that peace will be restored when the last cigarette smoker has been banished to the Alaskan tundra. Other products will be pressed into service as morally reprehensible. If you would know the future, look at California—the national leader in health fanaticism. After a long day in Los Angeles flagging a book I had written,

my wife and I sought relaxation with a drink at our hotel's outdoor bar. Our anticipation of pleasure was considerably diminished by a sign: "Warning! Toxic Substances Served Here." They were talking about my martini!

6   And martinis are a toxic substance, taken in any quantity sufficient to induce a sense of well-being. Why not, then, ban alcohol or at least require a death's head on every martini glass? Well, we did once outlaw alcohol; it was called Prohibition. The myth is that Prohibition increased the amount of drinking in this country; the truth is that it reduced it. There were, of course, some unfortunate side effects, like Al Capone and Dutch Schultz. But by and large the mobsters inflicted rigor mortis upon one another.

7   Why is it, then, that the end of Prohibition was welcomed joyously by the population? Not because alcohol is not dangerous. Not because the consumption of alcohol was not lessened. And not in order to save the lives of people with names like Big Jim and Ice Pick Phil. Prohibition came to an end because most Americans wanted to have a drink when and where they felt like it. If you insist on sounding like a law-and-economics professor, it ended because we thought the benefits of alcohol outweighed the costs.

8   That is the sort of calculation by which we lead our lives. Automobiles kill tens of thousands of people every year and disable perhaps that many again. We could easily stop the slaughter. Cars could be made with a top speed of ten miles an hour and with exteriors the consistency of marshmallows. Nobody would die, nobody would be disabled, and nobody would bother with cars very much.

9   There are, of course, less draconian measures available. On most highways, it is almost impossible to find anyone who observes the speed limits. On the theory of the tobacco precedent, car manufacturers should be liable for deaths caused by speeding; after all, they could build automobiles incapable of exceeding legal speed limits.

10   The reason we are willing to offer up lives and limbs to automobiles is, quite simply, that they make life more pleasant (for those who remain intact)—among other things, by speeding commuting to work, by making possible family vacations a thousand miles from home, and by lowering the costs of products shipped from a distance. The case for regulating automobiles far more severely than we do is not essentially different from the case for heavy regulation of cigarettes or, soon, alcohol.

11   But choices concerning driving, smoking, and drinking are the sort of things that ought to be left to the individual unless there are clear, serious harms to others.

12   The opening salvo in the drive to make smoking a criminal act is the proposed settlement among the cigarette companies, plaintiffs' lawyers, and the states' attorneys general. We are told that the object is to protect teenagers and children (children being the last refuge of the sanctimonious). But many restrictions will necessarily affect adults, and the tobacco pact contains provisions that can only be explained as punishment for selling to adults.

13   The terms of the settlement plainly reveal an intense hatred of smoking. Opposition to the pact comes primarily from those who think it is not severe enough. For example, critics say the settlement is defective in not restricting the marketing of cigarettes overseas by American tobacco companies. Connecticut's attorney general, Richard Blumenthal, defended the absence of such a provision: "Given our druthers we would have brought them to their knees all over the world, but there is a limit to our leverage." So much for the sovereignty of nations.

14   What the settlement does contain is bad enough. The pact would require the companies to pony up $60 billion; $25 billion of this would be used for public-health issues to be identified by a presidential panel and the rest for children's health insurance. Though the purpose of the entire agreement is punitive, this slice is most obviously so.

15   The industry is also required to pay $308 billion over 25 years, in part to repay states for the cost of treating sick smokers. There are no grounds for this provision. The tobacco companies have regularly won litigation against plaintiffs claiming injury on the grounds that everybody has known for the past forty years that smoking can cause health problems. This $308 billion, which takes from the companies what they have won in litigation, says, in effect, that no one assumed the risk of his own behavior.

16   The provision is groundless for additional reasons. The notion that the states have lost money because of cigarettes ignores the federal and state taxes smokers have paid, which cover any amount the states could claim to have lost. Furthermore, a percentage of the population dies early from smoking. Had these people lived longer, the drain on Medicare and Medicaid would have been greater. When lowered pension and Social Security costs are figured in, it seems certain that government is better off financially with smoking than without it. If we must reduce the issue to one of dollars, as the attorneys general have done, states have profited financially from smoking. If this seems a gruesome and heartless calculation, it is. But don't blame me. The state governments advanced the financial argument and ought to live with its consequences, however distasteful.

17   Other provisions of the settlement fare no better under the application of common sense. The industry is to reduce smoking by teenagers by 30 percent in five years, 50 percent in seven years, and 60 percent in ten years. No one knows how the industry is to perform this trick. But if those goals are not met, the industry will be amerced $80 million a year for each percentage point it falls short.

18   The settlement assumes teenage smoking can be reduced dramatically by requiring the industry to conduct an expensive anti-smoking advertising campaign, banning the use of people and cartoon characters to promote cigarettes, and similar tactics. It is entirely predictable that this will not work. Other countries have banned cigarette advertising, only to watch smoking increase. Apparently the young, feeling themselves invulnerable, relish the risk of smoking. Studies have shown, moreover, that teenagers are drawn to smoking not because of advertising but because their parents smoke or because of peer pressure. Companies advertise to gain or maintain market share among those who already smoke.

19   To lessen the heat on politicians, the pact increases the powers of the Food and Drug Administration to regulate tobacco as an addictive drug, with the caveat that it may not prohibit cigarette smoking altogether before the year 2009. The implicit promise is that the complete prohibition of cigarettes will be seriously contemplated at that time. In the meantime, the FDA will subject cigarettes to stricter and stricter controls on the theory that tobacco is a drug.

20   Another rationale for prohibiting or sharply limiting smoking is the supposed need to protect non-smokers from secondhand smoke. The difficulty is that evidence of causation is weak. What we see is a possible small increase in an already small risk which, as some researchers have pointed out, may well be caused by other variables such as misclassification of former smokers as non-smokers or such lifestyle factors as diet.

21   But the tobacco companies should take little or no comfort from that. Given today's product-liability craze, scientific support, much less probability, is unnecessary to successful lawsuits against large corporations.

22   The pact is of dubious constitutionality as well. It outlaws the advertising of a product it is legal to sell, which raises the problem of commercial speech protected by the First Amendment. The settlement also requires the industry to disband its lobbying organization, the Tobacco Institute. Lobbying has traditionally been thought to fall within the First Amendment's guarantee of the right to petition the government for the redress of grievances.

23   And who is to pay for making smoking more difficult? Smokers will have the price of cigarettes raised by new taxes and by the tobacco companies' costs of complying with the settlement. It is a brilliant strategy: Smokers will pay billions to have their pleasure taken away. But if the tobacco settlement makes little sense as public policy, what can be driving it to completion? The motivations are diverse. Members of the plaintiff's bar, who have signally failed in litigation against tobacco to date, are to be guaranteed billions of dollars annually. The states' attorneys general have a different set of incentives. They are members of the National Association of Attorneys General, NAAG, which is commonly, and accurately, rendered as the National Association of Aspiring Governors.

24   So far they have got what they wanted. There they are, on the front pages of newspapers all over the country, looking out at us, jaws firm, conveying images of sobriety, courage, and righteousness. They have, after all, done battle with the forces of evil, and won—at least temporarily.

25   Tobacco executives and their lawyers are said to be wily folk, however. They may find ways of defeating the strictures laid upon them. It may be too soon to tell, therefore, whether the tobacco settlement is a major defeat or a victory for the industry. In any case, we can live with it. But whenever individual responsibility is denied, government control of our behavior follows. After cigarettes it will be something else, and so on ad infinitum. One would think we would have learned that lesson many times over and that we would have had enough of it.

Writing Assignments

THE INVESTIGATIVE ARGUMENT

To develop any of the following topics, follow the guidelines in this chapter for writing an investigative paper or inductive argument. You will need to explain the methods used to collect evidence, to classify evidence in significant ways, to present it in several formats, and to explain its significance. The student paper (pp. 152–158) is your model.

1. Study print ads for one type of product (e.g., cars, cosmetics, cigarettes) and draw inferences about the dominant techniques used to sell that product. Remember that the more ads you study, the more support you have for your inferences. You should study at least 25 ads.

2. Study print ads for one type of product as advertised in different types of magazines clearly directed to different audiences to see how (or if) selling techniques

change with a change in audience. Remember that to demonstrate no change in technique can be just as interesting a conclusion as finding a change in techniques. Study at least 25 ads.

3. Select a major figure currently in the news and conduct your own study of bias in one of the news magazines (e.g., *Time, U.S. News & World Report,* or *Newsweek*). Use at least eight issues of the magazine from the last six months and study all articles on your figure in each of those eight issues.

4. Conduct your own study of violence on TV by analyzing, for one week, all prime-time programs that may contain violence. Try to devise some classification system for types of violence based on your prior TV viewing before you begin your week's study; count the number of times each type of violent act occurs and note also any violent acts that do not fit into your tentative classification system. You may also want to consider the total length of time (per program, per night, per type of violent act) of violence during the week you study. Give credit to Brandon Centerwall for any ideas you borrow from his article (p. 306).

5. An alternative topic to number 4 is to study the number and type of violent acts in children's programs on a Saturday morning. (The topics suggested in numbers 4 and 5 are best handled if you have access to a VCR so that you can tape and then replay the programs several times.)

6. Conduct a survey and analyze the results on some campus issue or current public-policy issues (e.g., gays in the military, use of the death penalty). Prepare questions that are without bias, and include questions about the participants that you may want to correlate answers with (e.g., age, sex, race, religion, proposed major in college, political affiliation). Decide before you begin if you want to survey students only or both students and faculty.

THE POSITION PAPER

Select an issue (1) that you care about and (2) that requires for its defense both evidence and an appeal to principles or moral judgments. Decide on your claim, list your evidence and reasons, and be certain to understand your warrant or assumptions. You may need to do some research to gather needed evidence. Many topics for debate are presented in the readings in Section IV. Here are just a few possibilities to start your thinking:

Voluntary euthanasia

The manufacture and sale of tobacco products

National standards for K–12 students

North American free trade agreements

National service

Affirmative action

Capital punishment

Preservation of endangered species

Preservation of historical landmarks

Pornography

Censorship on the Internet

THE DEFINITION ESSAY

Select an abstract term about which people disagree and develop an argument in support of your definition of the term. You will need to use a number of techniques to develop your definition, including examining the origin of the word, explaining its essential characteristics, giving examples, contrasting with words of similar, but not exactly the same, meaning. Some possible words include:

Obscenity

Pornography

Patriotism

Courtesy

Justice

Liberty

Equality

Hero

Community

THE PROBLEM-SOLUTION ARGUMENT

1. Think of a problem on your campus or in your community for which you have a workable solution. Organize your argument to include all relevant steps as described in this chapter. Although your primary concern will be to present your solution and show that it is a good and workable one, some preliminary steps may be necessary. (If, for example, your solution will cost a fair amount of money, you may need to begin by stressing the seriousness of the problem and the college's or community's need for some solution.)

2. Think of a situation that you consider serious but that apparently many people do not take seriously enough. Write an argument in which you emphasize, by providing evidence, that the situation is a serious problem. (You may need to do some research to gather good evidence.) You may conclude by suggesting a solution, but your chief purpose in writing will be to alert your audience to a problem.

THE REFUTATION ESSAY

Select an editorial, an op-ed column, a letter to the editor, or one of the essays in Section IV as an argument with which you disagree. Prepare a refutation of your opponent's logic, or evidence, or both. Follow the guidelines for organizing and developing your refutation that are explained in this chapter.

The Research Process

CHAPTER 6

Getting Started and Locating Sources (in the Library, Online, in the Field)

This section will help you sharpen skills in the research process and also give you a reference manual for preparing documented papers. Although the research process is in many ways just an extension of your work with one or two sources, there are some differences. A research project involves synthesizing information from several—or many—sources and using a formal documentation system. So, a research project will require some extra time (compared to other kinds of writing projects) and attention to detail. It will also provide some important rewards:

1. After your study, you will know something you did not know before.
2. When you share your new understanding, you will be participating in the academic community.
3. Doing research will improve critical thinking skills, for much of the process is asking the right questions and then finding ways to get the answers.

Defining the Research Process

WHAT RESEARCH IS

We do research all the time. You would not select a college or buy a car without doing research: gathering relevant information, analyzing that information, and drawing conclusions from your study. When you are assigned a research essay for a course, you will need to present the results in an organized way using formal documentation. You may also share your knowledge in a class presentation. Do not let the demands of researching and writing for a grade keep you from remembering the important goals of research:

1. New knowledge
   - The biochemical triggers of alcoholism

- A comparison of shopping habits in urban, suburban, and rural communities
- The discovery and publication of an artist's drawing notebook

2. New understanding
   - Better methods for preventing and treating alcoholism
   - A shopping-center plan based on the study of shopping habits
   - A reevaluation of the artist's work based on the study of the published notebook

TYPES OF RESEARCH PROJECTS

Not all research projects have the same purpose. Different purposes lead to papers that can be classified as primarily *expository*, *analytic*, or *argumentative*.

Expository

An expository or informative paper, often called a report, is an account of your study of a specific topic. The purpose is to share information, to explain to readers what the researcher has learned from the study. Market and technical reports are important kinds of informative writing in business. A good report reflects your critical judgment in the selection and arrangement of information. Instructors assign expository research papers when they want students to read widely on a topic, gain greater understanding of complex topics, or learn about the process of research.

Analytic

The analytic paper goes beyond an organized reporting of information to an examination of the implications of that information. A report on problems in education may assemble recent test scores and other data. An analysis will examine possible causes of the problem. Many literary studies are analyses.

Argumentative/Persuasive

The argumentative paper (often called an opinion or thesis paper) uses information and analysis to support a thesis, to argue for a claim. In an argumentative paper you cannot just report conflicting positions on your topic. You need to evaluate conflicting positions and refute those at odds with your position. To illustrate, compare the following topics to see how they differ in purpose:

Expository: Report of recent literature on infant speech development.

Analytic: Explanation of the process of infant speech development.

Argumentative: Argument for specific actions by parents to aid infant speech development.

WHAT DOES NOT COUNT AS RESEARCH

Defining the research process and looking at types of research projects can help us recognize what will not meet research paper expectations. The following is a cautionary list of kinds of writing to avoid when a research paper has been assigned:

1. A paper that merely strings together quotations from sources.
2. An essay drawn entirely from personal experiences and thoughts.
3. An entirely theoretical paper without any specifics from sources.
4. A paper in which information drawn from sources is not properly documented.

Stages in the Research Process

As you read through the following outline of stages in the research process, keep in mind that complex intellectual activities rarely fit into a rigid sequence. No one can map your particular thinking processes. Research writing means *re-searching, re-thinking,* and *re-writing* as well. Still, there is a basic process that can be described. Having an overview of this process will give you a sense of where you are headed. The following six stages provide that overview. Note, as you read, how the outline emphasizes the recursive nature of thinking, reading, and writing about a topic.

Stage 1. *Select and limit.* Select and limit a topic consistent with assignment guidelines. Review some sources as necessary to aid topic selection. Consider audience, purpose, and required length of paper.

Stage 2. *Focus and plan.* Choose an approach or focus for your research. Decide on a tentative thesis, hypothesis, or question to answer. Think, talk, and read to complete this stage. Write a statement of purpose or research proposal.

Stage 3. *Gather sources.* In a systematic manner locate potential sources from the library and other appropriate places.

Stage 4. *Read and think.* Read and evaluate sources (or study original data). Take notes on relevant information and ideas. Learn about the topic. Re-think what needs to be covered in your study. Re-search as necessary. Make a preliminary outline. Think some more.

Stage 5. *Organize and draft.* Plan in detail the structure of your paper. With notes arranged accordingly, write a first draft. Include documentation as you draft.

Stage 6. *Revise, edit, and format correctly.* First revise your draft and then edit to remove errors. Prepare the completed paper in an appropriate format with correct documentation of sources.

Finding a Workable Topic

As stage 1 indicates, to get started you need to select and limit a topic. One key to success is finding a *workable* topic. No matter how interesting or clever the topic, it is not workable if it does not meet the guidelines of your assignment. Begin with a thorough understanding of the writing context created by the assignment.

WHAT TYPE OF PAPER AM I PREPARING?

Study your assignment to understand the type of project. Is your purpose expository, analytic, or argumentative? How would you classify each of the following topics?

1. Explain the chief solutions proposed for increasing the Southwest's water supply.
2. Compare the Freudian and behavioral models of mental illness.
3. Find the best solutions to a current environmental problem.
4. Consider: What twentieth-century invention has most dramatically changed our personal lives?

Did you recognize that the first topic calls for a report? The second topic requires an analysis of two schools of psychology, so you cannot report on only one, but you also cannot argue that one model is better than the other. Both topics 3 and 4 require an argumentative paper. Just to report on what others have written will not meet the assignment guidelines.

WHO IS MY AUDIENCE?

If you are writing in a specific discipline, imagine your instructor as a representative of that field, a reader with knowledge of the subject area. If you are learning about the research process in a composition course, your instructor may advise you to write to a general reader, someone who reads newspapers but may not have the exact information and perspective you have. For a general reader, specialized terms and concepts need definition and illustration. In some courses students discuss their projects or present their papers to the class. In this situation you actually have the multiple readers you have prepared for in your reflections on audience.

> ✓ NOTE: Consider the expectations of readers of research papers. A research essay is not like a personal essay. A research essay is not about you; it is about a subject, so keep yourself more in the background than you might in a more informal piece of writing.

WHAT ARE THE ASSIGNMENT'S TIME AND LENGTH CONSTRAINTS?

The required length of the paper, the time you have to complete the assignment, and the availability of sources are three constraints you must consider when selecting a research topic. Most instructors will establish guidelines regarding length. Knowing the expected length of the paper is crucial to selecting an appropriate topic, so if an instructor does not specify, be sure to ask.

Suppose, for example, that you must argue for solutions to either an educational or environmental problem. Your paper needs to be about six pages and is due in three weeks. Do you have the space or the time to explore solutions to all the problems caused by overpopulation? Definitely not. Limit your study to one issue such as coping with trash. You could further limit this topic by exploring waste management solutions for your particular city or county.

WHAT KINDS OF TOPICS SHOULD I AVOID?

Here are several kinds of topics that are best avoided because they usually produce disasters, no matter how well the student handles the rest of the research process:

1. *Topics that are irrelevant* to your interests or the course. If you are not interested in your topic, you will not produce a lively, informative paper. If you select a topic far removed from the course content, you may create some hostility in your instructor, who will wonder why you are unwilling to become engaged in the course.

2. *Topics that are broad subject areas.* These result in general surveys that lack appropriate detail and support.

3. *Topics that can be fully researched with only one source.* You will produce a summary, not a research paper.

4. *Biographical studies.* Short undergraduate papers on a person's life usually turn out to be summaries of one or two major biographies.

5. *Topics that produce a strong emotional response in you.* If there is only one "right" answer to the abortion issue and you cannot imagine counterarguments, don't choose to write on abortion. Probably most religious topics are best avoided.

6. *Topics that are too technical for you* at this point in your college work. If you do not understand the complexities of the federal tax code, then arguing for a reduction in the capital gains tax may be an unwise topic choice.

HOW CAN I SELECT A GOOD TOPIC?

Choosing from assigned topics. At times students are unhappy with topic restriction. Looked at another way, your instructor has eliminated a difficult step in the research process and has helped you avoid the problem of selecting an unworkable topic. If topics are assigned, you will still have to choose from the list and develop your own thesis and approach.

Finding a course-related topic. This guideline gives you many options and requires more thought about your choice. Working within the guidelines, try to write about what interests you. Here are examples of assignments turned into topics of interest to the student:

Assignment	Interest	Topic
1. Trace the influence of any 20th-century event, development, invention.	Music	The influence of the Jazz Age on modern music
2. Support an argument on some issue of pornography and censorship.	Computers	Censorship of pornography on the Internet
3. Demonstrate the popularity of a current myth and then discredit it.	Science fiction	The lack of evidence for the existence of UFOs

When you are able to write on any course-related topic or on any subject at all, you will need to use some strategies for topic selection. You can begin by looking at your text's table of contents or index for subject areas that could be narrowed and focused.

Or look through your class notes and think about the subjects already covered that especially interest you. For this course, you can skim through the collection of readings in Section IV to see what topics attract your attention. If you select an issue discussed in one of the articles in this text, you have already located one source. Don't overlook college-based or local community issues as you search for a topic. The college or local newspapers may provide some sources, but you may also need to visit City Hall or find your own data through a questionnaire. Local topics can be fun and original.

Some people can generate good topics from thinking "in their heads," but others are more productive when they think "on paper." In selecting and focusing a topic, you may be aided by using such strategies as freewriting, brainstorming, or asking questions. *Freewriting* forces you to get some ideas on paper, because the "rule" is that you write for several minutes. *Brainstorming* is similar except that you make lists of possibilities and play around with that list rather than writing full sentences for a specific length of time. Most of us discover that once we get a few items on paper, other possibilities occur. A third strategy is *asking questions*. This strategy works well if you have a broad subject from which you need to create a more limited, focused topic. A student interested in Prohibition might develop these questions:

When was the law passed? When rescinded?

Who wanted Prohibition? Who opposed it?

What forces created the climate for the law's passage?

Where did the temperance movement originate? Where was it most influential?

Who benefited from Prohibition?

Why did people defy the law?

Observe that these questions include the *Who, What, Where, When,* and *Why* questions that reporters ask. For some topics a *How* question may also be appropriate.

If these strategies do not lead to a workable topic, then turn to various library sources for help. Search an electronic database for topics under a broad subject heading. If, for example, you need a controversial topic in a science field and you recall an early fascination with dinosaurs, type in *dinosaur* to see what subheadings might suggest a research topic. Subheadings under the word will include *dinosaur behavior* and *dinosaur extinction*.

WHAT IS THE "RIGHT" SIZE FOR A TOPIC?

Part of selecting a workable topic is making sure that the topic is sufficiently narrowed and focused. Students sometimes have trouble narrowing topics. Somehow it seems easier to write on a broad subject, such as education. You know there will be enough sources, all easy to find. But this line of thinking overlooks your purpose in doing research and what you know about good writing. You can piece together a generalized report on education in 6 to 12 pages, but you cannot support a thesis about the subject in such a short space. Consider the following list of increasingly narrower topics about education:

1. Education
2. Problems in education today

3. Problems in K–12 education today
4. Problems with testing students
5. Why standardized tests aren't fair for all students

The first three items are clearly too broad for a short research project. Do you recognize that topic 4 is also too broad? Remember that the more limited and focused your topic, the more concrete and detailed—and thus convincing and engaging—your study will be.

Writing a Tentative Thesis or Research Proposal

Once you have selected and narrowed a topic, you need to write a tentative thesis, research question, or research proposal to guide your planning and source selection. Some instructors will ask to see a statement—from a sentence to a paragraph long—to be approved before you proceed. Others may require as much as a one-page proposal that includes a tentative thesis, a basic organizational plan, and a description of types of sources to be used. Even if your instructor does not require anything in writing, you need to write something for your benefit—to direct your reading and thinking. Let's see how a topic on computers can illustrate the differences among subject, narrowed topic, thesis and research proposal.

Subject:	Computers
Topic:	The impact of computers on the 20th century
Thesis:	Computers have had the greatest impact of any technological development in the 20th century.
Research proposal:	I propose to show that computers have had the greatest impact of any technological development in the 20th century. I will show the influence of computers at work, in daily living, and in play to emphasize the breadth of influence. I will argue that other possibilities (such as cars) have not had the same impact as computers. I will check the library's book catalog and databases for sources on technological developments and on computers specifically. I will also interview a family friend who works with computers at the Pentagon.

This example illustrates several key ideas. First, the initial subject is both too broad and unfocused (What about computers?). Second, the thesis is more focused than the topic statement because it asserts a position, a claim the student must support. Third, the research proposal is more helpful than the thesis only because it includes some thoughts on developing the thesis and finding sources.

When you are less sure of your topic, write a research question rather than a thesis, or a more open-ended research proposal. Take, for example, a history student studying the effects of Prohibition. She is not ready to write a thesis, but she can write a research proposal that suggests some possible approaches to the topic:

Topic:	The effect of Prohibition
Research question:	What were the effects of Prohibition on the United States?

Research proposal: I will examine the effects of Prohibition on the United States in the 1920s (and possibly consider some long-term effects, depending on the amount of material on the topic). Specifically, I will look at the varying effects on urban and rural areas and on different classes in society.

Asking questions and working with fields of study (think of college departments) are two strategies you can use to focus a topic and develop a proposal. Suppose your assignment is to defend a position on a current social issue. You think you want to do something "on television." Using an electronic database to search for a narrowed topic, you decide on the following:

Topic: Television and violence

Research proposal: I will explore the problem of violence on TV. I will read articles in current magazines and newspapers and see what's on the Internet.

Do you have a focused topic and a proposal that will guide your thinking and research? Not yet. Raise questions by field of study.

Literary/humanities: What kinds of violence are found on TV? Children's cartoons? Cop and mystery shows? The news? How are they alike? How different?

Sociology: What are the consequences to our society of a continual and heavy dose of violence on television?

Psychology: What are the effects of television violence on children? Why are we drawn to violent shows?

Politics/government: Should violence on TV be controlled in any way? If so, how?

Education: What is the impact on the classroom when children grow up watching a lot of violence on TV? Does it impede social skills? Learning?

Structuring your thinking about the topic in these ways can help you focus your attention on a specific approach. After reflecting, you decide on the following more focused topic:

Topic: The negative effects of television violence on children and some solutions

Research proposal: I will demonstrate that children suffer from their exposure to so much violence on TV and propose some solutions. Until I read more, I am not certain of the solutions I will propose; I want to read arguments for and against the V-chip and ratings and other possibilities.

Do not settle for an unfocused topic and vague research proposal. To do so is only to put off the task of thinking about what you want to study and how you will proceed.

Locating Sources

To work effectively in this next stage in the research process you need to know:

Your search strategy—how and what to find to develop your topic.

Your choice of method and format for preparing a working bibliography.

Your library and the Internet—what is available and how to access it.

1. *Have a search strategy.* Reflect on the sample research proposals presented above. Each one includes some thoughts about what the student needs to cover or how to develop the topic. If you are writing on a course-related topic, your starting place may be your textbook for relevant sections and possible sources (if the text contains a bibliography). If you are in a composition course, you may find some potential sources among the readings in this text. Think about what you already know or have in hand as you plan your search strategy.

2. *Have a method for recording bibliographic information.* You have two choices: the always reliable 3 × 5 index cards or a bibliography file in your personal computer. If you will be composing on your PC and know how to combine files, you may want to compile a list of possible sources in a separate PC file. If your instructor requires bibliography cards, the decision has been made for you.

3. *Know which documentation format you will be using.* You may be assigned the Modern Language Association (MLA) format, or perhaps given a choice between MLA and the American Psychological Association (APA) documentation styles. In an upper-level course you may be expected to use the format common to that discipline. Once you select the documentation style, skim the appropriate pages in either Chapter 7 (for MLA) or Chapter 9 (for APA) to get an overview of both content and style.

Preparing a Working Bibliography

A list of possible sources is only a *working* bibliography because you do not yet know which sources you will use. (Your final bibliography will include only those sources you cite—actually refer to—in your paper.) A working bibliography will help you see what is available on your topic, note how to locate each source, and contain the information needed to properly document your paper. If you are using cards, put only one source on a card; also, avoid writing on the back because you might overlook that information. Whether you are using cards or computer files, follow these guidelines:

1. Check all reasonable catalogs and indexes for possible sources. (Use more than one reference source even if you locate enough sources there; you are looking for the best sources, not the first ones you find.)

2. Complete a card or prepare an entry for every potentially useful source. You won't know what to reject until you start a close reading of sources.

3. Copy (or download from an online catalog) all information needed to complete a citation and to locate the source. (When using an index that does not give all needed information, leave a space to be filled in when you actually read the source.)

4. Put bibliographic information in the correct format for every possible source; you will save time and make fewer errors. Do not mix or blend styles. When searching for sources, have your text handy and use the models in Chapter 7 or 9 as guides.

The following brief guide to correct form will get you started. Illustrations are for cards, but the information and order will be the same in your PC file. Guidelines are for MLA style only; use Chapter 9 if you have selected a different style.

BASIC FORM FOR BOOKS

As Figure 6–1 shows, the basic MLA form for books includes the following information in this pattern:

1. The author's full name, last name first.
2. The title (and subtitle if there is one) of the book, underlined.
3. The facts of publication: the city of publication (followed by a colon), the publisher (followed by a comma), and the date of publication.

Note that periods are placed after the author's name, after the title, and at the end of the citation. Other information, when appropriate (e.g., the number of volumes), is added to this basic pattern. (See pp. 230–45 for many sample citations.) Include, in your working bibliography, the book's classification number so that you can find it in the library.

BASIC FORM FOR ARTICLES

Figure 6–2 shows the simplest form for magazine articles. Include the following information, in this pattern:

1. The author's full name, last name first.
2. The title of the article, in quotation marks.
3. The facts of publication: the title of the periodical (underlined), the volume number (if the article is from a scholarly journal), the date (followed by a colon), and inclusive page numbers.

FIGURE 6–1   Bibliography Card for a Book

FIGURE 6–2   Bibliography Card for an Article

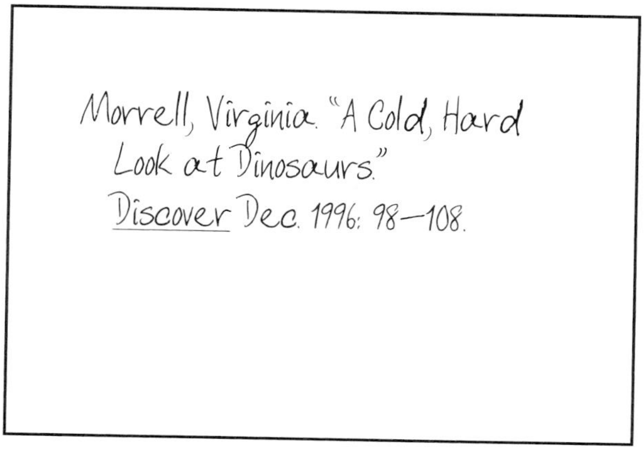

Morrell, Virginia. "A Cold, Hard
Look at Dinosaurs."
Discover Dec. 1996: 98–108.

Notice again that periods are placed after the author's name, after the article's title, and at the end of the citation.

As you search for sources, you will discover that indexes rarely present information in MLA format. Here, for example, is a source on animal rights found in an online database:

Planet of the free apes? Gail Vines.
   New Scientist June 5, 1993 vl38 n1876 p39(4)

To turn this information into a correct citation—if you read the article in the journal—you need to:

- Rearrange the information to put the author first.
- Eliminate bold type and place the article title in quotation marks, capitalizing the appropriate words.
- Underline the journal title and present the volume, date, and paging in MLA form.

The correct citation, as it would appear in your PC file, would look this way:

   Vines, Gail. "Planet of the Free Apes?" New Scientist 5 June 1993: 39–42.

If you obtain a full-text copy of the article from the online database, your citation requires additional information about the database. (See p. 240 for an example.)

✔   NOTE: A collection of printouts, slips of paper, and backs of envelopes is not a working bibliography! You may have to return to the library for missing information, and you risk making serious errors in documentation. Know the basics of your documentation format and follow that format faithfully.

Knowing Your Library

You also need to know your library, for many researchers their primary location for source material. If your knowledge of your campus library is limited, take a little time to learn about its hours, arrangement, and procedures. You will save time in the long run if you learn your way around at the beginning of your research project. What you will discover is that electronic technology has dramatically changed the appearance of and the procedures in most libraries. Instead of rows of drawers containing cards indexing the book catalog, you will probably find banks of computers. Although they may take a little getting used to, most computer applications make research easier and provide access to materials not previously available in many libraries.

All libraries contain books and periodicals, and a system for accessing them. A library's *book collection* is usually divided into three categories. First is the *general collection*, the books that circulate, usually for at least two weeks. Placed in a separate area or room is the *reference collection*, those books of a general nature essential to research that therefore cannot be checked out. The reference collection includes encyclopedias, atlases, handbooks, and manuals arranged by the book's classification number. The reference area also contains its most valuable resource, the reference librarian. Finally, there is the *reserve book collection*. The reserve collection consists of works that instructors consider essential aids to their courses. These books may be checked out for a brief period or placed on "closed" reserve, for use only in the library.

The library's *periodicals collection* consists of popular magazines, scholarly journals, and newspapers. Some libraries allow print periodicals to circulate, but most do not. Electronic databases with full texts of articles provide alternatives to the print periodicals collection. (See below.)

The book and periodicals collections are supplemented by audiovisual materials, including works on CD, tape, microfilm or microfiche, and online. Many libraries store back issues of periodicals on microfilm, so learn where the microfilm readers are and how to use them. Nonprint works can be valuable additions to many kinds of research projects.

Most libraries today provide coin- or card-operated photocopying machines. Using these gives you one way to study noncirculating materials outside the library. In addition, articles from electronic databases and Internet sources can be printed or, in many cases, e-mailed directly to your own PC.

> ✓ REMEMBER: All works, regardless of their source or the format in which you obtain them—and this includes online sources—must be fully documented in your paper. Also, there are certain restrictions on copyrighted materials; know the rules to avoid infringing on a copyright.

Once familiar with your library's services, you want to understand in detail how to use its major tools for locating sources.

LOCATING BOOKS

Your chief guide to the book (and audiovisual) collection is the catalog, once referred to as the "card catalog" because it used to consist of cards in drawers. Now your library's catalog is probably a computer database.

In a catalog there are at least three entries for each book: the author entry, the title entry, and one or more subject entries. Online catalogs continue to use these same access points plus a keyword option and possibly others, such as the book's International Standard Book Number (ISBN). When you go to your library's home screen and select the catalog, you will come to the search screen. Usually, keyword is the default. If you know the exact title, switch to title, type in the title, and click on "submit search." If instead you want a list of all of the library's books by Hemingway, for example, click on author and type in Hemingway. Remember:

- With a title search, do not type any initial article (a, an, the). Thus, to locate *The Great Gatsby*, type in "Great Gatsby."

- Use correct spelling. If you are unsure of a spelling, use a keyword instead of an author or title search.

- If you are looking for a list of possible books on your subject, do a keyword or subject search.

Reading Entries: Brief and Long View Screens

If you do an author search by last name only, you will get a list of all of the library's books written by writers with that last name. A keyword search will provide a list of all book titles containing your keyword. These "brief view" lists provide enough information to locate a book in the library: author, title, and classification number—the number by which the book is shelved (see Figure 6–3).

For books that look promising for your research, click on *View Record* to obtain the "long view" screen. This screen (see Figure 6–4) provides additional information, including bibliographic details needed for documentation and one or more subject listings that you can use to find other books on the same subject. For potentially useful books, copy all needed information into your working bibliography.

CLASSIFICATION OF BOOKS

Books are shelved according to either the Library of Congress classification system or the Dewey decimal system. You are probably familiar with the Dewey system used by many public libraries, especially small ones. Most colleges, however, use the Library of Congress system, so you will need to familiarize yourself with it.

OUTLINE OF THE LIBRARY OF CONGRESS CLASSIFICATION

Letters indicate the major subject divisions:

A—General Works
B—Philosophy and Religion
C—History, Auxiliary Sciences
D—History and Topography,
    except America

FIGURE 6–3   Online Catalog—Brief View Author List

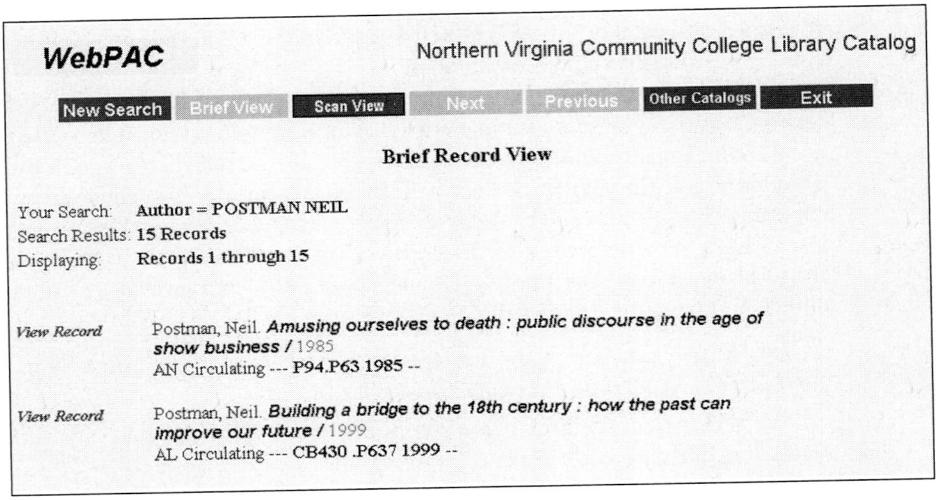

```
WebPAC                          Northern Virginia Community College Library Catalog

 New Search    Brief View    Scan View    Next    Previous   Other Catalogs   Exit

                              Brief Record View

Your Search:   Author = POSTMAN NEIL
Search Results: 15 Records
Displaying:    Records 1 through 15


View Record    Postman, Neil. Amusing ourselves to death : public discourse in the age of
               show business / 1985
               AN Circulating --- P94.P63 1985 --

View Record    Postman, Neil. Building a bridge to the 18th century : how the past can
               improve our future / 1999
               AL Circulating --- CB430 .P637 1999 --
```

> E—American History and General
>   U.S. History
> F—U.S. History (local), Latin
>   America, and Canada
> G—Geography and Anthropology
> H—Social Sciences
> J—Political Sciences
> K—Law
> L—Education
> M—Music
> N—Fine Arts
> P—Language and Literature
> Q—Science
> R—Medicine
> S—Agriculture, Forestry,
>   Hunting, and Fishing
> T—Technology
> U—Military Science
> V—Naval Science
> Z—Library Science and Bibliography

FIGURE 6–4 **Online Catalog Entry—Long View of One Book**

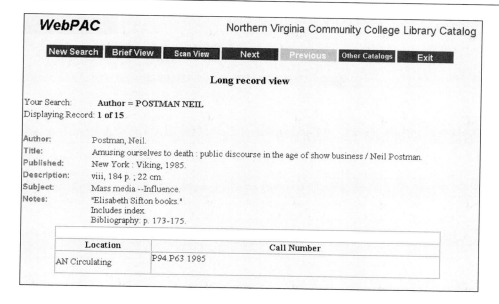

Major subdivisions within each general subject category are indicated by a second letter. For example, some subdivisions under D (History) are DC (French History) and DK (Russian History). Further subdivisions reflecting type, date, author, and specific work are indicated by Arabic numerals and the first initial of the author's last name. A specific British history text, for instance, George M. Trevelyan's *The English Revolution, 1688–1689,* would have the following number:

DA

452

.T7

ARRANGEMENT OF BOOKS ON THE SHELF

The classification or "call" number of each book is provided in the catalog entry and on the spine of the book, where it can be seen when the book is shelved. Be sure to copy the complete call number accurately before you look for a book.

As you search for sources, use every opportunity to add to your working bibliography. When using subject or keyword searches, make a bibliography card or entry for every book that might prove useful. Make a special note of books having bibliographies and examine those pages as soon as you locate the books. When in the stacks to obtain books, take a few minutes to look at the books near those you have listed, for they will be in the same subject category. If a book you want is not in its proper place on the shelf, look above and below—even behind other books—to see if the one you need is lurking in the wrong place. Successful researchers develop a "nose for books."

Using the Reference Collection

The research process often begins with the reference collection. Materials in this collection are invaluable because they provide information of a factual nature in a condensed format. You will find atlases, dictionaries, encyclopedias, general histories, critical studies, and biographies. In addition, various reference tools such as bibliographies and indexes are part of the reference collection.

Not surprisingly, many tools in the reference collection once only in print form are now also online. Some are now only online. Yet online is not always the way to go. Let's consider some of the advantages of each of the formats:

Advantages of the Print Reference Collection

1. The reference tool may be only in print—use it.
2. The print form covers the period you are studying. (Most online indexes and abstracts cover only from 1980 to the present.)
3. In a book, with a little scanning of pages, you can often find what you need without getting spelling or commands exactly right.
4. If you know the best reference source to use and are looking for only a few items, the print source can be faster than the online source.
5. All computer terminals are in use—or down—open a book!

Advantages of Online Reference Materials

1. Online databases are likely to provide the most up-to-date information.
2. You can usually search all years covered at one time.
3. Full texts (with graphics) are sometimes available, as well as indexes with detailed summaries of articles. Both can be printed or even e-mailed to your PC.
4. Through links to the Internet, you have access to an amazing amount of material. (Unless you focus your keyword search, however, you may be overwhelmed.)

Before using any reference work, take a few minutes to check its date, purpose, and organization. Before using reference sources that are online, go to your library's home page to see what reference materials and strategies for Internet searches are available. Also, if you are new to online searching, take a few minutes to learn about each reference tool by working through the online tutorial. (Go to the Help screen.) These strategies can supplement the following brief review of some key reference tools.

BASIC REFERENCE TOOLS

Use your library's reference collection as you need to for facts, for background information, and for indexes to possible sources.

Dictionaries

For the spelling of specialized words not found in your PC's dictionary, consult an appropriate subject dictionary; for foreign words, the appropriate foreign-language dictionary. If you need a word's origin or its definitions from an earlier time, use one of the unabridged dictionaries. Here are two to know:

Webster's Encyclopedic Unabridged Dictionary of the English Language. 1996.

The Oxford English Dictionary. 20 vols. in print. Also online.

General Encyclopedias

Two multi-volume encyclopedias to know are the *Encyclopedia Americana* and the *Encyclopaedia Britannica.* The *Britannica,* the *World Book,* and other encyclopedias are available online as well as in print.

Atlases

Atlases provide much more than simple maps showing capital cities and the names of rivers. Historical atlases show changes in politics, economics, and culture. Topographical atlases support studies in the earth sciences and many environmental issues. Here are just two:

Historical Atlas of the United States. National Geographic Society, 1988.

The Times Atlas of the World. 9th ed. 1992.

Check to see what atlases your library has on CD-ROM.

Quotations, Mythology, and Folklore

Use the following works to understand unfamiliar references:

*Bartlett's Familiar Quotations.*16th ed. 1992. In print and online.

Funk and Wagnall's Standard Dictionary of Folklore, Mythology, and Legend.

Edith Hamilton. *Mythology.*

Almanacs and Yearbooks

The following sources answer all kinds of questions about current events and provide statistical information on just about anything. Many of these works—and others like them—are both in print and online. Check to see which format your library offers.

Congressional Record. 1873 to date. Issued daily during sessions. Online.

Facts on File. 1940 to date. Digest of important news events. Online.

Statistical Abstract of the United States. 1978 to date. Annual publication of the Bureau of the Census. Much of this is free on the Internet.

World Almanac and Book of Facts. 1868 to date.

Biographical Dictionaries

Most libraries have an array of biographical dictionaries, some providing brief entries for many persons, others specializing by country or profession or providing lengthy essays about famous people. These are important tools for investigating authors with whom you are unfamiliar.

> *Contemporary Authors.* 1962 to date. A multivolume guide to current fiction and nonfiction writers and their books. Online.
>
> *International Who's Who.* 1935 to date. Contains brief biographies of important persons from almost every country.
>
> *American Men and Women of Science.* Provides brief sketches of more than 150,000 scientists. Lists degrees held and fields of specialization. Regularly updated.
>
> *Who's Who.* 1849 to date. English men and women.
>
> *Who's Who in America.* 1899 to date.
>
> *Who's Who in American Women.* 1958 to date.

Using Indexes to Periodicals

Periodicals (magazines, journals, and newspapers) provide good sources for research projects, especially for projects on current issues. The best way to access articles on your topic is to use one or more of the many periodical indexes. To be efficient, you want to select the most useful indexes for your particular study. Your library will maintain some print indexes to popular magazines, some for scholarly journals, and some to newspapers. In addition, your library probably provides many online databases. Online databases are more likely than older print indexes to blend magazines, journals, and newspaper articles, and many online databases include full texts of the articles. Often, online databases with full texts to some of the articles are replacing a library's subscriptions to print periodicals. So you will need to learn which of the indexes provide full texts and which indexes provide only lists of possibly useful articles that you must then locate in your library's paper collection of periodicals. Your library may also obtain a faxed copy of an article you need that is not available either online or in the library's periodicals collection, so be sure to ask if this service is available.

THE READER'S GUIDE TO PERIODICAL LITERATURE

Probably the most-used paper index, *The Reader's Guide to Periodical Literature* (1900 to date) combines author and subject headings that guide users to articles in about 200 popular magazines. The index is bound in hardcover volumes annually. As the sample entries in Figure 6–5 show, the information is heavily abbreviated. When using this index, study the explanation provided and check the list of periodicals found in the front of each volume for the complete title of each magazine. Use this index if you want articles written prior to 1980.

THE NEW YORK TIMES INDEX

Newspapers are a good source of information about both contemporary topics and historical events and issues. Since it is one of the most thorough and respected newspapers,

FIGURE 6–5   Entries in *The Reader's Guide to Periodical Literature*

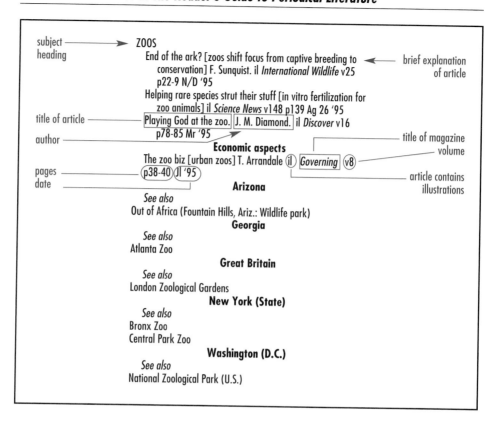

the *New York Times* is available in most libraries. So, when your topic warrants it, become familiar with the *New York Times Index*, for it can guide you to articles as far back as the mid-nineteenth century. (Back issues of the newspaper are on microfilm.) The print *NYT Index* (see Figure 6–6) is a subject index, cumulated and bound annually, with articles arranged chronologically under each subject heading. The *NYT Index* is also online; your library may have both formats. Articles in the *New York Times* are indexed in other online databases, but full texts of the articles are not usually available.

ONLINE DATABASES

You will probably access online databases by going to your library's home page and then clicking on the appropriate term or icon. (You may have found the book catalog by clicking on "library catalog"; you may find the databases by clicking on "periodicals databases" or "library resources" or some other descriptive label.) You will need to choose a particular database and then type in your keyword for a basic search or select "advanced search" to limit your search by date or periodical or to search for articles by

FIGURE 6–6   Explanation of Entries in the *New York Times Index*

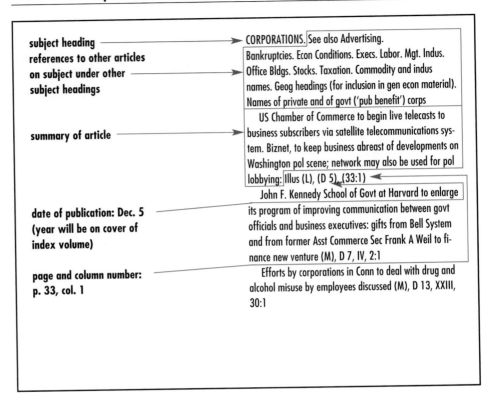

a specific author. Each library will create somewhat different screens, but the basic process of selecting among choices provided and then typing in your search commands remains the same. Figure 6–7 shows a first screen in response to the choice to search for magazine and newspaper articles. Notice that the librarians are suggesting four databases (*Infotrac, NewsBank Newsfile, Proquest Direct,* and *SIRS*) that are useful for many undergraduate research projects. If you do not want to work in one of these four, you can click to find an alphabetical list of databases or a subject list. (Note: Your library probably has hundreds of databases.)

If you select the first database, *Infotrac,* you will come to the list of specific choices within the *Infotrac* collection, complete with a brief description of the coverage for each one. (See Figure 6–8 for a partial list.) To begin your search for specific articles, select the database that seems most useful for your topic, click on "Start searching," and then

FIGURE 6–7   Beginning Screen to Search for Articles in Online Databases

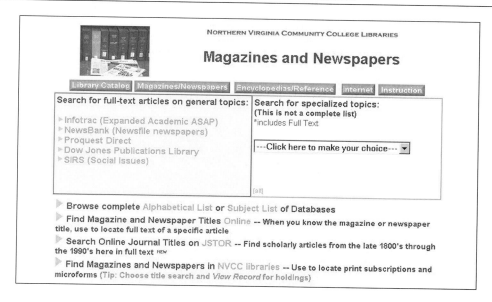

FIGURE 6–8   Partial List of Databases Available Through Infotrac

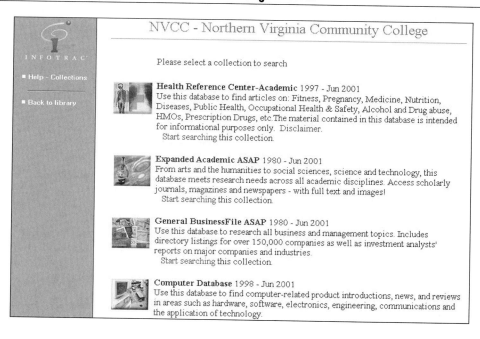

type in your keyword(s) on the next screen. Observe, in Figure 6–9, that in addition to a simple search, you can modify your search in several ways. The simple search for "zoos and animal rights," a combination of terms used to find only those articles that address both issues (rather than just zoos or just animal rights), yielded 12 articles. Figure 6–10 shows a partial list of those "hits." Study the annotations to Figure 6–10 to understand the information provided.

Keep these points in mind as you use online databases:

Guidelines for Using Online Databases

1. While some online databases provide full texts of all articles, others provide full texts of only some of the articles indexed. The articles not in full text will have to be located in a print collection of periodicals.

2. Articles indexed but not available in full text often come with a brief summary or abstract. This allows you to decide whether the article looks useful for your project. *Do not treat the abstract as the article. Do not use material from it and cite the author. If you want to use the article, find it in your library's print collection or obtain it from another library.*

3. The information you need for documenting material used from an article is not in correct format for any of the standard documentation styles. You will have to reorder the information and use the correct style for writing titles. If your instructor wants to see a list of possible sources in MLA format, do not hand in a printout of articles from an online database. (Follow MLA citation guidelines on pp. 230–45.)

4. Because no one database covers all magazines, you may want to search several databases that seem relevant to your project.

INDEXES TO ACADEMIC JOURNALS

The indexes to magazines and journals just reviewed provide many good articles for undergraduate research. At times, though, you may need to use articles exclusively from scholarly journals. Many of the more specialized indexes to journals began as print indexes but are now online as well. The following is a brief list of some of the more academic indexes students frequently use. Your reference librarian can recommend others appropriate to your study.

Applied Science and Technology Index   An index to periodicals covering engineering, data processing, earth sciences, space science, and more. Online through FirstSearch.

Book Review Digest   Begun in 1905 and now also online, this index is arranged by author of the book reviewed. It contains brief reviews of both fiction and nonfiction works.

FIGURE 6–9 **Search Screen for Online Database**

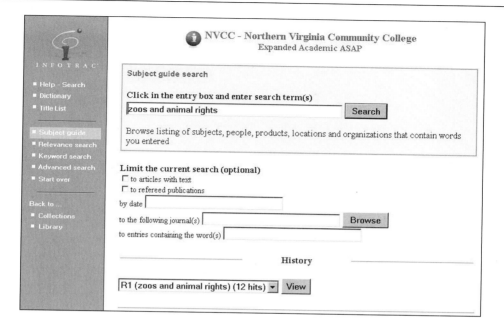

FIGURE 6–10 **Partial List of Articles Found on Search Topic**

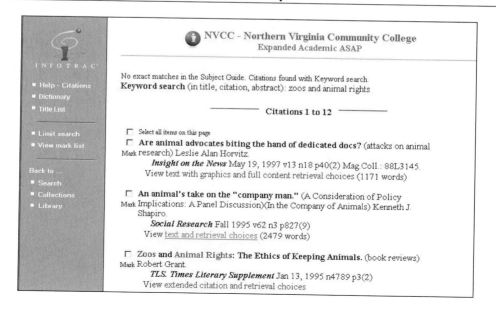

Essay and General Literature Index   An author and subject index, from 1900, this index includes references to both biographical and critical materials. Its chief focus is literary criticism.

Educational Research Information Center (ERIC)   In its print form, there are two sections, *Current Index to Journals in Education* and *Resources in Education*, a collection of unpublished reports on educational issues. *ERIC* is now online.

Humanities Index   This index lists articles on art, literature, philosophy, folklore, history, and related topics. Online.

MLA International Bibliography   The annual listing by the Modern Language Association of books, articles, and dissertations in language and literature. Online.

Public Affairs Information Service (PAIS)   Begun in 1915 and now online, this index covers books, pamphlets, reports, and articles on economics, government, social issues, and public affairs. It is international in scope and emphasizes works that are strong on facts and statistics.

Science Citation Index   An index (since 1961) of over 3,000 journals in mathematics and the natural, physical, and behavioral sciences. It includes an index to articles, a subject index based on keywords appearing in titles of articles indexed, and a citation index, arranged by author, that reveals which articles are referred to by other authors in their papers.

Social Sciences Citation Index   Like the *Science Citation Index*, this index includes a source index, a subject index by keywords, and a citation index.

Locating Government Documents and Related Publications

Each year, the U.S. government prints many thousands of documents ranging from pamphlets to maps to multivolume reports. Some are free; others are for sale; many are now available on the Internet. Most libraries subscribe to two kinds of indexes to government documents:

Monthly Catalog of U.S. Government Publications   Each monthly catalog is organized into four indexes: author, title, subject, and series report.

The GPO Publications Reference File or GPO Access (on the Web)   The former has been replaced by the regularly updated index on the Internet. You can reach *GPO Access* at www.access.gpo.gov/su_docs. (See Figure 6–11.)

Via the Internet, you have access to the *Congressional Record*, an index to the National Archives, the current federal budget, and much information through various department and agency home pages, to list only a few possibilities.

Searching the Internet

In addition to finding sources by using the online databases in your library, you can also search the Internet directly. If you are new to Internet searching, you may need to study online tutorials and practice to become efficient in your search for useful information. In addition, your college library may conduct workshops on searching—check it out.

FIGURE 6–11   Home Page of *GPO Access*

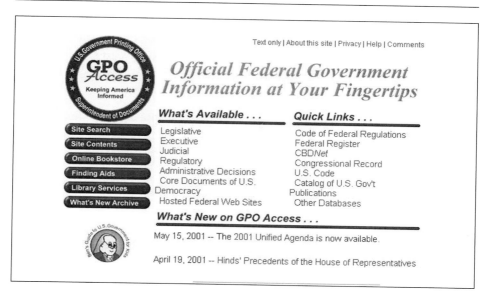

Keep in mind these realities about the Internet:

- The Internet is both disorganized and huge, so you can waste time trying to find information that is easily obtained in a reference book in your library.

- The Internet is best at providing current information such as news and movie reviews. It is also a great source of government information.

- Since anyone can create a website and put anything on it, you will have to use considerable ingenuity in evaluating Internet sources. Remember that articles in magazines and journals have been selected by editors and may also have been peer reviewed before publication, but no one selects or rejects material for the Web. (More on evaluating Internet sources can be found in Chapter 8.)

BASIC SERVICES AND FUNCTIONS OF THE INTERNET

When you have access to the Internet, you can obtain information in a variety of ways. The most common are described below.

E-mail

E-mail can be used instead of a printed letter to request information from a government agency or company.

Mailing Lists (Listservs)

You can sign up to receive, via your e-mail, continually updated bulletins on a particular subject. Listservs are essentially organized mailing lists. If you find one relevant to your project, you can subscribe for a while and unsubscribe when you are no longer interested.

Newsgroups

Newsgroups differ from listservs in that the discussions and exchanges are collected for you to retrieve; they are not sent to your e-mail address. Otherwise they are much the same: both are a type of discussion group. To find newsgroups on a specific subject, go to http://groups.google.com, a research tool sponsored by the search engine Google, that surveys all Usenet newsgroups.

World Wide Web

For most researchers, the Web provides more useful information than listservs or newsgroups. To access the Web from your library terminal or on your own PC through a hookup with your college library, you will, as with the catalog and online databases, start at your library's home-page. (If you work from your PC using your Internet service provider's home page, you probably already know something about selecting a search engine or initiating a search.) Usually selecting "search the Internet" will take you to a screen similar to the one shown in Figure 6–12. Observe the menu provided of various search engines and subject directories. Note as well the questions that you can click on to obtain information about the various search engines or guidelines for evaluating a website. You can see, in Figure 6–12, that there are many search engines and subject directories to use. Not all search engines are the same, and people differ on which are the best, so you may want to get some help selecting the best one for your search. Here are some sites to visit for help:

> *Librarians' Index to the Internet:* http://lii.org
>
> *Greg R. Notess's search engine comparison pages:* www.notess.com/search
>
> *Search Engine Watch:* www.searchenginewatch.com

FIGURE 6–12   Initial Screen for Internet Search

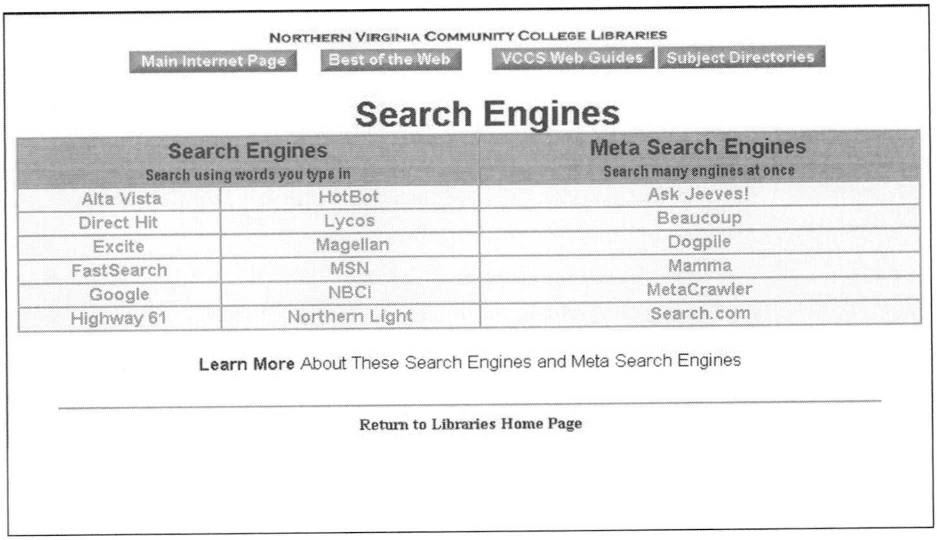

NORTHERN VIRGINIA COMMUNITY COLLEGE LIBRARIES

| Main Internet Page | Best of the Web | VCCS Web Guides | Subject Directories |

Search Engines

Search Engines Search using words you type in		Meta Search Engines Search many engines at once
Alta Vista	HotBot	Ask Jeeves!
Direct Hit	Lycos	Beaucoup
Excite	Magellan	Dogpile
FastSearch	MSN	Mamma
Google	NBCi	MetaCrawler
Highway 61	Northern Light	Search.com

Learn More About These Search Engines and Meta Search Engines

Return to Libraries Home Page

How much information you may find searching for a specific topic, and how useful it is, will vary from one research project to another. Here are some general guidelines to aid your research on the Internet:

Guidelines for Searching the Web

1. Bookmark sites you expect to use often so that you do not have to try to remember complicated Web addresses, or uniform resource locators (URLs).

2. Make your search as precise as possible to avoid getting overwhelmed with hits.

3. If you are searching for a specific phrase, put quotation marks around the words. This will reduce the number of hits and lead to sites more useful to your research. Examples: "Environmental Protection Agency" or "civil disobedience."

4. Learn to use Boolean connectors to make your search more precise.
   - AND: This connector limits results to those sites that contain both terms, for example, "zoos AND animal rights." A search term of "zoos" only will likely result in many hits that are not pertinent to the topic.
   - OR: This connector extends the hits to include all sites that contain one or the other search term. So, "zoos OR animal rights" will generate a list of sites containing either term.
   - NOT: This connector limits the search to only the first term, not the second. Thus, "zoos NOT animal rights" will give you sites only about zoo issues not involving animal rights.

5. If you are not successful with one search engine, try a different one. Remember that each search engine searches only a part of the Internet.

6. If you are not successful with a second search engine, check your spelling. Search engines cannot guess what you mean; spelling must be exact.

7. To get the best sites for most college research projects, try a directory of evaluated sites or subject guide rather than, say, Yahoo! (Yahoo! is better for news, people searches, and commercial sites.) Some of the best academic subject guides include:
   - The Argus Clearinghouse (www.clearinghouse.net)
   - The University of California's Infomine (http://infomine.ucr.edu)
   - Internet Scout Project (http://scout.cs.wisc.edu)

8. Be certain to complete a bibliography card—including the date you accessed the material—for each separate site from which you take information. Remember: All sources must be documented, including Internet sources. (See pp. 240–41 for documentation guidelines.)

---

behavior and attitudes of college students and/or faculty, and for topics on consumer habits. Prepare a brief list of questions with space for answers. Poll faculty through their mailboxes and students individually on campus or in your classes. When writing questions, keep these guidelines in mind:

- Use simple, clear language.
- Devise a series of short questions rather than only a few that have several parts to them. (You want to separate information for better analysis.)
- Phrase questions to avoid bias (wording that seeks to control the answer). For example, do *not* ask: How did you survive the *horrors* of the Depression? Do *not* write: Did you perform your civic duty by voting in the last election? These are loaded questions that prejudge the respondent's answers.

In addition to surveys and questionnaires, you can incorporate some original research. As you read sources on your topic, be alert to reports of studies that you could redo and update in part or on a smaller scale. Many topics on advertising and television give opportunities for your own analysis. Local-issue topics may offer good opportunities for gathering information on your own, not just from your reading. One student, examining the controversy over a proposed new shopping mall on part of the Manassas Battlefield, made the argument that the mall served no practical need in the community. He supported his position by describing existing malls, including the number and types of stores each contained and the number of miles each was from the proposed new mall. How did he obtain this information? He drove around the area, counting miles and stores. Sometimes a seemingly unglamorous approach to a topic turns out to be an imaginative one.

Exercises: Using the Library

Library Question Sheet

Take a library-sponsored tour, read your library's manual on its facilities and services, and make a thorough investigation of the library, asking questions when necessary, to learn where to find and how to use the library's resources. Then answer these questions:

1. What is the loan period for books?
2. Do periodicals circulate? If so, what is the loan period?
3. Where is the catalog of books? Is it a card, microform, or online catalog?
4. Where are the print periodical indexes?
5. Where is the collection of unabridged dictionaries?
6. Where are the *Book Review Digest* volumes? Are they also online?
7. Where are the encyclopedias? Are any online? If so, which ones?
8. Where is the *New York Times Index?*
9. Is there an audiovisual collection? Where is it kept?
10. Is your library open on Sundays? What are the hours?
11. Where are the microfilm readers located?

12. Where are the reserve books located?

13. Are the stacks (the bookshelves) open to students?

14. What classification system is used for arranging books?

15. Are there terminals for accessing the Internet? If so, where are they located?

Library Skills Practice

The following questions will test your ability to find and use or evaluate materials in the library. If you are unsure about any questions, restudy the appropriate sections of this chapter.

1. Interpret the following entry from an online database by answering questions a through f.

> **Are animal advocates biting the hand of dedicated docs?** (attacks on animal research) Leslie Alan Horvitz.
> **Insight on the News** May 19, 1997 v13 n18 p40(2) Mag.Coll.: 88L3145. View <u>text with graphics and full content retrieval choices</u>

   a. Who is the author?
   b. What is the name of the periodical?
   c. What is the title of the article?
   d. What is the date of publication?
   e. How many pages does the article have?
   f. Does the database provide full text of the article?

2. Interpret the following entry from *The Reader's Guide to Periodical Literature* by answering questions a through f.

> FEDERAL reserve banks
>   Can 2 + 2 = 5? A look at what voluntary
> membership in the Federal reserve system
> means to the economy. P. D. Nigro. bibl Intellect
> 103:48-50 O'74

   a. Who is the author?
   b. What is the name of the periodical?
   c. What is the subject heading?
   d. What is the title of the article?
   e. What is the volume number?
   f. What is the date of publication?

3. Select three journals in your field of interest (for example, *Science, Scientific American,* and the *Proceedings of the National Academy of Sciences*) or three journals that you could use in preparing your research paper. Examine the articles in at least one issue of each journal for the same year. Then write a brief report comparing the journals on these points:

   a. What kinds of topics are covered? How extensive is the range of topics?
   b. How technical are the articles? How would you characterize the style of writing?
   c. Who would you judge to be the anticipated audience for each journal?

    d. Under what circumstances, for what purposes, would you be likely to turn to each journal?

4. Choose a subject that interests you, or one that relates to your research project, or one from the list below, and look it up in both a general multivolume encyclopedia and a specialized reference work. Read both articles and write a brief report answering the four questions below. *Possible subjects:* Zen, ESP, the Federal Reserve System, DNA, Aphrodite, plate tectonics, naturalism, the Third Reich, jazz, the planet Jupiter, surrealism.

    a. Which reference work contains the longer entry on your subject?

    b. Which reference work contains a more technical or sophisticated discussion of the subject?

    c. What format is used by each work? (Formal essay? Briefer section with headings for each reference? Lists?)

    d. Under what circumstances would you be likely to use each reference work? What does each work seem best suited for?

Using Reference Materials

The left-hand column lists research problems. The right-hand column lists various indexes and reference materials that have been described in this chapter. Indicate the best source to use by placing the appropriate letter from the right-hand column next to the problem in the left-hand column.

_____ 1. Magazine articles on Prohibition from the 1920s

_____ 2. Billy Joel's birthdate

_____ 3. The author of "To err is human, to forgive divine"

_____ 4. The reception of the book *Chaos* by James Gleick

_____ 5. The birthplace of Coretta Scott King

_____ 6. A list of books and articles on *The Scarlet Letter*

_____ 7. Books in your library on advertising

_____ 8. The Senate vote on recent legislation

_____ 9. Newspaper coverage of the 1960 presidential election

a. book or online catalog

b. *MLA International Bibliography*

c. *Who's Who in American Women*

d. *New York Times Index*

e. *The Reader's Guide to Periodical Literature*

f. *Current Biography*

g. *Congressional Record*

h. *Book Review Digest*

i. *Bartlett's Familiar Quotations*

CHAPTER 7

Understanding Sources, Selecting Information, and Documenting (Using MLA)

Now you are ready to dig into your sources: to read, to learn about your subject, to select material to develop your paper, and to learn how to document that borrowed material. As you study in depth to learn about your topic, be sure to keep rethinking your purpose and approach. Keep testing your research proposal or tentative thesis against what you are learning about your topic. Remember: you can always change the direction and focus of your paper as new approaches occur to you, and you can even change your position as you reflect on what you are learning.

Using Sources Effectively

You will work with sources more effectively if you keep in mind why you are using them. What you are looking for will vary somewhat, depending on your topic and purpose, but there are several basic uses we can examine:

1. *Acquiring information and viewpoints firsthand.* Suppose that you are concerned about the mistreatment of animals kept in zoos. You do not want to just read what others have to say on this issue. First, visit a zoo, taking notes on what you see. Second, before you go, plan to interview at least one person on the zoo staff, preferably a veterinarian who can explain the zoo's guidelines for animal care. Only after gathering and thinking about these *primary sources* do you want to add to your knowledge by reading articles and books—*secondary sources*. Many kinds of topics require the use of both primary and secondary sources. If you want to study violence in children's TV shows, for example, you should first spend some time watching specific shows and taking notes. Then find some recent studies others have made. Literary analyses should be based, first or primarily, on your analysis, not exclusively on what others have written about your topic.

2. *Acquiring new knowledge.* Suppose you are interested in breast cancer research and treatment, but you do not know much about the choices of treatment and, in general, where we are with this medical problem. You will need to turn to sources first to learn about the topic. You should begin with sources that will give you an overview, perhaps a historical perspective of how knowledge and treatment have progressed in the last 30 years. Similarly, if your topic is the effects of Prohibition in the 1920s, you will need to read first for knowledge but also with an eye to ways to focus the topic and organize your paper.

3. *Learning about the issues.* Suppose you think that you know your views on gun control or immigration, so you intend to read only to obtain some useful statistical information to support your argument. Should you scan sources quickly, looking for facts you can use? This approach may be too hasty. As explained in Chapter 3, good arguments are built on a knowledge of counterarguments. You are wise to study sources presenting a variety of attitudes on your issue so that you understand—and can refute—the arguments of others. Remember, too, that with controversial issues often the best argument is a conciliatory one that presents a middle ground and seeks to bring people together. You may also want to consider interviewing an elected official or administering a questionnaire to fellow students.

Evaluating Sources

When you use facts and opinions from sources, you are saying to readers that the facts are accurate and the ideas credible. If you do not evaluate your sources before using them, you risk losing your credibility as a writer. (Remember Aristotle's idea of *ethos*, how your character is judged.) Just because they are in print does not mean that a writer's "facts" are reliable or ideas worthwhile. Judging both the usefulness and reliability of potential sources is always an essential part of the research process. Today, with access to so much material on the Internet, the need to evaluate is even more crucial. Here are some strategies for evaluating sources, with special attention to Internet sources:

Guidelines for Evaluating Sources

1. *Locate the author's credentials.* Periodicals often list their writers' degrees, current position, and other publications; books, similarly, contain an "about the author" section. If you do not see this information, check various biographical dictionaries (*Biography Index, Contemporary Authors*) for information about the author. If this strategy does not work, ask your instructor if he or she has heard of the author. Writers who have written several works on your topic and have been recognized by other writers in the field are ones you want to include in your study. For articles on the Web, look for the author's e-mail address or a link to a home page. Never use a Web source that does not identify the author or the organization

---

responsible for the material. *Critical question:* Is this author qualified to write on this topic? How do I know?

2. *Judge the credibility of the work.* For books, read how reviewers evaluated the book when it was first published. (Try the *Book Review Digest*—in paper and online.) For articles, judge the respectability of the magazine or journal. (Use the *New York Times*, not the *National Enquirer*, as a newspaper source.) Study the author's use of documentation as one measure of credibility. Scholarly works cite sources. Well-researched and reliable pieces in quality popular magazines will also make clear the sources of any statistics used or the credentials of any authority who is quoted. One good rule: Never use undocumented statistical information. Another judge of credibility is the quality of writing. Do not use sources filled with grammatical and mechanical errors. Also, ask yourself if the factual information makes sense: Is it logically presented and does it match your knowledge of the world? In addition, for Web sources, find out what institution hosts the site. If you have not heard of the company or university, find out more about it. You may want to see if you can verify website information or opinions in a print source. *Critical question:* Why should I believe information/ideas from this source?

3. *Select only those sources that are at an appropriate level for your research.* Avoid works that are either too specialized or too elementary for college research. You may not understand the former (and thus could misrepresent them in your paper), and you may gain nothing from the latter. You may want to pass on articles in the *Journal of Cell Biology*, but you also want to avoid many of the articles in popular magazines. These tend to be general reviews usually written by journalists, not experts in the field. *Critical question:* Will this source provide a sophisticated discussion for educated adults?

4. *Understand the writer's purpose.* Consider the writer's intended audience. Be cautious using works designed to reinforce biases already shared by the intended audience. Is the work written to persuade rather than to inform and analyze? (Examine the writing for strongly worded, emotionally charged language.) These works may be useful for understanding the views of opposing sides on a controversial issue, but the evidence presented must be evaluated carefully. For Internet sources, ask yourself why this person or institution decided to have a website or contribute to a newsgroup. *Critical question:* Can I trust the information from this source, given the apparent purpose of the work?

5. *In general, choose current sources.* Some studies published years ago remain classics, but many older works have become outdated. In scientific and technical fields, the "information revolution" has outdated some works published only five years ago. So look at publication dates (When was the website page last updated?) and pass over outdated sources in favor of current studies. *Critical question:* Is this information still accurate?

Documenting Sources to Avoid Plagiarism

Before beginning the process of taking notes, you need to understand why and how to document. Your use of sources is made clear to readers by the formal pattern of documentation you use. The need to document accurately and fully applies to all researchers, regardless of the particular pattern used. Proper documentation shows readers the breadth of your research and distinguishes between the work of others and your understanding of the topic.

Improper documentation of sources—plagiarism—is both unethical and illegal. To fail to document sources used is to lose your credibility and reputation. Ideas, new information, and wording belong to their author. To borrow them without acknowledgment is against the law and has led to many celebrated lawsuits. Paying for a paper from a service and submitting a friend's paper are clear examples of plagiarism. More often, though, students plagiarize unintentionally because they do not understand the requirements of documentation. Be certain that you know what constitutes appropriate documentation.

> ✔️   MLA documentation requires that precise page references be given for all ideas, opinions, and information taken from sources—except for common knowledge. Author and page references provided in the text are supported by complete bibliographic citations on the Works Cited page.

In sum, you are required to document the following:

- Direct quotations from sources
- Paraphrased ideas and opinions from sources
- Summaries of ideas from sources
- Factual information, except common knowledge, from sources

Understand that putting an author's ideas in your own words in a paraphrase or summary does not eliminate the requirement of documentation. To illustrate, consider the following excerpt from Thomas R. Schueler's report *Controlling Urban Runoff* (Washington Metropolitan Water Resources Planning Board, 1987: 3–4) and a student paragraph based on the report.

Source

The aquatic ecosystems in urban headwater streams are particularly susceptible to the impacts of urbanization . . . Dietemann (1975), Ragan and Dietemann (1976), Klein (1979) and WMCOG (1982) have all tracked trends in fish diversity and abundance over time in local urbanizing streams. Each of the studies has shown that fish communities become less diverse and are composed of more tolerant species after the surrounding watershed is developed. Sensitive fish species either disappear or occur very rarely. In most cases, the total number of fish in urbanizing streams may also decline.

Similar trends have been noted among aquatic insects which are the major food resource for fish . . . Higher post-development sediment and trace metals can interfere in their efforts to gather food. Changes in water temperature, oxygen levels, and substrate composition can further reduce the species diversity and abundance of the aquatic insect community.

Student Paragraph

Studies have shown that fish communities become less diverse as the amount of runoff increases. Sensitive fish species either disappear or occur very rarely, and, in most cases, the total number of fish declines. Aquatic insects, a major source of food for fish, also decline because sediment and trace metals interfere with their food-gathering efforts. Increased water temperature and lower oxygen levels can further reduce the species diversity and abundance of the aquatic insect community.

The student's opening words establish a reader's expectation that the student has taken information from a source, as indeed the student has. But where is the documentation? The student's paraphrase is a good example of plagiarism: an unacknowledged paraphrase of borrowed information that even collapses into copying the source's exact wording in two places. For MLA style, the author's name and the precise page numbers are needed for proper documentation. Additionally, most of the first sentence and the final phrase must be put into the student's own words or be placed within quotation marks. The following revised paragraph shows an appropriate acknowledgment of the source used.

Revised Student Paragraph

In *Controlling Urban Runoff*, Thomas Schueler explains that studies have shown "that fish communities become less diverse as the amount of runoff increases" (3). Sensitive fish species either disappear or occur very rarely and, in most cases, the total number of fish declines. Aquatic insects, a major source of food for fish, also decline because sediment and trace metals interfere with their food-gathering efforts. Increased water temperature and lower oxygen levels, Schueler concludes, "can further reduce the species diversity and abundance of the aquatic insect community" (4).

Students are often uncertain about what is considered common knowledge and wonder if most of their sentences will need documentation. In general, common knowledge includes:

- Undisputed dates.
- Well-known facts.
- Generally known facts, terms, and concepts in a field of study when you are writing in that field.

So, even if you had to check your history text for the exact dates of the American Revolution, you would not document that source. Such information is readily available in many reference works and known by many readers. If you are writing a paper for psychology, you would not cite your text when you use terms such as *ego* or *sublimation*. However, you must acknowledge a historian who analyzes the causes for England's loss to the American colonies or a psychologist who disputes Freud's ideas. *Opinions* about well-known facts must be documented. *Discussions* of debatable dates, terms, or concepts must be documented. If, after studying these guidelines or checking with your instructor, you are still uncertain, defend your integrity by documenting your source.

Selecting and Noting Material from Sources

As you read and learn, try to expand your research proposal in two ways. First, write a thesis that is as clear and focused as you can make it at this stage. Second, develop a preliminary outline. Keep the outline informal, but use it to think through your basic structure, the parts of your paper. Having an outline will guide your search for information and help you note how and where in your paper you plan to use the information.

You have several ways to note the material you plan to use. You can take notes from sources using your PC or note cards. You can also photocopy sources and work directly from these copies, annotating them as needed. If you are required to turn in note cards, then the format has been decided for you. Increasingly, instructors are letting (or encouraging) students to take keyboarded notes, but they may still ask to see the notes with the paper. If you are required to submit notes, you will have to print out copies, but you may want to do this anyway before drafting your paper. Instructors requiring notes probably will not accept annotated photocopies; they want to see how you have selected material from your sources. What follows are guidelines for these various methods of selecting material from sources:

Guidelines for Note Taking: Cards

1. *Use either 4 × 6 cards or half sheets of letter-size paper.* This size gives you ample space for writing and also may help you distinguish between note cards and bibliography cards.
2. *Write in ink.* Penciled notes will blur with shuffling and rearranging.

3. *Write only one item on each card.* Each card should contain only one idea, piece of information, or group of related facts. The flexibility of cards is lost if you do not follow this procedure. You want to be able to group cards according to your outline when you are ready to draft the paper.

Guidelines for Note Taking: With a Computer

1. *Make one file titled "notes" or make a separate file for each note.* Both strategies work. Think about which approach is easier for you to cut and paste and blend notes into a draft.

2. *Use clear headings and subheadings for notes so that you can find particular notes easily.*

3. *Consider printing copies of your notes and cutting them into separate "cards" for organizing prior to drafting.* When drafting, do not re-keyboard. Just use your printed notes as a guide to placement in the draft. Use the "cut and paste" or "move" features of your word processor to rearrange notes into the order you want.

Guidelines for Note Taking: Annotating Photocopies

1. *Do not endlessly highlight your photocopies.* Instead, carefully bracket those passages that contain information you want to use.

2. *Write a note in the margin next to bracketed passages indicating how and where you think you want to use that material.* Use the language of your informal outline to annotate marked passages (e.g., "causes," "effects," "rebuttal to counterargument," "solutions").

3. *Keep in mind that you will have to paraphrase most of the marked passages before using the material in your draft.*

Guidelines for Writing Notes: Cards or Keyboarded

1. *Study first; take notes later.* First, do background reading. Second, skim what appear to be your chief sources. Prepare summary notes and annotate photocopies of sources. Read so that you can develop your preliminary outline. Learn what the writers on your topic consider to be important facts, issues, and arguments. Keep in mind that taking too many useless notes is a frustrating, time-wasting activity.

2. *Before preparing any note, identify the source of the note.* Write or type the author's name, a shortened title if necessary, and the precise page number from which the material comes. *Remember: All borrowed information and ideas must be documented with precise page numbers if you are using MLA style—and for all direct quotations if you are using APA style.*

3. *Type or write an identifying word or phrase for each note.* Identifying words or phrases will help you sort cards or find notes when you are ready to draft. Select words carefully to correspond to the sections of your preliminary outline.

4. *Take down the information itself—accurately and clearly.* Be sure to put all directly quoted passages within quotation marks. To treat a direct quotation as a paraphrase in your paper is to plagiarize.

5. *Distinguish between fact and opinion.* Notes that contain opinion should be indicated with such phrases as "Smith believes that" or "Smith asserts that." Alternatively, label the note "opinion."

6. *Distinguish between information from sources and your own opinions, questions, and reactions to the recorded information.* Write notes to yourself so that you do not forget good ideas that come to you as you are reading. Just be certain to label your notes "my notes"—or draw (or type) a line between information from a source and your response.

Figure 7–1 shows a sample note card written according to these guidelines.

FORMAT FOR NOTES: QUOTING VERSUS PARAPHRASING VERSUS PHOTOCOPIES

A paper that is a string of quotations glued together with a few transitional sentences is mere patchwork, not your own paper. Many would argue that, since most of your paper should be in your own words, most of your notes should be paraphrases or summaries, not direct quotations. Others would argue that making many direct-quotation notes allows you to have the exact words to contemplate when you draft and that the time to move to paraphrase is at the writing stage. The latter argument, along with convenience, also justifies annotating photocopies of articles. Yet saving the task of paraphrasing for the writing stage may mean that you are doing this complicated process at a time when you are most pressed to complete your paper.

Probably some combination of strategies is appropriate. Photocopy (or download or e-mail to yourself) key articles so that you can work with them easily. Initially tab key passages in books with Post-it notes or slips of paper. Then, as you finish your studying of sources, make at least some paraphrased notes to start the process of moving away from the language of the original sources. Remember that you can spread out only so

FIGURE 7–1 **Sample Note Card**

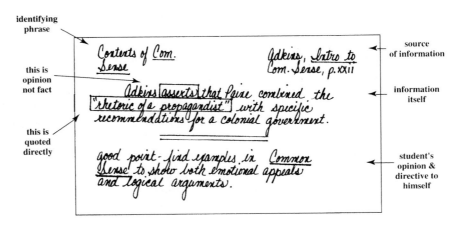

many sources on a desk as you draft your paper. It may be more efficient in the long run to prepare some paraphrased notes than to try to shift back and forth among a stack of books and articles.

Many students use too many direct quotations in their research papers. There are good reasons not to use too many quotations:

- Constantly shifting from your language to the language of your sources (not to mention seeing all those quotation marks) is difficult for readers.

- This is your paper and should sound like you.

- When you take a brief passage out of a larger context, you face the danger of misrepresenting the writer's views.

- You do not prove any point by quoting another person's opinion. All you indicate to your readers is that there is someone else who shares your views. Even if that person is an expert on the topic, your quoted material still represents the view of only one person. You support a claim with reasons and evidence, both of which can usually be presented in your own words.

So, no matter how you initially work with sources, you will need to paraphrase most borrowed information in your paper. If you must quote, keep the quotations brief and be sure to identify the author in your introduction of the quotation.

AVOIDING MISLEADING ACKNOWLEDGMENT OF SOURCES

If you are an honest student, you do not want to present a paper that is plagiarized, even though the plagiarism is unintentional. Unintentional plagiarism usually occurs in one of two ways:

1. A researcher takes notes carelessly, neglecting to indicate precise page references, but uses the information anyway, without proper documentation.

2. A researcher presents borrowed material in such a way that, even though the paper contains documentation, the researcher has misrepresented the degree of indebtedness to the source.

Good note-taking strategies will keep you from the first pitfall. The following discussion of appropriate documentation will help you avoid the second cause of plagiarism.

The best way to identify quoted or paraphrased material in your essay is by identifying the author. You may even include the author's credentials ("According to Dr. Hays, a geologist with the Department of the Interior, . . .") or the location of the material ("The president, as quoted by <u>Time</u> magazine, feels . . ."). These *introductory tags* give your reader a context for reading the borrowed material and also serve as part of the documentation in the paper. An introductory tag helps readers distinguish between your ideas and the ideas that you have borrowed. *Make certain that each tag clarifies rather than distorts an author's relationship to his or her ideas and your relationship to the source.* Here are three guidelines to follow to avoid misrepresenting borrowed material:

1. *Verbs in introductory tags.* Be careful when you vary such standard introductory tags as "Smith says" or "Jones states" that you do not select words that are misleading. Writing "Smith implies" rather than "Smith says" may misrepresent

Smith's attitude toward his work. (See pp. 257–58 for a discussion of varying word choice in introductory tags.)

2. *Location of introductory tags.* If you vary the pattern of mentioning Jones after you have mentioned her ideas in your paragraph, be sure that your reader can tell precisely which ideas in the passage belong to Jones. If your entire paragraph is a paraphrase of Jones's views, you are plagiarizing to conclude with "This idea is presented by Jones." Which of the several ideas in your paragraph is Jones's? Your reader will infer, incorrectly, that only the last idea has been taken from Jones.

3. *Proper paraphrasing.* Be sure that paraphrases are *in your own words* so that you do not bring Brown's ideas into your paper in his style of writing. To use Brown's words and/or sentence structure, even in a condensed version, is to plagiarize from Brown.

✔ Note: Putting a parenthetical page reference at the end of a paragraph is not sufficient if you have used the source throughout the paragraph. Use introductory tags to guide the reader through the material.

The paragraph below (from Franklin E. Zimring's "Firearms, Violence and Public Policy" [*Scientific American*, Nov. 1991]) provides material for the examples that follow of adequate and inadequate acknowledgment of sources. After reading Zimring's paragraph, study the three examples with these questions in mind: (1) Which example represents adequate acknowledgment? (2) Which examples do not represent adequate acknowledgment? (3) In exactly what ways is each plagiarized paragraph flawed?

Although most citizens support such measures as owner screening, public opinion is sharply divided on laws that would restrict the ownership of handguns to persons with special needs. If the U.S. does not reduce handguns and current trends continue, it faces the prospect that the number of handguns in circulation will grow from 35 million to more than 50 million within 50 years. A national program limiting the availability of handguns would cost many billions of dollars and meet much resistance from citizens. These costs would likely be greatest in the early years of the program. The benefits of supply reduction would emerge slowly because efforts to diminish the availability of handguns would probably have a cumulative impact over time. (page 54)

Student Paragraph 1

One approach to the problem of handgun violence in America is to severely limit handgun ownership. If we don't restrict ownership and start the costly task of removing handguns from our society, we may end up with around 50 million handguns in the country by 2040. The benefits will not be apparent right away but will eventually appear. This idea is emphasized by Franklin Zimring (54).

Student Paragraph 2

One approach to the problem of handgun violence in America is to restrict the ownership of handguns except in special circumstances. If we do not begin to reduce the number of handguns in this country, the number will grow from 35 million to more than 50 million within 50 years. We can agree with Franklin Zimring that a program limiting handguns will cost billions and meet resistance from citizens (54).

Student Paragraph 3

According to law professor Franklin Zimring, the United States needs to severely limit handgun ownership or face the possibility of seeing handgun ownership increase "from 35 million to more than 50 million within 50 years" (54). Zimring points out that Americans disagree significantly on restricting handguns and that enforcing such laws would be very expensive. He concludes that the benefits would not be seen immediately but that the restrictions "would probably have a cumulative impact over time" (54). Although Zimring paints a gloomy picture of high costs and little immediate relief from gun violence, he also presents the shocking possibility of 50 million guns by the year 2040. Can our society survive so much fire power?

Clearly, only the third student paragraph demonstrates adequate acknowledgment of the writer's indebtedness to Zimring. Notice that the placement of the last parenthetical page reference acts as a visual closure to the student's borrowing; then she turns to her response to Zimring and her own views on the problem of handguns.

MLA In-Text (Parenthetical) Citations

The student paragraphs above illustrate the most common form of parenthetical documentation in MLA style: parenthetical references to author and page number, or just to page number if the author has been mentioned in an introductory tag. Because a reference only to author and page number is an incomplete citation (readers could not find the source with such limited information), whatever is cited this way in the essay must refer to a specific source presented fully in a Works Cited list that follows the text of the paper. General guidelines for citing are given below, followed by examples and explanations of the required patterns of documentation.

✓   You need a 100 percent correspondence between the sources listed on your Works Cited page(s) and the sources you cite (refer to) in your paper. Do not omit from your Works Cited any sources you refer to in your paper. Do not include in your Works Cited any sources not referred to in your paper.

Guidelines for Using Parenthetical Documentation
- The purpose of documentation is to make clear exactly what material in a passage has been borrowed and from what source the borrowed material has come.
- Parenthetical documentation requires specific page references for borrowed material.
- Parenthetical documentation is required for both quoted and paraphrased material.
- Parenthetical documentation provides as brief a citation as possible consistent with accuracy and clarity.

THE SIMPLEST PATTERNS OF PARENTHETICAL DOCUMENTATION

The simplest parenthetical reference can be prepared in one of three ways:

1. Give the author's last name (full name in the first reference) in the text of your paper and place the relevant page number(s) in parentheses following the borrowed material.

   Frederick Lewis Allen observes that, during the 1920s, urban tastes spread to the country (146).

2. Place the author's last name and the relevant page number(s) in parentheses immediately following the borrowed material.

   During the 1920s, "not only the drinks were mixed, but the company as well" (Allen 82).

3. On the rare occasion that you cite an entire work rather than borrowing from a specific passage, give the author's name in the text and omit any page numbers.

   Barbara Tuchman argues that there are significant parallels between the fourteenth century and our time.

Each one of these in-text references is complete *only* when the full citation is found in the Works Cited, thus:

Allen, Frederick Lewis. <u>Only Yesterday: An Informal History of the Nineteen-Twenties</u>. New York: Harper, 1931.

Tuchman, Barbara W. <u>A Distant Mirror: The Calamitous 14th Century</u>. New York:

Knopf, 1978.

The three patterns just illustrated should be used in each of the following situations:

1. The work is not anonymous—the author is known.
2. The work is by one author.
3. The work cited is the only work used by that author.
4. No other author in your bibliography has the same last name.

PLACEMENT OF PARENTHETICAL DOCUMENTATION

The simplest placing of a parenthetical reference is at the end of the appropriate sentence *before* the period, but, when you are quoting, *after* the quotation mark.

During the 1920s, "not only the drinks were mixed, but the company as well" (Allen 82).

Do not put any punctuation between the author's name and the page number.

If the borrowed material ends before the end of your sentence, place the parenthetical reference *after* the borrowed material and before any subsequent punctuation. This placement more accurately shows what is borrowed and what is your own work.

Sport, Allen observes about the 1920s, had developed into an obsession (66),

another similarity between the 1920s and the 1980s.

If a quoted passage is long enough to require setting off in display form (block quotation), then place the parenthetical reference at the end of the passage, *after* the last period. (Remember that long quotations in display form do not have quotation marks.)

It is hard to believe that when he writes about the influence of science, Allen is

describing the 1920s, not the 1980s:

> The prestige of science was colossal. The man in the street and the woman
>
> in the kitchen, confronted on every hand with new machines and devices
>
> which they owed to the laboratory, were ready to believe that science
>
> could accomplish almost anything. (164)

And to complete the documentation for all three examples:

Works Cited

Allen, Frederick Lewis. <u>Only Yesterday: An Informal History of the Nineteen-</u>

<u>Twenties.</u> New York: Harper, 1931.

PARENTHETICAL CITATIONS FOR COMPLEX SOURCES

Not all sources can be cited in one of the three simplest forms described above, for not all meet the four criteria listed on page 227. Works by two or more authors, for example, will need somewhat fuller references. Each sample form of parenthetical documentation below would be completed with a full Works Cited reference, as illustrated above and in the next section of this chapter.

Two Authors, Mentioned in the Text

Richard Herrnstein and Charles Murray contend that it is "consistently . . .

advantageous to be smart" (25).

Two Authors, Not Mentioned in the Text

The advantaged smart group form a "cognitive elite" in our society (Herrnstein and

Murray 26–27).

A Book in Two or More Volumes

Sewall analyzes the role of Judge Lord in Dickinson's Life (2: 642–47).

OR

Judge Lord was also one of Dickinson's preceptors (Sewall 2: 642–47).

Note: The number before the colon always signifies the volume number: the number(s) after the colon represents the page number(s).

A Book or Article Listed by Title (Author Unknown)

According to the <u>Concise Dictionary of American Biography</u>, William Jennings

Bryan's 1896 campaign stressed social and sectional conflicts (117).

The <u>Times's</u> editors are not pleased with some of the changes in welfare programs

("Where Welfare Stands" 4:16).

Always cite the title of the article, not the title of the journal, if the author is unknown.

A Work by a Corporate Author

According to the report of the Institute of Ecology's Global Ecological Problems

Workshop, the civilization of the city can lull us into forgetting our relationship to the

total ecological system on which we depend (13).

Although corporate authors may be cited with the page number within the parentheses, your presentation will be more graceful if corporate authors are introduced in the text. Then only page numbers go in parentheses.

Two or More Works by the Same Author

During the 1920s, "not only the drinks were mixed, but the company as well" (Allen, Only Yesterday 82).

According to Frederick Lewis Allen, the early 1900s were a period of complacency in America (The Big Change 4–5).

In The Big Change, Allen asserts that the early 1900s were a period of complacency (4–5).

If your Works Cited list contains two or more works by the same author, the fullest parenthetical citation will include the author's last name, followed by a comma, the work's title, shortened if possible, and the page number(s). If the author's name appears in the text—or the author and title both, as in the third example above—omit these items from the parenthetical citation. When you have to include the title, it is best to simplify the citation by including the author's last name in the text.

Two or More Works in One Parenthetical Reference

Several writers about the future agree that big changes will take place in work patterns (Toffler 384–87; Naisbitt 35–36).

Separate each author cited with a semicolon. But if the parenthetical citation would be disruptively long, cite the works in a "See also" note rather than in the text.

Complete Publication Information in Parenthetical Reference

Occasionally you may want to give complete information about a source within parentheses in the text of your paper. Then a Works Cited list is not used. Square brackets are used for parenthetical information within parentheses. This approach may be appropriate when you use only one or two sources, even if many references are made to those sources. Literary analyses are one type of paper for which this approach to citation may be a good choice. For example:

Edith Wharton establishes the bleakness of her setting, Starkfield, not just through description of place but also through her main character, Ethan, who is described as "bleak and unapproachable" (Ethan Frome [New York: Scribner's, 1911] 3. All subsequent references are to this edition.). Later Wharton describes winter as "shut[ting] down on Starkfield" and negating life there (7).

ADDITIONAL-INFORMATION FOOTNOTES OR ENDNOTES

At times you may need to provide additional useful information, explanation, or commentary that is not central to the development of your paper. These additions belong in content footnotes or endnotes. However, use these sparingly and never as a way of advancing your thesis. Many instructors object to content footnotes or endnotes and prefer only parenthetical citations in student papers.

"SEE ALSO" FOOTNOTES OR ENDNOTES

More acceptable to most readers is the footnote that refers to other sources of evidence for or against the point to be established. Such footnotes (or endnotes) can be combined with parenthetical documentation. They are usually introduced with "See also" or "Compare," followed by the citation. For example:

Chekhov's debt to Ibsen should be recognized, as should his debt to Maeterlinck and

other playwrights of the 1890s who were concerned with the inner life of their

characters.[1]

---

[1]See also Eric Bentley, <u>In Search of Theatre</u> (New York: Vintage, 1959) 330; Walter Bruford, Anton <u>Chekhov</u> (New Haven: Yale UP, 1957) 45; and Raymond Williams, <u>Drama from Ibsen to Eliot</u> (New York: Oxford UP, 1953) 126–29.

Preparing MLA Citations for a "Works Cited" Page

As you have seen, parenthetical (in-text) citations are completed by a full reference to each source in a list presented at the end of the paper. To prepare your Works Cited page(s), alphabetize, by the author's last name, the sources you have cited and complete each citation according to the forms illustrated and explained in the following pages. The key is to find the appropriate model for each of your sources and then follow the model exactly. (Guidelines for formatting a finished Works Cited page are found on pages 273 and 279.)

FORMS FOR BOOKS: CITING THE COMPLETE BOOK

A Book by a Single Author

Fisher, David E. <u>Fire & Ice: The Greenhouse Effect, Ozone Depletion and Nuclear</u>

<u>Winter</u>. New York: Harper, 1990.

The subtitle is included, preceded by a colon, even if there is no colon on the book's title page.

A Book by Two or Three Authors

Yergin, Daniel, and Thane Gustafson. <u>Russia 2010: And What It Means for the</u>

<u>World</u>. New York: Random, 1993.

Second (and third) authors' names appear in signature form.

A Book with More Than Three Authors

Baker, Susan P., et al. <u>The Injury Fact Book</u>. Oxford: Oxford UP, 1992.

Use the name of the first author listed on the title page. The English "and others" may be used instead of "et al."

Two or More Works by the Same Author

Goodall, Jane. <u>In the Shadow of Man</u>. Boston: Houghton, 1971.

- - -. <u>Through a Window: My Thirty Years with the Chimpanzees of Gombe</u>. Boston: Houghton, 1990.

Give the author's full name with the first entry. For the second (and additional works), begin the citation with three hyphens followed by a period. Alphabetize the entries by the books' titles.

A Book Written under a Pseudonym with Name Supplied

Wrighter, Carl P. [Paul Stevens]. <u>I Can Sell You Anything</u>. New York: Ballantine, 1972.

Supply the author's name in square brackets.

An Anonymous Book

<u>Beowulf: A New Verse Translation</u>. Trans. Seamus Heaney. New York: Farrar, 2000.

Do not use "anon." Alphabetize by the book's title.

An Edited Book

Hamilton, Alexander, James Madison, and John Jay. <u>The Federalist Papers</u>. Ed. Isaac Kramnick. New York: Viking-Penguin, 1987.

Lynn, Kenneth S., ed. <u>Huckleberry Finn: Text, Sources, and Critics</u>. New York: Harcourt, 1961.

If you cite the author's work, put the author's name first and the editor's name after the title, preceded by "Ed." If you cite the editor's work (an introduction or notes), then place the editor's name first, followed by a comma and "ed."

A Translation

Schulze, Hagen. <u>Germany: A New History</u>. Trans. Deborah Lucas Schneider. Cambridge: Harvard UP, 1998.

Cornford, Francis MacDonald, trans. <u>The Republic of Plato</u>. New York: Oxford UP,

1945.

If the author's work is being cited, place the author's name first and the translator's name after the title, preceded by "Trans." If the translator's work is the important element, place the translator's name first, as in the second example above. If the author's name does not appear in the title, give it after the title. For example: By Plato.

A Book in Two or More Volumes

Spielvogel, Jackson J. <u>Western Civilization</u>. 2 vols. Minneapolis: West, 1991.

A Book in Its Second or Subsequent Edition

O'Brien, David M. <u>Storm Center: The Supreme Court and American Politics</u>. 2nd ed.

New York: Norton, 1990.

Sundqist, James L. <u>Dynamics of the Party System</u>. Rev. ed. Washington: Brookings,

1983.

Always include the number of the edition you have used, abbreviated as shown, if it is not the first edition.

A Book in a Series

Maclean, Hugh, ed. <u>Edmund Spencer's Poetry</u>. A Norton Critical Edition. New York:

Norton, 1968.

Waggoner, Hyatt H. <u>Nathaniel Hawthorne</u>. University of Minnesota Pamphlets on

American Writers, No. 23. Minneapolis: U of Minnesota P, 1962.

The series title—and number, if there is one— follows the book's title but is not underlined.

A Reprint of an Earlier Work

Cuppy, Will. <u>How to Become Extinct</u>. 1941. Chicago: U of Chicago P, 1983.

Twain, Mark. <u>Adventures of Huckleberry Finn</u>. 1885. Centennial Facsimile Edition.

Intro. Hamlin Hill. New York: Harper, 1962.

Faulkner, William. <u>As I Lay Dying</u>. 1930. New York: Vintage-Random, 1964.

Since the date of a work is often important, cite the original date of publication as well as the facts of publication for the reprinted version. Indicate any new material that is part of the reprinted book, as in the second example. The third example shows how to cite a book reprinted, by the same publisher, in a paperback version. (Vintage is a paperback imprint of the publisher Random House.)

A Book with Two or More Publishers

Green, Mark J., James M. Fallows, and David R. Zwick. <u>Who Runs Congress?</u> Ralph

Nader Congress Project. New York: Bantam; New York: Grossman, 1972.

If the title page lists two or more publishers, give all as part of the facts of publication, placing a semicolon between them, as illustrated above.

A Corporate or Governmental Author

California State Department of Education. <u>American Indian Education Handbook</u>.

Sacramento: California State Department of Education, Indian Education Unit, 1991.

Hispanic Market Connections. <u>The National Hispanic Database: A Los Angeles</u>

<u>Preview</u>. Los Altos, CA: Hispanic Market Connections, 1992.

List the institution as the author even when it is also the publisher.

A Book in a Foreign Language

Blanchard, Gerard. <u>Images de la musique au cinéma</u>. Paris: Edilig, 1984.

Gnüg, Hiltrud, ed. <u>Literarische Utopie-Entwürfe</u>. Frankfurt: Suhrkamp, 1982.

Capitalize only the first word of titles and subtitles and words normally capitalized in that language (e.g., proper nouns in French, all nouns in German). A translation in square brackets may be provided. Check your work carefully for spelling and accent marks.

The Bible

The Bible. [Always refers to the King James Version.]

The Bible. Revised Standard Version.

The Reader's Bible: A Narrative. Ed. with Intro. Roland Mushat Frye. Princeton:

Princeton UP, 1965.

Do not underline the title. Indicate the version if it is not the King James Version. Provide facts of publication for versions not well known.

A Book with a Title in Its Title

Piper, Henry Dan, ed. <u>Fitzgerald's</u> The Great Gatsby: <u>The Novel, the Critics, the</u>

<u>Background</u>. Scribner Research Anthologies. Gen. Ed. Martin Steinmann, Jr.

New York: Scribner's, 1970.

If a book's title contains a title normally placed in quotation marks, retain the quotation marks, but if it contains a title normally underlined, do not underline that title, as illustrated above.

FORMS FOR BOOKS: CITING PART OF A BOOK

A Preface, Introduction, Foreword, or Afterword

Sagan, Carl. Introduction. <u>A Brief History of Time: From The Big Bang to Black Holes</u>.

By Stephen W. Hawking. New York: Bantam, 1988. ix–x.

Use this form if you are citing the author of the preface, etc. Provide the appropriate identifying phrase after the author's name and give inclusive page numbers for the part of the book by that author at the end of the citation. The author of the book itself goes after the title, as illustrated.

An Encyclopedia Article

Ostrom, John H. "Dinosaurs." <u>McGraw-Hill Encyclopedia of Science and Technology</u>.

1987 ed.

"Prohibition." <u>New Encyclopaedia Britannica: Micropaedia</u>. 1988 ed.

When articles are signed or initialed, give the author's name. Complete the name of the author of an initialed article thus: K[enny], E[dward] J. Identify well-known encyclopedias and dictionaries by the year of the edition only. Give the complete facts of publication for less well-known works or those in only one edition.

"Benjamin Franklin." <u>Concise Dictionary of American Biography</u>. Mgr. Ed. Joseph

G. E. Hopkins. New York: Scribner's, 1964.

One or More Volumes in a Multivolume Work

James, Henry. <u>The Portrait of a Lady</u>. Vols. 3 and 4 of <u>The Novels and Tales of Henry

James</u>. 26 vols. New York: Scribner's, 1908.

When using a complete work that makes up one or more volumes of a multivolume work, cite the title and volume number(s) of that work followed by the title, editor (if appropriate), total number of volumes, and facts of publication for the multivolume work.

A Work Within One Volume of a Multivolume Work

Shaw, Bernard. <u>Pygmalion</u>. Vol 1. <u>The Complete Plays with Prefaces</u>. New York:

Dodd, 1963. 197–281. 6 vols.

Cite the author and title of the single work used, the volume number, and then the title and facts of publication for the multivolume work. Then give the inclusive page numbers for the specific work, in the format shown, followed by the total number of volumes.

A Work in an Anthology or Collection

Hurston, Zora Neale. <u>The First One</u>. <u>Black Female Playwrights: An Anthology of Plays

Before 1950</u>. Ed. Kathy A. Perkins. Bloomington: Indiana UP, 1989. 80–88.

Comstock, George. "The Medium and the Society: The Role of Television in

American Life." <u>Children and Television: Images in a Changing Sociocultural</u>

<u>World</u>. Eds. Gordon L. Berry and Joy Keiko Asamen. Newbury Park, CA:

Sage, 1993. 117–31.

Cite the author and title of the work you have used. Then give the title, the editor(s), and the facts of publication of the anthology or collection. Conclude by providing inclusive page numbers for the work used.

An Article in a Collection, Casebook, or Sourcebook

Welsch, Roger. "The Cornstalk Fiddle." <u>Journal of American Folklore</u> 77 (1964):

262–63. Rpt. in <u>Readings in American Folklore</u>. Ed. Jan Harold Brunvand.

New York: Norton, 1979. 106-07.

MacKenzie, James J. "The Decline of Nuclear Power." <u>engage/social</u> April 1986.

Rpt. as "America Does Not Need More Nuclear Power Plants" in <u>The</u>

<u>Environmental Crisis: Opposing Viewpoints</u>. Eds. Julie S. Bach and Lynn Hall.

Opposing Viewpoints Series. Ser. Eds. David L. Bender and Bruno Leone. St.

Paul: Greenhaven, 1986. 136–41.

Most articles in collections have been previously published, so a complete citation needs to include the original facts of publication (excluding page numbers if they are unavailable) as well as the facts of publication for the collection. The original facts of publication can be found at the bottom of the first page of the article or on an acknowledgments page in the front or back of the casebook. End the citation with inclusive page numbers for the article used.

Cross-References

If you are citing several articles from one collection, you can cite the collection and then provide only the author and title of specific articles used, with a cross-reference to the editor(s) of the collection:

Head, Suzanne, and Robert Heinzman, eds. <u>Lessons of the Rainforest</u>. San Francisco:

Sierra Club, 1990.

Bandyopadhyay, J., and Vandana Shiva. "Asia's Forest, Asia's Cultures." Head and

Heinzman 66–77.

Head, Suzanne. "The Consumer Connection: Psychology and Politics." Head and

Heinzman 156–67.

FORMS FOR PERIODICALS: ARTICLES IN JOURNALS

Article in a Journal with Continuous Paging Throughout the Issues of Each Year

Truman, Dana M., David M. Tokar, and Ann R. Fischer. "Dimensions of Masculinity:

Relations to Date Rape, Supportive Attitudes, and Sexual Aggression in Dating

Situations." Journal of Counseling and Development 76 (1996): 555-62.

Give the volume number followed by the year only, in parentheses, followed by a colon and inclusive page numbers. Neither issue number nor month (or season) is necessary to locate the article.

Article in a Journal with Separate Paging for Each Issue

Lewis, Kevin. "Superstardom and Transcendence." Arete: The Journal of Sport

Literature 2.2 (1985): 47–54.

When each issue of a journal begins with a new page 1, volume and year are not sufficient to locate the article, so give the issue number, immediately following the volume number, separated by a period. Alternatively, give the month or season with the year.

Lewis, Kevin. "Superstardom and Transcendence." Arete: The Journal of Sport

Literature 2 (Spring 1985): 47–54.

Article in a Journal That Uses Issue Numbers Only

Keen, Ralph. "Thomas More and Geometry." Moreana 86 (1985): 151-66.

If the journal uses only issue numbers, not volume numbers, treat the issue number as a volume number.

FORMS FOR PERIODICALS: ARTICLES IN MAGAZINES

Article in a Monthly Magazine

Zimring, Franklin E. "Firearms, Violence and Public Policy." Scientific American Nov.

1991: 48–54.

Articles in popular magazines are best identified by date, not volume number, so do not use volume or issue number, even if the magazine gives them. Instead, cite the month(s) and year after the title, followed by a colon and inclusive page numbers. Abbreviate all months except May, June, and July.

Article in a Weekly Magazine

Sowell, Thomas. "Race, Culture, and Equality." Forbes 5 Oct. 1998: 144–150.

Provide the complete date, after the magazine title, using the order of day, month, and year, followed by a colon and inclusive page numbers.

An Anonymous Article

"Death of Perestroika." <u>Economist</u> 2 Feb. 1991: 12–13.

The order is the same for any article. The missing name indicates that the article is anonymous. This citation would be alphabetized under D.

A Published Interview

Angier, Natalie. "Ernst Mayr at 93." Interview. <u>Natural History</u> May 1997: 8–11.

Follow the pattern for a published article, but add the identifying word "Interview" (followed by a period) after the article's title.

A Review

Bardsley, Tim. "Eliciting Science's Best." Rev. of <u>Frontiers of Illusion: Science,</u>

<u>Technology, and the Politics of Progress</u> by Daniel Sarewitz. <u>Scientific American</u>

June 1997: 142.

Shales, Tom. "A Chilling Stop in 'Nuremberg.' " Rev. of the movie <u>Nuremberg</u> TNT

16 July 2000. <u>Washington Post</u> 16 July 2000: G1.

If the review is signed, begin with the author's name, then the title of the review article. Since the review titles rarely make clear the work being reviewed, give the title of the work being reviewed and its author, preceded by "Rev. of." Alphabetize unsigned reviews by the title of the review. For reviews of art shows, videos, or computer software, provide place and date or descriptive label to make the citation clear.

An Article with a Quotation in the Title

Greenfield, Meg. " 'Colorizing' the News." <u>Newsweek</u> 18 Feb. 1991: 76.

Use single quotation marks around words or phrases, or a quoted title, in the title of the article you are citing.

Forms for Periodicals: Newspapers

An Article from a Newspaper

Arguila, John. "What Deep Blue Taught Kasparov—and Us." <u>Christian Science</u>

<u>Monitor</u> 16 May 1997: 18.

Newspapers are cited much the same as articles in weekly magazines, except for some additional information illustrated in the examples below. A newspaper's title should be cited as it appears on the masthead, excluding any initial article; thus *New York Times*, not *The New York Times*.

An Article from a Newspaper with Lettered Sections

Fiss, Owen M. "Affirmative Action: Beyond Diversity." <u>Washington Post</u> 7 May 1997:

A21.

Place the section letter immediately before the page number, without any spacing.

An Article from a Newspaper with Numbered Sections

Roberts, Sam. "Another Kind of Middle-Class Squeeze." <u>New York Times</u> 18 May

1997, sec. 4:1+.

Place the section number after the date, preceded by a comma and the abbreviation "sec."

An Article from a Newspaper with a Designated Edition

Pereira, Joseph. "Women Allege Sexist Atmosphere in Offices Constitutes

Harassment." <u>Wall Street Journal</u> 10 Feb. 1988, eastern ed.: 23.

If a newspaper is published in more than one edition each day, the edition used is cited after the date.

An Editorial

"Japan's Two Nationalisms." Editorial. <u>Washington Post</u> 4 June 2000: B6.

Add the descriptive label "Editorial" after the article title. Alphabetize by the title.

A Letter to the Editor

Wiles, Yoko A. "Thoughts of a New Citizen." Letter. <u>Washington Post</u> 27 Dec. 1995:

A22.

If the letter is titled, use the descriptive word "Letter" after the title. If the letter is untitled, place "Letter" after the author's name.

An Article from a Microform Collection Such As NewsBank

Birch, Doug. "Congress Acts to Save More Land for Historic Antietam." <u>Sun</u>

[Baltimore] 25 Sept. 1988. <u>NewsBank</u>, Housing and Land Development, 1988,

fiche 89, grid E9.

Give the facts of publication for the article and then the facts needed to locate the article in the NewsBank collection—your source of the article.

FORMS FOR ELECTRONIC SOURCES: GENERAL

Patterns for documenting electronic sources are still evolving, in part because the technology continues to evolve. As you study the following models, keep in mind that you are (1) still providing author, title, and the facts of publication, and (2) the formats are based on those for books and articles and then varied to accommodate the different media. CD-ROM and online sources are documented somewhat differently.

CITING CD-ROMs, DISKETTES, AND MAGNETIC TAPES

An Article Published Both in Print and on CD-ROM (or Diskette, etc.)

Sheridan, Mary Beth. "Americans Fuel Tejuana Drugstore Boom." <u>Los Angeles Times</u>

5 July 1996: A1. <u>CDNewsBank</u>. CD-ROM. <u>NewsBank</u>. April 1997.

Detweiler, Richard A. "Democracy and Decency on the Internet." <u>Chronicle of Higher</u>

<u>Education</u> 28 June 1996: A40. <u>General Periodicals Ondisc</u>. CD-ROM. UMI-

Proquest. April 1997.

For works published in print that you have obtained on CD-ROM, first cite the article in the standard format. Then add the following:

- Title of the database, underlined
- Publication medium (CD-ROM, diskette, etc.)
- Name of the vendor
- Electronic publication date (the latest date on the disk)

(Note: <u>NewsBank</u> is on both microfiche—see above—and CD-ROM. Compare the different citation patterns.)

A Work or a Part of a Work on CD-ROM, Diskette, or Magnetic Tape

"Surrealism." <u>Oxford English Dictionary</u>. 2nd ed. CD-ROM. New York: Oxford UP, 1992.

Eseiolonis, Karyn. "Georgio de Chirico's <u>Mysterious Bathers</u>." <u>A Passion for Art:</u>

<u>Renoir, Cezanne, Matisse and Dr. Barnes</u>. CD-ROM. Corbis Productions, 1995.

Barclay, Donald. *Teaching* <u>Electronic Information Literacy</u>. Diskette. New York: Neal-

Schuman, 1995.

Cite, in quotation marks, the portion of the "book" you have used, as you would with a print dictionary or encyclopedia. Give the publication medium before the facts of publication. If you cannot locate all information, give what you can find. You may need to ask a librarian to look on the CD-ROM itself, or the box it came in, to obtain the work's producer or date, for example. In the second example, each brief essay on one of the paintings in the Barnes collection concludes with the author's initials. The authors' full names are given at the end of the work, similar to movie credits at the end of a film.

CITING ONLINE SOURCES

MLA's updated guidelines for citing online sources list as many as 14 pieces of information that may be included to identify a specific source! Actually, most citations are not that complex. As always, begin with the author (or editor or translator, as appropriate), the title of a short work (within quotation marks), the title of a book (or journal, as appropriate), and the publication information for a work that has a print version. Then provide the title of the project, database, periodical, or site (e.g., home page); the editor (if relevant); any identifying number (if relevant); the date of electronic publication, latest update, or posting; the number of pages, paragraphs, or sections; the name of any institution sponsoring the site; the date you accessed the information; and the uniform resource locator (URL) in angle brackets. The following examples illustrate some common sources and patterns of documentation.

A Source from a Database of Previously Published Articles

"Breaking the Glass Ceiling." Editorial. <u>The Economist</u> 10 Aug. 1996: 13. <u>General</u>

<u>Business File ASAP</u>. Jan. 1998. 12 Jan. 1998

<http://sbweb2.med.iacnet.com/infotrac/session/460/259/2012624/

131xrn_39&kbm_13>.

Break URL's only after a slash.

Moffat, Anne Simon. "Resurgent Forests Can Be Greenhouse Gas Sponges." <u>Science</u>

18 July 1979: 315-16. <u>SIRS Researcher on the Web</u>. 1997. 24 Jan. 1998

<http://library2.cc.va.us>.

(Although the SIRS database is sold nationally, it is usually installed locally or regionally. The result is an address that is specific to a particular library or consortium of libraries. Your instructor can check your work, but you cannot locate SIRS with the above address.)

Abstracts of Articles in Online Databases

Many online indexes include the full texts of articles. For other articles, however, the database provides only an abstract, a brief summary of the article. In most cases, the author of the article did not write the abstract. As noted in Chapter 6, *never attribute these abstracts to the author. Never quote from these abstracts. Always try to find and study the complete article. If you cannot locate the article and must paraphrase some facts from the abstract, always indicate that you have used the abstract, not the original article.* Place the word "Abstract" (followed by a period) after the page numbers for the original facts of publication of the article.

Article from a Reference Database

"McGraw-Hill Five Year Financial Summary." <u>Dow Jones News Service</u>. 1998. 3

pars. 10 Jan. 1998 <telnet://telnet.exlibris.uls.vcu.edu>.

"Prohibition." <u>Britannica Online</u>. Vers. 98.1.1. Jan. 1998. <u>Encylopaedia Britannica</u>.

24 Jan. 1998 <http://www.eb.com:180>.

Online News Source

Associated Press. "Internet Regulators to Vote This Week on New Domain Suffixes."

CNN.com. 13 July 2000. 16 July 2000 <http://www.cnn.com>.

Article in an Online Magazine

Carnahan, Ira. "Is Voting Rational?" Slate. 12 July 2000. 11 pars. 17 July 2000

<http://slate.msn.com/Features/voting/voting.asp>.

Poem from a Scholarly Project

Keats, John. "Ode to a Nightingale." Poetical Works. 1884. Project Bartleby.

Columbia U. 15 Jan. 1998 <http://www.columbia.edu/

acis/bartleby/keats53.html>.

Information from a Government or Professional Site

U.S. Department of Health and Human Services. "The HHS Poverty Guidelines." 21 Jan.

1998. 23 Jan. 1998 <http://aspe.os/dhhs.gov/poverty/97/poverty.htm>.

Nolen-Hoeksema, Susan, Carla Grayson, and Judith Larson. "Explaining the Gender

Differences in Depressive Symptoms." Journal of Personality and Social

Psychology 77.5 (1999): 1061-72. American Psychological Association.

1999. 16 July 2000 http://www.apa.org/journals/psp/psp7751061.html>.

OTHER SOURCES

The materials in this section, although often important to research projects, do not always lend themselves to documentation by the forms illustrated above. Follow the basic order of author, title, facts of publication as much as possible and add whatever information is needed to make the citation clear and useful to a reader.

A Bulletin

Krasnowiecki, Jan, and others. Legal Aspects of Planned Unit Residential Development

with Suggested Legislation. Technical Bulletin No. 52. Washington: Urban Land

Institute, 1965.

Cartoons and Advertisements

Schulz, Charles M. "Peanuts." Cartoon. Washington Post 10 Dec. 1985: D8.

Give the cartoon title, if there is one; add the descriptive label "Cartoon"; then give the facts of publication. The pattern is similar for advertisements.

Halleyscope. "Halleyscopes Are for Night Owls." Advertisement. <u>Natural History</u>

Dec. 1985: 15.

Computer Software

Eysenck, H. J. <u>Know Your Own I.Q.</u> Computer software. Bantam Software, 1985.

Commodore 64, disk.

Give author, title, descriptive label, distributor, and year of issue. The computer that the software is designed for and the form can also be given.

Dissertation—Unpublished

Deepe, Marilyn J. "The Impact of Racial Diversity and Involvement on College

Students' Social Concern Values." Diss. Claremont Grad. Sch., 1989.

Dissertation—Abstract from Dissertation Abstracts

Deepe, Marilyn J. "The Impact of Racial Diversity and Involvement on College

Students' Social Concern Values." <u>DIA</u> 50 (1990): 2397A. Claremont Grad.

Sch., 1989.

Use this citation form when you cite *only* the abstract, not the dissertation itself. Include the appropriate letter following the page number to designate the volume from which the source comes. For the online version, use this form of citation:

Sieger, Thomas Martin. "Global Citizenship: A Model for Student Inquiry and

Decision-Making." 1996. <u>Dissertation Abstracts Online</u> Accession No.

AAG9720651. Online. FirstSearch. 1997.

Government Documents

U.S. President. <u>Public Papers of the Presidents of the United States</u>. Washington:

Office of the Federal Register, 1961.

United States. Senate. Committee on Energy and Natural Resources. Subcommittee on

Energy Research and Development. <u>Advanced Reactor Development Program:</u>

<u>Hearing, May 24, 1988</u>. Washington: GPO, 1988.

- - -. Environmental Protection Agency. <u>The Challenge of the Environment: A Primer on</u>

<u>EPA's Statutory Authority</u>. Washington: GPO, 1972.

Observe the pattern illustrated here. If the author of the document is not given, cite the name of the government first followed by the name of the department or agency. If you cite more than one document published by the United States government, do not repeat the name but use the standard three hyphens followed by a period instead. If you cite a second document prepared by the Environmental Protection Agency, use the following pattern:

United States. Senate . . .

- - -. Environmental Protection Agency . . .

- - -. - - -. [second source from EPA]

If the author is known, follow this pattern:

Geller, William. <u>Deadly Force</u>. U.S. Dept of Justice National Institute of Justice Crime

File Study Guide. Washington: U.S. Dept. of Justice, n.d.

If the document contains no date, use the abbreviation "n.d."

Hays, W. W., ed. <u>Facing Geologic and Hydrologic Hazards</u>. Geological Survey

Professional Paper 1240-B. Washington: GPO, 1981.

Abbreviate the U.S. Government Printing Office thus: GPO.

An Interview

Plum, Kenneth. Personal Interview. 5 Mar. 1995.

Alternative descriptive labels include "Interview" and "Telephone interview."

A Lecture

Bateson, Mary Catherine. "Crazy Mixed-Up Families." Lecture delivered at Northern

Virginia Community College, 26 Apr. 1997.

Legal Documents

U.S. Const. Art. 1, sec. 3.

The Constitution is referred to by article and section. Abbreviations are used; do not underline.

Turner v. Arkansas. 407 U.S. 366. 1972.

In citing a court case, give the name of the case (the plaintiff and defendant); the volume, name, and page of the report cited; and the date. The name of a court case is underlined (italicized) in the text but not in the Works Cited.

Federal Highway Act, as amended. 23 U.S. Code 109. 1970.

Labor Management Relations Act (Taft-Hartley Act). Statutes at Large. 61. 1947.

34 U.S. Code. 1952.

Citing laws is complicated, and lawyers use many abbreviations that may not be clear to nonexperts. Bills that become law are published annually in *Statutes at Large* and later in the *U.S. Code*. Provide the title of the bill and the source, volume, and year. References to both *Statutes at Large* and the *U.S. Code* can be given as a convenience to readers.

Unpublished Letter

McCulley, Cecil M. Letter to the author. 5 June 1968.

Treat a published letter as a work in a collection.

Maps and Charts

Hampshire and Dorset. Map. Kent, Eng.: Geographers' A-Z Map, n.d.

The format is similar to that for an anonymous book, but add the appropriate descriptive label.

Mimeographed or Photocopied Material

Burns, Gerald. "How to Say Some Interesting Things about Poems." Dittoed essay.

1972.

Plays or Concerts

Mourning Becomes Electra. By Eugene O'Neill. Shakespeare Theater. Washington

DC. 16 May 1997.

Include title, author, theater, city, and date of performance. Principal actors, singers, musicians, and/or the director can be added as appropriate.

Recordings

Stein, Joseph. Fiddler on the Roof. Jerry Bock, composer. Original-Cast Recording

with Zero Mostel. RCA, LSO-1093, 1964.

The conductor and/or performers help identify a specific recording. Also include manufacturer, catalog number, and date of issue.

A Report

Environment and Development: Breaking the Ideological Deadlock. Report of the

Twenty-first United Nations Issues Conference, 23–25 Feb. 1990. Muscatine,

Iowa: Stanley Foundation, n.d.

Television or Radio Program

"Breakthrough: Television's Journal of Science and Medicine." PBS series hosted by

Ron Hendren. 10 June 1997.

A Videocassette

The Killing Screens: Media and the Culture of Violence. Sut Jhaly, exec. prod. and
dir. Videocassette. Northampton, MA: Media Education, 1994.

Exercises: Presenting and Documenting Borrowed Information and Preparing Citations

1. Read the following passage and then the three plagiarized uses of the passage. Explain why each one is plagiarized and how it can be corrected.

   Original Text: Stanley Karnow, *Vietnam, A History. The First Complete Account of Vietnam at War*. New York: Viking, 1983, 319.

   Lyndon Baines Johnson, a consummate politician, was a kaleidoscopic personality, forever changing as he sought to dominate or persuade or placate or frighten his friends and foes. A gigantic figure whose extravagant moods matched his size, he could be cruel and kind, violent and gentle, petty, generous, cunning, naïve, crude, candid, and frankly dishonest. He commanded the blind loyalty of his aides, some of whom worshipped him, and he sparked bitter derision or fierce hatred that he never quite fathomed.

   a. LBJ's vibrant and changing personality filled some people with adoration and others with bitter derision that he never quite fathomed (Karnow 319).
   b. LBJ, a supreme politician, had a personality like a kaleidoscope, continually changing as he tried to control, sway, appease, or intimidate his enemies and supporters (Karnow 319).
   c. Often, figures who have had great impact on America's history have been dynamic people with powerful personalities and vibrant physical presence. LBJ, for example, was a huge figure who polarized those who worked for and with him. "He commanded the blind loyalty of his aides, some of whom worshipped him, and he sparked bitter derision or fierce hatred" from many others (Karnow 319).

2. Read the following passages and then each of the four sample uses of the passage. Judge each of the uses for how well they avoid plagiarism and if they are documented correctly. Make corrections as needed.

   Original Text: Stanley Karnow, *Vietnam, A History. The First Complete Account of Vietnam at War*. New York: Viking, 1983, 327.

   On July 27, 1965, in a last-ditch attempt to change Johnson's mind, Mansfield and Russell were to press him again to "concentrate on finding a way out" of Vietnam—"a place where we ought not be," and where "the situation is rapidly going out of control." But the next day, Johnson announced his decision to add forty-four American combat battalions to the relatively small U.S. contingents already there. He had not been deaf to Mansfield's pleas, nor had he simply swallowed the Pentagon's plans. He had waffled and agonized during his nineteen months in the White House, but eventually this was his final judgment. As he would later explain: "There are many, many people who can recommend and advise, and a few of them consent. But there is only one who has been chosen by the American people to decide."

a. Karnow writes that Senators Mansfield and Russell continued to try to convince President Johnson to avoid further involvement in Vietnam, "a place where we ought not to be" they felt. (327).

b. Though Johnson received advice from many, in particular Senators Mansfield and Russell, he believed the weight of the decision to become further engaged in Vietnam was solely his as the one " 'chosen by the American people to decide'" (Karnow 327).

c. On July 28, 1965, Johnson announced his decision to add forty-four battalions to the troops already in Vietnam, ending his waffling and agonizing of the past nineteen months of his presidency. (Karnow 357).

d. Karnow explains that LBJ took his responsibility to make decisions about Vietnam seriously (327). Although Johnson knew that many would offer suggestions, only he had " 'been chosen by the American people to decide' " (Karnow 327).

3. Turn the information printed below into correct bibliographic citations for each of the works. Pay attention to the order of information, the handling of titles, and punctuation. Write each citation on a separate index card, or, if your instructor requests, prepare the citations as an alphabetical listing of works.

a. On July 14, 1997, Newsweek magazine printed Robert J. Samuelson's article titled Don't Hold Your Breath on page 40.

b. Richard B. Sewell's book The Life of Emily Dickinson was published in 1974. His book was published in two volumes by the New York City publisher Farrar, Straus, & Giroux.

c. Richard D. Heffner has edited an abridged version of Democracy in America by Alexis De Tocqueville. This is a Mentor Book paperback, a division of (New York City's) New American Library. The book was published in 1956.

d. The Object Stares Back: On the Nature of Seeing by James Elkins is reviewed in an article titled Vision Reviewed by Luciano da F. Costa. The review appeared on pages 124 and 125 in the March 1997 issued of Scientific American.

e. Arthur Whimbey wrote the article Something Better Than Binet for the Saturday Review on June 1, 1974. Joseph Rubinstein and Brent D. Slife reprinted the article on pages 102–108 in the third edition of the edited collection Taking Sides. Taking Sides was published in 1984 by the Dushkin Publishing Company located in Guilford, Connecticut.

f. The Discovery of Superconductivity appeared in Physics Today on pages 40–42. The author of the article is Jacobus de Nobel. The article appeared in the September 1996 issue, volume 49, number 9.

g. You used a biographical article, titled Marc Chagall (1887–1985), from Britannica Online which you found on the Internet September 25, 1997. You used the 97.9.1 version, prepared September 1997, published by Encyclopaedia Britannica and available at <http://www.eb.com:180>.

h. An editorial appeared in the New York Times, on Sunday, September 7, 1997, with the title Protecting Children from Guns. The editorial could be found on page 16 of section 4.

i. Anthony Bozza's article "Moby Porn" appeared in the magazine Rolling Stone on June 26, 1977, on page 26. You obtained the text of the article from the September 1997 "edition" of <u>General Periodicals Ondisc</u>. The vendor is UMI-ProQuest.

j. A Letter to the Editor titled What Can We Do about Global Warming appeared in the Washington Post on July 24, 1997. The letter was written by S. Fred Singer and printed on page A24.

CHAPTER 8

Completing the Research Project

Although precise guidelines can be established for completing the early stages of the research process, no magic formula exists for merging all the parts into a unified, coherent paper. As you organize and draft, keep in mind that your skills in analytic and argumentative essays apply to the research paper as well. Do not let the more formal patterns of documentation distract you from your best use of critical thinking and writing skills.

Organizing the Paper

To make decisions about your paper's organization, a good place to begin is with the identifying phrases at the top of your notes. They represent subsections of your topic that emerged as you studied sources. They will now help you organize your paper. Here are some guidelines for getting organized to write:

1. *Arrange notes by identifying phrases and read them through.* Read personal notes as well. Work all notes into one possible order as suggested by the identifying phrases. In reading through all notes at one time, you may discover that some now seem irrelevant. Set them aside, but do not throw them away yet. Some additional note taking may be necessary to fill in gaps that have become apparent. You know your sources well enough by now to be able to find the additional material that you need.

2. *Reexamine your tentative thesis or research proposal and the preliminary outline that guided your research.* Consider: As a result of reading and reflection, do you need to alter or modify your thesis in any way? Or, if you began with a research question, what now is your answer to the question? What, for example, was the impact of Prohibition on the 1920s? Or, is TV violence harmful to children? You need to decide.

3. *Decide on a final thesis.* To produce a unified and coherent essay with a clear central idea and a "reason for being," you need a thesis that meets the following criteria:

   - *It is a complete sentence, not a topic or statement of purpose.*

     Topic: Rape on college campuses.

     Thesis: There are steps that both students and administrators can take to reduce incidents of campus rape.

- *It is limited and focused.*

  Unfocused: Prohibition affected the 1920s in many ways.

  Focused: Prohibition was more acceptable to rural than urban areas because of differences in religious values, in patterns of socializing, in cultural backgrounds, and in the economic impact of prohibiting liquor sales.

- *It can be supported by your research.*

  Unsupportable: *Time* magazine does not like George Bush.

  Supportable: A study of *Time's* coverage of President Bush during the 1990–91 winter months reveals a favorable bias during the Persian Gulf War but a negative bias after the war.

- *It establishes a new or interesting approach to the topic that makes your research worthwhile.*

  Not inventive: A regional shopping mall should not be built adjacent to the Manassas Battlefield.

  Inventive: Putting aside an appeal to our national heritage, one can say, simply, that the building of a regional shopping mall adjacent to the Manassas Battlefield has no economic justification.

4. *Write down the organization revealed by the way you have grouped notes and compare this organization with your preliminary plan.* If you have deleted sections or reordered them, justify those changes in your own mind. Consider: Does the new, fuller plan now provide a complete and logical development of your thesis?

The Formal Outline

Because a research paper is long and complex, many instructors expect a formal outline. Preparing a formal outline requires that you think through the entire structure of your paper and see the relationship of parts. Remember that the more you analyze your topic, the fuller and therefore more useful your outline will be. But do not expect more out of an outline than it can provide. A logical and clear organization does not result from a detailed outline; rather, a detailed outline results from a logical analysis of your topic.

The formal outline uses a combination of numbers and letters to show headings and subheadings. Keep in mind these three points about outlines: (1) the parts of the paper indicated by the same *types* of numbers or letters should be equally important; (2) headings and subheadings indicated by the same types of numbers or letters should be written in the same format or structure (e.g., A. Obtaining Good Equipment; B. Taking Lessons; C. Practicing); and (3) headings that are subdivided must contain at least *two* subsections (that is, if there is a 1 under A, there has to be a 2). A sample outline accompanies the first research paper at the end of this chapter.

Drafting the Paper

PLANNING YOUR TIME

Good writing takes time and a commitment to revision. Consider how much time you will need to draft the entire paper. Working with notes and being careful about documentation make research paper writing more time-consuming than writing undocumented essays. You will probably need two or three afternoons or evenings to complete a draft. You should start writing, then, at least five days before your paper is due to allow time between drafting and revising. You also need to calculate the time required to proofread the final version. Don't throw away weeks of library work by trying to draft, revise, and proof your paper in one day.

HANDLING DOCUMENTATION IN YOUR DRAFT

Although you may believe that stopping to include parenthetical documentation as you write will cramp your writing, you really cannot wait until you complete your draft to add the documentation. The risk of failing to document accurately is too great to chance. Remember that parenthetical documentation is brief and take the time to place in parentheses the author's name and the relevant page number(s) (or just the page numbers as appropriate) as you compose. Then, when your paper is finished and you are preparing your list of works cited, go through your paper carefully to make certain that there is a work listed for *every* parenthetical reference.

WRITING STYLE

Specific suggestions for composing the parts of your paper will follow, but first here are some general guidelines for research paper style.

Use the Proper Person

Research papers are written primarily in the third person (*she, he, it, they*) to create objectivity and to direct attention to the content of the paper. You are not likely to use the second person (*you*) at all, for the second person occurs in instructions. The usual question is over the appropriateness of the first person (*I, we*) in research essays. Although you want to avoid writing "as *you* can see," do not try to skirt around the use of *I* if you need to distinguish your position from others you have presented. It is better to write "I" than "it is the opinion of this writer" or "the researcher learned" or "this project analyzed." On the other hand, avoid qualifiers such as "I think." Just state your ideas.

Use the Proper Tense

When you are writing about people, ideas, or events of the past, the appropriate tense to use is the past tense. When writing about current times, the appropriate tense is the present. Both may occur in the same paragraph, as the following paragraph illustrates:

Fifteen years ago "personal" computers `were` all but unheard of. Computers

`were regarded` as unknowable, building-sized mechanized monsters that `required` a precise 68 degree air-conditioned environment and eggheaded technicians with thick glasses and white lab coats scurrying about to keep the temperamental and fragile egos of the electronic brains mollified. Today's generation of computers is accessible, affordable, commonplace, and much less mysterious. A computer that used to require two rooms to house is now smaller than a briefcase. A computer that cost hundreds of thousands of dollars fifteen years ago now has a price tag in the hundreds. The astonishing progress made in computer technology in the last few years has made computers practical, attainable, and indispensable. Personal computers are here to stay.

In the above example when the student moves from computers in the past to computers in the present, he shifts tenses accurately. When we write about sources, however, the convention is to use the present tense *even* for works or authors from the past. The idea is that the source, or the author, *continues* to make the point or use the technique into the present—that is, every time there is a reader. Use of the *historical present tense* requires that you write "Lincoln selects the biblical expression 'Fourscore and seven years ago' " and "King echoes Lincoln when he writes 'five score years ago.' "

WRITING GOOD BEGINNINGS

The best introduction is one that presents your subject in an interesting way to gain the reader's attention, states your thesis, and gives the reader an indication of the scope and limits of your paper. In a short research essay, you may be able to combine an attention-getter, a statement of subject, and a thesis in one paragraph. More typically, especially in longer papers, the introduction will expand to two or three paragraphs. In the physical and social sciences, the thesis may be withheld until the conclusion, but the opening introduces the subject and presents the researcher's hypothesis, often posed as a question. Since students sometimes have trouble with research paper introductions in spite of knowing these general guidelines, several specific approaches are explained and illustrated in the following pages:

1. Begin with a brief example or anecdote to dramatize your topic. One student introduced her study of the nightly news with this attention-getter:

   When I watched television in the first weeks after moving to the United States, I was delighted by the relaxing display of the news programs. It was different from what I was used to on German television, where one finds a stern-looking man reading the news without any emotion. Here the commentators laugh or show distress; their tone with each other is amiable. Watching the news in this country was a new and entertaining experience for me initially, but as my reading skills improved, I found that I preferred reading newspapers to watching television news. Then, reading Neil Postman's attack on television news shows in "Television News Narcosis" reminded me of my early experience with American TV and led me to investigate the major networks' presentation of the news.

In her second paragraph, the student completed her introduction by explaining the procedures used for analyzing network news programs.

2. In the opening to her study of car advertisements, a student, relating her topic to what readers know, reminds readers of the culture's concern with image:

Many Americans are highly image conscious. Because the "right" look is essential to a prosperous life, no detail is too small to overlook. Clichés about first impressions remind us that "you never get a second chance to make a first impression," so we obsessively watch our weight, firm our muscles, sculpt our hair, select our friends, find the perfect houses, and buy our automobiles. Realizing the importance of image, companies compete to make the "right" products, that is, those that will complete the "right" image. Then advertisers direct specific products to targeted groups of consumers. Although targeting may be labeled as stereotyping, it has been an effective strategy in advertising.

3. Challenging a popular attitude or assumption is an effective attention-getting opening. For a paper on the advantages of solar energy, a student began:

America's energy problems are serious, despite the popular belief that difficulties vanished with the end of the Arab oil embargo in 1974. Our problems remain because the world's supply of fossil fuels is not limitless.

4. Terms and concepts central to your project need defining early in your paper, especially if they are challenged or qualified in some way by your study. The following opening paragraph demonstrates an effective use of definition:

William Faulkner braids a universal theme, the theme of initiation, into the fiber of his novel <u>Intruder in the Dust</u>. From ancient times to the present, a prominent focus of literature, of life, has been rites of passage, particularly those of childhood to adulthood. Joseph Campbell defines rites of passage as "distinguished by formal, and usually very severe, exercises of severance." A "candidate" for initiation into adult society, Campbell explains, experiences a shearing away of the "attitudes, attachments and life patterns" of childhood (9). This severe, painful stripping away of the child and installation of the adult is presented somewhat differently in several works by American writers.

5. Begin with a thought-provoking question. A student, arguing that the media both reflect and shape reality, started with these questions:

Do the media just reflect reality, or do they also shape our perceptions of reality? The answer to this seemingly "chicken-and-egg" question is: They do both.

6. Beginning with important, perhaps startling, facts, evidence, or statistics is an effective way to introduce a topic, provided the details are relevant to the topic. Observe the following example:

Teenagers are working again, but not on their homework. Over 40 percent of teenagers have jobs by the time they are juniors (Samuelson A22). And their jobs do not support academic learning since almost two-thirds of teenagers are employed in sales and service jobs that entail mostly carrying, cleaning, and wrapping (Greenberger and Steinberg 62–67), not reading, writing, and computing. Unfortunately, the negative effect on learning is not offset by improved opportunities for future careers.

AVOIDING INEFFECTIVE OPENINGS

Follow these guidelines for avoiding openings that most readers find ineffective or annoying.

1. *Do not restate the title* or write as if the title were the first sentence in paragraph 1. First, the title of the paper appears at the top of the first page of text. Second, it is a convention of writing to have the first paragraph stand independent of the title.

2. *Do not begin with "clever" visuals* such as artwork or fancy lettering.

3. *Do not begin with humor* unless it is part of your topic.

4. *Do not begin with a question that is just a gimmick,* or one that a reader may answer in a way you do not intend. Asking "What are the advantages of solar energy?" may lead a reader to answer "None that I can think of." A straightforward research question ("Is *Death of a Salesman* a tragedy?") is appropriate.

5. *Do not open with an unnecessary definition quoted from a dictionary.* "According to Webster, solar energy means . . . " is a tired, overworked beginning that does not engage readers.

6. *Do not start with a purpose statement:* "This paper will examine . . . " Although a statement of purpose is a necessary part of a report of empirical research, such a report should open not with a purpose statement but rather with some interesting introduction to the research subject.

COMPOSING MAIN PARAGRAPHS

As you compose the body of your paper, keep in mind that you want to (1) maintain unity and coherence, (2) guide readers clearly through source material, and (3) synthesize source material and your own ideas. These are three demanding writing goals that take planning and practice on your part. Do not settle for paragraphs in which facts from notes are just loosely run together. Review the following discussion and study the examples to see how to present what you have learned and want others to understand.

Provide Unity and Coherence

Paragraph unity is achieved when every sentence in a paragraph relates to and develops the paragraph's main idea or topic sentence. If you have a logical organization, composing unified paragraphs is not a problem. Unity, however, does not automatically produce coherence; that takes attention to wording. Coherence is achieved when readers can follow the connection between one sentence and another and between each sentence and the topic sentence. Strategies for achieving coherence include repetition of key words, the use of pronouns that clearly refer to those key words, and the use of transition and connecting words. Observe these strategies at work in the following paragraph:

Perhaps the most important differences between the epiphanic initiations of Robin and Biff and that experienced by Chick are the facts that Chick's epiphany does not come all at once and it does not devastate him. Chick learns about adulthood —and enters adulthood —piecemeal and with support. His first eye-opening experience occurs as he tries to pay Lucas for dinner and is rebuffed (15–16). Chick learns, after trying again to buy a clear conscience, the impropriety and affront of his actions (24). Lucas teaches Chick how he should resolve his dilemma by setting him "free" (26–27). Later, Chick feels outrage at the adults crowding into the town, presumably to see a lynching, then disgrace and shame as they eventually flee (196–97, 210). As in most lives, Chick's passage into adulthood is a gradual process; he learns a little bit at a time and has support in his growing. Gavin is there for him, to act as a sounding board, to lay a strong intellectual foundation, to confirm his beliefs.

Chick's initiation is consistent with Joseph Campbell's explanation: "all rites of passage are intended to touch not only the candidate, but also every member of his circle" (9). Perhaps Gavin is affected the most, but Chick's mother and father, and Lucas as well, are influenced by the change in Chick.

Coherence is needed not only within paragraphs but between paragraphs. Submitting an outline does not eliminate the writer's responsibility to guide readers through your paper, connecting paragraphs and showing relationships by the use of transitions. Sometimes writers purposely avoid transition words or phrases because they seem awkward or heavy-handed, as they can be if writers unwisely choose "My first point is . . .," "My second point is . . .," and so on. But transitions can be smooth and still clearly signal shifts in the paper's subtopics from one paragraph to another. The following opening sentences of four paragraphs from a paper on solutions to rape on the college campus illustrate smooth transitions:

¶ 3 Specialists have provided a number of reasons why men rape.

¶ 4 Some of the causes of rape on the college campus originate with the colleges themselves and with how they handle the problem.

¶ 5 Just as there are a number of   for campus   , there are

a number of ways to help solve the problem of these rapes.

¶ 6 If these seem like common-sense solutions , why, then, is it so difficult to

significantly reduce the number of campus rapes ?

Without awkwardly writing "Here are some of the causes" and "Here are some of the solutions," the student guides her readers through a discussion of causes for and solutions to the problem of campus rape.

Guide Readers Through Source Material

To understand the importance of guiding readers through source material, consider first the following paragraph from a paper on the British coal strike in the 1970s:

The social status of the coal miners was far from good. The country blamed them for the

dimmed lights and the three-day work week. They had been placed in the position of

social outcasts and were beginning to "consider themselves another country." Some

businesses and shops had even gone so far as to refuse service to coal miners (Jones 32).

Who has learned that the coal miners felt ostracized or that the country blamed them? As readers we cannot begin to judge the validity of these assertions without some context provided by the writer. Most readers are put off by an unattached direct quotation or some startling observation that is documented correctly but given no context within the paper. Using introductory tags that identify the author of the source and, when useful, the author's credentials helps guide readers through the source material. The following revision of the paragraph above provides not only context but also sentence variety:

The social acceptance of coal miners, according to Peter Jones, British correspondent

for Newsweek , was far from good. From interviews both in London shops and in

pubs near Birmingham, Jones concluded that Britishers blamed the miners for the

dimmed lights and three-day work week. Several striking miners , in a pub on the

outskirts of Birmingham, asserted that some of their friends had been denied

service by shopkeepers and that they "consider[ed] themselves another country"

(32).

When you use introductory tags, try to vary both the words you use and their place in the sentence. Look, for example, at the first sentence in the sample paragraph above. The tag is placed in the middle of the sentence and is set off by commas. The sentence could have been written two other ways:

The social acceptance of coal miners was far from good, according to Peter Jones,

British correspondent for <u>Newsweek</u>

OR

According to Peter Jones, British correspondent for <u>Newsweek</u>, the social

acceptance of coal miners was far from good.

Whenever you provide a name and perhaps credentials for your source, you have these three sentence patterns to choose from. Make a point to use all three options in your paper. Word choice can be varied as well. Instead of writing "Peter Jones says" throughout your paper, consider some of the many options you have:

Jones *asserts*	Jones *contends*	Jones *attests to*
Jones *states*	Jones *thinks*	Jones *points out*
Jones *concludes*	Jones *stresses*	Jones *believes*
Jones *presents*	Jones *emphasizes*	Jones *agrees with*
Jones *argues*	Jones *confirms*	Jones *speculates*

Note: Not all the words in this list are synonyms; you cannot substitute *confirms* for *believes*. First, select the term that most accurately conveys the writer's relationship to his or her material. Then, when appropriate, vary word choice as well as sentence structure.

Readers need to be told how they are to respond to the sources used. They need to know which sources you accept as reliable and which you disagree with, and they need to see you distinguish clearly between fact and opinion. Ideas and opinions from sources need introductory tags and then some discussion from you.

Synthesize Source Material and Your Own Ideas

A smooth synthesis of source material is aided by an introductory tag and parenthetical documentation because they mark the beginning and ending of material taken from a source. But a complete synthesis requires something more: your ideas about the source and the topic. To illustrate, consider the problems in another paragraph from the British-coal-strike paper:

Some critics believed that there was enough coal in Britain to maintain enough

power to keep industry at a near-normal level for thirty-five weeks (Jones 30). Prime

Minister Heath, on the other hand, had placed the country's usable coal supply at

15.5 million tons (Jones 30). He stated that this would have fallen to a critical 7 million tons within a month had he not declared a three-day work week (Jones 31).

This paragraph is a good example of random details strung together for no apparent purpose. How much coal did exist? Whose figures were right? And what purpose do these figures serve in the paper's development? Note that the entire paragraph is developed with material from one source. Do sources other than Jones offer a different perspective? This paragraph is weak for several reasons: (1) it lacks a controlling idea (topic sentence) to give it purpose and direction; (2) it relies for development entirely on one source; (3) it lacks any discussion or analysis by the writer.

By contrast, the following paragraph demonstrates a successful synthesis:

Of course, the iridium could have come from other extraterrestrial sources besides an asteroid. One theory, put forward by Dale Russell, is that the iridium was produced outside the solar system by an exploding star (500). The theory of a nearby star exploding in a supernova is by far the most fanciful extraterrestrial theory; however, it warrants examination because of its ability to explain the widespread extinctions of the late Cretaceous Period (Colbert 205). Such an explosion, Russell states, could have blown the iridium either off the surface of the moon or directly from the star itself (500–01), while also producing a deadly blast of heat and gamma rays (Krishtalka 19). Even though this theory seems to explain the traces of iridium in the mass extinction, it does not explain why smaller mammals, crocodiles, and birds survived (Wilford 220). As Edwin Colbert explains, the extinctions of the late Cretaceous, although massive, were selective (205). So the supernova theory took a backseat to the other extraterrestrial theories: those of asteroids and comets colliding with the earth. The authors of the book The Great Extinction, Michael Allaby and James Lovelock, subtitled their work The solution to . . . the disappearance of the dinosaurs. Their theory: an asteroid or comet collided with earth around sixty-five million years ago, killing billions of organisms, and thus altering the course of evolution (157). This theory was hardly a new one when they wrote it; the Alvarezes came up with it nearly three years before. However, the fact that the theory of collision with a cosmic body warrants a book describing itself as the solution to the extinction of dinosaurs calls for some thought: is the asteroid or comet theory merely sensationalism, or is it rooted in fact? Paleontologist Leonard Krishtalka declares that few paleontologists have accepted the asteroid theory, himself calling "some catastrophic theories . . . small ideas injected with growth hormone" (22). However, other scientists, such as Allaby and Lovelock, see the cosmic catastrophic theory as a solid one based on more than guesswork (10–11).

This paragraph's synthesis is accomplished by several strategies: (1) the paragraph has a controlling idea; (2) the paragraph combines information from several sources; (3) the information is presented in a blend of paraphrase and short quotations; (4) information from the different sources is clearly indicated to readers; and (5) the student explains and discusses the information.

You might also observe the very different lengths of the two sample paragraphs just presented. Although the second paragraph is quite long, it is not unwieldy because it achieves unity and coherence. By contrast, body paragraphs of only three sentences are probably in trouble. To sum up, good body paragraphs need: (1) a controlling idea, (2) in most cases information from more than one source, and (3) analysis and discussion from the student writer.

WRITING GOOD CONCLUSIONS

Sometimes ending a paper seems even more difficult than beginning one. You know you are not supposed to just stop, but every ending that comes to mind sounds more corny than clever. Perhaps you are trying too hard for a "catchy" ending that really may not be appropriate for a complex and serious research essay. If you have trouble, try one of the following types of endings.

1. Do not just repeat your thesis as it was stated in paragraph 1, but expand on the original wording and emphasize the thesis's significance. Here is the conclusion of the solar energy paper:

The idea of using solar energy is not as far-fetched as it seemed years ago.

With the continued support of government plus the enthusiasm of research groups, environmentalists, and private industry, solar energy may become a household word quite soon. With the increasing cost of fossil fuel, the time could not be better for exploring this use of the sun.

2. End with a quotation that effectively summarizes and drives home the point of your paper. Researchers are not always lucky enough to find the ideal quotation for ending a paper. If you find a good one, use it. Better yet, present the quotation and then add your comment in a sentence or two. The conclusion to a paper on the dilemma of defective newborns is a good example:

Dr. Joseph Fletcher is correct when he says that "every advance in medical capabilities is an increase in our moral responsibility" (48). In a world of many gray areas, one point is clear. From an ethical point of view, medicine is a victim of its own success.

3. If you have researched an issue or problem, emphasize your proposed solutions in the concluding paragraph. The student opposing a mall adjacent to the Manassas Battlefield concluded with several solutions:

Whether the proposed mall will be built is clearly in doubt at the moment. What are the solutions to this controversy? One approach is, of course, not to build the mall at all. To accomplish this solution, now, with the rezoning having been approved, probably requires an act of Congress to buy the land and make it part of the National Park. Another solution, one that would please the County and the developer and satisfy citizens objecting to traffic problems, is to build the needed roads before the mall is completed. A third approach is to allow the office park of the original plan to be built, but not the mall. The local preservationists had agreed to this original development proposal, but now that the issue has received national attention, they may no longer be willing to compromise. Whatever the future of the William Center, the present plan for a new regional mall is not acceptable.

AVOIDING INEFFECTIVE CONCLUSIONS

Follow these guidelines to avoid conclusions that most readers consider ineffective and annoying.

1. *Do not introduce a new idea.* If the point belongs in your paper, you should have introduced it earlier.

2. *Do not just stop or trail off,* even if you feel as though you have run out of steam. A simple, clear restatement of the thesis is better than no conclusion.

3. *Do not tell your reader what you have accomplished:* "In this paper I have explained the advantages of solar energy by examining the costs . . ." If you have written well, your reader knows what you have accomplished.

4. *Do not offer apologies or expressions of hope.* "Although I wasn't able to find as much on this topic as I wanted, I have tried to explain the advantages of solar energy, and I hope that you will now understand why we need to use it more" is a disastrous ending.

5. *Do not end with a vague or confusing one- or two-sentence summary of complex ideas.* The following sentences make little sense: "These authors have similar and different attitudes and ideals concerning American desires. Faulkner writes with the concerns of man toward man whereas most of the other writers are more concerned with man toward money."

CHOOSING A TITLE

You should give some thought to your paper's title since that is what your reader sees first and what your work will be known by. A good title provides information and creates interest. Make your title informative by making it specific. If you can create interest through clever wording, so much the better. But do not confuse "cutesiness" with clever wording. Better to be just straightforward than to demean a serious effort with a "cutesy" title. Review the following examples of acceptable and unacceptable titles:

Vague:	A Perennial Issue Unsolved
	(There are many; which one is this paper about?)
Better:	The Perennial Issue of Press Freedom Versus Press Responsibility
Too Broad:	Earthquakes
	(What about earthquakes? This title is not informative.)
Better:	The Need for Earthquake Prediction
Too Broad:	<u>The Scarlet Letter</u>
	(Never use just the title of the work under discussion; you can use the work's title as a part of a longer title of your own.)
Better:	Color Symbolism in <u>The Scarlet Letter</u>

Cutesy: Babes in Trouble

(The slang "Babes" makes this title seem insensitive rather than clever.)

Better: The Dilemma of Defective Newborns

Revising the Paper: A Checklist

After completing a first draft, catch your breath and then gear up for the next step in the writing process: revision. Revision actually involves three activities that can best be approached as three separate steps. *Revising,* step 1, means *rewriting*—adding or deleting text, or moving parts of the draft around. Next comes *editing,* a rereading to correct errors from misspellings to incorrect documentation format. Finally, you need to *proofread* the typed copy. If you treat these as separate steps, you will do a more complete job of revision—and get a better grade on the completed paper!

REWRITING

Read your draft through and make changes as a result of answering the following questions:

Purpose and Audience
1. Is my draft long enough to fulfill assignment requirements and my purpose?
2. Are terms defined and concepts explained appropriately for my audience?

Content
1. Do I have a clearly stated thesis?
2. Have I presented sufficient evidence to support my thesis?
3. Are there any irrelevant sections that should be deleted?

Structure
1. Are paragraphs ordered to develop the topic logically?
2. Does the content of each paragraph help develop the thesis?
3. Is everything in each paragraph on the same subtopic to create paragraph unity?
4. Do body paragraphs have a balance of information and analysis, of source material and my own ideas?
5. Are there any paragraphs that should be combined? Are there any very long paragraphs that should be divided? (Check for unity.)

EDITING

Make revisions guided by your responses to the questions, make a clean copy, and read again. This time, pay close attention to sentences, words, and documentation format. Use the following questions to guide revisions.

Coherence

1. Have connecting words been used and key terms repeated to produce paragraph coherence?
2. Have transitions been used to show connections between paragraphs?

Sources

1. Have I paraphrased instead of quoted whenever possible?
2. Have I used introductory tags to create a context for source material?
3. Have I documented all borrowed material, whether quoted or paraphrased?
4. Are parenthetical references properly placed after borrowed material?

Style

1. Have I varied sentence length and structure?
2. Have I used my own words instead of quotations whenever possible?
3. Have I avoided long quotations?
4. Do I have correct form for quotations? For titles?
5. Is my language specific and descriptive?
6. Have I avoided inappropriate shifts in tense or person?
7. Have I removed any wordiness, deadwood, trite expressions, or clichés?
8. Have I used specialized terms correctly?
9. Have I avoided contractions as too informal for most research papers?
10. Have I maintained an appropriate style and tone for academic work?

PROOFREADING

When your editing is finished, prepare a completed draft of your paper according to the format described and illustrated below. Then proofread the completed copy, making any corrections neatly in ink. If a page has several errors, print a corrected copy. Be sure to make a copy of the paper for yourself before submitting the original to your instructor.

The Completed Paper

Your research paper should be double spaced throughout (including the Works Cited page) with one-inch margins on all sides. Your project will contain the following parts, in this order:

1. A *title page*, with your title, your name, the course name or number, your instructor's name, and the date, neatly centered, if required. Alternatively, place this information at the top of the first page, as shown on p. 275.
2. An *outline*, or statement of purpose, if required.

3. *The body or text of your paper.* Number all pages consecutively, including pages of works cited, using Arabic numerals. Place numbers in the upper right-hand corner of each page. You may also include your last name before each page number.

4. *A list of Works Cited,* placed on a separate page or pages after the text. Title the first of these pages "Works Cited." (Do not use the title "Bibliography.")

Sample Research Paper 1: A Current Problem

The following paper, in MLA style, illustrates a formal research essay format that includes a separate title page, an outline, and a Works Cited page. (Note: If you do not provide an outline, then you do not need a separate title page unless your instructor requires one. Use the second sample research essay as your model.) Notice, from the opening paragraph, that Connie Childress has selected a current issue of personal interest to her. Note, as well, that she has researched the issue and provides relevant facts and figures as well as value statements to advance her argument. The Works Cited page shows a range of types of sources used.

Good example of a title page format in a three-part pattern of title, author, and course information.

Adoption: An Issue of Love, Not Race

Connie Childress

English 112. Section 27N.

Dr. Pamela Monaco

November 2, 2001

Childress 2

Outline

Thesis: It is not society's place to decide for parents whether they are capable of parenting a child of a different race or ethnic background.

I.   The Issue of Transracial Adoptions

   A.   Discussion of Ashley's Adoption

   B.   Race or Ethnicity Should Not Be a Barrier to Adoption

II.   Transracial Adoption Problems

   A.   What the Numbers Show

   B.   Attitudes Toward Mixed-race Adoptions

   C.   Arguments Against Transracial Adoptions

   D.   Effects of Multiethnic Placement Act

III.   Some Consequences of Attitudes Against Transracial Adoptions

   A.   Different-race Children Taken from Foster Parents

   B.   U.S. Children Placed Overseas

IV.   What the Studies Show about Transracial Adoptions

V.   Solutions to the Problem

Last name and page number in upper right corner.

Repeat title on first page of text.

ADOPTION: AN ISSUE OF LOVE, NOT RACE

Double-space throughout.

Nine years ago when my daughter, Ashley, was placed in my arms, it marked the happy ending to a long, exhausting, and, at times, heartbreaking journey through endless fertility treatments and the red tape of adoption procedures. Ironically, she had not been in our home a day before we received a call from another adoption agency that specialized in foreign adoptions. The agency stated that it was ready to begin our home study. As I look at Ashley, with her brown hair, hazel eyes, and fair complexion, I have trouble imagining not having her in my life. I know in my heart that I would have this feeling about my daughter whether she came to us from the domestic agency or the agency bringing us a child from a foreign country. To us the issue was only the child, not his or her race or ethnic background. The issue of race or ethnicity should be considered by adoptive parents along with all the other issues needing thought when they make the decision to adopt. But race or ethnicity alone should not be a roadblock to adoption. It is not society's place to decide for parents if they are capable of parenting a child of a different race or ethnic background.

The student introduces her topic by referring to her own adopted daughter. Paragraph 1 concludes with her thesis.

Transracial adoptions are those adoptions involving a family and a child of a different race or ethnic background. Cultural differences occur when the family is of one racial or ethnic background and the adoptive child is of another. In 1996, according to the U.S. Department of Health and Human Services, "about 52 percent of children awaiting adoption through state placement services around the country are black" (Kuebelbeck). On average, black children wait longer to be adopted than white, Asian, or Hispanic children. Why should it be more difficult for a white family to adopt an African American child than a child from China or Russia? Or a Hispanic American or mixed-race child? Any of these combinations still results in a mixed-race adoption.

Student defines key term.

Although interracial adoptions are "statistically rare in the United States," according to Robert S. Bausch and Richard T. Serpe, who cite a 1990 study by

Student examines problems with U.S. adoptions.

Childress 4

Bachrach et al., the issue continues to receive attention from both social workers and the public (137). A New Republic editorial lists several articles, including a cover story in The Atlantic in 1992, to illustrate the attention given to transracial adoptions (6). All of the popular-press articles as well as those in scholarly journals describe the country's adoption and foster-care problems. While the great majority of families wanting to adopt are white, about half of the children in foster care waiting to be adopted are black ("All in the Family," 6). Robert Jackson estimates, in 1995, that about 440,000 children are being cared for in foster families (A26). The New Republic editorial reports on a 1993 study revealing that "a black child in California's foster care system is three times less likely to be adopted than a white child" (6). In some cases minority children have been in a single foster home with parents of a different race their entire life. They have bonded as a family. Yet, often when the foster parents apply to adopt these children, their petitions are denied and the children are removed from their care. For example, Beverly and David Cox, a white couple in Wisconsin, were asked to foster two young sisters, both African American. The Coxes provided love and nurturing for five years, but when they petitioned to adopt the two girls, not only was their request denied, but the girls

were removed from their home. Can removing the children from the only home they have ever known just because of their skin color really be in the best interest of the children? As Hillary Clinton has said, "Skin color [should] not outweigh the more important gift of love that adoptive parents want to offer" (Cole, Drummond, and Epperson 50).

> Words added to a quotation for clarity are placed in square brackets.

The argument against transracial adoption has rested on the concern that children adopted by parents of a different race or ethnic background will lose their cultural heritage and racial identity, and that these losses may result in adjustment problems for the children (Bausch and Serpe 136). The loudest voice against mixed-race adoptions has been the National Association of Black Social Workers (NABSW), who passed a resolution in 1972 stating their "vehement opposition to the practice of placing Black children with white families" and reaffirmed their position in 1994 (Harnack 188). Audrey T. Russell, speaking at the 1972 conference, described white adoption of black children as "a practice of genocide" (189).

Fortunately, for both children and families wanting to adopt, the NABSW has now reversed its position and concedes that placement in a home of a different race is far more beneficial to the child than keeping the child in foster care (Jackson A26). The NABSW's new position may have come in response to the passage of the Multiethnic Placement Act of 1994, legislation designed to facilitate the placement of minority children into adoptive homes. As Randall Kennedy explains, while this legislation continues to allow agencies to consider "the child's cultural, ethnic and racial background and the capacity of prospective foster or adoptive parents to meet the needs of a child of this background," it prohibits the delaying of an adoption solely for the purpose of racial matching (44). Kennedy objects to the law's allowing for even some consideration of race matching because he believes that this results in some children never being adopted, as agencies search for a race match (44). Sandra Haun, a social worker from Fairfax County, Virginia, said in an interview that she does not oppose transracial adoptions but that the best choice for a child is with a family of the same race, if the choice exists. Providing that both adoptive homes could offer the child the same environment in every other aspect, then clearly the same-race home may be the best choice. More often than not, however, placing a child in a home of the same race is not an option. How can we worry about a child's cultural identity when that child doesn't have a home to call his or her own? In the cases of minority children who have been with a foster family of a different race for most of their young lives, the benefits of remaining in a stable home far outweigh the benefits of moving to a family of the same race.

Student uses a personal interview as one source.

The emotional effects of removing a child from a home that he or she has lived in for an extended period of time is well illustrated in the movie Losing Isaiah. In the film, a black child is adopted by a white social worker and her husband after the child's birth mother has placed him in the garbage when he is three days old so that she can be free to search for drugs. When Isaiah is three, the courts return him to his birth mother, who is now off drugs. Is it fair to Isaiah for her reward to be at the expense of his emotional health? The attorney representing the adoptive parents sums up the plight of these children in one sentence: "The child is then wrenched from the only family they've ever known

The student refers to a recent movie on adoption.

and turned over to strangers because of the color of their skin." In the end, Isaiah's birth mother realizes that this system is unfair to him. She appeals to his adoptive parents to assist him in his adjustment to his new home.

To protect themselves from heartbreaking situations such as the one depicted in <u>Losing Isaiah</u>, potential adoptive couples in this country are seeking other alternatives. We know that many couples seeking to adopt often adopt children from foreign countries. One of the reasons for this is the assumed shortage of children in the United States available for adoption. What may be less widely known is that many American children of mixed race or African American are placed with adoptive families overseas. One of the reasons for this situation is the continued unwillingness of social workers to place black or mixed-race children with white couples (Blackman et al. 65). The NABSW's years of resistance to placing black children with white parents has left its mark, although Edmund Blair Bolles speculates that the rare placing of black— or American Indian—children with white couples may reflect racial prejudices rather than a great concern to preserve black or Indian identities (72). Whatever the explanation, it is ironic that American babies are being "exported" to adoptive homes in other countries while babies from other countries are being "imported" to American adoptive homes. The child social services system needs to be overhauled to remove the stigmas or concerns that keep American children from being adopted in the country of their birth. If one of the arguments against transracial adoptions is the possible loss of cultural identity, how can we tolerate a system which appears to prefer placing African American children outside their own country—their own cultural heritage?

The argument that adopted children may lose their cultural identity is no longer a justifiable objection to transracial adoptions. As Randall Kennedy asserts, "there exists no credible empirical support that substantiates" the idea that "adults of the same race as a child will be better able to raise that child than adults of a different race" (44). Bausch and Serpe cite four studies done between 1972 and 1992 that show that "most children of color adopted by white parents appear to be as well adjusted as children of color adopted by same-race parents" (137). Perhaps the most important study is one conducted over twenty years by Rita Simon, American University sociologist. She studied 204 interracial adoptees over the twenty-year period and found that many of the adoptees supported transracial adoptions (Davis A3).

Some did report that they felt isolated from other people of their own race, but we need to remember that those who participated in this study were adopted when adoptions were more secretive (and when races were more separated). At that time, most adoptees, regardless of race, may have felt isolated because of this lack of openness. Simon, in her book (with Howard Alstein and Marygold S. Melli) draws these conclusions:

> Transracial adoptees do not lose their racial identities, they do not appear to be racially unaware of who they are, and they do not display negative or indifferent racial attitudes about themselves. On the contrary, . . . transracially placed children and their families have as high a success rate as all other adoptees and their families. (204)

The student shortens the block quotation by using ellipses. Note format of block quotation.

With open adoptions becoming increasingly popular, more adoptees today are aware of their adopted state and often have knowledge of one or both of their birth parents. It is not only possible, but probably easier, to provide opportunities for today's adoptee to learn about his or her racial and cultural background. The fact that the child is being raised by a family of a different race or ethnic background does not condemn that child to a life of ignorance concerning his or her own racial and cultural identity.

A strong conclusion stressing the student's position on transracial adoptions.

There can be only one logical solution to the issues surrounding mixed-race adoptions. Children and their adoptive parents should be united as a family because they have passed the background investigations and screening interviews that show they are emotionally and financially able to provide loving and nurturing environments for the children. To keep children needing homes and loving parents apart because they are of different races or ethnic backgrounds is not fair to the children or the adoptive parents. Preventing or delaying such adoptions is detrimental to each child's development. Children require a consistent home environment to flourish, to grow into productive members of society. Legislation needs to support speedier adoptive placements for minority children to give them the same quality of life afforded other adoptees. Society needs to protect the rights of adoptive parents by not denying transracial adoptions as an option for couples seeking to adopt.

Childress 8

Works Cited

"All in the Family." Editorial. <u>New Republic</u> 24 Jan. 1994: 6–7.

Bausch, Robert S., and Richard T. Serpe. "Negative Outcomes of Interethnic Adoption of Mexican American Children." <u>Social Work</u> 42.2 (1997): 136–43.

Blackman, Ann, et al. "Babies for Export." <u>Time</u> 22 Aug. 1994: 64–65. <u>Time On-Disc</u>. CD-ROM. UMI-ProQuest. Sept. 1997.

Bolles, Edmund Blair. <u>The Penguin Adoption Handbook: A Guide to Creating Your New Family</u>. New York: Viking, 1984.

Cole, Wendy, Tamerlin Drummond, and Sharon E. Epperson. "Adoption in Black and White." <u>Time</u> 14 Aug. 1995: 50–51.

Davis, Robert. "Suits Back Interracial Adoptions." <u>USA Today</u> 13 Apr. 1995: A3.

Harnack, Andrew. Ed. <u>Adoption: Opposing Viewpoints</u>. San Diego: Greenhaven, 1995. 188.

Haun, Sandra. Personal Interview. 30 Sept. 1997.

Jackson, Robert L. "U.S. Stresses No Race Bias in Adoptions." <u>Los Angeles Times</u> 25 Apr. 1995: A26.

Kennedy, Randall, and Carol Moseley-Braun. "At Issue: Interracial Adoption—Is the Multiethnic Placement Act Flawed?" <u>ABA Journal</u> 81 (1995): 44–45. <u>ABA Journal On-Disc</u>. CD-ROM. UMI-ProQuest. Sept. 1997.

Kuebelbeck, Amy. "Interracial Adoption Debated." <u>AP US and World</u>. 31 Dec. 1996. 26 pars. 8 Oct. 1997 <http//www.donet.com/~brandyjc/p6at111.htm>.

<u>Losing Isaiah</u>. Howard W. Koch, Jr., Dir. Perf. Jessica Lange and Halle Berry. Paramount, 1995.

Russell, Audrey T. "Transracial Adoptions Should Be Forbidden." From <u>Diversity: Cohesion or Chaos—Mobilization for Survival: Proceedings of the Fourth Annual Conference of NABSW</u>, 1973. Harnack 189–96.

Simon, Rita J., Howard Altsteen, and Marygold S. Melli. "Transracial Adoptions Should Be Encouraged." From <u>The Case for Transracial Adoption</u>, 1994. Harnack 198–204.

Start a new page for the Works Cited. Include only works actually cited. Double-space throughout. Alphabetize and use hanging indentation.

Cites a CD-ROM database.

Cites an Internet news source.

Cross-reference citations.

Sample Research Paper 2: A Literary Research Essay

The following paper, in MLA style, illustrates the use of a few sources but many page references to one literary work. Alan's essay was written for a sophomore-level literature course and was based in part on class discussion of *Intruder in the Dust* as an example of an initiation novel. Alan demonstrates considerable skill in literary analysis and shows, by his references to Hawthorne and Miller, that he can make connections between other studied works and *Intruder*. Going beyond class discussion and making connections with other works or concepts will be rewarded in any field of study.

Peterson 1

Alan Peterson

American Literature 242

May 5, 1998

Appropriate heading when separate title page is not used. (See page 264.)

Center the title. Double-space throughout.

Faulkner's Realistic Initiation Theme

William Faulkner braids a universal theme, the theme of initiation, into the fiber of his novel <u>Intruder in the Dust</u>. From ancient times to the present, a prominent focus of literature, of life, has been rites of passage, particularly those of childhood to adulthood. Joseph Campbell defines rites of passage as "distinguished by formal, and usually very severe, exercises of severance." A "candidate" for initiation into adult society, Campbell explains, experiences a shearing away of the "attitudes, attachments and life patterns" of childhood (9). This severe, painful stripping away of the child and installation of the adult is presented somewhat differently in several works by American writers.

Opening ¶ introduces subject, presents thesis, and defines key term—initiation.

Student combines paraphrase and brief quotations in definition.

One technique of handling this theme of initiation is used by Nathaniel Hawthorne in his story "My Kinsman, Major Molineaux." The story's main character, Robin, is suddenly awakened to the real world, the adult world, when he sees Major Molineaux "in tar-and-feathery dignity" (Hawthorne 528). A terrified and amazed Robin gapes at his kinsman as the large and colorful crowd laughs at and ridicules the Major; then an acquiescent Robin joins with the crowd in the mirthful shouting (Hawthorne 529). This moment is Robin's epiphany, his sudden realization of reality. Robin goes from unsophisticated rube to resigned cynical adult in one quick scene. Hawthorne does hold out hope that Robin will not let this event ruin his life, indeed that he will perhaps prosper from it.

Summary and analysis combined to explain initiation in Hawthorne's story.

A similar, but decidedly less optimistic, example of an epiphanic initiation occurs in Arthur Miller's play <u>Death of a Salesman</u>. Miller develops an initiation theme within a flashback. A teenaged Biff, shockingly confronted with Willy's infidelity and weakness, has his boyhood dreams, ambitions—his vision—shattered, leaving his life in ruins, a truth borne out in scenes in which Biff is an adult during the play (1083–84, 1101).

Transition to second example establishes contrast with Hawthorne.

Biff's discovery of the vices and shortcomings of his father overwhelm him. His realization of adult life is a revelation made more piercing when put into the context of his naive and overly hopeful upbringing. A ravaged and defeated Biff has adulthood wantonly thrust upon him. Unlike Hawthorne's Robin, Biff never recovers.

¶ concludes with emphasis on contrast.

William Faulkner does not follow these examples when dealing with the initiation of his character Chick in <u>Intruder in the Dust</u>. In Robin's and Biff's cases, each character's passage into adulthood was brought about by realization of and disillusionment with the failings and weaknesses of a male adult playing an important role in his life. By contrast, Chick's male role models are vital, moral men with integrity. Chick's awakening develops as he begins to comprehend the mechanisms of the adult society in which he would be a member.

Transition to Faulkner's story by contrast with Hawthorne and Miller.

Faulkner uses several techniques for illustrating Chick's growth into a man. Early in the novel, at the end of the scene in which Chick tries to pay for his dinner, Lucas warns Chick to "stay out of that creek" (Faulkner 16).[1] The creek is an effective symbol: it is both a physical creek and a metaphor for the boy's tendency to slide into gaffes that perhaps a man could avoid. The creek's symbolic meaning is more evident when, after receiving the molasses, Chick encounters Lucas in town. Lucas again reminds Chick not to "fall in no more creeks this winter" (24). At the end of the novel, Lucas meets Chick in Gavin's office and states: "you ain't fell in no more creeks lately, have you?" (241). Although Lucas phrases this as a question, the answer is obvious to Lucas, as well as to the reader, that indeed Chick has not blundered into his naive boyhood quagmire lately. When Lucas asks his question, Chick's actual falling into a creek does not occur to the reader.

Footnote first parenthetical reference to inform readers that subsequent citations will exclude the author's name and give only the page number. (See pages 229–30.)

Another image Faulkner employs to show Chick growing into a man is the single-file line. After Chick gets out of the creek, he follows Lucas into the house, the group walking in single file. In the face of Lucas's much stronger adult will, Chick is powerless to get out of the line, to go to Edmonds's house (7). Later in the novel,

Note transition. (See pages 256–57 on transitions.)

---

[1] Subsequent references to Faulkner's novel cite page numbers only.

when Miss Habersham, Aleck Sander, and Chick are walking back from digging up the grave, Chick again finds himself in a single-file line with a strong-willed adult in front. Again he protests, then relents, but clearly he feels slighted and wonders to himself "what good that [walking single file] would do" (130). The contrast between these two scenes illustrates Chick's growth, although he is not yet a man.

Note interpolation in square brackets. (See page 25.)

Faulkner gives the reader other hints of Chick's passage into manhood. As the novel progresses, Chick is referred to (and refers to himself) as a "boy" (24), a "child" (25), a "young man" (46), "almost a man" (190), a "man" (194), and one of two "gentlemen" (241). Other clues crop up from time to time. Chick wrestles with himself about getting on his horse and riding away, far away, until Lucas's lynching is "all over finished done" (41). But his growing sense of responsibility and outrage quell his boyish desire to escape, to bury his head in the sand. Chick looks in the mirror at himself with amazement at his deeds (125). Chick's mother serves him coffee for the first time, despite the agreement she has with his father to withhold coffee until his eighteenth birthday (127). Chick's father looks at him with pride and envy (128–29).

Good use of brief quotations combined with analysis. (See pages 258–60.)

Perhaps the most important differences between the epiphanic initiations of Robin and Biff and that experienced by Chick are the facts that Chick's epiphany does not come all at once and it does not devastate him . Chick learns about adulthood —and enters adulthood —piecemeal and with support. His first eye-opening experience occurs as he tries to pay Lucas for dinner and is rebuffed (15–16). Chick learns , after trying again to buy a clear conscience, the impropriety and affront of his actions (24). Lucas teaches Chick how he should resolve *his* dilemma by setting him "free" (26–27). Later , Chick feels outrage at the adults crowding into the town, presumably to see a lynching, then disgrace and shame as they eventually flee (196–97, 210). As in most lives, Chick's passage into adulthood is a gradual process; he learns a little bit at a time and has support in his growing. Gavin is there for him , to act as a sounding board, to lay a strong intellectual foundation, to confirm his beliefs. Chick's initiation is consistent with Joseph Campbell's explanation: "all rites of passage are intended to touch not only the candidate,

Characteristics of Chick's gradual and positive initiation explained. Observe coherence techniques. (See pages 255–57.)

but also every member of his circle" (9). Perhaps Gavin is affected the most, but Chick's mother and father, and Lucas as well, are influenced by the change in Chick.

In <u>Intruder in the Dust</u>, William Faulkner has much to say about the role of and the actions of adults in society. He depicts racism, ignorance, resignation, violence, fratricide, citizenship, hope, righteousness, lemming-like aggregation, fear, and a host of other emotions and actions. Chick learns not only right and wrong, but that in order to be a part of society, of his community, he cannot completely forsake those with whom he disagrees or whose ideas he challenges. There is much compromise in growing up; Chick learns to compromise on some issues, but not all. Gavin's appeal to Chick to "just don't stop" (210) directs him to conform enough to be a part of the adult world, but not to lose sight of, indeed instead to embrace, his own values and ideals.

Student concludes by explaining the values Chick develops in growing up.

Works Cited

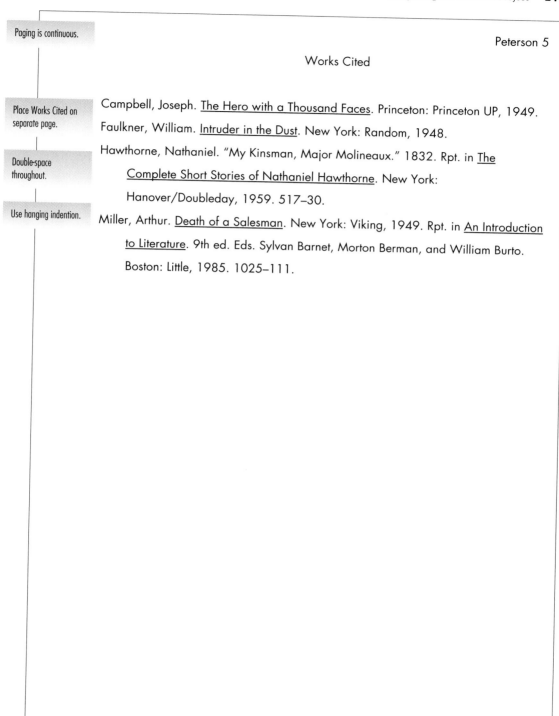

Campbell, Joseph. <u>The Hero with a Thousand Faces</u>. Princeton: Princeton UP, 1949.

Faulkner, William. <u>Intruder in the Dust</u>. New York: Random, 1948.

Hawthorne, Nathaniel. "My Kinsman, Major Molineaux." 1832. Rpt. in <u>The Complete Short Stories of Nathaniel Hawthorne</u>. New York: Hanover/Doubleday, 1959. 517–30.

Miller, Arthur. <u>Death of a Salesman</u>. New York: Viking, 1949. Rpt. in <u>An Introduction to Literature</u>. 9th ed. Eds. Sylvan Barnet, Morton Berman, and William Burto. Boston: Little, 1985. 1025–111.

Paging is continuous.

Place Works Cited on separate page.

Double-space throughout.

Use hanging indention.

CHAPTER 9

Other Styles of Documentation

Although the research process is much the same regardless of the area of study, the presentation of the results of research varies from one discipline to another. Because not all disciplines use MLA style, you need to be aware of other patterns of documentation, patterns that you will encounter in your reading and that you may use in some research projects.

Three common styles of documentation other than MLA are the author/year style, the footnote or endnote style, and the number style. The first two will be explained and illustrated in enough detail to allow you to use either one in a paper. The number style, used by scientists in several disciplines, will be explained only briefly, as it is the least likely pattern to be required of you during your undergraduate years.

Author/Year or APA Style

The *author/year system* identifies a source by placing the author's last name and the publication year of the source within parentheses at the point in the text where the source is cited. The in-text citations are supported by complete bibliographic information in an alphabetized list of sources at the end of the paper. Most disciplines in the social sciences, biological sciences, and earth sciences use some version of the author/year style. Of the various style manuals providing guidelines for the author/year style, the most frequently used is the *Publication Manual of the American Psychological Association* (5th ed., 2001). This style is often referred to as APA style.

APA STYLE: IN-TEXT CITATIONS

The simplest parenthetical reference can be presented in one of three ways:

1. Place the year of publication within parentheses immediately following the author's name in the text.

    In a typical study of preference for motherese, Fernald (1985) used an operant

    auditory preference procedure.

Within the same paragraph, additional references to the author do not need to repeat the year, if the researcher clearly establishes that the same source is being cited.

Because the speakers were unfamiliar subjects Fernald's work eliminates the possibility that it is the mother's voice per se that accounts for the preference.

2. If the author is not mentioned in the text, place the author's last name followed by a comma and the year of publication within parentheses after the borrowed information.

The majority of working women are employed in jobs that are at least 75 percent female (Lawrence & Matsuda, 1997).

3. Cite a specific passage by providing the page, chapter, or figure number following the borrowed material. *Always* give specific page references for quoted material.

- A brief quotation:

Deuzen-Smith (1988) believes that counselors must be involved with clients and "deeply interested in piecing the puzzle of life together" (p. 29).

- A quotation in display form:

Bartlett (1932) explains the cyclic process of perception:

Suppose I am making a stroke in a quick game, such as tennis or cricket. How I make the stroke depends on the relating of certain new experiences, most of them visual, to other immediately preceding visual experiences, and to my posture, or balance of posture, at the moment. (p. 201)

(Indent a block quotation five spaces from the left margin, do not use quotation marks, and double-space throughout. To show a new paragraph within the block quotation, indent the first line of the new paragraph an additional five spaces. Note the placing of the year after the author's name, and the page number at the end of the direct quotation.)

More complicated in-text citations should be handled as follows.

Two Authors, Mentioned in the Text

Kuhl and Meltzoff (1984) tested 4- to 5-month-olds in an experiment . . .

Two Authors, Not Mentioned in the Text

. . . but are unable to show preference in the presence of two mismatched modalities (e.g., a face and a voice; see Kuhl & Meltzoff, 1984).

Give both authors' last names each time you refer to the source. Connect their names with "and" in the text. Use an ampersand (&) in the parenthetical citation.

More Than Two Authors

For works coauthored by three, four, or five people, provide all last names in the first reference to the source. Thereafter, cite only the first author's name followed by "et al."

As Price-Williams, Gordon, and Ramirez have shown (1969), . . .

or

Studies of these children have shown (Price-Williams, Gordon, & Ramirez, 1969)

. . .

then

Price-Williams et al. (1969) also found that . . .

If a source has six or more authors, use only the first author's last name followed by "et al." every time the source is cited.

Corporate Authors

In general, spell out the name of a corporate author each time it is used. If a corporate author has well-known initials, the name can be abbreviated after the first citation.

First in-text citation: (National Institutes of Health [NIH], 1989)
Subsequent citations: (NIH, 1989)

Two or More Works Within the Same Parentheses

When citing more than one work by the same author in a parenthetical reference, use the author's name only once and arrange the years mentioned in order, thus:

Several studies of ego identity formation (Marcia, 1966, 1983) . . .

When an author, or the same group of coauthors, has more than one work published in the same year, distinguish the works by adding the letters *a*, *b*, *c*, and so on, as needed, to the year. Give the last name only once, but repeat the year, each one with its identifying letters; thus:

Several studies (Smith, 1990 a , 1990 b , 1990 c) . . .

When citing several works by different authors within the same parenthesis, list the authors alphabetically; alphabetize by the first author when citing coauthored works. Separate authors or groups of coauthors with semicolons; thus:

Although many researchers (Archer & Waterman, 1983; Grotevant, 1983;

Grotevant & Cooper, 1986; Sabatelli & Mazor, 1985) study identify

formation . . .

APA Style: Preparing a List of References

Every source cited parenthetically in your paper needs a complete bibliographic citation. These complete citations are placed on a separate page (or pages) after the text of the paper and before any appendices included in the paper. Sources are arranged alphabetically, and the first page is titled "References." Begin each source flush with the left margin and indent second and subsequent lines five spaces. Double-space throughout the list of references. Follow these rules for alphabetizing:

1. Organize two or more works by the same author, or the same group of coauthors, chronologically.

   Beck, A. T. (1991).

   Beck, A. T. (1993).

2. Place single-author entries before multiple-author entries when the first of the multiple authors is the same as the single author.

   Grotevant, H. D. (1983).

   Grotevant, H. D., & Cooper, C. R. (1986).

3. Organize multiple-author entries that have the same first author but different second or third authors alphabetically by the name of the second author or third and so on.

   Gerbner, G., & Gross, L.

   Gerbner, G., Gross, L., Jackson-Beeck, M., Jeffries-Fox, S., & Signorielli, N.

   Gerbner G., Gross, L., Morgan, M., & Signorielli, N.

4. Organize two or more works by the same author(s) published in the same year alphabetically by title.

FORM FOR BOOKS

A book citation contains these elements in this form:

Seligman, M. E. P. (1991). *Learned optimism.* New York: Knopf.

Weiner, B. (Ed.) (1974). *Achievement motivation and attribution theory.*

Morristown, NJ: General Learning Press.

Authors

Give all authors' names, last name first, and initials. Separate authors with commas, use the ampersand (&) before the last author's name, and end with a period. For edited books, place the abbreviation "Ed." or "Eds." in parentheses following the last editor's name.

Date of Publication

Place the year of publication in parentheses followed by a period.

Title

Capitalize only the first word of the title and of the subtitle, if there is one, and any proper nouns. Italicize the title and end with a period. Place additional information such as number of volumes or an edition in parentheses after the title, before the period.

> Butler, R., & Lewis, M. (1982). *Aging and mental health.*
>
> (3rd ed.)

Publication Information

Cite the city of publication; add the state (using the Postal Service abbreviation) or country if necessary to avoid confusion; then give the publisher's name, after a colon, eliminating unnecessary terms such as *Publisher*, *Co.*, and *Inc*. End the citation with a period.

> Newton, D. E. (1996). *Violence and the media.* Santa Barbara: ABC-Clio.
>
> Mitchell, J. V. (Ed.) (1985). *The ninth mental measurements yearbook.* Lincoln:
>
> University of Nebraska Press.
>
> National Institute of Drug Abuse. (1993, April 13). *Annual national high school*
>
> *senior survey.* Rockville, MD: Author.

(Give a corporate author's name in full. When the organization is both author and publisher, place the word "Author" after the place of publication.)

FORM FOR ARTICLES

An article citation contains these elements in this form:

> Changeaux, J-P. (1993). Chemical signaling in the brain. *Scientific American, 269,*
>
> 58–62.

Author

Same rules as for author(s) of books.

Date of Publication

Place the year of publication for articles in scholarly journals in parentheses, followed by a period. For articles in newspapers and popular magazines, give the year followed by month and day (if appropriate).

> (1997, March). (See also example below.)

Title of Article

Capitalize only the title's first word, the first word of any subtitle, and any proper nouns. Place any necessary descriptive information in square brackets immediately after the title.

Scott, S. S. (1984, December 12). Smokers get a raw deal [Letter to the Editor].

Publication Information

Cite the title of the journal in full, capitalizing according to conventions for titles. Underline the title and follow it with a comma. Give the volume number, underlined, followed by a comma, and then inclusive page numbers followed by a period. *If a journal begins each issue with a new page 1, then also cite the issue number in parentheses immediately following the volume number. Do not use "p." or "pp." before page numbers when citing articles from scholarly journals; do use "p." or "pp." in citations to newspaper and magazine articles.

Martin, C. L., Wood, C. H., & Little, J. K. (1990). The development of gender

stereotype components. *Child Development, 61,* 1891–1904.

Leakey, R. (2000, April–May). Extinctions past and present. *Time,* p. 35.

Form for an Article or Chapter in an Edited Book

Goodall, J. (1993). Chimpanzees—bridging the gap. In P. Cavalieri & P. Singer

(Eds.) *The great ape project: Equality beyond humanity* (pp. 10–18). New

York: St. Martin's.

Cite the author(s), date, and title of the article or chapter. Then cite the name(s) of the editor(s) in signature order after "In," followed by "Ed." or "Eds." in parentheses; the title of the book; the inclusive page numbers of the article or chapter, in parentheses, followed by a period. End with the place of publication and the publisher of the book.

A Report

U.S. Merit Systems Protection Board. (1988). *Sexual harassment in the federal*

workplace: An update. Washington, DC: U.S. Government Printing Office.

Electronic Sources

Many types of electronic sources are available on the Internet, and the variety can make documenting these sources complex. At a minimum, an APA reference for any type of Internet source should include the following information: a document title or description; dates—the date of publication or latest update and the date of retrieval—use (n.d.) for "no date" when a publication date is not available; an Internet address (the document's uniform resource locator, or URL) that works; and, whenever possible, an author name.

Unlike MLA style, APA style does not require that URLs appear within angle brackets (< >). Also do not place a period at the end of a reference when a URL concludes it. However, if you need to break an Internet address across lines, you should break the URL only after a slash. The basic forms for electronic references in APA style look like this:

Online periodical article:

> Author, A. (date). Title of article. *Title of Periodical, volume number or*
>
> > *equivalent,* page number(s). Retrieved month, day, year, from URL

Online document:

> Author, A. (date). Title of work. Retrieved month, day, year, from URL

Examples:

Electronic Daily Newspaper Article Available by Search

> Schwartz, J. (2002, September 13). Air pollution con game. *Washington*
>
> > *Times.* Retrieved September 14, 2002, from http://www.washtimes.com

Journal Article available from a Periodical Database (*Note that no URL is necessary; just provide the name of the database.*)

> Dixon, B. (2001, December). Animal emotions. *Ethics & the Environment,*
>
> > 6(2), 22. Retrieved August 26, 2002, from Academic Search Premier
> >
> > database/EBSCO Host Research Databases.

U.S. Government Report on a Government Web Site

> U.S. General Accounting Office. (2002, March). *Identity theft: Prevalence*
>
> > *and cost appear to be growing.* Retrieved September 3, 2002, from
> >
> > http://www.consumer.gov/idtheft/reports/gao-d02363.pdf

Sample Paper in APA Style

The following paper, Connie's argument for transracial adoptions, is reproduced here with the necessary changes to illustrate APA style. Use one-inch margins and double-space throughout, including any block quotations. Block quotations should be indented *five* spaces from the left margin (in contrast to the 10 spaces required by MLA style). The paper illustrates the following elements of papers in APA style: title page, running head, abstract, author/year in-text citations, subheadings within the text, and a list of references.

Sample title page for a paper in APA style.

Adoption: An Issue of Love, Not Race

Connie Childress

Northern Virginia Community College

Transracial Adoptions 2

Abstract

Over 400,000 children are in foster care in the United States. The majority of these children are non-white. However, the majority of couples wanting to adopt children are white. While matching race or ethnic background when arranging adoptions may be the ideal, the mixing of race or ethnic background should not be avoided, or delayed, when the matching of race is not possible. Children need homes, and studies of racial adoptees show that they are as adjusted as adoptees with new parents of their own race or ethnicity. Legislation should support speedier adoptions of children, regardless of race or ethnic background.

Adoption: An Issue of Love, Not Race

Nine years ago when my daughter, Ashley, was placed in my arms, it marked the happy ending to a long, exhausting, and, at times, heartbreaking journey through endless fertility treatments and the red tape of adoption procedures. Ironically, she had not been in our home a day before we received a call from another adoption agency that specialized in foreign adoptions. The agency stated that it was ready to begin our home study. As I look at Ashley, with her brown hair, hazel eyes, and fair complexion, I have trouble imagining not having her in my life. I know in my heart that I would have this feeling about my daughter whether she came to us from the domestic agency or the agency bringing us a child from a foreign country. To us the issue was only the child, not his or her race or ethnic background. The issue of race or ethnicity should be considered by adoptive parents along with all the other issues needing thought when they make the decision to adopt. But race or ethnicity alone should not be a roadblock to adoption. It is not society's place to decide for parents if they are capable of parenting a child of a different race or ethnic background.

Transracial adoptions are those adoptions involving a family and a child of a different race or ethnic background. Cultural differences occur when the family is of one racial or ethnic background and the adoptive child is of another. Amy Kuebelbeck (1996) reports that, according to the U.S. Department of Health and Human Services, "about 52 percent of children awaiting adoption through state placement services around the country are black." On average, black children wait longer to be adopted than white, Asian, or Hispanic children. Why should it be more difficult for a white family to adopt an African-American child than a child from China or Russia? Or a Hispanic American or mixed-race child? Any of these combinations still results in a mixed-race adoption.

Adoption Issues and Problems

Although interracial adoptions are "statistically rare in the United States," according to Robert S. Bausch and Richard T. Serpe (1997), who cite a 1990 study by Bachrach et al., the

---

Student introduces her paper by referring to her adoption experience.

The first paragraph concludes with her thesis.

Observe form of author/year citations.

issue continues to receive attention from both social workers and the public (p. 137). A *New Republic* editorial (1994) lists several articles, including a cover story in *The Atlantic* in 1992,

to illustrate the attention given to transracial adoptions. All of the popular-press articles as well as those in scholarly journals, the editors explain, describe the country's adoption and foster-care problems. While the great majority of families wanting to adopt are white, about half of the children in foster care waiting to be adopted are black. Robert Jackson (1995) estimates that, in 1995, about 440,000 children are being cared for in foster families. The *New Republic* editorial reports on a 1993 study revealing that "a black child in California's foster care system is three times less likely to be adopted than a white child" (p. 6). In some cases minority children have been in a single foster home with parents of a different race their entire life. They have bonded as a family. Yet, often when the foster parents apply to adopt these children, their petitions are denied and the children are removed from their care. For example, Beverly and David Cox, a white couple in Wisconsin, were asked to be foster parents to two young sisters, both African American. The Coxes provided love and nurturing for five years, but when they petitioned to adopt the two girls, not

only was their request denied, but the girls were removed from their home. Can removing the children from the only home they have ever known just because of their skin color really be in the best interest of the children? Cole, Drummond, and Epperson (1995) quote Hillary Clinton as saying that "skin color [should] not outweigh the more important gift of love that adoptive parents want to offer" (p. 50).

The argument against transracial adoption has rested on the concern that children adopted by parents of a different race or ethnic background will lose their cultural heritage and racial identity, and that these losses may result in adjustment problems for the children (Bausch & Serpe, 1997). The loudest voice against mixed-race adoptions has been the National Association of Black Social Workers (NABSW), who passed a resolution in 1972 stating their "vehement opposition to the practice of placing Black children with white families" and reaffirmed their position in 1994 (Harnack, 1995, p. 188). Audrey T. Russell (1993), speaking at the 1972 conference, described white adoption of black children as "a practice of genocide" (p. 189). Fortunately, for both children and families wanting to adopt, the NABSW has now reversed its position and concedes that placement in a home of a different race is far more beneficial to the child than keeping the child in foster care (Jackson, 1995). The NABSW's new position may have come in response to the passage of the Multiethnic Placement Act of 1994, legislation designed to facilitate the placement of minority children into adoptive homes. As Randall Kennedy (1995) explains, while this legislation continues to allow agencies to consider "the child's cultural, ethnic and racial background and the capacity of prospective foster or adoptive parents to meet the needs of a child of this background" (p. 44), it prohibits the delaying of an adoption solely for the purpose of racial matching. Kennedy objects to the law's allowing for even some consideration of race matching because he believes that this results in some children never being adopted, as agencies search for a race match. Sandra Haun (1997), a social worker from Fairfax County, Virginia, said in an interview that she does not oppose transracial adoptions but that the best choice for a child is with a family of the same race, if the choice exists. Providing that both adoptive homes could offer the child the same environment in every aspect, then clearly the same-race home may be the best choice. More often than not, however, placing a child in a home of the same race is not an option. How can we worry about a child's cultural identity when the child doesn't have a home to call his or her own? In the cases of minority children who have been with a foster family of a different race for most of their young lives, the benefits of remaining in a stable home far outweigh the benefits of moving to a family of the same race.

The emotional effects of removing a child from a home that he or she has lived in for an extended period of time is well illustrated in the movie *Losing Isaiah*. In the film, a black child is adopted by a white social worker and her husband after the child's birth mother has placed him in the garbage when he is three days old so that she can be free to search for drugs. When Isaiah is three, the courts return him to his birth mother, who is now off drugs. Is it fair to Isaiah for her reward to be at the expense of his emotional health? The attorney representing the adoptive parents sums up the plight of these children in one sentence: "The child is then wrenched from the only family they've ever known and turned over to strangers because of the color of their skin." In the end, Isaiah's birth mother realizes that

Good transition into
discussion of movie

this system is unfair to him. She appeals to his adoptive parents to assist him in his adjustment to his new home.

Some Consequences of Negative Attitudes toward Transracial Adoptions

Subheadings are often used in papers in the social sciences.

To protect themselves from heartbreaking situations such as the one depicted in *Losing Isaiah*, potential adoptive couples in this country are seeking other alternatives. We know that many couples seeking to adopt often adopt children from foreign countries. One of the reasons for this is the assumed shortage of children in the United States available for adoption. What may be less widely known is that many American children of mixed race or African American are placed with adoptive families overseas. One of the reasons for this situation is the continued unwillingness of social workers to place black or mixed-race children with white couples. The NABSW's years of resistance to placing black children with white parents has left its mark, although Edmund Blair Bolles (1984) speculates that the rare placing of black— or American Indian—children with white couples may reflect racial prejudices rather than a great concern to preserve black or Indian identities. Whatever the explanation, it is ironic that American babies are being "exported" to adoptive homes in other countries while babies from other countries are being "imported" to American adoptive homes. The child social services system needs to be overhauled to remove the stigmas or concerns that keep American children from being adopted in the country of their birth. If one of the arguments against transracial adoptions is the possible loss of cultural identity, how can we tolerate a system which appears to prefer placing African American children outside their own country—their own cultural heritage?

The argument that adopted children may lose their cultural identity is no longer a justifiable objection to transracial adoptions. As Randall Kennedy (1995) asserts, "there exists no credible empirical support that substantiates" the idea that "adults of the same race as the child will be better able to raise that child than adults of a different race" (p. 44). Bausch and Serpe (1997) cite four studies done between 1972 and 1992 that show that "most children of color adopted by white parents appear to be as well adjusted as children of color adopted by same-race parents" (p. 137). Perhaps the most important study is one conducted over twenty years by Rita Simon, American University sociologist. Davis (1995) reports that she studied 204 interracial adoptees over the twenty-year period and found that many of the adoptees supported

transracial adoptions. Some did report that they felt isolated from other people of their own race,

but we need to remember that those who participated in this study were adopted when

adoptions were more secretive (and when races were more separated). At that time, most

adoptees, regardless of race, may have felt isolated because of this lack of openness. Simon

(1994), in her book (with Howard Alstein and Marygold S. Melli) draws these conclusions:

> Transracial adoptees do not lose their racial identities, they do not appear to be racially
>
> unaware of who they are, and they do not display negative or indifferent racial attitudes
>
> about themselves. On the contrary, . . . transracially placed children and their families
>
> have as high a success rate as all other adoptees and their families. (p. 204)

With open adoptions becoming increasingly popular, more adoptees today are aware of their

adopted state and often have knowledge of one or both of their birth parents. It is not only

possible, but probably easier, to provide opportunities for today's adoptee to learn about his

or her racial and cultural background. The fact that the child is being raised by a family of a

different race or ethnic background does not condemn that child to a life of ignorance

concerning his or her own racial and cultural identity.

Conclusion

There can be only one logical solution to the issues surrounding mixed-race adoptions. Children

and their adoptive parents should be united as a family because they have passed the

background investigations and screening interviews that show they are emotionally and

financially able to provide loving and nurturing environments for the children. To keep children

needing homes and loving parents apart because they are of different races or ethnic

backgrounds is not fair to the children or the adoptive parents. Preventing or delaying such

Student restates her position in a concluding paragraph.

adoptions is detrimental to each child's development. Children require a consistent

home environment to flourish, to grow to be productive members of society. Legislation

needs to support speedier adoptive placements for minority children to give them the

same quality of life afforded other adoptees. Society needs to protect the right of adoptive

parents by not denying transracial adoptions as an option for couples seeking to adopt.

Transracial Adoptions 8

References

All in the family [Editorial]. (1994, Jan. 24). *New Republic*, pp. 6–7.

Bausch, R. S., & Serpe, R. T. (1997). Negative outcomes of interethnic adoption of Mexican American children. *Social Work, 42.2,* 136–43.

Blackman, A., et al. (1994, Aug. 22). Babies for export. *Time, Time On-disc* [CD-ROM], pp. 64–65.

Bolles, E. B. (1984). *The Penguin adoption handbook: A guide to creating your new family.* New York: Viking.

Cole, W., Drummond, T., & Epperson, S. E. (1995, Aug. 14). Adoption in black and white. *Time*, pp. 50–51.

Title the page *References.* Double-space throughout. In each citation indent all lines, after the first, five spaces. Note APA style placement of date and format for titles.

Davis, R. (1995, Apr. 13). Suits back interracial adoptions. *USA Today*, p. A3.

Harnack, A., Ed. (1995). *Adoption: Opposing viewpoints* (p. 188). San Diego: Greenhaven.

Haun, S. (1997, Sept. 30). Personal interview.

Jackson, R. L. (1995, Apr. 25). U.S. stresses no race bias in adoptions. *Los Angeles Times*, p. A26.

Kennedy, R., & Moseley-Braun, C. (1995). At issue: interracial adoption—is the multiethnic placement act flawed? *ABA Journal 81 ABA Journal On-Disc* [CD-ROM]. pp. 44–45.

Kuebelbeck, A. (1996, Dec. 31). Interracial adoption debated. *Ap US and World.* Retrieved October 10, 1999 from http://www.donet.com/~brandyjc/p6at111.htm.

Losing Isaiah (1995) [film].

Russell, A. T. (1995). Transracial adoptions should be forbidden. In A. Harnack, Ed., *Adoption: Opposing viewpoints* (pp. 189–96). San Diego: Greenhaven.

Simon, R. J., Alstein, H., & Melli, M. S. (1995). Transracial adoptions should be encouraged. In A. Harnack, Ed., *Adoption: Opposing viewpoints* (pp. 198–204). San Diego: Greenhaven.

Footnote or Endnote Style

Instructors in history, philosophy, and art history frequently prefer the footnote or endnote form of documentation to any pattern using parenthetical documentation. The two chief guides for this pattern are the *MLA Handbook* (4th ed., 1995) and the *Chicago Manual of Style* (14th ed., 1993). The required information and the order of that information in a footnote (or endnote) are the same in the two manuals, but they do differ in minor ways in format. Both manuals state a preference for endnotes (citations placed at the end of the paper) rather than footnotes (citations placed at the bottom of appropriate pages), but some instructors may want to see footnotes, so always be sure to determine the precise guidelines for your assignment. Further, learn your instructor's expectations with regard to a bibliography in addition to footnotes or endnotes. Because the first footnote (or endnote) reference to a source contains complete bibliographic information for the source, a list of works cited is not necessary. Still, some instructors want both complete documentation notes and the alphabetized Works Cited page(s) following the text (with footnotes) or after the endnotes.

The following guidelines adhere to the *Chicago Manual of Style*. The few differences in format found in the *MLA Handbook* are explained where appropriate.

IN-TEXT CITATIONS

Use a raised (superscript, such as this[2]) arabic numeral immediately following all material from a source, whether the borrowed material is quoted or paraphrased. The number follows all punctuation except the dash, and it always follows, never precedes, material needing documentation. Number footnotes or endnotes consecutively throughout the paper, beginning with "1." Use the same care to present material from sources with introductory tags and with a placing of superscript numbers so that readers can tell where borrowed material begins and where it ends. Regularly placing citation numbers only at the ends of paragraphs will not result in accurate documentation.

Location and Presentation of Footnotes

1. Place footnotes on the same page as the borrowed material. You need to calculate the number of lines needed at the bottom of the page to complete all the footnotes for that page. If you miscalculate, retype the page. (A word processor will make these calculations for you.)

2. Begin the first footnote four lines (two double spaces) below the last line of text.

3. Indent the first line of each footnote five spaces. Type the superscript numeral that corresponds to the one in the text, leave one space, and then type the reference information. (This is the most common practice in research papers, but the *Chicago Manual* shows online numerals followed by a period—for example: 1. Chicago style can be found in books and some journals, more commonly with endnotes than footnotes.)

4. If a footnote runs to more than one line of text, single-space between lines and begin the second line flush with the left margin.

5. If more than one footnote appears on a page, double-space between notes.

Location and Presentation of Endnotes

1. List endnotes in consecutive order corresponding to the superscript numbers in the text.

2. Indent the first line of each endnote five spaces. Type the raised number, leave one space, and then type the reference. (Again, this is the traditional pattern in research papers, but the *Chicago Manual* shows an online number followed by a period. See the alternative example below.)

3. If an endnote runs to more than one line, double-space between lines and begin the second line flush with the left margin.

4. Double-space between endnotes.

5. Start endnotes on a new page titled "Notes." Endnotes follow the text and precede a list of works cited, if such a list is included.

FOOTNOTE/ENDNOTE FORM: FIRST (PRIMARY) REFERENCE

Each first reference to a source contains all the necessary author, title, and publication information that would be found in a list of works cited or list of references. Subsequent references to the same source use a shortened form. Prepare all first-reference notes according to the following guidelines.

Form for Books

1. Cite the author's full name in signature order, followed by a comma.

2. Cite the title of the book and underline it. Include the complete subtitle, if there is one, unless a list of works cited is also provided. No punctuation follows the title.

3. Give the facts of publication in parentheses: city of publication followed by a colon, publisher followed by a comma, and year of publication.

4. Give the precise page reference. Do not use "p." or "pp." *MLA Handbook* style: Use no punctuation between the closing parenthesis and the page reference. *The Chicago Manual:* Place a comma after the closing parenthesis, before the page number.

   [1] Daniel J. Boorstin, <u>The Americans: The Colonial Experience</u> (New York: Vintage-Random, 1958), 46.

(The most common footnote/endnote pattern uses a superscript number and a comma after the closing parenthesis.)

Alternative

   1. Daniel J. Boorstin, <u>The Americans: The Colonial Experience</u> (New York: Vintage-Random, 1958), 46.

(If you use this less common style, do not indent the first line of the note.)

Form for Articles

1. Cite the author's full name in signature order, followed by a comma.
2. Cite the title of the article in quotation marks, and place a comma *inside* the closing quotation mark.
3. Give the facts of publication: the title of the journal, underlined; the volume in arabic numerals; and the date followed by a colon. Citations of scholarly journals require the volume number followed by the date in parentheses; citations of popular magazines and newspapers eliminate the volume number, giving the date only, not in parentheses.
4. Provide a precise page reference following the colon, without using "p." or "pp." All notes end with a period.

> [2] Everard H. Smith, "Chambersburg: Anatomy of a Confederate Reprisal," American Historical Review 96 (April 1991): 434.

SAMPLE FOOTNOTES/ENDNOTES

Additional information must be added as necessary to the simplest examples given above. Some of the common variations are illustrated here. Note that the examples are presented as endnotes; that is, the lines of each note are double-spaced. Remember that footnotes are single-spaced *within* each note but double-spaced *between* notes. The traditional style of indenting the first line, using a raised numeral, and placing a comma after the facts of publication in a book citation has been followed in these examples.

A Work by Two or Three Authors

> [3] Charles A. Beard and Mary R. Beard, The American Spirit (New York: Macmillan, 1942), 63.

A Work by More Than Three Authors

> [4] Lester R. Brown et al., State of the World 1990: A World-watch Institute Report on Progress Toward a Sustainable Society (New York: Norton, 1990), 17.

An Edited Work

> [5] The Autobiography of Benjamin Franklin, ed. Max Farrand (Berkeley: University of California Press, 1949), 6–8.

(Begin with the title—or the editor's name—if the author's name appears in the title.)

> [6] Bentley Glass, Orvsei Temkin, and William L. Straus, Jr., eds., Forerunners of Darwin: 1745–1859 (Baltimore: Johns Hopkins Press paperback edition, 1968), 326.

A Translation

[7] Allan Gilbert, trans. and ed., <u>The Letters of Machiavelli</u> (New York: Capricorn Books, 1961), 120.

[8] Jean-Jacques Rousseau, <u>The Social Contract and Discourses</u>, trans. with an introduction by G. D. H. Cole (New York: Dutton, 1950), 42–43.

A Preface, Introduction, or Afterword

[9] Ernest Barker, introduction, <u>The Politics of Aristotle</u>, trans. and ed. Ernest Barker (New York: Oxford University Press, 1962), xiii.

A Book in Two or More Volumes

[10] Paul Tillich, <u>Systematic Theology</u>, 3 vols. (Chicago: University of Chicago Press, 1951–63), 1:52.

(Make the page reference first to the volume number, followed by a colon, and then the page number.)

A Book in Its Second or Subsequent Edition

[11] Frank J. Sorauf and Paul Allen Beck, <u>Party Politics in America</u>, 6th ed. (Glenview, IL: Scott, Foresman/Little, Brown, 1988), 326.

A Book in a Series

[12] Charles L. Sanford, ed., <u>Benjamin Franklin and the American Character</u>, Problems in American Civilization (Lexington, MA: D.C. Heath, 1955), 4.

A Work in a Collection

[13] George Washington, "Farewell Address, 1796," in <u>A Documentary History of the United States</u>, ed. Richard D. Heffner (New York: New American Library, 1965), 64–65.

An Encyclopedia Article

[14] <u>The Concise Dictionary of American Biography</u>, 1964 ed., s.v., "Anthony, Susan Brownell."

(Do not cite a page number for reference works arranged alphabetically; rather, cite the entry in quotation marks after "s.v." [*sub verbo*—"under the word"]. The edition number or year is needed, but no other facts of publication are required for well-known reference works.)

An Article in a Scholarly Journal

[15] Ellen Fitzpatrick, "Rethinking the Intellectual Origins of American Labor History," <u>American Historical Review</u> 96 (April 1991): 426.

An Article in a Popular Magazine

[16] Richard Leakey, "Extinctions Past and Present," <u>Time</u>, April–May 2000: 35.

An Editorial

[17] "Means of Atonement," editorial, <u>Wall Street Journal</u>, 22 May 2000: A38.

A Review

[18] Gabriel P. Weisberg, "French Art Nouveau," rev. of <u>Art Nouveau in Fin-de-Siècle France: Politics, Psychology, and Style</u> by Deborah Silverman, <u>Art Journal</u> 49 (Winter 1990): 427.

An Online News Service

[19] Leslie Gevirtz, "US Leads 100-Year Game of Economic Development," <u>Reuters</u>, Nov/Dec. 1999. http://www.reuters. com/magazine/

FOOTNOTE/ENDNOTE FORM: SHORT FORMS

After the first full documentary footnote or endnote for a source, subsequent references to the same source should be shortened forms. The simplest short form for any source with an author or editor is the author's or editor's last name followed by a comma and a precise page reference; thus: [19]Fitzgerald, 425. If there is no author cited, use a short title and page number. If two sources are written by authors with the same last name, then add first names or initials to distinguish between them. For example, if you used "The Tendency of History" by Henry Adams and *The Founding of New England* by James T. Adams, then the short forms would be as follows:

> [20] Henry Adams, 16.

> [21] James T. Adams, 252.

If you use two or more sources by the same author, then add a short title to the note; thus:

> [22] Boorstin, <u>American Politics</u>, 167.

> [23] Boorstin, <u>The Americans</u>, 65–66.

The Latin abbreviations *loc. cit.* and *op. cit.* are no longer recommended, and ibid. is almost as obsolete, usually replaced now by the simple short form of author's last name and page number. Remember that ibid. can be used only to refer to the source cited in the immediately preceding note. The following footnotes, appearing at the bottom of a page from a history paper, illustrate the various short forms.

Sample Footnotes from a History Paper

While mid-twentieth-century historians may be more accurate, they may have lost the flavor of earlier American historians who had a clear ideology that shaped their writing.[20]

> [11] William Bradford, <u>Of Plymouth Plantation</u>, in <u>The American Puritans: Their Prose and Poetry</u>, ed. Perry Miller (New York: Anchor-Doubleday, 1956), 5.

> [12] Daniel J. Boorstin, <u>The Americans: The Colonial Experience</u> (New York: Vintage-Random, 1958), 16.

> [13] Ibid., 155.

> [14] James T. Adams, 136.

> [15] Henry Adams, <u>The Education of Henry Adams</u>, ed. D. W. Brogan (Boston: Houghton Mifflin, 1961), 342.

> [16] Boorstin, <u>American Politics</u>, 167.

> [17] Henry Adams, "The Tendency of History," 16.

> [18] Ibid., 71.

> [19] Henry Adams, <u>Education</u>, 408.

> [20] John Higham, "The Cult of the 'American Consensus': Homogenizing Our History," <u>Commentary</u> 27 (Feb. 1959): 94–96.

The Number System

The number system is really several number systems, depending on one's field of specialization in the sciences, engineering, medical sciences, and mathematics. *The Chicago Manual of Style* presents a number system but describes it as tedious for readers. Basically, the pattern requires that each source used be given a number as it is referred to the first time and that only the number appear within the text whenever reference is made to that source. In-text citation by numeral is supported by a complete list of references organized (usually) in the order in which the sources are referred to in the paper. (A variation of this pattern is to organize the reference list alphabetically.) Each reference will present the basics of author, title, and facts of publication, but the format for this information varies considerably from one discipline's style manual to another. Even the use of in-text numerals varies from a superscript number[1] to an online number in parentheses (2) to an online number in square brackets [3]. The Council of Biology Editors is calling for all scholars in the sciences to agree on one number system, but since this has not yet happened, the only good advice to student researchers is to be sure that you understand exactly which style manual you are to follow when documenting your paper. Style manuals, in addition to the *Chicago Manual of Style*, include *Scientific Style and Format: The CBE Manual for Authors, Editors, and Publishers* (6th ed., 1994), the *ACS Style Guide* (1986), published by the American Chemical Society, the *AIP Style Manual* (4th ed., 1990), published by the American Institute of Physics, and *A Manual for Authors of Mathematical Papers* (rev. ed., 1990), published by the American Mathematical Society.

A Collection of Readings

This section is divided into 14 chapters: each of the first 13 chapters on a current topic or set of interrelated issues open to debate and the last chapter a collection of some well-known arguments from the past. Although the number of articles varies in each chapter, all contain at least four articles in order to remind readers that complex issues cannot be divided into simple "for" or "against" positions. This point remains true even for the chapters on a rather specific topic, capital punishment for example. It is not sound critical thinking to be, simply, for or against any complicated public-policy issue.

There are questions following each article to aid your reading, analysis, and critical responses, and each chapter begins with a brief introduction and set of questions to focus your thinking as you read. Each introduction concludes with a list of a few websites that are relevant to the chapter's topic and may be of interest to you. However, please keep these two thoughts in mind as you read: (1) there is no way to include all possibly relevant Web addresses, and (2) the Internet is ever-changing. Although every effort has been made to include sites that are expected to last, websites in existence when this text was prepared may no longer be available.

Here are some general questions to guide your critical thinking as you read and reflect on the various issues:

1. What are my views on this issue? Do I already have a coherent position? If so, what can I gain by studying the writers who present a different point of view?

2. Which writers rely primarily on facts to support their claims? Which combine facts and logic? Which also use persuasive strategies? Which ones seem to be primarily interested in "pushing emotional buttons" in readers who are assumed to be in agreement with the author? Do I recognize any logical fallacies?

3. Which type of argument usually works best for me? Does my answer to this question depend in part on the particular issue?

CHAPTER 10

The Media:
Image and Reality

Although we may not agree with Marshall McLuhan that the medium itself is the message, we must still recognize the ways that the various media influence us, touching our emotions, shaping our vision of the world, altering our lives. The essays in this chapter debate the effects of television, advertising, and the press on the way we imagine and then live our lives. Surely we are influenced by media images, by the "reality" they bombard us with. The questions become, first, how extensive is the influence, given the other influences in our lives, and, second, what, if any, controls should be placed on the media to guard us, particularly children, from their influence. The writers here do not answer these questions in the same way.

As you read these articles, reflect on the following questions:

1. What are the effects of television images? How have they altered our views of "reality"?
2. What groups seem especially vulnerable to influence by the media?
3. Are those concerned about media influences taking their concerns too seriously, or do they have justification?
4. What solutions do the writers offer? If you were media czar, what would you do?

Websites Related to This Chapter's Topic

Terry Sanford Institute of Public Policy

www.pubpol.duke.edu

Site maintained by someone at the institute. Contains many good links.

Lion and Lamb

www.lionlamb.org

Site of national advocacy organization seeking to affect the selling of violence to children, either through toys or the media.

Baby Bag

www.babybag.com/articles/amaviol.htm

Facts about media violence; directed to parents, but useful for others as well.

Kansas State University Site
  www.ksu.edu/humec/tele.htm
  Contains articles and book excerpts on television violence.

Interact/Jesuit Communication Project Site at the University of Oregon
  http://interact.uoregon.edu/MediaLit/JCP/violence.html
  Contains bibliographies and a list of video resources on media violence.

Television and Violent Crime

Brandon S. Centerwall

Brandon Centerwall (b. 1954) holds a medical degree from the University of California, San Diego, and a master's in public health, with a specialty in epidemiology, from Tulane University. He did his residency in psychiatry at the University of Washington and is currently a professor there in the department of epidemiology. Centerwall has testified before Congressional committees on television violence and has published articles on various psychological issues, including the impact of television violence on behavior. The following article appeared in the Spring 1993 issue of *Public Interest.*

1   Children are born ready to imitate adult behavior. That they can, and do, imitate an array of adult facial expressions has been demonstrated in newborns as young as a few hours old, before they are even old enough to know that they have facial features. It is a most useful instinct, for the developing child must learn and master a vast repertoire of behavior in short order.

2   But while children have an instinctive desire to imitate, they do not possess an instinct for determining whether a behavior ought to be imitated. They will imitate anything, including behavior that most adults regard as destructive and antisocial. It may give pause for thought, then, to learn that infants as young as fourteen months demonstrably observe and incorporate behavior seen on television.

3   The average American preschooler watches more than twenty-seven hours of television per week. This might not be bad if these young children understood what they were watching. But they don't. Up through ages three and four, most children are unable to distinguish fact from fantasy on TV, and remain unable to do so despite adult coaching. In the minds of young children, television is a source of entirely factual information regarding how the world works. There are no limits to their credulity. To cite one example, an Indiana school board had to issue an advisory to young children that, no, there is no such thing as Teenage Mutant Ninja Turtles. Children had been crawling down storm drains looking for them.

4   Naturally, as children get older, they come to know better, but their earliest and deepest impressions are laid down at an age when they still see television as a factual source of information about the outside world. In that world, it seems, violence is common and the commission of violence is generally powerful, exciting, charismatic, and effective. In later life, serious violence is most likely to erupt at moments of severe stress—and it is precisely at such moments that adolescents and adults are most likely

to revert to their earliest, most visceral sense of the role of violence in society and in personal behavior. Much of this sense will have come from television.

The Seeds of Aggression

5   In 1973, a remote rural community in Canada acquired television for the first time. The acquisition of television at such a late date was due to problems with signal reception rather than any hostility toward TV. As reported in *The Impact of Television* (1986), Tannis Williams and her associates at the University of British Columbia investigated the effect of television on the children of this community (which they called "Notel"), taking for comparison two similar towns that already had television.

6   The researchers observed forty-five first- and second-graders in the three towns for rates of inappropriate physical aggression before television was introduced into Notel. Two years later, the same forty-five children were observed again. To prevent bias in the data, the research assistants who collected the data were kept uninformed as to why the children's rates of aggression were of interest. Furthermore, a new group of research assistants was employed the second time around, so that the data gatherers would not be biased by recollections of the children's behavior two years earlier.

7   Rates of aggression did not change in the two control communities. By contrast, the rate of aggression among Notel children increased 160 percent. The increase was observed in both boys and girls, in those who were aggressive to begin with and in those who were not. Television's enhancement of noxious aggression was entirely general and not limited to a few "bad apples."

8   In another Canadian study, Gary Granzberg and his associates at the University of Winnipeg investigated the impact of television upon Indian communities in northern Manitoba. As described in *Television and the Canadian Indian* (1980), forty-nine third-, fourth-, and fifth-grade boys living in two communities were observed from 1973, when one town acquired television, until 1977, when the second town did as well. The aggressiveness of boys in the first community increased after the introduction of television. The aggressiveness of boys in the second community, which did not receive television then, remained the same. When television was later introduced in the second community, observed levels of aggressiveness increased there as well.

9   In another study conducted from 1960 to 1981, Leonard Eron and L. Rowell Huesmann (then of the University of Illinois at Chicago) followed 875 children living in a semirural U.S. county. Eron and Huesmann found that for both boys and girls, the amount of television watched at age eight predicted the seriousness of criminal acts for which they were convicted by age thirty (Figure 1). This remained true even after controlling for the children's baseline aggressiveness, intelligence, and socioeconomic status. Eron and Huesmann also observed second-generation effects. Children who watched much television at age eight later, as parents, punished their own children more severely than did parents who had watched less television as children. Second- and now third-generation effects are accumulating at a time of unprecedented youth violence.

10   All seven of the U.S. and Canadian studies of prolonged childhood exposure to television demonstrate a positive relationship between exposure and physical aggression. The critical period is preadolescent childhood. Later exposure does not appear to produce any additional effect. However, the aggression-enhancing effect of exposure in

FIGURE 1

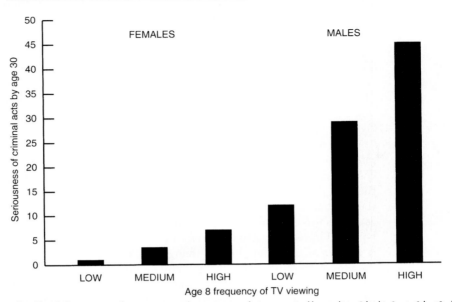

Relationship of television viewing frequency at age eight to seriousness of crimes committed by age thirty. Columbia County Cohort Study, 1960–1981. (Reprinted by permission from Leonard D. Eron and L. Rowell Huesmann, "The control of aggressive behavior by changes in attitudes, values, and the conditions of learning," Advances in the Study of Aggression. Orlando, Florida: Academic Press, 1984.)

preadolescence extends into adolescence and adulthood. This suggests that any interventions should be designed for children and their caregivers rather than for the general adult population.

11   These studies confirmed the beliefs of most Americans. According to a Harris poll at the time of the studies, 43 percent of American adults believe that television violence "plays a part in making America a violent society." An additional 37 percent think it might. But how important is television violence? What is the effect of exposure upon entire populations? To address this question, I took advantage of an historical accident—the absence of television in South Africa prior to 1975.

The South African Experience

12   White South Africans have lived in a prosperous, industrialized society for decades, but they did not get television until 1975 because of tension between the Afrikaner- and English-speaking communities. The country's Afrikaner leaders know that a South African television industry would have to rely on British and American shows to fill out its programming schedule, and they felt that this would provide an unacceptable cultural advantage to English-speaking South Africans. So, rather than negotiate a complicated compromise, the government simply forbade television broadcasting. The entire population of two million whites—rich and poor, urban and rural, educated and

FIGURE 2

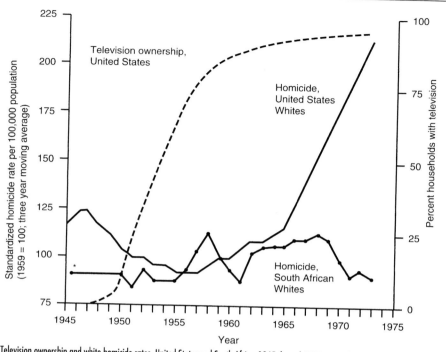

Television ownership and white homicide rates, United States and South Africa, 1945 through 1973. Asterisk denotes six-year average. Note that television broadcasting was not permitted in South Africa prior to 1975. (Reprinted by permission from Brandon S. Centerwall, "Exposure to television as a cause of violence," Public Communication and Behavior, Vol. 2, Orlando, Florida: Academic Press, 1989.)

uneducated—was thus excluded from exposure to television for a quarter century after the medium was introduced in the United States.

13   In order to determine whether exposure to television is a cause of violence, I compared homicide rates in South Africa, Canada, and the United States. Since blacks in South Africa live under quite different conditions than blacks in the United States, I limited the comparison to white homicide rates in South Africa and the United States, and the total homicide rate in Canada (which was 97 percent white in 1951).* I chose the homicide rate as a measure of violence because homicide statistics are exceptionally accurate.

14   From 1945 to 1974, the white homicide rate in the United States increased 93 percent. In Canada, the homicide rate increased 92 percent. In South Africa, where television was banned, the white homicide rate declined by 7 percent (Figure 2).

---

*   The "white homicide rate" refers to the rate at which whites are the victims of homicide. Since most homicide is intra-racial, this closely parallels the rate at which whites commit homicide.

Controlling for Other Factors

15   Could there be some explanation other than television for the fact that violence increased dramatically in the U.S. and Canada while dropping in South Africa? I examined an array of alternative explanations. None is satisfactory:

- *Economic growth.* Between 1946 and 1974, all three countries experienced substantial economic growth. Per capita income increased by 75 percent in the United States, 124 percent in Canada, and 86 percent in South Africa. Thus differences in economic growth cannot account for the different homicide trends in the three countries.

- *Civil unrest.* One might suspect that anti-war or civil-rights activity was responsible for the doubling of the homicide rate in the United States during this period. But the experience of Canada shows that this was not the case, since Canadians suffered a doubling of the homicide rate without similar civil unrest.

16   Other possible explanations include changes in age distribution, urbanization, alcohol consumption, capital punishment, and the availability of firearms. As discussed in *Public Communication and Behavior* (1989), none provides a viable explanation for the observed homicide trends.

17   In the United States and Canada, there was a lag of ten to fifteen years between the introduction of television and a doubling of the homicide rate. In South Africa, there was a similar lag. Since television exerts its behavior-modifying effects primarily on children, while homicide is primarily an adult activity, this lag represents the time needed for the "television generation" to come of age.

18   The relationship between television and the homicide rate holds *within* the United States as well. Different regions of the U.S., for example, acquired television at different times. As we would expect, while all regions saw increases in their homicide rates, the regions that acquired television first were also the first to see higher homicide rates.

19   Similarly, urban areas acquired television before rural areas. As we would expect, urban areas saw increased homicide rates several years before the occurrence of a parallel increase in rural areas.

20   The introduction of television also helps explain the different rates of homicide growth for whites and minorities. White households in the U.S. began acquiring television sets in large numbers approximately five years before minority households. Significantly, the white homicide rate began increasing in 1958, four years before a parallel increase in the minority homicide rate.

21   Of course, there are many factors other than television that influence the amount of violent crime. Every violent act is the result of a variety of forces coming together—poverty, crime, alcohol and drug abuse, stress—of which childhood TV exposure is just one. Nevertheless, the evidence indicates that if, hypothetically, television technology had never been developed, there would today be 10,000 fewer homicides each year in the United States, 70,000 fewer rapes, and 700,000 fewer injurious assaults. Violent crime would be half what it is.

The Television Industry Takes a Look

22   The first congressional hearings on television and violence were held in 1952, when not even a quarter of U.S. households owned television sets. In the years since, there have been scores of research reports on the issue, as well as several major government investigations. The findings of the National Commission on the Causes and Prevention of Violence, published in 1969, were particularly significant. This report established what is now the broad scientific consensus: Exposure to television increases rates of physical aggression.

23   Television industry executives were genuinely surprised by the National Commission's report. What the industry produced was at times unedifying, but physically harmful? In response, the network executives began research programs that collectively would cost nearly a million dollars.

24   CBS commissioned William Belson to undertake what would be the largest and most sophisticated study yet, an investigation involving 1,565 teenage boys. In *Television Violence and the Adolescent Boy* (1978), Belson controlled for one hundred variables, and found that teenage boys who had watched above-average quantities of television violence before adolescence were committing acts of serious violence (e.g., assault, rape, major vandalism, and abuse of animals) at a rate 49 percent higher than teenage boys who had watched below-average quantities of television violence. Despite the large sum of money they had invested, CBS executives were notably unenthusiastic about the report.

25   ABC commissioned Melvin Heller and Samuel Polsky of Temple University to study young male felons imprisoned for violent crimes (e.g., homicide, rape, and assault). In two surveys, 22 and 34 percent of the young felons reported having consciously imitated crime techniques learned from television programs, usually successfully. The more violent of these felons were the most likely to report having learned techniques from television. Overall, the felons reported that as children they had watched an average of six hours of television per day—approximately twice as much as children in the general population at that time.

26   Unlike CBS, ABC maintained control over publication. The final report, *Studies in Violence and Television* (1976), was published in a private, limited edition that was not released to the general public or the scientific community.

27   NBC relied on a team of four researchers, three of whom were employees of NBC. Indeed, the principal investigator, J. Ronald Milavsky, was an NBC vice president. The team observed some 2,400 schoolchildren for up to three years to see if watching television violence increased their levels of physical aggressiveness. In *Television and Aggression* (1982), Milavsky and his associates reported that television violence had no effect upon the children's behavior. However, every independent investigator who has examined their data has concluded that, to the contrary, their data show that television violence did cause a modest increase of about 5 percent in average levels of physical aggressiveness. When pressed on the point, Milavsky and his associates conceded that their findings were consistent with the conclusion that television violence increased physical aggressiveness "to a small extent." They did not concede that television violence actually caused an increase, but only that their findings were consistent with such a conclusion.

FIGURE 3

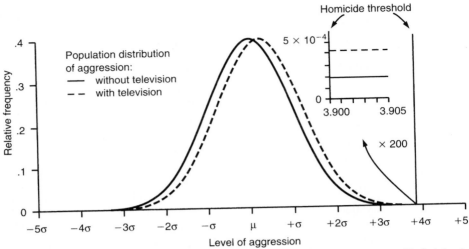

Relationships between television, aggression, and homicide in the general population: a model. (Reprinted by permission of Academic Press.)

28   The NBC study results raise an important objection to my conclusions. While studies have repeatedly demonstrated that childhood exposure to television increases physical aggressiveness, the increase is almost always quite minor. A number of investigators have argued that such a small effect is too weak to account for major increases in rates of violence. These investigators, however, overlook a key factor.

29   Homicide is an extreme form of aggression—so extreme that only one person in 20,000 committed murder each year in the United States in the mid-1950s. If we were to rank everyone's degree of physical aggressiveness from the least aggressive (Mother Theresa) to the most aggressive (Jack the Ripper), the large majority of us would be somewhere in the middle and murderers would be virtually off the chart (Figure 3). It is an intrinsic property of such "bell curve" distributions that small changes in the average imply major changes at the extremes. Thus, if exposure to television causes 8 percent of the population to shift from below-average aggression to above-average aggression, it follows that the homicide rate will double. The findings of the NBC study and the doubling of the homicide rate are two sides of the same coin.

30   After the results of these studies became clear, television industry executives lost their enthusiasm for scientific research. No further investigations were funded. Instead, the industry turned to political management of the issue.

The Television Industry and Social Responsibility

31   The television industry routinely portrays individuals who seek to influence programming as un-American haters of free speech. In a 1991 letter sent to 7,000 executives of consumer product companies and advertising agencies, the president of the Network Television Association explained:

Freedom of expression is an alienable right of all Americans vigorously supported by ABC, CBS, and NBC. However, boycotts and so-called advertiser "hit lists" are attempts to manipulate our free society and democratic process.

32   The letter went on to strongly advise the companies to ignore all efforts by anyone to influence what programs they choose to sponsor. By implication, the networks themselves should ignore all efforts by anyone to influence what programs they choose to produce.

33   But this is absurd. All forms of public discourse are attempts to "manipulate" our free society and democratic process. What else could they be? Consumer boycotts are no more un-American than are strikes by labor unions. The Network Television Association is attempting to systematically shut down all discourse between viewers and advertisers, and between viewers and the television industry. Wrapping itself in patriotism, the television industry's response to uppity viewers is to put them in their place. If the industry and advertisers were to actually succeed in closing the circle between them, the only course they would leave for concerned viewers would be to seek legislative action.

34   In the war against tobacco, we do not expect help from the tobacco industry. If someone were to call upon the tobacco industry to cut back production as a matter of social conscience and concern for public health, we would regard that person as simpleminded, if not frankly deranged. Oddly enough, however, people have persistently assumed that the television industry is somehow different—that it is useful to appeal to its social conscience. This was true in 1969 when the National Commission on the Causes and Prevention of Violence published its recommendations for the television industry. It was equally true in 1989 when the U.S. Congress passed an anti-violence bill that granted television industry executives the authority to hold discussions on the issue of television violence without violating antitrust laws. Even before the law was passed, the four networks stated that there would be no substantive changes in their programming. They have been as good as their word.

35   For the television industry, issues of "quality" and "social responsibility" are peripheral to the issue of maximizing audience size—and there is no formula more tried and true than violence for generating large audiences. To television executives, this is crucial. For if advertising revenue were to decrease by just 1 percent, the television industry would stand to lose $250 million in revenue annually. Thus, changes in audience size that appear trivial to most of us are regarded as catastrophic by the industry. For this reason, industry spokespersons have made innumerable protestations of good intent, but nothing has happened. In the more than twenty years that levels of television violence have been monitored, there has been no downward movement. There are no recommendations to make to the television industry. To make any would not only be futile but could create the false impression that the industry might actually do something constructive.

36   On December 11, 1992, the networks finally announced a list of voluntary guidelines on television violence. Curiously, reporters were unable to locate any network producers who felt the new guidelines would require changes in their programs. That raises a question: Who is going to bell the cat? Who is going to place his or her career in jeopardy in order to decrease the amount of violence on television? It is hard to say,

but it may be revealing that when Senator Paul Simon held the press conference announcing the new inter-network agreement, no industry executives were present to answer questions.

Meeting the Challenge

37   Television violence is everybody's problem. You may feel assured that your child will never become violent despite a steady diet of television mayhem, but you cannot be assured that your child won't be murdered or maimed by someone else's child raised on a similar diet.

38   The American Academy of Pediatrics recommends that parents limit their children's television viewing to one or two hours per day. But why wait for a pediatrician to say it? Limiting children's exposure to television violence should become part of the public health agenda, along with safety seats, bicycle helmets, immunizations, and good nutrition. Part of the public health approach should be to promote child-care alternatives to the electronic babysitter, especially among the poor.

39   Parents should also guide what their children watch and how much. This is an old recommendation that can be given new teeth with the help of modern technology. It is now feasible to fit a television set with an electronic lock that permits parents to preset the channels and times for which the set will be available; if a particular program or time of day is locked, the set will not operate then. Time-channel locks are not merely feasible; they have already been designed and are coming off the assembly line.

40   The model for making them widely available comes from closed-captioning circuitry, which permits deaf and hard-of-hearing persons access to television. Market forces alone would not have made closed-captioned available to more than a fraction of the deaf and hard-of-hearing. To remedy this problem, Congress passed the Television Decoder Circuitry Act in 1990, which requires that virtually all new television sets be manufactured with built-in closed-captioning circuitry. A similar law should require that all new television sets be manufactured with built-in time-channel lock circuitry—and for a similar reason. Market forces alone will not make this technology available to more than a fraction of households with children and will exclude most poor families, the ones who suffer the most from violence. If we can make television technology available to benefit twenty-four million deaf and hard-of-hearing Americans, surely we can do no less for the benefit of fifty million American children.

41   A final recommendation: Television programs should be accompanied by a violence rating so that parents can judge how violent a program is without having to watch it. Such a rating system should be quantitative, leaving aesthetic and social judgments to the viewers. This approach would enjoy broad popular support. In a *Los Angeles Times* poll, 71 percent of adult Americans favored the establishment of a TV violence rating system. Such a system would not impinge on artistic freedom since producers would remain free to produce programs with high violence ratings. They could even use high violence ratings in the advertisements for their shows.

42   None of these recommendations would limit freedom of speech. That is as it should be. We do not address the problem of motor vehicle fatalities by calling for a ban on cars. Instead, we emphasize safety seats, good traffic signs, and driver education. Similarly, to address the problem of television-inspired violence, we need to promote

time-channel locks, program rating systems, and viewer education about the hazards of violent programming. In this way we can protect our children and our society.

References
Following is a partial list of studies and articles on this topic.

William A. Belson, *Television Violence and the Adolescent Boy.* Westmead, England: Saxon House (1978).

Brandon S. Centerwall, "Exposure to Television as a Cause of Violence," *Public Communication and Behavior*, Vol. 2. Orlando, Florida: Academic Press (1989), pp. 1–58.

Leonard D. Eron and L. Rowell Huesmann, "The Control of Aggressive Behavior by Changes in Attitudes, Values, and the Conditions of Learning," *Advances in the Study of Aggression*. Orlando, Florida: Academic Press (1984), pp. 139–171.

Gary Granzberg and Jack Steinbring (eds.), *Television and the Canadian Indian*. Winnipeg, Manitoba: University of Winnipeg (1980).

L. Rowell Huesmann and Leonard D. Eron, *Television and the Aggressive Child*. Hillsdale, New Jersey: Lawrence Erlbaum Associates (1986), pp. 45–80.

Candace Kruttschnitt, et al., "Family Violence, Television Viewing Habits, and Other Adolescent Experiences Related to Violent Criminal Behavior," *Criminology*, Vol. 24 (1986), pp. 235–267.

Andrew N. Meltzoff, "Memory in Infancy," *Encyclopedia of Learning and Memory*. New York: Macmillan (1992), pp. 271–275.

J. Ronald Milavsky, et al., *Television and Aggression*. Orlando, Florida: Academic Press (1982).

Jerome L. Singer, et al., "Family Patterns and Television Viewing as Predictors of Children's Beliefs and Aggression," *Journal of Communication*, Vol. 34, No. 2 (1984), pp. 73–89.

Tannis M. Williams. (ed.), *The Impact of Television*. Orlando, Florida: Academic Press (1986).

Questions for Reading and Analysis

1. Centerwall begins with some facts. How much television do preschoolers watch? How well do they understand what they are watching? What impressions of the world will they retain from TV?

2. In his four-paragraph opening, Centerwall does not state a thesis, or even announce a purpose in writing. What subject is established? What thesis is implied?

3. What type of argument is this?

4. To make his argument successful, what causal relationship must Centerwall establish?

5. What evidence of increased aggression from viewing TV violence does the author present? Summarize each study.

6. What does Centerwall seek to accomplish in the section "Controlling for Other Factors"?

7. What did the television-sponsored studies reveal? How does the TV industry now feel about research?

8. What is the industry's strategy now for avoiding control over its programming? What is the author's attitude toward the industry's argument?

9. What strategy does Centerwall use in paragraph 34 to express the idea that we should not expect help from the TV industry? What motivates television executives?

10. List Centerwall's proposed solutions.

11. Analyze the author's argument. Is his tone appropriate? Is his evidence clearly presented? Relevant and effective? Are potential counterarguments considered and met? Are conciliatory strategies used?

Questions for Discussion and Response

1. Which of Centerwall's reasons or evidence do you find most compelling? Why?

2. Which of Centerwall's recommendations have been adopted or made available? Are they making a difference?

3. Do you agree with Centerwall's recommendations? Do you think that they will make a difference? Why or why not?

4. Are there other suggestions that you would offer?

Caution: Children Watching

Suzanne Braun Levine

A graduate of Radcliffe College, Suzanne Levine (b. 1941) has held various reporting and editorial positions with magazines. She has edited the *Columbia Journalism Review* since 1989 and is co-editor of *The Decade of Women, a Ms. History of the Seventies* (1989). The following article appeared in the July/August 1994 issue of *Ms.* magazine. Here Levine combines her experience as a mother with the results of research to explore the problem of violence on television.

1   I am very proud of the fact that I have never (well, hardly ever) actually sent my kids off to watch TV just to get them out of my hair. I'm less proud of the fact that I don't exert very strong controls over what they watch; and there have even been times when I have caught an image of a horrendous act of violence out of the corner of my eye . . . and kept walking. When they were little, they were content to mellow out over endless reruns of *Mister Rogers' Neighborhood*, but as they got older—they are now eight and ten—and once we acquired a remote control, they began to graze around the dial and learned to snap back to something safe at the sound of an approaching adult.

Hours vs. Content

2   I do try to limit the number of hours they watch, and I'm pretty good at enforcing the no-TV-before-homework rule; overall my children certainly watch less than the national average of three and a half hours a day. (That is probably due as much to full-time child care as to my moral authority. Parents caught between the demands of a workday

and the obscenely outdated 3:00 P.M. school dismissal time have every reason to argue that watching TV—any kind of TV—is preferable to most of the alternatives.) But I must confess it makes me tired just to achieve that level of control; so when it comes to restricting content, I don't always have it in me to take on the philosophical questions of why violence is bad (because it rarely solves anything; because innocent people get hurt; because it is damaging to the soul) and why violence on TV is also bad, but in a different way (because by making it entertaining, TV shows trivialize it; because on TV violence is both glorified and simplified; and because it even gives people ideas).

3   When I have tried to engage them in dialogue over the issue, I find my children's sophistry daunting: *Teenage Mutant Ninja Turtles* is not violent, they claim, because it is a cartoon and cartoons are funny; *MacGyver* is not harmful, because the hero doesn't carry a gun; and, besides, they argue, both of the above are hard to distinguish from the news shows grownups watch. They would not be impressed, although I am, by statistics assembled in a 1992 *TV Guide* study, that put cartoons at the top of the list of violent fare, followed by toy commercials(!). And although MacGyver may be unarmed, the promotions for his show were cited as having among the highest number of incidents of gunplay and physical assault; the newscasts aired only a tame fraction of the same.

The Connection between Television and Violence

4   The National Center for Juvenile Justice estimates that there were 247,000 violent crimes committed by minors in 1992 (the most recent year for which data are available). We know that before they are out of grade school, most of our children have seen some 8,000 murders and 100,000 acts of violence on television. Any parent can tell you that there is a connection between these numbers, regardless of the ongoing debate among experts. In a poll of 71,000 *USA Weekend* readers, 86 percent said that they "notice changes in [their] kids' behavior after they've seen a violent show." While some parents I know witness increased aggressiveness, there are other responses; I have found that sometimes my kids become more passive, detached, "spaced out." It seems that boys are more drawn to the shows and more agitated by them; girls, for the most part, are repelled, even saddened by them.

5   Whether these differences in children's responses are a function of nature or environment is a perplexing issue for parents, one that highlights the gray area between cause and effect—and therefore complicates the debate over suggested remedies. For example, a bill proposed by Senators Daniel Inouye (D.-Hawaii) and Ernest Hollings (D.-S.C.) to limit the kinds of shows broadcast during peak viewing hours for children raises important questions about freedom and responsibility. Proponents of the bill point to studies that show children exposed to a heavy diet of blood and guts become desensitized to real violence and, at the same time, excessively fearful of becoming victims. But the very persuasive arguments against such legislation center around the risks of censorship. Television's First Amendment protection *is* limited by a federal statute that instructs the Federal Communication Commission to make sure that TV stations operate in the "public interest." But any further effort to restrict content opens a Pandora's box.[1] Whenever I say to myself, "Children shouldn't be allowed to see this

---

[1]   In Greek myth, Pandora opened a box containing all the evils of human life.—Ed.

stuff!" I am reminded that the same motives were behind efforts I deplored to remove from library shelves such "offensive material" as *The Diary of Anne Frank*, *The Adventures of Tom Sawyer*, and *Our Bodies, Ourselves*.

Necessary Violence

6   Efforts to explain the relationship between violence imagined and violence committed lead into other mazes. World-renowned child psychologist Bruno Bettelheim made the disturbing observation that the ghoulish fairy tales that show up in every culture are necessary vehicles for children to work out their violent impulses and to come to terms with their own hearts of darkness.

7   My own childhood experience with grim fairy tales (Hans Christian Andersen, in my case) has made me leery of parental prudishness. I remember my mother reading me a story called "The Girl Who Trod on a Loaf." It went something like this: "There was a very vain girl who loved her beautiful clothes. One muddy day she went out to buy bread, and on the way home, she came across a big puddle. She didn't want to get her party shoes dirty so she put the loaf down and stepped on it instead . . ." And? And nothing. I must have seen that there were more pages to the story, or perhaps I sensed my mother's internal censor cutting the narrative off, because soon after I was able to read, I went back to that story and found that indeed it goes on into a horrendous climax in which the girl is sucked through the mud puddle into a subterranean hell where she is punished for her vanity. To this day it is the only fairy tale I remember, and the horror of the story is compounded by the distress I felt at uncovering my mother's subterfuge.

8   The Television Violence Reduction Through Parental Empowerment Act—better known as the V-Chip Bill[2]—proposed by Edward Markey (D.-Mass.) would do just what my mother tried to do: banish the bad stuff. There is something too neat and clean about putting a microchip in the TV that would alert parents to violent programming and allow them to block it out. It has obvious immediate appeal, but does it give parents the false confidence that by pushing a button, they have fulfilled their responsibility to articulate and "sell" their values to their children? And how would you protect your children from the promos for the off-limits violent movies and series that, according to the *TV Guide* study, "have become a major source of televised violence"? On a strictly pragmatic level, I know that the Girl-Who-Trod-on-a-Loaf principle will ensure that my children will ultimately see the proscribed show—most likely at a friend's house—at which time they will probably pay closer attention than usual because of the taboo at home.

9   The instructive power of violent images is evoked by Walter Wink, a professor of biblical interpretation at Auburn Theological Seminary in New York City. In his book, *Engaging the Powers*, Wink writes that "violence is so successful as a myth precisely because it does not appear to be mythic in the least. Violence simply appears to be the nature of things." Children's entertainment, says Wink, reflects the "myth of redemptive violence" as played out in the classic plot line:

---

2   The V-chip bill has been passed. A ratings system has also been established.—Ed.

Children identify with the good guys so that they can think of themselves as good. This enables them to project out onto the bad guy their own repressed anger, violence, rebelliousness, or lust and then vicariously to enjoy their own evil by watching the bad guy initially prevail. . . . When the good guy finally wins, viewers are then able to reassert control over their own inner tendencies, repress them, and reestablish a sense of goodness. Salvation is guaranteed through identification with the hero.

10   The redemptive value of this morality play is challenged by such real-life findings as those of Leonard Eron, a professor of psychology at the University of Michigan who monitored a group of kids for over 20 years. He concluded that the more frequently they watched violent television at age 8, the more serious were the crimes they were convicted of by 30, the more aggressive their behavior when drinking, and the harsher the punishment they inflicted on their own children.

11   The crusading founder of Action for Children's Television, Peggy Charren, responds to such studies with characteristic directness: "Poverty is what you fix if you want to do something about violence." She spoke at a *TV Guide* symposium on television violence and children, where she described the work she has done to bring about changes in children's programming; although her group no longer exists, its mission has been picked up by the Washington, D.C.-based Center for Media Education. Meanwhile, public anxiety is rising to a desperate level. A Times Mirror Center for the People & the Press study has found that 80 percent of those interviewed felt violence on TV was "harmful to society." I am among that 80 percent. What can we do?

What the Public Can Do

12   First of all, we can protest—to the stations, the producers, the advertisers. (We should also praise, with equal vigor, shows that please us.) We can urge them to adopt a rating system that will alert parents to particularly lethal shows—ABC announced an 800-number to call for parental advisories on specific programming. We can try harder to monitor the programs that our kids watch. And we can try to put simulated violence into a larger moral context.

13   A recurrent worry expressed at the congressional hearings was that young viewers are seeing a sensitized kind of punching, stabbing, and killing. How to reconstruct violence with pain and suffering in their minds? "Make it grisly," advises TV critic Marvin Kitman. When Gloucester is blinded in the 1983 Granada TV production of *King Lear*, Kitman reminds us, we are forced to focus on "those bloody rags" he uses to cover the ravaged eye sockets, which "said something special about the enormity of the violence wrought." Kitman may have identified a positive use for "if it bleeds, it leads" format embraced by most local TV news programs: a reality fix on violence. When we invite our children to join us watching the news (after stressing to them that the world is not a uniformly violent place, that good and peaceful deeds are taking place all the time, only not on camera) we might be able to use the litany of crime and cruelty as "bloody rags"—reminders that when violence strikes, real people bleed and suffer and die, and real people mourn them. One local television station—WCCO in Minneapolis—is trying out a "family sensitive" five o'clock news broadcast that reports crime but saves the

pictures for eleven. This format has possibilities, but it remains to be seen whether newswriters will take the opportunity to create an instructive context that could help families deal with the crime stories.

14   In the opposite vein, we can find ways to heighten a child's awareness of the artifice that makes a pretend punch look real and a real actor appear to be blown apart by a sub-machine gun. I would welcome a violence counterpart to a very effective aid I have found for explaining advertising to my kids. I taped an HBO special called *Buy Me That* that demystifies the techniques used by makers of commercials for children's toys. One segment begins by showing an ad in which several kids are hopping happily on a sort of pogo stick, as if it were the easiest thing in the world; then the toy is given to a group of real kids who try to hop. They fall off; they hurt themselves; many give up. In another segment, the maker of cereal commercials explains that glue is poured onto cereal (yuk!) because it looks whiter than milk. My kids watch the show over and over and are experts at detecting similar gimmicks on TV commercials. The spell has clearly been broken.

Remedial Programming

15   It would certainly be possible to do the same with scenes of violence: to explain exactly how blood shows up on the clean white shirt of a victim or how the noise of a punch is made or how a retractable knife blade simulates a stabbing; and it would be great to interview a stunt man or woman about the athletic expertise it takes to jump from a building or simply to fall down dead.

16   Another kind of remedial programming would dramatize convincing alternatives to a body blow. We know that, in the same way that violent families produce violent children, a limited vocabulary of alternatives for conflict resolution produces a reflexive use of violence. Elizabeth Thoman, executive director of the Center for Media Literacy in Los Angeles, advises parents to explore with their children alternatives to stories that focus on violence as the solution to interpersonal conflict. In the same vein, Kitman proposes a policy modeled on the fairness doctrine, which used to require giving equal airtime to conflicting political points of view. It would mandate a balance of programs that deal with conflict and anger in ways that are nonviolent.

17   Kitman's suggestion recalls the truism that television's weakness is also its strength: it is one of the most effective teaching tools we have. Dr. Deborah Prothrow-Stith of the Harvard School of Public Health is thinking of ways to use the best of the medium to combat the worst. She suggests the campaign against smoking as an analogy. "We went from thinking it was the most glamorous thing in the world to finding it offensive and unhealthy," she points out at the *TV Guide* symposium. "How did we do that? It was education in the classroom. It was working with the media. We banned the advertising of cigarettes on television." She thinks we can perform a similar change of attitudes about violence. So does Charren, who has an imaginative suggestion of her own, a "media-literacy merit badge" for Girl and Boy Scouts. "It's a way to teach kids that the violence you see on television is not the solution to problems," she says.

18   While such ideas are building toward a nationwide campaign to heal the bruised hearts and minds of our children, I take my hat off to one innovative father I have heard about. He would let his child watch *Teenage Mutant Ninja Turtles* cartoons, but only if the child would imagine a fifth turtle named Gandhi. Later they would discuss how

"Ninja Gandhi" might get the turtles out of trouble without violence. I am equally impressed by the legendary parent who lures her kids away from the evil box with an invitation to an impromptu spring picnic. But my true (and secret) role model is the one who can effectively command "Turn the TV off—*now* . . . because I say so!" I am none of the above. But I'm trying. And I believe that as long as we keep struggling with the system and with our children, we are teaching at the only level that really counts—by what we do, not what we say.

Questions for Reading and Analysis

1. What is the author's purpose in writing? That is, what does she want to accomplish?

2. State the essay's thesis so that Levine's purpose is clear.

3. How do Levine's children try to justify their watching some violent shows?

4. What is the author's attitude toward government control of TV programming? What problem does she see with the V-chip?

5. Where does Levine stand on the connection between violent television shows and violence in society?

6. List the author's proposals for coping with violence on television.

7. In addition to mentioning three books that some people have wanted to censor, Levine refers to a story her mother read her. What is the point of her reference to "The Girl Who Trod on a Loaf"? What makes this an effective example?

8. Examine Levine's three "role model" parents in her closing paragraph. What does she accomplish by admitting that she is "none of the above"? What makes her final paragraph an effective conclusion?

Questions for Discussion and Response

1. When expressing her understanding of how parents can use the TV as a babysitter, Levine refers to "the obscenely outdated 3:00 P.M. school dismissal time." Should the school day be extended to more closely match parents' work schedules? Why or why not?

2. Is Levine right in asserting that the V-chip gives parents "false confidence" that they have fulfilled their responsibility? Is she right that children will find ways to see prohibited shows? Do these statements "ring true" based on your experience?

3. Levine argues that censorship is more damaging than being exposed to violent TV shows. How can it be more damaging? Do you agree that it is more damaging? Why or why not?

4. Which of the author's proposed solutions seem most sensible, most likely to be effective? Explain your position. Are there other proposals you would make? Explain.

Feds vs. First Amendment

Michael Grebb

Michael Grebb (b. 1970) holds a degree in journalism from Ohio University and is a senior editor at *Cablevision* magazine. The following article was published in *Cablevision* on June 28, 1999.

1   Forget V-chips. More draconian measures may be on the way.

2   Now that everyone agrees that violent movies and television shows are the previously unreported Eighth Sign that will hasten the Apocalypse, the feds have decided to move into publicity mode. This is the time when Washington power brokers start trying to get their names in the papers and news shows with promises to clamp down on the evil media.

3   The latest chapter in this saga is all about checking IDs. Really. The Clinton Administration has convinced the National Association of Theater Owners to require photo identification for young people trying to get into "R" rated movies. In addition, the theater owners have agreed to support a national study on the causes of violence and help out with a planned educational campaign to teach parents about the movie-ratings system. Despite the fact that movie ratings have been around for decades, "I think people don't really know the ratings system entirely," insists Tom Freedman, special assistant to the President and senior director of public policy.

4   Then there's the V-chip. The Federal Communications Commission held a self-congratulatory seance on June 9 to announce that new TV sets will indeed contain the V-chip as promised. FCC Commissioner Gloria Tristani, who heads the FCC's internal V-chip task force, quipped that in Washington, "when someone does what they're supposed to do when they say they're going to do it, that's news." FCC Chairman Bill Kennard made the most salient observation at the event when he noted, "We can't hope to be the national censor for everything that's going out over the airwaves and via satellite."

5   Interestingly, just as the V-chip gets ready to hit the streets, Sens. John McCain (R-Ariz.) and Joseph Lieberman (D-Conn.) have introduced the "21st Century Media Responsibility Act" pushing the makers of video games, TV shows, movies and music to come up with a uniform ratings system. How that will affect V-chips, which were made for today's rating system, is anyone's guess.

6   Of course, movie theaters were already supposed to be checking IDs. The V-chip rollout schedule is the same it always was. There are already ratings for video games, movies, TV shows and music. So why all the announcements? Well, Washington just loves window dressing. But that doesn't mean that more draconian measures—with real teeth—won't come in the future.

7   Luckily for us, the First Amendment—like those newly vigilant theater owners—always cards at the door. True, the feds usually figure out a way to sneak in the back service entrance, which is often left unlatched by incidents like the tragedy in Littleton, Colo. But once inside, they seldom take a drink. Rest assured that if no one is watching them closely, before long they will start drinking and the First Amendment could be too late to bounce them onto the street.

8   So far, nothing appears to be on the horizon that would amount to government censorship or coercion, but it's clear that a growing culture of potential demagoguery is

taking shape. In the coming months, more pressure will come to bear on the industry as the government floats countless trial balloons. Food for thought as the feds snoop around the bar, waiting to grab a drink when one of us isn't looking.

Questions for Reading and Analysis

1. What is Grebb's subject? What is his claim?
2. Grebb says that checking IDs at the movies and V-chips for TV are not new. Why, then, is he writing about these issues?
3. What is the author's view of a bill to extend V-chip ratings to video games and music?
4. What evidence does Grebb present to support his concern over possible government coercion or censorship? What is the primary support for his argument?
5. Examine the author's word choice. What are "draconian measures"? What image does he use in the last two paragraphs? How would you describe the essay's tone?

Questions for Discussion and Response

1. Think about the author's writing context. Does he expect his readers to share his views? How do you know?
2. If you were going to refute this argument, how would you proceed?
3. Do you find Grebb's argument to be convincing? Why or why not?

It's Not Just a Toy, It's an Indoctrination

Daphne White

A freelance writer and staff reporter for several periodicals, including *Higher Education Daily*, Daphne White (b. 1955) is currently founder and director of the Lion and Lamb Project, a non-profit organization seeking to inform parents and influence Congress on media and advertising actions, especially as they affect children. White's article on video-game advertising was published in the *Washington Post* on August 13, 2000.

1   The action figure your preschooler is clamoring for looks innocent enough, as these things go: "Primagen" is a green creature with five tentacles plus one lobster-like claw and one three-fingered hand. Its blue face—a cross between that of a turtle and ET— looks a bit sad. The label on the package says Primagen is a Turok character—not that you know what Turok is—suitable for "ages 4 and up."

2   So maybe you buy one.

3   If you do, you will be bringing home a Trojan horse. For inside Primagen's box is a "game code," or tip sheet, for Turok 2: Seeds of Evil—which is, in fact, an explicitly gory, frighteningly violent video game that is industry-rated "M"—for "mature" players at least 17 years old.

4   Certainly there is a significant distance between the plastic doll in the toy store and the adrenaline-pumping interaction of the video game. But there is no question that the cross-marketing of brands—in this case, the video game developer Acclaim licensing its Turok characters to the kiddie-toy maker Playmates—is a way to get 4-year-olds to bridge that distance, to make friends at an early age with characters most parents wouldn't want them to know.

5   It reminds me of Joe Camel, the swaggering cartoon hipster that R.J. Reynolds employed to sell cigarettes to "adults" (nudge, wink) until 1997. But to me, these toy-store action figures are even more sinister than smokin' Joe, because they're not making an understandable pitch in the public marketplace. Instead, they are stealth-marketing violence in a techno-world of video games that few parents comprehend.

6   Joe Camel was fired only after he was criticized at congressional hearings, denounced before the Federal Trade Commission, and highlighted in the Food and Drug Administration's proposal to regulate tobacco. The same kind of forceful public activism is justified against the marketing of violent entertainment to children.

7   Turok is far from the only super-bloodthirsty game with a kiddie connection: Quake, Metal Gear Solid, Resident Evil, Mortal Kombat and others have related action figures or hand-held electronic games for small children. None of these products carry any warnings that they are based on M-rated games. Like most toys, the only warning they might bear refers to possible choking hazards, as mandated by the Consumer Product Safety Commission.

8   As for "suitable for ages . . . " ratings, they are in many ways meaningless. Take the Duke Nukem action figure, based on an M-rated game that takes the player into porn theaters and strip bars (among other places), killing all the way. The action figure is labeled "for ages 10 and up." The reality is that today's pre-teens don't play with action figures. Little boys do.

9   Game companies introduce children to a brand early in the hope that they will identify with it and grow up with it. And they're certainly growing up fast.

10   "We're seeing kids going from Teletubbies to Sesame Street to Barney to Power Rangers," Michael Tabakin, director of sales promotion at Toys R Us, told the trade publication Kidscreen. "There is a natural progression. But from Teletubbies to Power Rangers, there isn't an awful lot of years there."

11   From Power Rangers to Seeds of Evil is also a quick jump. Marketers have a shorthand expression for the fast-forward nature of modern childhood: KAGOY, as in "kids are getting older younger." In a KAGOY world, no child is too tiny to be targeted: I've heard marketers talk about aiming products at children beginning at "age zero." By the age of 6—according to Kidscreen, as well as many toy marketers—children begin moving away from action figures and into hand-held electronic games such as Game Boy. By the time they are 8 or 10, the kids consider themselves ready for games rated Teen— supposedly aimed at ages 13 and older. And 12-year-olds get into Mature-rated computer games, the forbidden fruit that has been advertised to them since kindergarten.

12   There are few safeguards to prevent children from buying or downloading these games. (Several experts who have studied them say we shouldn't even use the word "games," but should call them what they are: "murder simulations." In fact, the U.S. military has increasingly been using simulation games to train soldiers. There is even a

version of the M-rated game "Doom" that has been adapted for military training—it's called "Marine Doom.") Most parents don't even know that video games have a rating system.

13   Like most mothers, I have no idea how to actually play video games. So to find out just what lurks inside Turok 2: Seeds of Evil, I rented it. Then I borrowed some experienced players of M-rated games—Mike, 13, and his brother Jeff, 15. Several girls were visiting, making up a sort of a peanut gallery. This is what we saw.

14   Turok is a "first-person shooter" game—in other words, the player sees the world through Turok's eyes and wields his weapon, which is visible at all times at the bottom of the screen. At first the weapon is a talon. The player uses it to rip up the Primagens, who gush bright red blood copiously onto the screen. After successfully disemboweling a few, the player is rewarded with an upgraded weapon: a pistol.

15   The visuals are darkly Gothic, the music ominous. One of the 15-year-old girls, who is not accustomed to playing video games, screamed whenever one of the Primagens burst onto the screen. "It's so dark and scary," she said, covering her eyes and hugging her knees to her chin. After a while, she left the room.

16   As more enemies are gruesomely killed, the player earns more weapons: a flying razor-blade disc, a grenade launcher, eventually a hand-held nuclear weapon. The grenade launcher leaves gaping holes in the victims' chests, and the ribs protrude. There is also a "cerebral bore," which drills into the enemies' skulls, sending their brains spewing out in a glutinous red mass.

17   "The whole point is to kill everybody," Mike explained, saying the game didn't really have enough of a plot for him. Jeff said it gave him a headache.

18   There's a Game Boy version of Turok 2, rated E for Everyone over age 6. It has the same name as the adult version, and the same basic plot, although the graphics are more cartoon-like and less explicit. The music is downright cheerful, as opposed to the dark, suspense-filled soundtrack of the M-rated game. There is no question that the E game is a playable advertisement for the M version. If it is not, why call them both Turok 2?

19   Too often, both government and the entertainment industry place all responsibility for monitoring the games children play on the shoulders of their parents. Certainly, parents need to be vigilant and provide their kids with guidance. But in a culture where $1 billion a year is spent by industries of all sorts to advertise their products directly to children, parents can't stem the tide of "entertainment" violence on their own.

20   Some tentative first steps have been taken. The Federal Trade Commission, under a request from President Clinton, is studying the marketing of violent "entertainment" to children—through video games, movies and music—with a report expected out next month. Congress—often under the leadership of Sen. Sam Brownback (R-Kan.)—has held a series of informational hearings on the issue.

21   More concretely, Sen. John McCain (R-Ariz.) and Sen. Joseph Lieberman (D-Conn.) have introduced a Uniform Ratings Bill and are planning to hold hearings on it after the FTC report comes out. This bill would mandate an end to the current hodge-podge of ratings systems and require that Hollywood, the video game industry and music industry work together to create a single ratings system. If the industries fail to come up with such a system, the FTC would be authorized to establish one.

22   This bill would be a large step forward in making the ratings clear and understandable to parents—but it does not address the advertising or marketing issues.

23 Toys and other products promoting adult-rated video games and movies to children need to be clearly labeled as such. Requiring a warning label in the style of the health warning label that appears on cigarettes would be a good start.

24 There's an obvious problem with these solutions: Any Internet-savvy kid can go online and download demo versions of truly violent games. If they're *really* savvy, kids can figure out how to get whole games. The way the Internet works, I don't see any practical way for government to keep them from doing that. But Congress and the FTC, which already have sought to limit children's access to online pornography, should at least seek the same limits on their access to violent video games.

25 Parents, of course, can and should try to monitor their children's online activity—but I know all too personally how difficult that is. I've been actively opposed to violent children's media since my own son was 2. But a few years ago, when he was in third grade, I mentioned that I lacked the computer gaming skills to study products that I was concerned about, and he cheerfully offered to help. "Mom, I can download Blood or Thrill Kill for you," he said—and he did.

26 We need government's help to keep such products out of our children's hands. At least it is worth the effort to put in some safeguards. To make a similar comparison, children under 18 aren't legally allowed to buy cigarettes. The fact that many younger children start smoking doesn't make that law less worthwhile.

27 The need for action was made clear last month, when four major public health groups—the American Medical Association, the American Psychological Association, the American Academy of Pediatrics and the American Academy of Child and Adolescent Psychiatry—issued a joint statement to Congress saying that "viewing entertainment violence can lead to increases in aggressive attitudes, values and behavior, particularly in children. Its effects are measurable and long-lasting. Moreover, prolonged viewing of media violence can lead to emotional desensitization toward violence in real life."

28 Significantly, the statement noted: "Although less research has been done on the impact of violent interactive entertainment [such as video games] on young people, preliminary studies indicate that the negative impact may be significantly more severe than that wrought by television, movies or music."

29 Like the tobacco industry of old, the entertainment and toy industries generally deny any responsibility and are unlikely to make changes on their own. Joe Camel did not disappear because concerned parents told their children to "just say no" to cigarettes. It took sustained legal and government action. This issue deserves no less.

Questions for Reading and Analysis

1. What is White's subject? What is her claim? Where does she state it?

2. White compares the marketing of action figures from video games to the cigarette advertising figure of Joe Camel. How are the two situations similar? How do they differ? How does this comparison serve as a persuasive strategy?

3. What product information is provided with action figures? What is not provided? How helpful are the age guidelines, according to White?

4. What is the new expression marketers use to emphasize the need to market to young children? At what age do children start playing handheld games? At what age are some into mature, violent video games?

5. What happens in the Turok 2 game?

6. What, in the author's view, should we call these games?

7. How does the Game Boy version differ from the M-rated version? What seems to be the purpose of the Game Boy version?

8. What is Congress doing to address what White sees as a problem? Why, according to White, is this action not enough?

9. What, according to various public-health groups, are the consequences of "entertainment violence" in general and video games in particular?

10. What are White's recommendations?

Questions for Discussion and Response

1. Have you played Turok 2 or other adult video games? If so, when did you start playing? Does your experience, direct or indirect, confirm what White says about the age progression from action figures to adult games?

2. If you have seen the adult video games, would you agree with White and the public-health groups that these games are violent—and violent enough to do some harm to heavy users? Why or why not?

3. Who seems to be White's targeted audience? Has she developed her argument effectively to influence that audience? (Consider her use of Joe Camel, her reporting of playing Turok 2, and her reference to the views of public-health groups.)

4. Do you agree with White's proposed solutions? Are there proposals you would reject? Add?

5. Should violent video games be restricted only to those 18 and over? Why or why not?

Lovely to Look Upon—Or Else

Gloria Steinem

Editor, writer, and lecturer, Gloria Steinem (b. 1934) has been cited in *World Almanac* as one of the 25 most influential women in America. She is the co-founder of *Ms.* magazine and of the National Women's Political Caucus and is the author of a number of books. She continues her association with *Ms.* as contributing editor. Her article on the media's treatment of women was published in the *New York Times* on January 16, 2000.

1   Just when you think it's safe to dislike a truly dislikable woman, she is treated so unfairly that you have to empathize. I'm speaking of the merciless humiliation of Linda Tripp.

2   For nearly two years, the media have focused almost totally on her looks, not her acts. I, too, wish she could have had a character transplant. But being born less than conventionally attractive is hardly a bigger crime than taping the confidences of a friend (plus entertaining your bridge group with them). Taken together, however, her

cosmetic and moral sins have been used to justify anything. Presidential wannabe Donald Trump called her "the personification of evil."

3   This hostility was her reported reason for undergoing unnecessary plastic surgery, a body carving so drastic that Lucianne Goldberg, her friend and co-conspirator, told *The National Enquirer;* "It looks like she's had a head transplant." As a well-socialized woman, Linda Tripp had internalized the fault—"I was responsible for the portrayal in the media by the way I looked," she told *People* magazine—rather than challenge the fault finders.

4   Most tragically, Ms. Tripp's transformation seems to have been in vain. John Goodman, the beefy comic, has said he will go right on donning drag and a fright wig to do his portrayal of Ms. Tripp, pre-surgery and weight loss, on *Saturday Night Live*.

5   Such ridicule may be new in scope, but not in purpose. It has long been the most popular way of disheartening and dehumanizing women, as well as less powerful groups of men. Think of the 19th century cartoons of ape-like Negroes and Irish, the portrayal of suffragists as "unnatural women," or the buck-toothed Japanese in World War II comic books. Powerful men may be lampooned, too, but not with the goal of proving their inferiority by looks alone. For example, think of all the funny-looking white guys who have been given a comparatively free ride, from paunchy robber barons to chicken-necked anchormen. There are also media moguls with one strand of hair twirled around their heads, and United States senators who look like turtles without shells. (Does this offend you? Of course. No one should be judged by the vulnerabilities of the flesh.)

6   Women are also attacked as a way of demeaning the men they are attached to. It's the civilized form of raping the enemy's women. Thus, Eleanor Roosevelt's looks were ridiculed because of her husband's controversial policies as well as her own, while less attractive and active wives of status quo presidents were left alone or praised.

7   Hillary Clinton and Monica Lewinsky reaped the whirlwind of hatred for Bill Clinton. And ridiculing Linda Tripp and Paula Jones was easier than taking on Kenneth Starr, the independent prosecutor.

8   It's not just the so-called unattractive woman who pays a price. No matter how long and hard she may work, a pretty woman often finds her success attributed to her looks, even to sleeping her way to the top. (If this were possible, there would be many more women at the top.) Compliments about her appearance may go to her husband or boss, as if she were an artwork or acquisition.

9   What is new is the all-pervasiveness and acceptability of cruel external judgments. In this media-saturated era, our every response is mediated. Since the media are also financed by products sold on insecurity, there has never been so much rating and berating of people, especially female people, for looks alone.

10   In recent years of backlash against women's advances—a free-floating hostility that stretches from rock lyrics to bombed abortion clinics, from Internet pornography to obstructionists in Congress—this attention has become suffused with meanness. Linda Tripp, Monica Lewinsky, and Hillary Clinton are just exaggerated versions of what may be in store for anyone.

11   Despite 30 years of feminism, for example, a reporter for *The Washington Post* can get away with writing of Monica Lewinsky, "She was born to be a voluptuous cartoon." Later in the same article, he claims that the female judge in Linda Tripp's trial "giggles."

12   Despite John McCain's status as a presidential candidate—and a media darling whose voting record on women's issues resembles that of Jesse Helms—he made a

homophobic joke about the looks of Hillary and Chelsea Clinton and Janet Reno. He wrote a letter of apology to President Clinton, but not to the women, telling the press that apologizing to Ms. Reno was unnecessary.

13 Jay Leno, whose wife campaigns admirably for the rights of women in Afghanistan, ridicules women's bodies with such anything-for-a-joke ferocity that an Afghan veil might seem a refuge. Still, he congratulates himself for not mentioning Chelsea Clinton. As he told Maureen Dowd, "Political humor is like the Mafia—everything's open game as long as you don't go after the families."

14 This seems to be the closest that a media power has come to a guideline for self-restraint. Call me crazy, but I think the media might aim for a higher standard than the Mafia. I have some other suggestions: Actions are fair game, but conditions of birth are not. Consider whether the ridicule of a woman would be directed against a man—whether the characterization of someone without power would be made of someone with it.

15 More to the point: what if the same style of reporting were directed at you?

Questions for Reading and Analysis

1. What is Steinem's general subject? Who are her particular examples?

2. What is Steinem's thesis, the claim of her argument? Where does she state it?

3. What did Linda Tripp do in response to media treatment of her? Did her actions appear to make any difference in her treatment?

4. Historically, what groups have been ridiculed by the media? What people are not lampooned?

5. What do these media attacks tell us about power in our society?

6. What reasons does Steinem give for the "all-persuasiveness and acceptability" of media attacks?

7. What are the standards that Steinem recommends?

Questions for Discussion and Response

1. Have you been aware of the media's treatment of women, particularly unattractive women? If so, what has been your reaction? If not, has Steinem made you alert to this condition?

2. Do you agree with the author that this treatment by the media is a serious problem? If you disagree, what explanation would you give to Steinem, Tripp, and Lewinsky?

3. How would you explain the media's abusive treatment of some people? Why do they do this?

4. What are the consequences to a society that lives with the constant cruel treatment of selected people by the media?

5. Do you agree with Steinem's recommended standards? If you do, how do you suggest that we get the media to adhere to them?

CHAPTER 11

Euthanasia

In this chapter four writers explore the issues associated with euthanasia. Currently, doctor-assisted suicide is illegal in the United States, but that has not kept some physicians from at least speeding up the end of a life by heavy doses of morphine. And Dr. Jack Kevorkian continues to challenge this law, spending time in prison after aiding patients who want to end their lives. As Drs. Peter A. Singer and Mark Siegler, and Rosalynn Carter make clear, though, the issue is not as simple as granting a patient's right to choose death. There are moral, medical, and public-policy issues wrapped up in the term *euthanasia*. Philosopher Peter Singer takes a unique approach of calling for an entirely new set of commandments—of ethical guidelines—for our time.

Reflect on the following questions before you read to enrich your analysis of and responses to the following articles on this timely topic:

1. Do you have a current position on doctor-assisted suicide? If so, what is your view?
2. What are the main sources of influence on your position: your reading and thinking, family, friends, religious beliefs? How strong are these influences on your life and values?
3. How much thought have you given to this issue? Do you think that the issue deserves more thought on your part?
4. Have you had the experience of losing a loved one who suffered at the end of his or her life? If so, how has that experience shaped your thinking?

Websites Related to This Issue

Euthanasia and Physician Assisted Suicide

www.religioustolerance.org/euthanas.htm

Good definitions of terms and broad overview of topic; claims to represent all sides.

Euthanasia World Directory

www.finalexit.org

Good links to legal decisions, books on the right to die, and right-to-die societies worldwide.

International Anti-Euthanasia Task Force

www.iaetf.org

Good links to articles and legal decisions.

Euthanasia.com
www.euthanasia.com
Contains many links to articles and to organizations related to the issue.

Euthanasia—A Critique*

Peter A. Singer and Mark Siegler

A graduate of the University of Toronto Medical School and holding a master's in public health from Yale University, Dr. Peter A. Singer (b. 1960) is assistant professor of medicine and associate director of the Center for Bioethics at the University of Toronto. He is the author of many articles on bioethics, end-of-life care, and euthanasia. Dr. Mark Siegler (b. 1941) obtained his medical degree from the University of Chicago, where he is director of the Center of Clinical Medical Ethics. Dr. Siegler is a recognized authority in the field of clinical medical ethics, having written more than 100 articles, six books, and the chapters on clinical ethics in two standard texts on internal medicine. In the following article, published in the *New England Journal of Medicine* on June 20, 1990, the authors provide a good review of the issues that are central to the debate on euthanasia and present their views on this issue.

1   A vigorous medical and political debate has begun again on euthanasia, a practice proscribed 2500 years ago in the Hippocratic oath.[1-4] The issue has been publicized recently in three widely divergent settings: a journal article, a legislative initiative in California, and public policy in the Netherlands.

2   The case of "Debbie" shows that euthanasia can be discussed openly in a respected medical journal. "It's Over, Debbie" was an anonymous, first-person account of euthanasia, published on January 8, 1988, in the *Journal of the American Medical Association*,[5-8] that stimulated widespread discussion and elicited spirited replies. Later in 1988, perhaps as a result, the Council on Ethical and Judicial Affairs of the American Medical Association reaffirmed its opposition to euthanasia.[9]

3   In California, a legislative initiative[10,11] has shown that in the near future euthanasia may be legalized in certain U.S. jurisdictions. A bill proposing a California Humane and Dignified Death Act was an attempt to legalize euthanasia through the referendum process, which allows California voters to approve controversial issues directly. Public-opinion polls reported that up to 70 percent of the electorate favored the initiative, and many commentators flatly predicted that the initiative would succeed. Nevertheless, the signature drive failed, collecting only 130,000 of the 450,000 required signatures. Attributing the failure to organizational problems, the proponents vowed to introduce the legislation again in California and in other states in 1990.

4   Experience in the Netherlands has shown that a liberal democratic government can tolerate and defend the practice of euthanasia. Although euthanasia is technically illegal in the Netherlands, in fact it is part of Dutch public policy today.[1,12-16] There is agreement at all levels of the judicial system, including the Supreme Court, that if physicians follow the procedural guidelines issued by a state commission, they will not

be prosecuted for performing euthanasia.[16] The Dutch guidelines emphasize five requirements: an explicit, repeated request by the patient that leaves no doubt about the patient's desire to die; very severe mental or physical suffering, with no prospect of relief; an informed, free, and consistent decision by the patient; the lack of other treatment options, those available having been exhausted or refused by the patient; and consultation by the doctor with another medical practitioner (and perhaps also with nurses, pastors, or others).[13] The usual method of performing euthanasia is to induce sleep with a barbiturate, followed by a lethal injection of curare.[1] An estimated 5000 to 10,000 patients receive euthanasia each year in the Netherlands.[16]

5   In view of these developments, we urge physicians to consider some reasons for resisting the move toward euthanasia. This article criticizes the main arguments offered by proponents and presents opposing arguments. The case for euthanasia is described in detail elsewhere.[10,17]

Critique of the Case for Euthanasia

6   In the debate about euthanasia, imprecision of language abounds. For the purposes of this article, euthanasia is defined as the deliberate action by a physician to terminate the life of a patient. The clearest example is the act of lethal injection. We distinguish euthanasia from such other acts as the decision to forgo life-sustaining treatment (including the use of ventilators, cardiopulmonary resuscitation, dialysis, or tube feeding—the issue raised in the Cruzan case[18]); the administration of analgesic agents to relieve pain; "assisted suicide," in which the doctor prescribes but does not administer a lethal dose of medication; and "mercy killing" performed by a patient's family or friends. The Dutch guidelines described above and the terms proposed in the California initiative represent two versions of euthanasia.

7   The case for euthanasia is based on two central claims.[10,17] First, proponents argue that patients whose illnesses cause them unbearable suffering should be permitted to end their distress by having a physician perform euthanasia. Second, proponents assert that the well-recognized right of patients to control their medical treatment includes the right to request and receive authanasia.

Relief of Suffering

8   We agree that the relief of pain and suffering is a crucial goal of medicine.[19] We question, however, whether the care of dying patients cannot be improved without resorting to the drastic measure of euthanasia. Most physical pain can be relieved with the appropriate use of analgesic agents.[20] Unfortunately, despite widespread agreement that dying patients must be provided with necessary analgesia,[21] physicians continue to underuse analgesia in the care of dying patients because of concern about depressing respiratory drive or creating addiction. Such situations demand better management of pain, not euthanasia.

9   Another component of suffering is the frightening prospect of dying shackled to a modern-day Procrustean bed, surrounded by the latest forms of high technology. Proponents of euthanasia often cite horror stories of patients treated against their will. In the past, when modern forms of live-saving technology were new and physicians were just learning how to use them appropriately, such cases occurred often; we have begun to move beyond that era. The law, public policy, and medical ethics now

acknowledge the right of patients to refuse life-sustaining medical treatment, and a large number of patients avail themselves of this new policy.[22-24] These days, competent patients may freely exercise their right to choose or refuse life-sustaining treatment; to carry out their preferences, they do not require the option of euthanasia.

10   We acknowledge that some elements of human suffering and mental anguish—not necessarily related to physical pain—cannot be eliminated completely from the dying process. These include the anticipated loss of important human relationships and membership in the human community, the loss of personal independence, the feeling of helplessness, and the raw fear of death. Euthanasia can shorten the duration of these emotional and psychological hardships. It can also eliminate fears about how and when death will occur. Finally, euthanasia returns to the patient a measure of control over the process of dying. These are the benefits of euthanasia, against which its potential harms must be balanced.

Individual Rights

11   The second argument in favor of euthanasia is based on the rights of the individual. Proponents contend that the right of patients to forgo life-sustaining medical treatment should include a right to euthanasia. This would extend the notion of the right to die to embrace the concept that patients have a right to be killed by physicians. But rights are not absolute. They must be balanced against the rights of other people and the values of society. The claim of a right to be killed by a physician must be balanced against the legal, political, and religious prohibitions against killing that have always existed in society generally and in medicine particularly. As the President's Commission for the Study of Ethical Problems in Medicine and Biomedical and Behavioral Research has observed, "Policies prohibiting direct killing may also conflict with the important value of patient self-determination. . . . The Commission finds this limitation on individual self-determination to be an acceptable cost of securing the general protection of human life afforded by the prohibition of direct killing."[22] We agree. In our view, the public good served by the prohibition of euthanasia outweighs the private interests of the persons requesting it.

The Case Against Euthanasia

12   The arguments against euthanasia are made from two perspectives: public policy and the ethical norms of medicine.

Euthanasia Is Perilous Public Policy

13   Proponents of euthanasia use the concept of individual rights to support their claim, but this same concept can be used for the opposite purpose. The argument against euthanasia on grounds of civil rights involves a consideration of the rights not just of those who would want euthanasia themselves but of all citizens. As public policy, euthanasia is unacceptable because of the likelihood, or even the inevitability, of involuntary euthanasia—persons being euthanized without their consent or against their wishes.

14   There are four ways in which the policy of voluntary euthanasia could lead to involuntary euthanasia. The first is "crypthanasia" (literally, "secret euthanasia").[15] In the Netherlands, for instance, it is alleged that vulnerable patients are euthanized without

their consent. Dutch proponents of euthanasia disavow these reports and claim that they are unrelated to the toleration of voluntary euthanasia. We suggest, however, that a political milieu in which voluntary euthanasia is tolerated may also foster involuntary euthanasia and lead to the killing of patients without consent. The second way in which involuntary euthanasia may occur is through "encouraged" euthanasia, whereby chronically ill or dying patients may be pressured to choose euthanasia to spare their families financial or emotional strain.[25] The third way is "surrogate" euthanasia. If voluntary euthanasia were permissible in the United States, the constitutional guarantees of due process, which tend to extend the same rights to incompetent as to competent patients, might permit euthanizing incompetent patients on the basis of "substituted judgment" or nebulous tests of "burdens and benefits." Finally, there is the risk of "discriminatory" euthanasia. Patients belonging to vulnerable groups in American society might be subtly coerced into "requesting" euthanasia. In the United States today, many groups are disempowered, disenfranchised, or otherwise vulnerable: the poor, the elderly, the disabled, members of racial minorities, the physically handicapped, the mentally impaired, alcoholics, drug addicts, and patients with the acquired immunodeficiency syndrome. In a society in which discrimination is common and many citizens do not have access even to basic health care, the legalization of euthanasia would create another powerful tool with which to discriminate against groups whose "consent" is already susceptible to coercion and whose rights are already in jeopardy.

15   The proponents of euthanasia contend that procedural safeguards, such as the five provisions of the Dutch guidelines noted above, will prevent involuntary euthanasia. They claim further that society permits many dangerous activities if adequate procedural safeguards are provided to reduce risk and protect the public. We agree that safeguards would reduce the risk of involuntary euthanasia, but they would not eliminate it entirely. In the case of euthanasia, safeguards have not been adequately tested and shown to be effective. Even in their presence, we are concerned that patients could be euthanized without their consent or even against their wishes. Even one case of involuntary euthanasia would represent a great harm. In the current era of cost containment, social injustice, and ethical relativism, this risk is one our society should not accept.

Euthanasia Violates the Norms of Medicine

16   In addition to being perilous as public policy, euthanasia violates three fundamental norms and standards of medicine. First, as noted above, it diverts attention from the real issues in the care of dying patients—among them, improved pain control, better communication between doctors and patients, heightened respect for the patient's right to choose whether to accept life-sustaining treatment, and improved management of the dying process, as in hospice care. The hospice movement has demonstrated that managing pain appropriately and allowing patients control over the use of life-sustaining treatments reduce the need for euthanasia.

17   Second, euthanasia subverts the social role of the physician as healer. Historically, physicians have scrupulously avoided participating in activities that might taint their healing role, such as capital punishment or torture. Physicians should distance themselves from euthanasia to maintain public confidence and trust in medicine as a healing profession.

18   Third, euthanasia strikes at the heart of what it means to be a physician.[26] Since the time of Hippocrates, the prohibition against it has been fundamental to the medical profession and has served as a moral absolute for both patients and physicians. This prohibition has freed physicians from a potential conflict of interest between healing and killing and in turn has enabled patients to entrust physicians with their lives. It has enabled physicians to devote themselves singlemindedly to helping patients achieve their own medical goals. This prohibition may even have encouraged medical research and scientific progress, because physicians, with the consent of patients, are motivated to perform risky, innovative procedures that are aggressive and sometimes painful, with a total commitment to benefit the patient.

Conclusions

19   Pressure to legalize euthanasia will surely increase in an era of spiraling health care costs, but it must be resisted. Euthanasia represents a development that is dangerous for many vulnerable patients and that threatens the moral integrity of the medical profession. Physicians must become more responsive to the concerns of patients that underlie the movement for euthanasia and must provide better pain management, more compassionate terminal care, and more appropriate use of life-sustaining treatments. But physicians need to draw the line at euthanasia. They and their professional associations should defend the integrity of medicine by speaking out against the practice. Finally, even if euthanasia is legalized in some jurisdictions, physicians should refuse to participate in it, and professional organizations should censure any of their members who perform euthanasia.

References

[1]Angell M. Euthanasia. N Engl J Med 1988; 319:1348–50.

[2]Singer PA. Should doctors kill patients? Can Med Assoc J 1988; 138:1000–1.

[3]Kinsella TD, Singer PA, Siegler M. Legalized active euthanasia: an Aesculapian tragedy. Bull Am Coll Surg 1989; 74(12):6–9.

[4]Wanzer SH, Federmann DD, Adelstein SJ, et al. The Physician's responsibility toward hopelessly ill patients: A second look. N Engl J Med 1989; 320:844–9.

[5]It's over, Debbie. JAMA 1988; 259:272.

[6]Vaux KL. Debbie's dying: mercy killing and the good death. JAMA 1988; 259:2140–1.

[7]Gaylin W, Kass LR, Pellegrino ED, Siegler M. 'Doctors must not kill' JAMA 1988; 259:2139–40.

[8]Lundberg GD. 'It's over, Debbie' and the euthanasia debate. JAMA 1988; 259:2142–3.

[9]The Council on Ethical and Judicial Affairs of the American Medical Association. Euthanasia. Report: C (A-88). AMA council report. Chicago: American Medical Association, 1988:1.

[10]Risley RL. A humane and dignified death: a new law permitting physician aid-in-dying. Glendale, Calif.: Americans Against Human Suffering, 1987.

[11]Parachini A. Mercy, murder, & mortality: perspectives on euthanasia: the California Humane and Dignified Death Initiative. Hastings Cent Rep 1989; 19(1):Suppl:10–2.

[12]Pence GE. Do not go slowly into that dark night: mercy killing in Holland. Am J Med 1988; 84:139–41.

[13]Rigter H, Borst-Eilers E, Leenen HJJ. Euthanasia across the North Sea. BMJ 1988; 297:1593–5.

[14]Rigter H. Mercy, murder, & morality: euthanasia in the Netherlands: distinguishing facts from fiction. Hastings Cent Rep 1989; 191(1):Suppl:31–2.

[15]Fenigsen R. Mercy, murder & morality: perspectives on euthanasia: a case against Dutch euthanasia. Hastings Cent Rep 1989; 19(1):Suppl:22–30.

[16]de Wachter MAM. Active euthanasia in the Netherlands. JAMA 1989; 262:3316–9.

[17]Humphry D. Wickett A. The right to die: understanding euthanasia. New York: Harper & Row, 1986.

[18]Angell M. Prisoners of technology: the case of Nancy Cruzan. N Eng J Med 1990; 322:1226–8.

[19]Cassell EJ. The nature of suffering and the goals of medicine. N Engl J Med 1982; 306:639–45.

[20]Foley KM. The treatment of cancer pain. N Engl J Med 1985; 313:84–95.

[21]Angell M. The quality of mercy. N Engl J Med 1982; 306:98–9.

[22]President's Commission for the Study of Ethical Problems in Medicine and Biomedical and Behavioral Research. Deciding to forgo life-sustaining treatment: a report on the ethical, medical, and legal issues in treatment decisions. Washington, D.C.: Government Printing Office, 1983.

[23]The Hastings Center. Guidelines on the termination of life-sustaining treatment and the care of the dying: a report. Briarcliff Manor, N.Y.: Hastings Center, 1987.

[24]Emanuel EJ. A review of the ethical and legal aspects of terminating medical care. Am J Med 1988; 84:291–301.

[25]Kamisar Y. Some non-religious views against proposed "mercy-killing" legislation. Minn Law Rev 1958; 42:969–1042.

[26]Kass LR. Neither for love nor money: why doctors must not kill. Public Interest 1989; 94(winter):25–46.

Questions for Reading and Analysis

1. What debate do the authors join in with their essay?

2. Examine the format of this essay; what kind of paper is it?

3. How many people in the Netherlands apparently employ euthanasia each year? Summarize the required guidelines physicians must follow to use euthanasia there without prosecution.

4. What do the authors want to accomplish in their opening references to the article, the California initiative, and the practice of euthanasia in the Netherlands?

5. What position do Singer and Siegler take on euthanasia?

6. Analyze the essay's organization, indicating the paragraphs that belong in each part.

7. How do Singer and Siegler define *euthanasia*? What is not included in their definition?

8. What are the two reasons of those who argue for euthanasia? Summarize the authors' rebuttal of each reason.

9. What do the authors accomplish in paragraph 10?

10. What two approaches do Singer and Siegler take in arguing against euthanasia?

11. Why is euthanasia bad public policy? What could voluntary euthanasia lead to? What characteristics of modern society make, in the authors' view, legalizing euthanasia too risky?

12. Why is euthanasia inconsistent with the norms of medicine? What do the authors want physicians to do?

Questions for Discussion and Response

1. Do you agree that interest in euthanasia is increasing? What evidence would you cite to support your answer?

2. Which of the two arguments supporting euthanasia is the most convincing, in your view? Which of the arguments against euthanasia is the most convincing? Why?

3. Do you agree that we live in an "era of cost containment, social injustice, and ethical relativism"? Why or why not? The authors do not provide evidence for this assertion; what evidence can you provide either to support or to challenge the assertion?

4. Where do you stand on the issue of legalizing euthanasia? Be prepared to defend your position.

In Defense of Voluntary Euthanasia

Sidney Hook

A philosopher, educator, and author, Sidney Hook (1902–1989) taught philosophy at New York University and was a senior research fellow at the Hoover Institution. He published numerous articles and books on philosophy throughout his busy career, and his autobiography, *Out of Step: An Unquiet Life in the Twentieth Century,* appeared in 1987. The following emotional argument for euthanasia, incorporating his personal experience with grave illness, was published in the *New York Times* in 1987.

1 A few short years ago, I lay at the point of death. A congestive heart failure was treated for diagnostic purposes by an angiogram that triggered a stroke. Violent and painful hiccups, uninterrupted for several days and nights, prevented the ingestion of food. My left side and one of my vocal cords became paralyzed. Some form of pleurisy set in, and I felt I was drowning in a sea of slime. At one point, my heart stopped beating; just as I lost consciousness, it was thumped back into action again. In one of my lucid intervals during those days of agony, I asked my physician to discontinue all life-supporting services or show me how to do it. He refused and predicted that someday I would appreciate the unwisdom of my request.

2 A month later, I was discharged from the hospital. In six months, I regained the use of my limbs, and although my voice still lacks its old resonance and carrying power I no

longer croak like a frog. There remain some minor disabilities and I am restricted to a rigorous, low sodium diet. I have resumed my writing and research.

3 My experience can be and has been cited as an argument against honoring requests of stricken patients to be gently eased out of their pain and life. I cannot agree. There are two main reasons. As an octogenarian, there is a reasonable likelihood that I may suffer another "cardiovascular accident" or worse. I may not even be in a position to ask for the surcease of pain. It seems to me that I have already paid my dues to death—indeed, although time has softened my memories they are vivid enough to justify my saying that I suffered enough to warrant dying several times over. Why run the risk of more?

4 Secondly, I dread imposing on my family and friends another grim round of misery similar to the one my first attack occasioned.

5 My wife and children endured enough for one lifetime. I know that for them the long days and nights of waiting, the disruption of their professional duties and their own familial responsibilities counted for nothing in their anxiety for me. In their joy at my recovery they have been forgotten. Nonetheless, to visit another prolonged spell of helpless suffering on them as my life ebbs away, or even worse, if I linger on into a comatose senility, seems altogether gratuitous.

6 But what, it may be asked, of the joy and satisfaction of living, of basking in the sunshine, listening to music, watching one's grandchildren growing into adolescence, following the news about the fate of freedom in a troubled world, playing with ideas, writing one's testament of wisdom and folly for posterity? Is not all that one endured, together with the risk of its recurrence, an acceptable price for the multiple satisfactions that are still open even to a person of advanced years?

7 Apparently those who cling to life no matter what, think so. I do not.

8 The zest and intensity of these experiences are no longer what they used to be. I am not vain enough to delude myself that I can in the few remaining years make an important discovery useful for mankind or can lead a social movement or do anything that will be historically eventful, nor less event-making. My autobiography, which describes a record of intellectual and political experiences of some historical value, already much too long, could be posthumously published. I have had my fill of joys and sorrows and am not greedy for more life. I have always thought that a test of whether one had found happiness in one's life is whether one would be willing to relive it—whether, if it were possible, one would accept the opportunity to be born again.

9 Having lived a full and relatively happy life, I would cheerfully accept the chance to be reborn, but certainly not to be reborn again as an infirm octogenarian. To some extent, my views reflect what I have seen happen to the aged and stricken who have been so unfortunate as to survive crippling paralysis. They suffer, and impose suffering on others, unable even to make a request that their torment be ended.

10 I am mindful too of the burdens placed upon the community, with its rapidly diminishing resources, to provide the adequate and costly services necessary to sustain the lives of those whose days and nights are spent on mattress graves of pain. A better use could be made of these resources to increase the opportunities and qualities of life for the young. I am not denying the moral obligation the community has to look after its disabled and aged. There are times, however, when an individual may find it pointless to insist on the fulfillment of a legal and moral right.

11   What is required is no great revolution in morals but an enlargement of imagination and an intelligent evaluation of alternative uses of community resources.

12   Long ago, Seneca observed that "the wise man will live as long as he ought, not as long as he can." One can envisage hypothetical circumstances in which one has a duty to prolong one's life despite its costs for the sake of others, but such circumstances are far removed from the ordinary prospects we are considering. If wisdom is rooted in knowledge or the alternatives of choice, it must be reliably informed of the state one is in and its likely outcome. Scientific medicine is not infallible, but it is the best we have. Should a rational person be willing to endure acute suffering merely on the chance that a miraculous cure might presently be at hand? Each one should be permitted to make his own choice—especially when no one else is harmed by it.

13   The responsibility for the decision, whether deemed wise or foolish, must be with the chooser.

Questions for Reading and Analysis

1. What subject is introduced in Hook's opening two paragraphs? What strategy does he use as an introduction?

2. What have some people seen in his experience? For what two reasons does Hook disagree with them?

3. What is Hook's position on euthanasia? Where does he state his claim?

4. Analyze the nature of the author's argument. What kind of evidence does he provide?

5. When others observe the pleasures of life the author can still experience, what are Hook's responses? Summarize his reasons for not wanting to continue to live on in his eighties.

Questions for Discussion and Response

1. Hook argues that he should be free to make choices about his life—or death—as long as he does not harm others. Do you agree with this philosophy, in general? Do you agree that it applies to the choice of euthanasia? Why or why not?

2. What is your position on euthanasia? What are your reasons?

3. Hook writes of "intelligent evaluation," of "wisdom," "knowledge," and "a rational person." How would you describe his philosophy? What does he value as essential to being human?

4. The article before Hook's—by Drs. Singer and Siegler—and this essay by Hook make for interesting comparisons beyond their differing views on euthanasia. Do a comparative analysis of the style and approach of the two pieces. Which approach to this particular issue do you find most effective? How does the answer to this question depend in part on the particular audience for each piece?

A Quality End of Life

Rosalynn Carter

The former First Lady from Plains, Georgia, Rosalynn Carter (b. 1927) holds several honorary degrees and has won many awards for her work, especially in the area of mental health. She has written *First Lady from Plains* (1984) and *Helping Yourself Help Others: A Book for Caregivers* (1994) and serves as honorary chair of Last Acts, a national coalition to improve care for the terminally ill. The following article, reflecting her interest in how the dying are cared for, appeared in the *Washington Post* on June 30, 1997.

1   The Supreme Court's refusal to grant physician-assisted suicide as a constitutional right for all Americans obviously is a crucial decision that will affect thousands of people in this country. But the court's decision must be viewed separately from an equally important question: What will we as a society demand as a standard for good care at the end of life? Properly given, such care might substantially reduce the number of patients considering physician-assisted suicide.

2   The overwhelming evidence from the largest clinical study ever conducted with dying people shows that Americans too often face death in pain and attached to machines. That study, published in the *Journal of the American Medical Association* in 1995, was a wake-up call to many who are concerned about improving care at the end of life. This goal is attainable and should be a much higher priority for medical schools, hospitals, insurance companies, the clergy, and other groups. And if these professionals are to help us, as a society and as individuals, we must overcome our fears about discussing death.

3   I helped care for my father and grandfather, who, like many people, died from prolonged illnesses. My experiences taught me that the unpleasant prospect of our deaths does not preclude meaningful experiences at the end of our lives. Although some people may be sad and physically compromised during their last months and years, these days also can be an opportunity to appreciate life's last chapter and to reach out again to loved ones.

4   We must focus not on whether we have the right to ask a doctor to end our lives prematurely, but on the changes that need to take place to ensure that systems exist to help us die with dignity.

5   Doctors should be encouraged to devote at least part of their training to nursing homes and hospices as well as hospital emergency rooms.

6   Insurance companies, managed-care organizations and the federal government should be obliged to pay for long-term care that supports people's emotional needs as well as their physical needs.

7   Clergy and others who address spiritual needs could collaborate more with medical-service providers to address health needs of patients that cannot be addressed by tests or surgeries.

8   Hospitals and lawyers can stop being fearful of lawsuits, and let doctors prescribe the dosages that are required for pain relief.

9   Jimmy and I have written living wills, but legal documents to express our wishes are not enough to prepare us for our final days. We must talk honestly with our loved ones, our clergy, and our doctors and nurses about the choices we would make if confronted with a chronic or terminal illness.

10   The old cliché is true: Dying is part of living. Any definition of "dying well" must include respecting patient's wishes, reducing pain, involving care givers throughout the process, minimizing financial burden and encouraging spiritual growth until the very moment of death.

Questions for Reading and Analysis

1. What was the occasion that led to Carter's writing? Where do you find the answer to this question?

2. What is her subject? What is her thesis?

3. How does her claim connect to the issue of euthanasia? Instead of asking for a doctor to end life, what should we focus on?

4. According to a recent study, how do many Americans face death?

5. What must we, as individuals, do as a first step to improving end-of-life care?

6. What do those involved in health care need to do?

7. What kinds of positive experiences may be a part of the last months of life?

Questions for Discussion and Response

1. Instead of arguing specifically for or against euthanasia, Carter comes at this issue from a different perspective. Do you think that her approach contributes usefully to the discussion? Why or why not? (Before responding to this question, you may want to review what Singer and Siegler and Sydney Hook have to say about managing a patient's pain.)

2. Do you find it difficult to talk to loved ones about end-of-life care? If so, has this article helped at all to get you to act? Have you prepared a living will? If so, why did you do it? If not, why not?

3. Imagine that you, or a loved one, has a terminal illness. What is your idea of "dying well"? What would you like to provide a loved one, or what would you like to have, in the final months of life?

Rethinking Life and Death

Peter Singer

With degrees from Melbourne and Oxford Universities, Peter Singer (b. 1946) is a philosophy professor at Monash University in Australia. He is the editor of a book on ethics as well as *The Great Ape Project*, a collection of articles defending the rights of primates, a concern he is best known for. The following material comes from Singer's book *Rethinking Life and Death: The Collapse of Our Traditional Ethics,* published in 1994.

1   Like cosmology before Copernicus, the traditional doctrine of the sanctity of human life is today in deep trouble. Its defenders have responded, naturally enough, by trying to patch up the holes that keep appearing in it. They have redefined death so that they can remove beating hearts from warm, breathing bodies, and give them to others with better prospects, while telling themselves that they are only taking organs from a corpse. They have drawn a distinction between "ordinary" and "extraordinary" means of treatment, which allows them to persuade themselves that their decision to withdraw a respirator from a person in an irreversible coma has nothing to do with the patient's poor quality of life. They give terminally ill patients huge doses of morphine that they know will shorten their lives, but say that this is not euthanasia, because their declared intention is to relieve pain. They select severely disabled infants for "non-treatment" and make sure that they die, without thinking of themselves as killing them. By denying that an individual human being comes into existence before birth, the more flexible adherents of the sanctity of life doctrine are able to put the life, health, and well-being of a woman ahead of that of a fetus. Finally, by putting a taboo on comparisons between intellectually disabled human beings and nonhuman animals, they have preserved the species boundary as the boundary of the sanctity of life ethic, despite overwhelming evidence that the differences between us and other species are differences of degree rather than of kind.

2   The patching could go on, but it is hard to see a long and beneficial future for an ethic as paradoxical, incoherent and dependent on pretense as our conventional ethic of life and death has become. New medical techniques, decisions in landmark legal cases and shifts of public opinion are constantly threatening to bring the whole edifice crashing down . . .

3   It is time for another Copernican revolution. It will be, once again, a revolution against a set of ideas we have inherited from the period in which the intellectual world was dominated by a religious outlook. Because it will change our tendency to see human beings as the centre of the *ethical* universe, it will meet with fierce resistance from those who do not want to accept such a blow to our human pride. At first, it will have its own problems, and will need to tread carefully over new ground. For many the ideas will be too shocking to take seriously. Yet eventually the change will come. The traditional view that all human life is sacrosanct is simply not able to cope with the array of issues that we face. The new view will offer a fresh and more promising approach.

Rewriting the Commandments

4   What will the new ethical outlook be like? I shall take . . . [three] commandments of the old ethic . . . and show how they need to be rewritten for a new ethical approach to life and death. But I do not want the . . . [three] new commandments to be taken as something carved in stone. I do not really approve of ethics carved in stone anyway. There may be better ways of remedying the weaknesses of the traditional ethic. The title of this book suggests an ongoing activity: we can rethink something more than once. The point is to start, and to do so with a clear understanding of how fundamental our rethinking must be.

First Old Commandment:
Treat all human life as of equal worth

5   Hardly anyone really believes that all human life is of equal worth. The rhetoric that flows so easily from the pens and mouths of popes, theologians, ethicists and some doctors is belied every time these same people accept that we need not go all out to save a severely malformed baby; that we may allow an elderly man with advanced Alzheimer's disease to die from pneumonia, untreated by antibiotics; or that we can withdraw food and water from a patient in a persistent vegetative state. When the law sticks to the letter of this commandment, it leads to what everyone agrees now is an absurdity, like Joey Fiori's survival for almost two decades in a persistent vegetative state, or the continuation of respirator support for the anencephalic Baby K. The new approach is able to deal with these situations in the obvious way, without struggling to reconcile them with any lofty claims that all human life is of equal worth, irrespective of its potential for gaining or regaining consciousness.

First New Commandment:
Recognise that the worth of human life varies

6   This new commandment allows us frankly to acknowledge . . . that life without consciousness is of no worth at all. We can reach the same view—. . . as British judges did in considering the condition of Baby C—about a life that has no possibility of mental, social or physical interaction with other human beings. Where life is not one of total or near total deprivation, the new ethic will judge the worth of continued life by the kind of balancing exercise recommended by Lord Justice Donaldson in the case of Baby J, taking into account both predictable suffering, and possible compensations.

7   Consistent with the first new commandment, we should treat human beings in accordance with their ethically relevant characteristics. Some of these are inherent in the nature of the being. They include consciousness, the capacity for physical, social and mental interaction with other beings, having conscious preferences for continued life, and having enjoyable experiences. Other relevant aspects depend on the relationship of the being to others, having relatives for example who will grieve over your death, or being so situated in a group that if you are killed, others will fear for their own lives. All of these things make a difference to the regard and respect we should have for a being.

8   The best argument for the new commandment is the sheer absurdity of the old one. If we were to take seriously the idea that all human life, irrespective of its capacity for consciousness, is equally worthy of our care and support, we would have to root out of medicine not only open quality of life judgments, but also the disguised ones. We would then be left trying to do our best to prolong indefinitely the lives of anencephalics, cortically dead infants, and patients in a persistent vegetative state. Ultimately, if we were really honest with ourselves, we would have to try to prolong the lives of those we now classify as dead because their brains have entirely ceased to function. For if human life is of equal worth, whether it has the capacity for consciousness or not, why focus on the death of the brain, rather than on the death of the body as a whole?

9   On the other hand, if we do accept the first new commandment, we overcome the problems that arise for a sanctity of life ethic in making decisions about anencephalics, cortically dead infants, patients in a persistent vegetative state, and those who are declared to be brain dead by current medical criteria. In none of these cases is the really

important issue one of how we define death. That question has had so much attention only because we are still trying to live with an ethical and legal framework formed by the old commandment. When we reject that commandment, we will instead focus on ethically relevant characteristics like the capacity for enjoyable experiences, for interacting with others, or for having preferences about continued life. Without consciousness, none of these are possible; therefore, once we are certain that consciousness has been irrevocably lost, it is not ethically relevant that there is still some hormonal brain function, for hormonal brain function without consciousness cannot benefit the patient. Nor can brain-stem function alone benefit a patient, in the absence of a cortex. So our decisions about how to treat such patients should not depend on lofty rhetoric about the equal worth of all human life, but on the views of families and partners, who deserve consideration at a time of tragic loss. If a patient in a persistent vegetative state has previously expressed wishes about what should happen to her or him in such circumstances, they should also be taken into account. (We may do this purely out of respect for the wishes of the dead, or we may do it in order to reassure others, still alive, that their wishes will not be ignored.) At the same time, in a public health-care system, we cannot ignore the limits set by the finite nature of our medical resources, nor the needs of others whose lives may be saved by an organ transplant.

Second Old Commandment:
Never intentionally take innocent human life

10   The second commandment should be rejected because it is too absolutist to deal with all the circumstances that can arise. We have already seen how far this can be taken, in the Roman Catholic Church's teaching that it is wrong to kill a fetus, *even if that would be the only way to prevent both the pregnant woman and the fetus dying.* For those who take responsibility for the consequences of their decisions, this doctrine is absurd. It is horrifying to think that in the nineteenth and early twentieth century it was probably responsible for the preventable and agonising deaths of an unknown number of women in Roman Catholic hospitals or at the hands of devout Roman Catholic doctors and midwives. This could occur if, for example, the head of the fetus became stuck during labour, and could not be dislodged. Then the only way of saving the woman was to perform an operation known as a craniotomy, which involves inserting a surgical implement through the vagina and crushing the cranium, or skull, of the fetus. If this was not done, the woman and fetus would die in childbirth. Such an operation is obviously a last resort. Nevertheless, in those difficult circumstances, it seems appalling that any well-intentioned healthcare professional could stand by while both woman and fetus die. For an ethic that combines an exceptionless prohibition on taking innocent human life with the doctrine that the fetus is an innocent human being, however, there could be no other course of action. If the Roman Catholic Church had said that performing a craniotomy is permissible, it would have had to give up either the absolute nature of its prohibition on taking innocent human life, or its view that the fetus is an innocent human being. Obviously, it was—and remains—willing to do neither. The teaching still stands. It is only because the development of obstetric techniques now allows the fetus to be dislodged and removed alive that the doctrine is no longer causing women to die pointlessly.

11   Another circumstance in which the second old commandment needs to be abandoned is—as the British law lords pointed out in deciding the Bland case—when life

is of no benefit to the person living it. But the only modification to the absolute pro-hibition on taking human life that their lordships felt able to justify in that case—to allow a life to be taken intentionally by withholding or omitting treatment—still leaves the problem of cases in which it is better to use active means to take innocent human life. The law found Dr Nigel Cox guilty of the attempted murder of Mrs Lillian Boyes, despite the fact that she begged for death, and knew that she had nothing ahead of her but a few more hours of agony. Needless to say, no law, no court, and no code of medical ethics, would have required Dr. Cox to do everything in his power to prolong Mrs Boyes' life. Had she suddenly become unable to breathe on her own, for instance, it would have been quite in accordance with the law and the traditional ethical view not to put her on a respirator—or if she was already on one, to take it away. The very thought of drawing out the kind of suffering that Mrs Boyes had to en-dure is repugnant, and would have been regarded as wrong under the traditional ethic as well as the new one. But this only shows how much weight the traditional ethic places on the fine line between ending life by withdrawing treatment, and ending it by a lethal injection. The attitude of the traditional ethic is summed up in the famous couplet:

> Thou shalt not kill; but need'st not strive
> Officiously to keep alive.

12   These lines are sometimes uttered in revered tones, as if they were the wisdom of some ancient sage. One doctor, writing in the *Lancet* to defend the non-treatment of infants with spina bifida, referred to the lines as "The old dictum we were taught as med-ical students".[1] This is ironic, for a glance at the poem from which the couplet comes—Arthur Hugh Clough's "The Latest Decalogue"—leaves no doubt that the intention of this verse, as of each couplet in the poem, is to point out how we have failed to heed the spirit of the original ten commandments. In some of the other couplets, this is un-mistakable. For example:

> No graven images may be
> Worshipped, except the currency.

13   Clough would therefore have supported an extended view of responsibility. Not killing is not enough. We are also responsible for the consequences of our decision not to strive to keep alive.[2]

Second New Commandment:
Take responsibility for the consequences of your decisions

14   Instead of focusing on whether doctors do or do not intend to end their patients' lives, or on whether they end their patients' lives by withdrawing feeding tubes rather than giving lethal injections, the new commandment insists that doctors must ask whether a decision that they foresee will end a patient's life is the right one, all things considered.

15   By insisting that we are responsible for our omissions as well as for our acts—for what we deliberately don't do, as well as for what we do—we can neatly explain why the doctors were wrong to follow the Roman Catholic teaching when a craniotomy was the only way to prevent the deaths of both mother and fetus. But there is a price to pay

for this solution to the dilemma too: unless our responsibility is limited in some way, the new ethical approach could be extremely demanding. In a world with modern means of communication and transport, in which some people live on the edge of starvation while others enjoy great affluence, there is always something that we could do, somewhere, to keep another sick or malnourished person alive. That all of us living in affluent nations, with disposable incomes far in excess of what is required to meet our needs, should be doing much more to help those in poorer countries achieve a standard of living that can meet their basic needs is a point on which most thoughtful people will agree; but the worrying aspect of this view of responsibility is that there seems to be no limit on how much we must do. If we are as responsible for what we fail to do as we are for what we do, is it wrong to buy fashionable clothes, or to dine at expensive restaurants, when the money could have saved the life of a stranger dying for want of enough to eat? Is failing to give to aid organisations really a form of killing, or as bad as killing?

16   The new approach need not regard failing to save as equivalent to killing. Without some form of prohibition on killing people, society itself could not survive. Society can survive if people do not save others in need—though it will be a colder, less cohesive society. Normally there is more to fear from people who would kill you than there is from people who would allow you to die. So in everyday life there are good grounds for having a stricter prohibition on killing than on allowing to die. In addition, while we can demand of everyone that he or she refrain from killing people who want to go on living, to demand too much in the way of self-sacrifice in order to provide assistance to strangers is to confront head-on some powerful and near-universal aspects of human nature. Perhaps a viable ethic must allow us to show a moderate degree of partiality for ourselves, our family and our friends. These are the grains of truth within the misleading view that we are responsible only for what we do, and not for what we fail to do.

17   To pursue these questions about our responsibility to come to the aid of strangers would take us beyond the scope of this book—but two conclusions are already apparent. First, the distinction between killing and allowing to die is less clear-cut than we commonly think. Rethinking our ethic of life and death may lead us to take more seriously our failure to do enough for those whose lives we could save at no great sacrifice to our own. Second, whatever reasons there may be for preserving at least a part of the traditional distinction between killing and allowing to die—for example, maintaining that it is worse to kill strangers than to fail to give them the food they need to survive—these reasons do not apply when, like Lillian Boyes, a person wants to die, and death would come more swiftly and with less suffering if brought about by an act (for example, giving a lethal injection) than by an omission (for example, waiting until the patient develops an infection, and then not giving antibiotics).

Third Old Commandment:
Never take your own life, and always try to prevent others taking theirs
18   For nearly two thousand years, Christian writers have condemned suicide as a sin. When we should die, said Thomas Aquinas, is God's decision, not ours.[3] That view became so deeply embedded in Christian nations that to attempt suicide was a crime, in some cases punished—ideologues lack a sense of irony—by death. The prohibition on suicide was one element of a general view that the state should enforce morality and act paternalistically towards its citizens.

19   This view of the proper role of the state was first powerfully challenged by the nine-teenth-century British philosopher John Stuart Mill, who wrote in his classic *On Liberty:* "The only purpose for which power can be rightfully exercised over any member of a civilised community, against his will, is to prevent harm to others. His own good, either physical or moral, is not a sufficient warrant."[4]

20   Incurably ill people who ask their doctors to help them die at a time of their own choosing are not harming others. (There could be rare exceptions, for example if they have young children who need them; but people who are so ill as to want to die are generally in no position to care adequately for their children.) The state has no grounds for interfering, once it is satisfied that others are not harmed, and the decision is an enduring one that has been freely made, on the basis of relevant information, by a competent adult person. Hence the new version of the third commandment is the direct opposite of the original version.

Third New Commandment:
Respect a person's desire to live or die

21   John Locke . . . defined a "person" as a being with reason and reflection that can "consider itself as itself, the same thinking thing, in different times and places." This concept of a person is at the centre of the third new commandment. Only a person can *want* to go on living, or have plans for the future, because only a person can even understand the possibility of a future existence for herself or himself. This means that to end the lives of people, against their will, is different from ending the lives of beings who are not people. Indeed, strictly speaking, in the case of those who are not people, we cannot talk of ending their lives against or in accordance with their will, because they are not capable of having a will on such a matter. To have a sense of self, and of one's continued existence over time, makes possible an entirely different kind of life. For a person, who can see her life as a whole, the end of life takes on an entirely different significance. Think about how much of what we do is oriented towards the future—our education, our developing personal relationships, our family life, our career paths, our savings, our holiday plans. Because of this, to end a person's life prematurely may render fruitless much of her past striving.

22   For all these reasons, killing a person against her or his will is a much more serious wrong than killing a being that is not a person. If we want to put this in the language of rights, then it is reasonable to say that only a person has a right to life.[5]

Notes

[1]Dr. L. Haas, from a letter in the *Lancet*, 2 November 1968; quoted from S. Gorovitz (ed.), *Moral Problems in Medicine*, Prentice-Hall, Englewood Cliffs, NJ, 1976, p. 351.

[2]Clough's "The Latest Decalogue" can be found in Helen Gardner (ed.), *The New Oxford Book of English Verse*, Oxford University Press, Oxford, 1978.

[3]Thomas Aquinas, *Summa Theologica*, II, ii, Question 64, Article 5.

[4]John Stuart Mill, *On Liberty*, J.M. Dent & Sons, London, 1960, pp. 72–3.

[5]This position is associated with Michael Tooley's influential article, "Abortion and Infanticide," *Philosophy and Public Affairs*, vol.2, 1972, pp. 37–65; for a slightly different argument to the same conclusion, see also Michael Tooley, *Abortion and*

Infanticide, Oxford University Press, Oxford, 1983. Similar views have been defended by several philosophers and bioethicists, among them H. Tristram Engelhardt, Jr, *The Foundations of Bioethics*, Oxford University Press, New York, 1986; R. G. Frey, *Rights, Killing and Suffering*, Blackwell, Oxford, 1983; Jonathan Glover, *Causing Death and Saving Lives*, Penguin, Harmondsworth, 1977; John Harris, *The Value of Life*, Routledge and Kegan Paul, London, 1985; Helga Kuhse, *The Sanctity of Life Doctrine in Medicine: A Critique*, Oxford University Press, Oxford, 1987; James Rachels, *The End of Life*, Oxford University Press, Oxford, 1986 and *Created from Animals*, Oxford University Press, Oxford, 1991. See also my own *Practical Ethics*, Cambridge University Press, Cambridge, 1979, 2nd ed., 1993.

Questions for Reading and Analysis

1. What is Singer's subject?

2. What are the key concepts of the traditional ethic of human life? Why does Singer believe that the revolution against the traditional views of life and death will succeed?

3. What is Singer's claim?

4. What is the author's attitude toward his new commandments?

5. What is the first old commandment? What is Singer's first new commandment?

6. What is the second old commandment? What is Singer's second new commandment?

7. What is the third old commandment? What is Singer's third new commandment? Explain the distinction he makes about a person and a non-person.

8. Consider Singer's approach. How clever and/or helpful is it to organize his argument by old and new commandments?

Questions for Discussion and Response

1. Evaluate the strength of the argument for each new commandment. Do you think that all arguments are equally effective, or do you find one stronger than the others? Explain.

2. Is your evaluation influenced by your own position on euthanasia? If so, how?

3. What is your reaction to Singer's emphasis on taking responsibility for one's actions as part of the second new commandment?

4. If you disagree with any of the author's new commandments, how would you refute his argument?

CHAPTER 12

Guns and Society

The four articles on the issue of gun control take both different positions *and* different approaches to this controversial issue. Reflecting on these questions before you read will enrich your study of this issue:

1. What does the expression "gun control" mean to you? Do you think that what you mean by the term is about the same as what most people mean by it? Do you have evidence for your answer to this question?
2. Is part of the conflict over this issue generated by differing ideas of the meaning of the expression?
3. Do you have a position on this issue? If so, what is it?
4. What are the main sources of influences on your position—your reading and thinking, family, friends, religious beliefs? How strong are these influences?
5. What, if anything, do you think you may be able to learn from someone whose views on this issue differ from yours?

Websites Related to This Chapter's Topic

Handgun Control and the Center to Prevent Handgun Violence

www.handguncontrol.org

A grass-roots organization founded in 1974 by Sarah Brady, this organization's home page provides links to recent articles, news headlines, and facts about guns.

GunCite

www.guncite.com

Provides a long list of links to all aspects of the issue.

Center for Responsive Government

www.opensecrets.org/news/guns/index.htm

The center's Web page called Gun Control vs. Gun Rights provides information on congressional votes and contributions by lobbies to representatives.

National Rifle Association

www.nra.org

This large gun lobby provides commentary and news updates on gun-control issues.

America's Unchecked Epidemic

Richard Harwood

Richard Harwood has been a syndicated columnist writing about both national and international issues. His column on violence and guns appeared on December 1, 1997.

1   Americans have invested a great deal of wealth and effort in this century to keep death at bay, and they have had a lot of success. Cholera, smallpox, typhoid have been eliminated in this country. Other diseases that once killed millions now are cured easily or prevented. The average American's life span has been extended by nearly 30 years.

2   Health and medical care have become our leading industry. We spend more on these services than we spend for food, housing, automobiles, clothes or education.

3   But neither money nor science has brought us any closer to solving or even moderating one epidemic in American life: violence. For at least a century and probably longer we have been the most murderous "developed" society on earth. Since 1980 nearly 400,000 Americans have died at the hands of fellow citizens—more than the number of Americans who died on the battlefields of World War I and World War II combined. It would take eight Vietnams to fill as many graves.

4   Our propensity to violence cannot be explained by the cliché that America is a uniquely "lawless" society. Franklin Zimring and Gordon Hawkins of the University of California write: "The reported rates [per 100,000 people] of both violent and nonviolent crime in the United States . . . are quite close to those found in countries like Australia, Canada and New Zealand." The rate of criminal assault is higher in those countries than here. In robberies, the United States is second to Poland and similar in rate to Italy, Australia, Czechoslovakia, Canada and England. Scandinavian robbery rates are not strikingly lower than those in this country. A study in 1992 revealed that London had a higher overall crime rate than New York City, including 66 percent more thefts and 57 percent more burglaries. But New York has 11 times as many murders.

5   So it is not crime that sets us apart. We have no more pickpockets, shoplifters, burglars, robbers or brawlers than Western Europe or the British Isles. But we have a surplus of killers—a large surplus. Our homicide rate is 20 times the rate in England and Wales, 10 times the rate in France and Germany and is exceeded only by a few Latin American countries, notably Colombia, Mexico and Brazil.

6   Why this is so is a mystery to medical scientists (psychiatrists and psychologists included) and to anthropologists and social scientists as well. Politicians have no answers. They wage futile "wars" on crime, expand the police forces and the offenses punishable by death, keep a million citizens in prison, beef up law enforcement agencies and equip them with everything from tanks to helicopter gunships. Through it all, the homicide rate remains almost constant—roughly eight to 10 murders for every 100,000 people in the course of a year.

7   When 20,000 to 25,000 people are being murdered every year, you've got a problem. It's not a huge problem in the context of death in America; more than 2.25 million of us die every year from all causes—including 30,000 to 40,000 from AIDS, 40,000 or so in automobile accidents and about 30,000 as a result of suicide.

8   But even in that context, murder is a serious problem. It poisons society with fear and suspicion, turns large areas of our cities into combat zones and contributes to urban flight.

9   Still, despite our cowboy image in much of the world, it is irrational to assume that a propensity for murder is rampant in the American character; 99.99 percent of us never murder anyone. And there is no uniformity among those who do. Some regions have more violent traditions than others, the South in particular: Louisiana's murder rate today is 20 times the rate in Vermont. Men are more murderous than women. Cities have proportionately more murders than suburbs and rural areas. The 20 largest U.S. cities have 11.5 percent of the American population but account for 34 percent of the reported homicides.

10   African Americans, heavily concentrated in these cities, are at far more risk of death by homicide than nonblacks. They are 13 percent of the American population, but they account for 45 percent of homicide victims and 55 percent of suspects charged with homicide, according to calculations by Zimring and Hawkins. Many theories are offered to explain the relatively high level of lethal violence in these urban communities, but none has been validated. Whatever the "causal" factors, the number and percentage of blacks charged with homicide in the age groups most prone to violence—15 to 34— is tiny, roughly a tenth of one percent. And if black homicides were ignored in the calculations, the U.S. homicide rate still would be three to five times greater than the rates in Europe and Britain.

11   Zimring and Hawkins conclude that the one "causal" factor that sets us apart from the rest of the world is the huge arsenal of handguns—estitmated at from 50 million to 70 million—that makes it possible to settle with finality the passionate domestic arguments and street disputes that produce most of our homicides. Eliminating handguns would not eliminate rage or conflict but certainly would lower the life-threatening consequences of these encounters.

12   People will argue that other deadly weapons—knives, blunt instruments, poison and the noose—will remain available to people who want to kill. Sure. They're available all over the world, too, but nowhere else is murder so commonplace.

13   It would take political courage to do anything about the gun problem, and it is in short supply in Washington. But no other remedy—medical, chemical, technological or spiritual—is at hand or even on the horizon.

Questions for Reading and Analysis

1. What is America's "unchecked epidemic"?

2. How many Americans have died at the hands of other citizens since 1980? How does this number compare to those who died in Vietnam?

3. Can America's violent deaths be explained by America's being a lawless society? What evidence does Harwood provide to answer this question?

4. What is the United States' homicide rate compared to England's? How many Americans are murdered each year?

5. What are some of the social consequences of our murder rate?

6. What areas of the country have the highest murder rate? What racial group is most at risk?

7. What causal explanation does Harwood give to account for our murder rate?

8. What claim are we to infer from Harwood's concluding paragraphs?

9. Consider the author's opening two paragraphs. What does he gain by his approach?

10. In paragraph 10, Harwood explains that the black murder rate is not significant in making the United States such a murderous country. Why does he include this information?

Questions for Discussion and Response

1. Do any of Harwood's statistics surprise you? If so, which ones are most surprising? Why?

2. Many people get "exercised" over the gun-control issue. How would you describe Harwood's approach and tone? Is his argument enhanced by his approach and style? Why or why not?

3. Does Harwood make a convincing argument for gun control? Explain your response.

Gun Registration: It's Common Sense

Sarah Brady

An advocate for gun-control legislation since her husband was shot and severely disabled when President Ronald Reagan was shot, Sarah Brady (b. 1942), a graduate of the College of William and Mary and a former teacher, is chair of Handgun Control and the Center to Prevent Handgun Violence. This article was published June 11, 1999, shortly after the student shootings in Littleton, Colorado.

1   In an interview on *Good Morning, America* last week, the president said that we should consider registering guns just as we register cars. He's right, of course. In the same way that we require the registration of cars, we should require that the sale or transfer of firearms—at least handguns—be reported to law enforcement authorities.

2   Registration is a vital law enforcement tool. It's a crime-solver. By permitting guns to be readily traced back to their last lawful owner, police can more readily identify who pulled the trigger and, if the shooter is a prohibited purchaser, who illegally sold or transferred the gun to the shooter. When police are unable to trace a gun, a criminal and his accomplice can, quite literally, get away with murder. And that's what happens all too often.

3   It took law enforcement officials two weeks to determine who sold the TEC-9 assault pistol to the two shooters in Littleton, Colo. And if the seller hadn't identified

himself, the police might never have made the link. The police in Littleton were not searching for the killers; the two killed themselves. But in many criminal investigations, the shooters and their accomplices are not identified and, thanks in part to weak gun laws, they may never be caught.

4 The gun lobby will insist that the president has made a critical miscalculation. No sitting president since Lyndon B. Johnson has dared suggest that firearms should be registered. The NRA would like everyone to believe that gun registration, in whatever form, is the third rail of American politics.

5 Some third rail. A public opinion survey conducted last year by the National Opinion Research Center found that 85 percent of Americans, including 75 percent of gun owners, support mandatory registration of handguns.

6 It all comes down to common sense. Almost everywhere else in the world, sales or transfers of firearms must be recorded. Some countries, such as Japan and Great Britain, have banned handguns altogether.

7 Meanwhile, in this country, it took a massacre the size of Littleton for congressional leaders to acknowledge that background checks should be conducted at gun shows. And it was regarded as a giant step forward when the Senate a few weeks ago voted to prohibit the sale of AK-47s and Uzis to children. Requiring gun manufacturers to provide a simple safety lock with every handgun they sell was, by American standards, a major accomplishment.

8 So as the House of Representatives prepares to consider the Senate-passed gun legislation, congressional leaders are urging caution. Some on both sides are suggesting that going beyond the Senate-passed bill may be going too far. Establishing a minimum 72-hour waiting period on handgun purchases so that law enforcement can do a more thorough background check? Not likely. Limiting handgun purchases to one handgun per month so that professional gun traffickers cannot go around buying 50 or 100 guns a month? Forget it, too controversial.

9 And while the House might consider prohibiting the sale of handguns at gun shows to those between the ages of 18 and 21, it might stop short of prohibiting 18-year-olds from actually possessing handguns. It doesn't seem to matter that 18- and 19-year-olds lead the nation in homicides. These youth shouldn't be limited, so the argument goes, to possessing rifles and shotguns. They need handguns.

10 Is it any wonder that the president seemed upset the other day when he was questioned about his commitment to tougher gun laws? This president has done far more than any other to advance our thinking about guns, and yet Congress is still playing political games. When the Senate took up the issue of guns a few weeks ago, the first amendment that passed was one that would have gutted our gun laws, stopping Brady background checks on criminals reclaiming guns at pawn shops and permitting federally licensed gun dealers to sell at gun shows in all 50 states. Now some in the House want to limit the time that can be taken for background checks at gun shows—even if the records are showing a problem, such as a felony arrest, that needs more investigation. Allowing felons to get guns in the interest of promoting quick gun sales makes no sense.

11 When is this insanity going to end? Anyone who bemoans the "inconvenience" that these new gun-show restrictions might impose on gun-show promoters should be

required to talk to as many victims of gun violence as I have. Let them start with some of the 13 mothers who every day lose a child to gun violence. And then let them talk to some of the many children who have lost classmates.

12   The simple truth is that we don't need to ban guns in this country to reduce gun violence. All we need are common-sense gun laws. Since the Brady Law was passed in 1993, gun crimes have dropped sharply. But we still have so far to go. Common sense, when it comes to guns, remains in short supply. At least in Congress.

Questions for Reading and Analysis

1. How can gun registration help police solve crimes?
2. What percentage of Americans support handgun registration? What percentage of gun owners support such registration?
3. What countries ban all handguns? How common are records of gun sales and transfers?
4. How many mothers lose a child to gun violence each day?
5. When Brady writes, in paragraph 8, "Not likely" and "Forget it, too controversial," what is she really saying? Does she agree with members of Congress who have doubts about passing gun legislation?
6. What is Brady's claim? Where does she state it?
7. Brady is, of course, associated with lobbying for gun control. What does she gain by asserting that "we don't need to ban guns in this country to reduce gun violence"?

Questions for Discussion and Response

1. Are you among the 85 percent who support gun registration? Why or why not?
2. Should sales of semi-automatics to children be banned? Should ownership be banned except for military personnel? Explain you position.
3. Should 18- or 19-year-olds be allowed to buy handguns? Why or why not?
4. Should those attending gun shows be limited to the purchase of one gun? Why or why not?
5. How would you account for America's fascination with guns and the country's murder rate?

Sliding Down the Slippery Slope

Tanya K. Metaksa

A graduate of Smith College, Tanya Metaksa has served as a member of the National Rifle Association Board of Directors and is currently Executive Director of the NRA Institute for Legislative Action. She is the author of many articles in defense of the right to own guns and a book on self-protection, *Safe, Not Sorry* (1997). The following article was published in the June 1997 issue of *American Hunter*.

1   If you doubt for a second how this [the Clinton] Administration regards our right to keep and bear arms, forget it fast. We now have in black and white what Bill Clinton, Al Gore and Janet Reno think of your right to keep and bear arms.

2   The following is from a letter written on behalf of the president by Ronnie L. Edelman, a Department of Justice official:

3   "The Second Amendment, whether in regard to handguns or all guns, is a matter of growing scholarly debate. The current state of federal law does not recognize that the Second Amendment protects the right of private citizens to possess firearms of any type. Instead, the Second Amendment is deemed to be a collective right belonging to the state and not to an individual. Accordingly, the Second Amendment is interpreted by this administration as prohibiting the federal government from preventing a state government from forming or having a state-recognized militia force. With this understanding in mind, the sources of citizens' authority to possess a handgun have never been particularly identified in American law. Since the beginning of the creation of various gun control laws, beginning in 1934, no administration has sought to clarify this ambiguity."

4   I suggest, Mr. Edelman, that you read the Gun Control Act of 1968. Congress affirmed the gun-owning rights of the individual citizen, stating that the law was not intended to "place any undue or unnecessary Federal restrictions or burdens on law-abiding citizens with respect to the acquisition, possession, or use of firearms appropriate to the purpose of hunting, trap-shooting, target shooting, personal protection, or any other lawful activity. . . ."

5   Edelman did manage to stumble onto the truth—the Second Amendment is a matter of growing scholarly debate. But if Edelman or his bosses had bothered to follow that debate over the past two decades, they'd know that it is rather one-sided. They'd also know their side, the "collective right" side, is losing and losing overwhelmingly.

6   As historian Joyce Lee Malcolm told Congress in 1955: "It is very hard to find an historian who now believes it [the Second Amendment] is only a collective right. As it has become more thoroughly researched, there is general consensus that in fact it is an individual right. There is no one for me to argue against anymore."

7   Unfortunately, the Clinton-Gore Administration doesn't let the facts slow down its drive to vilify gun owners, such as those hunters and target shooters who own cartridges that President Clinton shamelessly says "cut through a police vest like a hot knife through butter." Nor does this Administration worry about facts in its rush to add new groups of citizens, such as those guilty of *misdemeanor* domestic abuse offenses, to the Gun Control Act's prohibited list.

8   To further its civil liberties-trashing agenda, this Administration encourages political rather than scientific research at the Federal Centers for Disease Control and Prevention. One of the latest gunowner smears appears in the February 1997 issue of *The American Journal of Public Health*. It would be laughable if it were not so serious.

9   The authors of this taxpayer-funded propaganda masquerading as science suggest that those of us who own "automatic or semi-automatic firearms are more likely . . . to binge drink frequently," than those who prefer other types of guns. The authors not only admit that there is "no strong consensus within the alcohol research community on the

definition of binge drinking," they also show shocking ignorance of the technical features of firearms. "What distinguishes automatic and semi-automatic firearms" from other types of firearms, they write, "is that they can be spray fired."

10   The authors are smart enough to leave themselves an out. They write: "[I]t is doubtful that binge drinking causes an individual to purchase a certain type of firearm or that owning a particular type of firearm causes one to drink heavily." But you can see where this latest "research" is heading. One night Peter Jennings or Dan Rather will dramatically announce: "According to government research, semi-automatic firearms are not only more deadly than other types, they also are the guns of choice of those who drink in excess."

11   It won't matter that millions of responsible American gunowners know that guns and alcohol don't mix, and that we constantly preach that fact. Facts won't matter to the Clinton crowd when it next seeks to deprive another whole category of citizens of their Second Amendment rights.

12   The fact that as responsible gunowners, we make responsible choices in our lives doesn't matter much in some offices on Capitol Hill either. Rep. Charles Schumer (D-NY) demands to know "Who needs to buy more than one handgun a month?" Schumer, along with Sen. Barbara Boxer (D-CA) and others, also think it's the government's business to dictate how you store property in your home. In their eyes you can't be trusted to be responsible enough to store your guns safely. Do it their way or one day in the future you'll be held criminally liable if a thief breaks into your home, steals a gun and then misuses it in a crime.

13   We will never lose our civil liberties all at once, by dictator decree. If the day ever comes in America when we lose our guns, it will be because once we compromised our beliefs and started down the slippery slope of waiting periods, gun bans, mandatory storage laws and the like. It became easier and easier just to go along for the ride.

Questions for Reading and Analysis

1. Based on information in the headnote, what views on gun control do you expect to find in this article? What details in the headnote contribute to your expectations?

2. What is Edelman's explanation of the meaning of the Second Amendment?

3. What does the Gun Control Act of 1968 say about individual ownership of guns? Does this law alter or render incorrect what Edelman says about the Bill of Rights?

4. What new group did the Clinton administration want to prohibit from owning guns?

5. The author objects to recent research that shows a correlation between ownership of semi-automatic firearms and binge drinking. Does she provide any evidence that the research is careless or inaccurate?

6. Has the author answered the concerns of researchers, or of elected officials who want to restrict gun sales or require proper storage, by saying that millions of Americans are responsible gun owners? What kind of argument strategy is she using?

7. What is Metaksa's thesis? Where does she state it?

8. What is the author's tone? What specific word choice helps to create her tone?

Questions for Discussion and Response

1. Is it, in your opinion, a good idea to restrict those convicted of domestic abuse from gun ownership? Why or why not?

2. Do you think Metaksa's argument will be convincing to many of her intended readers? If so, why? If not, why not?

3. Is Metaksa's argument effective for you? Why or why not? Is your answer affected by your position on gun control?

4. What seems to be her purpose in writing? What does she want to accomplish?

All Fired Up; The NRA Makes a Lot of Noise, but That Doesn't Help the Gun Owners of America

Osha Gray Davidson

Osha Davidson is an adjunct associate professor at the University of Iowa and a freelance writer. He is regularly published in newspapers and magazines and is the author of several books, including *Under Fire: The NRA and the Battle for Gun Control* (1993) and *The Enchanted Braid: Coming to Terms with Nature on the Coral Reef* (1998). His article on gun-control issues was published by the *Washington Post* on June 4, 2000.

1   I was 10 years old the first time I fired a gun. It was love at first shot.

2   I loved the heft of the well-made .22-caliber bolt-action rifle. I loved the loud crack of the explosion when I squeezed the trigger, and the puff of smoke from the muzzle. I even grew to love the acrid smell of the spent gunpowder.

3   But most of all, I loved that I was able to hit the target dead center nearly every time. I was something of a Wunderkind at Camp Esther K. Newman on the Nebraska prairie in the summer of 1964. Being the top marksman was an intoxicating experience for a boy who had previously associated sports with a single emotion: humiliation. And then there were the shiny brass medals I earned as I steadily shot my way up the ranking system: Pro-Marksman, Marksman, Marksman-First Class. Stamped across each medal were three words: National Rifle Association.

4   Today those words are freighted with political baggage—both self-generated and imposed by outsiders—but back then I barely noticed them. All I knew about the NRA was that it sponsored the camp shooting program. And, in fact, there wasn't a whole lot more to know about the gun group of that era. It did some lobbying against gun control measures, but by and large the NRA was then primarily a hunting and sport-shooting organization. In 1968, when Congress was considering banning mail-order gun sales, the NRA's leader, retired Army general Franklin Orth, testified before a House committee—in favor of the bill. "We do not think any sane American, who calls himself an American," declared the general, "can object to placing into this bill the instrument

which killed the president of the United States." Orth was referring to long rifles like the Mannlicher-Carcano that Lee Harvey Oswald used to kill John F. Kennedy. As it happens, Oswald bought the weapon through a mail-order ad in the NRA's *American Rifleman* magazine.

5   One wonders what Orth, a model of spit-and-polish military rectitude, would think of today's NRA, whose leaders malign federal law enforcement officers as "jack-booted government thugs," allege that the president of the United States is "willing to accept a certain level of killing to further his political agenda" and oppose virtually all gun control legislation.

6   My guess? He'd think they're nuts. He'd also raise an eyebrow, I bet, over the NRA's decision to thrust itself squarely into the fall [2000] elections by attacking Vice President Gore's presidential run and by launching a multimillion-dollar stealth campaign in support of George W. Bush and congressional candidates in 20 states.

7   I come to those conclusions as a former NRA member, and as a journalist who spent a decade researching the group and writing a book about its tumultuous, fascinating and increasingly radical history.

8   Whatever your opinion of the gun lobby, let's stipulate this fact: In the past 25 years, the group has been extraordinarily effective in preventing the enactment of meaningful gun laws, especially after hard-core extremists took over the NRA in 1977 and booted out the more moderate hunters and sport shooters in the leadership at the group's annual meeting in Cincinnati. To gauge the NRA's success, just look at the only gun control legislation pending in Congress. Partisans have been battling for more than a year over a bill that would. . .what? Require background checks on prospective purchasers at gun shows. Ye gods! For all the hyperbolic rhetoric, you'd think this wisp of a bill called for the immediate confiscation of all guns—right down to my old .22.

9   Which is exactly what the NRA tells its members.

10   The NRA's power comes in large part from convincing its membership of this axiomatic deception: that any gun bill, no matter how mild or reasonable, is the first step down a slippery slope that ends in total gun confiscation and the establishment of a police state. This NRA-induced paranoia explains the bizarre T-shirt so popular at the group's annual convention last month in Charlotte. The shirt features a picture of Adolf Hitler striking the Sieg Heil salute, over the caption "All in Favor of Gun Control, Raise Your Right Hand."

11   Gun Control = Nazi tyranny. Not a bad equation for whipping up the troops. Or for recruiting members who'll fork over a minimum of $35 a year to stop National Socialism, er, gun control. That fee is just the first installment in this crusade. Members are subject to a never-ending barrage of fundraising letters, known as "action alerts," each a variation on the same apocalyptic theme: Without your immediate help (check, cash or credit card accepted), the barbarians will be goose-stepping through the gates by nightfall!

12   If you haven't seen these appeals and think I'm exaggerating, here are a few examples:

13   "[O]ur government creeps toward authoritarian rule. . . . Wake up, America! Little by little, your freedom and safety are being robbed. . . ."

14   "[G]ood people . . . could have their doors kicked in and their property taken by a police state driven by masters of deceit. . . ."

15 "[T]he time has come for the showdown of the century. Will you fight, or will you fold?"

16 Most NRA members don't know that for many members of the group's top leadership, the fight isn't really about government tyranny. It's largely about increasing the NRA's revenue stream.

17 Take the NRA's top staffer, Executive Vice President Wayne LaPierre. He wrote the infamous fundraising letter (mailed a month before one-time NRA member Timothy McVeigh bombed the Alfred P. Murrah Federal Building in Oklahoma City, killing 168 people) that called Bureau of Alcohol, Tobacco and Firearms agents "jackbooted government thugs." And he recently claimed that [former] President Clinton desires a certain number of gun deaths each year. Pretty extreme stuff.

18 But when LaPierre and I sat down for a one-on-one interview several years ago, I found that in person he is soft-spoken, and, in his hand-tailored suit, wingtips and aviator-style glasses, looks more like the CEO of a Fortune 500 company than the head of a gun lobby. Even more surprising, LaPierre was far less familiar with guns than I was at Camp Newman. He's the first NRA leader who came to the group with a love not of firearms, but of politics. A former campaign manager, he was on the board of the American Association of Political Consultants. With LaPierre at the helm, it's clear that the NRA's metamorphosis from a sportsmen's group to a political lobby is complete. In recent years, the shift in priorities has meant a shift in resources from traditional NRA programs, such as hunting clinics and assistance in setting up target ranges, to the group's lobbying wing, causing disaffection among its more traditional members.

19 But the NRA's fear-mongering appears to be paying off. The organization boasts that it raised $10 million in a recent six-week period, money it plans to use to help put Bush in the White House in November [2000].

20 The NRA also claims its membership rolls have skyrocketed from 2.6 million members in 1998 to a record of 3.6 million today. I don't doubt that the group has added some members as the debate on gun control has heated up. But the numbers deserve closer scrutiny. First, what the NRA doesn't mention is that in 1994 it had more than 3.5 million members, and then lost 25 percent of them over the next four years as gun owners abandoned the group for a variety of reasons, including embarrassment over the NRA's extremist rhetoric, which was publicly scrutinized following the Oklahoma City bombing. So today's "all-time high" figure, as the NRA calls it, is only a slight improvement over its 1994 figures. And as a proportion of the American population, membership is down.

21 There are far more serious problems with the figures. Two years ago, David Gross, then an NRA board member, confided to me that a substantial number of the group's 1 million Life Members are, well, dead—an assertion reported in my book. "There just isn't that much incentive to go find out when someone passes away," Gross explained. "Not when the cost of maintaining [a dead member] is minimal and when they add to your membership list."

22 Then there's the fact that not long ago the NRA switched accounting methods, including on its roster anyone who had made an installment payment toward life membership, where previously it had counted only fully paid members. Only the NRA knows how much the switch boosted its membership. Who else is included in that

figure of 3.6 million? I may be—although I haven't been a member for years. Not long ago, I received an NRA form letter stating that in recognition of my previous commitment to the Second Amendment, the gun group had granted me an honorary membership. The mailing even included an NRA membership card embossed with my name.

23   Partial members, former members, dead members: It's all part of the NRA's campaign of smoke and mirrors to make itself appear more formidable in Washington, where appearance often trumps reality. The NRA leadership must offer a silent prayer of thanks to the gods of journalistic sloth and credulity every time a reporter repeats that figure of 3.6 million members and the words "record high."

24   But let's forget the problem of membership inflation and, for the sake of argument, just accept the NRA's assertion that things have never been better. With that concession, a far more important question emerges: Is what's good for the NRA good for gun owners? I don't think so.

25   It's true that in the short term the NRA's fortunes and the interests of gun owners sometimes do converge. A powerful NRA has managed to shoot down most recent gun control legislation, but some of the NRA's victories have hurt gun owners—sometimes literally. For example: Thanks to the NRA's efforts, the Consumer Product Safety Commission is prohibited from regulating firearms. Through that NRA-engineered loophole passed the Ruger Old Model six-shooter, which, because of a design defect, has a history of firing when dropped. The company sold 1.5 million of the guns before it halted production in 1972. More than 600 people (mostly the guns' owners) have been accidentally shot by this defective handgun, for which—again thanks to the NRA—there exists no recall provisions. That's because the NRA opposes any laws making gun manufacturers accountable to gun owners, citing the familiar "slippery slope" theory. This bias toward manufacturers owes more to the bottom line than it does to the Second Amendment. Gun makers are well represented on the NRA board and a significant portion of NRA revenue comes from advertisements bought by this industry.

26   It's in the long term, however, that the NRA's interests and those of the average gun owner diverge most. For decades, polls have indicated that a majority of Americans favor stronger gun control legislation. But proponents weren't as committed to passing laws as NRA members were to blocking them. As NRA board member Robert Brown (whose day job is publishing *Soldier of Fortune*, a magazine for mercenaries) observed: "It doesn't matter what the mainstream is. What is important is, who will vote?"

27   The NRA is betting that the future will forever mirror the past, with gun control advocates unable to harness mainstream sentiment on Election Day. But this confidence appears more misplaced all the time. Americans, particularly women, and even more particularly suburban women who vote, have grown increasingly impatient with congressional inaction after a string of schoolyard massacres culminating last year in 13 dead at Columbine. The NRA spin doctors have tried to downplay the significance of the recent Million Mom March, dubbing the event that brought several hundred thousand people to Washington calling for more stringent gun control, the Misinformed Mom March.

28   The wise gun owner, however, will see the march for what it was—a symptom of widespread and growing frustration with the NRA's extremism and unwillingness to compromise on common-sense, reasonable gun control measures. There have been

other signs, including one a year ago in gun-friendly Missouri, where voters rejected a "concealed carry" bill—despite the fact that the NRA had poured millions into that referendum.

29   The NRA's response to this groundswell is shrill and predictable: The Second Amendment is under attack! Circle the wagons! Send money! But this tactic merely heightens polarization on this already divisive issue, a situation that benefits no one—except the NRA. It certainly doesn't help responsible gun owners, who are increasingly perceived as being outside the mainstream, thanks to the gun lobby's histrionics. When NRA President Charlton Heston hoisted a musket over his head at the group's convention last month and roared "from my cold dead hands!" he merely reinforced the view that all gun owners are cliché-spouting buffoons, unable or unwilling to discuss rationally how to balance gun rights with responsibilities.

30   Gun owners should understand that the will of the majority can be bottled up for only so long. And when it breaks through, as it inevitably will, the results might be gun control measures far tougher than anything advocated today by mainstream groups such as Handgun Control. By constantly fighting a battle against an illusory slippery slope, the NRA is leading gun owners over a very real cliff of Draconian gun legislation, demanded by a citizenry sick and tired of gun violence, disgusted by the NRA's extremism and no longer in the mood to compromise.

31   And then, the NRA will gnash its teeth and scream bloody murder, crying, "We told you so!" But, for all the NRA's protestations, the political landscape it will deplore will be of its own making. And gun owners who didn't speak up and protest the NRA's extremism will share the blame.

Questions for Reading and Analysis

1. What was Davidson's early connection with the NRA? What is his view of the organization now?

2. What argument does the NRA use with its members? What emotional strategies? What does the NRA seem to want most from its members?

3. What does LaPiere represent to Davidson? How has he changed the NRA?

4. Explain Davidson's account of the NRA's 3.6 million "members."

5. What is the relationship between the NRA and gun manufacturers?

6. How have some of the NRA's rejections of gun control backfired on the organization's members?

7. How do mainstream Americans view the NRA?

8. What is the author's prediction regarding gun legislation? Who should be blamed for what will happen, according to Davidson?

9. What is Davidson's claim?

10. Examine the author's opening. What does he accomplish in the first three paragraphs?

Questions for Discussion and Response

1. What is your reaction to Davidson's examples of the NRA's language?
2. What is your reaction to his account of the NRA's explanation of its membership figures?
3. What is your attitude toward the NRA as a lobbying organization? Has Davidson influenced your thinking in any way?
4. Has Davidson made an effective case against the NRA? Why or why not?

CHAPTER 13

Capital Punishment

The following four articles examine the relevant issues and present arguments for or against the use of the death penalty. The first two writers examine the practical, social, and philosophical or moral issues that may be considered in forming a position on capital punishment. Each writer will demand your close attention, but for an issue so significant—so ultimate—only arguments of this seriousness are justified. The next two writers examine the issue of mistakenly putting innocent people to death—and the role of DNA evidence—thereby adding currency to the debate on this topic.

Reflect on the following questions to enrich your reading on this issue:

1. Do you have a position on capital punishment? If so, what is your position? If not, do you think that you ought to have a position on this issue?

2. On what should your position be based? On social/political concerns? On moral or religious beliefs? On practical considerations—including human error? On some blending of these? (As you read, watch for the ways that the authors choose and argue for the *basis* on which a position should, in their view, rest.)

3. In capital cases, what kinds of evidence do we need in order to decide on guilt beyond a reasonable doubt?

4. What are the current laws on the use of the death penalty?

5. If you wanted to change any of the current laws to make them reflect your position, how would you go about trying to get the laws changed?

Websites Related to This Chapter's Topic

Justice Center Web Site: Focus on the Death Penalty

www.uaa.alaska.edu/just/death/index.html

From the University of Alaska/Anchorage, a site that gives information—statistics and court decisions—as well as many good links to other sources.

Ohio ESL

www.ohio.edu/esl/project/penalty/index.html

Ohio University site providing definitions relevant to the topic and links to sites on both sides of the debate.

Cornell Law School—Cornell Death Penalty Project
www.lawschool.cornell.edu/library/death
Contains information on court decisions and results of relevant studies.

University of San Diego, Ethics Across the Curriculum
http://ethics.acusd.edu/death_penalty.html
Site with legislative information, statistics, and links to other sites.

The Ultimate Punishment: A Defense

Ernest van den Haag

A naturalized citizen born in 1914 in the Netherlands, Ernest van den Haag holds a doctorate from New York University and has been a psychoanalyst. In addition, he has written many articles in both American and European journals and several books on sociological issues, including violence and crime. "The Ultimate Punishment: A Defense" is reprinted (with some footnotes omitted) from the May 7, 1986, issue of the *Harvard Law Review*. Van den Haag effectively organizes his defense around the arguments put forward by his opponents.

1   In an average year about 20,000 homicides occur in the United States. Fewer than 300 convicted murderers are sentenced to death. But because no more than thirty murderers have been executed in any recent year, most convicts sentenced to death are likely to die of old age.[1] Nonetheless, the death penalty looms large in discussions: it raises important moral questions independent of the number of executions.

2   The death penalty is our harshest punishment. It is irrevocable: it ends the existence of those punished, instead of temporarily imprisoning them. Further, although not intended to cause physical pain, execution is the only corporal punishment still applied to adults. These singular characteristics contribute to the perennial, impassioned controversy about capital punishment.

I. Distribution

3   Consideration of the justice, morality, or usefulness, of capital punishment is often conflated with objections to its alleged discriminatory or capricious distribution among the guilty. Wrongly so. If capital punishment is immoral *in se*, no distribution among the guilty could make it moral. If capital punishment is moral, no distribution would make it immoral. Improper distribution cannot affect the quality of what is distributed, be it punishments or rewards. Discriminatory or capricious distribution thus could not justify abolition of the death penalty. Further, maldistribution inheres no more in capital punishment than in any other punishment.

4   Maldistribution between the guilty and the innocent is, by definition, unjust. But the injustice does not lie in the nature of the punishment. Because of the finality of the death penalty, the most grievous maldistrubution occurs when it is imposed upon the innocent. However, the frequent allegations of discrimination and capriciousness refer to maldistribution among the guilty and not to the punishment of the innocent.

5   Maldistribution of any punishment among those who deserve it is irrelevant to its justice or morality. Even if poor or black convicts guilty of capital offenses suffer capital

punishments, and other convicts equally guilty of the same crimes do not, a more equal distribution, however desirable, would merely be more equal. It would not be more just to the convicts under sentence of death.

6   Punishments are imposed on persons, not on racial or economic groups. Guilt is personal. The only relevant question is: does the person to be executed deserve the punishment? Whether or not others who deserved the same punishment, whatever their economic or racial group, have avoided execution is irrelevant. If they have, the guilt of the executed convicts would not be diminished, nor would their punishment be less deserved. To put the issue starkly, if the death penalty were imposed on guilty blacks, but not on guilty whites, or, if it were imposed by a lottery among the guilty, this irrationally discriminatory or capricious distribution would neither make the penalty unjust, nor cause anyone to be unjustly punished, despite the undue impunity bestowed on others.

7   Equality, in short, seems morally less important than justice. And justice is independent of distributional inequalities. The ideal of equal justice demands that justice be equally distributed, not that it be replaced by equality. Justice requires that as many of the guilty as possible be punished, regardless of whether others have avoided punishment. To let these others escape the deserved punishment does not do justice to them, or to society. But it is not unjust to those who could not escape.

8   These moral considerations are not meant to deny that irrational discrimination, or capriciousness, would be inconsistent with constitutional requirements. But I am satisfied that the Supreme Court has in fact provided for adherence to the constitutional requirement of equality as much as possible. Some inequality is indeed unavoidable as a practical matter in any system.[2] But, *ultra posse neo obligatur*. (Nobody is bound beyond ability.)

9   Recent data reveal little direct racial discrimination in the sentencing of those arrested and convicted of murder. The abrogation of the death penalty for rape has eliminated a major source of racial discrimination. Concededly, some discrimination based on the race of murder victims may exist; yet, this discrimination affects criminal victimizers in an unexpected way. Murderers of whites are thought more likely to be executed than murderers of blacks. Black victims, then, are less fully vindicated than white ones. However, because most black murderers kill blacks, black murderers are spared the death penalty more often than are white murderers. They fare better than most white murderers. The motivation behind unequal distribution of the death penalty may well have been to discriminate against blacks, but the result has favored them. Maldistribution is thus a straw man for empirical as well as analytical reasons.

II. Miscarriages of Justice

10   In a recent survey Professors Hugo Adam Bedau and Michael Radelet found that 7000 persons were executed in the United States between 1900 and 1985 and that 25 were innocent of capital crimes. Among the innocents they list Sacco and Vanzetti as well as Ethel and Julius Rosenberg. Although their data may be questionable, I do not doubt that, over a long enough period, miscarriages of justice will occur even in capital cases.

11   Despite precautions, nearly all human activities, such as trucking, lighting, or construction, cost the lives of some innocent bystanders. We do not give up these activities, because the advantages, moral or material, outweigh the unintended losses.

Analogously, for those who think the death penalty just, miscarriages of justice are off-set by the moral benefits and the usefulness of doing justice. For those who think the death penalty unjust even when it does not miscarry, miscarriages can hardly be decisive.

III. Deterrence

12   Despite much recent work, there has been no conclusive statistical demonstration that the death penalty is a better deterrent than are alternative punishments. However, deterrence is less than decisive for either side. Most abolitionists acknowledge that they would continue to favor abolition even if the death penalty were shown to deter more murders than alternatives could deter. Abolitionists appear to value the life of a con-victed murderer or, at least, his nonexecution, more highly than they value the lives of the innocent victims who might be spared by deterring prospective murderers.

13   Deterrence is not altogether decisive for me either. I would favor retention of the death penalty as retribution even if it were shown that the threat of execution could not deter prospective murderers not already deterred by the threat of imprisonment.[3] Still, I believe the death penalty, because of its finality, is more feared than imprisonment, and deters some prospective murderers not deterred by the threat of imprisonment. Sparing the lives of even a few prospective victims by deterring their murderers is more important than preserving the lives of convicted murderers because of the possibility, or even the probability, that executing them would not deter others. Whereas the lives of the victims who might be saved are valuable, that of the murderer has only negative value, because of his crime. Surely the criminal law is meant to protect the lives of po-tential victims in preference to those of actual murderers.

14   Murder rates are determined by many factors; neither the severity nor the probabil-ity of the threatened sanction is always decisive. However, for the long run, I share the view of Sir James Fitzjames Stephen: "Some men probably abstain from murder because they fear that if they committed murder they would be hanged. Hundreds of thousands abstain from it because they regard it with horror. One great reason why they regard it with horror is that murderers are hanged." Penal sanctions are useful in the long run for the formation of the internal restraints so necessary to control crime. The severity and finality of the death penalty is appropriate to the seriousness and the finality of murder.

IV. Incidental Issues: Cost, Relative Suffering, Brutalization

15   Many nondecisive issues are associated with capital punishment. Some believe that the monetary cost of appealing a capital sentence is excessive. Yet most comparisons of the cost of life imprisonment with the cost of execution, apart from their dubious rele-vance, are flawed at least by the implied assumption that life prisoners will generate no judicial costs during their imprisonment. At any rate, the actual monetary costs are trumped by the importance of doing justice.

16   Others insist that a person sentenced to death suffers more than his victim suf-fered, and that this (excess) suffering is undue according to the *lex talionis* (rule of re-taliation). We cannot know whether the murderer on death row suffers more than his victim suffered; however, unlike the murderer, the victim deserved none of the suffer-ing inflicted. Further, the limitations of the *lex talionis* were meant to restrain private vengeance, not the social retribution that has taken its place. Punishment—regardless of the motivation—is not intended to revenge, offset, or compensate for the victim's

suffering, or to be measured by it. Punishment is to vindicate the law and the social order undermined by the crime. This is why the kidnapper's penal confinement is not limited to the period for which he imprisoned his victim; nor is a burglar's confinement meant merely to offset the suffering or the harm he caused his victim; nor is it meant only to offset the advantage he gained.[4]

17 Another argument heard at least since Beccaria is that, by killing a murderer, we encourage, endorse, or legitimize unlawful killing. Yet, although all punishments are meant to be unpleasant, it is seldom argued that they legitimize the unlawful imposition of identical unpleasantness. Imprisonment is not thought to legitimize kidnapping; neither are fines thought to legitimize robbery. The difference between murder and execution, or between kidnapping and imprisonment, is that the first is unlawful and undeserved, the second a lawful and deserved punishment for an unlawful act. The physical similarities of the punishment to the crime are irrelevant. The relevant difference is not physical, but social.[5]

V. Justice, Excess, Degradation

18 We threaten punishments in order to deter crime. We impose them not only to make the threats credible but also as retribution (justice) for the crimes that were not deterred. Threats and punishments are necessary to deter and deterrence is a sufficient practical justification for them. Retribution is an independent moral justification. Although penalties can be unwise, repulsive, or inappropriate, and those punished can be pitiable, in a sense the infliction of legal punishment on a guilty person cannot be unjust. By committing the crime, the criminal volunteered to assume the risk of receiving a legal punishment that he could have avoided by not committing the crime. The punishment he suffers is the punishment he voluntarily risked suffering and, therefore, it is no more unjust to him than any other event for which one knowingly volunteers to assume the risk. Thus, the death penalty cannot be unjust to the guilty criminal.

19 There remain, however, two moral objections. The penalty may be regarded as always excessive as retribution and always morally degrading. To regard the death penalty as always excessive, one must believe that no crime—no matter how heinous—could possibly justify capital punishment. Such a belief can be neither corroborated nor refuted; it is an article of faith.

20 Alternatively, or concurrently, one may believe that everybody, the murderer no less than the victim, has an imprescriptible (natural?) right to life. The law therefore should not deprive anyone of life. I share Jeremy Bentham's view that any such "natural and imprescriptible rights" are "nonsense upon stilts."

21 Justice Brennan has insisted that the death penalty is "uncivilized," "inhuman," inconsistent with "human dignity" and with "the sanctity of life," that it "treats members of the human race as nonhumans, as objects to be toyed with and discarded," that it is "uniquely degrading to human dignity" and "by its very nature, [involves] a denial of the executed person's humanity." Justice Brennan does not say why he thinks execution "uncivilized." Hitherto most civilizations have had the death penalty, although it has been discarded in Western Europe, where it is currently unfashionable probably because of its abuse by totalitarian regimes.

22 By "degrading," Justice Brennan seems to mean that execution degrades the executed convicts. Yet philosophers, such as Immanuel Kant and G.F.W.Hegel, have insisted that,

when deserved, execution, far from degrading the executed convict, affirms his humanity by affirming his rationality and his responsibility for his actions. They thought that execution, when deserved, is required for the sake of the convict's dignity. (Does not life imprisonment violate human dignity more than execution, by keeping alive a prisoner deprived of all autonomy?)

23   Common sense indicates that it cannot be death—our common fate—that is inhuman. Therefore, Justice Brennan must mean that death degrades when it comes not as a natural or accidental event, but as a deliberate social imposition. The murderer learns through his punishment that his fellow men have found him unworthy of living; that because he has murdered, he is being expelled from the community of the living. This degradation is self-inflicted. By murdering, the murderer has so dehumanized himself that he cannot remain among the living. The social recognition of his self-degradation is the punitive essence of execution. To believe, as Justice Brennan appears to, that the degradation is inflicted by the execution reverses the direction of causality.

24   Execution of those who have committed heinous murders may deter only one murder per year. If it does, it seems quite warranted. It is also the only fitting retribution for murder I can think of.

Notes

1.   Death row as a semipermanent residence is cruel, because convicts are denied the normal amenities of prison life. Thus, unless death row residents are integrated into the prison population, the continuing accumulation of convicts on death row should lead us to accelerate either the rate of executions or the rate of commutations. I find little objection to integration.

2.   The ideal of equality, unlike the ideal of retributive justice (which can be approximated separately in each instance), is clearly unattainable unless all guilty persons are apprehended, and thereafter tried, convicted and sentenced by the same court, at the same time. Unequal justice is the best we can do; it is still better than the injustice, equal or unequal, which occurs if, for the sake of equality, we deliberately allow some who could be punished to escape.

3.   If executions were shown to increase the murder rate in the long run, I would favor abolition. Sparing the innocent victims who would be spared, *ex hypothesi*, by the nonexecution of murderers would be more important to me than the execution, however just, of murderers. But although there is a lively discussion of the subject, no serious evidence exists to support the hypothesis that executions produce a higher murder rate. *Cf.* Phillips, *The Deterrent Effect of Capital Punishment: New Evidence on an Old Controversy*, 86 AM. J. Soc. 139 (1980) (arguing that murder rates drop immediately after executions of criminals).

4.   Thus restitution (a civil liability) cannot satisfy the punitive purpose of penal sanctions, whether the purpose be retributive or deterrent.

5.   Some abolitionists challenge: If the death penalty is just and serves as a deterrent, why not televise executions? The answer is simple. The death even of a murderer, however well-deserved, should not serve as public entertainment. It so served in earlier centuries. But in this respect our sensibility has changed for the better, I believe. Further, television unavoidably would trivialize executions, wedged in, as they would be, between game shows, situation comedies and the like. Finally,

because televised executions would focus on the physical aspects of the punishment, rather than the nature of the crime and the suffering of the victim, a televised execution would present the murderer as the victim of the state. Far from communicating the moral significance of the execution, television would shift the focus to the pitiable fear of the murderer. We no longer place in cages those sentenced to imprisonment to expose them to public view. Why should we so expose those sentenced to execution?

Questions for Reading and Analysis

1. What does van den Haag mean by "distribution"? That is, what issue in the death-penalty debate does the author examine in section one?

2. On what grounds does van den Haag dismiss the issue of possible maldistribution of death sentencing among the guilty? State his argument in your own words.

3. Does van den Haag believe that a significant racial bias can be found in the distribution of capital punishment? Does he offer evidence to support his views?

4. According to van den Haag, what kind of logical fallacy is illustrated by the argument of maldistribution?

5. On what two grounds does the author dismiss challenges to the death penalty based on miscarriages of justice?

6. Consider the author's word choice in the second section. What words does he avoid using that a writer opposed to the death penalty might use instead of "miscarriage of justice" or to refer to the persons executed because of the miscarriage?

7. What do studies show about the death penalty's potential as a deterrent to murder?

8. What is the position on deterrence of those who oppose the death penalty? What does van den Haag conclude about the values of abolitionists?

9. Why does van den Haag dismiss deterrence as an issue in the debate?

10. Why should costs be considered an irrelevant issue?

11. What is the purpose of punishing a criminal, according to van den Haag? Why is this purpose important to our understanding of death sentencing?

12. How does the author refute the idea that death sentencing legitimizes murder? Those who make this claim are using what type of argument? What strategy does van den Haag use to reveal a weakness in this type of argument?

13. What, finally, is the author's justification of legal punishment, including the death penalty?

14. To argue that the death penalty is always excessive, what must one believe? Why does van den Haag believe that the death penalty does not degrade? Explain his argument in your own words.

15. Where does the author place his claim, the thesis of his essay? What does he accomplish by this choice?

Questions for Discussion and Response

1. Van den Haag is prepared to accept some miscarriages of justice (some innocent people will be punished) to achieve the advantages of capital punishment. Are you? If you agree with the author, explain why. If you disagree, how would you challenge van den Haag?

2. Van den Haag argues that capital punishment is a form of retribution for murder; it is not revenge but justice. Do you agree with his distinction between retribution and revenge? Explain your views.

3. Evaluate van den Haag's argument. Is it reasoned, thorough, and appropriately serious? Is it logical? Do you think he is right? Why or why not?

Death is Different

Hugo Adam Bedau

A native of Oregon with a doctorate from Harvard University, Hugo Adam Bedau (b. 1926) has taught for many years in the philosophy department at Tufts University. He is the author of articles and books on justice and capital punishment, including *The Courts, the Constitution and Capital Punishment* (1977) and *Death Is Different* (1987). In the following essay, the concluding chapter of *Death Is Different*, Bedau provides a thorough review of the debating points in the argument over capital punishment.

1   Insofar as fundamental moral questions are raised by the death penalty, their resolution does not turn on what a majority of the Supreme Court says the Constitution permits or forbids. Nor does it rest on what the tea leaves of public-opinion polls can be construed to mean. Morally speaking, what are at stake are the *reasons* that can be brought forward to support or to criticize this punishment. These reasons—familiar from public debates, letters to the editor, and radio and television talk shows—have not significantly altered over the past generation, and perhaps not even during the past century.

2   In order of increasing importance, the main reasons for support seem to me to be these six: (1) the death penalty is a far less expensive method of punishment than the alternative of life imprisonment; the death penalty is more effective in preventing crime than the alternative because (2) it is a more effective deterrent, and because (3) it more effectively incapacitates; (4) the death penalty is required by justice; (5) in many cases there is no feasible alternative punishment; and (6) the death penalty vindicates the moral order and thus is an indispensable symbol of public authority. I want to evaluate each of these reasons and elaborate especially on those of salient current importance.

The Taxpayer's Argument

3   Is the death penalty really so much less expensive than long-term imprisonment? The answer depends on how one allocates the costs imposed under the two alternatives. The few attempts that have been made to do this in a manner comparable to the way economists try to answer other questions about the costs of alternative social policies are in agreement. In the words of the most recent study, "A criminal justice system that includes the death penalty costs more than a system that chooses life imprisonment."[1]

Why this is true is easily understood. It is mainly a consequence of the commendable desire to afford every protection to a defendant whose life is at stake, and virtually every such defendant avails himself of all these protections. If the defendant is indigent, as are most of those accused of crimes that put them in jeopardy of the death penalty, then society has to foot the bill for the defendant's attorney as well as for the costs involved in the prosecution, jury selection, trial, and appeals. Although in theory these costs would need to be paid even if the defendant were not on trial for his life, in practice the evidence shows that non-death-penalty trials and appeals are generally less protracted and therefore less expensive. So the taxpayer's argument, as I have called it, is simply wrong on the facts.

4   But, of course, even if it were sound, no decent citizen or responsible legislator would support the death penalty by relying on this argument alone. Those who seriously advance it do so only because they also believe that the criminals in question ought to be executed whatever the cost to society and however galling the expenditure may be. As a consequence, the taxpayer's argument is really no more than a side issue, since defenders and critics of the death penalty agree that economic costs should take a back seat to justice and social defense where human life is concerned.

Uniquely Effective Deterrent

5   No one has ever offered any scientific evidence that the death penalty is an effective deterrent, or more effective than the alternative of long-term imprisonment, to any such crime as rape, arson, burglary, kidnapping, aircraft hijacking, treason, espionage, or terrorism (which itself typically involves one or more of these other crimes). All arguments for the death penalty that rest on belief in its superior deterrent capacity to prevent or reduce the incidence of these crimes depend entirely on guesswork, common sense, or analogy to its allegedly superior deterrent effects on the crime of murder.

6   What, then, is the evidence that the death penalty is an effective deterrent to murder? There is little or none. Murder comes in many different forms (gangland killings, murder among family members, murder during armed robbery or burglary, murder in jail or prison, murder for hire, murder to escape custody or avoid arrest), but very little of the research on deterrence has concentrated exclusively on one of these types to the exclusion of all the rest. The threat of executions is conceivably a much better deterrent to some types of murder than to others; but no research currently exists to confirm such a hypothesis.

7   It doesn't really matter. Deterrence is increasingly a make-weight in the argument for the death penalty. Public opinion surveys indicate that most of those who profess support for the death penalty would support it even if they were convinced—contrary to what they believe—that it is not a better deterrent than life imprisonment.[2] I find this plausible. Although from time to time there is sporadic evidence in favor of the deterrent power of executions (hardly anyone who thinks about it attaches much differential deterrent efficacy to the death penalty *statutes*, all by themselves), none of it survives careful scrutiny very long.[3] If anything, there is a steadily accumulating body of evidence to suggest that on balance the death penalty may cause (or encourage, or set the example for) more homicides than it prevents, because its "brutalizing" effect outperforms its deterrent effect.[4]

8   Furthermore, and quite apart from the status of the evidence on the issue of deterrence vs. brutalization, one would expect that the rationale for deterrence in our society is of slowly declining importance. In previous centuries and up to a generation ago, when our society punished many *non*homicidal crimes with death, deterrence was the most plausible reason for hanging a counterfeiter or a horse thief or a claim jumper. Today, however, with the death penalty applied exclusively to murder, nondeterrent considerations naturally play an increasingly prominent role all the time. Indeed, social science research, public opinion, and Supreme Court rulings all neatly converge at this point. Despite more than a decade of effort to obtain convincing support for rational belief in the superior deterrent power of the death penalty, the evidence points the other way. During the same period, advocates of capital punishment—both those who are and those who are not aware of this lack of evidence—shifted the basis of their support for executions from deterrence to other reasons. Meanwhile, the Supreme Court has said in effect that the death penalty is unconstitutional except where it is not disproportionate to the crime and regardless of its deterrent effects.

9   From a public-policy perspective, one can say this: During the past fifteen years, the legislative re-enactment of death penalty statutes has been no more than a series of stabs in the dark, insofar as these laws have been predicated on their supposed superior deterrence. A legislature ought to have better reasons than this for trying to protect the life of its citizens by imposing the threat of the death penalty. On moral grounds, general deterrence is certainly a legitimate function of the criminal law and therefore a justifiable basis on which to construct a system of punishments under law. Nevertheless, the choice of more rather than less severity in punishment for particular crimes on grounds of better deterrence alone encounters two different objections. One is that we violate moral principles if we are willing to use punitive methods, regardless of their savagery, in order to secure slight improvements in deterrence; the other is that there simply is no adequate evidence in favor of the superior deterrent efficacy of the death penalty.

Incapacitation and Prevention

10   No one can dispute that capital punishment, when carried out, does effectively incapacitate each offender who is executed. (This has nothing to do with deterrence, however, because deterrence operates by threat and intimidation, not by destroying the capacity to break the law.) Does this incapacitation make a significant dent in the crime rate? The Department of Justice has reported that as of the end of 1984 "approximately 2 of every 3 offenders under sentence of death had a prior felony conviction; nearly 1 out of 10 had previously been convicted for homicide."[5] These data indicate that more than a hundred of those currently under sentence of death may be some of the worst offenders in the nation—and that several hundred more served a prison term for robbery, assault, or some other crime, and then, after their release, went on to commit the even graver crime of murder. (Of course, these data simultaneously show that the vast majority of condemned prisoners are *not* recidivist murderers.) But do these data also show that society needs the incapacitating power of death to prevent more crimes from being committed by convicted capital offenders?

11   If parole boards and release authorities knew in advance which inmates would murder after their release, the inmates in question would obviously be prevented from committing these offenses by being kept in some form of custody. Yet we have no reliable

methods for predicting future dangerousness, and especially not for the propensity of a convicted murderer to murder again.[6] Consequently, the only effective general-policy alternatives to the present one are a system of mandatory death penalties and a system of mandatory prison terms for life. Even then, if the Bureau's own statistics are reliable, this would prevent only a tiny fraction of the twenty thousand or so murders committed in this nation each year. The truth is, as all release statistics agree, very few of the persons convicted of homicide and sent to prison are ever convicted of homicide again. Either to kill all those convicted of murder or to keep them all in prison forever, because of a few exceptions that cannot be identified in advance, would be an expensive and unjustified policy that very few of us, on reflection, would want to support.

12   Opponents of the death penalty encounter their stiffest objections when they try to explain why even the multiple or serial or recidivist murderer should not be executed. Few would disagree that "the thirst for revenge is keenest in the case of mass murder, . . . especially when it includes elements of sadism and brutality against innocent victims."[7] Revenge apart, incapacitation probably has its most convincing application in such cases. It is hardly surprising that many who generally oppose the death penalty would be willing to make an exception for such killers.

13   Let us note first that if the death penalty were confined to such cases, abolitionists would have scored a major victory. The immediate consequence of such a policy would be an unprecedented reduction in the annual number of death sentences—a drop from more than two hundred per year to fewer than twenty, if we can rely on the Bureau of Justice Statistics report quoted above. Any policy change that reduced death sentences by more than 90 percent should be welcomed by opponents of the death penalty as a giant step in the right direction.

14   More controversial is whether abolitionists could accommodate such an exception on moral grounds. The best way to do so, it seems to me, is to argue much as George Bernard Shaw did earlier in this century in his little book *The Crime of Imprisonment* that the execution of such murderers is society's only alternative—we have no nonlethal methods of sedation or restraint that suffice to make certain that such offenders will not and cannot kill yet again. However, this is a factual question, and I (unlike Shaw) think that once the offender is in our custody, we are never in the position where our only recourse is to lethal methods. Others who have studied the problem more carefully agree;[8] there are reasonably humane methods at our disposal for coping with the most difficult and dangerous prisoners.

15   In the end, however, I think one must admit that the refusal to execute a murderer who has repeated his crime—not to mention those who embody murderous evil on a gigantic scale, such as an Adolph Eichmann or a Lavrenti Beria—is evidence of a position on the death penalty that owes something to fanatic devotion as well as to cool reason. Dedicated pacifists and devoutly religious opponents of the death penalty may well be able to embrace such categorical opposition to executions without fear of rebuke from reason. Conscientious liberals, however, cannot so easily refuse to compromise. Do they not already compromise on other life-and-death issues—often tolerating suicide, euthanasia, abortion, the use of lethal force in social and self-defense—thereby showing that they refuse to accept any moral principle that categorically condemns all killing? If so, what is so peculiarly objectionable, from the moral point of view as they see it, in an occasional state-authorized killing of that rare criminal, the murderer who

has murdered more than once? I cannot point to any clear and defensible moral principle of general acceptability that is violated by such a compromise, a principle that *absolutely forbids* such executions. If one nonetheless opposes all executions, as I do, then it must be on other grounds.

Retributive and Vindictive Justice

16   Today there is substantial agreement that retribution is an essential aspect of the criminal justice system, and that a general policy of punishment for convicted criminals is the best means to this end. Less argument exists on whether retribution alone justifies the practice of punishment; and there is no consensus on how to construct a penalty schedule on retributive grounds, matching the severity of punishments to the gravity of crimes. Regrettable confusion of the dangerous (though normal) emotion of anger and the desire for revenge it spawns—neither of which has any reliable connection to justice—with moral indignation at victimization—which does—often clouds the thinking of those who defend the "morality" of capital punishment.[9] There is also disagreement on whether other considerations of justice—such as equality, fairness of administration, and respect for the rights of the accused—should yield or prevail when they conflict with the demands of retribution.

17   These issues are inescapably philosophical, and I have my own views on them, which I have explained elsewhere.[10] In a word, the most that principles of retribution can do for the death penalty is to *permit* it for murder; principles of retribution are strained beyond their capacity if they are invoked to justify the death penalty for any other crime. Thus if retribution is the moral principle on which defenders of the death penalty want to rest their case, then morality requires that nonhomicidal crimes must be punished in some less severe manner. However, the principles of retribution do not *require* us to punish murder by death; what they require is the severest punishment for the gravest crime consistent with our other moral convictions. Consequently, the appeal to retribution in the present climate of discussion—and it is a widespread appeal—fails to justify the death penalty.

18   In fact I think there is considerable self-deception among those who think they rest their defense of the death penalty on the moral principles of just retribution. Those principles cannot explain why society actually executes those few whom it does, and why it sentences to death no more than a small percentage of the murderers it convicts. Retribution is another fig leaf to cover our nakedness, I am afraid, even if it appears to be a respectable line of moral reasoning when taken in the abstract.

19   In recent years, neo-conservative writers of various sorts—such as columnist George F. Will, New York's Mayor Edward Koch, and academicians Walter Berns and Ernest van den Haag—have made much of the vindictive powers of the death penalty and of the civilizing and moralizing influence it thus wields. Van den Haag writes, "The [death] penalty is meant to vindicate the social order."[11] Berns elaborates the point: "The criminal law must be made awful, by which I mean, awe-inspiring. . . . It must remind us of the moral order by which alone we can live as *human* beings, and in our day the only punishment that can do this is capital punishment."[12] The language is resonant, but the claim is unconvincing.

20   One purpose of *any* system of punishment is to vindicate the moral order established by the criminal law—and properly so, because that order protects the rights of

the law-abiding and because in a liberal society those rights are the basis for self-esteem and mutual respect. To go further, however, and insist that lethal punishment is the "only" appropriate response by society to the gravest crimes is wrong on two counts. The claim itself relies on naked moral intuitions about how to fit punishment to crimes, and such intuitions—with their deceptive clarity and superficial rationale—are treacherous. The least bit of historical sophistication would tell us that our forebears used the same kind of intuitive claims on behalf of maiming and other savageries that we would be ashamed to preach today. Furthermore, the claim makes sense only against the background of a conception of the state as a mystical entity of semi-divine authority, a conception that is hardly consistent with our pluralistic, liberal, nontheocratic traditions.

The Alternative

21   Imprisonment as it is currently practiced in this country is anything but an ideal alternative to the death penalty. Life imprisonment without the possibility of parole has been opposed by all experienced prison administrators as a virtually unmanageable option. The more one knows about most American prisons the more one judges long-term imprisonment to be a terrible curse for all concerned.[13] Defenders of the death penalty rightly point out that persons in prison can and sometimes do murder other inmates, guards, or visitors—although such crimes occur much less frequently than some of those defenders imply. (Nor do they occur with greater frequency in the prisons of states that do not punish these crimes with death than in the prisons of states that do.[14]) So imprisonment for ten or twenty years, not to mention for life, is vulnerable to many objections. Indeed, a cynic might even go so far as to say that one of the best reasons for the death penalty is the alternative to it. Nevertheless, I think this alternative is still superior to execution—and will have to suffice until something better is proposed—for at least three important reasons.

22   First, society avoids the unsolvable problem of picking and choosing among the bad to try to find the worst, in order to execute them. Experience ought long ago to have taught us that it is an illusion to expect prosecutors, juries, and courts to perform this task in a fashion that survives criticism. Deciding not to kill any among the murderers we convict enables us to punish them all more equitably, just as it relieves us of the illusion that we can choose the worst among the bad, the irredeemable from the others, those who "deserve to die" from those who really do not.

23   Second, we avoid the risk and costly error of executing the innocent, in favor of the equally risky but far less costly error of imprisoning the innocent. Arresting, trying, convicting, and punishing the innocent is an unavoidable problem, whose full extent in our history is only now beginning to be understood. Recent research on persons erroneously convicted of capital crimes in this century in the United States has identified some 350 such cases.[15] Scores of these convictions occurred in states where there was no death penalty; dozens of these errors were corrected and in some instances the wrongly convicted defendant was indemnified. Not so in all cases in the death penalty states. Where is the necessity—moral or empirical—to run the risk of executing the innocent?[16]

24   Third, there is a crucial symbolic significance in drawing the line at punishments that deprive the offender of his liberty. Just as we no longer permit the authorities to use torture to secure confessions or to attack the body of the convicted offender with whips, branding irons, or other instruments that maim and stigmatize, nor to carry out the

death penalty by the cruelest means our fevered imaginations can devise—even though some still cry out that social defense and just retribution require it—so we should repudiate the death penalty. It belongs alongside these other barbaric practices, which our society has rejected in principle.

25   For at least these reasons, the alternative of imprisonment is preferable to death as punishment in all cases.[17]

The Symbolism: Death or Life?

26   During earlier centuries, the death penalty played a plausible, perhaps even justifiable, role in society's efforts to control crime and mete out just deserts to convicted offenders. After all, the alternative of imprisonment—the modern form of banishment—had yet to be systematically developed. Consequently, society in an earlier age could tolerate the death penalty with a clearer conscience than we can today. For us, however, the true dimension in which we assess this mode of punishment is neither its crime-fighting effectiveness nor its moral necessity, but its symbolism. Mistaken faith in deterrent efficacy, confusion over the requirements of justice, indifference to unfair administration, ignorance of nonlethal methods of social control—all these can explain only so much about the current support for the death penalty. The rest of the explanation lies elsewhere, in what executions symbolize, consciously or unconsciously, for those who favor them.

27   This symbolism deserves a closer look.[18] The death penalty, today as in the past, symbolizes the ultimate power of the state, and of the government of society, over the individual citizen. Understandably, the public wants visible evidence that the authority of its political leaders is intact, their powers competent to deal with every social problem, and their courage resolute in the face of any danger. Anxiety about war, fear of crime, indignation at being victimized provoke the authorities to use the power of life and death as a public gesture of strength, self-confidence, and reassurance. Not surprisingly, many are unwilling to abandon the one symbol a society under law in peacetime has at its disposal that, above all others, expresses this power with awe-inspiring finality: the death penalty.

28   This is precisely why, in the end, we should oppose the death penalty in principle and without exception. As long as capital punishment is available under law for any crime, it is a temptation to excess. Tyrannical governments, from Idi Amin's Uganda to the Ayatollah's Iran, teach this lesson. At best the use of the death penalty here and elsewhere has been and continues to be capricious and arbitrary. The long history of several of our own states, notably Michigan and Wisconsin, quite apart from the experience of other nations, proves that the government of a civilized society does not *need* the death penalty. The citizenry should not clamor for it. Their political leaders should know better—as, of course, the best of them do—than to cultivate public approval for capital statutes, death sentences, and executions. Instead a civilized government should explain why such practices are ill-advised, and why they are ineffective in reducing crime, removing its causes, and responding to victimization.

Notes

1.   Comment, "The Cost of Taking a Life: Dollars and Sense of the Death Penalty," *U. C. Davis Law Review* 18 (1985):1221–74, at 1270.

2. See *The Gallup Report*, January-February 1986, nos. 244–45, pp.10–16; and Phoebe C. Ellsworth and Lee Ross, "Public Opinion and Capital Punishment: A Closer Examination of the Views of Abolitionists and Retentionists," *Crime & Delinquency* 29 (1983):116–69, at 147.

3. The findings reported by Isaac Ehrlich, "The Deterrent Effect of Capital Punishment: A Question of Life and Death," *American Economic Review* 65 (1975):397–417 ("[each] additional execution . . . may have resulted . . . in 7 or 8 fewer murderers") have been extensively criticized; see, e.g., Lawrence R. Klein, Brian Forst, and Victor Filatox, "The Deterrent Effect of Capital Punishment: An Assessment of the Estimates," in Alfred Blumstein, Jacqueline Cohen, and Daniel Nagin, eds., *Deterrence and Incapacitation: Estimating the Effects of Criminal Sanctions on Crime Rates* (1978), pp. 336–60. The findings reported by James A. Yunker, "Is the Death Penalty a Deterrent to Homicide? Some Time Series Evidence," *Journal of Behavioral Economics* 5 (1976):45–81 ("one execution will deter 156 murders") have been evaluated and found wanting by James Alan Fox, "The Identification and Estimation of Deterrence: An Evaluation of Yunker's Model," *Journal of Behavioral Economics* 6 (1977):225–42. The findings reported by David P. Phillips, "The Deterrent Effect of Capital Punishment: New Evidence on an Old Controversy," *American Journal of Sociology* 86 (1980):139–48 (". . . in the two weeks following a public execution the frequency of homicide drops by 35.7%") has been refuted by William J. Bowers, "Deterrence or Brutalization: What Is the Truth About Highly Publicized Executions?" (unpublished). The latest claims in this vein are by Stephen K. Layson, "Homicide and Deterrence: A Reexamination of the United States Time-Series Evidence," *Southern Economic Journal* 52 (1985):68–89 ("the tradeoff of executions for murders is approximately—18.5," i.e., each execution results in a net decrease of 18.5 murders); for criticism see James Alan Fox, "Persistent Flaws in Econometric Studies of the Death Penalty: A Discussion of Layson's Findings," testimony submitted to the Subcommittee on Criminal Justice, House of Representatives, U.S. Congress, 7 May 1986.

4. See Bowers, "Deterrence or Brutalization."

5. United States, Department of Justice, Bureau of Justice Statistics, *Capital Punishment* 1984 (1985), p. 1.

6. Mark H. Moore et al., *Dangerous Offenders: The Elusive Target of Justice* (1984), and Ted Honderich et al., "Symposium: Predicting Dangerousness," *Criminal Justice Ethics* 2 (Winter/Spring 1983):3–17.

7. Jack Levin and James Alan Fox, *Mass Murder: America's Growing Menace* (1985), p.222. The authors do not support the death penalty for serial, mass, or recidivist murderers.

8. See especially Norval Morris, *The Future of Imprisonment* (1974), pp. 85–121.

9. This is especially true of Walter Berns, *For Capital Punishment: Crime and the Morality of the Death Penalty* (1979), pp.153ff. The arousal of "anger" is not evidence that anything morally wrong is its cause. There is no reason to believe that the punitive policies adopted by a society "angry" at criminals will be fair or effective in reducing crime. The revenge that "anger" can motivate has no claim as such to the title of just retribution. Moral indignation is another matter. As a feeling, it may be indistinguishable from anger, but its claim for a different status rests on its essential

connection to a moral principle; one's indignation is aroused only if an important moral principle has been violated. Even when this happens, the policies inspired by moral indignation are not thereby guaranteed to be just or effective; and the capacity for self-deception about the legitimacy of one's indignation is legendary.

10. See Bedau, "Classification-Based Sentencing: Some Conceptual and Ethical Problems," *New England Journal of Criminal and Civil Confinement* 10 (1984):1–26; Bedau, "Prisoners' Rights," *Criminal Justice Ethics* 1 (Winter/Spring 1982):26–41; Bedau, "Retribution and the Theory of Punishment," *Journal of Philosophy* 75 (1978):601–20; Bedau, "Penal Theory and Prison Reality Today," *Juris Doctor* 2 (December 1972):40–83.

11. Ernest van den Haag, "The Death Penalty Vindicates the Law," *American Bar Association Journal* 71 (April 1985):38–42 at 42; cf. van den Haag, "Refuting Reiman and Nathanson," *Philosophy & Public Affairs* 14 (1985):165–76 ("punishment must vindicate the disrupted public order").

12. Berns, *For Capital Punishment*, p. 173.

13. See, e.g., Robert Johnson and Hans Toch, eds., *The Pains of Imprisonment* (1982).

14. See Wendy Phillips Wolfson, "The Deterrent Effect of the Death Penalty upon Prison Murder," in Bedau, ed., *The Death Penalty in America*, 3d ed. (1982), pp. 159–73.

15. Hugo Adam Bedau and Michael L. Radelet, "Miscarriages of Justice in Potentially Capital Cases," presented at the annual meeting of the American Society of Criminology, November 1985.

16. Ernest van den Haag argues, with evident complacency, that the death penalty does "lead to the unintended death of some innocents in the long run"; he goes on to add that this leaves the death penalty precisely where other things of the same sort are: "in the long run nearly all human activities are likely to lead to the unintended deaths of innocents." Van den Haag, "The Death Penalty Vindicates the Law," p. 42. This tends to obscure three important points. First, lawful activities that take "statistical lives" (e.g., coal mining) are not designed to kill anyone, whereas every death by capital punishment (whether of a guilty or an innocent person) is intentional. Second, society permits dangerous commercial and recreational activities on various grounds—it would be wrongly paternalistic to interfere with what people choose to do at their own risk (e.g., scaling dangerous cliffs), and society can better afford the cost of the risky activity than the cost of its complete prevention or stricter regulation (e.g., public highways crowded with long truck-trailer rigs rather than separate highways for cars and trucks). But these reasons have no bearing on the choice between the death penalty and imprisonment, unless the combined deterrent/incapacitative effects of executions are demonstrably superior to those of the alternative. Since no defender of the death penalty has sustained the burden of the proof on this point—see the papers cited in n. 3 supra—van den Haag's argument is undermined. Van den Haag's position would be less vulnerable to objection if the only executions he favored were of persons convicted of several—serial, multiple, or recidivist—murders. But he does not confine his support for the death penalty to such cases.

17. Michael Davis has recently argued that the death penalty is no more "irrevocable," in any important sense of that term, than many other punishments, including life in prison. See Davis, "Is the Death Penalty Irrevocable?" *Social Theory and Practice*

10 (1984):143–56. Insofar as he addresses the arguments I put forward in Chapter 1, to explain why death is a "more severe" punishment than imprisonment, he does not seem to disagree. On his interpretation, however, the issue of revocability has nothing to do with severity (see p. 147). Basic to his argument that the punishments of death and of life in prison are equally (ir)revocable is the idea that (a) an irrevocable punishment is such that if it is erroneously imposed on someone, then there is no way to compensate the person for the injustice he suffers, and (b) anyone has interests that are not extinguished with the end of natural life (see p. 146). But as compensating a person is not always identical with conferring a benefit on something he is interested in—rather, it is sometimes a matter of benefiting *him*, directly and in his own person—the truth of (a) and (b) do not entail that there is no difference, relative to irrevocability, that distinguishes the punishment of death from a life behind bars.

18. See Barbara Ann Stolz, "Congress and Capital Punishment: An Exercise in Symbolic Politics," *Law & Policy Quarterly* 5 (1983):157–80; and Tom R. Tyler and Renee Weber, "Support for the Death Penalty: Instrumental Response to Crime or Symbolic Attitude?" *Law & Society Review* 17 (1982):21–45. Tyler and Weber bifurcate all defenses of the death penalty into the "instrumental" and the "symbolic." Thus a retributive defense of the death penalty is, for them, merely "symbolic." Nor do they make it clear whether the "symbolic" role of this punishment is a conscious and intentional one. Stolz is concerned with the conscious symbolism of enacting national (more precisely, federal) criminal penalties; how much of what she reports could be transferred without loss to the reasons for enactment of state death penalty laws or to the reasons the public supports executions (state or federal) is not clear.

Questions for Reading and Analysis

1. According to Bedau, on what should the resolution of the death-penalty debate rest? Why?

2. How does Bedau organize his discussion?

3. What are the six arguments in support of capital punishment? Compare these to the arguments of van den Haag. Has Bedau covered the arguments presented by van den Haag?

4. What are two reasons for dismissing the "taxpayer's argument"? Compare Bedau and van den Haag on the role of cost in one's position on the death penalty. Do they agree? What might you conclude from your comparison?

5. What is Bedau's position on deterrence? Is there evidence that the death penalty deters murder? Is deterrence a justifiable use of criminal law? Is capital punishment justifiable as a possible deterrent?

6. What are the facts on recidivist murderers? What kind of murderer do many people want executed, even those who generally oppose the death penalty? What would be accomplished if only this kind of murderer were executed? Which group of people will still be unhappy? Why?

7. Does retribution *allow* for the death penalty? Does it *require* it? What distinction does Bedau make between *retribution* and *revenge*? What does the author's distinctions among words illustrate about the nature of good argument?

8. What are Bedau's arguments for rejecting capital punishment as the necessary response to grave crimes?

9. Bedau begins his discussion of the alternative to the death penalty by agreeing that it is not an ideal alternative. By so doing, what does he accomplish? How does this strengthen his argument?

10. The author gives three reasons for preferring imprisonment to death. Explain each in your own words.

11. What does the death penalty symbolize, according to Bedau? Why is that the very reason to oppose the death penalty?

Questions for Discussion and Response

1. Compare Bedau's views on deterrence to van den Haag's. Who makes the better case? Why?

2. Which of the three reasons for supporting imprisonment over death sentencing do you think is the strongest? Why?

3. Could you accept the compromise position of death sentencing only for multiple murders? Is this a position we should work to make the practice in this country? Why or why not?

4. Do you think that the motive of revenge justifies the death penalty? If so, how would you refute Bedau on this issue?

5. Has Bedau led you to change your views on capital punishment in any way? Explain.

Innocent on Death Row

George F. Will

George Will (b. 1941) has been a syndicated columnist since 1974. He is the author of several books, one about his great love—baseball. He is also a regular participant on television programs of political analysis. Will published the following column on April 6, 2000.

1   "Don't you worry about it," said the Oklahoma prosecutor to the defense attorney. "We're gonna needle your client. You know, lethal injection, the needle. We're going to needle Robert."

2   Oklahoma almost did. Robert Miller spent nine years on death row, during six of which the state had DNA test results proving his sperm was not that of the man who raped and killed the 92-year-old woman. The prosecutor said the tests only proved that another man had been with Miller during the crime. Finally, the weight of scientific evidence, wielded by an implacable defense attorney, got Miller released and another man indicted.

3   You could fill a book with such hair-curling true stories of blighted lives and justice traduced. Three authors have filled one. It should change the argument about capital

punishment and other aspects of the criminal justice system. Conservatives, especially, should draw this lesson from the book: Capital punishment, like the rest of the criminal justice system, is a government program, so skepticism is in order.

4   Horror, too, is a reasonable response to what Barry Scheck, Peter Neufeld and Jim Dwyer demonstrate in *Actual Innocence: Five Days to Execution and Other Dispatches from the Wrongly Convicted*. You will not soon read a more frightening book. It is a catalog of appalling miscarriages of justice, some of them nearly lethal. Their cumulative weight compels the conclusion that many innocent people are in prison, and some innocent people have been executed.

5   Scheck and Neufeld (both members of O. J. Simpson's "dream team" of defense attorneys) founded the pro-bono Innocence Project at the Benjamin N. Cardozo School of Law in New York to aid persons who convincingly claim to have been wrongly convicted. Dwyer, winner of two Pulitzer Prizes, is a columnist for the *New York Daily News*. Their book is a heart-breaking and infuriating compendium of stories of lives ruined by:

6   ■ Forensic fraud, such as that by the medical examiner who, in one death report, included the weight of the gallbladder and spleen of a man from whom both organs had been surgically removed long ago.

7   ■ Mistaken identifications by eyewitnesses or victims, which contributed to 84 percent of the convictions overturned by the Innocence Project's DNA exonerations.

8   ■ Criminal investigations, especially of the most heinous crimes, that become "echo chambers" in which, because of the normal human craving for retribution, the perceptions of prosecutors and jurors are shaped by what they want to be true. (The authors cite evidence that most juries will convict even when admissions have been repudiated by the defendant and contradicted by physical evidence.)

9   ■ The sinister culture of jailhouse snitches, who earn reduced sentences by fabricating "admissions" by fellow inmates to unsolved crimes.

10   ■ Incompetent defense representation, such as that by the Kentucky attorney in a capital case who gave his business address as Kelley's Keg tavern.

11   The list of ways the criminal justice system misfires could be extended, but some numbers tell the most serious story: In the 24 years since the resumption of executions under Supreme Court guidelines, about 620 have occurred, but 87 condemned persons—one for every seven executed—had their convictions vacated by exonerating evidence. In eight of these cases, and in many more exonerations not involving death row inmates, the evidence was from DNA.

12   One inescapable inference from these numbers is that some of the 620 persons executed were innocent. Which is why, after the exoneration of 13 prisoners on Illinois' death row since 1987, for reasons including exculpatory DNA evidence, Gov. George Ryan, a Republican, has imposed a moratorium on executions.

13   Scheck, Neufeld and Dwyer note that when a plane crashes, an intensive investigation is undertaken to locate the cause and prevent recurrences. Why is there no comparable urgency about demonstrable, multiplying failures in the criminal justice system? They recommend many reforms, especially pertaining to the use of DNA and the prevention of forensic incompetence and fraud. Sen. Patrick Leahy's Innocence Protection Act would enable inmates to get DNA testing pertinent to a conviction or death sentence, and ensure that courts will hear resulting evidence.

14   The good news is that science can increasingly serve the defense of innocence. But there is other news.

15   Two powerful arguments for capital punishment are that it saves lives, if its deterrence effect is not vitiated by sporadic implementation, and it heightens society's valuation of life by expressing proportionate anger at the taking of life. But that valuation is lowered by careless or corrupt administration of capital punishment, which *Actual Innocence* powerfully suggests is intolerably common.

Questions for Reading and Analysis

1. What is Will's subject? (Do not answer "the death penalty"; be more precise.)
2. What is the occasion for his column? That is, what has led him to write on this subject?
3. What kinds of stories are found in *Actual Innocence?*
4. How many people have received capital punishment since we resumed the death penalty 24 years ago? How many persons convicted of capital crimes had their convictions overturned during that time? What inference does Will draw from these numbers?
5. What is the critical new evidence that is being used to challenge some convictions?
6. Will says that there are two arguments for capital punishment; what are they? Which argument is weakened by miscarriages of justice?
7. What is Will's claim? Is it correct to say that he opposes the death penalty? Explain.

Questions for Discussion and Response

1. How effective are Will's statistics in supporting his argument?
2. Will is appalled by what he has read in *Actual Innocence*. What is your reaction to his list of stories? Why did you react that way?
3. Has Will affected your position on capital punishment in any way? If so, why? If not, why not?
4. Illinois has stopped capital punishment for the moment. Should all states place a moratorium on the death penalty at least until better procedures are in place for handling DNA and other forensic evidence? Why or why not?

The Death Penalty Is Fairer Than Ever

Eugene H. Methvin

A graduate of the University of Georgia, Eugene Methvin (b. 1934) is the author of two books (*The Riot Makers* and *The Rise of Radicalism*) and many articles. He is currently contributing editor to *Reader's Digest*. His article on the death penalty appeared in *The Wall Street Journal* May 10, 2000.

1   If there's been a change in the death-penalty winds, it's because capital punishment opponents have been fanning a national panic over the chance that we might be putting innocent people to death. The truth is, we've never been better positioned to ascertain guilt or innocence.

2   Last month, Illinois Gov. George Ryan declared a moratorium on executions in his state. A Republican who favors capital punishment, Mr. Ryan nonetheless said Illinois had a "shameful record" of condemning innocent people to die. He based his decision in part on the case of Steve Manning, a former Chicago cop who in January became the 13th man exonerated from Illinois's death row since 1976.

3   Mr. Ryan isn't the only Republican calling for a rethinking of the death penalty. In April televangelist Pat Robertson joined the ACLU in asking for a nationwide moratorium on executions. Widespread coverage has followed a new book, *Actual Innocence: Five Days to Execution and Other Dispatches from the Wrongly Convicted*, written by two lawyers and a journalist who claim DNA is proving appalling miscarriages of justice. And just this week, New York Gov. George Pataki proposed a state DNA review committee to examine all convictions overturned because of new genetic evidence.

Rarity of Error

4   Some of the scrutiny is justified. Illinois has set a national record over the past decade for convicting cops and judges in federal corruption probes, and the state has had some close calls—one death-row prisoner came within two days of execution before he was exonerated. And certainly no one can say unequivocally that no innocent person in the U.S. has been wrongly executed, or that it can't happen.

5   But so far no one has demonstrated that it has. Quite the opposite. With the average time consumed by appeals between sentencing and execution now at about 10 years, and with the arrival of DNA testing in the 1990s, the likelihood of wrongful executions is less than ever.

6   Opponents of capital punishment have pointed to the work of two abolitionist scholars, Hugo Bedau and Michael Radelet, who claimed they found 23 instances of convicts executed between 1900 and 1986 who were later proved innocent. But only one of these executions occurred after 1976, when the Supreme Court radically revamped death-penalty procedures. Moreover, the scholars appear to have based their conclusions on defendants' briefs, newspaper stories, defense-attorney claims or lapses in prosecutor conduct or trial procedure.

7   Stephen Markman and Paul Cassell, two Justice Department lawyers during the Reagan administration, reviewed 13 of the 23 cases—every one since 1950, the date after which they could get original court records. Based on these actual transcripts, they demonstrated that the alleged executed innocents were "guilty as sin," and that, at least since 1950, there was no documented case of innocent individuals executed. In all 13 cases, they noted, the trial records contained eyewitness testimony, confessions, or circumstantial and physical evidence demonstrating guilt. If anything, said Mr. Markman, the Bedau-Radelet study "speaks eloquently about the extraordinary rarity of error in capital punishment."

8   Virginia's 1992 execution of Roger Keith Coleman illustrates the point. An articulate liar and manipulator, Coleman had already served a 20-month prison term for attempted rape. Yet after an unspeakable rape-murder, he mobilized America's vocal

abolitionist minority and conned the media into portraying him as the innocent victim of backwoods justice.

9   On March 10, 1981, Coleman went to the home of his sister-in-law, whose husband was at work, cut her throat and raped her. Blood stains on his pants, semen matching Coleman's rare blood type, and witnesses' testimony—not to mention his own lies about his movements that night—persuaded a jury to convict him.

10   In 1990 Kitty Behan, a former ACLU lawyer with the high-powered Washington law firm of Arnold & Porter, mounted a legal and media blitz to save him. Ms. Behan got a court order requiring a newly developed DNA test on the semen. But the highly respected expert she chose found the test pointed unmistakably to Coleman. She then hired another "expert" to dispute these findings. She issued press releases accusing another man of the murder. The man sued for libel, and Ms. Behan's law firm reportedly paid an out-of-court settlement.

11   Still, Ms. Behan's media blitz had an effect. Both *Newsweek* and *Time* ran stories portraying Coleman as an innocent victim. Neither magazine mentioned the damning DNA evidence. When U.S. District Judge Glen Williams reviewed the evidence, he declared: "This court finds the case against Coleman as strong or stronger than the evidence adduced at trial." Eleven years after he murdered his sister-in-law, Coleman was executed. But he left millions fearing an innocent man had been murdered by the justice system.

12   Many death-row convictions are overturned not on questions of guilt but on procedural grounds, in a judicial war against the death penalty. The Georgia Supreme Court in March overturned the death sentence of a killer who nearly decapitated a former girlfriend. The court found the prosecutor had wrongly urged jurors to follow the biblical mandate: "All they who take up the sword shall die by the sword." Departing from prior decisions approving biblical arguments, Justice Norman Fletcher decreed: "Biblical references . . . improperly appeal to the religious beliefs of jurors."

13   Other judges have voided death sentences because jurors weren't told the killer would otherwise get life without parole. Prosecutors, however, are forbidden to argue that killers might escape, which they do, even from high-security facilities.

14   Multiple appeals not only make executing the innocent more unlikely than ever, they make it hard to execute the clearly guilty. Illinois executed John Wayne Gacy in 1994 for murdering 33 young men. He had confessed, and his guilt was never in the slightest doubt. Yet his lawyers consumed 14 years with legal delays. "He had 523 separate appeals," fumes House Judiciary Chairman Henry Hyde (R., Ill.). "And none were based on a claim of innocence."

15   Things haven't changed much since then. On the first anniversary of the Oklahoma City bombing, Congress passed the Antiterrorism and Effective Death Penalty Act. For the first time in 128 years, legislators used their constitutional authority to strip the Supreme Court and lower federal judges of jurisdiction to hear appeals for a certain class of case.

16   Even under this change, a state convict can still have 10 appeals (in some cases 12), before the new law affects him. He can go through five or six state and federal courts on direct appeal, then go through them again with habeas corpus petitions. But for a second federal habeas corpus review, Congress decreed, convicts must get permission from

a three-judge federal appeals panel. If he is turned down, the Supreme Court can grant only one further review, and only in rare circumstances.

17   As for DNA, it is doing much more than just helping re-evaluate convictions. At least 64 U.S. criminal convictions have been set aside as a result of DNA testing, according to the Innocence Project of the Cardozo Law School at Yeshiva University. But DNA testing also allows investigators to eliminate many suspects early on, and concentrate on pursuing the real perpetrators.

False Sentimentality

18   Even Hugo Bedau, a professor at Tufts University and a leading abolitionist, has admitted that it is "false sentimentality to argue that the death penalty ought to be abolished because of the abstract possibility that an innocent person might be executed when the record fails to disclose that such cases occur." That drunk drivers kill thousands of innocents, that airplanes fall, that pedestrians get smashed by cars, does not prevent us from drinking, flying or crossing the street. But the possibility that an innocent person may be executed is supposed to make us give up capital punishment because "death is irrevocable."

19   Compelled to administer justice in an imperfect world, we should not allow a utopian yearning for perfect certainty to render us moral eunuchs. As George Washington wrote a friend on the eve of the Constitutional Convention, "Perfection falls not to the lot of mortal man. We must take men as we find them."

Questions for Reading and Analysis

1. What is Methvin's claim? Where does he state it?

2. Is it possible to say that no innocent person has been executed?

3. Is there good evidence, in Methvin's view, that few if any innocent persons have been executed since 1953?

4. What does the author seek to accomplish with the detailed example of Coleman?

5. How has recent federal legislation changed the appeals process for those on death row? How many years of appeals are available to death-row inmates?

6. DNA evidence can be used to determine innocence and overturn incorrect convictions. What, as the author points out, can it also be used for?

7. What does Methvin expect to accomplish by quoting Bedau's "false sentimentality" comments?

8. Evaluate Methvin's argument in paragraphs 17 and 18. Is it logical? Is it effective?

Questions for Discussion and Response

1. Compare Methvin's response to the book *Actual Innocence* with George Will's response. Which writer's response seems more logical, more appropriate, in your

view? Why? Find one or two reviews of the book and compare the reviewers' comments with Methvin's and Will's.

2. Has Methvin affected your position on capital punishment in any way? If so, why? If not, why not?

3. Has Methvin presented a convincing argument? Why or why not?

4. In spite of seemingly convincing DNA evidence in the O. J. Simpson trial, Simpson was not convicted. Do jurors too often misunderstand DNA? Is it possible to get a fair trial with a "jury of one's peers" given the complexity of today's forensic evidence and the parade of "expert" witnesses? What suggestions do you have for the courts (and society) to deal with these issues?

CHAPTER 14

Censorship, Pornography, and the Arts

Four writers in this chapter explore contemporary situations that generate debates about censorship—and First Amendment rights. These situations include censoring books in school libraries, removing some controversial passages in assigned books, "policing" the Internet, and restricting campaign funding and flag desecration. As you explore these specific issues, keep in mind that the Supreme Court continues to hand down rulings that shape our interpretation of First Amendment rights, so what is protected speech under the First Amendment is never absolute—it continues to evolve or be reinterpreted, depending on your point of view. Also keep in mind that many would argue that there is no such thing as absolute freedom in a society, and the First Amendment does not pretend to offer absolute freedoms. For example, you cannot go into a crowded theater and yell "Fire!" when there is no fire. You will be arrested for this behavior that puts others at risk.

Reflecting on the following questions before you read will enrich your reading on this always-troublesome collection of issues we label censorship or First Amendment issues:

1. Do you have a position on censorship? If so, what is it?
2. What restrictions of free speech—and publication—are part of current laws?
3. Have you considered positions between the extremes of absolutely no censorship of published materials (in any medium) and of laws prohibiting the publication of obscene, pornographic, or treasonable works or hate speech? What are some possible restrictions that may be agreed upon by most people?
4. What are some ways to control what is published (in any medium) without always resorting to legal restrictions? Are any of these possibilities feasible?

Websites Relevant to This Chapter's Topic

MIT Student Association for Freedom of Expression (SAFE)
http://web.mit.edu/safe/www/safe
Good information and links; site opposes censorship.

Index on Censorship
www.oneworld.org/index_oc
A bi-monthly magazine supporting freedom of speech.

National Coalition Against Censorship (NCAC)

www.ncac.org

Organization promoting free speech. Site contains articles and news alerts.

The Censorship Pages, Sponsored by Books A to Z

www.booksatoz.com/censorship

Contains links to resources and lists of frequently banned books.

Expelling *Huck Finn*

Nat Hentoff

A staff writer for the *Village Voice* and a syndicated columnist for many years, Nat Hentoff (b. 1925) is also an author of articles and books on jazz and education. He is perhaps best known for his "Sweet Land of Liberty" columns on First Amendment issues. "Expelling *Huck Finn*" was published in the *Washington Post* on November 27, 1999.

1   The Pennsylvania State Conference of the NAACP has instructed its branches to file grievances with the state's human rights commission demanding that local school boards and district superintendents remove Mark Twain's *Adventures of Huckleberry Finn* from mandatory reading lists.

2   The charge, supported by the national NAACP, is that "tax dollars should not be used to perpetuate a stereotype that has psychologically damaging effects on the self-esteem of African American children."

3   Some years ago I was talking to African American eighth-graders in a Brooklyn public school who had been reading *Huckleberry Finn* in class—along with the history of racism in such towns as Hannibal, Mo., where Twain had grown up.

4   The students recently had been discussing the passage in which Huck, on the raft with Jim, was tormented by what he had been raised to believe—that he would go to hell if he did not report this runaway slave to the owner.

5   Huck wrote a note doing just that, but finally, destroying the note, he said to himself, "All right, then, I'll *go* to hell!"

6   "Do you think we're so dumb," one of the Brooklyn eighth-graders said to me, "that we don't know the difference between a racist book and an anti-racist book? Sure, the book is full of the word 'Nigger.' That's how those bigots talked back then."

7   As Twain said years later, Huck, after writing the note, was struggling between "a sound heart" and "a deformed conscience" that he had to make right.

8   "The people whom Huck and Jim encounter on the Mississippi"—Russell Baker wrote in the *New York Times* in 1982—"are drunkards, murderers, bullies, swindlers, lynchers, thieves, liars, frauds, child abusers, numskulls, hypocrites, windbags and traders in human flesh. All are white. The one man of honor in this phantasmagoria is 'Nigger Jim,' as Twain called him to emphasize the irony of a society in which the only true gentleman was held beneath contempt."

9   Michael Meyers—assistant national director of the NAACP under Roy Wilkins from 1975 to 1984—wrote to Julian Bond, the present NAACP chairman, about the organization's desire to censor *Huck Finn*.

10   Calling the book "a great anti-slavery classic," Meyers—now the executive director of the New York Civil Rights Coalition—asked Bond whether there is an actual NAACP policy "that encourages NAACP branches to either support or seek book banning or censorship." Bond, as Meyers noted in his letter, is on the ACLU's national advisory council, as is the NAACP's president, Kweisi Mfume. If such a policy exists, Meyers wrote, "what are you doing—or what are you prepared to do—to change such a policy?"

11   Bond answered that "the NAACP does not have a policy for every occasion. Might I ask you for a policy we might adopt that could allow the NAACP to express outrage at racist expression while protecting free speech?"

12   Meyers was puzzled by the response because, he says, *Huckleberry Finn*—as the youngsters in Brooklyn emphatically understood—is *anti*-racist.

13   In 1998 Judge Stephen Reinhardt, writing for a unanimous three-judge panel of the 9th Circuit Court of Appeals, rejected a lawsuit by an African American parent, who is also a teacher, asking that *Huckleberry Finn* be removed from mandatory reading lists in the Phoenix, Ariz., schools.

14   "Words can hurt, particularly racist epithets," Reinhardt wrote, "but a necessary component of any education is learning to think critically about offensive ideas. Without that ability, one can do little to respond to them." Part of learning to think critically about offensive speech is to understand the context in which it is used.

15   Bond might consider sending Judge Reinhardt's decision (*Kathy Monteiro v. the Tempe Union High School District*) to the Pennsylvania State Conference of the NAACP. He might also inform it of "The Jim Dilemma: Reading Race in *Huckleberry Finn*" by Jocelyn Chadwick-Joshua, an African American who has been instructing black and white teachers about the book for years.

16   She writes: "Without the memory of what a word once meant and what it can continue to mean, we as a society are doomed to repeat earlier mistakes about ourselves, each other, and serious issues involving us all."

Questions for Reading and Analysis

1. What is Hentoff's subject?

2. What is the occasion for Hentoff's column? That is, what has happened to lead the author to write?

3. Hentoff devotes four paragraphs to his experience in a Brooklyn school. What are we to infer from his experience with Brooklyn students?

4. What is Meyers's view of the novel? Is the issue really a conflict between censorship and racist writing? What, in Hentoff's view, does the NAACP need to understand?

5. What is Hentoff's claim?

Questions for Discussion and Response

1. Have you read *Huck Finn*? If so, was your understanding similar to that of the Brooklyn students—or were you offended by the novel? Explain your reactions.

2. Many scholars of American literature and culture will argue that *Huck Finn* is essential reading. Should books that are so important be required reading?

3. Some parents have worked to ban *Huck Finn* from school libraries. Should it be banned? Should any book be banned from a library? Explain your views.

If You Assign My Book, Don't Censor It

Mark Mathabane

A former White House Fellow at the Department of Education, Mark Mathabane is best known for his widely read—and at times controversial—novel *Kaffir Boy*. Mathabane lives and writes in North Carolina; his most recent novel is *Ubuntu*. The following article appeared in the *Washington Post* on November 28, 1999.

1   A few weeks ago, school officials at Kearsley High School in Flint, Mich., decided to censor *Kaffir Boy*, my story of growing up in a South African ghetto during apartheid. On the recommendation of a special committee of administrators, teachers and staff, the school has begun taping over several sentences and parts of sentences in its copies of the book after a half-dozen parents objected to my graphic description of one of the most harrowing experiences of my life: When I was 7 years old and trapped in the poverty-stricken ghetto of the Alexandra township, 10 miles north of Johannesburg, hunger drove me to tag along with a ring of boys who prostituted themselves for food. One parent called my description "pornography," according to the *Flint Journal*, adding that *Kaffir Boy* belonged in an adult bookstore rather than in a 10th-grade English class.

2   I wasn't altogether surprised by the parents' objections. The raw emotions and experiences in *Kaffir Boy*, which constitute the core of its power and appeal, have made the book controversial ever since its publication in the United States in 1986. When it became required reading for thousands of high school students nationwide several years ago, it was challenged by parents in school districts in a dozen states and, in some cases, withdrawn. No, what surprises—and disturbs—me is the decision at Kearsley to censor the text, altering a passage that marks a crucial turning point in the book—and in my life.

3   As a parent of three public school students, ages 6, 8 and 10, I pay attention to what they are assigned to read. I've read them portions of *Kaffir Boy* and my other books, which deal with issues of hunger, child abuse, poverty, violence, the oppression of women and racism. I'm always careful to provide context, to talk to them in a language they can understand.

4   Every year I also talk to thousands of students about my work and my life in South Africa. I tell them how fortunate they are to live in America, how important it is not to take this nation's freedoms for granted. I recall for them how my peers and I were forbidden by the government in Pretoria to read the U.S. Constitution and the Bill of Rights. I recall how empowered I felt after I clandestinely secured a copy of the Declaration of Independence. And I recall how, during the Soweto uprising of 1976, hundreds of students died fighting for recognition of their unalienable rights to "life, liberty and the pursuit of happiness."

5   When I came to America in 1978, I was stunned—and exhilarated—to find out that I could walk into any library and check out books that were uncensored and read them without fear of being harassed, thrown in jail or killed.

6   I have that experience in mind when I think about my own children's reading lists. In large part, I trust their teachers to have the judgment to assign books that are not only consistent with educational goals, but also with my children's maturity level. Should my children bring home a book I find objectionable, the responsible thing for me to do would be to request that my child be assigned a different one.

7   That's why I have no problem with parents who make such a request about *Kaffir Boy*. The parents of a sophomore at West Mecklenburg High School in Charlotte, N.C., where the book has also been challenged, did just that. They were not only uncomfortable with the prostitution scene, but also with my use of racially graphic language such as the word "kaffir" (a pejorative term for "black").

8   But I strongly disagree with censoring portions of the book. They have no right to decide the issue for other students. Should those students be deprived of what I believe is a key scene in order to make a few parents comfortable?

9   I don't think so. Books aren't written with the comfort of readers in mind. I know I didn't write *Kaffir Boy* that way. I wrote it to reflect reality, to show the world the inhumanity of the apartheid system. It wasn't an easy book for me to write. The memories gave me nightmares. What's more, after the book was published in the United States, members of my family in South Africa were persecuted by the Pretoria regime, which subsequently banned the book there.

10   *Kaffir Boy* is disturbing, but it isn't pornographic. As Kari Molter, chairwoman of the English department at Kearsley High, said, the prostitution scene, which makes up three pages, is "frightening," but it is "an important scene." I included it in the book not to titillate readers, but to reveal a disturbing truth about life under apartheid.

11   That disturbing truth included the terror and helplessness I felt as a child during brutal midnight police raids; the grinding, stunting poverty in which I, my family and millions of other blacks were steeped; the emasculation of my father by a system that denied him the right to earn a living in a way that gave him dignity; the hopelessness and psychic pain that led me to contemplate suicide at age 10; the sacrifices and faith of my long-suffering mother as she battled to save me from the dead-end life of the street and its gangs.

12   Not the least disturbing of those truths is the passage about prostitution. My father, the only breadwinner in a family of nine, had been arrested for the crime of being unemployed. There was no food in our shack, and my mother couldn't even get the usual cattle blood from the slaughterhouse to boil as soup. Desperate for food, one afternoon I linked up with a group of 5-, 6- and 7-year-old boys on the way to the nearby men's hostel. Their pimp, a 13-year-old boy named Mphandlani, promised that at the hostel we would get money and "all the food we could eat" in exchange for playing "a little game" with the migrant workers who lived there.

13   Once inside the hostel, I stood by in confusion and fear as the men and boys began undressing. In the book, I give some physical descriptions of what happened. When Mphandlani told me to undress, too, I refused. One of the men came after me, and I bolted out of the hostel. I fled because I knew that what the men were doing to the boys

was wrong, and recalled my parents telling me never to do wrong things. I was called a fool—and shunned—by those boys afterward.

14   Resisting peer pressure is one of the toughest things for young people to do. That is the lesson of the prostitution scene. It's a lesson that seems to be lost on the people who want to censor my book. Teenagers understand what peer pressure is. They confront tough choices every day, particularly if they happen to live in environments where child abuse, poverty, violence and death are commonplace, where innocence dies young, and where children can't afford to be children.

15   Many students have connected powerfully with the story of *Kaffir Boy*. The book, they've told me in letters and e-mail, teaches them to never give up in the face of adversity, not to take freedom—or food—for granted, to regard education as a powerful weapon of hope, and always to strive to do the right thing.

16   Could *Kaffir Boy* have had this impact without the prostitution scene? I doubt it. It was an event that changed me forever. Could I have made that point using less graphic language? Perhaps. But language is a very sacred thing for a writer. When I write, I strive for clarity and directness, so the reader understands precisely what I mean. To fudge language in order to avoid offending the sensibilities of one group or another leads to doublespeak, which is the death of honesty.

17   That very honesty is what prompted a senior from Sentinel High School in Missoula, Mont., to send me a letter a few days ago. In it she wrote that *Kaffir Boy* made her realize "that no matter what, there is always hope." It is this hope that I'm seeking to keep alive with my books.

18   I owe my life to books. While I was in the ghetto, groaning under the yoke of apartheid, wallowing in self-pity, believing that I was doomed to die from the sheer agony of frustrated hopes and strangled dreams, books became my best friends and my salvation. Reading broadened my horizons, deepened my sensibilities and, most importantly, made me think. Books liberated me from mental slavery and opened doors of opportunity where none seemed to exist.

19   Censorship is not the solution to the legitimate concern some parents have about what is appropriate for their children to read. I wish child abuse and racism weren't facts of life, but they are. Only by knowing about them can we combat them effectively.

20   What's more, there are alternatives to censorship. One possible solution lies in schools developing reading-list guidelines, such as those being drawn up by the Charlotte-Mecklenburg school system in the wake of objections to *Kaffir Boy*. Under the guidelines, teachers will still choose their own books, but they will be required to give students and parents a summary of the contents and potential concerns, such as profanity or sexually explicit scenes. I don't mind if my book doesn't make the list, or if some parents choose another title for their offspring, but if students do read it, let them read it the way I wrote it.

Questions for Reading and Analysis

1. What is the author's occasion for writing? What is the specific issue with regard to *Kaffir Boy*?

2. What is Mathabane's claim?

3. What does the author seek to accomplish in paragraphs 3–7 when he writes of his children and the U.S. freedoms that he admired from a distance in South Africa?

4. What does Mathabane approve of parents doing? What does he object to?

5. Why is the prostitution scene disturbing? Why is it not, in the author's view, pornographic? What definition of pornography emerges from Mathabane's discussion?

6. How does the author defend his choice of language in *Kaffir Boy*?

7. What did books do for the author?

8. What can schools do, instead of censoring, to help parents guide their children's reading?

Questions for Discussion and Response

1. Have you read *Kaffir Boy*? If so, did you find it disturbing? Did you find it moving and encouraging, as the author suggests?

2. Are there other assigned readings that bothered you—or that your parents did not want you to read? If so, how did you handle the situation?

3. Do you agree with Mathabane's definition of pornography? If not, why not?

4. Mathabane would rather students not read his book than read it with parts removed. Can you understand his position? Why does he think it inappropriate to change someone's words?

5. Has the author presented an effective argument against altering books? Against censorship? Explain.

Freedom's Fair-Weather Friends

Robyn E. Blumner

A graduate of Cornell University and New York University (J.D.), Robyn Blumner (b. 1961) is currently a columnist and editorial writer for the *St. Petersburg Times*. Her article on First Amendment issues appeared March 31, 2000, in *The Wall Street Journal*.

1   Clarity is a rare thing in politics, but this week, as the Senate debated two proposed constitutional amendments, one thing was made perfectly clear: In Congress, the First Amendment has few true friends.

2   Who is a true friend to free speech? Just like in real life, it's a person who can be counted on through thick and thin, good times and bad—what Thelma was to Louise, or Bebe Rebozo to Richard Nixon.

3   True friends of free speech understand that freedom is an all-or-nothing proposition. Regardless of the issue—pornography on the Internet, violent video games, support of political candidates or flag burning—the important question is not whether speech is good or bad, but who has the power to decide. In a free society, the individual makes his own choices about which political causes to advocate and what entertainment to enjoy. It's a simple idea, but one that seems to elude our political leaders on

both the left and right. For them, the First Amendment is like dim sum—take what you want, and leave the rest.

4   Both of the amendments the Senate rejected this week would have limited the Bill of Rights. One would give Congress the power to prohibit the physical desecration of the American flag. The other, proposed by Sen. Ernest Hollings (D., S.C.), would allow the government to set spending and contribution limits on campaigns, giving Congress the switch to turn off political speech.

5   Each was introduced as a response to Supreme Court rulings striking down, on free-speech grounds, statutes with similar provisions. A constitutional amendment is the only way at Congress' disposal to trump the court's ruling. While both amendments ultimately failed, the senators' highly partisan voting patterns demonstrate that many see their vow to uphold the Constitution as a marriage of convenience.

6   Democrats voted 33–12 against the flag amendment, which Republicans supported 51–4. Democrats supported the campaign-finance amendment by a margin of 30–15, whereas Republicans deep-sixed it, 52–3.

7   Democrats may wring their hands over the sacredness of free speech when flag burning is on the line, but they don't want to invoke the First Amendment when the conversation shifts to campaign-finance reform. Republicans take an equally disingenuous approach, waving the First Amendment around when political contributions are on the chopping block, then putting it aside when political dissent includes treading on the Stars and Stripes.

8   Thus Sen. Orrin Hatch (R., Utah), lead sponsor of the flag-desecration amendment, spoke of his deep conviction for the First Amendment in the context of campaign finance reform. "Without free speech, " Sen. Hatch warned, "our republic would become a tyranny."

9   This kind of hypocrisy doesn't surprise Paul McMasters, First Amendment ombudsman at the Freedom Forum in Arlington, Va., who notes resignedly that "friends of the First Amendment in Congress are inconsistent and inconstant."

10   Republicans try to outlaw expression they see as unpatriotic rather than communicate the concept that love of country is more profoundly expressed by protecting the principles of freedom than by a piece of cloth. Democrats, meanwhile, talk about "getting the money out of politics," but don't want to be bothered with the disturbing reality that the campaign-finance limits they propose would give government the power to stifle a challenge to the status quo.

11   Politicians learn quickly that standing up for our nation's first principles doesn't always play with their constituents. Rather than show some leadership and teach the voters why the Bill of Rights is worth protecting, they pander, trotting out the First Amendment when it serves them and ignoring it the rest of the time.

12   Sen. Mitch McConnell (R., Ky.) was one of the heroes this week, but even he has a blind spot. Mr. McConnell, a staunch opponent of campaign-finance limits, changed his view on the flag amendment from pro to con because he wanted to take a consistent stance on the First Amendment. During the debate on the Hollings campaign-finance amendment, Mr. McConnell berated his Senate colleagues for forcing him to spend time and energy "defending the Constitution, not from foreign enemies . . . but from Congress itself."

13   Yet Mr. McConnell has voted twice to censor the Internet. In 1996 he supported the Communications Decency Act, which would have stripped universally accessible Internet sites of any content deemed unsuitable for a five-year-old. Then, after the Supreme Court struck down the CDA on the grounds that it severely infringed the free speech of adults, Mr. McConnell joined his colleagues in passing the 1998 Child Online Protection Act.

14   The lesson of all this is that representative bodies can't be counted on to protect individual rights. The tyranny of the majority is as real a danger today as it was in 1791, when the Bill of Rights was ratified. On the left, in addition to campaign finance reform, come efforts to control violence in the media, tobacco advertising, hate speech and sexual speech at the workplace. The right's bugaboos are flag burning, pornography and radical activism. In other words, no matter who's in control in Congress, the First Amendment is always in someone's sight.

15   As friends to free speech, members of Congress take their cues from Monica and Linda rather than Thelma and Louise.

Questions for Reading and Analysis

1. What is Blumner's subject? (Do not answer "the First Amendment"; be more precise.)

2. What are the two specific amendments rejected by the Senate?

3. How did the Senate vote by party? What does the author infer about politicians from the voting pattern?

4. What does the example of Senator McConnell illustrate?

5. What does the political left want to control? What does the political right want to control?

6. What is Blumner's claim?

Questions for Discussion and Response

1. Blumner asserts that "freedom is an all-or-nothing proposition." Is this a realistic assertion—or an overstatement for dramatic effect? Explain your reaction.

2. Blumner lists the favorite issues of the left and right. Do you lean to the left or the right? Do you share the views that the author attributes to your side of the political spectrum?

3. The author lists control of "sexual speech at the workplace" (usually called sexual harassment) as a limitation of First Amendment rights. Is this a new idea for you? Do you agree with Blumner? If so, why? If not, how would you challenge her view?

4. Campaign-finance changes would limit political advertising. Do you see this issue as a First Amendment issue? If so, why? Is there another way to approach campaign-finance changes? On what basis can one defend the need for change?

Protecting Our Children from Internet Smut: Moral Duty or Moral Panic?

Julia Wilkins

Julia Wilkins (b. 1968) holds a master's degree in social policy and is currently a special education teacher. She has published several articles on education and is the author of two books: Math Activities for Young Children: A Resource Guide for Parents and Teachers (1995) and Non-Competitive Motor Activities: A Guide for Elementary Classroom Teachers (1996). In the following article, which appeared in the September/October 1997 issue of The Humanist, Wilkins applies the sociological concept "moral panic" to Internet pornography.

1   The term *moral panic* is one of the more useful concepts to have emerged from sociology in recent years. A moral panic is characterized by a wave of public concern, anxiety, and fervor about something, usually perceived as a threat to society. The distinguishing factors are a level of interest totally out of proportion to the real importance of the subject, some individuals building personal careers from the pursuit and magnification of the issue, and the replacement of reasoned debate with witchhunts and hysteria.

2   Moral panics of recent memory include the Joseph McCarthy anti-Communist witchhunts of the 1950s and the satanic ritual abuse allegations of the 1980s. And, more recently, we have witnessed a full-blown moral panic about pornography on the Internet. Sparked by the July 3, 1995, *Time* cover article "On a Screen Near You: Cyberporn," this moral panic has been perpetuated and intensified by a raft of subsequent media reports. As a result, there is now a widely held belief that pornography is easily accessible to all children using the Internet. This was also the judgment of Congress, which, proclaiming to be "protecting the children" voted overwhelmingly in 1996 for legislation to make it a criminal offense to send "indecent" material over the Internet into people's computers.

3   The original *Time* article was based on its exclusive access to Marty Rimm's *Georgetown University Law Journal* paper, "Marketing Pornography on the Information Superhighway." Although published, the article had not received peer review and was based on an undergraduate research project concerning descriptions of images on adult bulletin board systems in the United States. Using the information in this paper, *Time* discussed the type of pornography available online, such as "pedophilia (nude pictures of children), hebephelia (youths) and . . . images of bondage, sadomasochism, urination, defecation, and sex acts with a barnyard full of animals." The article proposed that pornography of this nature is readily available to anyone who is even remotely computer literate and raised the stakes by offering quotes from worried parents who feared for their children's safety. It also presented the possibility that pornographic material could be mailed to children without their parents' knowledge. *Time*'s example was of a ten-year-old boy who supposedly received pornographic images in his e-mail showing "10 thumbnail size pictures showing couples engaged in various acts of sodomy, heterosexual intercourse and lesbian sex." Naturally, the boy's mother was shocked and concerned, saying, "Children should not be subject to these images." *Time* also quoted another mother who said that she wanted her children to benefit from the vast amount of knowledge available on the Internet but was inclined not to allow access, fearing that

her children could be "bombarded with X-rated pornography and [she] would know nothing about it."

4   From the outset, Rimm's report generated a lot of excitement—not only because it was reportedly the first published study of online pornography but also because of the secrecy involved in the research and publication of the article. In fact, the *New York Times* reported on July 24 1995, that Marty Rimm was being investigated by his university, Carnegie Mellon, for unethical research and, as a result, would not be giving testimony to a Senate hearing on Internet pornography. Two experts from *Time* reportedly discovered serious flaws in Rimm's study involving gross misrepresentation and erroneous methodology. His work was soon deemed flawed and inaccurate, and *Time* recanted in public. With Rimm's claims now apologetically retracted, his original suggestion that 83.5 percent of Internet graphics are pornographic was quietly withdrawn in favor of a figure less than 1 percent.

5   *Time* admitted that grievous errors had slipped past their editorial staff, as their normally thorough research succumbed to a combination of deadline pressure and exclusivity agreements that barred them from showing the unpublished study to possible critics. But, by then, the damage had been done: the study had found its way to the Senate.

Government Intervention

6   Senator Charles Grassley (Republican—Iowa) jumped on the pornography bandwagon by proposing a bill that would make it a criminal offense to supply or permit the supply of "indecent" material to minors over the Internet. Grassley introduced the entire *Time* article into the congressional record, despite the fact that the conceptual, logical, and methodological flaws in the report had already been acknowledged by the magazine.

7   On the Senate floor, Grassley referred to Marty Rimm's undergraduate research as "a remarkable study conducted by researchers at Carnegie Mellon University" and went on to say:

> The university surveyed 900,000 computer images. Of these 900,000 images, 83.5 percent of all computerized photographs available on the Internet are pornographic. . . . With so many graphic images available on computer networks, I believe Congress must act and do so in a constitutional manner to help parents who are under assault in this day and age.

8   Under the Grassley bill, later known as the Protection of Children from Pornography Act of 1995, it would have been illegal for anyone to knowingly or recklessly transmit indecent material to minors. This bill marked the beginning of a stream of Internet censorship legislation at various levels of government in the United States and abroad.

9   The most extreme and fiercely opposed of these was the Communications Decency Act, sponsored by former Senator James Exon (Democrat—Nebraska) and Senator Dan Coats (Republican—Indiana). The CDA labeled the transmission of "obscene, lewd, lascivious, filthy, indecent, or patently offensive" pornography over the Internet a crime. It was attached to the Telecommunications Reform Act of 1996, which was then passed by Congress on February 1, 1996. One week later, it was signed into law by

President Clinton. On the same day, the American Civil Liberties Union filed suit in Philadelphia against the U.S. Department of Justice and Attorney General Janet Reno, arguing that the statute would ban free speech protected by the First Amendment and subject Internet users to far greater restrictions than exist in any other medium. Later that month, the Citizens Internet Empowerment Coalition initiated a second legal challenge to the CDA, which formally consolidated with *ACLU v. Reno*. Government lawyers agreed not to prosecute "indecent" or "patently offensive" material until the three-judge court in Philadelphia ruled on the case.

10   Although the purpose of the CDA was to protect young children from accessing and viewing material of sexually explicit content on the Internet, the wording of the act was so broad and poorly defined that it could have deprived many adults of information they needed in the areas of health, art, news, and literature—information that is legal in print form. Specifically, certain medical information available on the Internet includes descriptions of sexual organs and activities which might have been considered "indecent" or "patently offensive" under the act—for example, information on breast-feeding, birth control, AIDS, and gynecological and urinological information. Also, many museums and art galleries now have websites. Under the act, displaying art like the Sistine Chapel nudes could be cause for criminal prosecution. Online newspapers would not be permitted to report the same information as is available in the print media. Reports on combatants in war, at the scenes of crime, in the political arena, and outside abortion clinics often provoke images or language that could be constituted "offensive" and therefore illegal on the net. Furthermore, the CDA provided a legal basis for banning books which had been ruled unconstitutional to ban from school libraries. These include many of the classics as well as modern literature containing words that may be considered indecent.

11   The act also expanded potential liability for employers, service providers, and carriers that transmit or otherwise make available restricted communications. According to the CDA, "knowingly" allowing obscene material to pass through one's computer system was a criminal offense. Given the nature of the Internet, however, making service providers responsible for the content of the traffic they pass on to other Internet nodes is equivalent to holding a telephone carrier responsible for the content of the conversations going over that carrier's lines. So, under the terms of the act, if someone sent an indecent electronic comment from a workstation, the employer, the e-mail service provider, and the carrier all could be potentially held liable and subject to up to $100,000 in fines or two years in prison.

12   On June 12, 1996, after experiencing live tours of the Internet and hearing arguments about the technical and economical infeasibility of complying with the censorship law, the three federal judges in Philadelphia granted the request for a preliminary injunction against the CDA. The court determined that "there is no evidence that sexually oriented material is the primary type of content on this new medium" and proposed that "communications over the Internet do not 'invade' an individual's home or appear on one's computer screen unbidden. Users seldom encounter content 'by accident.' " In a unanimous decision, the judges ruled that the Communications Decency Act would unconstitutionally restrict free speech on the Internet.

13   The government appealed the judges' decision and, on March 19, 1997, the U.S. Supreme Court heard oral arguments in the legal challenge to the CDA, now known as

Reno v. ACLU. Finally, on June 26, the decision came down. The Court voted unanimously that the act violated the First Amendment guarantee of freedom of speech and would have threatened "to torch a large segment of the Internet community."

14   Is the panic therefore over? Far from it. The July 7, 1997, *Newsweek,* picking up the frenzy where *Time* left off, reported the Supreme Court decision in a provocatively illustrated article featuring a color photo of a woman licking her lips and a warning message taken from the website of the House of Sin. Entitled "On the Net, Anything Goes," the opening words by Steven Levy read, "Born of a hysteria triggered by a genuine problem—the ease with which wired-up teenagers can get hold of nasty pictures on the Internet—the Communications Decency Act (CDA) was never really destined to be a companion piece to the Bill of Rights." At the announcement of the Court's decision, anti-porn protesters were on the street outside brandishing signs which read, "Child Molesters Are Looking for Victims on the Internet."

15   Meanwhile, government talk has shifted to the development of a universal Internet rating system and widespread hardware and software filtering. Referring to the latter, White House Senior Adviser Rahm Emanuel declared, "We're going to get the V-chip for the Internet. Same goal, different means."

16   But it is important to bear in mind that children are still a minority of Internet users. A contract with an Internet service provider typically needs to be paid for by credit card or direct debit, therefore requiring the intervention of an adult. Children are also unlikely to be able to view any kind of porn online without a credit card.

17   In addition to this, there have been a variety of measures developed to protect children on the Internet. The National Center for Missing and Exploited Children has outlined protective guidelines for parents and children in its pamphlet, *Child Safety on the Information Superhighway.* A number of companies now sell Internet newsfeeds and web proxy accesses that are vetted in accordance with a list of forbidden topics. And, of course, there remain those blunt software instruments that block access to sexually oriented sites by looking for keywords such as *sex, erotic,* and *X-rated.* But one of the easiest solutions is to keep the family computer in a well-traveled space, like a living room, so that parents can monitor what their children download.

Fact or Media Fiction?

18   In her 1995 CMC magazine article, "Journey to the Centre of Cybersmut," Lisa Schmeiser discusses her research into online pornography. After an exhaustive search, she was unable to find any pornography, apart from the occasional commercial site (requiring a credit card for access), and concluded that one would have to undertake extensive searching to find quantities of explicit pornography. She suggested that, if children were accessing pornography online, they would not have been doing it by accident. Schmeiser writes: "There will be children who circumvent passwords, Surfwatch software, and seemingly innocuous links to find the 'adult' material. But these are the same kids who would visit every convenience store in a five-mile radius to find the one stocking *Playboy.*" Her argument is simply that, while there is a certain amount of pornography online, it is not freely and readily available. Contrary to what the media often report, pornography is not that easy to find.

19   There *is* pornography in cyberspace (including images, pictures, movies, sounds, and sex discussions) and several ways of receiving pornographic material on the

Internet (such as through private bulletin board systems, the World Wide Web, news-groups, and e-mail). However, many sites just contain reproduced images from hardcore magazines and videos available from other outlets, and registration fee restrictions make them inaccessible to children. And for the more contentious issue of pedophilia, a recent investigation by the *Guardian* newspaper in Britain revealed that the majority of pedophilic images distributed on the Internet are simply electronic reproductions of the small output of legitimate pedophile magazines, such as *Lolita*, published in the 1970s.

20   Clearly the issue of pornography on the Internet is a moral panic—an issue perpetuated by a sensationalistic style of reporting and misleading content in newspaper and magazine articles. And probably the text from which to base any examination of the possible link between media reporting and moral panics is Stanley Cohen's 1972 book, *Folk Devils and Moral Panic*, in which he proposes that the mass media are ultimately responsible for the creation of such panics. Cohen describes a moral panic as occurring when "a condition, episode, person or group of persons emerges to become a threat to societal values and interests; . . . the moral barricades are manned by editors . . . politicians and other 'right thinking' people." He feels that, while problematical elements of society can pose a threat to others, this threat is realistically far less than the perceived image generated by mass media reporting.

21   Cohen describes how the news we read is not necessarily the truth; editors have papers to sell, targets to meet, and competition from other publishers. It is in their interest to make the story "a good read"—the sensationalist approach sells newspapers. The average person is likely to be drawn in with the promise of scandal and intrigue. This can be seen in the reporting of the *National Enquirer* and *People*, with their splashy pictures and sensationalistic headlines, helping them become two of the largest circulation magazines in the United States.

22   Cohen discusses the "inventory" as the set of criteria inherent in any reporting that may be deemed as fueling a moral panic. This inventory consists of the following:

Exaggeration in Reporting

23   Facts are often overblown to give the story a greater edge. Figures that are not necessarily incorrect but have been quoted out of context, or have been used incorrectly to shock, are two forms of this exaggeration.

24   Looking back at the original *Time* cover article, "On a Screen Near You: Cyberporn," this type of exaggeration is apparent. Headlines such as "The Carnegie Mellon researchers found 917,410 sexually explicit pictures, short stories and film clips online" make the reader think that there really is a problem with the quantity of pornography in cyberspace. It takes the reader a great deal of further exploration to find out how this figure was calculated. Also, standing alone and out of context, the oft-quoted figure that 83.5 percent of images found on Usenet Newsgroups are pornographic could be seen as cause for concern. However, if one looks at the math associated with this figure, one would find that this is a sampled percentage with a researcher leaning toward known areas of pornography.

The Repetition of Fallacies

25   This occurs when a writer reports information that seems perfectly believable to the general public, even though those who know the subject are aware it is wildly

incorrect. In the case of pornography, the common fallacy is that the Internet is awash with nothing but pornography and that all you need to obtain it is a computer and a modem. Such misinformation is integral to the fueling of moral panics.

26   Take, for example, the October 18, 1995, *Scotland on Sunday*, which reports that, to obtain pornographic material, "all you need is a personal computer, a phone line with a modem attached and a connection via a specialist provider to the Internet." What the article fails to mention is that the majority of pornography is found on specific Usenet sites not readily available from the major Internet providers, such as America Online and Compuserve. It also fails to mention that this pornography needs to be downloaded and converted into a viewable form, which requires certain skills and can take considerable time.

Misleading Pictures and Snappy Titles

27   Media representation often exaggerates a story through provocative titles and flashy pictorials—all in the name of drawing in the reader. The titles set the tone for the rest of the article; the headline is the most noticeable and important part of any news item, attracting the reader's initial attention. The recent *Newsweek* article is a perfect example. Even if the headline has little relevance to the article, it sways the reader's perception of the topic. The symbolization of images further increases the impact of the story. *Time*'s own images in its original coverage—showing a shocked little boy on the cover and, inside, a naked man hunched over a computer monitor—added to the article's ability to shock and to draw the reader into the story.

28   Through sensationalized reporting, certain forms of behavior become classified as *deviant*. Specifically, those who put pornography online or those who download it are seen as being deviant in nature. This style of reporting benefits the publication or broadcast by giving it the aura of "moral guardian" to the rest of society. It also increases revenue.

29   In exposing deviant behavior, newspapers and magazines have the ability to push for reform. So, by classifying a subject and its relevant activities as deviant, they can stand as crusaders for moral decency, championing the cause of "normal" people. They can report the subject and call for something to be done about it, but this power is easily abused. The *Time* cyberporn article called for reform on the basis of Rimm's findings, proclaiming, "A new study shows us how pervasive and wild [pornography on the Internet] really is. Can we protect our kids—and free speech?" These cries to protect our children affected the likes of Senators James Exon and Robert Dole, who took the *Time* article with its "shocking" revelations (as well as a sample of pornographic images) to the Senate floor, appealing for changes to the law. From this response it is clear how powerful a magazine article can be, regardless of the integrity and accuracy of its reporting.

30   The *Time* article had all of Cohen's elements relating to the fueling of a moral panic: exaggeration, fallacies, and misleading pictures and titles. Because certain publications are highly regarded and enjoy an important role in society, anything printed in their pages is consumed and believed by a large audience. People accept what they read because, to the best of their knowledge, it is the truth. So, even though the *Time* article was based on a report by an undergraduate student passing as "a research team from Carnegie Mellon," the status of the magazine was great enough to launch a panic that continues unabated—from the halls of Congress to the pulpits of churches, from public schools to the offices of software developers, from local communities to the global village.

Questions for Reading and Analysis

1. What does the term *moral panic* mean?

2. What is Wilkins's subject? What is her thesis? What is she *not* arguing?

3. What events have led to the current "moral panic" over Internet pornography? What, eventually, was *Time* magazine's position on the Rimm study?

4. What law was passed by Congress? What would the law have banned on the Internet? What has happened to this law?

5. Has the moral panic over Internet pornography faded away? How does the author answer this question?

6. In what ways are children best protected from Internet pornography? How serious is the problem of children accessing porn on the Internet, according to Lisa Schmeiser?

7. In his book *Folk Devils and Moral Panic*, where does Stanley Cohen place the blame for moral panic?

8. What strategies are used to fuel a moral panic?

Questions for Discussion and Response

1. How does Wilkins's argument differ significantly from the other three on censorship? How does her purpose differ?

2. Does the author convince you that media coverage of Internet pornography represents an example of moral panic? Why or why not?

3. Have you found pornography on the Internet? If so, was it easy to access? Do you consider it damaging—relative to *Playboy* or X-rated films? Explain.

4. Will a "decency" law work for the Internet? Why or why not? What are the potential problems?

5. Should there be an Internet V-chip for parents? Other strategies to block access? Explain your position.

CHAPTER 15

Internet Issues: Privacy, Ownership, Entrapment

New technologies bring changes, not all of them unquestionably good. Six writers in this chapter examine some of the characteristics—or problems, depending on your perspective—of Internet technology. With more of the world run by computers, is there any way to keep privacy? This question is debated, specifically, by the first two writers and in more general terms by the last author. The other three writers examine entrapment and intellectual rights: ways a boss can use your office e-mail to "set you up," to test your loyalty or adherence to the company's rules, and what to do with music downloading sites such as Napster. Whether you are a novice with your PC or a real "techie," you can benefit from reflecting on the tasks, good and bad, that computers now perform—and the concerns some have for the "wired world" of this new century.

Reflecting on the following questions before you read will enrich your reading and thinking about this topic:

1. Do you think that it is possible for the code makers to stay ahead of the hackers, or will "secure" sites always be reachable by gifted "techies"? Is your answer to this question influenced in any way by your degree of sophistication with computers?

2. You are probably aware of the role that the Internet has played in expanding the global economy. But, the global economy can seem quite distant from the lives of many of us. How does the computer affect your life in more immediate ways? Try listing the many ways that computers affect your daily life.

3. Do you shop online? If so, does that mean that you believe your credit-card number is secure? If not, why not? Have you downloaded music from Napster or a similar site? Do you think that such downloading should be legal? Do you think it is moral? Why or why not?

4. In this age of cell phones and Palm Pilots, how far away is the world of *Star Trek?* How do you envision computer applications affecting your life in the next twenty years? In the next fifty years? Will the effects be good or bad? Why?

Websites Relevant to This Chapter's Issues

Electronic Privacy Information Center: Internet Censorship

www.epic.org/free_speech/censorship/

This site focuses on legislation and court cases related to Internet censorship.

Internet Freedom

www.netfreedom.org

This site supports a position against all forms of censorship and content regulation on the Internet.

The Privacy Pages

www.2020tech.com/maildrop/privacy.html

Sponsored by the Orlando Mail Drop, this site contains many links to organizations and periodicals; it gives current news updates and information on security software and other privacy issues.

If All the World's a Computer

Peter McGrath

Peter McGrath holds a Ph.D. from the University of Chicago and is editor of New Media at *Newsweek* magazine. This article appeared in *Newsweek* January 1, 2000.

1   Any time, anywhere: that is the promise the captains of technology make us, even as we struggle with our existing machines, our cranky software and our creaky Internet. They mean it too. Imagine this: computers that enfold you, like a second skin. Rooms that come alive with sensors, cameras and embedded chips, allowing them to "know" you and adjust to your preferences when you arrive. Cars that monitor not only traffic but also your vital signs, and tell you when you're not fit to be on the road.

2   These all belong to a family of devices on the drawing board at places like IBM, Xerox's Palo Alto Research center (PARC) and the Media Lab at the Massachusetts Institute for Technology. Some are in advanced stages of prototyping. They include such things as microchips farmers till into the soil to measure moisture and acidity; building materials that adjust resistance to wind and earthquake; insulation that changes according to weather conditions. The idea is simple: computing must become ubiquitous, pervasive. And nowhere will it be more pervasive than when it is closest to us. As Michael Hawley put it in the mission statement for his Things That Think project at the MIT Media Lab, "We wear clothes, put on jewelry, sit on chairs and walk on carpets that all share the same profound failing: they are blind, deaf and very dumb. Cuff links don't, in fact, link with anything else . . . Glasses help sight, but they don't see."

3   They will if the engineers have their way. Eyeglasses are the medium of choice for an idea variously called BodyNet and the Personal Area Network, or PAN. You would wear glasses with a camera in the frame, a photodiode sensor to monitor your eye movements, a voice transmitter in the earpiece and a short-range radio connection to a pagerlike device worn on a belt or in a handbag. That device would contain whole libraries of personal information, about both you and everyone you've ever met while wearing the BodyNet.

4   One effect would be to displace at a smaller size the multiple electronic devices we carry today, such as laptops, mobile phones and personal digital assistants. But BodyNet goes further. Thus equipped, you could be prompted with the name and business of an

acquaintance approaching on the street. (The device would compare the image with its database, and your glasses would whisper the result in your ear.) You could, with the help of a phased array of microphones embedded in the fabric of your jacket—what Hawley calls "underware"—respond knowingly to conversations: if your acquaintance mentions an investment opportunity, your device could connect to the Internet and call up all relevant information about the company in question, using your glasses as a display screen. Dinner parties would never be the same.

5   Sound good? It certainly does to the digerati. They are prone to such statements as "If computers are everywhere, they better stay out of the way" (Mark Weiser and John Seely Brown, senior scientists at Xerox PARC), and "The idea is nothing less than to make the world itself programmable" (Alan Daniels, then of Georgia Tech).

6   In their view, computing will, by the year 2005, shift decisively from domination by the personal computer to reliance on a variety of "information appliances." At first most of these devices will be handheld: Web-ready telephones and palmtops, for example. Increasingly, though, they will be embedded in the background in ways almost invisible to us. Wearable computers will arrive soon after, though it will take some time to make them small and light enough to actually embed them in clothing. Cameras will be everywhere, feeding visual data to the Internet, and some researchers believe that by 2020 we will be on camera nearly nonstop.

7   The world of ubiquitous computing raises a number of questions. High among them is the issue of inescapability. "In practice," says Ann Livermore, president of enterprise computing at Hewlett-Packard, "the slogan 'Any time, anywhere' means 'All the time, everywhere.' " Even greater, though, is the problem of privacy, when pervasive in fact means invasive. There is no precedent for the idea of self-executing devices that are ubiquitous, networked and always on. If your car knows when you're intoxicated, why can't it also inform a police car? If a communicating pacemaker can tell your doctor that you're on the verge of a cardiac event, why can't it also tell your insurance company?

8   All such devices will, of course, be presented as having benefits so obvious as to pre-empt objection. It's hard to quarrel with a car that deters drunk driving, even at the cost of a little self-incrimination. It's even harder to argue against a networked pacemaker, if it saves lives. But, says Coralee Whitcomb, president of Computer Professionals for Social Responsibility, it never stops there: "All these things develop other uses . . . Any time you create a technology that is inherently invasive, it'll get used that way. And there's always a million good reasons for it."

9   Technologists do expect resistance to such devices, at least at first. "We are naturally squeamish about ideas like electronics that are worn, ingested, implanted," says Hawley. "Maybe it's rooted in our deep fear [of] being eaten, or disgust at being the host for a parasite. But once we cross these bridges they seem to become second nature." Health care is only the most immediate use of ubiquitous computing, he says. He envisions a world in which the ability to put entire systems on a single chip, creating such devices as voice-activated "metaphones" the size of a lapel pin, effectively abolishes distance as a barrier to human interaction.

10   Some high hurdles remain. Power supplies must be miniaturized. Current network-management tools are wholly inadequate to ubiquitous computing. Nor will there be enough network capacity for another 10 years. But these are susceptible to engineering attack. The same might be said of privacy: protection will come from some combination

of encryption and digital fingerprinting, in which people who gain access to your personal data leave electronic traces of their presence, allowing you to hold them accountable. These technical fixes aren't durable, though. As David Brin, a scientist and author of *The Transparent Society*, notes, "Each year's 'unbreakable' encryption standard is broken within less than three years by groups of amateurs." A new and stronger standard then emerges, only to be itself broken, in a permanent game of digital leapfrog.

11   In any case, privacy is not just a condition. It's also a state of mind, a feeling of security that owes more to the possibility of anonymity than anything else. And anonymity is one thing that the next wave of computing will abolish.

Questions for Reading and Analysis

1. Where are some of the "cutting-edge" computer uses being developed?
2. What would BodyNet do for you?
3. What are some people predicting for the role of computers by 2005? By 2020?
4. If computers are everywhere and always on, what may be lost?
5. Why may people resist embedded computers?
6. What technological challenges remain to produce the age of ubiquitous computers?
7. Does McGrath think that digital privacy is possible?
8. Is this an informative essay only, or is it an argument? If it is an argument, what is McGrath's claim? (Consider: What seems to be the author's attitude toward computers everywhere? How do you know?)

Questions for Discussion and Response

1. How many computer-related "gadgets" do you own and use (e.g., PC, PalmPilot, laptop, computer games, and so forth)?
2. Can you imagine wearing a BodyNet? Do you think you would like a world of "embedded" computers? Why or why not?
3. Do you agree that privacy is in part a state of mind and based on anonymity? Explain your reaction to this idea.
4. Do you believe that advantages of new computer technology will outweigh losses in privacy? Why or why not?

Technology Will Solve Web Privacy Problems

Lawrence Lessig

Lawrence Lessig is a professor at the Stanford University Law School. He is the author of *Code and Other Laws of Cyberspace* (1999). His article on Web privacy was published May 31, 2000, in *The Wall Street Journal*.

1   The privacy showdown has come. After years of waiting for the high-tech industry to voluntarily enforce "fair information practices," the Federal Trade Commission's patience is at an end. While the number of Web sites sporting privacy policies has increased significantly, only 20% even partially implement the fair-information recommendations. The FTC is now insisting that Congress enforce compliance.

2   We are lucky the industry so far has ignored the FTC. And until the agency's privacy recommendations change, Congress should turn a cold shoulder as well.

3   The privacy problem in cyberspace has a very specific source—how the Internet is designed. The code of cyberspace—the software and hardware that make up the Internet—makes privacy a problem. This code makes it extremely easy for data about individuals to be collected and profiled; it makes it extremely difficult for individuals to know that this profiling and tracking is taking place.

4   The solution to this problem with code is better code. Specifically, we need code that helps consumers make more informed choices. But so far the FTC has ignored code. It remains fixated on a standard Washington strategy—more privacy policies. More words won't advance privacy in cyberspace. Consumers will simply ignore the clutter.

5   The aim of the FTC's "fair information policy" is sensible enough. It requires that sites give notice about information practices and offer consumers a choice about how their information is used. It demands consumer access to information the site has collected and adequate protection of such data.

6   Many sites already comply. Hertz Rental is one example. A privacy policy page on Hertz's Web site dutifully explains how an individual's data will be used by Hertz (in short, to Hertz's maximal commercial benefit); it explains that individuals can limit, to some degree, how their data is used (you can, for example, stop the sale of some data or halt junk mail to you); it explains that visitors have the right to correct mistakes (call the local Hertz office; no number provided); and it describes how data is kept safe (through a "Secure Socket Layer"; don't worry, no one else understands, either).

7   In the FTC's eyes, Hertz is a success. It believes that if everyone followed Hertz's example, privacy policies would flourish, consumers would be informed, choice would be meaningful and confidence would return. But to ordinary users the policies are meaningless. Does anyone really believe that consumers have the time to wade through privacy policies? Are we to build a chart reminding us of how Yahoo's privacy policy differs from Excite's?

8   It's not enough for the government to identify the principles it wants adopted. Rather, the law must be sensitive to how those principles get implemented. The cost of processing words in cyberspace is already too high. Multiplying legalese will increase these costs without doing anything to improve consumer privacy.

9   The answer is better code. There have already been a flood of code-based solutions to the problem of cyberspace privacy. The most promising of these builds upon the work of the World Wide Web Consortium's Platform for Privacy Preferences. P3P establishes a framework for standardized, computer-readable privacy policies. This framework would make it easy for companies to explain their practices in a form that computers could read, and make it easy for consumers to express their preferences in a way that computers would automatically respect.

10   Companies such as PrivacyBot.com, for example, provide a $30 tool that allows companies to make their Web sites P3P compliant. Microsoft is creating similar tools and promises to integrate P3P into its browser. Consumers would then tell the browser the level of privacy they want, and the browser would automatically steer the consumer away from privacy-abusing sites. Rather than consumers reading Hertz's words, browsers would read the Hertz P3P code and warn the consumer if the site fails to match consumer preferences.

11   P3P is neither perfect nor yet complete. Neither is it the only code-based solution to the privacy problem, nor a substitute for strong privacy legislation. But P3P is at least a step toward a world where consumers make their own privacy choices at relatively low cost to business.

12   The FTC, however, has said little about the potential of code-based solutions. Instead, it has simply said the government should remain "technologically neutral." But there is a big difference between being neutral among different technological solutions and being neutral about whether technology is part of a solution. Only technology can lower the cost of expressing and enforcing privacy preferences. Without that cost lowered, the principles the FTC promotes will never effectively be realized.

13   There is a role for Congress in facilitating these code-based solutions to Internet privacy. The invisible hand won't solve this privacy gap any more than it led steel mills to scrub soot from their smokestacks. But if the government created incentives for code-based solutions—by either subsidizing code or insisting that code is part of any solution—the market would quickly supply them.

14   Congress should embrace the FTC's principles, but insist on compliance through code. Neither words nor code alone will solve the problem of privacy in cyberspace. But at the moment we need fewer words, and better code.

Questions for Reading and Analysis

1. What is Lessig's subject? What is his claim? Where does he state it?
2. How does the nature of the Internet make privacy a problem in two ways?
3. What does Lessig think is the answer to the privacy problem?
4. What is ineffective, according to Lessig, about the FTC's privacy policy information regulations? How does the Hertz example demonstrate his point?
5. How does P3P work? What are its advantages?
6. Why does Lessig assert that a technological solution is the only viable approach to privacy on the Internet?

Questions for Discussion and Response

1. What are some of the ways your privacy can be invaded if you surf the Internet? Why is this troubling to people?
2. Has Lessig convinced you that privacy problems can be solved with technology? Why or why not?

3. Do you think that his argument would convince Peter McGrath, author of "If All the World's a Computer"? Why or why not?

4. What, currently, can you do to protect your privacy when online?

E-Mail or E-Sting? Your Boss Knows, but He's Not Telling

Michael Schrage

Holding a bachelor's degree in economics and computer science, Michael Schrage is co-director of the MIT Media Lab's eMarkets Initiative and executive director of Merrill Lynch's Innovation Grants Competition. He writes a column for *Fortune* magazine and has published in a number of newspapers and magazines. He is also the author of several books, including *Serious Play: How the World's Best Companies Simulate to Innovate* (1999). The following *Fortune* column appeared on March 20, 2000.

1   Before announcing key promotions, a top manager at a mid-sized technology firm decided to run a loyalty check on his subordinates. He persuaded a buddy in IT to forge an e-mail to look like a personalized inquiry from a prestigious consulting firm. The information requested seemed innocuous enough, but the e-mail coyly invited the recipients to attach a "bio" to their response. At least two people bit. Guess who didn't move up?

2   Sleazy and deceitful? Absolutely. Atypical behavior? Absolutely not. In fact, the techno-tactic was tacitly condoned when it came to the attention of the operating committee. The more Machiavellian types admired the ruse. Everyone in the company is now a lot more circumspect about responding to outside e-mail. Is that such a bad thing?

3   There has probably never been a better time or technology for management to use guile, deception, and trickery to catch employees in the act of disloyalty or dishonesty. The passive surveillance of e-mail and Net usage has already become a corporate norm. But as matters of both individual practice and institutional policy, companies increasingly must decide whether to resort to more active measures to exorcise bad actors.

4   In other words, we will see a surge of "cyberstings" as organizations realize that networks make testing human integrity even easier than testing data integrity. Law enforcement agencies already embrace "e-stings" as essential to their crime-fighting initiatives. Cops regularly make markets on eBay to see who is willing to sell or buy illicit and/or stolen goods. The FBI and other agencies have successfully run stings to flush out sexual predators who would use the Internet to seduce underage boys and girls. Is this such a bad thing? Does it truly make criminals out of otherwise honest people? Not bloody likely.

5   As e-commerce proliferates and evolves, so will the cybersting. The feds and the Interpreneurs will cheerfully collaborate to set traps to catch next-generation perps aspiring to launch the next round of "denial of service" site attacks. Cybercops and binary billionaires are gonna become better buddies.

6   Is this errant speculation about the future of entrapment? Well, to quote one CEO who obviously believed he was entrapped, it depends on what the meaning of "is" is. The legal and ethical issues surrounding "entrapment" guarantee noisy debate about just what level of deceitfulness is necessary to uncover deceit.

7   When the *New York Times* sacked 22 employees for circulating pornographic e-mails in clear violation of company policy, the high-profile terminations provoked global comment about whether the punishment fit the crime. Certainly, no outraged employees had reported the offenders; *Times* management stumbled across those e-mails by accident.

8   But suppose a manager had sent—or had caused to be sent—a pornographic e-mail to an employee explicitly to test if she would observe the corporate policy of immediately reporting inappropriate messages. If the employee simply deleted the e-mail without reporting the offense, should she be punished? Does deliberately sending that e-mail constitute a loathsome attempt to entrap, or is it a thoroughly legitimate effort to see if an employee is prepared to honor the rules?

9   Pro-active management might use their networks to test all manner of legal, ethical and organizational compliance. An employee could receive e-mails containing "humorous" ethnic epithets or a sleazy but legal request from a key supplier or customer. A hard-nosed manager might contrive an outright illegal request to an employee to see what she would do. What should she disclose, and when should she disclose it? Managers can figure out all kinds of creative ways to challenge their employees. Sometimes, testing managerial integrity can be as important as testing managerial skill. No one wants to work for a company with a *Stasi*-like rat's nest of squealers and informers. On the other hand, one company's rat-fink is another firm's whistle blower. And if you think companies don't need to act like law enforcement agencies sometimes, talk to the wealthy lawyers who sue them for harassment, discrimination, and other alleged misconduct on the part of their employees.

10   So don't bet on too many organizations scrambling to the moralistic high ground by promising never, ever to lead their employees into temptation. It's all too easy to imagine how even the best-intentioned corporate cybersting could be abused to set up employees targeted for dismissal or disrepute. Yet it's understandable why organizations feel they have not only the right but also the obligation to see how rigorously their policies—and the law—are followed.

11   Ronald Reagan's admonition about nuclear arms control comes to mind: "Trust but verify." The ethical problems arise because active verifications can be so much more effective than passive ones. As organizations become more Net-centric, the aggressiveness of the verification and the strength of that trust are sadly guaranteed to be at odds. The Net truly puts the "e" in entrapment.

Questions for Reading and Analysis

1. What is Schrage's subject?
2. What is a "cybersting"?
3. What do employers want to test with their cyberstings? What do the police want to do?
4. What is Schrage's claim? What does he predict? Does he state an opinion on his topic? Does he imply one?

Questions for Discussion and Response

1. Do you think the *New York Times* employees should have been fired? Why or why not?

2. Should employers set up scams to test employee loyalty? To test employees on the company's rules about using the Net? Why or why not?

3. Should the police set up stings to catch pornographers and child abusers on the Net? Why or why not?

4. Do you agree with the author that more companies are likely to use cyberstings? Do you find this acceptable? Or unethical? Explain.

Napster Should Be Playing Jailhouse Rock

Paul Kedrosky

A professor of business at the University of British Columbia, Paul Kedrosky (b. 1956) has published widely on business topics and has written a book, about to be published, on the dot-com revolution, *The Market of Oz*. His views on Napster appeared in *The Wall Street Journal* on July 31, 2000.

1   An appeals court has stayed a federal judge's ordering shutting down Napster. Too bad. I would happily flip the switch myself.

2   Sure it's cool that you can get all the music you want, gratis, through the Napster online service. When I was in college, I had a roommate who liked to steal flags. He was good at it, and we had so many flags that we could have run our own United Nations sessions. But he didn't get fawning press coverage, and he couldn't steal flags any further from campus than he could get on his bicycle.

3   The Internet has assuredly changed things. It has made innocent, college-style theft possible on a global scale. And that's interesting—in the same way that it would be interesting if some college kids created a global garage-door opener and ignition-starter. You might be momentarily impressed, but you would also want to bust the punks, college kids or not.

4   Let's be blunt: Napster-style file-sharing is theft. But for some reason commentators don't see it that way. Instead, we hear all sorts of tripe about waves of change, the inevitability of the Internet, and so on. Theft ends up sounding somehow okay. Commentators are falling all over themselves saying that the forces Napster has set loose cannot be stopped.

5   Why do so-called opinion leaders so smirkingly dismiss theft? In a nutshell, it's because aging would-be hipsters are trying to demonstrate their technology bona fides to amoral technologists. It is a sad sight, kind of like watching drunken 45-year-olds at a 20-year reunion chasing freshman women.

6   Opinioneers aside, the rest of us should know better. So why don't we treat online music theft the same way we treat offline theft? In part, because it doesn't feel like theft. After all, you're just sitting at home downloading files. It's not as if you slipped a CD from Sam Goody into your coat pocket, then scrambled out the door.

7   It also has to do with the perceived seriousness of the crime. Imagine that instead of sharing music, Napster was used to share semiconductor designs. Engineers at companies

like Intel and AMD could throw designs up on Napster and blithely pass blueprints around the planet. While it might be great for engineering graduate students, and even better for Intel and AMD's upstart competitors, Intel and AMD would be understandably upset. And they would sue—and win.

8   Some Napster enthusiasts even say that the recording industry is doing artists ill. They are, they argue, actually helping artists by destroying the music industry, or at least forcing it to restructure. What childish nonsense. All they are really saying is that the ends justify the means.

9   So we (apparently) applaud Napster because of three flawed premises. One, we think that theft is subjective: It depends on the seriousness of the thing being stolen. Two, theft also depends on how much theft feels like theft. And three, it depends, Robin Hood style, on who we're stealing from. The recording industry is rich; they can afford to give up a few songs for free, can't they?

10   For what it's worth, Napster has done little to dissuade people from thinking otherwise. After standing blithely by while millions of dollars in pirated music flowed over its servers, Napster is now insisting that it has a role to play. It has, it insists, market presence and could be a new means of distribution for music. In other words, it is saying "Just pay us!" Sound familiar? It should. It's a classic shakedown, right out of Mafia 101.

11   Technologists disavow any responsibility for their electronic fencing ring. Information, they say, wants to be free. Not their own, of course, but other people's. As a recent article in this newspaper pointed out, Napster, the company, gets agitated in a hurry when people start sharing its assets, from logos to its underlying file structures. Share? Sure, but not us!

12   All the while, technologists insist that people need to decide what is right and wrong for themselves. That's fair enough when the issues are subtle or nuanced, but not when the illegality is obvious and egregious. Insisting that individuals need to decide about right and wrong in such cases is childish, a species of society-wide infantilization. A clearer example of moral abdication would be hard to find.

13   We have let our love of technological change unseat our moral centers. It is one thing to stand on the sidelines applauding while new technologies transform industries. That is classic Schumpeterian economic change, the kind of upheaval that makes economies dynamic and vital. But it is something else altogether to applaud, or even cock an amused eye, while technology turns our friends, neighbors and families into petty criminals.

14   Shut Napster down—for good.

Questions for Reading and Analysis

1. What is Napster?
2. What is Kedrosky's claim? Where does he state it?
3. What is the author's objection to Napster?
4. Why, in Kedrosky's view, do "opinion leaders" downplay what Napster does?

5. Why do ordinary people fail to recognize that "Napster-style file-sharing is theft"?

6. What has been Napster's response to its critics? What is the response of "technologists" to the business of file-sharing? How does Kedrosky label their approach?

Questions for Discussion and Response

1. Kedrosky's essay appeared in 2000, when Napster was facing a court case threatening to shut down the site. What is the current situation for companies such as Napster?

2. Whether or not the courts have shut down music file-sharing sites such as Napster, how are the issues raised by Kedrosky still relevant?

3. Is our response to new technologies often one of "moral abdication"? Do we reason that if it can be done, it must be all right? Do you see this kind of reasoning in other areas of modern science?

4. Do you agree with Kedrosky that music file sharing is theft? Why or why not?

5. Do you agree that the music companies are too wealthy and do not treat artists fairly? If so, what can be done about this problem without justifying file sharing?

6. If you disagree with Kedrosky's argument, how would you go about refuting him?

Hear Me Play, but Respect My Rights

Jenny Toomey

A musician and activist, Jenny Toomey has played in bands, managed an independent record label, and written about music and Internet technology. You can find her at www.futureofmusic.com. Her take on the Napster issue appeared in the *Washington Post*, June 4, 2000.

1   As an independent musician and label owner, I've struggled to release music in a market that's dominated by the big-time corporate labels. You might think I'd be thrilled about the Internet and the possibility that it would allow me to distribute my art without going broke on manufacturing and distribution costs—and without aligning myself with such industry giants as Sony and Time Warner. I'd love to think that rapper Chuck D was right when he told a congressional committee last month that digital download technology was a meteor speeding toward the heads of those major record label dinosaurs.

2   But logically, I can't get past the fact that if a meteor is about to hit the industry, it will land with the impartiality of . . . well, a meteor. And that means it could crush the independent musicians as well as those fossils at the major labels. I don't know about Chuck D, but I'm looking for a shield. I believe indie musicians can survive and prosper in this digital revolution, but not unless our dot-com buddies show some respect for copyright and creativity.

3   At the heart of the debate today lies the service Napster. With an ordinary desktop computer and a modem, even the clumsiest computer user can sign up with Napster

to download high-quality recordings, from the Beatles to Beck to Brahms, from any other Napster member without spending a dime on either software or music. Add a high-speed Internet connection to reduce download time and a program that allows users to share files among hundreds of thousands of potential users worldwide, and it's not difficult to see that the future of music is going digital.

4   The obvious problem is that more than 90 percent of the music tracks that are being shared for free through services like Napster are copyright-protected works. Napster, however, makes no provision for collecting royalties for the owners of these copyrights, nor does it provide any other means of compensating artists and record labels.

5   This oversight has already led to several lawsuits, which I suspect the company will lose: Existing copyright law is likely to lead to a finding that Napster is responsible for enabling piracy. But similar programs such as Gnutella and Freenet are waiting to step into the vacuum left by a deflating Napster; more importantly, the sheer volume of users underscores the fact that a form of technology this clever and convenient will not simply be legislated away. That is why I believe the only workable response to these technologies is one that will adapt them to serve both copyright owners and customers.

6   My position is rarely reflected in the media coverage of Napster, in which musicians and music fans are generally presented with a false choice: support traditional notions of artists' rights and be called a money-grubbing Luddite or support new technology solutions and be accused of ignoring the plight of those artists left behind.

7   Like Chuck D, I am an advocate of advances in digital download technology *because* they allow artists to distribute their music independently and inexpensively across the Internet, therefore removing the pressure for artists to work within the major label system. His dinosaur metaphor is an apt one. The big five labels (BMG Entertainment, EMI Music, Sony Music Entertainment, Universal Music Group, Warner Music Group) have spent much of the past 50 years dominating the media landscape. Fat and contented, they failed to evolve, underestimating the power of digital download technology, and believing their reign would last forever.

8   I can't help but smile at the thought of them dying a fiery death. It's easy to see the monopoly these corporations have over international media and distribution channels. According to the congressional testimony of Tom Silverman, who is the CEO of a large independent label called Tommy Boy Records, only 20 percent of the 38,857 records released in the United States last year were major label releases. But that same 20 percent constitutes the overwhelming majority of the music played on the radio.

9   I have always understood that it would be impossible to get my indie rock music into the regular rotation at any commercial radio station. I also knew that it would be difficult to get my records sold in chain stores. It wouldn't be my posters hanging in the windows of Tower Records, or my videos featured on MTV. This was not just because I was selling far fewer records than those other bands. It was because I didn't have the money to buy the advertising that would allow me to compete; because I couldn't imagine being able to pay $20,000 for a video, let alone the $1 million that some cost; because I don't have the resources it takes to convince the program directors at increasingly consolidated radio stations to take a chance on talent over cash.

10   So, instead of competing in the major label world where I was destined to fail—or giving up control to work within it—I, and musicians like me, have created a parallel universe of "mom and pop" stores, mail-order customers and college radio programming

where we build audiences and sell records. These independent niches succeed on a much smaller scale and help musicians earn or supplement a living. For the past 15 years, I have worked in this world. I play guitar in several bands—Tsunami, Grenadine, Liquorice—and the record label, Simple Machines, of which I am an owner, has released more than 75 projects.

11   The Internet offers independent musicians many ways to save money, to connect with fans and even to level the playing field between mainstream and niche markets. With a simple home page and an e-mail-based ordering system, independent musicians are potentially as accessible as the major labels. There are sites that allow bands to put up videos that MTV would never broadcast. Hundreds of Internet radio stations like *www.3wk.com* offer diverse programming that gives indie bands exposure. Even controversial programs like Napster are seen in Internet circles as being a sort of "new radio" where music lovers can hear music that isn't commercially broadcast.

12   The downside of all this is loss of control. There's a saying in the Internet community that goes, "If you can hear it, you can copy it." While this has been true since the advent of tape recorders, high-quality digital copies are something new. With easily downloadable and free software and CD burners running as low as $200, anyone can amass a free archive of music via the Web. As more and more music fans sign up with services like Napster and offer their favorite tracks for trade, more and more music is made available for free.

13   Within the Internet community, this is often seen as a sort of karmic payback to the major labels that have artificially inflated the cost of CDs. Sometimes it is seen as a backlash to commercial radio's bottom-line programming. I understand these arguments. But as an indie musician who has already tallied up more than $10,000 in expenses against my unfinished solo album, I can't help but worry about future lost sales. When I began squirreling away money from my paycheck last year (I also work in *The Post*'s advertising department) with plans to book time in King-size, my favorite Chicago studio, I wasn't worried that innovations in digital download technology might make it impossible to recoup my investment.

14   Now I worry that someone with an advance copy might offer the entire album via Napster before it's for sale. It is becoming increasingly clear that selling download tracks in the Napster environment is like trying to sell 50-cent beer next to a table that's giving it away.

15   Worse still, the great majority of independent rock releases are sold to college-age consumers—the very people who are consistently trading files. While many college-age music fans say that they only download files to try them out and then go on to purchase CDs, I can't help but wonder what happens as we move away from CDs toward downloads as the standard distribution format for music.

16   The Recording Industry Association of America suggests that the best solution to this problem is a secure digital format, which would allow files to be downloaded once but not pirated. In order to develop this standard, it created a group called the Secure Digital Music Initiative (SDMI) and invited a group of powerful consumer electronics manufacturers, PC manufacturers and record labels to develop alternative copyright-enabled technologies.

17   Aside from questions about the viability of the encryption idea, I wonder what is lost in standardizing encryption software, which more than likely will be owned and

enforced by the same dinosaurs that controlled the monopolies digital downloads were supposed to unseat.

18   I hate to think of hard-working Simple Machines artists like Danielle Howle or Ida losing potential royalties. Still, I only need to look at the dedication of their fans to see where the true solution lies: Not in SDMI, which would place the controls back into the hands of the majors, but in the development of legal payment strategies and the education of fans who would gladly pay for tracks to support the artists they love.

19   The Internet music entrepreneurs who operate with business models that do not compensate musicians should be held accountable for enabling piracy. They should be held accountable not only by the courts that protect intellectual property rights, but by the fans who want access and recognize the need to compensate artists.

20   I believe fans would pay if they had a means of doing so. The swift creation of a digital download technology that builds a method of compensation for the artist into the program is the only shield that might protect the independent labels from the meteors. That protection will only come about if the new technology remains decentralized and freely accessible to musicians, regardless of money or power. Only then can we ensure that future Internet links revenue goes directly to the artists who create the music—and not to some reestablished distribution channel of *majorlabeldinosaur.com*.

Questions for Reading and Analysis

1. What issue does Toomey explore? What is her particular perspective on the topic?

2. Toomey writes in June 2000 that she believes Napster will lose in court. Why? File sharing of music involves ignoring what?

3. What false choice have we been given on this issue?

4. Toomey devotes several paragraphs to exploring the music business and her roles in it. What does she accomplish in these paragraphs? What is her attitude toward the big music companies? Toward Internet technology? What does this technology offer independent musicians? What is the downside of the Internet for musicians?

5. What is SDMI? Who gains from SDMI? Who stands to lose if it is developed?

6. What is Toomey's claim? What is her solution to the problem for musicians created by Napster and similar sites?

Questions for Discussion and Response

1. Compare Toomey's debate of the music-sharing issue with Paul Kedrosky's. In what ways do they agree? How do they disagree?

2. What has been your view of Napster and similar sites? Are they good because they get around the big music companies? Are they bad because file sharing is theft? Have you given thought to the problems they raise for independent musicians such as Toomey?

3. Now that you have read Toomey's argument, have you changed your views on this issue in any way? Why or why not?

4. Toomey does more than complain; she offers a solution. How does her solution compare, in general, to Lessig's approach to Internet privacy? Does her solution make sense to you? Why or why not?

5. If you disagree with Toomey's argument, how would you go about refuting her position?

Will We Have Any Privacy Left?

David Gelernter

A professor of computer science at Yale University, David Gelernter (b. 1955) is also chief scientist at Mirror Worlds Technologies and art critic of the *Weekly Standard*. He has published numerous articles and books on a wide range of scientific and cultural topics, including *1939: The Lost World of the Fair* (1995), *Machine Beauty* (1997), and *Drawing Life: Surviving the Unabomber* (1997). His views on privacy in this new century appeared in the February 21, 2000, issue of *Time* magazine.

1   Our bad dreams about the haunted house called "Privacy, Circa 2025" are likely to focus on those all-seeing orbiting spy cameras that are always peering at us. They already exist, capable of observing from miles overhead that your lawn could use mowing and your dog needs a shampoo. By 2025, they will be *really* good. Audio spy technology has been advancing fast too. But the biggest threat to privacy doesn't even exist yet. By 2025 it will be in full bloom.

2   Today we are engulfed by the signal-carrying waves of broadcast radio and TV. Come 2025, we will be engulfed by a "cybersphere" in which billions of "information structures" will drift (invisible but real, like radio waves) bearing the words, sounds and pictures on which our lives depend. That's because the electronic world will have achieved some coherence by 2025. Instead of phone, computer and TV networks side by side, one network will do it all. TVs and phones and computers will all be variations on one theme. Their function will be to tune in these information structures in the sense that a radio tunes in station WXYZ.

3   These cyberstructures will come in many shapes and sizes, but one type, the "cyberstream," is likely to be more important than any other. A cyberstream is an electronic chronicle of your daily life, in which records accumulate like baroque pearls on an ever lengthening string—each arriving phone call and e-mail message, each bill and bank statement, each Web bookmark, birthday photo, Rolodex card and calendar entry.

4   An irresistible convenience: your whole life in one place. Tune in anywhere, using any computer, phone or TV. Just put your card in the slot, pass a security test (supply your password and something like a fingerprint) and you're in. You see your electronic life onscreen or hear a description over the phone, starting with the latest news and working back.

5   By feeding all this information into the food processor of statistical analysis, your faithful software servants will be able to make smooth, creamy, startlingly accurate

guesses about your plans for the near future. They will find patterns in your life that you didn't know were there. They will respond correctly to terse spoken commands ("Call Juliet," "Buy food," "Print the news") because they will know exactly who Juliet is, what food you need and what news stories you want to read.

6   So it's 2025, and the living is easy. You glide forward on a magic carpet woven out of detailed data and statistical analyses. But should anyone seize access to your electronic life story, "invasion of privacy" will take on a whole new meaning. The thief will have stolen not only your past and present but also a reliable guide to your future.

7   Such information structures are just beginning to emerge. They are likely to be far safer and more private than anything we have ever put on paper. Nonetheless, by 2025, a large proportion of the world's valuable private information will be stored on computers that are connected to a global network, and if a thief can connect his computer to that same global network, he will have—in principle—an electronic route from his machine to yours.

8   The route will be electronically guarded and nearly impassable, unless the intended target has given out information he should not have—as people do. And unfortunately, electronic thievery and invasion of privacy are jackpots that keep growing. They are just the crimes for shameless, cowardly, clever crooks. No need to risk life or limb; just tiptoe over wires and through keyholes.

9   So what else is new? Technology always threatens privacy. Those threats usually come to nothing. They have been defeated before, and will be in the future, by a force that is far more powerful than technology—not Congress, the law or the press, not bureaucrats or federal judges, but morality.

10   You could, after all, get a pair of high-power binoculars and start spying on your neighbor tomorrow morning. But you won't. Not because you can't, not because it's illegal, not because you're not interested; to be human is to be a busybody. You won't do it because it is beneath you. Because you know it is wrong, and you would be ashamed of yourself if you did it.

11   Laws are bad weapons in the fight to protect privacy. Once we invoke the law, the bad deed has ordinarily been done, and society has lost. Attempting to restrain technological progress is another bad strategy—it's a fool's game and won't work. The best method for protecting privacy in 2025 is the same method we have always used: teaching our children to tell right from wrong, making it plain that we count on them to do what is right.

12   Outrageously naive advice for a high-tech future? Think again. It has been field-tested, and it works. All over the country, people leave valuable private papers in unlocked mailboxes along the street. Astonishing! Suburban mail is a vastly easier mark than anything in cyberspace will ever be. But our mailboxes are largely safe because we are largely honest. Some technology pundits have been startled by people's willingness to confide their credit-card numbers to websites. But for years we have been reciting those numbers over the phone. And we have all sorts of other long-standing habits (paying our taxes, for example) that reflect our confidence in the honor of our fellow citizens.

13   As we venture further into the deep waters of technology, temptations increase. When it comes to temptation resistance, we are admittedly not at the top of our game

in early 2000. This is an age of moral confusion. We love to talk about law; we hate morality talk. But we will snap out of this dive, as we have snapped out of others before. Among our characteristic American obsessions, two have been prominent since 1776—our technological inventiveness and our stubborn desire to know and do what is right.

14   And by 2025, the issue will be framed differently. We are obsessed with privacy because we have temporarily mislaid a more important word: dignity. We talk about our "right to privacy," but we don't really mean it. This broken-down, ramshackle idea falls apart the moment you blow on it. Privacy to commit murder? To beat a wife or child? To abuse an animal? To counterfeit money? To be insane, refuse treatment and suffer never-endingly? Privacy is no absolute right; it is a nice little luxury when we can get it. Dignity is a necessity to fight for. And come 2025, life will be better: not because of the technology revolution but because of a moral rebirth that is equally inevitable and far more important.

Questions for Reading and Analysis

1. Explain Gelernter's concept of a "cybersphere" that will engulf us in 2025. Explain his image of a "cyberstream."

2. How will we connect to the cyberstream? What will be its advantages for us?

3. What is the danger of the cybersphere? What can happen? How?

4. What is Gelernter's topic? (Do not answer "the future of technology"; look at his title and at paragraph 9 and answer more precisely.)

5. What is the author's claim?

6. Why are laws "bad weapons in the fight to protect privacy"?

7. What evidence does Gelernter provide to support his claim?

8. Gelernter asserts that we live in an age of "moral confusion." What evidence does he provide that we will move out of this period of moral confusion?

9. When the author says that we are "not at the top of our game," what does he mean? What writing strategy is he using?

10. Gelernter asserts that privacy is not an absolute right. What is it that we really want instead?

Questions for Discussion and Response

1. Lessig, a law professor, believes that technology itself will solve the privacy problems created by technology. Gelernter, a computer science professor, takes a quite different approach. Are you surprised by his solution to the problem of privacy created by computer technology? Why or why not?

2. Have you argued in the past for the "right to privacy"? If so, are you prepared to agree with Gelernter that you really meant the right to dignity?

3. Do you agree that this is an age of moral confusion? Why or why not? Are we too focused on the law and not enough on morality?

4. Do you agree that we will snap out of our current moral morass and get back to "the top of our game" by 2025? If you do not agree that this is inevitable, do you agree that it is even more important than the ongoing technology revolution? Why or why not?

5. If you wanted to refute Gelernter's claim or evidence, how would you proceed? If you basically agree with his argument, what additional evidence or reasons would you offer in support of his claim?

CHAPTER 16

The Animal Rights Debate

The animal rights debate is really a series of debates, but debates that intersect and overlap in key ways. Primate researchers and activists such as Jane Goodall, for example, seek, first, the public's acceptance of our close connections with the other primates. If that acceptance is forthcoming, then, these activists reason, it will follow that we will not abuse chimpanzees in research, in zoos, or in the wild. Indeed, our sense of affiliation with the other primates may extend to all animals, bringing us to oppose the use of fur coats or the eating of meat. Others take a more legalistic approach, examining the "rights" of primates. What rights, if any, should they be accorded under the law, these writers ask. Still others focus specifically on the issue of using animals, particularly chimpanzees, in medical research.

Reflecting on the following questions before you read will enrich your reading and thinking about this topic:

1. Do you already have a position on animal-rights issues? If so, what might you gain from reading the articles in this chapter? If not, do you think that you should have a position on this issue? Why or why not?

2. Does the demand for ongoing advances in human medicine justify the use of animals in research? Is the use of animals ethical so long as they are not abused? What constitutes "abuse"?

3. Why do we have zoos? Is it possible to oppose abuse of animals and still justify the existence of zoos? If so, why? If not, why not?

4. In many states there are no laws regarding the private ownership of wild animals; that is, you can keep a tiger in a cage in your backyard. Should individuals be allowed to own wild animals? If so, why? If not, why not?

Websites Related to This Chapter's Topic

Animal Rights Watch

www.lbbs.org/animal_rights_watch.htm

Part of the ZNet political site, this site, supporting animal rights, includes definitions, information on a vegan diet, and links to useful sources.

Animal Rights vs. Animal Welfare

www.dandy-lions.com/animal_rights.html

Part of the Stop Animal Rights Madness Web Ring, this site expresses the views of those who oppose the work of animal rights activists. It contains many good links to resources, articles, other groups.

Chimpanzees — Bridging the Gap

Jane Goodall

Ethologist, author, and activist on behalf of primates, Jane Goodall (b. 1934) has performed field studies of chimpanzees since 1960 at the Gombe Stream Research Centre in Tanzania. Two of her many books based on her field experience are *Through a Window: My Thirty Years with the Chimpanzees of Gombe* (1990) and *The Chimpanzee: The Living Link Between "Man" and "Beast"* (1992). The following is a chapter in *The Great Ape Project,* edited by Paola Cavalieri and Peter Singer (1993).

1   She was too tired after their long, hot journey to set to on the delicious food, as her daughters did. She had one paralysed arm, the aftermath of a bout of polio nine years ago, and walking was something of an effort. And so, for the moment, she was content to rest and watch as her two daughters ate. One was adult now, the other still caught in the contrariness of adolescence—grown up one moment, childish the next. Minutes passed. And then her eldest, the first pangs of her hunger assuaged, glanced at the old lady, gathered food for both of them and took it to share with her mother.

2   The leader of the patrol, hearing the sudden sound, stopped and stared ahead. The three following froze in their tracks, alert to the danger that threatened ever more sinister as they penetrated further into neighbouring territory. Then they relaxed: it was only a large bird that had landed in a tree ahead. The leader looked back, as though seeking approval for moving on again. Without a word the patrol moved on. Ten minutes later they reached a lookout place offering a view across enemy territory. Sitting close together, silent still, they searched for sign or sound that might indicate the presence of strangers. But all was peaceful. For a whole hour the four sat there, uttering no sound. And then, still maintaining silence, the leader rose, glanced at the others and moved on. One by one they followed him. Only the youngest, a youth still in his teens, stayed on for a few minutes by himself, reluctant, it seemed, to tear himself away from the prospect of violence. He was at that age when border skirmishes seemed exhilarating as well as challenging and dangerous. He couldn't help being fascinated, hoping for, yet fearing, a glimpse of the enemy. But clearly there would be no fighting that day and so he too followed his leader back to familiar haunts and safety.

3   We knew her as 'Auntie Gigi'. She had no children of her own, but two years ago she had more or less adopted two youngsters who had lost their own mother in an epidemic—pneumonia, probably. They were lucky, those two. Not that Gigi was all sweet and motherly, not at all. She was a tough old bird, somewhat mannish in many ways. But she made a perfect guardian for she stood no nonsense, not from anyone, and had high standing in her society. If anyone picked a quarrel with either of these two kids, he or she had Auntie Gigi to reckon with. Before Gigi came into the picture, one of the orphans, little Mel, had been cared for by Sam, a teenage youth. It was quite extraordinary—it

wasn't even as though Sam was related to the sickly orphan. He had not even been close with Mel's mother during her life. Yet after she passed away, Sam and Mel became really close, like a loving father and child. Sam often shared his food with Mel, usually carried him when they went on long trips together, and even let the child sleep with him at night. And he did his best to keep him out of harm's way. Maybe it was because Sam's mother had got sick and died in that same epidemic. Of course, he'd not been spending much time with her then—he'd been out and about with the boys mostly. Even so, it is always a comfort if you can sneak off to Mum for a while when the going gets tough, and the big guys start picking on you. And suddenly, for Sam, his old mother wasn't there. Perhaps his closeness with that dependent little child helped to fill an empty place in his heart. Whatever the reason, Mel would almost certainly have died if Sam hadn't cared for him as he did. After a year Sam and Mel began spending less time together. And that was when Auntie Gigi took over.

4   Those anecdotes were recorded during our thirty-one years of observation of the chimpanzees of Gombe, in Tanzania. Yet the characters could easily be mistaken for humans. This is partly because chimpanzees do behave so much like us, and partly because I deliberately wrote as though I were describing humans, and used words like 'old lady', 'youth', and 'mannish'. And 'Sam' was really known as 'Spindle'.

5   One by one, over the years, many words once used to describe human behaviour have crept into scientific accounts of nonhuman animal behaviour. When, in the early 1960s, I brazenly used such words as 'childhood', 'adolescence', 'motivation', 'excitement', and 'mood' I was much criticised. Even worse was my crime of suggesting that chimpanzees had 'personalities'. I was ascribing human characteristics to non-human animals and was thus guilty of that worst of ethological sins—anthropomorphism. Certainly anthropomorphism can be misleading, but it so happens that chimpanzees, our closest living relatives in the animal kingdom, do show many human characteristics. Which, in view of the fact that our DNA differs from theirs by only just over 1 per cent, is hardly surprising.

6   Each chimpanzee has a unique personality and each has his or her own individual life history. We can speak of the history of a chimpanzee community, where major events—an epidemic, a kind of primitive 'war', a 'baby boom'—have marked the 'reigns' of the five top-ranking or alpha males we have known. And we find that individual chimpanzees can make a difference to the course of chimpanzee history, as is the case with humans. I wish there was space to describe here some of these characters and events, but the information, for those interested, can be found in my most recent book, *Through a Window*.[1]

7   Chimpanzees can live more than fifty years. Infants suckle and are carried by their mothers for five years. And then, even when the next infant is born, the elder child travels with his or her mother for another three or four years and continues to spend a good deal of time with her thereafter. The ties between family members are close, affectionate and supportive, and typically endure throughout life. Learning is important in the individual life cycle. Chimpanzees, like humans, can learn by observation and imitation, which means that if a new adaptive pattern is 'invented' by a particular individual, it can be passed on to the next generation. Thus we find that while the various chimpanzee groups that have been studied in different parts of Africa have many behaviours in common, they also have their own distinctive traditions. This is particularly well

documented with respect to tool-using and tool-making behaviours. Chimpanzees use more objects as tools for a greater variety of purposes than any creature except ourselves and each population has its own tool-using cultures. For example, the Gombe chimpanzees use long, straight sticks from which the bark has been peeled to extract army ants from their nests; 100 miles to the south, in the Mahale Mountains, there are plenty of the same ants, but they are not eaten by the chimpanzees. The Mahale chimpanzees use small twigs to extract carpenter ants from their nests in tree branches; these ants, though present, are not eaten at Gombe. And no East African chimpanzee has been seen to open hard-shelled fruits with the hammer and anvil technique that is part of the culture of chimpanzee groups in West Africa.

8   The postures and gestures with which chimpanzees communicate—such as kissing, embracing, holding hands, patting one another on the back, swaggering, punching, hair-pulling, tickling—are not only uncannily like many of our own, but are used in similar contexts and clearly have similar meanings. Two friends may greet with an embrace and a fearful individual may be calmed by a touch, whether they be chimpanzees or humans. Chimpanzees are capable of sophisticated co-operation and complex social manipulation. Like us, they have a dark side to their nature: they can be brutal, they are aggressively territorial, sometimes they even engage in a primitive type of warfare. But they also show a variety of helping and care-giving behaviours and are capable of true altruism.

9   The structure of the chimpanzee brain and central nervous system is extraordinarily like ours. And this appears to have led to similar emotions and intellectual abilities in our two species. Of course, it is difficult to study emotion even when the subjects are human—I can only guess, when you *say* you are sad and *look* sad, that you *feel* rather as I do when I am sad. I cannot know. And when the subject is a member of another species, the task is that much harder. If we ascribe human emotion to nonhuman animals we are, of course, accused of anthropomorphism. But given the similarities in the anatomy and wiring of the chimpanzee and human brains, is it not logical to assume that there will be similarities also in the feelings, emotions and moods of the two species? Certainly all of us who have worked closely with chimpanzees over extended periods of time have no hesitation in asserting that chimpanzees, like humans, show emotions similar to—sometimes probably identical to—those which we label joy, sadness, fear, despair and so on.

10   Our own success as a species (if we measure success by the extent to which we have spread across the world and altered the environment to suit our immediate purposes) has been due entirely to the explosive development of the human brain. Our intellectual abilities are so much more sophisticated than those of even the most gifted chimpanzees that early attempts made by scientists to describe the similarity of mental process in humans and chimpanzees were largely met with ridicule or outrage. Gradually, however, evidence for sophisticated mental performances in the apes has become ever more convincing. There is proof that they can solve simple problems through process of reasoning and insight. They can plan for the immediate future. The language acquisition experiments have demonstrated that they have powers of generalisation, abstraction, and concept-forming along with the ability to understand and use abstract symbols in communication. And they clearly have some kind of self-concept.

11   It is all a little humbling, for these cognitive abilities used to be considered unique to humans: we are not, after all, quite as different from the rest of the animal kingdom as we used to think. The line dividing 'man' from 'beast' has become increasingly blurred. The chimpanzees, and the other great apes, form a living bridge between 'us' and 'them', and this knowledge forces us to re-evaluate our relationship with the rest of the animal kingdom, particularly with the great apes. In what terms should we think of these beings, nonhuman yet possessing so very many human-like characteristics? How should we treat them?

12   Surely we should treat them with the same consideration and kindness as we show to other humans; and as we recognise human rights, so too should we recognise the rights of the great apes? Yes — but unfortunately huge segments of the human population are *not* treated with consideration and kindness, and our newspapers inform us daily of horrific violations of human rights in many countries around the world.

13   Still, things have got better in some Western-style democracies. During the past 100 years we have seen the abolition of enforced child and female labour, slavery, the exhibiting of deformed humans in circuses and fairs and many other such horrors. We no longer gather to gloat over suffering and death at public hangings. We have welfare states so that (theoretically) no one needs to starve or freeze to death and everyone can expect some help when they are sick or unemployed. Of course there are still a myriad of social injustices and abuses, but at least they are not publicly condoned by the government and, once public sympathy has been aroused, they are gradually addressed. We are trying, for example, to abolish the last traces of the old sadism in mental institutions.

14   Finally, there is a growing concern for the plight of nonhuman animals in our society. But those who are trying to raise levels of awareness regarding the abuse of companion animals, animals raised for food, zoo and circus performers, laboratory victims and so on, and lobbying for new and improved legislation to protect them, are constantly asked how they can devote time and energy, and divert public monies, to 'animals' when there is so much need among human beings. Indeed, in many parts of the world humans suffer mightily. We are anguished when we read of the millions of starving and homeless people, of police tortures, of children whose limbs are deliberately deformed so that they can make a living from begging, and those whose parents force them—even sell them—into lives of prostitution. We long for the day when conditions improve worldwide—we may work for that cause. But we should not delude ourselves into believing that, so long as there is human suffering, it is morally acceptable to turn a blind eye to nonhuman suffering. Who are we to say that the suffering of a human being is more terrible than the suffering of a nonhuman being, or that it matters more?

15   It is not so long ago, in historical perspective, that we abolished the slave trade. Slaves were taken from 'savage' tribes that inhabited remote corners of the earth. Probably it was not too difficult for slave traders and owners to distance themselves, psychologically, from these prisoners, so unlike any people their 'masters' had known before. And although they must have realised that their slaves were capable of feeling pain and suffering, why should that matter? Those strange, dark, heathen people were so *different*—not really like human beings at all. And so their anguish could be ignored. Today we know that the DNA of all ethnic groups of humans is virtually the same, that we are all—yellow, brown, black and white—brothers and sisters around the globe. From our superior

knowledge we are appalled to think back to the intelligent and normally compassionate people who condoned slavery and all that it entailed. Fortunately, thanks to the perceptions, high moral principles and determination of a small band of people, human slaves were freed. And they were freed *not* because of sophisticated analysis of their DNA, but because they so obviously showed the same emotions, the same intellectual abilities, the same capacity for suffering and joy, as their white owners.

16   Now, for a moment, let us imagine beings who, although they differ genetically from *Homo sapiens* by about 1 per cent and lack speech, nevertheless behave similarly to ourselves, can feel pain, share our emotions and have sophisticated intellectual abilities. Would we, today, condone the use of those beings as slaves? Tolerate their capture and export from Africa? Laugh at degrading performances, taught through cruelty, shown on our television screens? Turn a blind eye to their imprisonment, in tiny barren cells, often in solitary confinement, even though they had committed no crimes? Buy products tested on them at the cost of their mental or physical torture?

17   Those beings exist and we *do* condone their abuse. They are called chimpanzees. They are imprisoned in zoos, sold to anyone who cares to buy them as 'pets', and dressed up and taught to smoke or ride bicycles for our entertainment. They are incarcerated and often tortured, psychologically and even physically, in medical laboratories in the name of science. And this is condoned by governments and by large numbers of the general public. There was a time when the victims in the labs would have been human; but thanks to a dedicated few who stood up to the establishment and who gradually informed the general public of the horrors being perpetrated behind closed doors, the insane and other unfortunates are now safe from the white-coated gods. The time has come when we must take the next step and protect our closest living relatives from exploitation. How can we do this?

18   If we could simply argue that it is morally wrong to abuse, physically or psychologically, any rational, thinking being with the capacity to suffer and feel pain, to know fear and despair, it would be easy—we have already demonstrated the existence of these abilities in chimpanzees and the other great apes. But this, it seems, is not enough. We come up, again and again, against that non-existent barrier that is, for so many, so real—the barrier between 'man' and 'beast'. It was erected in ignorance, as a result of the arrogant assumption, unfortunately shared by vast numbers of people, that humans are superior to nonhumans in every way. Even if nonhuman beings are rational and *can* suffer and feel pain and despair it does not matter how we treat them provided it is for the good of humanity—which apparently includes our own pleasure. They are not members of that exclusive club that opens its doors only to bona fide *Homo sapiens*.

19   This is why we find double standards in the legislation regarding medical research. Thus while it is illegal to perform medical experiments on a brain-dead human being who can neither speak nor feel, it is legally acceptable to perform them on an alert, feeling and highly intelligent chimpanzee. Conversely, while it is legally permitted to imprison an innocent chimpanzee, for life, in a steel-barred, barren laboratory cell measuring five foot by five foot by seven foot, a psychopathic mass murderer must be more spaciously confined. And these double standards exist only because the brain-dead patient and the mass murderer are *human*. They have souls and we cannot, of course, prove that chimpanzees have souls. The fact we cannot prove that *we* have souls, or that chimps do not, is, apparently, beside the point.

20 So how can we hope to procure improved legal standing for the great apes? By trying to prove that we are 'merely' apes, and that what goes for us, therefore, should go for them also? I see no point in altering our status as humans by constantly stressing that we differ from the apes *only* in that our brains are bigger and better. Admittedly at our worst we can outdo the Devil in wickedness, but at our best we are close to the angels: certain human lives and accomplishments vividly illustrate the human potential. As we plod from cradle to grave we need all the encouragement and inspiration we can get and it helps, sometimes, to know that wings and halos *can* be won. Nor do I think it useful to suggest reclassifying the great apes as *human*. Our task is hard enough without the waving of red flags.

21 Fortunately there are some heavy-duty people (like the editors of this book) out there fighting for the rights of the great apes, along with those fighting for the rights of humans. If only we could march under one banner, working for apes and humans alike, and with our combined intelligence and compassion—our humanity—strive to make ever more people understand. To understand that we should respect the individual ape just as we should respect the individual human; that we should recognise the right of each ape to live a life unmolested by humans, if necessary helped by humans, in the same way as we should recognise these rights for individual human beings; and that the same ethical and moral attitudes should apply to ape beings and human beings alike. Then, as the thesis of this book proposes, we shall be ready to welcome them, these ape beings, into a 'moral community' of which we humans are also a part.

22 Let me end with a combined message from two very special members of this moral community. The first is a chimpanzee being named Old Man. He was rescued from a lab when he was about twelve years old and went to Lion Country Safaris in Florida. There he was put, with three females, on an artificial island. All four had been abused. A young man, Marc Cusano, was employed to care for them. He was told not to get too close—the chimps hated people and were vicious. He should throw food to the island from his little boat. As the days went by Marc became increasingly fascinated by the human-like behaviour of the chimps. How could he care for them if he did not have some kind of relationship with them? He began going closer and closer. One day he held out a banana—Old Man took it from his hand. A few weeks later Marc dared step on to the island. And then, on a never to be forgotten occasion, Old Man allowed Marc to groom him. They had become friends. Some time later, as Marc was clearing the island, he slipped, fell and scared the infant who had been born to one of the females. The infant screamed, the mother, instinctively, leapt to defend her child and bit Marc's neck. The other two females quickly ran to help their friend; one bit his wrist, the other his leg. And then Old Man came charging towards the scene—and that, thought Marc, was the end. But Old Man pulled each of those females off Marc and hurled them away, then kept them at bay while Marc, badly wounded, dragged himself to safety.

23 'There's no doubt about it,' Marc told me later, 'Old Man saved my life'.

24 The second hero is a human being named Rick Swope. He visits the Detroit zoo once a year with his family. One day, as he watched the chimpanzees in their big new enclosure, a fight broke out between two adult males. Jojo, who had been at the zoo for years, was challenged by a younger and stronger newcomer—and Jojo lost. In his fear he fled into the moat: it was brand new and Jojo did not understand water. He had got over the barrier erected to prevent the chimpanzees from falling in—for they cannot

swim—and the group of visitors and staff that happened to be there stood and watched in horror as Jojo began to drown. He went under once, twice, three times. And then Rick Swope could bear it no longer. He jumped in to try to save the chimp. He jumped in despite the onlookers yelling at him about the danger. He managed to get Jojo's dead weight over his shoulder, and then he crossed the barrier and pushed Jojo on to the bank of the island. He held him there (because the bank was too steep and when he let go Jojo slid back to the water) even when the other chimps charged towards him, screaming in excitement. He held him until Jojo raised his head, took a few staggering steps, and collapsed on more level ground.

25   The director of the institute called Rick. 'That was a brave thing you did. You must have known how dangerous it was. What made you do it?'

26   'Well, I looked into his eyes. And it was like looking into the eyes of a man. And the message was, "Won't *anybody* help me?" '

27   Old Man, a chimpanzee who had been abused by humans, reached across the supposed species barrier to help a human friend in need. Rick Swope risked his life to save a chimpanzee, a nonhuman being who sent a message that a human could understand. Now it is up to the rest of us to join in too.

Note

1. J. Goodall, *Through a Window: My Thirty Years with the Chimpanzees of Gombe* (Houghton Mifflin, Boston, 1990).

Questions for Reading and Analysis

1. Goodall begins with three brief anecdotes describing the behavior of chimpanzees. What does she seek to accomplish with this introduction?

2. What "human" traits are revealed in the three stories?

3. What is meant by "anthropomorphism"? Does Goodall believe that she is being anthropomorphic in her descriptions of chimpanzees?

4. List the specific "human" traits ascribed to chimpanzees by Goodall. What is the source of her information about chimps?

5. How closely are we related to chimpanzees? What regarding emotions does Goodall infer based on human/chimpanzee similarities in brains and nervous systems?

6. How should we treat other animals, particularly other primates, according to the author?

7. How does Goodall answer the challenge to animal activists that they should worry more about human suffering around the world?

8. What is Goodall's claim? How does she defend it? What reasons, evidence, or other strategies does she employ?

9. Why has a moral argument not been sufficient to stop the mistreatment of animals? What should we do?

Questions for Discussion and Response

1. Do you find the opening and concluding stories effective strategies in support of Goodall's claim? Why or why not?

2. Do you find the evidence of human traits and DNA similarities convincing arguments for Goodall's claim? Why or why not?

3. Do you hold the view that there is a barrier between "human" and "nonhuman"? If so, does this barrier justify human uses of nonhumans in any way that is helpful or amusing for humans? Why or why not?

4. Is it possible to be sympathetic to Goodall's position and still support the use of animals in medical research? If so, how would you defend that position? If not, how would you demonstrate that the two positions cannot be held?

On the Rights of an Ape

Daniel W. McShea

An assistant professor of zoology at Duke University, Daniel McShea (b. 1956) holds a Ph.D. from the University of Chicago and did postdoctoral studies at the Michigan Museum of Paleontology and the Santa Fe Institute. His interests include large-scale evolutionary trends and the philosophy of science. He has published articles for both scholarly journals and popular magazines. The following article appeared in *Discover* in February 1994.

1   Life, liberty, and the pursuit of happiness. The Declaration of Independence holds these rights to be self-evident, unalienable. In the eighteenth century, when the words were written, they were called natural rights; today we call them human rights. Whatever we call these rights, it has long seemed obvious to most people that only human beings have them. But now a group of human beings—headed by philosopher Peter Singer and backed by a number of prominent anthropologists, biologists, lawyers, psychologists, and ethicists—has challenged our basic assumptions on the subject, insisting that we reconsider this limitation. In the preface to their book, *The Great Ape Project*, they set forth a Declaration on Great Apes. "We demand the extension of the community of equals to include all great apes: human beings, chimpanzees, gorillas, and orangutans," they write. " 'The community of equals' is the moral community within which we accept certain basic moral principles or rights as governing our relations with each other and enforceable at law."

2   The moral principles or rights they mean are life, liberty, and the necessary precursor to the pursuit of happiness: freedom from torture. Their demand will undoubtedly ignite a hot debate. Some people will protest that rights should not be extended to apes when most human beings do not enjoy them. But denying rights to apes will not help oppressed people in their struggle to achieve them, Singer and his colleagues contend. And that argument assumes that apes have a lesser worth than humans—an assumption they strenuously dispute throughout the book.

3   There is also a fundamental difficulty with the concept of "rights." The rules of chess grant me the right to move my bishop diagonally; the U.S. legal system—a set of

rules—grants me the right to a speedy trial. Rights only exist, or make sense, under a set of rules. But under what set of rules do apes—or human beings, for that matter—have rights? And even if such rules exist, how do we know what they are? Who has access to them? Who interprets them?

4   This is arguably just a theoretical problem. As a practical matter, the word rights is part of our everyday political language. Badly treated individuals or groups use this word to seek special protection, and we know what they mean even if we don't agree on how to respond. There is little doubt that nonhuman apes have been treated badly in the past, and that they are harmed or killed routinely even today. As a practical matter, then, the question is whether they too deserve some sort of special protection.

5   The Great Ape Project's resounding Yes! is backed by a number of arguments. Two are especially salient. One is that apes are intelligent: they solve puzzles, they learn and use language, and they can recognize and think about themselves. The second is our kinship. Orangutan DNA differs from ours by less than 4 percent, on average; chimps and gorillas are closer yet. We're separated, at most, by a mere 16 million years of evolution. They are very nearly us.

6   Yet no matter how close we are genetically, many people will argue that they're just not us. They'll acknowledge ape intelligence and our close kinship but insist that humans come first, especially when important human interests—such as our health—are at stake. To many, humans are obviously special, and there is something unserious, unthinking, or overly emotional about such a high level of concern for other species. This usually unspoken charge must lie at the heart of many people's skepticism about the animal welfare movement in general; it will doubtless influence views on ape rights. To answer it, I suggest a different sort of argument than the one based on intelligence and kinship, an argument that speaks to us more directly. This argument for ape rights is based on our concern for our own well-being, our own feelings.

7   Feelings are basic human equipment, like legs and livers. They're the driving force behind all human behavior that requires thought. Some behavior is automatic, or reflexive, and requires no thought to be performed properly. Heartbeats are reflexive, as are digestion and even the mechanics of walking. Earthworms reflexively crawl up out of the ground to avoid drowning when it rains; cats go limp when grasped by the scruff of the neck.

8   Other behaviors, however, are what might be called motivated. Motivated behavior requires a combination of two equally essential ingredients: intelligence and feelings. Intelligence is the ability to reason; feelings are the internal states of tension or dissatisfaction that motivate reasoning and ultimately behavior. A house cat meowing at the door is experiencing an internal state of dissatisfaction, a feeling—it wants to go out. A human mother hearing her newborn baby crying experiences a state of dissatisfaction, a feeling of empathy—she wants to help somehow.

9   Clearly such behavior is intelligent. The cat meows at the outside door, not the oven door; the mother tries rocking her newborn, she doesn't sneak up behind it and pop a balloon. But intelligence is only half the story. Without motivation, intelligence can do nothing. Consider one of the most rational creatures ever, the home computer. Plugged in and humming, packing multimegabytes of memory and multimegahertz of speed, it sits on the desk doing only what it is told. It worries about nothing and takes no interest in anything. It has no preferences, not even a preference for survival. It is a

completely reflexive beast. The defect is not a failure of reason—as a logician the home computer is almost flawless—but an absence of motives.

10 The link between intelligence and motivation, reason and feelings, is often misunderstood. Feelings tell us what we want, usually in very unspecific terms; culture fills in the specifics. Our intelligence computes how to get it. The Scottish philosopher David Hume recognized this in the eighteenth century when he wrote, "Reason is and ought to be the slave of the passions."

11 Yet most of us assume that reason is supposed to dominate. The person who trips over a loose floor tile, then turns angrily to kick it, is said to be behaving irrationally, to be momentarily carried away by his or her feelings. But what has really happened is that one feeling—pain-evoked anger—has temporarily won out over calmer feelings that might have motivated a repair project. All motivations are feelings.

12 Rationality, on the other hand, motivates nothing. A truly rational Mr. Spock (of the old *Star Trek* series) or Mr. Data (of the newer series) would have no motivations and thus would never do anything, including get up in the morning. That's why scriptwriters surreptitiously infuse these characters with feelings like curiosity or loyalty. They're calm feelings but feelings nonetheless.

13 Feelings are just as central in the nonhuman great apes. In chimpanzee society, for instance, relative peace is maintained by a complex dominance hierarchy. Occasionally, subordinate males recruit allies and attempt coups. In captive chimp populations, females will take sides in these coups, but they will also attempt to orchestrate reconciliations between the combatants. All this social maneuvering requires each chimp to be able to read the feelings of others, to act to alter those feelings, and to respond emotionally in ways that can be understood. To pull this off, a chimp needs, at the very least, a complete package of chimpanzee motivational equipment—chimpanzee feelings. Nothing less will do. An orangutan, a mainly solitary ape, could never arrange a reconciliation between chimps. Neither could an emotionally deficient chimp.

14 Apes have feelings, but the case for protecting apes doesn't hinge on the damage done to their feelings by maltreatment. Rather, it hinges on the damage that their maltreatment does to our feelings. In particular, it hinges on the damage done to one of these feelings—the one Hume called "natural sympathy."

15 It's hard to define natural sympathy, but it's easy to trigger. Visual cues work well: just the sight of a baby—with its large eyes, large head, and tiny legs and toes is enough to evoke immediate feelings of affection and protectiveness. A kitten, a baby seal, and E.T. can do the same. That's natural sympathy.

16 Emotional cues can be equally evocative. The sight of another human being in need or distress—the Midwest's flood victims, California's fire victims, starving Somalis—triggers natural sympathy. Hollywood plays on our natural sympathy all the time. How easy it was to feel affection for the kindly ant in the movie *Honey, I Shrunk the Kids* after it rescued the children from a much less sympathetic scorpion, even though both are insects, creatures more likely to trigger natural revulsion than natural sympathy. And how easy to sympathize with the murderous, bloblike silicon creature—the horta—in the old *Star Trek* series when we learned that it had been killing only to protect its unhatched eggs. Recognition of familiar passions evokes sympathy, regardless of appearance. On the other hand, what could be less sympathetic than the

Terminator (in the first movie): intelligent and human in appearance, but mechanical and dispassionate, not to mention homicidal.

17   Natural sympathy makes Darwinian sense. Parents who feel great affection for their children doubtless care for them better and thus leave behind more surviving offspring. Individuals who respond sympathetically to other adults are likely to have the favor returned one day; such favors might also translate into more surviving offspring.

18   Most large, furry animals trigger sympathy in us, but none more than the great apes. They look like us and they often act like us. They play. They grieve. They feel. Free-living chimpanzees have been known to go out of their way to sit and watch the sunset. One famous chimpanzee, Washoe, supposedly leapt over an electric fence to rescue a drowning young chimp she'd never met. The apes' intellectual accomplishments—such as self-recognition, tool use, and language acquisition—are impressive, but the displays of feeling affect us far more profoundly.

19   Like any other vital organ, however, our feelings, our natural sympathy, can be damaged. Horrifying sights or situations can dull any emotion. Soldiers who've seen excessive brutality in battle and children who are constantly bombarded by violence on television or on the streets risk having their feelings numbed. Natural sympathy can take only so much battering before it ceases to function.

20   Similarly, any human being can become inured to the plight of an injured or confined ape just by seeing it often enough. Eventually one can look at a laboratory chimp with paralyzed limbs or electrodes buried in its skull and not feel sympathy. Some will call this a triumph of rationality over emotion or feeling. But that would be impossible, because rationality has no motivating force. What happens is that one feeling, curiosity, which motivates the search for knowledge, overrides another, our natural sympathy for apes. This sort of suppression brutalizes us, damaging our ability to live in a cooperative society and have normal, nonneurotic interpersonal relationships.

21   The argument is that we need to protect apes to protect ourselves. It follows, then, that we should treat apes better than we do. What's not clear is how far this protection should go. Certain measures present no problem. For example, if we prohibited the removal of any more apes from the wild and eliminated private ownership of apes, the gains for apes and thus for us would be great, and the losses trivial. But other possible protections—such as the elimination of all medical research on apes—are more troubling.

22   Medical research on apes has resulted in real human gains in the past; many scientists believe that a cure for AIDS will come from research on apes. If that promise is fulfilled, human suffering will be reduced. Apes may engage our natural sympathy, but so do other humans, particularly sick, suffering humans. The choice is difficult. Vital feelings will be sacrificed either way, and this argument offers no easy way to choose.

23   The argument leaves another question dangling as well: Why protect only the great apes? Why stop there? We have natural sympathy for pandas and dolphins—why not include them? And what about the millions of unfeeling and unpleasant-looking species in the world? Mosquitoes, for example, hardly engage my natural sympathy. Yet the range of creatures to which our natural sympathy extends seems to widen over time, perhaps as our perspective widens. Today few people could witness slavery with indifference, although once many could. And while it's unlikely that our sympathy will ever be much aroused by mosquitoes, it makes little sense to rule out the possibility.

24 So where—in the huge gray area between apes and mosquitoes—should we draw the line? Unfortunately this is not a subject that lends itself to drawing lines, because our sympathy is not an all-or-nothing phenomenon. Some people cheerfully bait their hooks with earthworms and feel no compassion, while others recoil in horror at the thought of driving a piece of barbed steel through the sensitive flesh of a living organism. Obviously, in the gray area, how far natural sympathy extends will vary from person to person. But this variability should not affect our judgment in the clear-cut cases like apes. Milk is indigestible only to some people, but cyanide is poisonous to all.

25 The theoretical problems with ape rights are serious, and the legal problems could be worse. The apes can't speak for themselves, so who would defend their rights? If apes have rights to life and liberty, do they also have rights to property? These difficulties, however, are not reasons to abandon the Great Ape Project. They are reasons to get to work ironing out the ambiguities and devising workable laws. To protect apes, to protect one of our most vital feelings—natural sympathy—we need to take bold steps. According apes the basic protections of life, liberty, and freedom from torture is a first step in the right direction.

Questions for Reading and Analysis

1. What is McShea's topic?

2. Animal activists want basic rights awarded to all great apes. What is the problem with the concept of "rights"? In spite of a philosophical debate we could have over terms, what is the basic point of the Great Ape Project?

3. What are two reasons usually given to support ape rights? How do many respond to these reasons?

4. What is McShea's reasoning based on?

5. What does motivated behavior require?

6. What are McShea's examples of "people" or objects lacking human motivation? What are these examples missing? How does this discussion connect to primates?

7. What is "natural sympathy"? Why do we have natural sympathy? How can it be damaged in us?

8. How, according to McShea, should we treat apes? Why should medical research on apes be stopped? Why?

9. What is McShea's claim?

Questions for Discussion and Response

1. Analyze this argument by using Toulmin's terms, noting McShea's qualifiers, warrant, backing, and rebuttal.

2. Evaluate his argument in terms of style and tone, logic and evidence.

3. Evaluate this as a conciliatory argument. Does McShea succeed in establishing common ground? Why or why not?

The Next Rights Revolution?

Richard A. Epstein

A professor of law at the University of Chicago, Richard Epstein (b. 1943) has published widely—and produced controversy—on a number of legal topics, including issues of private property and labor law. Two of his recent books are *Simple Rules for a Complex World* (1995) and *Private and Common Property* (2000). His contribution to the animal-rights debate appeared in the *National Review* on November 8, 1999.

1   "Fur is murder!" is a slogan you didn't hear very much until recently. In part, it is because the world used to face other forms of outrage, in which human beings lost their lives because of their religious beliefs or, closer to home, were kept out of public places because of their skin color. Against this grim background, the advocates of civil rights and civil liberties had a proper mission: to ensure that all human beings enjoy the full and equal protection of the laws.

2   Now come the animal-rights advocates, who ask the following provocative question: Has the civil-rights revolution gone far enough by attacking invidious distinctions based on race, color, or religious beliefs? Or should it be regarded as backward and incomplete because it fails to recognize legal rights in (nonhuman) animals? Is discrimination against animals, as many animal-rights advocates repeatedly insist, like discrimination against blacks? That the law was so wrong, for so long, on the scope of its protection in the prior case raises challenges that we cannot ignore in the second. In what way, exactly, is the law justified in preferring the status of human beings to that of lower animals?

3   Both sides must be heard on this critical debate. It is unfortunate, therefore, that many of the law courses that address this issue are courses in animal "rights," taught by advocates on one side of the issue, as opposed to animal "law," which offers a more fruitful and historically grounded approach.

4   The treatment of animals did not suddenly pop onto the social agenda. Rather, it has been with us from the beginning of human society. In ancient times, animals were already crucial to the survival of society. Domesticated animals were the source of food, clothing, agricultural muscle-power, and even (through cavalry) military and strategic strength. Animals were treated as an animate type of property. People acquired ownership of wild animals by capturing them; once acquired, these animals ceased to be free and became the property of owners, to use, breed, consume, or sell. The Romans, for example, reserved their most solemn form of conveyance for certain key draft animals, which they recognized as critical capital assets. Only land rivaled them in value.

5   In the 19th and 20th centuries, one weakness of this system of animal law became apparent. Its property-based rules provided no mechanism to prevent the systematic extinction of wild animals through over-hunting and over-fishing. To counter this risk, legal systems instituted, with varying degrees of success, statutes that limited the catch of whales, fish, and wild game in order to counteract the "tragedy of the commons" that results when a hunter keeps his entire quarry, but suffers only a tiny fraction of the losses caused by the eventual extinction of the herd. More recently, stringent protections afforded to endangered species have generated controversy, as farmers have claimed—

rightly in my view—that they have been unfairly forced to stand aside while protected animals decimate their sheep and cattle, for which they receive not a dime in compensation from the government.

6   Behind these traditional debates lies one key assumption: *The animal itself cannot be recognized as a holder of property rights valid against human beings.* Today's vocal defenders of animal rights brand this assumption "species-ist." Sometimes the classical view made animals property; at other times, they were the object of public regulation. In both cases, the legal rules were imposed largely for the benefit of human beings, either as owners of animals or as part of the public at large that benefited from their preservation.

7   Today's animal-rights activists want to overturn this "species-ist" consensus; they call for a declaration of independence of animals from their owners. While this clarion call generates tremendous emotional resonance, it is intellectually dangerous. Last August, I asked in the *New York Times*: "Would even bacteria have rights? There would be nothing left of human society if we treated animals not as property but as independent holders of rights."

8   The animal-rights activists were unhappy with that comment, but they are philosophically misguided on several grounds. First, they claim that our understanding of the complex behavior of animals has been revolutionized in such a way that the status of animals must be changed. But although the field of animal behavior has made enormous strides in recent years, the basic understanding has not changed. The law has understood for a long time that animals have extensive powers of anticipation and rationalization; they can form, and break, alliances; they can show anger, annoyance, and remorse; they can store food for later use; they respond to courtship and aggression; they can engage in acts of rape and acts of love; they respect, and violate, territories. In many ways, their repertory of emotions is quite broad, rivaling that of human beings. But the fact remains that they do not have the higher capacity for language and thought that characterizes human beings as a species.

9   We should never pretend that the case against recognizing animal rights is easier than it really is; by the same token, we cannot accept the facile argument that our new understanding of animals must lead to a new appreciation of their rights. The fundamentals of animal behavior were well known to the men who fashioned the old legal order.

10   Second, animal-rights activists claim that because people today do not need to rely on animal labor in order to survive, greater animal rights must be recognized. They tend to phrase this claim in a universalistic way, as if it were true uniformly of all societies, when, in fact, less fortunate societies would suffer greatly from the loss of animal-based food and clothing. There would be serious harm even in the prosperous lands that could survive without using animals for consumption or labor, because the demands of the activists cut far deeper. For them, the mere ownership of animals is a sin: no pets, no circuses, no milk, no cheese, no horses to ride, no dogs, cats, birds, or fish around the house. These relationships are based on an inequality of power and are thus condemned; the animals who seem to like being cared for suffer from, as it were, a form of false consciousness!

11   An even more ominous consequence would forbid the use of animals for medical science. The argument here is moral, for no one would dispute the proposition that animals should not be used in research if the same results could be achieved at the same cost by test tubes or computer simulations alone. Nor would many people want future

surgeons to try out new techniques on animals if they could be performed, without risk, on human beings. Sadly, however, these animal tests are necessary. We have a dreadful shortage today of human organs for transplantation, and unless we are prepared to do studies on pigs and perhaps chimpanzees, we shall never develop an understanding of how to overcome the problem of organ rejection. And unless we are prepared to harvest animal organs, then all research done in this area will prove idle.

12   I think any delay in this testing would be undesirable. If that be species-ism, I plead guilty—because, while I do care about the welfare of animals, I consider the welfare of humans a higher concern.

13   If parity between animal rights and human rights is ever acknowledged, more than medical research will suffer. Our entire system of property allows owners to transform the soil and to exclude others. Now, if the first human being on the scene may exclude subsequent arrivals, what happens when animals are given similar rights? Their dens, burrows, nests, and hives long antedate human arrival. The principle of first possession might therefore block us from clearing the land for farms, homes, and factories—unless we can find a way to make just compensation to each animal for its losses. But I fail to see how this system would work, for to transfer animals from one habitat to another only impermissibly displaces animals at the second location.

14   The blunt truth is that the arrival of human beings necessarily results in the death of some earlier animal occupants, even if it increases the welfare of others. So if prior in time is higher in right, then we should fold up our tents right now and let the animals fight it out for territory, just as if we had never arrived on the face of the globe.

15   The defenders of animal rights shrink, at least publicly, from the stark implications of their position, and choose to dwell instead on their victories in court. But the legal arguments the activists make in these court cases are credible precisely because they have nothing whatsoever to do with their broader claims. Animal owners have recovered large awards for the malpractice of veterinarians. The damages paid are meant to cover not only the market value of the animal, but the loss of companionship to the owner. This is good law and solid economics, because it recognizes that when these non-monetary elements are included, the *actual* losses to the owner exceed the market value. It is commonplace today to allow one spouse to sue for the damages that result from the loss of companionship when the other spouse is injured or dies. But, whether for human beings or pets, the interests vindicated are those of the party who suffers the emotional loss and the loss of companionship, not the interests of the person or animal who has died or been injured. These cases derive their power from a property-rights conception. It is hard, then, to see how they augur a new judicial age in which animals will have rights of their own against owners. It is not as though offspring of the deceased animal have an action for wrongful death.

16   A similar logic applies to a recent federal-court decision in Washington, D.C., in which a zoo visitor was held to have "standing" to sue under a federal law requiring that zookeepers confine primates in such a way that the animals' "psychological well-being" is assured. That objective is certainly laudable in simple human terms. But the recognition of the zoo visitor's standing to sue makes it crystal clear that the rights vindicated by the action were those of the individual plaintiff, and not those of the animal.

17   No one can deny the enormous political waves created by animal rights activists. It is also easy to understand how their anti-property theme gains adherents among those

who, for other reasons, don't like private property. But even though it's understandable, we have to recognize that the results of a victory by animal-rights extremists would be pernicious. Rules that prevent gratuitous cruelty to animals should be supported, because animals suffer. But it is one thing to raise social consciousness about the plight of animals and another to raise their status to an asserted parity with human beings. That move, if systematically implemented, would pose a mortal threat to society that few human beings will, or should, accept.

[18]   We have quite enough difficulty in persuading or coercing human beings to respect the rights of their fellows, so that all can live in peace. By treating animals as our moral equals, we would undermine the liberty and dignity of human beings—making the slaughters of Hitler, Stalin, or Pol Pot seem no worse than the daily activity of preparing cattle for market. That is one kind of moral equivalence we must never allow. Animals are properly property. To misunderstand the rights of animals is to cheapen the rights of human beings.

Questions for Reading and Analysis

1. In his introductory two paragraphs, Epstein establishes his topic—the animal-rights debate. Although he does not state his position, can you tell by his introduction what his position may be? If so, by what clues?

2. What distinction does Epstein make between courses in animal rights and courses in animal law? What does paragraph 3 serve to introduce?

3. What has animal law established in the past? What are animals unable to do under current laws?

4. What is the author's reaction to changes in animal law desired by animal-rights activists? How does he rebut two of their arguments?

5. What is Epstein's position on using animals for research? How does he support his position?

6. How else would human life be altered if all animals were given rights under our laws?

7. Malpractice suits are based on what concept?

8. What is Epstein's claim?

Questions for Discussion and Response

1. Locate several places where Epstein seeks a conciliatory approach. Are these passages successful in finding a middle ground, given the rest of Epstein's argument? Why or why not?

2. Examine Epstein's word choice when he refers to the opposition. What do his language and tone suggest to you about his perception of his audience? That is, does he expect most of his readers to agree or disagree with him?

3. Epstein concludes by asserting that if we treat animals as our equals, we "undermine the liberty and dignity of human beings" and make no distinction between the slaughters of tyrants and the slaughter of the cattle farmer. Do you agree with these assertions? Why or why not?

4. Who has the stronger argument—Epstein or Goodall—in your view? Why? Is your position influenced by a previously held position on animal rights?

Animal Rights v. Animal Research: A Modest Proposal

Joseph Bernstein

Dr. Joseph Bernstein is an assistant professor of orthopaedics at the University of Pennsylvania's hospital and a senior fellow at the Leonard Davis Institute of Health Economics, also at the University of Pennsylvania. Bernstein's "modest proposal" for animal research appeared in the *Journal of Medical Ethics* in 1996 along with Timothy Sprigge's response.

1   Many people love animals. Some animal lovers, though, in the name of their love, oppose the use of any animals in any medical research, regardless of the care given, regardless of the cause. Of course, many other animal lovers acknowledge the need for animal subjects in some medical studies, as long as no alternatives exist, and provided that care, respect and dignity are applied at all times. Unhappily, between the opponents of animal research and the researchers themselves lies no common ground, no place for an agreement to disagree: the opponents are not satisfied merely to abstain from animal experimentation themselves—they want everyone else to stop too.

2   Despite that, I would argue that in this case (to a far greater extent than, say, in the case of abortion) the animal rights question can be answered by exactly that tactic: the abstention of the opposition. Of course, I do not advocate abstention from debate; and, of course, abstention from performing research by those who are not researchers is not meaningful. Rather, I propose that the protesters—and every citizen they can enlist—abstain from the benefits of animal research. I say let the proponents of animal rights boycott the products of animal research. Let them place fair market-place pressure on ending activities they find reprehensible. Let them mobilise the tacit support they claim. Let the market for therapies derived from animal research evaporate, and with it much of the funding for such work. Let the animal lovers attain their desired goal without clamour, and without violence.

3   To assist them, I offer a modest proposal.

4   I suggest that we adopt a legal release form, readily available to all patients, which will enable them to indicate precisely which benefits of animal research they oppose—and from which, accordingly, they refuse to benefit. This form could be sent to all hospitals and physicians, and would be included in the patient's chart, much like operative consent forms, or Do Not Resuscitate instructions. It should resolve the issue once and for all.

5   This "Animal Research Advance Directive" would look something like this:

6   Dear Doctor:

Animals deserve the basic freedom from serving as experiment subjects against their will. Today, we who are committed to seeing the world's scientific laboratories free from unwilling and innocent animals, hereby refuse to benefit from research performed on these victims.

7   Accordingly, I ask that you care for me to the best of your abilities, but request that: (CHECK ALL THAT APPLY)

8   ☐ You do not perform on me a coronary bypass operation, or fix any heart defect my child may be born with, as these operations and the heart lung machine used during the procedures were developed using dogs. In fact, since the entire field of cardiology has been polluted by animal research for nearly a century, I cannot in good conscience accept any cardiological care.

9   ☐ You treat my child for any disease she may develop, but do not give her a vaccine that was tried first on a blameless animal. As I am not aware of any vaccines that were not animal-tested, please skip them all.

10   ☐ You avoid offering any suggestions regarding my diet and habits, when that information was derived from animal studies. This includes salt and fat intake, tobacco smoke, and various cancer-causing food additives. Do not bother to test my cholesterol levels, as the association between high cholesterol and heart disease is knowledge stolen from the suffering of the innocent.

11   ☐ Should I develop a malignancy, you do not give me chemotherapy, as those drugs were administered first to animals. I must also decline surgical treatment as well, since modern surgical technique and equipment owes its existence to sinful animal research. Finally, do not treat my disease with radiation, since that field, too, was contaminated by dog studies.

12   ☐ You amputate my leg or arm should I break it in such fashion that it requires surgery. Fracture fixation devices were designed through the suffering of dogs, so I must refuse repair of the bone. That probably will hurt a lot, but since I must refuse all pain medicine studied on rats (and that includes just about all of them), it is best if you just remove the damaged limb.

13   Needless to say, I will not accept an AIDS vaccine should one be developed, as unwilling Rhesus monkeys have been used in AIDS research.

14   Thank you for considering my wishes. Only through the concerted avoidance of these ill-gotten technologies can we halt the barbaric practice of animal research. Of course, I have no objection to studying disease on humans. To that end, I pledge my body to science upon my death. It probably will occur a lot sooner than I'd like.

Questions for Reading and Analysis

1. What is Bernstein "proposing"? Does he seriously expect to see the use of an "Animal Research Advance Directive"? How do you know the answer to this question?

2. Why does he include such a long checklist? What does he want to make clear to readers?

3. What is the tone of this essay? What language and strategies help to create the tone?

Questions for Discussion and Response

1. Bernstein asserts that there is no common ground for animal-rights activists and researchers. Do you agree with this assertion? If so, why? If not, what common ground would you propose?

2. Has Bernstein presented a convincing argument? Are his persuasive strategies effective? Explain your response.

3. If you wanted to refute Bernstein's argument, how would you proceed?

A Reply to Joseph Bernstein

Timothy Sprigge

Endowment fellow in philosophy at the University of Edinburgh, Timothy Sprigge (b. 1932) has contributed articles to scholarly journals of philosophy and published several books of philosophy, including *Theories of Existence* (1985) and *Rational Foundations of Ethics* (1990). His argument on the animal-rights debate, a response to Joseph Bernstein's argument, also appeared in the *Journal of Medical Ethics* in 1996.

1   Dr Bernstein's "A modest proposal" lays down a witty challenge to opponents of animal experimentation. However, matters are rather less clear cut than he evidently realises and there are various reasons, which I list below, why an anti-vivisectionist may feel no obligation to sign such directives under present conditions. Things would be different if (1) adequately funded facilities on the National Health Service were introduced which would make no use of further medical advances based on painful animal experimentation; (2) public funding for (painful) animal research and "alternative" research henceforth reflected the proportion of those who would not, and those who would, opt for these facilities.

2   (1) A first point is that Dr Bernstein does not distinguish between the use of animals in research which does, and that which does not, involve serious suffering for them (including that imposed by their housing, such as the extremes of boredom, but obviously not including being painlessly killed). The original anti-vivisection societies were, as their names imply, opposed to the cutting up of conscious live animals rather than to human use of animals in general (as may be the case with many animal rightists nowadays) and it seems to me reasonable to use "vivisection" today in a broader sense to cover all research which involves serious animal suffering (something worse, for example, than we feel when we receive an injection). Opponents of this are not necessarily opponents of all use of animals in medical research and it is not clear how many of the medical procedures Dr Bernstein lists were developed through work involving such serious suffering (as opposed, for example, to painless killing). It would facilitate rational debate if both defenders and critics of animal research were clearer on this point than they usually are.

3   (2) Even if, in practice, most of these procedures have been developed in ways which did involve serious animal suffering, it is another question whether they could

have been developed without this. The anti-vivisectionist who believes that they could have been, or even probably could have been, developed (by now) by other means has no reason to avoid them because of their unfortunate and, as he thinks, (probably) un-necessary history. In fact, I suggest, no one really knows how far medicine could have advanced had work of a kind which most anti-vivisectionists would condemn, been avoided.[1] If this is so, there is no bad faith in the anti-vivisectionists making use of ad-vances in medicine which he/she guesses would probably have been gained in other ways had the ethics of the past been more like theirs now.

4   The autobahnen in Germany were originally developed for their utility in trans-porting troops for aggressive war. Should those against aggressive war therefore not use those built in the Hitler period? Likewise Volkswagen cars were developed as cars for the people in the Third Reich as part of a plan to encourage love of that regime. Is one wrong to drive or travel in one today?

5   Many nations established their present borders in wars which involved all manner of what we would now regard as atrocities. Should its decent citizens refuse loyalty to any country with such a past?

6   Few people would answer these questions affirmatively, doubtless believing that, since we cannot change past history, refusing to benefit from its evils, especially where similar benefits could probably have been won otherwise, would be a pointless sacrifice.

7   In short, one may avail oneself of knowledge and techniques which exist now, how-ever first acquired, with a clear conscience even if they were developed in ways which fall below what one would like to be the moral standards of today. Where procedures rely on very recent research he/she should perhaps avoid benefiting from it, if he/she can, because this is likely to be part of a current research programme which he/she should be attempting to discourage. But even here if one believes that similarly useful developments in medicine could have occurred without such pain for animals it is not unreasonable or inconsistent to avail oneself of it, in the absence of alternatives (either of procedures or research) which might have been developed instead in a society less ready to base itself on animal suffering.

8   (3) If our society had long been based on a culture which outlawed the causing of serious pain to animals for human benefit it would have been so different through and through that no one can tell whether humans would have been better off or worse off now than they are. After all, we are the product of a history which, in innumerable ways, depended on behaviour which we would now dub immoral, and we just have to accept that for better or for worse. The moral question now is whether these practices can be justified in the light of the moral ideals to which we now aspire and the knowl-edge we now possess. So there is no more call on those of us who argue for the cessation of such animal experimentation as involves serious suffering to reject what was acquired in the past by means of it than there is for us to distance ourselves from most of our in-stitutions with their morally mixed past.

9   (4) Judgments about whether people in the past are to be morally condemned for what they did are highly problematic. People act in a historical context and cannot be expected to live by standards which have been developed since. The anti-vivisection-ist thinks that we are now ready for higher standards, in our relations with animals. For one thing the technologies of discovery are more sophisticated and need not be so phys-ically intrusive or painful as perhaps they were bound to be in the past. For another

thing, surgery was so dreadful for everyone until the development of anaesthetics, that perhaps people could not be expected to be too sensitive about animals amidst so much inevitable pain for themselves. But, with medical advances meaning so much less pain for us humans of today (when the groups to which we belong behave themselves, as admittedly too few do), it is surely time to be more sensitive about the suffering of animals for our advantage.

10   It would clarify the whole debate enormously if the following were sharply distinguished: animal-based research which 1) must involve serious animal suffering; 2) does involve it but which could be replaced by research (whether using animals or not) which does not; 3) does not involve it. All sides might then agree that 2) is wrong (inasmuch as the suffering would be uncontentiously unnecessary) and attention could then be paid to how much falls into the first category and whether the benefits it may bring justify the harm both to animals and those who must render themselves callous to their suffering. As for category 3) that divides into various types the morality of which is, indeed, important but much less urgent. At any rate, I see no reason why an anti-vivisectionist should feel the need to avoid the benefits of research other than what he/she is sure is of the first type.

Reference

1 Balls M. Recent progress towards reducing the use of animal experimentation in biomedical research. In: Garratini S, van Bekkum DW, eds. *The importance of animal experimentation for safety and biomedical research.* Dordrecht: Kluwer Academic Publishers, 1990: 228–9.

Questions for Reading and Analysis

1. In replying to Bernstein's argument, Sprigge makes several distinctions. What distinctions does he make regarding use of animals in research? What distinction does he make with regard to the past and the present?

2. What is Sprigge's position with regard to the use of medical science based on animal research in the past?

3. To support his argument, Sprigge makes several analogies. Do they provide effective reasoning in support of his argument?

4. What does the author assert regarding the behavior of people in the past? Have we opposed the use of animals for human advantages in the past?

5. What distinctions does he recommend for the present use of animals in medical research? How will these distinctions clarify the debate?

Questions for Discussion and Response

1. Does Sprigge make a convincing argument for animal-rights activists benefiting from medical science based on animal experiments in the past? Do you agree with him on this point? Why or why not?

2. Analyze the differences in approach of Bernstein and Sprigge. What strategies of debate does each use? Which do you find the most effective? Why?

3. Is Sprigge effective in establishing some common ground for both sides? If so, what is that common ground? If you think that he has failed to do this, explain why.

4. What are your responses to Sprigge's three categories of current animal-based research? Do you agree that number 2 is wrong? Do you agree that number 3 is not as urgent for debate as number 1? What is your position on number 1? Why?

CHAPTER 17

Immigration and Immigrants

The four articles in this chapter explore issues regarding immigration into the United States and noncitizens in this country. The articles differ not only in their "position"—stated or implied—on immigrants but also in their approach to the several issues we collect under the heading "immigration."

Reflecting on the following questions before you read will enrich your reading and thinking about this topic:

1. What do you know about immigration laws and the status and problems of current immigrants in the United States?
2. How much of what you know is based on study? On experience? On ideas expressed by family and friends? On what you have seen/heard on TV?
3. What do we gain by welcoming new immigrants to the United States?
4. Who gains and who loses from illegal aliens?
5. If you are a recent immigrant, or if your parents were immigrants, reflect on ways that your views on this topic may differ from those families who have been U.S. citizens for at least two generations. If you and your parents are U.S. citizens, reflect on ways that your views on this topic may differ from those individuals or families who have only recently come to this country.

Websites Relevant to This Chapter's Topic

Yahoo! News Full Coverage

http://dailynews.yahoo.com/fc/US/Immigration

This site contains many links to articles and debates on immigration.

Federation for American Immigration Reform (FAIR)

http://www.fairus.org

This is a source of facts, legislation, and issues; FAIR is an advocate for more restricted and controlled immigration.

The Border Patrol State

Leslie Marmon Silko

An English professor (University of Arizona) and writer, Leslie Marmon Silko (b. 1948) is the recipient of several grants and awards for her poetry. Her first novel, *Ceremony* (1977) was praised for its portrayal of life on an Indian reservation. Other works include *Storyteller* (1981), a collection of her poems and short stories, and the novel *Almanac of the Dead* (1991). "The Border Patrol State," based in part on her own experience driving in the Southwest, was published on October 17, 1994, in *Nation* magazine.

1   I used to travel the highways of New Mexico and Arizona with a wonderful sensation of absolute freedom as I cruised down the open road and across the vast desert plateaus. On the Laguna Pueblo reservation, where I was raised, the people were patriotic despite the way the U.S. government had treated Native Americans. As proud citizens, we grew up believing the freedom to travel was our inalienable right, a right that some Native Americans had been denied in the early twentieth century. Our cousin, old Bill Pratt, used to ride his horse 300 miles overland from Laguna, New Mexico, to Prescott, Arizona, every summer to work as a fire lookout.

2   In school in the 1950s, we were taught that our right to travel from state to state without special papers or threat of detainment was a right that citizens under communist and totalitarian governments did not possess. That wide open highway told us we were U.S. citizens; we were free. . . .

3   Not so long ago, my companion Gus and I were driving south from Albuquerque, returning to Tucson after a book promotion for the paperback edition of my novel *Almanac of the Dead*. I had settled back and gone to sleep while Gus drove, but I was awakened when I felt the car slowing to a stop. It was nearly midnight on New Mexico State Road 26, a dark, lonely stretch of two-lane highway between Hatch and Deming. When I sat up, I saw the headlights and emergency flashers of six vehicles—Border Patrol cars and a van were blocking both lanes of the highway. Gus stopped the car and rolled down the window to ask what was wrong. But the closest Border Patrolman and his companion did not reply; instead, the first agent ordered us to "step out of the car." Gus asked why, but his question seemed to set them off. Two more Border Patrol agents immediately approached our car, and one of them snapped, "Are you looking for trouble?" as if he would relish it.

4   I will never forget that night beside the highway. There was an awful feeling of menace and violence straining to break loose. It was clear that the uniformed men would be only too happy to drag us out of the car if we did not speedily comply with their request (asking a question is tantamount to resistance, it seems). So we stepped out of the car and they motioned for us to stand on the shoulder of the road. The night

was very dark, and no other traffic had come down the road since we had been stopped. All I could think about was a book I had read—*Nunca Más*—the official report of a human rights commission that investigated and certified more than 12,000 "disappearances" during Argentina's "dirty war" in the late 1970s.

5   The weird anger of these Border Patrolmen made me think about descriptions in the report of Argentine police and military officers who became addicted to interrogation, torture and the murder that followed. When the military and police ran out of political suspects to torture and kill, they resorted to the random abduction of citizens off the streets. I thought how easy it would be for the Border Patrol to shoot us and leave our bodies and car beside the highway, like so many bodies found in these parts and ascribed to "drug runners."

6   Two other Border Patrolmen stood by the white van. The one who had asked if we were looking for trouble ordered his partner to "get the dog," and from the back of the van another patrolman brought a small female German shepherd on a leash. The dog apparently did not heel well enough to suit him, and the handler jerked the leash. They opened the doors of our car and pulled the dog's head into it, but I saw immediately from the expression in her eyes that the dog hated them, and that she would not serve them. When she showed no interest in the inside of our car, they brought her around back to the trunk, near where we were standing. They half-dragged her up into the trunk, but still she did not indicate any stowed-away human beings or illegal drugs.

7   Their mood got uglier; the officers seemed outraged that the dog could not find any contraband, and they dragged her over to us and commanded her to sniff our legs and feet. To my relief, the strange violence the Border Patrol agents had focused on us now seemed shifted to the dog. I no longer felt so strongly that we would be murdered. We exchanged looks—the dog and I. She was afraid of what they might do, just as I was. The dog's handler jerked the leash sharply as she sniffed us, as if to make her perform better, but the dog refused to accuse us: She had an innate dignity that did not permit her to serve the murderous impulses of those men. I can't forget the expression in the dog's eyes; it was as if she were embarrassed to be associated with them. I had a small amount of medicinal marijuana in my purse that night, but she refused to expose me. I am not partial to dogs, but I will always remember the small German shepherd that night.

8   Unfortunately, what happened to me is an everyday occurrence here now. Since the 1980s, on top of greatly expanding border checkpoints, the Immigration and Naturalization Service and the Border Patrol have implemented policies that interfere with the rights of U.S. citizens to travel freely within our borders. I.N.S. agents now patrol all interstate highways and roads that lead to or from the U.S.-Mexico Border in Texas, New Mexico, Arizona and California. Now, when you drive east from Tucson on Interstate 10 toward El Paso, you encounter an I.N.S. check station outside Las Cruces, New Mexico. When you drive north from Las Cruces up Interstate 25, two miles north of the town of Truth or Consequences, the highway is blocked with orange emergency barriers, and all traffic is diverted into a two-lane Border Patrol checkpoint—ninety-five miles north of the U.S.-Mexico border.

9   I was detained once at Truth or Consequences, despite my and my companion's Arizona driver's licenses. Two men, both Chicanos, were detained at the same time, despite the fact that they too presented ID and spoke English without the thick Texas accents of the Border Patrol agents. While we were stopped, we watched as

other vehicles—whose occupants were white—were waved through the checkpoint. White people traveling with brown people, however, can expect to be stopped on suspicion they work with the sanctuary movement, which shelters refugees. White people who appear to be clergy, those who wear ethnic clothing or jewelry and women with very long hair or very short hair (they could be nuns) are also frequently detained; white men with beards or men with long hair are likely to be detained, too, because Border Patrol agents have "profiles" of "those sorts" of white people who may help political refugees. (Most of the political refugees from Guatemala and El Salvador are Native American or mestizo [of mixed Indian and European heritage] because the indigenous people of the Americas have continued to resist efforts by invaders to displace them from their ancestral lands.) Alleged increase in illegal immigration by people of Asian ancestry means that the Border Patrol now routinely detains anyone who appears to be Asian or part Asian, as well.

10   Once your car is diverted from the Interstate Highway into the checkpoint area, you are under the control of the Border Patrol, which in practical terms exercises a power that no highway patrol or city patrolmen possesses: They are willing to detain anyone, for no apparent reason. Other law-enforcement officers need a shred of probable cause in order to detain anyone. On the books, so does the Border Patrol; but on the road, it's another matter. They'll order you to stop your car and step out; then they'll ask you to open the trunk. If you ask why or request a search warrant, you'll be told that they'll have to have a dog sniff the car before they can request a search warrant, and the dog might not get there for two or three hours. The search warrant might require an hour or two past that. They make it clear that if you force them to obtain a search warrant for the car, they will make you submit to a strip search as well.

11   Traveling in the open, though, the sense of violation can be even worse. Never mind high-profile cases like that of former Border Patrol agent Michael Elmer, acquitted of murder by claiming self-defense, despite admitting that as an officer he shot an "illegal" immigrant in the back and then hid the body, which remained undiscovered until another Border Patrolman reported the event. (Last month, Elmer was convicted of reckless endangerment in a separate incident, for shooting at least ten rounds from his M-16 too close to a group of immigrants as they were crossing illegally into Nogales in March 1992.) Or that in El Paso, a high school football coach driving a vanload of his players in full uniform was pulled over on the freeway and a Border Patrol agent put a cocked revolver to his head. (The football coach was Mexican-American, as were most of the players in his van; the incident eventually caused a federal judge to issue a restraining order against the Border Patrol.) We've a mountain of personal experiences like that which never make the newspapers. A history professor at U.C.L.A. told me she had been traveling by train from Los Angeles to Albuquerque twice a month doing research. On each of her trips, she had noticed that the Border Patrol agents were at the station in Albuquerque scrutinizing the passengers. Since she is six feet tall and of Irish and German ancestry, she was not particularly concerned. Then one day when she stepped off the train in Albuquerque, two Border Patrolmen accosted her, wanting to know what she was doing, and why she was traveling between Los Angeles and Albuquerque twice a month. She presented identification and an explanation deemed "suitable" by the agents, and was allowed to go about her business.

¹²   Just the other day, I mentioned to a friend that I was writing this article and he told me about his 73-year-old father, who is half Chinese and had set out alone by car from Tucson to Albuquerque the week before. His father had become confused by road construction and missed a turnoff from Interstate 10 to Interstate 25; when he turned around and circled back, he missed the turnoff a second time. But when he looped back for yet another try, Border Patrol agents stopped him and forced him to open his trunk. After they satisfied themselves that he was not smuggling Chinese immigrants, they sent him on his way. He was so rattled by the event that he had to be driven home by his daughter.

¹³   This is the police state that has developed in the southwestern United States since the 1980s. No person, no citizen, is free to travel without the scrutiny of the Border Patrol. In the city of South Tucson, where 80 percent of the respondents were Chicano or Mexicano, a joint research project by the University of Wisconsin and the University of Arizona recently concluded that one out of every five people there had been detained, mistreated verbally or nonverbally, or questioned by I.N.S. agents in the past two years.

¹⁴   Manifest Destiny may lack its old grandeur of theft and blood—"lock the door" is what it means now, with racism a trump card to be played again and again, shamelessly, by both major political parties. "Immigration," like "street crime" and "welfare fraud," is a political euphemism that refers to people of color. Politicians and media people talk about "illegal aliens" to dehumanize and demonize undocumented immigrants, who are for the most part people of color. Even in the days of Spanish and Mexican rule, no attempts were made to interfere with the flow of people and goods from south to north and north to south. It is the U.S. government that has continually attempted to sever contact between the tribal people north of the border and those to the south.*

¹⁵   Now that the "Iron Curtain" is gone, it is ironic that the U.S. government and its Border Patrol are constructing a steel wall ten feet high to span sections of the border with Mexico. While politicians and multinational corporations extol the virtues of NAFTA [the North American Free Trade Agreement] and "free trade" (in goods, not flesh), the ominous curtain is already up in a six-mile section of the border crossing at Mexicali; two miles are being erected but are not yet finished at Naco; and at Nogales, sixty miles south of Tucson, the steel wall has been all rubber-stamped and awaits construction. Like the pathetic multimillion-dollar "antidrug" border surveillance balloons that were continually deflated by high winds and made only a couple of meager interceptions before they blew away, the fence along the border is a theatrical prop, a bit of pork for contractors. Border entrepreneurs have already used blowtorches to cut passageways through the fence to collect "tolls" and are doing a brisk business. Back in Washington, the I.N.S. announces a $300 million computer contract to modernize its record-keeping and Congress passes a crime bill that shunts $255 million to the I.N.S. for 1995, $181 million earmarked for border control, which is to include 700 new partners for the men who stopped Gus and

---

*   The Treaty of Guadalupe Hidalgo, signed in 1848, recognizes the right of the Tohano O'Odom (Papago) people to move freely across the U.S.-Mexico border without documents. A treaty with Canada guarantees similar rights to those of the Iroquois nation in traversing the U.S.-Canada border.

me in our travels, and the history professor, and my friends' father, and as many as they could from South Tucson.

16   It is no use; borders haven't worked, and they won't work, not now, as the indigenous people of the Americas reassert their kinship and solidarity with one another. A mass migration is already under way; its roots are not simply economic. The Uto-Aztecan languages are spoken as far north as Taos Pueblo near the Colorado border, all the way south to Mexico City. Before the arrival of the Europeans, the indigenous communities throughout this region not only conducted commerce, the people shared cosmologies, and oral narratives about the Maize Mother, the Twin Brothers and their Grandmother, Spider Woman, as well as Quetzalcoatl the benevolent snake. The great human migration within the Americans cannot be stopped; human beings are natural forces of the Earth, just as rivers and winds are natural forces.

17   Deep down the issue is simple: The so-called "Indian Wars" from the days of Sitting Bull and Red Cloud have never really ended in the Americas. The Indian people of southern Mexico, of Guatemala and those left in El Salvador, too, are still fighting for their lives and for their land against the "cavalry" patrols sent out by the government of those lands. The Americas are Indian country, and the "Indian problem" is not about to go away.

18   One evening at sundown, we were stopped in traffic at a railroad crossing in downtown Tucson while a freight train passed us, slowly gaining speed as it headed north to Phoenix. In the twilight I saw the most amazing sight: Dozens of human beings, mostly young men, were riding the train; everywhere, on flat cars, inside open boxcars, perched on top of boxcars, hanging off ladders on tank cars and between boxcars. I couldn't count fast enough, but I saw fifty or sixty people headed north. They were dark young men, Indian and mestizo; they were smiling and a few of them waved at us in our cars. I was reminded of the ancient story of Aztlán, told by the Aztecs but known in other Uto-Aztecan communities as well. Aztlán is the beautiful land to the north, the origin place of the Aztec people. I don't remember how or why the people left Aztlán to journey farther south, but the old story says that one day, they will return.

Questions for Reading and Analysis

1. What does the author accomplish in her first two paragraphs? Can you predict what kind of discussion or argument development will follow her opening?

2. What feelings did Silko sense among the Border Patrolmen? How is the mood of her experience developed by the details regarding the dog?

3. Where are drivers being stopped? What kinds of people are detained? What do they have in common?

4. What is Silko's thesis?

5. What, in Silko's view, is the political purpose in reference to immigration and illegal aliens?

6. Why, according to the author, will borders fail to work in the Southwest?

Questions for Discussion and Response

1. In the closing paragraph, Silko describes Mexicans riding on a train from Tucson to Phoenix. For her, the picture is a positive one. Why? Is it likely to be a positive picture for all readers? Was it for you? Why or why not?

2. What type of evidence does the author present to support her thesis? Is her approach effective? Why or why not?

3. In your view, what images are especially powerful in this essay? Why?

4. Should Americans of color be harassed by police officers in situations in which they might be breaking the law? Why or why not?

5. Should the Mexican-American border be open? Explain your position.

Revolution in America

William Norman Grigg

William Grigg (b. 1963), a graduate of Utah State University in political science and a former newspaper columnist, is currently a senior editor at the *New American*, a bi-weekly conservative journal. He is the author of *Freedom on the Altar* (1995), a study of the United Nations' family policy. "Revolution in America," a study of the problems and issues related to immigration, was published (in a somewhat longer version) in the February 19, 1996, issue of *New American*.

1   "I am not an American. There is nothing about me that is American. I don't want to be an American, and I have just as much right to be here as any of you." Thus spoke one individual identified as a "Latino activist" during a session of the "National Conversation on American Pluralism and Identity," a $4 million project funded by the National Endowment for the Humanities (NEH). NEH Director Sheldon Hackney reacted to this hateful outburst by cooing, "What an American thing to say—squarely in the great tradition of American dissent. He was affirming his American identity even as he was denying it."

2   From Hackney's perspective, there are none so American as those who hate this country. Unfortunately, a similar concept of the American identity governs our present immigration policies. Guided by the dogma of "diversity," the political establishment has rejected the traditional goal of assimilation, choosing instead to create a Babel of querulous ethnic interest groups squabbling over government largesse and united only through the political power of the state. . . .

3   To understand how the present state of affairs came about, and how it may be remedied, it is necessary to review America's traditional immigration policy.

4   Throughout its history, America's philosophy of God-given individual rights and institutions of ordered liberty have attracted many immigrants from around the globe. However, from our nation's founding until 1965, American policymakers understood that immigration is a *privilege*, not an unalienable *right*—and that this nation, like every sovereign nation, may properly regulate immigration in its own interests. Dr. Charles Rice, a professor of law at Notre Dame University, observes that "with respect to nonresident

aliens, their admission to the country is subject to the virtually plenary power of Congress."

5   This is not to say that Congress may regard aliens as "non-persons"; rather, it is to acknowledge that such people do not possess the procedural rights and immunities which are enjoyed by American citizens, and that their admission to this country is contingent on their qualifications for productive citizenship. In his report on immigration to the First Congress, James Madison urged that America "welcome every person of good fame [who] really means to incorporate himself into our society, but repel all who will not be a real addition to the wealth and strength of the United States."

6   America's political system, economy, and cultural institutions are derivative of Anglo-European traditions; accordingly, American immigration policies traditionally favored English-speaking immigrants from Europe who could be readily assimilated into our society. Additionally, during the last "great wave" of immigrations (which lasted roughly from 1890 to 1920), the absence of a welfare state made assimilation a necessity. Peter Brimelow estimates, "At the turn of the century, 40 percent of all immigrants went home, basically because they failed in the work force." However, millions of immigrants succeeded in America's economy and embraced American ideals.

7   Even before the advent of the welfare state, however, social pressures attendant to the great wave created support for tighter immigration controls. The Immigration Acts of 1921 and 1924 were intended to preserve a stable *status quo* by imposing a national origins quota system. The McCarran-Walter Act of 1952 retained the basic structure of the 1924 measure, while adding important provisions intended to prevent the admission of known subversives to America's shores.

Inverted Priorities

8   However, the passage of the Immigration Reform Act of 1965 infused an entirely different set of values and priorities into our basic immigration law. Simply put, the effect of the 1965 immigration law was to define American immigration policies by our nation's supposed obligation to the rest of the world, rather than by a sound definition of our own national interest. As Senator Robert F. Kennedy (D-NY) stated during the debate over the 1965 law, the measure assumed that "the relevant community is not merely the nation, but all men of goodwill."

9   One expressed intention of the measure was proportionately to increase immigration from non-Western nations; this was accomplished by abolishing the national origins quota system. Furthermore, although the formal immigration quota was raised only slightly, the measure allowed for theoretically unlimited "non-quota" immigration for refugees, asylum seekers, and relatives of naturalized citizens for purposes of "family reunification" (also known as "chain immigration").

10   Many critics of the 1965 measure predicted that its passage would result in a torrential surge of unassimilable immigrants, resulting in profound social dislocations. Senator Edward Kennedy (D-MA), who served as Senate floor manager for S. 500 (the Senate version of the measure), parried such objections by offering these assurances of what the bill supposedly would not do:

> First, our cities will not be flooded with a million immigrants annually.
> Under the proposed bill, the present level of immigration remains

substantially the same. . . . Secondly, the ethnic mix of this country will not be upset. . . . Contrary to the charges in some quarters, S. 500 will not inundate America with immigrants from any one country or area, or the most populated and economically deprived nations of Africa and Asia. . . . In the final analysis, the ethnic pattern of immigration under the proposed measure is not expected to change as sharply as the critics seem to think.

The Post-1965 Influx

11   . . . As Peter Brimelow observes, "*Every one* of Senator Kennedy's assurances has proven false. Immigration levels *did* surge upward. They *are* now running at around a million a year, not counting illegals. Immigrants *do* come predominantly from one area—some 85 percent of the 16.7 million legal immigrants arriving in the United States between 1968 and 1993 came from the Third World: 47 percent from Latin America and the Caribbean; 34 percent from Asia. . . . Also, immigrants *did* come disproportionately from one country—20 percent from Mexico." Nearly two million immigrants arrived in 1991 alone, and the 1990s rate is at least one million immigrants per year—a figure which exceeds the number of immigrants admitted by the rest of the industrialized nations combined.

12   Taken by itself, such an influx would have enormously unsettling social, cultural, and economic effects. However, when coupled with the welfare state and racial spoils system which presently exist in this country, the post-1965 immigrant wave has proven to be uniquely disruptive. Liberal commentator Michael Lind, who does not reject the welfare/affirmative action state in principle, points out, "As a proportion of the U.S. population, the groups eligible for racial preference benefits are rapidly growing, thanks to mass immigration from Latin America and Asia."

13   While earlier European immigrants were under the necessity of assimilating quickly, Lind observes that "today's Hispanic and Asian immigrants are tempted by a variety of rewards for retaining their distinctive racial identities, even their different languages:

> The moment a Mexican or Chinese immigrant becomes a naturalized citizen of the United States, he can qualify for special consideration in admission to colleges and universities, at the expense of better-qualified white Americans; expect and receive special treatment in employment; apply for minority business subsidies denied to his neighbors; and even demand to have congressional district lines redrawn to maximize the likelihood of electing someone of his race or ethnic group. . . .

14   These perks and privileges are sources of ethnic tensions and considerable public expense. In a 1993 study, economist Donald Huddle of Rice University documented that "immigrants cost the American taxpayer more than $42.5 billion in 1992 alone" for services such as subsidized education, Medicaid, health and welfare services, bilingual education, and Aid to Families with Dependent Children. Should the present immigration policies remain in place, Huddle asserted, the cost of welfare subsidies to immigrants between 1993 and 2002 would average "$67 billion per year in 1992 dollars, a net total of $668.5 billion after taxes over the decade."

Breakdown at the Border

15   Beyond the problems created by legal immigration are those precipitated by the breakdown of the "thin green line"—the Immigration and Naturalization Service (INS) and its Border Patrol, which are supposed to maintain the integrity of our borders against illegal immigration. "Illegal immigrants come from all over the world," reported the November 26, 1993, *Los Angeles Times.* "They come in rickety boats. They arrive on jetliners with valid business, student or tourist visas and then ignore the expiration date and stay here illegally. They enter on forged documents or fraudulent employment visas. They contract sham marriages to U.S. citizens." Most illegal immigrants enter the U.S. across our 2000-mile border with Mexico.

16   How many illegals enter the U.S. every year? "We don't know—that's the bottom line," says INS spokesman Robert Stiev. It's almost as if we were asked, 'How many fish didn't you catch?' " An INS study in 1992 estimated that 3.4 million illegal immigrants had taken up residence in the United States, with another 300,000 arriving every year. To stem this tide, the Border Patrol has been assigned fewer than 5,000 agents and allocated a budget of $584 million—a pitiful pool of resources when compared, for example, to the 32,000 U.S. servicemen and $2 billion to $3 billion which has been set aside to patrol the artificial border of the "nation" of Bosnia. . . .

Ethnic Separatism

17   Immigration reform advocate Richard Estrada observes that unrestrained immigration is producing "a leveling down of American society, which in turn could be accompanied by an intensification of tribalist politics, ethnic and linguistic separatism, and finally the further debasement of the coin of individual initiative, freedom, and liberty." The fissiparous [divisive] tendencies which concern Estrada are most pronounced along America's border with Mexico.

18   According to Henry Cisneros, the Clinton Administration's [first] Secretary of Health and Human Services, the effective breakdown of the border between the U.S. and Mexico is resulting in "the Hispanization of America. . . . It is already happening and it is inescapable." Less sanguine observers would refer to this development as an *invasion.* While some might shrink from using the term, "invasion" was the word used to describe the Mexican exodus to the U.S. in a 1982 article published in *Excelsior,* Mexico's equivalent of the *New York Times.* In "The Great Invasion: Mexico Recovers Its Own," *Excelsior* columnist Carlos Loret de Mola examined the cultural and political implications of uncontrolled Mexican immigration to the U.S.:

> A peaceful mass of people . . . carries out slowly and patiently an unstoppable invasion, the most important in human history. You cannot give me a similar example of such a large migratory wave by an ant-like multitude, stubborn, unarmed, and carried on in the face of the most powerful and best-armed nation on earth. . . . [Neither] barbed-wire fences, nor aggressive border guards, nor campaigns, nor laws, nor police raids against the undocumented, have stopped this movement of the masses that is unprecedented in any part of the world.

19   According to Loret, the migrant invasion "seems to be slowly returning [the southwestern United States] to the jurisdiction of Mexico without the firing of a single shot,

nor requiring the least diplomatic action, by means of a steady, spontaneous, and uninterrupted occupation." The effects of Mexico's immigration invasion were even then visible in Los Angeles, which Loret cheekily referred to as "the second largest Mexican city in the world."

20 Loret's essay invoked the irredentist fantasy that California, Arizona, New Mexico, Colorado, and Texas—the states created in the territory obtained from Mexico through the Treaty of Guadalupe Hidalgo in 1848—compose "Aztlan," the mythical homeland of the Aztec Indians, and that those states must be wrested from the United States in order to create a new Chicano homeland. More than a quarter of a century ago, political analyst Patty Newman warned that "the basic concept of El Plan de Aztlan is endorsed by most of the major Mexican-American organizations on campus and off, liberal and supposedly conservative." Believers in the Aztlan legend insist upon the indivisibility of "*la Raza*" (the Mexican race) and the need to abolish the border between the U.S. and Mexico; one of their preferred slogans is, "We didn't cross the border—the border crossed us.". . .

Mexican Meddling

21 Although the literature of radical Chicano activists is replete with criticism of the Mexican government, . . . the Mexican establishment is actually pursuing the same ends which define the Chicano movement in the U.S.: The effective eradication of the border and the political consolidation of Mexicans within this country. The December 10, 1995, *New York Times* reported that the Mexican regime "is campaigning hard for an amendment to the Mexican Constitution that would allow Mexicans living in the United States to retain Mexican nationality rights even when they adopt American citizenship."

22 Like their supposed enemies in the radical Chicano movement, Mexican officials do not shy away from expressions of racial and ethnic solidarity with Hispanics residing in this country. During a speech to Mexican-American politicians in Dallas, Mexican President Ernesto Zedillo declared, "You're Mexicans—Mexicans who live north of the border." Jose Angel Gurria, Mexico's foreign minister, has explained that the "double nationality amendment [is] designed to stress our common language . . . culture, [and] history" across national borders. The proposed amendment is intended to create a political fifth column under the influence of the Mexican regime. As Rodolfo O. de la Garza, a professor of government at the University of Texas, observes, "As Mexican-Americans become more powerful, the Mexican government wants them to defend Mexican interests here in the United States."

23 The next logical step would be to extend the voting franchise to immigrants who are not citizens—a possibility which is being openly discussed by open borders activists in California and elsewhere. Jorge Casteñada, an influential Mexican intellectual and a columnist for the *Los Angeles Times*, defends the idea in his book *The Mexican Shock: Its Meaning for the U.S.*:

> Immigration from Mexico is likely to continue regardless of what enthusiasts of free trade, peace in Central America, or the closing of the border may say or do. The only realistic way to alter the negative effect of Mexican influence on California, then, is to change the nature of its origin by

legalizing immigration [that is, extending another amnesty to illegals] and giving foreigners the right to vote in state and local elections.

24   In his book *Importing Revolution: Open Borders and the Radical Agenda,* William Hawkins of the Hamilton Center for National Strategy observes, "Non-citizen voting for local government has already been implemented in the liberal suburban enclave of Tacoma Park, Maryland. . . . Nearby in Washington, DC, City Councilman Frank Smith has endorsed legislation to allow non-citizens to vote in local elections in the nation's capital." Jamin Raskin, a law professor at American University, has noted, "Increasingly, advocates for immigrants in New York—as in Washington, Los Angeles and several smaller cities across the nation—have begun exploring the sensitive issue of securing voting privileges for immigrants who are not citizens." Raskin insists that "noncitizen voting is the suffrage movement of the decade" and predicts:

> [I]f picked up by large cities—like Los Angeles, Washington, New York and Houston—it could strengthen American democracy by including in the crucial processes of local government many hundreds of thousands of people born elsewhere. . . . There are 10 million legal immigrants who are not United States citizens. In number, at least, they represent a potential political force of some diversity and dimension, particularly in such cities as New York.

25   The enfranchisement of foreigners would lead to the literal "unmaking" of America as a sovereign, independent nation. While such a prospect is presently shocking, it is not in principle significantly different from the logic of our post-1965 immigration policy. After all, if everyone has an unconditional "right" to come to America and feast at the welfare trough, why should there be any defining advantages to citizenship? Why not eliminate our borders altogether, and extend all of the rights and privileges of citizenship to anyone who happens to occupy our nation at any given time?

Questions for Reading and Analysis

1. What is Grigg's subject? What is the claim of his argument?

2. After reading paragraph 3, you should be able to classify his argument. What type of argument is this?

3. What used to be America's immigration policy? On what concept was it based?

4. In Grigg's view, on the what basis should people be admitted to this country? Prior to 1965, what group was most frequently allowed to enter? Why?

5. How has immigration changed since 1965?

6. What is the author's attitude toward the number of immigrants in the 1990s? What current public policies complicate immigration in the 1990s?

7. What is the author's attitude toward illegal immigrants? How do you know?

8. What, according to Grigg, is happening in the American Southwest? What is the response of some Mexican politicians? How do these issues advance Grigg's argument?

9. Is voting rights for non-citizens a "next logical step"? In our history, has granting voting rights to non-Americans been seriously considered?

10. What kind of argument does the author seem to be making in the final paragraph? What does he want to accomplish here?

Questions for Discussion and Response

1. Should the problem of illegal immigration be discussed in the context of immigration policies? Why do some people, Grigg included, introduce illegal aliens into their discussion? What do they hope to accomplish? Is this effective argument?

2. What solutions does Grigg offer to the problems he sees with immigration policy? What solutions does he imply?

3. What is your position on immigration? Explain.

4. Who has the better argument: Silko or Grigg? Why? Is your answer influenced by your views on the issue prior to your reading?

Saved by Immigrants

Charles Krauthammer

A graduate of Harvard Medical School and board certified in psychiatry, Charles Krauthammer (b. 1950) is a syndicated columnist and a regular on the political talk show *Inside Washington*. He has won a Pulitzer Prize for political commentary. His column on immigrants appeared July 17, 1998.

1   For decades now, the prospect of world overpopulation—and the impoverishment, resource depletion and ecological damage associated with it—have dominated our nightmares and permeated our politics. Population control, particularly Third World population, is something on which we all reflexively, vaguely agree. We may argue over whether abortion should be included among the means to achieve it. But the end— fewer mouths to feed—is not in dispute.

2   Maybe it should be. A startling and unjustly overlooked article by Nick Eberstadt in the *Public Interest* (Fall 1997) explodes the conventional wisdom. Drawing on the United Nations' 1996 report, "World Population Prospects," Eberstadt finds a quite plausible scenario that shows world population stabilizing in 40 years at 7.7 billion (it is just under 6 billion today) and, even more astonishing, declining thereafter.

3   This scenario posits no war or epidemic or other scourge to do the job. It simply assumes that today's radical decline in fertility worldwide continues. And radical it is. In the developed nations, the rate has fallen from 2.8 children per woman in the early '50s to 1.5 today. In the less-developed nations, it has fallen from 6 to just under 3.

4   In America, where full-page ads for ZPG (zero population growth) still grace our tonier political magazines, awareness of this historic change has been slow in coming. It has taken a while for Ben Wattenberg's warning about *The Birth Dearth*, the name of his 1987 book on the dwindling population of the West, to take hold. On July 10, however, it received the imprimatur of the *New York Times* in a front-page article highlighting the unprecedented population implosion now taking place in Europe.

5   Not a single country on the continent has a fertility rate high enough to maintain its current population. Italy, for example, is now the first nation ever with more people over 60 than under 20. In Bologna, there will soon be 25 people over 50 for every child under 5.

6   Eberstadt estimates that in 1900 the median age in the world was about 20. In the mid-21st century, it will be about 42. And in such countries as Japan, Italy and Germany, the median age will be in the mid-fifties!

7   Result? Social disaster: children with no blood relatives but their parents; no brothers, sisters, aunts, uncles, cousins. (That's what happens when you have two consecutive generations of single-child families.) Historic disaster: countries losing half their population every two generations. And economic disaster: Not enough working young people to pay the pensions of the old.

8   And while Europe is committing suicide, what happens to the United States? Here the fertility rate is barely at replacement level. But we are saved—by immigration.

9   Immigration is a lifesaver not just for bulking up our numbers. (And raw numbers matter: You can have the highest per capita income in the world, but if you've got no capita, you've got no income.) It illuminates one of the great paradoxes in American life: How is it that our schools are consistently among the worst in the developed world and yet we lead the world in science and technology and R&D in just about every field?

10   The answer is simple. We import many of our best brains. Walk down any corridor in the laboratories of the National Institutes of Health, for example, and you'll meet the best young minds from every corner of the globe. And many of them stay. Indeed, our computer industry is now begging Congress for an increase in the quota of skilled immigrants to cover our huge shortfall in high-tech workers.

11   The anti-immigrant demagogues warn that immigration is the road to Balkanization. They are wrong. At the start of this century there were (as a percentage of the population) 50 percent more foreign-born U.S. residents than there are today. And yet the Irish and Italians and Jews and Poles and Chinese and Japanese of that immigrant wave assimilated so remarkably into the American mainstream that today *they* are the American mainstream.

12   The problem today is not unassimilable immigrants but an American educational elite that, in the name of ethnic authenticity and multiculturalism, would like them to be unassimilable. Hence the imposition of such devices as bilingual education—a euphemism for slighting and delaying English instruction—that not just celebrate but perpetuate ethnic separatism.

13   California's Proposition 227, effectively abolishing bilingual education, marks a welcome resurgence of American common sense. Immigrants are our future. We owe a duty to them—and to ourselves as a nation—to make them American as quickly as possible. We'd better. Immigrants are the magic cure—the American cure—for the birth dearth.

Questions for Reading and Analysis

1. What is happening to world population? What is the current fertility rate in developed countries? In undeveloped countries?

2. What are the social, historic, and economic consequences of a fertility rate under 2.0?

3. Why does the author begin his column with a detailed discussion of world population figures? How does this introduction connect to Krauthammer's topic?

4. What, according to Krauthammer, are the advantages to the United States from immigrants?

5. What does the author mean by the term *Balkanization?* Why is it not true that immigration will produce Balkanization?

6. What is the author's view of bilingual education? How does this issue connect to his argument?

7. What is Krauthammer's claim?

Questions for Discussion and Response

1. Have you been aware of the decrease in the fertility rate—of the "birth dearth"? If not, what is your reaction to these numbers?

2. Krauthammer opposes bilingual education. What is your view on this educational strategy? Does bilingual education hold some students back and slow assimilation?

3. Krauthammer encourages a positive view of immigrants both for their numbers and for their skills. Do you support the selection of immigrants based on education and skills? Why or why not?

4. Many immigrants today are poor and poorly educated Hispanics. Do you think that the United States should have quotas based on education? Based on race or ethnicity? Explain your position.

Illegal Aliens

George J. Borjas

An immigrant from Cuba, George Borjas (b. 1950) is a professor of public policy at Harvard University's John F. Kennedy School of Government and a research associate at the National Bureau of Economic Research. He has written numerous articles, a textbook (*Labor Economics*), and *Heaven's Door* (1999), from which the following excerpt is taken.

1   Five million illegal aliens lived in the United States in 1996 (see Table 11–2).[1] Their number grows by about 300,000 per year. And these numbers are on top of the three million illegal aliens who were granted amnesty in the late 1980s.

2   The common perception of an illegal alien is of someone who avoided inspection at the time of entry because he or she lacked the necessary documents for legal entry (such as a passport and a visa). The Immigration and Naturalization Service refers to these persons as EWIs, for "entry without inspection." The stereotypical EWI is a Mexican immigrant running across the border. Many illegal aliens, however, had a legal visa when they first entered, such as a student's visa or a tourist's visa, but simply remained in the country long after their visas expired. The illegal alien flow, therefore, can originate anywhere. And, in fact, almost half of the illegal alien population is *not* of Mexican origin.

TABLE 11–2

Illegal Immigration in the United States, October 1996

	Number of illegal aliens
Total	5,000,000
"Top five" countries of origin	
Mexico	2,700,000
El Salvador	335,000
Guatemala	165,000
Canada	120,000
Haita	105,000
"Top five" states of residence	
California	2,000,000
Texas	700,000
New York	540,000
Florida	350,000
Illinois	290,000

Source: U.S. Immigration and Naturalization Service, *Statistical Yearbook of the Immigration and Naturalization Service, 1996* (Washington, D.C., 1997), p. 198.

3   The United States attracts illegal aliens for many reasons. First, persons originating in many source countries have strong economic incentives to enter the United States—regardless of whether they can get a visa or not. Per capita income in the United States is at least three times larger than in Mexico. Even after netting out the cost of illegal immigration, such as getting to the U.S. border and payments to *coyotes* (the experienced guides who help the illegal aliens across the border), the income differential between the two countries remains exceptionally high.

4   Second, black markets arise whenever government regulations prevent people from voluntarily exchanging goods and services. Although it is illegal to buy drugs and sex, many people still desire those goods, and black markets arise to satisfy the illicit demand. Illegal immigration is no different. Immigration policy prohibits the entry of many persons, but these persons still wish to live in the United States. As long as the potential immigrants believe that the cost of participating in this black market is relatively low, they will come. In fact, there are few penalties imposed directly on the illegal aliens who are caught by the Border Patrol. When they are apprehended, they are simply put on the first plane or bus that goes back to their source country. Once there, the aliens are free to try to reenter the United States whenever the opportunity arises.

5   Third, it is no secret that many American employers benefit greatly from the entry of illegal aliens. This vast pool of workers lowers wages and increases profits in the affected industries. Even though it is illegal for employers to "knowingly hire" illegal aliens, the chances of getting caught are negligible and the penalties are trivial.[2] Newly hired workers must offer proof that they are U.S. citizens, are permanent legal residents, or have visas permitting them to work in the United States. Employers must then complete forms for each new employee certifying that the relevant documents were reviewed. The

statutes, however, have a huge loophole, one that essentially permits anyone to hire an illegal alien. Employers need only to certify that they reviewed the documents that described the legal status of job applicants. The employer is not required to keep copies of these documents for inspection. Hence there is practically no chance of detecting employers who decide to hire illegal aliens after "reviewing" the documents provided by willing co-conspirators.[3]

6   Finally, the United States does a notoriously poor job at controlling its borders. In fact, few other countries have been so lackadaisical about border control. Although the number of agents in the Border Patrol rose rapidly in the 1990s (from about three thousand in 1990 to near ten thousand by 1998), the Mexican–U.S. border is 1,950 miles long.[4]

7   A number of highly publicized Border Patrol operations in the mid-1990s, such as Operation Hold the Line in El Paso and Operation Gatekeeper in San Diego, attempted to curtail illegal immigration by providing an around-the-clock Border Patrol presence in some of the stretches that illegal aliens typically used to cross the border.[5] These operations seem to have been effective in the targeted areas, but many observers suspect that some of the illegal aliens eventually entered the United States by crossing the border in those areas that were less heavily patrolled. A Binational Study of Migration, commissioned by the governments of Mexico and the United States, concluded that "the United States border enforcement strategies begun in 1994 are affecting migration patterns, but not preventing unauthorized entry."[6] Moreover, tighter controls on the U.S.–Mexico border do not address the problem of how to curtail the number of visa overstayers, who account for about half of the illegal aliens in the United States.

8   Any serious reform of immigration policy—and any attempt to adopt a skills-based point system—is doomed to failure unless the problem of illegal immigration is also resolved. A well-designed immigration policy may not have the desired effect on the social welfare of the United States if the border is porous. Illegal immigration can effectively unravel the social and economic effects of that policy. Illegal immigration is also unfair and unjust. Both the moral and the political legitimacy of immigration restrictions come into question if one can get to the front of the immigration queue by simply breaking the law. Finally, illegal immigration may be the root cause of substantial social and ethnic conflict, particularly in California, where the voters, fed up with government inaction on this issue, enacted Proposition 187 in 1994. This proposition denied many locally provided benefits to illegal aliens—including a public education.[7]

9   Proposition 187, in fact, raises fundamental questions about how far the United States can go—or *should* go—in controlling the illegal alien flow. Much has been made, for instance, about the rights and wrongs of denying a public education to the children of illegal aliens. The supporters of Proposition 187 argued that illegal aliens should not be entitled to attend public schools, that illegal immigration has unalterably lowered the quality of education in California schools, and that such a ban might reduce the incentives for illegal aliens to migrate to the United States. After all, illegal immigration from Mexico responds to the price of *tomatoes* in the United States—apprehensions rise when the price is high and American farms pay more to harvest the crops.[8] If aliens respond to the price of tomatoes, they would surely respond to the cut in education benefits.

10   The opponents of the proposition argued that it is morally wrong to kick children out of school and that, in any case, it makes economic sense to provide illegal aliens

with free schooling. Preventing illegal aliens from getting a high school diploma today will only buy the United States more poverty, welfare, and crime in the future.

11   Putting the moral issues aside, barring illegal aliens from public schools may not be the most effective way of stopping the illegal flow. Many of the children who live in households headed by illegal aliens were born in the United States and are American citizens—courtesy of the Fourteenth Amendment to the Constitution.[9] The denial of public education affects a relatively small part of the illegal population, and would likely not deter the migration of single persons and childless couples.

12   The United States could probably deter many more illegal aliens by imposing substantial penalties on the employers who hire them. These firms—large agricultural enterprises, sweatshops, and native households that hire illegal aliens as maids or nannies—get the bulk of the gains from illegal immigration, but bear few of the costs. The demand for illegal aliens would probably drop dramatically if the government began to bill the owners of the fields where the aliens toil and the families who hire illegal servants for the expenses incurred by public schools and Medicaid.

13   There should also be some penalties assessed on the illegal aliens themselves. It is sometimes recommended that illegal aliens, when caught, should be sent for a few days to some type of detention center, so that they can pay for their crime through a short incarceration. The problem with this proposal is that it is very expensive to send a person to jail. In 1997, it cost $59.83 to send a person for one day to a federal prison.[10] If every apprehended illegal alien (and there were 1.6 million of them in 1996) were forced to spend two weeks in a federal prison, the total bill would be around $1.3 billion—assuming that no new prisons have to be built. It is unclear, therefore, whom this incarceration actually punishes, the illegal alien or the taxpayer.

14   One alternative might be to punish the illegal aliens by hitting them where it hurts the most, in the pocketbook. Federal law, for example, routinely allows the confiscation of much of the property used by drug dealers in their illegal business activities. The application of this principle to illegal immigration would imply that the aliens could be fined for their illegal activities (such as working in the United States) through the confiscation of their assets prior to deportation. The assets that would revert to the U.S. treasury could include bank accounts, cash, automobiles, and the right to collect social security benefits upon retirement (if the illegal alien had somehow been issued a valid social security number). These penalties would probably move the economic activities of the illegal alien population further into the underground economy. But the financial penalties—if accompanied by a strong effort at detecting and apprehending the aliens—could trim the economic benefits associated with migrating to the United States, and reduce the size of the illegal alien flow.

15   Ultimately, any serious attempt to resolve the illegal alien problem faces a crucial obstacle. There must be a simple way of determining who is an illegal alien, and who is not. After all, it is unreasonable to increase the penalties on employers who hire illegal aliens if it is difficult for employers to determine the legal status of a particular job applicant. The United States has yet to grapple with this troublesome detail, which raises the specter of a national identification system.

16   The United States has a somewhat paradoxical attitude on this issue. Most Americans probably have a libertarian streak that immediately rejects the notion of living in a country where one has to carry a card that provides information to potential

employers about whether one is legally entitled to work. Yet most Americans carry credit cards that are scanned regularly whenever goods and services are purchased. The information provided by that scanning—including the type of purchase, the amount, and the location—triggers a computer "prediction" of whether the credit card actually belongs to the person who is carrying it. If, given the past consumption history of the authorized credit card holder, the computer concludes that the person at the store is buying the wrong things, or buying them in the wrong place, or going on an unexplained shopping spree, it will signal the shopkeeper to check for identification.

[17]   Regardless of one's position on the critical issue of a national identification system, the basic dilemma is clear. The illegal alien problem will remain a problem as long as the United States skirts the central question of how to identify who is a legal resident and who is not.

[18]   Finally, it may be possible to encourage the parties involved in the immigration debate to take illegal immigration more seriously by linking the point system for legal immigration with the size of the illegal alien flow. Suppose, for example, that the United States were to adopt a system that granted 500,000 legal visas each year. Each of these slots would become much more valuable if the government "taxed" the number of legal visas available every time an illegal alien entered the country. The Immigration and Naturalization Service might report that 200,000 illegal aliens had entered the country in any given year. The point system could then be adjusted so that only 300,000 legal visas would be granted.

[19]   This "tax" would introduce a number of important incentives into the enforcement of immigration policy. First, it would make the country aware of the opportunity cost of illegal immigration. In other words, by looking the other way and letting in 200,000 illegal aliens, Americans would be forgoing the economic benefits that could be provided by 200,000 well-chosen immigrants. Second, firms that employ immigrants would have to "compete" over their share of entrants. Even though some firms might benefit from the less-skilled illegal aliens, many other firms would want to see the entry of the skilled legal immigrants that they prefer to hire. Finally, the immigrant community already in the United States would have a strong incentive to stop the illegal alien flow, since each illegal alien who entered the country would make it that much harder for the relatives of current U.S. residents to enter, even if the relatives were highly skilled.

Notes

1. A good description of the methodologies used to calculate the number of illegal aliens is given in U.S. General Accounting Office, *Illegal Aliens: Despite Data Limitations, Current Methods Provide Better Population Estimates,* GAO/PEMD-93–25 (Washington, D.C., August 1993).

2. Remarkably, it was not illegal for firms to hire illegal aliens until 1988. Even though it was illegal for some persons to be in the United States, and it was illegal for those persons to work, firms were free to hire the illegal aliens. Since 1988, first-time offenders have been liable for fines ranging from $250 to $2,000 per illegal alien hired. Criminal penalties can be imposed on repeated violators when there is a "pattern and practice" of hiring illegal aliens, including a fine of $3,000 per illegal alien and up to six months in prison.

3. Many studies have attempted to determine if the 1986 Immigration Reform and Control Act slowed down the illegal alien flow. These studies typically conclude that the legislation was a dismal failure; see Katherine M. Donato, Jorge Durand, and Douglas S. Massy, "Stemming the Tide? Assessing the Deterrent Effects of the Immigration Reform and Control Act," *Demography* 29 (May 1992): 139–157.

4. Most of the illegal crossings, however, take place over a relatively small area, stretching for about 165 miles. See Robert J. Caldwell, "Grading Gatekeeper: Tougher Border Enforcement Shows Promise but Remains Incomplete," *San Diego Union-Tribune*, August 10, 1997, p. G-1.

5. See Robert Suro, *Strangers among Us: How Latino Immigration Is Transforming America* (New York: Knopf, 1998), chap. 16, for a detailed discussion of the El Paso operation.

6. Quoted ibid., p. 273.

7. In the 1982 *Plyer v. Doe* decision, the U.S. Supreme Court ruled narrowly (on a 5-to-4 vote) that illegal aliens were entitled to a public education.

8. S.J. Torok and Wallace E. Huffman, "U.S.–Mexican Trade in Winter Vegetables and Illegal Immigration," *American Journal of Agricultural Economics* 68 (May 1986): 246–260. See also Gordon H. Hanson and Antonio Spilimbergo, "Illegal Immigration, Border Enforcement, and Relative Wages: Evidence," *American Economic Review*, forthcoming 1999.

9. This amendment states: "All persons born or naturalized in the United States, and subject to the jurisdiction thereof, are citizens of the United States and of the State wherein they reside." The amendment was enacted in 1868 to grant citizenship to the newly freed slave population.

10. Public Affairs Office, Federal Bureau of Prisons, telephone conversation with author.

Questions for Reading and Analysis

1. How do illegal aliens get into the United States? What is incorrect about the stereotypical image of illegal aliens?

2. What reasons does Borjas give for our attracting illegal aliens?

3. What, according to Borjas, are the serious problems with illegal aliens?

4. What are the arguments for and against Proposition 187 in California?

5. Why does Borjas think that denying public education to the children of illegals will not do much to reduce the flow of illegals?

6. Who benefits the most from illegal aliens?

7. What are Borjas's proposed solutions to the problem of illegal aliens?

8. What is a key problem to implementing Borjas's proposed solutions? How might we identify legals?

9. Why does the author begin with specifics about who illegal aliens are? What does he want to accomplish?

Questions for Discussion and Response

1. What is the most surprising detail, for you, in Borjas's discussion? Why?

2. Has Borjas convinced you that California's Proposition 187 is not useful to the United States? Why or why not?

3. In order to identify illegals and control this problem, Borjas recommends a national ID. What is your response to this proposal?

4. Evaluate Borjas's proposed solutions. Are they workable? Are they right? Why or why not?

5. If you do not agree with the author's solutions, what would you recommend?

Issues in Education

To say that the issues in education are both numerous and serious is certainly an understatement. In the 2000 presidential debates, and in many state elections, proposals for educational reform were endlessly presented and argued. So where do we start? America's best schools and colleges attract students from around the world. But, the variation in funding, facilities, quality teachers, and test scores from one school to the next should be unacceptable to politicians and parents alike. Elite colleges have demanding entrance requirements, but the majority of colleges have few requirements beyond a high school diploma. At many colleges, up to one-third of the freshman class is taking at least one remedial course, and fewer than half of those who start college actually graduate. Are we failing at the goal of universal education? Is this goal unrealistic? Can we make changes that will improve K–12 education? Can we revitalize higher education? These questions—and others raised by the six authors in this chapter—should be the concern of all citizens, for we all benefit—economically and socially—from an educated citizenry.

The first three authors in this chapter examine issues relevant to K–12 education: testing the teaching strategies to judge what works, testing the teachers to improve instruction, recognizing the problem of dumbing down learning. The last three authors explore issues specifically connected to college education: the ease of acceptance, the demographic changes taking place, the impact of distance learning made possible by computers. These six specific topics are connected, in various ways, to the larger questions about U.S. education raised here. Think about each author's particular argument, but also reflect on the ways that each one comments on the larger educational issues facing us at the beginning of this new century.

Websites Relevant to This Chapter's Topic

U.S. Department of Education

www.ed.gov

This government site contains links to many resources on educational issues.

National Education Association

www.nea.org

This site contains definitions, resources on education, links to debates on bilingual education, charter schools, vouchers, and more.

American Federation of Teachers

www.aft.org

This union's site contains many resources and links. Go to their higher education page for resources on college issues, including distance learning.

Educational Policy Studies

http://w3.ed.uiuc.edu/EPS/Ed_Resources/category.lasso?

This site, maintained by the University of Illinois, contains a wealth of information on the many philosophies of education.

But Does It Work?

Alan B. Krueger

A former chief economist of the Department of Labor, Alan Krueger is the Bendheim Professor of Economics and Public Affairs at Princeton University. He has published *Education Matters* (2000, with Joshua Angrist) and wrote the following essay on testing educational strategies for the Education Section of the *New York Times* on November 7, 1999.

1   We run from one fad to another in education, from phonics to whole language and back to phonics, from subject-based to holistic learning, from curriculum-based to child-centered learning, from neighborhood to magnet to charter schools, from old to new to whole math, from English-only to bilingual education to language immersion.

2   With education growing as a voter concern, politicians have been quick to martial dueling remedies of their own. Republicans propose expanding charter schools and diverting funds from failing schools to finance vouchers. Democrats want to reduce class size and install computers in the classroom.

3   Indeed, how we teach our children shifts with the winds of philosophies and politics, leaving many observers dizzy and dismayed.

4   "The sad truth is," the Rev. Dr. Martin Luther King Jr. once lamented, "American schools, by and large, do not know how to teach. The ineffectiveness in teaching reading skills to many young people, whether white or black, poor or rich, strongly indicts foundations and government for not spending funds effectively to find out what different kinds of reading experiences are needed by youth with various learning styles at various points in their life."

5   Thirty years later, we still know little about the effectiveness of the tools in vogue: school vouchers, charter schools, school-to-work transition programs, summer school, year-round schooling, extended-day schooling, tracking, school uniforms and small schools.

6   Dr. King was correct to look to research to shed light on this darkness. But therein lies the problem: education suffers from a lack of scientifically sound studies.

7   The federal government spent $14 billion on space exploration last year, but less than $300 million on research to improve education. The primary research function of the Department of Education has been to administer tests and collect data. Less than 1 percent of its budget goes to research, with even less to conduct and evaluate studies.

8   Controlled experiments are especially rare. With insufficient funds and little tradition in experimental methods, most researchers rely only on observations in a handful of classrooms, without any concrete measure of results. Findings are weak or inconclusive.

9   Take, for example, the decades of seesawing over automatic promotion, the practice of passing students to the next grade so they can remain with their peers, whether or not they have mastered the material. The National Research Council and various studies have found that students who are held back, with little additional tutoring, continue their academic slide and are more likely to drop out. But those studies don't tell how those children would have fared if they *had* been promoted. They might have done even worse, justifying an end to the policy once and for all.

10   Or consider the nationwide rush to wire schools, despite the contradictory claims about the effectiveness of computer-based instruction. Should computers be a priority for inner-city fourth graders who read at the first-grade level? Or do they need more books and less software?

11   By randomly selecting some classrooms to receive computers and some to go without—or some districts to practice automatic promotion and some to hold back failing students—the effects could be measured under scientifically appropriate conditions. Random assignment ensures a balance in terms of variables like students' intelligence, motivation and parental involvement.

12   Such research is not unheard of. In the late 1980's, in a Tennessee study by a consortium of universities, 11,600 students in kindergarten through third grade were randomly assigned to regular-size classes of 22 to 25 students, to regular-size classes with teacher's aides or to smaller classes of 13 to 17 students. The results, gleaned from tracking the students for four years, showed that attending a smaller class increased average test scores. Students did not score higher when their classes had teacher's aides; and the teacher's experience and whether he or she had an advanced degree were also irrelevant to scores. Two recent follow-up studies showed that students assigned to smaller classes were more likely to graduate from high school and apply to college.

13   Although these results have made a case for reducing class size, leading to billions of dollars in additional federal, state and local spending, they shouldn't be the end of the story.

14   The largest improvement occurred the first year. The gain remained about the same for four years, while the students were in smaller classes, but the advantage shrank when they returned to regular classes. Think of it as that first aspirin that makes a headache go away; the second and third keep it at bay, and when you're off the aspirin, it comes back, but not as badly.

15   Further experiments might show that it isn't necessary to reduce class size for all grades—an expensive proposition. One dose might suffice. And it may not be necessary to reduce them everywhere but to concentrate efforts in districts where the study found the most improvement—areas with many low-income and minority students.

16   Another reform sweeping the country is just beginning to be tested. In 1997, Mathematica, a nonprofit research company in Princeton, N.J., conducted a lottery to randomly select 1,300 low-income public schoolchildren in New York City to receive vouchers to attend private elementary schools. After the first year, the students scored, on average, only 2 percentile points higher on math and reading tests than those who remained in public schools—a difference that was just barely discernible statistically.

By comparison, the gain for low-income Tennessee students after one year of small classes was 7 percentile points. The voucher experiment is to continue for another two years, and it will be interesting to see if the private school students ultimately show meaningful gains.

17   Naturally, experiments involving children raise a host of ethical dilemmas. Some fear that members of a control group are denied the advantages of a sound education. But without conducting a controlled study, it wouldn't be clear which students were harmed—say, those who were given computers or those who weren't. And some students would be denied computers anyway, because they aren't being installed in all schools at once.

18   Enough progress has been made since Dr. King's day that we don't need to take radical, untested steps to try to improve education. American public schools have educated the most productive work force in the world, test scores are rising, and a higher proportion of students graduate from high school than ever. Educators should demand compelling evidence before making wholesale changes.

19   The Food and Drug Administration requires scientific testing before new drugs are prescribed. Why should we treat children's minds differently from their bodies? Just as that agency has created an impressive body of medical knowledge, the Education Department can lead the way to a greater understanding of what works and what doesn't by requiring experimental evaluations before federal dollars are thrown to the philosophical and political winds.

Questions for Reading and Analysis

1. What is the educational problem addressed by Krueger?

2. Why has research in education not aided our understanding of what works?

3. What two examples does the author use to illustrate our lack of good evidence of what works?

4. What did the Tennessee study reveal? What has the study of vouchers for private schooling revealed so far?

5. In paragraph 17, Krueger discusses the use of children in experiments. Why does he bring up this point? What is his argument for doing controlled experiments?

6. What does Krueger seek to accomplish in paragraph 18? In his concluding paragraph?

7. The author uses an analogy to explain the impact of smaller classes. What is his analogy? Is it effective?

8. What is Krueger's claim?

Questions for Discussion and Response

1. Has Krueger surprised you at all by his charge that educators do not have good evidence for many of the decisions they make? If not, what experiences have led you not to be surprised?

2. Has the class size study convinced you? Why or why not? What further studies might be useful?

3. Politicians are debating private school vouchers. Does this seem like a good idea to you? Why or why not? If you think vouchers are a good idea, how do you account for the study referred to by Krueger?

4. How valuable are computers in the classroom? And in what classrooms? Is it enough that students are interested in them, even if they take time away from "reading, writing, and arithmetic"? How would you argue for computers in all K–12 classrooms? How would you argue for limiting computers—and what limitations would you seek?

Put Teachers to the Test

Diane Ravitch

Educated at Wellesley College and Columbia University, Diane Ravitch (b. 1938) has been an adjunct professor at Columbia's Teachers College and an assistant secretary in the Department of Education in the first Bush administration. Currently she teaches at New York University and is a visiting fellow at the Brookings Institution. Ravitch has written extensively, in articles and books, on the problems in American schools. The following article was published on February 25, 1998, in the *Washington Post*.

1   Last summer, a suburban school district in New York advertised for 35 new teachers and received nearly 800 applications. District officials decided to narrow the pool by requiring applicants to take the 11th-grade state examination in English. Only about one-quarter of the would-be teachers answered 40 of the 50 multiple-choice questions correctly.

2   As Congress considers reauthorization of the Higher Education Act, teacher education has emerged as a major issue. Many states—and now President Clinton—are clamoring to reduce class size, but few are grappling with the most important questions: If we are raising standards for students, don't we also need to raise standards for teachers? Shouldn't state and local officials make sure that teachers know whatever they are supposed to teach students?

3   Almost every state claims that it is strengthening standards for students, but the states have been strangely silent when it comes to ensuring that teachers know what they are supposed to teach. Most instead certify anyone with the right combination of education courses, regardless of their command of the subject they expect to teach, and many states require future teachers to pass only a basic skills test.

4   Today, in some states it may be harder to graduate from high school than to become a certified teacher. Something is wrong with this picture.

5   Last summer the U.S. Department of Education reported that approximately one-third of the nation's public school teachers of academic subjects in middle school and high school were teaching "out of field," which means that they had earned neither an undergraduate major nor a minor in their main teaching field.

6   Fully 39.5 percent of science teachers had not studied science as a major or minor; 34 percent of mathematics teachers and 25 percent of English teachers were similarly

teaching "out of field." The problem of unqualified teachers was particularly acute in schools where 40 percent or more of the students were from low-income homes; in these schools, nearly half the teaching staff was teaching "out of field."

7   Many states now routinely certify people who do not know what they are supposed to teach. No one should get a license to teach science, reading, mathematics or anything else unless he or she has demonstrated a knowledge of what students are expected to learn.

8   A majority of the nation's teachers majored in education rather than an academic subject. This is troubling, even though most of those who majored in education are elementary teachers. There is a widely accepted notion that people who teach little children don't need to know much other than pedagogical methods and child psychology; that is wrong. Teachers of little children need to be well-educated and should love learning as much as they love children. Yes, even elementary school teachers should have an academic major.

9   The field of history has the largest percentage of unqualified teachers. The Department of Education found that 55 percent of history teachers are "out of field," and that 43 percent of high school students are studying history with a teacher who did not earn either a major or minor in history. This may explain why nearly 60 percent of our 17-year-olds scored "below basic" (the lowest possible rating) on the most recent test of U.S. history administered by the federally funded National Assessment of Educational Progress. Only one out of every five teachers of social studies has either a major or minor in history. Is it any wonder that today's children have no idea when the Civil War occurred, what Reconstruction was, what happened during the progressive era, who FDR was, what the *Brown* decision decided, or what Stalin did? Many of their teachers don't know those things either.

10   There are many conditions over which school officials have no control, but they have complete control over who is allowed to teach. Why should anyone be certified to teach science or history who doesn't know what he or she is expected to teach the children?

11   Many state officials say that they have an abundance of people who want to teach and that this is actually an excellent time to raise standards. For career-changers with a wealth of experience in business or the military, however, obsolete certification requirements get in the way. Instead of requiring irrelevant education courses, states should examine prospective teachers for their knowledge of their academic field and then give them a chance to work in the schools as apprentice teachers.

12   As Congress ponders ways to improve the teaching profession, it should consider incentives for colleges of liberal arts to collaborate with schools of education in preparing future teachers. Representatives from both parts of the same campus should sit down together, study state academic standards and figure out how to prepare teachers who know both their subject and how to teach it well. Teachers need a strong academic preparation as well as practical classroom experience to qualify for one of the toughest jobs in America.

13   Every classroom should have a well-educated, knowledgeable teacher. We are far from that goal today. Congress can address this problem by focusing on the quality, not quantity, of the nation's teaching corps.

Questions for Reading and Analysis

1. What strategy does Ravitch use in her opening paragraph? What makes her opening effective?

2. What is the claim of Ravitch's argument? What type of argument is this?

3. What kinds of evidence does Ravitch provide to support her claim? What key assumption is a part of her argument?

4. What solutions does the author present? What should school officials do? The states? Congress? How does she defend the feasibility of her solutions?

Questions for Discussion and Response

1. Are you surprised by any of Ravitch's statistics? Why or why not?

2. Did you have any teachers teaching "out of field"? If so, how effective were they?

3. Do you agree that K–6 teachers should have a major in an academic subject? Why or why not? (What does Ravitch think they will gain from an academic major?)

4. Should all teachers have to pass a basic test in reading, writing, math, history, and science? If not, why not? If so, at what level? Think of some representative types of questions that you would put on such a test.

The Dumbing Down of Education Is Becoming an International Trend

Thomas Sowell

Thomas Sowell (b. 1930) is a senior fellow at the Hoover Institution at Stanford University. He writes a syndicated column in addition to a biweekly column in *Forbes* magazine. His articles appear in newspapers and magazines as well as scholarly journals, and he is the author of several books, including *Inside American Education* (1992) and *Migrations and Cultures: A World View* (1996). The following article was published on January 24, 2000, in *Insight on the News*.

1   If you have been appalled by the low test scores of students in our public schools, you also should know that it is not always good news when the test scores go up. Investigators have charged dozens of teachers and principals in New York City with helping students cheat on tests. This was done to make their schools look good—or at least not as bad as they would have looked with honest test results.

2   This is just one of many ways in which our academically failing schools are very successful in doing something other than what they are supposed to be doing. They are most successful in serving the interests of "educators" who do not educate.

3   While American students often come in at or near the bottom on international tests, ours is not the only country that is dumbing down—or even misleading the public about it. New Zealand's minister of education declared: "The fact is that New Zealand has a world-class education system—other country's envy us."

4   Let's hope they are not envying this minister's knowledge of English. Nor are New Zealand's test scores in international competition anything to envy, even though they are better than ours.

5   Like other English-speaking countries, New Zealand uses murky standards for evaluating students and schools, standards "which are capable of a wide range of interpretation," according to Roger Kerr of the New Zealand Business Roundtable.

6   These are the kinds of "standards" known in America as outcome-based education—with the outcomes being defined in vague pieties, rather than with serious criteria that would distinguish success from failure. The educator's report on New Zealand education "is full of banalities and ducks all the tough issues," says Kerr. Sound familiar?

7   Kerr adds that the problem is not with incidental issues in education, but with "the tough but ultimately critical issues, such as how to get rid of poor teachers and attract and retain good ones." In other words, you can't make a silk purse out of a sow's ear in New Zealand, any more than you can in the United States.

8   If you wonder why students from so many Asian countries, even poor ones, do better on international tests than students from affluent English-speaking countries, this is part of the reason. All is not lost everywhere, or even everywhere in the English-speaking world. Britain's Education and Employment secretary, David Blunkett, has come out for special programs for gifted children, as well as a policy of throwing disruptive students out, and basing teachers' pay at least in part on performance.

9   These may seem like modest goals, but they are meeting raucous resistance from the teachers' union and from education gurus. Some are already objecting that "daily homework could harm a child's development" and that "focusing on literacy could curb creativity."

10   But Blunkett isn't buying it. He says his vision of education has no room for the "ill-disciplined, anything-goes philosophy which did so much damage in the last generation."

11   It is much too early to know whether Blunkett will be able to carry out his policies over the opposition of the educational establishment. However, it is encouraging just to see someone in a position of authority willing to talk sense in plain English about what the real problems are in the trendy education of our times.

12   It won't be easy. Another government official named Tony Millns, responsible for the curriculum in British classrooms, declared on national radio that students don't need to know exactly where Paris is. "What we are saying," Millns explained, "is that you only need a certain number of facts before you can move on to interpretation, understanding, hypotheses and the real skills which grow out of geography." In other words, you can wing it and shoot off your mouth—which is exactly what American schools encourage.

13   The big problem in the long process of dumbing down the schools—whether in the United States, Britain or New Zealand—is that you can reach a point of no return. How are parents who never received a decent education themselves to recognize that their children are not getting a decent education?

14   Old codgers like yours truly, who can remember when schools had tough academic standards, even in working-class neighborhoods, are going to pass from the scene and be replaced by people who think our education is so good that "other country's envy us."

CHAPTER 18 Issues in Education   **477**

Questions for Reading and Analysis

1. What is Sowell's subject?
2. What is one way some New York City schools are "improving" test scores?
3. Explain how the quotation in paragraph 3 calls into question New Zealand's "world-class education system."
4. What are the problems with New Zealand's standards and handling of other issues in education?
5. What does Britain's education secretary want to do in the schools? What are some of the objections to Blunkett's goals?
6. Why does Sowell include examples from New Zealand and England?
7. What is Sowell's claim? What is his concern for the future of U.S. education?

Questions for Discussion and Response

1. You have probably heard the expression "dumbing down of education." Look over Sowell's examples and comments and then list some of the elements of dumbing down—the attitudes toward knowledge and homework and teacher/school accountability.
2. Does Sowell's concern at the end of his essay make sense to you? That is, after a couple of generations of dumbed-down education, will anyone know that schools used to be different?
3. Do you agree that U.S. schools have dumbed down K–12 education? What evidence do you have to support your reaction?
4. If it is true that public schools are not offering a rigorous education to all students, what do you think we should do to address this problem?

Cakewalk to College

Jackson Toby

Jackson Toby (b. 1925) has been a longtime member of the sociology faculty at Rutgers University. He is the recipient of many research grants and the author of numerous articles and several books, including *Social Problems in America* (1972, with Harry Bredemeier) and *Contemporary Society* (1971). "Cakewalk to College" was published on March 2, 2000, in the *Washington Post*.

1   The most important contributors to the miserable performance of students in high school and, to a lesser extent, in the lower grades are the country's colleges. What have the colleges got to do with it? Simple: They're too easy to get into.

2   Oh, yes, Harvard, Yale, Princeton, Swarthmore, Brown, Wesleyan, MIT and a handful of other colleges and universities have 10 or more applicants for every place in the freshman class. Students aiming at such institutions keep their eye on their prized

goal—admission to a selective college. They study hard in high school and compete desperately to produce an outstanding resume.

3   But they are a tiny segment of the 9 million students enrolled in four-year colleges and the 5 1/2 million in two-year colleges. For most high school students, getting into college is not a problem. For the bulk of American colleges a warm body is sufficient.

4   Consequently, American high schools contain many students who spend more time at malls than doing homework, which many of their teachers have given up trying to assign. Prof. Laurence Steinberg concluded after a monumental survey of more than 20,000 American high school students that about 40 percent were just going through the motions. Steinberg pointed out the consequences of being "disengaged" from the educational process:

5   "The amount of time American teenagers devote to more intellectual or academic pursuits is quite meager. On average, American adolescents spend less than 1 hour each week reading for pleasure, and one-fourth of high school students say they never read at all. Seventy percent of high school students devote less than 5 hours weekly to homework, while only 5 percent spend 20 hours or more each week on their studies outside of school."

6   At the same time, at least 40 percent work at part-time jobs and spend most or all of their earnings on personal expenses: clothes, recreation, cars. So a third of all college entering freshmen require remedial courses.

7   The late president of the American Federation of Teachers, Albert Shanker, put his finger on the culprit, the colleges. They do not provide strong incentives for students to do well in high school:

8   "If they know they have to work hard, listen in class and come to school every day with their homework done in order to get into college, they'll do that. If they know they can get by with less and still get into college, that is what they'll do."

9   Shanker rightly assumed that a majority of American youngsters want to attend college, partly because they have been told that they need higher education to get a good job later, partly because college is where young people go. (Two-thirds of American high school graduates enroll in college, although fewer than half actually graduate.)

10   Contrast the American system of higher education with the Japanese university system, where every university requires a rigorous entrance examination. As a result, Japanese youngsters expend tremendous effort in the primary and secondary schools in order to prepare for college entrance exams. They are convinced that their futures depend on admission to a good college; they know that this requires learning a lot in primary and secondary school, and they believe that, with effort, they can learn what is necessary. As a result, Japanese high school students do two and three times as much homework, on average, as American high school students and know a great deal more when they arrive at college.

11   This being so, what will help more than the billions to be spent on "fixing" the problems at the primary and secondary levels is reducing, not increasing, access to college. The trouble with Pell Grants and other forms of "financial aid" to high school graduates who want to attend college is that they promiscuously help everybody: good students as well as students who can barely read and write. Thus the existence of

financial aid that does not depend on academic performance either in high school or college undermines a major incentive for studying. An honest political candidate might want to point out this truth sometime, but sad to say, he'd never get elected.

Questions for Reading and Analysis

1. What is Toby's subject? What is his claim?

2. What kind of argument is this? (Consider the various kinds of arguments discussed in Chapter 4.)

3. How does Toby account for the "cakewalk to college"? What is a major cause for American high school students not studying and learning?

4. How does the author qualify his assumption that high school graduates know they can get into college?

5. Summarize the facts: how many high school grads attend college? How many graduate? How many are in college? How many high schoolers have jobs? How many need remedial courses in college?

6. By contrast, how do Japanese students behave?

7. If we know the cause of a problem, we often know the solution. What is Toby's recommendation for improving high school performance?

Questions for Discussion and Response

1. Which of Toby's statistics are most surprising to you? Why?

2. Does your experience confirm Toby's argument that high school students do little work because they know they can go to college anyway? If it doesn't, can you account for your different experience?

3. Should Pell grants be tied to academic performance? Why or why not?

4. Are Toby and Sowell correct in their concerns for American education, or are they making a problem out of nothing? Explain and defend your views.

Affirmative Action for Men?

Katha Pollitt

Associate editor at *The Nation*, Katha Pollitt (b. 1949) contributes to periodicals, has collected essays in *Reasonable Creatures: Essays on Women and Feminism* (1994), and has a book of poetry *Antarctic Traveller* (1982). "Affirmative Action for Men?" appeared in *The Nation* on December 27, 1999.

[1] Women today constitute 54 percent of college students 24 and younger, and 56 percent of college students overall. Some people have a problem with that. At a conference held in November [1999] at Goucher College titled "Fewer Men on Campus,"

an array of education experts put forth a variety of gloomy explanations: a lack of smart role models for boys in popular culture; the prevalence of female teachers in elementary grades; a lack of attention to boys' developmental needs. Tom Mortenson, the education analyst who is the torchbearer for the issue, blamed single-parent families and the increasing "disengagement" of men from family, work and civic life. Others mentioned boys' greater physicality, their impatience with rules and instructions, social taboos on male expressivity.

2   Some of these explanations are clearly wrong—elementary school teaching has been in the hands of women for more than a century, but female undergrads started consistently outnumbering males only in the late eighties. Still, the Goucher conference represented the reasonable end of an often acrimonious conversation. On a *Chronicle of Higher Education* Web discussion board, a male professor claimed campus feminists have driven men to avoid college; another said men are discouraged by having to deal with more and more female registrars and administrators.

3   Are "fewer men" going to college, though—or more women? "More of everybody is going to college, actually," Jacqueline King of the American Council on Education (ACE) told me. A far higher percentage of kids are graduating from high school than in, say, 1960, when 54 percent of boys went directly to college and 38 percent of girls—a situation that aroused no worryfests, by the way. Of today's larger high school grad population, a higher percentage of boys (64 percent) is going on to college—but the percentage of girls is even higher (70 percent). Why? It's possible, of course, that girls are just smarter and, with the toppling of formal barriers to education, can finally reap the rewards of their brainpower. More likely, though, it's economics that drives women to college.

4   For all we hear about the decline of high-paid blue-collar jobs, women with a college degree average barely more than men with a high school diploma—$35,400 versus $31,200. (Women with only a high school diploma average $22,000.) Women are mostly shut out of the high-tech industries in which Bill Gates, a college dropout, made himself the world's richest man. A boy can get a certificate from Microsoft or Intel and earn a decent living. As former Georgia Governor Zell Miller said, "Who in his right mind would want to go into debt for the privilege of reading *Beowulf* when he can make $30,000 a year in air-conditioner maintenance straight out of high school?" *Beowulf* doesn't look so bad when the alternative is waitressing or cleaning bedpans in a nursing home. If women could earn as much as men without a college degree, lots of them would probably give it a pass too.

5   As the above suggests, class is often a buried issue when we talk about gender—and so is race. According to ACE, among non-Hispanic white students 24 and younger, it's a nearly even split between men (49 percent) and women (51 percent) enrolled in college. It's among nonwhites that the gap shows up. Among black college students, only 37 percent are male as against 63 percent who are female. Among Hispanics, 45 percent are male and 55 percent are female. That minority girls, despite poverty, inferior schools and all the other strikes against them, are more likely to make it to college than their brothers is a tribute to their determination. But mostly their achievement is presented as yet another problem: They will have to marry less-educated men—or remain single.

6   Nobody worried about unequal education levels in marriage when it was the man who typically had the BA. No college over the many long decades of greater male

enrollment would have considered lowering its standards to admit more women to improve the dating scene or engineer more intellectual compatibility in marriage. Indeed,
until the seventies colleges routinely and openly discriminated in favor of men, whether
by formally limiting the number of female students, admitting women to smaller single-
sex colleges affiliated with larger all-male institutions (Harvard-Radcliffe, Columbia-
Barnard, Rutgers-Douglass) or, most commonly, demanding higher qualifications of female applicants. Nowadays that kind of preference would be illegal. Yet that colleges
today admit less-qualified men over more-qualified women is higher education's dirty
little secret. "I'm sure it happens," political scientist Andrew Hacker told me, and every
expert I talked with agreed, including Tom Mortenson, who said the practice outraged
him. In one of the few cases that made the papers, the University of Georgia was forced
to abandon its practice of giving male applicants extra points after a female applicant
sued for being denied admittance.

7   Are some boys disadvantaged in education today—maybe not more than girls, as
Mortenson argues, but in different ways? In poor neighborhoods, where special education functions as a dumping ground for kids with disciplinary problems, the vast majority of kids in special ed are boys. More broadly, minority boys are targeted by police, and
often end up in jail instead of school. It's true, too, that boys, like girls, are victims of a
cult of masculinity. A society that makes a hero of Stone Cold Steve Austin shouldn't
be too surprised if boys scorn intellectual pursuits.

8   Opponents of affirmative action haven't had much to say about admissions policies
that give boys a break. Maybe they're embarrassed. After all, one reason girls do better is
that they work harder. But if it's acceptable to admit less-qualified white, middle-class boys
to make for a happier campus social scene, or increase the number of potential husbands,
why can't a similar rationale be used to dip further into the applicant pool of minorities? A
racially and ethnically integrated campus serves important social functions too—as students from heavily white campuses will discover when they move out into the big world.

9   Right now the moral on campus seems to be: If white men can't jump, lower the
basket.

Questions for Reading and Analysis

1. What educational situation is Pollitt's subject?

2. Some people think this situation is a problem; does Pollitt?

3. How does the author respond to some of the causes offered as explanations?

4. What percentage of boys graduating from high school go on to college? What percentage of girls?

5. Why does Pollitt think so many girls are going to college? What evidence does she present?

6. What is another set of statistics that helps explain why there are more women than men at college?

7. It is now illegal to discriminate against women in admissions. Does this still happen? What evidence does Pollitt offer to support her view on this?

8. What are some of the facts about boys that may explain why fewer of them than girls go to college?

9. Does Pollitt think that girls should be discriminated against in selection? What is her claim?

Questions for Discussion and Response

1. Which statistics in this article are most surprising to you? Why?

2. Pollitt asserts that maybe those opposing affirmative action are embarrassed by policies favoring boys at college because "girls . . . work harder." Pollitt does not provide evidence for this assertion. Should she assume that everyone understands this? Do you agree that girls, as a group, work harder than boys in school? Why or why not?

3. How would you describe Pollitt's tone in this essay? Is it an appropriate tone for her topic and audience?

4. Should colleges admit students in part to accomplish some social engineering? Should less qualified boys be admitted to improve the dating/marriage situation? Should less qualified minorities be admitted to reflect America's diversity? Explain and defend your views.

Cyber U: What's Missing

Michele Tolela Myers

Born in Morocco in 1941, Michele Tolela Myers is currently president of Sarah Lawrence College. She has published in her field—sociology and communications—with co-author Gail E. Myers, *The Dynamics of Human Communication* (a textbook), *Communicating When We Speak* (1978), and *Managing by Communication* (1982). The following article was published by the *Washington Post* on May 21, 2000.

1   The scramble is on to respond to the easy access to knowledge and financial opportunities that computers can provide. Earlier this year the U.S. Department of Education reported that distance education programs had almost doubled in the past three years. Every week another college, university or private individual seeks to establish online education—whether for-profit like Michael Milken's online university, Unext, or Michael Saylor's projected non-profit online university whose motto would be "free education for everyone on earth, forever."

2   If education were only as simple as reading, then libraries would have replaced schools long ago. We educators are in the business of forming minds—not just filling them.

3   Gutenberg's invention of printing in the 15th century essentially ended up removing priests as the only gatekeepers of information and knowledge. In the same way, the computer and the Web are allowing larger and larger numbers of people direct access to more information and may well take the more traditional middlemen and gatekeepers (our teachers and educators) out of the system. Readily available technology is good for society and good for education because it will bring ever more information from the

wider world to everyone. Every academic institution will clearly want to embrace this new technology to enhance the learning experience in the classroom and to reach those who do not have the money or time to attend school.

4   The principal role of a university or college is not, however, to transmit information. If it were, then our goal would be the most "productive" way of passing on information. Logically, the larger the auditorium the better, with one teacher lecturing hundreds of students. Distance learning and virtual education are clearly even better vehicles for transmitting information, with the computer screen delivering a prepackaged syllabus to thousands, possibly millions at a time. It makes great economic sense, and predictions may be right that classrooms will go the way of the hand-scribed text.

5   But higher education in the 21st century is in a different business—a business made even more imperative precisely because of the ubiquity of information technology. More than ever, we need to teach our young people to learn how to learn, to sort and evaluate information, to make judgments about evidence and sources. They must learn how to separate the important from the trivial and, most important, they must learn to think analytically and creatively, to have ideas, to write and speak intelligently about ideas, and to know how to go from ideas to actions. It is not enough for our students to know; rather, they should know what to know and have the capacity to imagine.

6   There is no better way to form good minds than in one-on-one interactions. Research tells us that the two most significant factors that contribute positively to learning among college students are their interaction with each other and their interaction with teachers. Is there any doubt that for children and adolescents, face-to-face time is important? Parenting and teaching both require human physical contact and creative individual responses to a singular individual to be most effective.

7   More than ever, then, we are going to need liberal arts preparation at the undergraduate level, the kind of education liberal arts colleges are best positioned to offer. This kind of education may not be the most efficient, but it is clearly the most effective. A liberal arts college offers the most contact time between teachers and students. It offers time for students to actually practice writing, speaking, arguing, evaluating and researching in small classes with real professors who care about them as individuals and care about their work, who will critique them and hold them accountable. It is here that students hone their skills to communicate effectively—the number one quality that corporations seek when they are interviewing candidates. No computer can sharpen the mind as well as a cross-fire discussion among students with their teacher. In human affairs, there is ultimately no substitute for real human contact.

8   The emergence of computers challenges us to know what our business is. We must respond that we are in the business of ideas, not information, of forming minds, not filling them.

Questions for Reading and Analyzing

1. What is Myers's subject? What is the claim of her argument?

2. How does Myers use a conciliatory approach? Where does she state common ground?

3. How does the author use the book/library analogy as evidence to support her claim?

4. Put in your own words what Myers asserts about the "business" of a college education.

5. What, according to Myers, is the best format for fulfilling the "business" of a college education?

6. What is "the number one quality" that businesses are looking for in hiring college graduates?

Questions for Discussion and Response

1. Observe Myers's opening and concluding paragraphs. What makes each one effective?

2. Some of the writers in this chapter offer statistics as part of their evidence. Myers uses reasons. Analyze her argument, explaining how her reasons connect to build support for her claim.

3. Do you agree that higher education is not primarily about gaining knowledge? Why or why not?

4. Do you think that you are getting the kind of education that Myers describes? If not, how do you account for this?

5. Would you want to do college through an online university? Why or why not?

CHAPTER 19

Race, Gender, and Identity

There are actually many points of debate within the general category of race, gender, and identity issues. It can be helpful, though, to see how many of the separate debate issues intersect and overlap. They overlap at times because the issues turn on prejudice and stereotyping; they intersect over concepts of government's roles in protecting minority interests, over adjusting to social change, over struggles for power.

One of the issues still getting attention is affirmative action because, as Charles Lawrence and Mari Matsuda note, there is a backlash to affirmative action policies. Indeed, changes have been made in state laws as a result of lawsuits and, in California, because of voter-approved propositions. Affirmative action issues connect directly to college students, as we see in an essay by Gregory Rodriguez and Ronald Takaki and another by Shelby Steele, both reacting to California's Proposition 209.

In addition to the stresses and arguments generated by affirmative action, we see more municipalities and private companies providing equal benefits to heterosexual and homosexual partnerships—while the Boy Scouts exclude gay leaders. And we have two writers examining the power that race still has over behavior in this country.

Reflecting on the following questions before you read articles in this chapter will enrich your reading on these multifaceted issues:

1. What does the term *affirmative action* mean to you? Does it produce strong emotions in you? If so, why do you think that is so?
2. Do you have a position on affirmative action? If so, what is it?
3. Do you understand how elite colleges select their students? Did they select on merit long before affirmative action guidelines came into effect?
4. Why do we categorize and stereotype people? What do we gain from this way of responding to the world? What do we lose?
5. Will we ever "get over" race in America?

Websites Relevant to This Chapter's Topic

Office of Affirmative Action, Equal Opportunity, and Diversity

www.uri.edu/affirmative_action

This site, maintained by the University of Rhode Island, contains definitions, legislation, news, and resources outside this university's program.

Office of Affirmative Action/Equal Opportunity

www.uvm.edu/~aaeo

The University of Vermont's "Affirming Diversity" page provides good links to relevant legislation.

National MultiCultural Institute

www.nmci.org

This site provides links to resources related to education, race, health, crime, conflict resolution, and more; the organization promotes multiculturalism in education and business.

Extending the Reach of Affirmative Action

Charles R. Lawrence III and Mari J. Matsuda

Charles Lawrence and Mari Matsuda are law professors at Georgetown University. They are co-authors (with Kimberle Williams Crenshaw and Richard Delgado) of *Words That Wound: Critical Race Theory, Assaultive Speech and the First Amendment* (1992) in addition to *We Won't Go Back: Making the Case for Affirmative Action* (1997), from which the following excerpt is taken.

1   A colleague of ours, who is sympathetic to the goals of affirmative action, tells us that he believes we and other progressives should drop affirmative action as a political goal. "This issue is killing us," he says. The overwhelming mood of the country, he argues, is opposed to affirmative action. A principled stand in favor of it is political suicide. We will lose not only on affirmative action, but on a range of civil rights and human rights initiatives if we demand something that the majority is unprepared to give. This is not the time, he believes, to defend affirmative action.

2   We disagree. Where the resistance is great is the exact location of the struggles we choose. The current backlash against affirmative action, the confusion and the anger aroused by feminist and antiracist struggles, are markers alerting us to important work.

3   In friendship, in love, in families, this is so. There are the things we are not supposed to talk about, subjects we draw lines around, marking where we should not venture. Carefully crossing those lines is often what cements relationships and makes love true.

4   The social and cultural lines that delimit race and gender privilege are much the same. The private clubs that require women to enter through a side door are more than remnants of an old era. They mark the locations of patriarchal power and privilege—places where deals are made and assumptions formed. The women in cities across the country who walked through front doors, either in open defiance or after successful campaigns to drop gender bars, were changing a culture and demanding a share of power.[1] Joining an exclusive club, of course, is not the goal of feminism. The point is that the resistance these trailblazers encountered signaled tangible consequences.

5   The animosity affirmative action spawns is not a reason for retreat. Rather, it is a reason to expand demands for affirmative action. Affirmative action has not gone far enough. We must reinvigorate and enlarge existing programs.

6   When we say affirmative action has not gone far enough, we use as our measure the goal of equal participation in economic, political, and social life. In every institution of power, there is continued exclusion of women and people of color, and disparities in power are marked by gender and race lines. The following widely reported statistics[2] portray this inequality. Only about 30 percent of all scientists are women, and in certain specialties the numbers are even more drastic—only 16 percent of physicists, for example, are women. There are fewer women doctors than men, and in every medical specialty women earn less. Between 30 and 40 percent of associate attorneys in law firms are women, but only 11 percent of partners are women. Women make up 50 percent of entry-level accountants, but less than 20 percent of accounting firm partners. They represent 48 percent of journalists, but hold only 6 percent of the top editorial jobs. Forty percent of college professors are women, but they make up only 11 percent of tenured staff. Seventy-two percent of elementary school teachers are women, but they represent only 29 percent of school principals.

7   Similar statistics reveal the exclusion of people of color. For example, African Americans, 12 percent of the population, hold only 2.5 percent of the managerial jobs "above the glass ceiling." In fact, a white woman with a high school degree has as good a chance as a Black person with a college degree to obtain a managerial position.[3]

8   Overall, the number of women and minorities in executive or management positions is paltry. Over the past decade there were two women CEOs in fifteen hundred top companies. Ninety-five to 97 percent of the senior managers (corporate vice presidents and up) were men, and of those men, 97 percent were white. The little progress that women made in upper corporate echelons was virtually reserved for white women: 95 percent of women senior managers are white. Among the women who have made it to the senior management level, 95 percent report that a glass ceiling exists to this day for all women.[4]

9   Most employed women are clustered in occupations that are 75 percent or more women. It's not news that female-dominated occupations pay far less, have fewer benefits, and frequently offer tenuous job security. Moreover, sex discrimination exists even within female-dominated occupations: male nurses earn an average of 10 percent more than female nurses, and male bookkeepers earn an average of 16 percent more than female bookkeepers.[5]

10   At the slow pace of existing reform, the landscape of privilege—where economically well-off white men run Congress, major corporations, unions, the newspapers and television stations, publishing firms, law, accounting, investment firms, and banks—will remain the prevailing picture well into the next generation. Unless we initiate radical changes now, the gender gap in wealth and earnings will not close, and the feminization of poverty will continue. Affirmative action has made small gains in the direction of equality, but small is not enough. Every corporate board, every university, every union, every branch of the media, should make full integration its goal and should accelerate affirmative action initiatives to achieve that goal today. There is no reason, given the wealth of talent available, to continue exclusion in these institutions.

11   We oppose subordination on all axes. We have focused on race and gender in particular both because of our own experiences and because those were the first categories in the affirmative action plans generated by the civil rights movement of the 1960s and 1970s, the plans currently under attack.

12   Race and gender, however, are only part of the story of how some human beings are made lesser. Failure to see the whole story is one of the reasons the civil rights movement has not brought about widespread equality. A just vision of affirmative action would include our lesbian and gay citizens, who are afraid that whom they love will define what jobs and opportunities they will have; our citizens with disabilities, who are asking not for pity but for liberation in the tradition of civil rights struggles; and the growing ranks of the poor and the working poor, to whom the basic security of adequate food, shelter, and medical care is denied and to whom decent education is largely unavailable. As advocates of expanded affirmative action, we embrace them all.

13   In committing to expand affirmative action, we face the complaint that now "everyone is a minority," and only straight white men are left out. This familiar inversion of the truth is contradicted by the statistical reality of extraordinary white male advantage. Others complain that affirmative action seeks "special rights" for minorities when equal rights are enough. *We demand whatever rights are necessary to achieve equality.*

14   To our colleague, and many like him, who counsel scaling down demands for affirmative action as the "special rights" rhetoric generates, for example, antigay legislation in states like Colorado, we answer that retreat rarely ensures safety. Backlash is exactly what we should expect when we attempt to move a culture forward. People don't always cooperate, even when their souls are at stake, in making positive social change. Even as they complain, however, they eventually do change and adjust to new demands. The requested change that seems outlandish today seems probable tomorrow and inevitable the day after that. Thus, we choose a politics of vision over one that asks, "What can we realistically hope to obtain?"

15   One of the most frequent attacks on affirmative action is that it fails to take into account the poor. As a prominent former mayor once exclaimed at a congressional hearing:

> How galling it is for white males to know that the children of Bill Cosby and Cosby himself are entitled to preferential treatment in a whole host of programs simply because they and he are black. It is unacceptable to fair-minded people that a poor white male from Appalachia, or other parts of the United States, or some Asians, are placed at an enormous disadvantage because of the concept of group rights. Affirmative action laws, executive orders, and regulations have created group rights in the name of equality, a contradiction in terms.[6]

16   While critics of affirmative action often use the "what about poverty" question as a diversion tactic, the issue of affirmative action based on economic need is an important one. Affirmative action should include the economically disadvantaged, and many of the best programs already do. The University of California, long before Governor Pete Wilson's attack on affirmative action, included in its plan the category of economic disadvantage. Many other universities, including all of the Ivy League schools, consider overcoming economic disadvantage a plus in the admissions process. A student who attains high grades and test scores in spite of growing up poor and going to low-quality public schools is considered a particularly good candidate for admission. This moderately expanded form of affirmative action, however, does not go to the heart of what is needed to overcome economic obstacles to education and opportunity, for it

is exceedingly rare for students to come through circumstances of abject poverty with the ability to meet traditional admission criteria.

17   Real affirmative action for the "poor white male from Appalachia" and for others growing up in poverty must begin with the redistribution of educational resources. We know that intervention in the early years works to open up educational opportunity. A joint study by the University of North Carolina at Chapel Hill and the University of Alabama in Birmingham reveals that poor children who went through supportive preschool programs had higher intelligence test scores, better achievement in math and reading, fewer cases of having to repeat grades, and less special education placement than a comparable group without the benefit of such programs.[7] The academic differences between the two groups of children widened as the children got older: the preschool education had visible, lasting benefits at the ages of eight, twelve, and fifteen. Study after study shows that poor children who are exposed to programs like Headstart obtain educational benefits that last into adulthood. Headstart children are more likely than poor children who do not go to Headstart, for instance, to graduate from high school, stay out of the criminal justice system, go on to college, get a job, and stay off welfare.[8]

18   The proven success of early intervention programs is well known. Given this success rate, one wonders where all the affirmative action foes who lament the fate of the "poor white male from Appalachia" go when, year after year, Congress refuses full funding for social programs like Headstart, turning away thousands of families of all races who are seeking a better education for their children.

19   The Children's Defense Fund has reported that a child who has lived in poverty for one year or more is 3.2 times more likely to drop out of high school than a child who was never poor.[9] Poor children live around more crime but have less access to high-quality recreation, which develops positive social skills and puts children in regular contact with supportive adults.[10] Recreation programs and teen job training are labeled "pork" by the Republican Congress, which reduced or eliminated such programs as part of its crime bill revisions.[11]

20   In every state in the nation, there are children who go hungry when we cut school breakfast programs, who are turned away from overcrowded Headstart classrooms, whose public libraries are closed half the week because of funding cuts. For these children, the affirmative action debate is largely academic. Saying, "We will set aside 1 percent of government contracts for you if you manage to start your own business," or "We will hold a place for you at the university if you can score in the 85 percent range of the SATs" is a cruel jest. If one is denied a fighting chance to obtain the skills necessary to enter the door, no setaside can help.

21   Affirmative action for the economically disadvantaged must take two forms. First, we should expand existing programs to include economic disadvantage as a category. This would provide a point of entry for the exceptions, the rare individuals who—often because of significant nonmaterial resources, such as a loving and supportive family— are able to overcome poverty and obtain the minimal qualifications for employment and higher education opportunities. We must make special efforts to include such individuals in all of our public and private institutions.

22   Second, we must make antipoverty, literacy, and remedial education programs a significant part of our affirmative action efforts. Some colleges, such as the prestigious

City College in New York, have made this commitment, saying to students, "If you will work hard, we will meet you halfway. If you had a lousy preparatory education through no fault of your own, we will set up the courses and tutorials that can bring you up to speed so that you can compete in a rigorous university environment."

23   This type of program recognizes the effects of poverty and exclusion from opportunity and does something about it. Talented, hard-working individuals who grow up poor are not always able to show their talents and sometimes lack skills that they could attain with help. Giving them this help is a fair way to open doors.

24   Why don't we do it more often? First, it costs. Remedial education and early intervention, unlike set-asides and quotas, require upfront expenditures. Second, these expenditures are seen as redistributions—taking from the haves to give to the have-nots—which go against America's tenets of individualism, private property, and capitalism. Finally, a successful propaganda campaign has convinced even those concerned about poverty that no government antipoverty program will work. Stories of inept bureaucracies and intransigent, congenitally lazy poor people have permeated the culture, to the point where many who would give a dollar to a homeless person on a cold night would not vote to spend a government dollar on a poverty program.

25   To these reasons for avoiding affirmative action for the economically disadvantaged, we charge prevarication. From our mothers, who made lifelong vocations of teaching and healing young children, we learned this truth: what you give to a child is returned tenfold. The teachers who know how to do this already exist, they are good at what they do, and they could train others to do it. But they are underpaid and unsupported in their efforts.

26   In these days of budget-cutting madness, Congress has made a cowardly surrender in the War on Poverty. To save tax dollars today, they have committed us to untold billions of future expenditures to pay for multiplying ravages: more child abuse, more crime, more imprisonment, more untrained and unemployable workers, more citizens who believe, and quite dangerously so, that there is nothing to be gained by entering into the social compact. To live among fellow citizens who care nothing for their own lives, or ours, is a scary thing. This is the world we are creating by cutting prenatal care, cutting Aid to Families with Dependent Children (AFDC), and refusing full funding for Headstart.

27   Certainly there is a cost to fighting poverty, but it is far exceeded by the cost of expanding poverty. The punishment exacted on poor children is borne by society time and again. A high school dropout, for example, will secure a low-paying job at best, will pay fewer taxes, is more likely to commit a crime, and more likely to get sick.[12] One estimate shows that each dollar cut from AFDC reduces future economic output by up to $1.51, making the cost to society $177 billion for each year that our nation's 14.6 million poor children spend in poverty.[13] Ironically, the Census Bureau estimates that it would cost only about $39.4 billion to end child poverty today.[14]

28   Are antipoverty programs contrary to American virtues of individualism, private property, and capitalism? The premise of taxation is that any government must collect revenues from individuals and distribute them for the benefit of the collective. We understand this when our tax money is invested in roads and highways or police and fire departments. Education is no less essential to the life of the Republic.

29   Two of our nation's great philosophers of education, John Dewey and Alexander Meiklejohn, stressed the importance of educational opportunity for all in a democracy. It is not just the ideal of fairness that requires this equality, but the maintenance of democracy itself. Dewey wrote that "a government resting upon popular suffrage cannot be successful unless those who elect and who obey their governors are educated. Since a democratic society repudiates the principal of external authority, it must find a substitute in voluntary disposition and interest; these can be created only by education."[15]

30   Alexander Meiklejohn, the educational experimentalist and constitutional theorist, understood that participation in democracy's objective, which is self-governance, presupposes education. "All human beings should have the same essential education,"[16] he argued.

31   Democracy works when all citizens are educated and able to participate actively in self-governance. Under this rationale, our public schools were once the world's finest, but today a devastating effect of America's racism has been the abandonment of public schools. Communities that in days past would have voted inevitably for school bonds, and in support of expanded funding to schools, now reject such proposals. In many parts of the country those with resources send their children to private schools, while public schools—other than enclaves of prestige public schools in wealthy neighborhoods—have become the domain of less privileged "others."

32   The notion that funding education and antipoverty programs takes from haves to give to have-nots is a perversion of individualism. It does not require confiscatory takings to right the wrongs of which we speak, but it does require that each person see self-interest as tied to the collective. We are born with great gifts of empathy for others, and we can use these gifts to see that each individual has the potential to flourish.

Notes

1. Cf. Sally Frank, "The Key to Unlocking the Clubhouse Door: The Application of Antidiscrimination Laws to Quasi-Private Clubs," 2 *Michigan Journal of Gender Law* 27 (1994).
2. Statistics and facts about women in the workplace referred to in this paragraph are from the Federal Glass Ceiling Commission, *Good for Business: Making Full Use of the Nation's Human Capital* (Washington, D.C.: Bureau of National Affairs, 1995); The American Association of University Women, "The Time for Affirmative Action Has Not Passed," March 15, 1994; Edward Frost and Margaret Cronin Smith, "The Profession after Fifteen Years," *National Law Journal,* Aug. 9, 1993, p. 1; Mark J. McGarry, "Short Cuts," *Newsday,* June 14, 1994, p. A42; *Statistical Abstract of the United States,* 1993, Table No. 637, p. 426; Arden Moore, "Women in Education Review Gains," *Orlando Sentinel,* March 11, 1994, p. C5; Testimony of Marcia Greenberger, to House Judiciary Committee on the Constitution, Dec. 7, 1995; Marion Crain, "Between Feminism and Unionism: Working-Class Women, Sex Equality and Labor Speech," 82 *Georgia Law Journal* 1993, 1913–1914 (1994).
3. Ibid.
4. Ibid.
5. Ibid.

6. Prepared testimony of Edward I Koch, before the Senate Judiciary Committee Subcommittee on Constitution, Federalism, and Property Rights of Affirmative Action, Oct. 23, 1995.

7. Craig T. Ramey and Sharon Landesman Ramey, *At Risk Does Not Mean Doomed*, National Health/Education Consortium Occasional Paper #4, Civitan International Research Center, June 1992, p. 5 ("children who received early education intervention had, on average, IQ scores that were 20 points higher than those in the control condition"); p. 6 ("the children who received the full day, 5 day a week center-based program, supplemented by home visits as well, showed much higher intellectual performance than did the children in the home-based only treatment group or the control group"); Sharon Landesman Ramey and Craig T. Ramey, "Early Educational Intervention with Disadvantaged Children—to What Effect?" *Applied & Preventive Psychology*, 1:131–140 (1992), p. 135 (citing Abecedarian Project's finding that at age twelve, "children who had received the early educational intervention continued to show benefits in terms of both academic achievement and IQ scores and a reduction of nearly 50 percent in the rate of repetition of at least one grade in the elementary school years"). Cf. Frances A. Campbell and Craig T. Ramey, "Effects of Early Intervention on Intellectual and Academic Achievement: A Follow-up Study of Children from Low-Income Families," *Child Development*, 65, 684–698 (1994).

8. See, e.g., Lawrence J. Schwineheart, Helen V. Barnes, David P. Weikart, *Significant Benefits: The High/Scope Perry Preschool Study through Age 27* (Ypsilanti, MI: High/Scope Press, 1993), p. 59 ("the program group had a significantly higher regular high school graduation rate than did the no-program group"); p. 83 ("As compared with the no-program group, the program group averaged a significantly lower number of lifetime [juvenile and adult] criminal arrests . . . and a significantly lower number of adult criminal arrests"); p. 60 ("38 percent of the program group and 21 percent of the no-program group had at some time enrolled in what appeared to be academic or vocational post-secondary programs"); p. 97 ("The most recent evidence . . . indicates that, compared with the no-program group, the program group at age 27 . . . had significantly higher monthly earnings . . . [and] nearly significantly higher annual earnings"); p. 106 ("significantly fewer members of the program group than of the no-program group had received social services sometime in the ten years before the age-27 interview and records searches").

9. Children's Defense Fund, *Wasting America's Future: The Children's Defense Fund Report on the Costs of Child Poverty* (Boston: Beacon Press, 1994), p.xxiii.

10. Ibid., pp.29–38.

11. Joe Donnelly, "A Run at Night Basketball," *Washington Post*, Aug. 18, 1994, p.A1.

12. Children's Defense Fund, *Wasting America's Future*, pp.105–115.

13. Ibid.

14. Ibid, p.116.

15. John Dewey, *Democracy and Education: An Introduction to the Philosophy of Education* (New York: Macmillan Co., 1916), p.101.

16. Alexander Mieklejohn, *Education Between Two Worlds* (New York: Harper Bros., 1942), p. 282.

Questions for Reading and Analysis

1. What is the authors' claim? Where do they stand on the issue of affirmative action? Where do they state their claim?

2. What evidence do the authors provide to show that affirmative action has not gone far enough? Summarize the data.

3. Lawrence and Matsuda acknowledge that affirmative action has traditionally addressed race and gender inequities. What other groups should, in their view, be included?

4. What is one program for the disadvantaged that the authors want expanded? How does it make a difference? What other programs help poor children improve their lives through education?

5. Why aren't these programs and services more widely available?

6. In paragraphs 25–27, Lawrence and Matsuda offer what kind of argument in defense of programs for poor children? What do they want to show with the data they provide?

7. In paragraphs 28–32, the authors refute what challenge to government spending on education? How do they respond to their opposition?

8. How would you describe the essay's tone? Are the authors angry? Reflective? Analytic? Serious? Something else? Have they selected an effective tone for their subject and purpose? Explain.

Questions for Discussion and Response

1. In paragraph 13, the authors seek to refute challenges made to affirmative action. Are the challenges (or complaints) familiar to you? Do the authors answer the challenges successfully? Why or why not?

2. Lawrence and Matsuda devote most of their argument to social, economic, and political self-interest appeals: we will all benefit from affirmative action and the educational programs that will provide genuine equal opportunity. Are there other arguments that can be made in support of affirmative action? Of equal quality schools?

3. Does democracy require an educated citizenry? Why might democracy collapse without widespread education? Explain your answers.

California's Big Squeeze

Gregory Rodriguez and Ronald Takaki

Gregory Rodriguez is a senior fellow at Pepperdine University's Public Policy Institute and an associate editor at Pacific News Service. Ronald Takaki is an Ethnic Studies professor at the University of California at Berkeley and the author of a number of books, including *Strangers from a Different Shore: A History of Asian Americans* (1989) and *Iron Cages: Race and Culture in 19th Century America* (1979/2000). The Editors of *The Nation* magazine asked each author to comment on California's approval of Proposition 209, a proposition that eliminates affirmative action in the selection of students for the state's public colleges. The authors' comments appeared in *The Nation* on October 5, 1998.

1   With the implementation this year of voter-approved Proposition 209, affirmative action in California public university system passed into history. As predicted by opponents, the measure was followed by a drop-off in minority admissions. How should progressives respond to the new situation? Following are two provocative and differing views. —The Editors

Gregory Rodriguez

2   The recent news that the University of California admitted fewer African-American and Latino students into this fall's freshman class than it had in 1997 provoked a wave of alarmist headlines and editorials that mirrored the worst fears of opponents of the victorious Proposition 209, passed two years ago. Prop 209, which prohibits public universities from considering race in their admissions decisions, had now borne its first fruit, and its opponents were quick to pounce on admissions data to declare that California had indeed regressed to the era of separate and unequal.

3   On *The NewsHour With Jim Lehrer,* California State Assembly Speaker Antonio Villaraigosa said he thought Prop 209 was "going to close the door of opportunity on children of California." Meanwhile, a lawyer for the NAACP publicly warned of the return of "race-exclusive" campuses.

4   National news coverage focused on the precipitate drop of 57 percent and 36 percent in black and Latino admissions at, respectively, UCLA and UC Berkeley—the two flagship campuses of the system. "Acceptance of Blacks, Latinos to UC Plunges," screamed a front-page headline in the *Los Angeles Times.* "Proposition 209 Shuts the Door" read a lead editorial in the *New York Times.* But there's been a misreading of the numbers. The elitist and narrow focus fixation on UC's two flagship campuses obscured the far less dramatic drop in minority admissions to the entire eight-campus system. When you look at numbers for the entire system, you find that the UC campuses admitted only 18 percent fewer black students and only 7 percent fewer Latinos.

5   Let's be clear. Even these reduced numbers are nothing to cheer about. On the other hand, they hardly amount to racial exclusion. Indeed, to put these statistics in context, the University of California system, with a total undergraduate enrollment of about 129,000, admitted a total of 294 fewer black and 392 fewer Latino undergraduates this year as compared with last.

6   It's lamentable that even this small number of minority students is being excluded. But the UC system has always been about exclusion—even in the heyday of affirmative action. The top level of California's public higher education system, UC has always been the destination for only a very select group of students. On average, fewer than a quarter of California students in four-year colleges attend the University of California. In 1995, before Prop 209, nearly twice as many undergraduates were enrolled in the less-celebrated California State University system, and many more attended private four-year colleges.

7   Despite the outcry, post-209 admissions data don't highlight gross racial inequity at the University of California. If anything, the data reveal how traditional selectivity

has evolved into an exclusionary elitism at the system's flagship campuses. No matter what one's background, the odds of being admitted to UC Berkeley these days are pretty slim. Fully 21,500 of the 30,000 applicants this year were rejected. Almost a third of these "rejects" had unblemished, straight-A 4.0 grade-point averages. Consider this: In 1996, before implementation of Prop 209, even students with GPAs between 3.0 and 3.99 and SATs between 1200 and 1390 had only a 33 percent chance of getting into Berkeley.

8   Moreover, the students with the highest rate of acceptance are not white, but Asian-American. While only 15 percent of California's public high school graduates, Asian-American students made up 37 percent of UC's 129,000 undergraduates and 41 percent of the Berkeley campus last year. Twenty-eight percent of all students admitted to the UC system this year were Asian-American.

9   Another figure that got lost in the post-209 debate is that the number of self-identified white students admitted to UC this year fell 9 percent. Another is that the percentage (14.5) of students who declined to state their ethnicity or race was nearly triple last year's rate. In other words, statistical comparisons between the two years are rendered problematic by the 8,814 rebellious applicants who opted out of the racial head count.

10   Affirmative action at the University of California was long a cosmetic program that obscured the system's low minority retention rates and the deterioration and deeper inequities in the state's primary education system—the principal UC "feeder" schools. Post-209 admissions numbers appear to indicate that the disparities exist not so much along racial but rather class lines. Funding varies greatly from school district to district. Urban schools are falling apart. Largely middle-class districts have many more of the honors courses that give high schoolers the extra boost in their GPA necessary for UC applications.

11   This fall, concerned students and faculty will be spearheading a movement for a proposed ballot initiative to reverse Proposition 209 as far as it applies to higher education. They should also be talking about building more UC campuses—campuses that could accommodate not only the few hundred black and Latino students who were rejected this year but also the nearly 16,000 Californians of all backgrounds who are being turned away by increasingly elitist academic barriers.

Ronald Takaki

1   I no longer wish to say "No to Prop 209." The time has come to be proactive.

2   Support for affirmative action is substantial. A December 1997 poll by the *New York Times* showed that a majority of Americans want to retain or mend affirmative action, not abolish it. California's Prop 209 did not present the issue clearly or honestly. Purposely avoiding the term "affirmative action," this initiative described the policy as "preferential treatment." Its supporters also misled the voters when they promoted it as the California "Civil Rights" Initiative. Furthermore, they racialized affirmative action, covering over the fact that the primary beneficiaries of these programs have been women.

3   The people of California are entitled to have another opportunity to vote on the issue of affirmative action. Here is a suggested draft of the "California Equality Initiative" for the 2000 election: "In order to act affirmatively in promoting equality of opportunity, it shall be lawful for the state to consider race, gender or socioeconomic

class disadvantage in the selection of qualified individuals for university admission, employment and contracting. This law does not permit the use of quotas, but does allow the use of considerations based on the above three categories."

4   There are good reasons why pursuing this proposition is necessary and timely.

5   1. CEI's signature-gathering campaign would stir minority voter registration in California, where minorities are rapidly becoming the majority.

6   2. CEI would provoke useful dialogues on why we need affirmative action in the university. The current devastating drop in black and Latino admissions at Berkeley and UCLA is not morally acceptable in a nation "dedicated" to the principle of equality. The highlighting of the overall low decline of black and Latino admissions for the "entire" UC system only hides the creation of a two-tier university with preponderantly Asian and white student bodies (90 percent) at the two flagship campuses. This exclusivity is not politically acceptable in a state where blacks and Latinos together total nearly 40 percent of the population.

7   3. CEI would compel a critical examination of the existing admissions system and expose policies that produce inequality.

Questions for Reading and Analysis

Gregory Rodriguez

1. Rodriguez devotes most of his first three paragraphs to presenting responses to the changes in minority enrollments in the UC system as a result of California's rejection of race as a factor in admissions policies. Why does he do this? What does he seek to accomplish?

2. What is Rodriguez's reaction to all the news coverage? How should we understand the changes in minority enrollment?

3. What should we understand about the UC system in general and UC–Berkeley in particular?

4. Which race has the highest rate of acceptance into the UC system?

5. What is also happening that affects our understanding of the breakdown of UC's student body by race?

6. Instead of affirmative action, what does Rodriguez want to see? What is the real problem, in his view? What solutions does he state or imply?

Ronald Takaki

1. How does Takaki justify a second vote on affirmative action for Californians? What would he call his recommended new proposition?

2. State the idea of Takaki's proposition in your own words.

3. What are the author's three reasons in support of a new proposition?

Questions for Discussion and Response

1. These writers have responded differently to the California proposition, not just in their views but in their writing styles. How would you describe the style and tone of each piece?

2. Examine the writers' uses of statistics. How does Rodriguez present numbers to support his position that the rejection of affirmative action has not resulted in a significant loss of black and Latino students? What is Takaki's key statistic to support his position?

3. How does Takaki specifically rebut a point made by Rodriguez? Which writer has the better argument on this point? Why?

4. Can you find any common ground in these two arguments? What do the writers agree on? Do you agree with their common views? Why or why not?

5. How have these writers influenced your thinking on affirmative action in college admissions?

X-Percent Plans

Shelby Steele

Holding a Ph.D. from the University of Utah, Shelby Steele (b. 1947) has been a professor of English and is a research fellow at Stanford University's Hoover Institution. He has written many essays on race, some of which have been collected in his book *The Content of Our Character* (1990). His latest book is *A Dream Deferred: The Second Betrayal of Black Freedom in America* (1998). "X-Percent Plans" was published in the *National Review* on February 7, 2000.

1   We are a society exhausted and polarized by the affirmative-action impasse. So it was not surprising to see excitement over Florida governor Jeb Bush's new best-of-both-worlds plan to have diversity in Florida's state universities without racial preferences. In place of the usual preferences, Bush proposes to make the top 20 percent of graduates in each Florida high school eligible for university admission. This, he argues, may bring in even more minorities than the current regime of preferences. In Texas, where racial preferences were eliminated by court decision, the University of Texas already claims some success with a 10 percent plan implemented last year. In California, despite a system-wide increase in minority enrollments after Proposition 209 ended preferences in that state, the University of California still hopes an upcoming 4 percent plan will bring more minorities into its two most selective campuses, Berkeley and UCLA. So, do "X-percent" plans, with their promise of minority inclusion without racial preferences, offer the longed-for relief from our withering affirmative-action debate?

2   Sadly, I think not. Some problems with these plans are immediately obvious. Under racial preferences, lower academic standards were effectively isolated to minorities, so that standards elsewhere were not much affected. But X-percent plans spread

lowered standards far past the minority track where low grade-point averages and high dropout rates have long been tolerated. These plans lower the academic norm of the entire student body so that schools must come down in standards simply to meet their students. The University of Texas has already had to come up with remedial classes for premed students with SAT scores as much as 200 points below the university average. When competitive admissions give way to guaranteed percentages, great universities—as the famous decline of CCNY after open enrollments makes clear—slide into mediocrity. Good faculty go elsewhere. Research money follows. Graduates become less competitive. Funding declines.

3   This diminishes precisely the first-rate state universities that have historically offered superb educations to hardworking students from modest backgrounds. And, over time, these plans will be yet another pressure to relegate equality to the public sector and excellence to the private sector. This could extend to universities the sort of class divide and white flight that has already taken hold in K–12 education. Unencumbered by a percent requirement, private universities and colleges could simply continue to maintain competitive admissions for whites and Asians by targeting only blacks and Hispanics for lowered standards. This capacity to isolate (or seem to isolate) academic mediocrity strictly to a minority track would give even second- and third-tier private institutions a great advantage over their public competitors.

4   All of this raises a timeless question: Must equality always come at the expense of excellence? My answer is no. I believe it is quite possible to have racial equality without destroying our public institutions. Moreover, this can be an equality not just of rights but also of performance levels. This does not happen now because we have pursued equality in education more by engineering unequals into institutions than by insisting on their development to parity with others. We have conceived of equality as mere "inclusion" rather than as an equality of skills between the races.

5   And this engineering works by one all-important mechanism: a tolerance for levels of academic mediocrity in blacks and Hispanics that are rarely tolerated in whites and Asians. The racial preference is simply a willingness to tolerate more mediocrity in some races than in others. Thus the engineering method can relegate many minority students to an academic limbo in which there are neither serious expectations nor serious consequences. And in this limbo there is no clear link between one's skill development and one's advancement. One's presence on campus is tied at least as much to a racial politics as to one's own efforts. Which does one do: develop skills or hone a politicized racial identity?

6   Conversely, a developmental model—in which minorities are asked to become competitive with others—restores the natural incentives of life. Excellence becomes the mechanism of inclusion and academic weakness the reason for exclusion. In this model, disadvantage is not exculpatory; it is a prod to excellence. Where this model prevails—sports, music, entertainment—blacks thrive.

7   So why do we keep trying to engineer rather than asking for development? Because American institutions and their largely white leaders lack the moral authority to insist on true excellence from blacks in the way that they insist on it from whites and Asian-Americans. These institutions and leaders must seek racial moral authority—must prove the negative, that they are not racist—simply to function in a society greatly shamed by its racist history.

⁸   The problem is that this moral authority invariably comes at the expense of minority development. And this, I believe, is the single greatest problem in American racial reform.

⁹   This profound neediness determines all, and it drives the society over and over again into engineering and away from the slower but effective struggle of development. Affirmative action and X-percent plans may not close skills gaps between the races and may injure our best institutions, but they display that posture of repentance that moral authority requires. Because this problem of moral authority affects all whites, it is distinctly nonpartisan. If Democrats engineer with affirmative action, many Republicans now want to engineer with X-percent plans. The need for racial moral authority is so absolute and urgent for white men on both sides of the political divide that they simply cannot risk a developmental approach to equality. Out of the white mouth, development—with all its disproportionate yet necessary demands on former victims—plays as mean and victim-blaming. Neither Gore, Bradley, Bush, nor McCain can ask minorities for the sacrifices that parity with other groups demands. All four are engineers. Even when they support development in earlier grades—as G. W. Bush does—they favor college admissions programs that tolerate the very mediocrity that keeps minorities from becoming truly equal.

¹⁰   They will likely justify this by saying that minority disadvantages are exculpatory. The disadvantage explains the weakness and therefore the weakness should be tolerated. But of course, in the long run, reality does not tolerate weakness even when it is caused by a legacy of slavery and segregation. And here is the nub of the problem. Just at the moment when this truth—made clear by centuries of black suffering—might be allowed to become a powerful motivation to excellence in black life, it is muted by white institutions and leaders who protect blacks from it as a way of asserting their own moral authority.

¹¹   In a free society, inequalities will be overcome primarily by the will of those who suffer them. This truism does not "let society off the hook" so much as point toward reform that asks a lot of the people it tries to help. It is only the obsession with moral authority in those who never suffered inequality that makes this seem harsh.

Questions for Reading and Analysis

1. What are "X-percent" plans designed to accomplish at colleges?

2. What is Steele's view of X-percent plans? Will they bring about the desired result? What would be the consequences of X-percent plans, in the author's view?

3. What kind of "equality," according to Steele, have we produced through racial preferences? What difficult choice has this given to black and Hispanic students?

4. What is the difference between engineering and development models? Why do political and educational leaders keep choosing engineering instead of development?

5. What is Steele's claim? Summarize his argument.

Questions for Discussion and Response

1. Does Steele explain, to your satisfaction, how X-percent plans will lead to low-ered standards at public colleges? (At your state university, what percent of high school graduates are admitted?)

2. Do you agree with Steele that we have been using the engineering model? Do you agree that this model does not produce genuine equality? Why or why not?

3. Evaluate Steele's evidence. Are there some audiences that would be most recep-tive to Steele's argument? Are there some likely to reject his argument?

The Problem of the Color Line

Anna Quindlen

Anna Quindlen (b. 1953) is a syndicated columnist with the *New York Times*. She has published several novels, including *Black and Blue* (1998), and a collection of her columns in *Thinking Out Loud* (1994). The following "Last Word" column of *Newsweek* appeared on March 13, 2000.

1   Here's a riddle: Why was the internationally known Princeton professor stopped for driving too slowly on a street where the speed limit was 25 miles per hour? How come a Maryland state trooper demanded to search the car of a lawyer who graduated from Harvard? And why were an accomplished actor, a Columbia administrator, a grad-uate student and a merchandiser for Donna Karan arrested together in New York al-though none of them had done anything wrong?

2   The answer is elementary: all of the men were black. In some twisted sense, they were the lucky ones. They were only humiliated. Not, like Rodney King, beaten bloody. Not, like Abner Louima, sodomized with a broken broomstick. Not, like Amadou Diallo, killed in a gray blizzard of bullets.

3   The verdict is in. The jury has spoken. The death of Diallo, a hardworking African immigrant, was adjudged a terrible accident, not murder, not manslaughter. Louima's assailant is in jail. Two of the officers who beat King went to prison. There have been commissions, investigations, demonstrations, public reaction, prayer vigils, op-ed pieces, television segments, classroom dialogues. And so Americans ricochet from event to event, speaking of reasonable doubt and prosecutorial competence and ignor-ing the big picture, the real thing, the most important issue in this country that we try not to talk about. That is, race.

4   "The problem of the 20th century is the problem of the color line," summed up W.E.B. Du Bois in 1903. How dispiriting to realize it is the problem of the 21st century as well. "Our truncated public discussions of race suppress the best of who and what we are as a people because they fail to confront the complexity of the issue in a candid and critical manner," wrote Cornel West, that suspiciously slow-moving Princeton profes-sor, in his aptly titled monograph "Race Matters." But in truth there are really no pub-lic discussions of race. There are discussions of affirmative action, and single parent-hood, and, in the wake of human tragedies like the Diallo killing, of police training and procedures. These are discussions designed to cause the least amount of discomfort to the smallest possible number of white people.

⁵   Police officers are just us wearing uniforms. The assumptions they make, the prejudices they carry with them, are the assumptions and prejudices of their roots, their neighborhoods, their society. These are not necessarily the excesses of the egregious bigots, but the ways in which race changes everything, often in subtle or unconscious fashion. It is an astonishing dissonance in a nation allegedly based on equality, that there is a group of our citizens who are assumed, simply by virtue of appearance, to be less. Less trustworthy. Less educated or educable. Less moral. What we need to talk about candidly is something more difficult to apprehend than 41 shots in an apartment-house vestibule. It is the unconscious racial shorthand that shapes assumptions so automatic as to be a series of psychological tics: that the black prep-school kid must be on scholarship, that the black woman with a clutch of kids is careless instead of devoted to the vocation of motherhood. Not the shouts of "nigger" but the conclusions about everything from family background to taste in music, based on color alone, which blunt the acceptance of individuality and originality that is the glory of being human.

⁶   Some of this is easy to see, and to deride. A black electrician gets on the train at night and there is the barely perceptible embrace of purses on the laps of women around him. A black lawyer stands with upraised hand and watches the cabs whiz by. A mall security guard trails the only black customer through a store. When police officers looking for drug dealers in New York threw four professional men in jail—including, ironically, the black actor who played Coalhouse Walker, harassed by bigots in the musical *Ragtime*—they became suspects by virtue of color alone. On the highways, being stopped because of race is so commonplace that there's even a clever name for it: DWB, or "driving while black." Amadou Diallo's mother is asked to accept that the police who shot her son thought his wallet was a gun. I have two teenage sons, and when they roam the streets of New York City, I never assume that they will be arrested for something they did not do, or shot, or killed. Their wallets will be seen as wallets.

⁷   Poll after poll shows a great gap in understanding, between a white America that believes things are ever so much better and a black America that thinks that is delusional. And that gap mirrors a gap more important than numbers, between what many of us believe we believe, and the subtle assumptions that creep into our consciousness, and which we are often unwilling to admit are there. For a long time we blamed this chasm on black men and women. We who are white expected them to teach us what it was like to be them, to make us comfortable, and we complained when they did not. *Why Are All the Black Kids Sitting Together in the Cafeteria?* Beverly Daniel Tatum called her book about the black experience. America is a nation riven by geographic apartheid, with precious few truly intergrated neighborhoods, particularly in the suburbs. The great divide between black and white yawns wide with the distance of ignorance, and the silence of shame.

⁸   So the sophistry of the margins continues, the discussions of the LAPD or the foster-care system or the failure of black leadership. The flagrant bigotries are discussed; the psychology of how we see one another and what that does to us too often is not. The most talkative nation on earth falls silent in the face of the enormity of the failure, of being two nations across a Mason-Dixon line of incomprehension and subtle assumptions. Oscar Wilde once called homosexuality "the love that dare not speak its name." But we speak its name all the time now. Sex. Religion. Politics. We talk about them all. But what race means, in all its manifestations large and small, is too often a whisper, our great unspoken issue.

Questions for Reading and Analysis

1. Examine Quindlen's opening. What does she accomplish in her first three paragraphs?

2. What is America's problem in the twenty-first century? How are we "dealing" with this problem?

3. What evidence for the existence of this problem does Quindlen cite? According to the polls, how do blacks and whites view race relations in the United States?

4. Analyze the author's tone and style. How would you describe her tone? Look especially at word choice, metaphors, and sentence patterns in her concluding paragraph to comment on elements of style.

Questions for Discussion and Response

1. How might Steele use Quindlen's essay as support for his views that whites do not dare to use a developmental model for educational equality?

2. Have you had any direct experience with racial profiling? If so, what was your reaction to the experience?

3. What are some of the causes of racial profiling—not just by police officers but by people like you and me? Where does the stereotyping come from? What leads us to prejudging any group?

4. Do you have any solutions to offer to remove the "color line"?

It's Time We Rejected the Racial Litmus Test

Cecelie Berry

Holding both undergraduate and law degrees from Harvard, Cecelie Berry (b. 1961) is currently a freelance writer whose articles have been published in both newspapers and magazines. She has also been a National Public Radio *Morning Edition* commentator. The following "My Turn" article was published by *Newsweek* on February 7, 2000.

1   I recognize the sassy swivel of the head, the rhythmic teeth sucking and finger snapping. My son Spenser has come home from kindergarten talking like he's black. Never mind that he *is* black; somehow his skin color is no longer adequate to express his racial identity. Sometimes, in diverse schools like the one he attends, black children feel pressure to "act" black. My 8-year-old son Sam asks me to tell Spenser not to use "that phony accent" around his friends. "I'll talk to him," I say with a sigh.

2   "Be yourself" seems insufficient at times like this. I know from my experience with integration that it takes a long time to own your identity. In an all-black elementary school in Cleveland, I carried around a dogeared copy of *A Little Princess* and listened to Bach on my transistor radio. Nobody paid attention. When my family moved to Shaker Heights, an affluent suburb known for its successfully integrated schools, I encountered the war over who was authentically black. I had hoped that when I raised my

own children there wouldn't be any more litmus tests, that a healthy black identity could come in many styles. But the impulse to pigeonhole each other endures.

3   As I considered what to say to Spenser, I recalled my own struggles over my accent. In seventh grade, I was rehearsing a play after school when a group of black girls passed by. "You talk like a honky," their leader said. "You must think you're white." In the corner of my eye, I could see her bright yellow radio, shaped like a tennis ball, swinging like a mace. A phrase I'd found intriguing flashed through my mind: "The best defense is a good offense." I stepped forward and slapped her hard.

4   I was suspended for that fight, but I felt I deserved a medal. My true reward came later, when I heard two girls talking about me in the hallway. "I heard she's an oreo," one said. "Don't let her hear you say that," the other replied, "'cause she'll kick your butt!"

5   I hesitate to tell Spenser to be himself because I know it's not that simple. From integration, I learned that you have to fight for the right to be yourself, and often, your opponents have the same color of skin as you. My sons will discover, as I did, that you can feign a black accent, but your loyalty will continue to be tested as long as you allow it.

6   In high school, I enhanced my reputation as an "oreo" by participating in activities that most black students didn't: advanced-placement classes, the school newspaper and the debate team. Mostly, I enjoyed being different. It put me in a unique position to challenge the casually racist assumptions of my liberal classmates. I remember a question posed by my social-studies teacher, "How many of you grew up addressing your black housekeepers by their first names?" Many students raised their hands. "And how many of you addressed white adults that way?" The hands went down. One girl moaned: "That's not racist. Everybody does that."

7   "We never addressed our housekeeper that way," I said. In the silence that followed, I could feel myself being reassessed. I'd challenged my classmate on the fairness of a privilege she had, like many whites, taken completely for granted. I had defied the unspoken understanding of how blacks in white settings are supposed to be: transparent and accommodating.

8   If black students inflicted upon each other a rigid code of "blackness," liberal whites assumed that the blacks in their midst would not dispute their right-mindedness. Being myself, I found, could be lonely. In high school, I grew weary of walking the tightrope between black and white.

9   By college, I was eating regularly at the controversial "black tables" of Harvard's Freshman Union. I talked black, walked black and dated black men. My boyfriend, an Andover graduate, commented on my transformation by saying that I had never been an oreo; I was really a "closet militant." I laughed at the phrase; it had an element of truth. I had learned that people—black or white—tend to demonize what they don't understand and can't control. So I sometimes hid the anger, ambition and self-confidence that provoked their fear. Integration taught me to have two faces: one that can get along with anybody and one that distrusts everybody.

10   I've seen both sides, now. I've "hung" white and I've "hung" black, and been stereotyped by both groups. I choose integration for my children, not out of idealism, but a pragmatic assessment of what it takes to grow up. When it comes to being yourself—and finding out who that person is—you're on your own. Experimentation is a prerequisite, trying on various accents and dress styles, mandatory. Diversity is the best laboratory for building individuality.

11   I am about to explain this to Spenser, when I see him change, like quicksilver, into someone else. Playfully, he stretches his arm out toward my face, turns his gap-toothed smile in the opposite direction and, in a tone as maddening as it is endearing, he says, "Mom, talk to the hand."

Questions for Reading and Analysis

1. How would you categorize this essay as a "type" of essay? What are the characteristics of this type of essay?

2. What does Berry accomplish by writing about her sons and her own experiences?

3. This essay is also an argument. What is Berry's claim? Where does she state it?

4. What did Berry do in high school that was perceived by some blacks as acting white? What did she do in college to act black?

5. What would she like for her sons?

Questions for Discussion and Response

1. Has your experience in high school or college matched Berry's in any way? Do you think that there is greater acceptance of diversity today? Support your response.

2. Berry writes that she had to hide her ambition and self-confidence. Should any person have to hide these traits, regardless of race or ethnicity? Why would some young people fear these traits in others? Why would whites fear these traits in blacks?

3. What can young people do to encourage accepting diversity and individuality in high school and college?

The Scouts Take Their Stereotypes to Court

John Shelby Spong

The former Episcopal bishop of Newark, New Jersey, the Right Reverend Spong (b. 1931) is the William Belden Nobel lecturer at Harvard University and the author of many books on religion and ethics, including *Beyond Moralism* (2000, with Denise Haines). His article on gay leaders in the Boy Scouts appeared in the *Washington Post* on March 27, 2000, before the Supreme Court ruling that the Scouts could exclude gays from leadership roles.

1   The U.S. Supreme Court is the latest battleground on which the historic prejudice against gay people is being engaged. The contenders are the Boy Scouts of America and James Dale, an ousted Eagle Scout. As happens with all dying prejudices, a smoke screen of rhetoric is being used to cover the issues in this debate. The basic question is whether a citizen of this country can be penalized for what a person "is," when everything he or she has ever "done" has been proper and even laudatory.

2   Prejudice has a long shelf life and an incredibly powerful effect on social mores. Stereotypes, even false ones, die slowly. And strangely, prejudice seems to die most slowly when it is found in religious and patriotic settings. In this case, the Boy Scouts of America uses its affiliation with religious and law-and-order organizations as sustenance for its anti-gay policies. So it is disappointing but not surprising that the issue of justice for gay people is being fought out in this deeply traditional, overtly patriotic, and religiously affiliated organization.

3   Behind the conflict are two mutually incompatible definitions about what it means if someone is gay. One is old and traditional. It has shaped our consciousness for thousands of years. The other is relatively new, arising in recent centuries. The new definition challenges the old one at its very core.

4   The old definition stubbornly holds that homosexuality is a sickness or character flaw, a distortion of God's plan. This definition allows other humans to see homosexuals as "other"—as unnatural, perverted or "queer"—and, as such, to be dangerous to social order, untrustworthy or threatening in some way. Based on this view, many religious bodies righteously proclaim that God shares in their condemnation of homosexual people, quoting biblical texts such as those found in Leviticus 18 and 20 and in Paul's Epistle to the Romans.

5   Some religious organizations holding these views—as well as many that do not—are involved in scouting. The Boy Scouts argue that they officially embrace this same definition—or accommodate those who do—and dismiss outstanding Scout leaders, not because of anything they have done but because they are known to be or have acknowledged being gay. Boy Scouts of America does so without laying claim to an anti-gay agenda or to whatever constitutional protection may grudgingly exist for those who organize to propagate bigotry.

6   A new and radically contrary understanding of homosexuality has arisen slowly but steadily over the past 100 years or so, primarily because of work done in medical and scientific circles, amplified by sociological and anthropological studies. This definition suggests that homosexuality is a normal aspect of the human experience; that it is a "given" in life, not a "chosen"; and that it is more like left handedness, something to which a person awakens, than something that people elect to become. Significant data also establish that homosexuals constitute a stable and consistent minority, present at all times in the human population.

7   In James Dale, we have a classic example of a gay person living out what appears to be an unquestionably moral, responsible and admirable life. And yet there are those who would look past what his life presents and attribute to him an unworthy or even dangerous aspect, in many cases with a sense of full righteousness. In the face of science and of what lives like Dale's indisputably teach, this righteousness sadly is misplaced.

8   No one, certainly not I, would suggest that all sexual behavior is healthy or without risk. Some homosexuals engage in behaviors that are quite destructive. Some heterosexual behavior is violent, unhealthy and life denying. HIV infection, for example, knows no boundaries based on sexual orientation, and in our society, children are far more at risk of being molested by heterosexual men than they are by homosexual persons. Yet no one has ever suggested that heterosexuals might not be proper choices to be school teachers or scoutmasters. Heterosexual misconduct is viewed as an individual deviation

from a collective good. But all homosexual conduct is viewed as inevitably a manifestation of something that is both evil and dangerous to be around.

9   So we have a strange anomaly in this particular court case. An Eagle Scout who has served scouting nobly and well without a single breach of propriety is removed because of who he is, notwithstanding all he has done. Certainly the government may demand that a person not be penalized for who he is when his record contravenes all he is miscast to represent. If the Supreme Court should decide in favor of the Boy Scouts of America in this case it would be symptomatic of the fact that the definitions, stereotypes and prejudices of the past are still operating and that the profound ignorance on which they are based is still encouraged to flourish.

10   One can only hope that the court will not vote to victimize people living today by revitalizing attitudes that are so clearly wrong and should be allowed to die out.

Questions for Reading and Analysis

1. What is Spong's subject? What is his attitude toward the issue? What language in paragraphs 1 and 2 reveal his position?

2. Who are the combatants in the lawsuit? The Supreme Court has ruled since Spong wrote; what was its decision?

3. What are the two definitions of homosexuality that are in conflict?

4. Where does Spong find prejudice lingering?

5. On what bases have views of homosexuality been altered in the minds of many in this century?

6. On what basis is James Dale judged by the Scouts? On what basis does Spong want all people to be judged?

7. Where do you find Spong using a conciliatory approach—noting common ground?

8. How would you describe Spong's tone? What words help to shape his tone?

Questions for Discussion and Response

1. Do you agree with Spong that people should be judged on what they do, how they live, not on who they are? Why or why not?

2. Do you believe that homosexuality is inherently wrong, or do you believe that it is simply a minority sexual orientation? Is your answer to that question consistent with your answer to question 1? If not, do you think that this is a problem in reasoning? Explain.

3. Should Boy Scout troops be denied use of public buildings and campgrounds because of their policy of discrimination? Why or why not?

4. Are you surprised that Spong—who not only has had a religious vocation but is married—is making this argument? Do (or should) his words carry special weight because of his religious vocation? Explain your views.

The Dissension of Species

Lisa Mundy

Lisa Mundy (b. 1960) holds a M.A. degree in English literature from the University of Virginia and is a staff writer and columnist for the *Washington Post*. The following article, employing a time-honored strategy for commenting on human behavior, appeared in the Sunday *Washington Post Magazine* on October 5, 1997.

1   The dogs couldn't call a meeting because, as everyone knew, dogs couldn't have meetings anymore. That is to say, they couldn't have dogs-only meetings. If they had a meeting, they were obliged to admit cats. There was some talk about legislation that would make them accept birds, too, but fortunately nothing had come of that. At least not yet. Even so, some dogs privately grumbled that soon they'd be required to make room for *fish*, and to bring in water and filtration systems and all those expensive things you need to accommodate fishes' special needs.

2   Yet even without the right to have private meetings, word quickly got around. Another dog had been given away, by a neighborhood family. Apparently the family's son had left for college, and both husband and wife worked, and nobody was at home all day, and it seemed cruel to keep a dog in such lonely conditions, and so the family gave the dog away. Now they were talking about getting a cat.

3   Of course. Of course they were, the neighborhood dogs agreed when they found themselves together at fire hydrants and parks and the like, the only places, now, where dogs could have a decent dog-to-dog talk. Of course, the family was thinking about getting a cat. Who wasn't getting a cat? Every darn family had to have its cat! After all, cats didn't care if the family was home; all cats wanted, the whole world knew even if nobody would admit it, was a comfy couch and a plate of tuna. Yes, the dogs agreed, here was new evidence—if evidence was needed—that cats were unfairly favored, and if time permitted, the dogs would keep talking, and inevitably one would remind the others that cats now outnumber dogs in America, and then collectively the dogs would try to figure out when, exactly, the world started to decline for dogs. There was some disagreement on this point. Some dogs believed that the problem was the two-income family, specifically working women, who were no longer home to let the dog in and out, with the result that dogs were seen as too much trouble. So working women were bad; but worse still were leash laws.

4   Yes, the dogs would agree, growling, leash laws must be abolished! Time was when it was a glorious thing to be a dog; time was when, if you were lucky enough to be born a dog, you could run through yards with impunity, poop anywhere, even bite the odd child, and nothing would happen. Dogs would be dogs; everybody knew that; why, time was when dogs regularly killed cats, and it was accepted that this was part of a dog's inevitable nature!

5   Now, that was bad, the dogs admitted. It was bad to kill cats, but the thing is—and here's what lawmakers refuse to believe—dogs *know* that now. No dogs, these days, would kill a cat, even if they sometimes still feel a faint delicious urge to do so. Everybody knows better than to kill cats—dogs may resent cats sometimes, but they don't dislike them—and no normal dog would ever bite a child, good grief, it's common

knowledge that biting children is a crime. So why do you need leash laws? Here you have dogs confined like prisoners, while everywhere you see cats running amok, killing birds, sullying gardens, and heck, the law doesn't stop them, it encourages them! Every now and then, it's true, dogs enjoy a small victory: Some local jurisdiction will get tired of bird-killing and garden-sullying and pass a leash law for cats, and then you have the quiet satisfaction of seeing cats with leashes around their necks, leaping and strangling. Or better yet, some cat will try to enroll, disastrously, in obedience class, proving that all the laws in the world can't help cats when it comes to real competition; and dogs, if they could write, would pen triumphant editorials about how this shows the bankruptcy of special treatment for cats.

6   Well, maybe not all dogs. Because sometimes in these conversations—which were just conversations, mind you, just venting sessions—a progressive-minded dog, usually a small dog with a nervous bark, would get up the courage to point out that there were, in fact, bad things about the old unfettered days, and that those things weren't just dead cats—there were dead dogs, too. In the days before leash laws, many was the owner who came out to fetch the paper only to find his dog's stiff body by the side of the road. These days, the small dog would point out, pets in general tend to be safer and healthier. The law hasn't benefited just a single species, it has extended its protection to all; old, weak dogs benefit from leash laws, as do—ahem—smaller dogs; and even if owners complain about being over regulated with regard to both dogs and cats (just try to adopt a stray!), most animals are better for it. The small dog would go on and on, pointing out that kittens still don't command the price puppies do, that cats are still more likely to be abandoned or drowned, even suggesting that dogs have much in common with cats—four legs, teeth, a tail—and a mutual enemy—cars—but by then the dogs would have stalked away, and the cats, who were eavesdropping, would have fled, and the standoff between the species would have continued, bitter and sad and unresolved.

Questions for Reading and Analysis

1. What situation has the author created in which the "words" come to us? Whose "words" and "thoughts" are these?

2. What kind of life did dogs used to have? How has their life changed?

3. What law makes them most unhappy? Why do they think they don't need the law?

4. What kind of dog challenges the others in their venting sessions? How does he challenge their complaints? Who has benefited from the new laws?

5. How do these conversations end? Do any animals change their thinking?

6. What kind of story is this? Who is it really about? Can you assign a gender to the dogs? To the cats? On what basis? What might the leash law represent?

7. How would you describe the tone of the piece?

Questions for Discussion and Response

1. How do you read Mundy's fable? What attributes of people does she present? What issues or conflicts or changes is she writing about?

2. Does she see much hope for the "dogs" and "cats" to listen to and understand and get along with one another? Do you share her thinking? If so, why? If not, why not?

3. If you were a wise dog, what would you say during the conversations by the hydrant?

CHAPTER 20

Examining Marriage and Family

Seven articles compose this chapter, providing you with much to learn about, reflect on, and debate over with regard to marriage and family. No topic is more closely tied to all of us than the topic of family, for, as Betty Carter and Joan K. Peters point out, we are all members of a family—for better or for worse. (Those who choose to leave a family circle are, of course, being shaped by their alienation from their family, so "family" still influences much of their lives.)

This chapter's writers look at the incredible changes that the twentieth century has brought to the institutions of marriage and family. Some approach these changes—and their effects on our lives—from a therapeutic perspective; others take a more jocular or satiric approach. Some write from the perspective of research data; others develop their arguments from emotion or a religious persuasion. Some express strongly held views; others seek common ground. All, however, consider the changes of the last 30 years to have a profound influence on our lives, an influence that not all are recognizing or considering when trying to make sense of their overly busy, stressful, or disturbing days.

Reflecting on the following questions before you read will enrich your reading of this chapter.

1. Do you have a position on gay marriage? If so, what is it, and what is its source?
2. Do you think that you have anything to learn from arguments presenting opposing views on gay marriage? Why or why not?
3. Do you have a position on abortion rights? If so, what is it, and what is its source? Do you believe that there is any common ground to explore on this issue?
4. Do you expect to have a career? To have a spouse and children? Should society support both men and women having these choices? If so, how?
5. What can the business world, the government, and the community do to enrich family life for all?

Websites Relevant to This Chapter's Topic

Same-Sex Marriage & Domestic Partnerships

http://fullcoverage.yahoo.com/fc/US/same_sex_marriage

This Yahoo! Full Coverage site contains news, opinion, and useful links.

Topics on Abortion

www.nrlc.org/abortion

This page of the National Right to Life Committee's Site provides information, contains an anti-abortion position.

National Abortion and Reproductive Rights Action League

www.naral.org

This site provides current news, legislative updates, and links. NARAL is a pro-choice activist group.

American Psychological Association: Family and Relationships

http://helping.apa.org/family/index.html

This URL takes you directly to the index of articles on marriage and family issues made available on the APA's information-packed website.

Daughters of the Revolution

Patricia Dalton

Patricia Dalton is a clinical psychologist with a practice in Washington, D.C. Her sobering look at some of the consequences of the feminist revolution appeared in the Outlook Section of the *Washington Post* on May 21, 2000.

1   If popular culture both shapes and reflects the way women's lives have changed over the past few decades, it provides a sobering image. While the television programs of 30 years ago like *That Girl* and *The Mary Tyler Moore Show* depicted fairly sanitized versions of the travails of being young, single and female, is there anyone who would rather have the neurotic, date-desperate life of their contemporary counterpart, Ally McBeal? Or, worse still, those of the hardened sexual sophisticates Carrie and friends in HBO's *Sex and the City?*

2   I ask myself that question whenever I see an Ally McBeal in my office, trying to come to grips with the reality of her life. And, like other therapists I know, I have seen too many. An attractive, intelligent woman of 32 came in a few years ago, troubled about the lack of direction in her love life and concerned that she was running out of time. She told me that she had "hooked up" with a lot of guys since she was in high school, even lived with two of them, but nothing had worked out. She had tried everything—new clothes, new haircut, regular trips to the gym. She was convinced that something was wrong—or not quite right—with her.

3   She would be mistaken to think that she has some undiagnosed psychological illness; but she is a fine example of someone who has picked up all the wrong messages from our culture. The sexual revolution of four decades ago was meant to liberate women. Instead, it has left too many of them flailing around with a faulty blueprint for life. I remember an unhappy teenager who told me in all seriousness that her New Year's resolution was not to sleep with anyone until she had known them at least three months. Her definition of restraint reminded me of a letter to the editor I'd seen in *Glamour* magazine, commenting on an article titled, "Men You've Slept With." "At

21," the letter writer said, "I have had 17 partners—too many, I think." Her uncertainty gave me as much pause as the number.

4   On television and in women's magazines, in restaurants and after happy hours, women's lamentations about sex and cynical complaints that men are jerks leave out the other side of the equation: Women today are being led willingly and blindly down the garden path—and some are doing the leading.

5   Many of the women who come to me for therapy have an almost breathtaking lack of awareness of the price they stand to pay for casual sex. And the price they pay can be high indeed. It's as if they need a detailed informed consent form about the risks attached to sexual decision making, just like the ones medical patients sign before agreeing to treatment.

6   Therapists can help a woman examine her upbringing, her relationships with her parents, siblings and peers, and her sense of self. We can help her make decisions about how to handle her problems. But we can't magically restore the hope, optimism and innocence that these world-weary women have lost.

7   It is not by chance that both the sexual revolution and the feminist movement were launched in the '60s, with the development of an effective birth control pill. Women no longer felt they needed to act as sexual gatekeepers. Pregnancy could be prevented, and antibiotics could cure most of the sexually transmitted diseases (STDs) known at the time, which were predominantly bacterial, not viral. Sex was suddenly thought to be free of adverse consequences. "Whatever turns you on" was the vernacular of the day. Women went on to challenge and change many constraints that the fact of being female had imposed on their work and personal lives.

8   I feel very fortunate to have grown up during the '50s and '60s, in time to reap the benefits of many of these developments. I have a family and a career, and both mean a great deal to me. But some of the wholesale changes in behavior that accompanied both the sexual revolution and women's movement have had largely unacknowledged drawbacks.

9   For example, in reaction to the notion that sexual differences can be used to discriminate against women, a countervailing idea was put forth: that the sexual natures of men and women are basically identical. The folly of that way of thinking has been dawning on behavioral experts, as well as the rest of us.

10   Take the two basic realities that shape women's sexual lives in very different ways from men's. First, a woman's child-bearing years are finite, while men have the luxury of time. As women age, their chances of becoming pregnant drop steadily, while the possibility of multiple births, congenital defects and complications rises. While male sperm counts drop with advancing age, men can and do father children well into advanced age. (Whether this is desirable is another question.)

11   Second, there is the social convention, found all over the world, that men seek mates the same age or younger, while women mate with men close to their age or older. (There are exceptions to this pattern—Bill and Ernestine Bradley, and Susan Sarandon and Tim Robbins, for example—but they're a minority.) What this means is that the pool of potential partners increases for men as they age, and shrinks for women.

12   Young women ignore these realities at their peril. Those women who have embraced both word and deed of the sexual revolution can find that the years of fertility pass pretty quickly. There are women who have sex with no thought to commitment;

others entertain a hope of commitment that may or may not pan out. I would be hard-pressed to say which one costs more.

13   One 31-year-old female patient, who is having trouble extricating herself from a relationship, recently came to this clear-eyed conclusion: "I figured it out. I've been acting like a wife, and he's been acting like a boyfriend." A woman in her late thirties whom I once saw in therapy was involved in a 10-year affair with a married man with children who ultimately decided to stay with his wife. He was vaguely, and I do mean vaguely, apologetic; she was distraught—and childless. Then she had to face the terrible truth that she had not just him but also herself to blame.

14   Most young adults know that casual sex is associated with STDs, the list of which keeps growing, and includes AIDS. But their ignorance about the specific risks is alarming. I've seen female patients who do not know that male-to-female transmission of HIV is far more common than female-to-male transmission; that hepatitis B and C have been linked to liver cancer; or that certain strains of human papilloma virus, which causes genital warts, have recently been associated with cervical cancer in women as young as their early twenties.

15   Some years ago, when I described the deleterious effects STDs can have on women's fertility to a group of seniors at an all-girls' high school, you could have heard a pin drop. They did not know about chlamydia, a symptomless disease that has been found so frequently in inner-city adolescent girls that the Centers for Disease Control now recommends yearly testing of this population. They did not know that, like gonorrhea, it can cause scarring of the fallopian tubes, which can seriously jeopardize fertility.

16   If one of the consequences of casual sex is cohabitation, recent research on that custom is not encouraging, either. Cohabitation is associated with more cheating and physical abuse than marriages, and couples who have cohabited appear to have a higher divorce rate when they do marry. A large, methodologically sound survey detailed in the 1994 book *Sex in America* reported that couples who knew each other longer before having sex were more likely to get married than those who reported short intervals.

17   Then there are the emotional costs of breaking up over and over, which are hard to calculate. If "You've Lost That Loving Feeling" by the Righteous Brothers is the classic male lament, then "I Can't Make You Love Me" by Bonnie Raitt is the female counterpart. I am convinced that break-ups are much harder when unmarried couples have had sex to bring them closer. That's what sex is supposed to do, after all, in evolutionary terms: promote pair bonding and thereby provide a secure environment for raising offspring.

18   And if there is a disease of our time, it's got to be loneliness. According to the late social historian Christopher Lasch, the '80s version was narcissism, and maybe the sex-as-sport I've described has been its natural consequence. Psychiatrist Frank Pittman describes the curious phenomenon of adults who behave like juveniles in his book *Grow Up!* If marriage has always been one rite of passage to adulthood, sex without commitment makes it possible to put off that step. (I've heard countless patients comment with apparent amazement that when their parents were their age, they had two or three kids and a mortgage.) People are marrying considerably later than in previous generations, and they are also having fewer children. In addition, the divorce rate, which doubled between 1966 and 1978 and then leveled off to something over 50 percent, leaves more women alone, since men are much more likely to remarry after divorce. A higher percentage of adults live alone today than ever before in the history of the United States.

19 Finally, there is the emotional price that many children of these divorced adults pay. That was brought home to me once again while watching the film *Reality Bites*, about a group of so-called Generation Xers who are avoiding commitment in a variety of creative, unsatisfying ways. There is a segment in which each main character flashes on the screen and says, "My parents divorced when I was _" (he or she fills in the age). I've often seen the aimlessness and the inability to take hold of life that the film was depicting. Some of my patients have real difficulty trusting the people they date. They are afraid of the future, having seen so much go wrong in their own families.

20 I don't want to imply that the sexual revolution has had only unfortunate results. It was fueled by understandably serious discontent with the sexual strait-jacketing of previous times. Many who filtered these ideas through some common sense and moderation have benefited from a more relaxed feeling about sex. There are probably more marriages today in which sex is an important part of the communication between partners than in more repressive times. Sex therapists do report fewer cases of severe sexual inhibition than they used to, and that is good news. On the other hand, they see more cases of problems of sexual desire, in both men and women, gay and straight, which have coincided with the sex-saturation of our culture.

21 On particularly bad days at the office when the human toll of the sexual revolution is especially apparent, I've thought of it as a sexual devolution. Yes, it has made us more familiar and comfortable with our animal nature, but have we put too much faith in our hormones and not enough on our frontal cortex? After all, our higher brain functions are what distinguish us from the rest of the animal kingdom. As Katharine Hepburn said dryly to Humphrey Bogart in *The African Queen:* "Nature, Mr. Allnut, is what we are put into this world to rise above."

Questions for Reading and Analysis

1. How does Dalton introduce her topic? How does she cleverly move from her opening paragraph into her subject?
2. What, in Dalton's view, has been the actual, not intended, result, for women, of the sexual revolution?
3. How does Dalton characterize many of today's women?
4. How are women's sexual lives significantly different from men's?
5. What do many young women today not understand about the health risks of sex?
6. What do the statistics reveal about cohabitation?
7. What are some of the emotional consequences of relationships that end?
8. What can be good about the sexual revolution? How can women help themselves to find the benefits rather than the disadvantages?

Questions for Discussion and Response

1. What is the most surprising information—for you—in this essay? Why?

2. Have you experienced any of the emotional consequences described by Dalton? If so, what are your thoughts on this experience?

3. How does Dalton seek to avoid the charge of overstating the problem, of being too negative? Does she succeed? Explain your response.

4. Dalton offers some general solutions to the problem. What additional solutions do you have to offer?

Will Women Still Need Men?

Barbara Ehrenreich

Barbara Ehrenreich (b. 1940), whose focus is women's studies and social commentary, publishes frequently in popular magazines and is the author of several books, the most recent a book on poverty to be published in 2001. Other books include *Blood Rites: Origins and History of the Passions of War* (1997) and *Talking about a Revolution* (1998). Her provocative essay on relations between the sexes in the future was published in *Time* on February 21, 2000.

1   This could be the century when the sexes go their separate ways. Sure, we've hung in there together for about a thousand millenniums so far—through hunting-gathering, agriculture and heavy industry—but what choice did we have? For most of human existence, if you want to make a living, raise children or even have a roaring good time now and then, you had to get the cooperation of the other sex.

2   What's new about the future, and potentially more challenging to our species than Martian colonization or silicon brain implants, is that the partnership between the sexes is becoming entirely voluntary. We can decide to stick together—or we can finally say, "Sayonara, other sex!" For the first time in human history and prehistory combined, the choice will be ours.

3   I predict three possible scenarios, starting with the Big Divorce. Somewhere around 2025, people will pick a gender equivalent of the Mason-Dixon Line and sort themselves out accordingly. In Guy Land the men will be free to spend their evenings staging belching contests and watching old Howard Stern tapes. In Gal Land the women will all be fat and happy, and no one will bother to shave her legs. Aside from a few initial border clashes, the separation will for the most part be amicable. At least the "battle of the sexes," insofar as anyone can remember it, will be removed from the kitchens and bedrooms of America and into the U.N.

4   And why not? If the monosexual way of life were counter to human nature, men wouldn't have spent so much of the past millennium dodging women by enlisting in armies, monasteries and all-male guilds and professions. Up until the past half-century, women only fantasized about their version of the same: a utopia like the one described by 19th century feminist Charlotte Perkins Gilman, where women would lead placidly sexless lives and reproduce by parthenogenesis. But a real separation began to look feasible about 50 years ago. With the invention of TV dinners and drip-dry shirts, for the first time the average man became capable of feeding and dressing himself. Sensing their increasing dispensability on the home front, and tired of picking up dropped socks, women rushed into the work force. They haven't achieved full economic independence

by any means (women still earn only 75% of what men do), but more and more of them are realizing that ancient female dream—a room, or better yet, a condo of their own.

5   The truly species-shaking change is coming from the new technologies of reproduction. Up until now, if you wanted to reproduce, you not only had to fraternize with a member of the other sex for at least a few minutes, but you also ran a 50% risk that any resulting baby would turn out be a member of the foreign sex. No more. Thanks to in vitro fertilization, we can have babies without having sex. And with the latest techniques of sex selection, we can have babies of whatever sex we want.

6   Obviously women, with their built-in baby incubators, will have the advantage in a monosexual future. They just have to pack up a good supply of frozen semen, a truckload of turkey basters and go their own way. But men will be catching up. For one thing, until now, frozen-and-thawed ova have been tricky to fertilize because their outer membrane gets too hard. But a new technique called intracytoplasmic sperm injection makes frozen ova fully fertilizable, and so now Guy Land can have its ovum banks. As for the incubation problem, a few years ago feminist writer Gena Corea offered the seemingly paranoid suggestion that men might eventually keep just a few women around in "reproductive brothels," gestating on demand. A guy will pick an ovum for attractive qualities like smart, tall and allergy-free, then have it inserted into some faceless surrogate mother employed as a reproductive slave.

7   What about sex, though, meaning the experience, not the category? Chances are, we will be having sex with machines, mostly computers. Even today you can buy interactive CD-ROMS like Virtual Valerie, and there's talk of full-body, virtual-reality sex in which the pleasure seeker wears a specially fitted suit—very specially fitted—allowing for tactile as well as audiovisual sensation. If that sounds farfetched, consider the fact that cyber-innovation is currently in the hands of social skills–challenged geeks who couldn't hope to get a date without flashing their Internet stock options.

8   Still, there's a reason why the Big Divorce scenario isn't likely to work out, even by Y3K: we love each other, we males and females—madly, sporadically, intermittently, to be sure—but at least enough to keep us pair bonding furiously, even when there's no obvious hardheaded reason to do so. Hence, despite predictions of the imminent "breakdown of the family," the divorce rate leveled off in the 1990s, and the average couple is still hopeful or deluded enough to invest about $20,000 in their first wedding. True, fewer people are marrying: 88% of Americans have married at least once, down from 94% in 1988. But the difference is largely made up by couples who set up housekeeping without the blessing of the state. And an astounding 16% of the population has been married three times—which shows a remarkable commitment to, if nothing else, the institution of marriage.

9   The question for the new century is, Do we love each other *enough*—enough, that is, to sustain the old pair-bonded way of life? Many experts see the glass half empty: cohabitation may be replacing marriage, but it's even less likely to last. Hearts are routinely broken and children's lives disrupted as we churn, ever starry-eyed, from one relationship to the next. Even liberal icons like Hillary Rodham Clinton and Harvard Afro-American studies professor Cornel West have been heard muttering about the need to limit the ease and accessibility of divorce.

10   Hence, perhaps, Scenario B: seeing that the old economic and biological pressures to marry don't work anymore, people will decide to replace them with new forms of coercion. Divorce will be outlawed, along with abortion and possibly contraception.

Extramarital hanky-panky will be punishable with shunning or, in the more hard-line jurisdictions, stoning. There will still be sex, and probably plenty of it inside marriage, thanks to what will be known as Chemically Assisted Monogamy: Viagra for men and Viagra-like drugs for women, such as apomorphine and Estratest (both are being tested right now), to reignite the spark long after familiarity has threatened to extinguish it. Naturally, prescriptions will be available only upon presentation of a valid marriage license.

11   It couldn't happen here, even in a thousand years? Already, a growing "marriage movement," including groups like the Promise Keepers, is working to make divorce lawyers as rare as elevator operators. Since 1997, Louisiana and Arizona have been offering ultratight "covenant marriages," which can be dissolved only in the case of infidelity, abuse or felony conviction, and similar measures have been introduced in 17 other states. As for the age-old problem of premarital fooling around, some extremely conservative Christian activists have launched a movement to halt the dangerous practice of dating and replace it with parent-supervised betrothals leading swiftly and ineluctably to the altar.

12   But Scenario B has a lot going against it too. The 1988 impeachment fiasco showed just how hard it will be to restigmatize extramarital sex. Sure, we think adultery is a bad thing, just not bad enough to disqualify anyone from ruling the world. Meanwhile, there have been few takers for covenant marriages, showing that most people like to keep their options open. Tulane University sociologist Laura Sanchez speculates that the ultimate effect of covenant marriages may be to open up the subversive possibility of diversifying the institution of marriage—with different types for different folks, including, perhaps someday, even gay folks.

13   Which brings us to the third big scenario. This is the diversity option, arising from the realization that the one-size-fits-all model of marriage may have been one of the biggest sources of tension between the sexes all along—based as it is on the wildly unrealistic expectation that a single spouse can meet one's needs for a lover, friend, co-parent, financial partner, reliably, 24-7. Instead there will be renewable marriages, which get re-evaluated every five to seven years, after which they can be revised, re-celebrated or dissolved with no, or at least fewer, hard feelings. There will be unions between people who don't live together full-time but do want to share a home base. And of course there will always be plenty of people who live together but don't want to make a big deal out of it. Already, thanks to the gay-rights movement, more than 600 corporations and other employers offer domestic-partner benefits, a 60-fold increase since 1990.

14   And the children? The real paradigm shift will come when we stop trying to base our entire society on the wavering sexual connection between individuals. Romantic love ebbs and surges unaccountably; it's the bond between parents and children that has to remain rocklike year after year. Putting children first would mean that adults would make a contract—not to live together or sleep together but to take joint responsibility for a child or an elderly adult. Some of these arrangements will look very much like today's marriages, with a heterosexual couple undertaking the care of their biological children. Others will look like nothing we've seen before, at least not in suburban America, especially since there's no natural limit on the number of contracting caretakers. A group of people—male, female, gay, straight—will unite in their responsibility for the children they bear or acquire through the local Artificial Reproduction Center.

Heather may routinely have two mommies, or at least a whole bunch of resident aunts—which is, of course, more or less how things have been for eons in such distinctly unbohemian settings as the tribal village.

15 So how will things play out this century and beyond? Just so you will be prepared, here's my timeline:

16 Between 2000 and 2339: geographical diversity prevails. The Southeast and a large swath of the Rockies will go for Scenario B (early marriage, no divorce). Oregon, California and New York will offer renewable marriages, and a few states will go mono-sexual, as in Scenario A. But because of the 1996 Defense of Marriage Act, each state is entitled to recognize only the kinds of "marriages" it approves of, so you will need a "marriage visa" to travel across the country, at least if you intend to share a motel room.

17 Between 2340 and 2387: NATO will be forced to intervene in the Custody Wars that break out between the Polygamous Republic of Utah and the Free Love Zone of the Central Southwest. A huge refugee crisis will develop when singles are ethnically cleansed from the Christian Nation of Idaho. Florida will be partitioned into divorce-free and marriage-free zones.

18 In 2786: the new President's Inauguration will be attended by all five members of the mixed-sex, multiracial commune that raised her. She will establish sizable tax reductions for couples or groups of any size that create stable households for their children and other dependents. Peace will break out.

19 And in 2999: a scholar of ancient history will discover these words penned by a gay writer named Fenton Johnson back in 1996: "The mystery of love and life and death is really grander and more glorious than human beings can grasp, much less legislate." He will put this sentence onto a bumper sticker. The message will spread. We will realize that the sexes can't live without each other, but neither can they be joined at the hip. We will grow up.

Questions for Reading and Analysis

1. What is Ehrenreich's subject? What is her claim? Where is it stated?

2. What changes about 50 years ago began to make a separation of the sexes a possibility? What current technologies will really let men and women go their separate ways?

3. In spite of new technologies, what may keep men and women together? What evidence does the author provide?

4. What is Ehrenreich's "Scenario B"? What evidence suggests that this plan will not materialize?

5. What is the third possibility? What is critical to this scenario?

6. Summarize the author's "timeline" for change. How serious is she regarding this timeline? (Examine her word choice and think about her tone.)

Questions for Discussion and Response

1. What, for you, is the most startling idea in Ehrenreich's scenarios for the next few centuries? Why? Be prepared to discuss your choice with classmates.

2. What, for you, is the most startling new fact or example (including new technologies) mentioned in this essay? Why? Be prepared to discuss your choice with classmates.

3. Which scenario is most appealing to you? Which most unappealing? Why?

4. The author hopes that eventually we will "grow up." What elements are a part of her idea of growing up with regard to marriage/partnerships/children? Do you agree with her views of growing up? If not, how would you define growing up with regard to gender issues?

Will Gay Marriage Be Legal?

John Cloud

John Cloud (b. 1970) is a graduate of Harvard University and a Rhodes Scholar. He is currently a staff writer at *Time* magazine, which published his article on February 2, 2000.

1   Gay marriage is already legal in some sense: Michael and I recently bought a set of All-Clad pans together. We watch *The Sopranos* and split the HBO bill every month. We shave with the same razor.

2   Slightly more important, we both work for companies that offer health insurance to their workers' sweethearts, whether legally married or not. If we wanted them to, our families would come to one of those precious pseudo-weddings you've seen on sit-coms. Ours would involve tuna tartare and Madonna remixes, followed by a trip downtown to register with New York City as "domestic partners."

3   In fact, Michael and I can't really marry—not in New York and not even in Norway or Hawaii, which have thought about allowing same-sex marriages in recent years but ultimately decided not to. I shouldn't trivialize the perks we miss: law books at all levels contain thousands of statutes pertaining to spouses. If I were struck by a drunk driver, for instance, Michael wouldn't have the legal standing to sue the bastard or help decide on my medical treatment.

4   Will he in 2025? Almost certainly. In fact, within a decade, gay couples—at least those who live in progressive states—will probably enjoy all the rights, responsibilities and daily frustrations of married life, even if they don't have a marriage license. In Vermont the state supreme court has already ruled that the state must start providing the same benefits to all couples, gay and straight, except the title of marriage itself. Vermont legislators now have the option of granting same-sex couples the M word too. If they do—and it doesn't seem likely—they will ignite a federal case over whether other states have to honor Vermont's licenses. (Congress has said states can ignore others' gay marriages, but that law hasn't been tested in court.)

5   Ultimately, of course, the battle for gay marriage has always been about more than winning the second-driver discount at the Avis counter. In fact, the individual who has done most to push same-sex marriage—a brilliant 43-year-old lawyer-activist named Evan Wolfson—doesn't even have a boyfriend. He and the others who brought the marriage lawsuits of the past decade want nothing less than full social equality, total validation—not just the right to inherit a mother-in-law's Cadillac. As Andrew Sullivan, the (also persistently single) intellectual force behind gay marriage,

has written, "Including homosexuals within marriage would be a means of conferring the highest form of social approval imaginable."

6   In this light, the Vermont decision looks more like *Plessy v. Ferguson*, the 1896 Supreme Court ruling that allowed "separate but equal" facilities for blacks, than *Brown v. Board of Education*, the 1954 decision that finally required meaningful equality. If that analogy stands, it will be another half-century before gay couples can, in all 50 states, stand in the same line for marriage licenses as others.

7   By that time, Michael and I will be in our 80s, too old to stand in line for anything but mashed peas. He and I will have had a "gay marriage," probably one without an official certificate. Tomorrow's gay kids will enjoy simply marriage—without qualifiers.

Questions for Reading and Analysis

1. What can gay partnerships do now?
2. What are they not able to do?
3. What rights will gays have by 2025, in Cloud's view?
4. Why do gays want the opportunity for a legal marriage? What is attached to this official act?
5. Is Cloud simply analyzing social norms and predicting the future? What is his position on gay marriages? How do you know?

Questions for Discussion and Response

1. Do you think that Cloud's predictions are correct about the changes ahead? If you think that he is incorrect, what evidence do you have to challenge his predictions?
2. What are your views on these predictions? Should gay partnerships have health benefits? Adoption rights as a couple? (An individual gay or lesbian person can now adopt a child.) All rights except a legally sanctioned marriage? Legally sanctioned marriage itself? Explain your views.

Gay Marriage, an Oxymoron

Lisa Schiffren

A speech writer for former vice president Dan Quayle, Lisa Schiffren began her career at the *Detroit News*. She now writes on public policy and social issues in popular magazines and newspapers. Her article on gay marriage was published in the *New York Times* on March 23, 1996—before Hawaii decided not to sanction gay marriages.

1   As study after study and victim after victim testify to the social devastation of the sexual revolution, easy divorce, and out-of-wedlock motherhood, marriage is fashionable again. And parenthood has transformed many baby boomers into advocates of bourgeois norms.

2   Indeed, we have come so far that the surprise issue of the political season is whether homosexual "marriage" should be legalized. The Hawaii courts will likely rule that gay marriage is legal, and other states will be required to accept those marriages as valid.

3   Considering what a momentous change this would be—a radical redefinition of society's most fundamental institution—there has been almost no real debate. This is because the premise is unimaginable to many, and the forces of political correctness have descended on the discussion, raising the cost of opposition. But one may feel the same affection for one's homosexual friends and relatives as for any other and be genuinely pleased for the happiness they derive from relationships while opposing gay marriage for principled reasons.

4   "Same-sex marriage" is inherently incompatible with our culture's understanding of the institution. Marriage is essentially a lifelong compact between a man and woman committed to sexual exclusivity and the creation and nurture of offspring. For most Americans, the marital union—as distinguished from other sexual relationships and legal and economic partnerships—is imbued with an aspect of holiness. Though many of us are uncomfortable using religious language to discuss social and political issues, Judeo-Christian morality informs our view of family life.

5   Though it is not polite to mention it, what the Judeo-Christian tradition has to say about homosexual unions could not be clearer. In a diverse, open society such as ours, tolerance of homosexuality is a necessity. But for many, its practice depends on a trick of cognitive dissonance that allows people to believe in the Judeo-Christian moral order while accepting, often with genuine regard, the different lives of homosexual acquaintances. That is why, though homosexuals may believe that they are merely seeking a small expansion of the definition of marriage, the majority of Americans perceive this change as a radical deconstruction of the institution.

6   Some make the conservative argument that making marriage a civil right will bring stability, an end to promiscuity, and a sense of fairness to gay men and women. But they miss the point. Society cares about stability in heterosexual unions because it is critical for raising healthy children and transmitting the values that are the basis of our culture.

7   Whether homosexual relationships endure is of little concern to society. That is also true of most childless marriages, harsh as it is to say. Society has wisely chosen not to differentiate between marriages, because it would require meddling into the motives and desires of everyone who applies for a license.

8   In traditional marriage, the tie that really binds for life is shared responsibility for the children. (A small fraction of gay couples may choose to raise children together, but such children are offspring of one partner and an outside contributor.) What will keep gay marriages together when individuals tire of each other?

9   Similarly, the argument that legal marriage will check promiscuity by gay males raises the question of how a "piece of paper" will do what the threat of AIDS has not. Lesbians seem to have little problem with monogamy or the rest of what constitutes "domestication," despite the absence of official status.

10   Finally, there is the so-called fairness argument. The government gives tax benefits, inheritance rights, and employee benefits only to the married. Again, these financial

benefits exist to help couples raise children. Tax reform is an effective way to remove distinctions among earners.

[11]   If the American people are interested in a radical experiment with same-sex marriages, then subjecting it to the political process is the right route. For a court in Hawaii to assume that it has the power to radically redefine marriage is a stunning abuse of power. To present homosexual marriage as a fait accompli, without national debate, is a serious political error. A society struggling to recover from thirty years of weakened norms and broken families is not likely to respond gently to having an institution central to most people's lives altered.

Questions for Reading and Analysis

1. What is Schiffren's topic? What is her claim? Where is it stated?

2. What is Schiffren's definition of marriage? What is the source of our society's ideas about marriage?

3. What does the Judeo-Christian tradition say about homosexual unions?

4. How does Schiffren organize her argument? Briefly summarize the main points of her argument.

5. If same-sex marriages are to be approved, by what process should this occur, in the author's view?

6. How does the author use conciliatory strategies in her argument? Are they effective?

Questions for Discussion and Response

1. The author asserts that "marriage is fashionable again." Does she provide any evidence to support this assertion? Has the number of marriages in the United States increased in recent years? (How might you obtain such information?)

2. How does the author explain why there has been no debate about same-sex marriages? Does her explanation match your experience? Has the debate of this topic increased since Schiffren wrote in 1996?

3. Schiffren asserts that society does not care about stability in gay relationships, only in marriages with children. Does she offer evidence that this is how most citizens feel? Or are we to believe that she is speaking in a legal sense—the state's interest? Should society—we—care about the stability of all relationships? Why or why not? Since "society's" concern has not kept the divorce rate from being slightly more than 50 percent, is this a meaningful argument? Why or why not?

4. Schiffren also asserts that gay males are promiscuous, presumably more so than both lesbians and heterosexuals. Is there evidence for this assertion? Do Schiffren's unsupported assertions affect the quality of her argument? Why or why not?

Remaking Marriage and Family

Betty Carter and Joan K. Peters

A family therapist and author of academic books and articles and textbooks, Betty Carter (b. 1929) is director of the Family Institute of Westchester in White Plains, New York. She is the author, with Joan Peters (b. 1945)—a freelance journalist and author of the novel *Manny and Rose* (1985)—of *Love, Honor & Negotiate: Making Your Marriage Work* (1996). The following article, an excerpt from *Love, Honor & Negotiate*, initially appeared in the November/December 1996 issue of *Ms.* magazine.

1   When I started my work with couples in the seventies, I assumed that since women now worked and considered themselves the equals of men, we'd solved the gender problems I had struggled with in the early years of my own marriage. In therapy, I treated every marriage as if it were as unique as a snowflake. But as I began to notice the repetition of complaints, I couldn't help but realize that I was caught in a blizzard of sex-role issues that had not gone away.

2   The more I explored couples' "communication" problems, the more I found that one of the main things they can't communicate about is the power to make decisions. The more I questioned younger couples, the more I heard about their constant arguments. The more I questioned them about the content of their arguments, the more I heard about who spends what money, who does what housework and child care, and—if both partners work—whose work comes first. Or else I heard about the backlash from these conflicts in their sex lives—if they still had any. Older couples complained about the emptiness between them or argued bitterly about every detail of their lives. But the more I questioned them, the more I heard from the women about how much they resented their husbands' high-handedness or indifference to family life. The men, on the other hand, were defensively dismissive of these complaints.

3   Finally, I began to see the reason for this pattern—*most American couples backslide into traditional sex roles as soon as their children are born*. Women cut back at work, quit, or play superwoman because they are *automatically* the ones in charge of children. Meanwhile, men toil even more to "be good providers," ending up the bewildered breadwinner. Many are just furious because of what they see as their spouse's incessant complaints. And the divorce rates skyrocket.

4   I saw all this, but I was stymied. There was no way to use traditional family therapy theory to respond to the problems of gender. So, with a few like-minded colleagues—Marianne Walters, Peggy Papp, and Olga Silverstein—in 1977 I cofounded the Women's Project in Family Therapy, where we developed our own techniques. But it meant thinking in an entirely new way for a family systems therapist. To explain the new thinking, though, I should first describe what family systems therapy is.

5   Family systems therapy was developed in the fifties as an improvement on individual therapy. The classic Freudian approach treats the individual in a vacuum, as if a person has an emotional problem within himself or herself. Family systems theorists say that the individual doesn't exist alone emotionally but in dynamic relationship with other family members. This means that emotional problems exist not inside the person who happens to exhibit or experience the problem but among all the family members.

6 Except for rare circumstances, the family is the most powerful emotional system we ever belong to. It shapes and continues to determine the course and outcome of our lives. A three- or four-generation family operates as a finely tuned system with roles and rules for functioning as a unit. For example, if one member behaves "irresponsibly," an "overresponsible" member will step in and pick up the slack; if one person is silent and withdrawn, another is usually the one to talk and engage, and vice versa—the sequences are circular.

7 Everyone in the family maintains problem behavior, such as that of an alcoholic father or depressed mother or runaway son. They don't do this because they want or need to but because their "common sense" responses to the problem are also part of the problem. The wife who empties her husband's bottles of scotch, the husband who suggests his wife go on antidepressants, and the parents who send their runaway son to therapy to "get fixed" are all trying to be helpful. But they're only making the problem worse, partly because these "solutions" imply that the person's symptom is the problem. Instead of looking for the factors in the family system that are producing the person's anxiety or depression, they try to get rid of the symptoms.

8 Most people don't realize the extent to which the marriage and family we create is a product of the family we were raised in, whether we are trying to re-create that original family or do the opposite. Our family relationships—the gears that run the clock, so to speak—are highly patterned and reciprocal. Rules are spoken and unspoken. They are based on our family history, which produces themes, stories, taboos, myths, secrets, heroes, and rebels. This history is passed on, consciously and unconsciously, to the next generation and to all new marriages.

9 That's what we mean when we say that family relationships aren't optional. They're also not equal or fair. You might say that our original family is like a hand of cards dealt by fate. And that our life's task, emotionally, is dealing with this hand.

10 For all these reasons, the family therapist will help patients actively work out problems with their parents on the assumption that, as I always put it, if you can work them out with your parents, you can work them out with anyone. And you'd better, I tell them, because your parents will always play a significant, if silent, part in all your relationships, particularly in your marriage. The more unresolved the problems of the past, the more they influence the present.

11 Even when people flee their "families of origin," as we call them, the impact of the family doesn't end. In fact, it actually increases. Not speaking to family members who caused us difficulty may temporarily relieve the pain of trying to deal with them. But the poison of the cutoff spreads throughout the family as members expend enormous emotional energy taking sides, justifying some people's actions and vilifying others. Every subsequent family event takes place in the shadow of the cutoff, and when the conflict that supposedly caused it is almost forgotten, what remains are families whose members are disconnected from one another and who live with broken hearts or hearts covered with calluses. Worst of all, the legacy suggests to future generations that family members we disagree with should be discarded. This is not a healthy resolution of conflict.

12 The other side of the coin—what we call enslavement or fusion—comes up when family members become overinvolved and entangled in their relationships, taking inappropriate responsibility for one another, wanting peace at any price, insisting on ignoring differences through denial and compromise. There is no "live and let live" in this smothering system.

13   Family therapists normally believe that for a person to have a mature relationship with family members, he or she must be authentically true to self—even in ways that may break the family rules—while still having a meaningful personal connection. Of course, as anyone who has ever tried to achieve this with parents, spouses, and siblings knows, it is very difficult to do. Most of us will spend a lifetime trying to do it. Family therapy just helps us move in that direction.

14   But the family context wasn't enough to explain the gender complaints I was constantly hearing. So I had to discover on my own that family systems therapy—like Freudian therapy—wasn't drawing a large enough picture. Marriages, I realized, were not only two people enmeshed in family structures, they were also families enmeshed in cultural structures—structures that often exert unbearable pressures on these families, making spouses blame each other for what are really social problems.

15   Each family tries to teach its members the "right way" to live in our time and the "right values" to have about things like money, marriage, work, parenting, and sex. A family does this without realizing the degree to which these "truths" are dictated by the family's place in our very stratified culture—for example, their race, gender, ethnicity, social class, or sexual orientation—and how those values play out not only against the family, but also within it.

16   Without an understanding of the impact of family and cultural beliefs, couples are left with the crazy idea that they are inventing themselves and their lives, or that they could, if only their spouses would change. It is this false notion of independence that leads to natural power struggles and, often, divorce.

17   Improved communication is supposed to solve a couple's problems, but in the majority of cases, it cannot. For example, if a woman who works outside the home still does the lion's share of housework and child care, communication can only name the problem or identify the source of the wife's unhappiness. Unless the talk leads to a change in how the couple divide up housework and child care, it won't help at all. Too often, "communication" can become an argument without end and lead to mutual blame and psychological name-calling. With a cultural perspective on their problems, as well as a psychological one, couples can start to evaluate their problems in the context of their families and our culture.

18   American culture intrudes upon the inner sanctum of marriage. On one hand, it has given us new expectations of marriage; on the other, it has failed to allow the new marriage to fulfill these expectations. The American economy requires that most husbands and wives work outside the home but offers little workplace or social support for the two-earner family. And couples have changed—but not enough.

19   That's why I've come to believe in resolutions that combine the personal, social, and political. First, we have to give up the myths that women can't have it all except by doing it all and that men don't have to do it all but can have it all. We seriously have to question the idea that men's careers must never be disturbed and that mothering is different from—and more involving than—fathering.

20   The problem with contemporary marriage is that the lives of men and, especially, women have changed dramatically, radically, in this century, but the rules about marriage have not. Partly because of economics and partly because of the women's movement, women's behavior has changed drastically since the sixties. The vast majority of women are now in the workforce and half of them are providing as much—or more—

of the family's income as their husbands. But men's behavior has changed far less. For personal, social, and economic reasons, they have not accommodated themselves to women's working by participating equally in the home. Although they now "accept" that a woman will work, they also "expect" her to be a homemaker. It is this lag in men's role change (combined with women's ambivalence about insisting on greater change) that results in contradictory wishes that weaken so many marriages.

21   In addition to blaming their husbands, women in this predicament often blame the women's movement for "taking away their 'right' to stay home." Instead of joining with other women to find support and solutions, they join the backlash that paints feminism as the enemy of men and family. Some may end up losing themselves in the excesses of the self-help movement, focusing on their "codependency" or their "inner child," as if these were the real problems in their marriages.

22   Men in these harried marriages also blame women. Instead of helping men to become more involved with the daily emotional and practical lives of their families, the men's movement blames contemporary women for "making them marginal." Spokesmen encourage men to take back their rightful place at the "head" of the family. As my colleague and friend Marianne Walters points out, the men's movement is about "male bonding" against women's "domination," not about developing men's capacities for emotional connection with wives and children and adjusting to equal partnership.

23   The changes women have made by coming into the world of work and politics have been a step up for them, a gain of power. For men, however, family involvement seems like a step down, a loss of power. This standstill reflects our continued valuing of power over connectedness and the continued association of power and money. Yet men have everything to gain by being more emotionally engaged in their lives.

24   While the traditional definition of masculinity is surely being challenged, it still holds sway in most men's lives. And the rules for "man the provider" are still very slippery. Is his wife fully committed to being a coprovider for life, or will she suddenly decide she has to stay home with the children? If his children are a priority for him, will he be penalized at work for taking paternity or family emergency leaves?

25   Men are also often afraid of the intimacy of family life. They are afraid that they don't know how to be intimate, and they're afraid of their own feelings, which they've been taught to suppress. Intimacy and connection have traditionally been the feminine sphere. Recognizing that "feminine" part of himself threatens a man's identity.

26   Unfortunately, avoiding intimacy also means that men cut themselves off from their deepest feelings, from their spouses, and from their children. Men who don't "feel" are as haunted and unhappy as women who aren't autonomous. They might grin and bear it, drink, gamble, have affairs, or become TV zombies, but escape is never satisfying. The demons are there when the high or the numbness wears off.

27   What does finally motivate men to change? Recognizing their own pain. Most men I work with begin to realize how much they suffered because their own fathers were distant and overworked. In their own longing and pain, they find the will to be a different kind of husband and father.

28   Men's reluctance to change has certainly been an obstacle to family life today. But to a large extent, society hasn't allowed them to change. It certainly hasn't helped them. If there is a villain in the contemporary marriage problem, it is our society. Women at work and men in the family are this century's revolution and problem.

Society pays lip service to equality and to marriage, but there has been so little support of the two-paycheck marriage that I've come to think of the American workplace as the iron vise squeezing the life out of otherwise resilient, viable couples.

29   It's taken me a lifetime to realize that how we live and work as a nation is our own choice. And mostly I feel as if we don't even try to make our lives better, though it wouldn't be so very difficult to do so; we did it in the early part of the twentieth century by legislating an eight-hour workday and workplace safety standards. But now, women—who suffer most—don't dare challenge the status quo for fear we might sound "unrealistic" or "unable to make the grade in a man's world."

30   The Family and Medical Leave Act of 1993 sounded good, but it didn't actually change our lives. In the first place, the legislation only applies to companies with more than 50 employees, while most Americans work for smaller ones. Second, employers can exempt "key employees," so women and men who want to take parental leave can kiss the best jobs good-bye. Third, the provision is for three months of unpaid leave with the birth of a child or a medical emergency. If parents need the income, they can't take off. But still, we don't join together to challenge the workplace rules that leave no time for family. And one thing we need, desperately, is more time with our families.

31   The real reason most parents don't take sufficient time off when a child is born or a family member is ill is because they are afraid of losing their jobs. Justifiably. As much talk as there has been in the business community about the "work-family" problem, there's been precious little action. Why?

32   • Because many companies believe that work-family programs are too costly, even though it has been proven that companies don't actually lose money.

33   • Because most bosses are male, and they just don't see what the problem is. Or if there is some problem for working mothers, their bosses believe it's up to the mothers to solve it.

34   • Because women don't yet have enough power in the business community to change the work-family conflict.

35   Add to these problems several more: over half of all working women still earn less than $25,000 a year; child care is expensive and often of very poor quality; there are few after-school programs, no elder care for infirm parents, and no coverage on school holidays. And giving in to economic pressure, or careerism, or greed, parents work so much overtime that they often can't be home to put their children to sleep, let alone eat dinner with them.

36   In the past, the Puritan work ethic caused no conflict because the wife was the homemaker. Now that nearly everyone works, home life is often as hectic as work. Work has become the center of our universe, our raison d'être, even though most salaries today no longer buy either the free time or the upward mobility enjoyed by many of our parents. Today both partners usually have to work just to stay in place. But—and here's the shock—most don't really have to work as hard as they do.

37   And so here we are, striving so fiercely and working such long hours for security, only to find ourselves feeling lost in an obsessive concern with marketplace values and an out-of-control whirlwind of activity that we don't know how to stop long enough to take care of our relationships.

38   Whenever asked, people here in the United States say that family life and betterment of society are more important than having a nice home, car, and clothes. Clearly, our beat-the-clock lives are not in sync with our deep belief in family and community.

The result is that not only do we suffer from overwork, but we also betray ourselves daily. Overworked Americans cannot raise their children well, cannot contribute to their communities, and cannot sustain the companionship they once found in their marriages. They also can't live according to their expressed values; they just don't have the time.

39   Society also drives us. We don't want to be workaholics, but we just can't stop. In a *Los Angeles Times* survey, nearly 40 percent of men say they would change jobs to have more family and personal time; and in another survey, cited by *Time* magazine, half of the men interviewed said they would refuse a promotion that involved sacrificing family time. The problem is they can't work fewer hours or refuse the promotion and hold on to their jobs. Even more women than men would give up money and status if they could have more family time. But they can't.

40   The lucky few can work shorter hours if they let themselves, but the average couple have to work outside the home at inflexible jobs, confronting a terrible choice between work and family. Clearly, sweeping changes are necessary.

41   What would improve the workplace for people who also want fulfilling personal and family lives? In the last several years, social critics and workers have come up with a list of suggestions. These are the most frequently cited:

42   • On-Site Day Care. Or: subsidies or discounts at child care centers near the workplace.

43   • Flextime. This allows employees to choose their hours and days. Compressed workweeks help, too, especially when there's a long commute.

44   • No Mandatory Overtime.

45   • Family Leave. What would a really supportive plan look like? Swedes are guaranteed 15 months of paid parental leave after the birth or adoption of a child, four months paid leave for sick children under 12, and the right to work part-time without losing their job or benefits until their children are 12.

46   • Telecommuting. Many companies are now experimenting with employees working at home two or more days a week. Some companies go a step further to the "ultimate flexibility" of the virtual office. With laptops, e-mail, cellular phones, and beepers, people can work wherever they work best.

47   Given how much better family support programs could make the lives of today's men, women, and children, wouldn't it be wonderful if the men's movement turned its energies to advocating such programs? Men could bond by sharing fathering problems and the challenges of their new roles. Men's groups could explore the work-family problem to see how business today might support them as fathers and equal partners in their marriages. Finally, men could use the very real power they have to campaign for changes in the workplace.

48   The clients who come to my office to try to repair their family relationships want to believe that their lives have some meaning beyond their own narrow self-interest. Caught up, like the rest of us, in the scramble and the individualism of the competitive marketplace, they nevertheless readily acknowledge that "there must be more to life than this."

49   The positive side of any crisis that brings a couple to therapy is the opportunity to reflect in just this way: Is my life meaningful? Do my relationships work? Are we teaching our children what they need to know? Do I like my work? Is money as important as I thought it was? Do I have caring connections? Do I belong? Among my clients and

friends, some search for this kind of meaning or spirituality through religion, but many seek it through a connection with others in a positive, mutually helpful way. That is, by being part of a caring community.

50   To thrive, couples have to repair their deep emotional connections to their original families and also put out new shoots into the community, whose support may make a life-or-death difference to their relationships. So few people seem to understand how interconnected the personal and public levels of experience are. So few couples make the time to invest themselves beyond their family and friends, beyond their own ambition and pleasure. And most couples suffer because they don't. Ending the isolation of marriage is as important as changing the emotions and behavior within it. We have overloaded the marital circuits by expecting one relationship to meet all of our needs.

51   It may seem odd that a family therapist should issue a call for social and political involvement, but it is precisely the misaligned connection between marriage and society that has put marriage in such jeopardy and will continue to do so if the social contract isn't repaired. We must recognize the degree to which we are all interdependent. Just as we benefit from understanding how a family functions as a system, we can benefit from understanding how society functions as a system and how, as individuals and couples, we are all a part of it.

52   I teach my therapist trainees that it is their job to connect the clients' complaints not only to what is going on in the family system, but also to what is happening in the social system they live in. A truly systematic therapy encourages clients to question their role in every system they belong to. Alienation, cynicism, and despair poison relationships, whether their source is the family system or the larger systems of society, or typically, both.

53   As a culture, we have begun to understand the importance of connectedness and what we have lost by devaluing it. This is one of the reasons why the issue of "family values" strikes home for so many people. But family values need not be defined according to a notion of rigid family forms and traditional sex roles. Real family values are more appropriately defined as those created by parents who are as involved in their marriage and their children as they are in their own achievement. Real family values are reflected by a family's involvement in society and by a society that supports the needs of its families whatever those families might look like: two-paycheck marriages, single-parent households, remarried couples with their children, gay and lesbian couples with children, as well as traditional wage earner-homemaker partners.

54   The so-called family values debate now raging has become a code phrase to signify support for the traditional family structure of yesterday. But wage-earner father/stay-at-home mother is a family structure few of today's families want or can afford. Nor do women want the contemporary variation on that structure that "allows" wives to work if the family needs the income but preserves the traditional role of husband-money manager and wife-homemaker. We cannot turn the clock back to a marriage contract meant for a different social system. But we can certainly uphold family values. Who could possibly be against "family values" if it means what it always has: adults caring about each other and teaching their children to be loving, responsible, productive people? Bad values, an equal opportunity problem, can be learned from family or peers in the slums, in the heartland, in school, in the corporation or the country club.

55   The traditional nuclear family structure led to an extremely high divorce rate, and certainly produced at least as much alcoholism, drug addiction, incest, and physical abuse as any other family structure. It could exist only through the sacrifice of women's autonomy. We need to strengthen the family values in the actual present-day structures of the American family. And this view was upheld recently by the men and women interviewed in a national survey. The vast majority of them did not define family values as having a traditional family. Nine out of ten of the women interviewed said, "Society should value all types of families." And the families that make up these new structures must in turn make their voices heard in their local communities and in the American polity.

56   That may sound very grandiose, but as Madeline Kunin, three-time governor of Vermont and current U.S. Ambassador to Switzerland, has said, "The difference between community activities and political action is merely one of scale." As Kunin organized to better her children's lives, she took the next obvious step and got involved in local politics. But she never deviated from her family focus. The result of her efforts and the efforts of so many idealistic young families that settled in Vermont during the sixties and seventies was that Vermont was ranked the number one state for environmental policy, children's services, and mental health during much of Kunin's tenure as governor. And Kunin was rated one of the nation's top ten education governors. I am reminded of my favorite quotation, something credited to Margaret Mead: "Never doubt that a small group of thoughtful, committed citizens can change the world. Indeed, it's the only thing that ever has."

57   The more that men are involved with the daily workings of family life, the easier it will be to get legislation that supports family needs. And the more that women learn to translate their personal needs into political action, the more that public policy will reflect real American values. There has seldom been a time when we have so urgently needed to return an ethos of caring about others to the American dialogue. We need a new vision of communal life that we can relate to—one that calls forth our caring, not our fears; one that describes more than the "information highway" that lies ahead. And this new vision should include an extension of family values into the larger society, such values as taking responsibility for ourselves and being responsible toward others, particularly those in need. As someone once said, we are not here to see through each other, but to see each other through.

Questions for Reading and Analysis

1. What basic problem did Carter find when working with couples in therapy?

2. What is the concept of "family systems therapy"? How does it differ from therapy based on Freudian psychology?

3. What role does the family play in each person's life?

4. What structures other than family structures also play an important role in our lives?

5. How have men's and women's lives changed? What element of marriage has not changed? What results?

6. In many modern marriages, whom do men blame? Why? What are some trying to do? Do they have the right approach?

7. Why do many women want to work? Why do many men not want to do more in the home? What do men fear?

8. What contributes to the "work-family conflict"? Why don't we just work less?

9. What suggestions have been made for easing the stress between work and family?

10. Besides finding more time for family relationships, what else do we need to do to enrich our lives?

Questions for Discussion and Response

1. The authors suggest that the family you are born into is like a "hand of cards" that you are stuck having to "play" with. Does this comparison seem apt? Are you happy with the hand you have been dealt? If not, what can you do?

2. The authors also argue for accepting the many forms that families take today and supporting them. Do you agree with the authors? Do you think only the "traditional" nuclear family is "right"? If you want a return to the traditional family, how would you try to accomplish that goal? Is this a realistic goal, given the number of women who work?

3. Do you see any hope in some of the authors' suggestions for workplace changes? Are there other suggestions you would make?

4. In a society that places so much value on money and job prestige, and that insists on each individual's right to self-fulfillment, how do we get people to see the good—to themselves—of spending more time with family and in their communities? What suggestions do you have?

Social Science Finds: "Marriage Matters"

Linda J. Waite

A former senior sociologist at the Rand Corporation, Linda Waite (b. 1947) is currently a professor at the University of Chicago. She has co-authored several books, including *Teenage Motherhood* (1979) and *New Families, No Families?* (1991). In this article, published in *The Responsive Community* in 1996, Waite pulls together various studies to explore the effects that marriage has on married people.

1   As we are all too aware, the last few decades have witnessed a decline in the popularity of marriage. This trend has not escaped the notice of politicians and pundits. But when critics point to the high social costs and taxpayer burden imposed by disintegrating "family values," they overlook the fact that individuals do not simply make the decisions that lead to unwed parenthood, marriage, or divorce on the basis of what is good for society. Individuals weigh the costs and benefits of each of these choices to themselves—and sometimes their children. But how much is truly known about these costs and benefits, either by the individuals making the choices or demographers like

myself who study them? Put differently, what are the implications, for individuals, of the current increases in nonmarriage? If we think of marriage as an insurance policy—which it is, in some respects—does it matter if more people are uninsured, or are insured with a term rather than a whole-life policy? I shall argue that it does matter, because marriage typically provides important and substantial benefits, benefits not enjoyed by those who live alone or cohabit.

2   A quick look at marriage patterns today compared to, say, 1950 shows the extent of recent changes. Figures from the Census Bureau show that in 1950, at the height of the baby boom, about a third of white men and women were not married. Some were waiting to marry for the first time, some were divorced or widowed and not remarried. But virtually everyone married at least once at some point in their lives, generally in their early twenties.

3   In 1950 the proportion of black men and women not married was approximately equal to the proportion unmarried among whites, but since that time the marriage behavior of blacks and whites has diverged dramatically. By 1993, 61 percent of black women and 58 percent of black men were not married, compared to 38 percent of white men and 41 percent of white women. So, in contrast to 1950 when only a little over one black adult in three was not married, now a majority of black adults are unmarried. Insofar as marriage "matters," black men and women are much less likely than whites to share in the benefits, and much less likely today than they were a generation ago.

4   The decline in marriage is directly connected to the rise in cohabitation—living with someone in a sexual relationship without being married. Although Americans are less likely to be married today than they were several decades ago, if we count both marriage and cohabitation, they are about as likely to be "coupled." If cohabitation provides the same benefits to individuals as marriage does, then we do not need to be concerned about this shift. But we may be replacing a valuable social institution with one that demands and offers less.

5   Perhaps the most disturbing change in marriage appears in its relationship to parenthood. Today a third of all births occur to women who are not married, with huge but shrinking differences between blacks and whites in this behavior. One in five births to white mothers and two-thirds of births to black mothers currently take place outside marriage. Although about a quarter of the white unmarried mothers are living with someone when they give birth, so that their children are born into two-parent—if unmarried—families, very few black children born to unmarried mothers live with fathers too.

6   I believe that these changes in marriage behavior are a cause for concern, because in a number of important ways married men and women do better than those who are unmarried. And I believe that the evidence suggests that they do better because they are married.

Marriage and Health

7   The case for marriage is quite strong. Consider the issues of longevity and health. With economist Lee Lillard, I used a large national survey to follow men and women over a 20-year period. We watched them get married, get divorced, and remarry. We observed the death of spouses and of the individuals themselves. And we compared deaths of married men and women to those who were not married. We found that once we took other factors into account, married men and women faced lower risks of dying at any

point than those who have never married or whose previous marriage has ended. Widowed women were much better off than divorced women or those who had never married, although they were still disadvantaged when compared with married women. But all men who were not currently married faced significantly higher risks of dying than married men, regardless of their marital history. Other scholars have found disadvantages in death rates for unmarried adults in a number of countries besides the United States.

8   How does marriage lengthen life? First, marriage appears to reduce risky and un-healthy behaviors. For example, according to University of Texas sociologist Debra Umberson, married men show much lower rates of problem drinking than unmarried men. Umberson also found that both married men and women are less likely to take risks that could lead to injury than are the unmarried. Second, as we will see below, mar-riage increases material well-being—income, assets, and wealth. These can be used to purchase better medical care, better diet, and safer surroundings, which lengthen life. This material improvement seems to be especially important for women.

9   Third, marriage provides individuals—especially men—with someone who moni-tors their health and health-related behaviors and who encourages them to drink and smoke less, to eat a healthier diet, to get enough sleep and to generally take care of their health. In addition, husbands and wives offer each other moral support that helps in dealing with stressful situations. Married men especially seem to be motivated to avoid risky behaviors and to take care of their health by the sense of meaning that marriage gives to their lives and the sense of obligation to others that it brings.

More Wealth, Better Wages—for Most

10   Married individuals also seem to fare better when it comes to wealth. One com-prehensive measure to financial well-being—household wealth—includes pension and Social Security wealth, real and financial assets, and the value of the primary residence. According to economist James Smith, in 1992 married men and women ages 51–60 had median wealth of about $66,000 per spouse, compared to $42,000 for the widowed, $35,000 for those who had never married, $34,000 among those who were divorced, and only $7,600 for those who were separated. Although married couples have higher incomes than others, this fact accounts for only about a quarter of their greater wealth.

11   How does marriage increase wealth? Married couples can share many household goods and services, such as a TV and heat, so the cost to each individual is lower than if each one purchased and used the same items individually. So the married spend less than the same individuals would for the same style of life if they lived separately. Second, mar-ried people produce more than the same individuals would if single. Each spouse can de-velop some skills and neglect others, because each can count on the other to take re-sponsibility for some of the household work. The resulting specialization increases efficiency. We see below that this specialization leads to higher wages for men. Married couples also seem to save more at the same level of income than do single people.

12   The impact of marriage is again beneficial—although in this case not for all in-volved—when one looks at labor market outcomes. According to recent research by economist Kermit Daniel, both black and white men receive a wage premium if they are married: 4.5 percent for black men and 6.3 percent for white men. Black women re-ceive a marriage premium of almost 3 percent. White women, however, pay a marriage

penalty, in hourly wages, of over 4 percent. In addition, men appear to receive some of the benefit of marriage if they cohabit, but women do not.

13   Why should marriage increase men's wages? Some researchers think that marriage makes men more productive at work, leading to higher wages. Wives may assist husbands directly with their work, offer advice or support, or take over household tasks, freeing husbands' time and energy for work. Also, as I mentioned earlier, being married reduces drinking, substance abuse, and other unhealthy behaviors that may affect men's job performance. Finally, marriage increases men's incentives to perform well at work, in order to meet obligations to family members.

14   For women, Daniel finds that marriage and presence of children together seem to affect wages, and the effects depend on the woman's race. Childless black women earn substantially more money if they are married but the "marriage premium" drops with each child they have. Among white women only the childless receive a marriage premium. Once white women become mothers, marriage decreases their earnings compared to remaining single (with children), with very large negative effects of marriage on women's earnings for those with two children or more. White married women often choose to reduce hours of work when they have children. They also make less per hour than either unmarried mothers or childless wives.

15   Up to this point, all the consequences of marriage for the individuals involved have been unambiguously positive—better health, longer life, more wealth, and higher earnings. But the effects of marriage and children on white women's wages are mixed, at best. Marriage and cohabitation increase women's time spent on housework; married motherhood reduces their time in the labor force and lowers their wages. Although the family as a whole might be better off with this allocation of women's time, women generally share their husbands' market earnings only when they are married. Financial well-being declines dramatically for women and their children after divorce and widowhood; women whose marriages have ended are often quite disadvantaged financially by their investment in their husbands and children rather than in their own earning power. Recent changes in divorce law—the rise in no-fault divorce and the move away from alimony—seem to have exacerbated this situation, even while increases in women's education and work experience have moderated it.

Improved Intimacy

16   Another benefit of married life is an improved sex life. Married men and women report very active sex lives—as do those who are cohabiting. But the married appear to be more satisfied with sex than others. More married men say that they find sex with their wives to be extremely physically pleasurable than do cohabiting men or single men say the same about sex with their partners. The high levels of married men's physical satisfaction with their sex lives contradicts the popular view that sexual novelty or variety improves sex for men. Physical satisfaction with sex is about the same for married women, cohabiting women, and single women with sex partners.

17   In addition to reporting more active and more physically fulfilling sex lives than the unmarried, married men and women say that they are more emotionally satisfied with their sex lives than do those who are single or cohabiting. Although cohabitants report levels of sexual activity as high as the married, both cohabiting men and women

report lower levels of emotional satisfaction with their sex lives. And those who are sexually active but single report the lowest emotional satisfaction with it.

18   How does marriage improve one's sex life? Marriage and cohabitation provide individuals with a readily available sexual partner with whom they have an established, ongoing sexual relationship. This reduces the costs—in some sense—of any particular sexual contact, and leads to higher levels of sexual activity. Since married couples expect to carry on their sex lives for many years, and since the vast majority of married couples are monogamous, husbands and wives have strong incentives to learn what pleases their partner in bed and to become good at it. But I would argue that more than "skills" are at issue here. The long-term contract implicit in marriage—which is not implicit in cohabitation—facilitates emotional investment in the relationship, which should affect both frequency of and satisfaction with sex. So the wife or husband who knows what the spouse wants is also highly motivated to provide it, both because sexual satisfaction in one's partner brings similar rewards to oneself and because the emotional commitment to the partner makes satisfying him or her important in itself.

19   To this point we have focused on the consequences of marriage for adults—the men and women who choose to marry (and stay married) or not. But such choices have consequences for the children born to these adults. Sociologists Sarah McLanahan and Gary Sandefur compare children raised in intact, two-parent families with those raised in one-parent families, which could result either from disruption of a marriage or from unmarried childbearing. They find that approximately twice as many children raised in one-parent families than children from two-parent families drop out of high school without finishing. Children raised in one-parent families are also more likely to have a birth themselves while teenagers, and to be "idle"—both out of school and out of the labor force—as young adults.

20   Not surprisingly, children living outside an intact marriage are also more likely to be poor. McLanahan and Sandefur calculated poverty rates for children in two-parent families—including stepfamilies—and for single-parent families. They found very high rates of poverty for single-parent families, especially among blacks. Donald Hernandez, chief of marriage and family statistics at the Census Bureau, claims that the rise in mother-only families since 1959 is an important cause of increases in poverty among children.

21   Clearly poverty, in and of itself, is a bad outcome for children. In addition, however, McLanahan and Sandefur estimate that the lower incomes of single-parent families account for only half of the negative impact for children in these families. The other half comes from children's access—or lack of access—to the time and attention of two adults in two-parent families. Children in one-parent families spend less time with their fathers (this is not surprising given that they do not live with them), but they also spend less time with their mothers than children in two-parent families. Single-parent families and stepfamilies also move much more frequently than two-parent families, disrupting children's social and academic environments. Finally, children who spend part of their childhood in a single-parent family report substantially lower quality relationships with their parents as adults and have less frequent contact with them, according to demographer Diane Lye.

Correlation Versus Causality

22   The obvious question, when one looks at all these "benefits" of marriage, is whether marriage is responsible for these differences. If all, or almost all, of the benefits

of marriage arise because those who enjoy better health, live longer lives, or earn higher wages anyway are more likely to marry, then marriage is not "causing" any changes in these outcomes. In such a case, we as a society and we as individuals could remain neutral about each person's decision to marry or not, to divorce or remain married. But scholars from many fields who have examined the issues have come to the opposite conclusion. Daniel found that only half of the higher wages that married men enjoy could be explained by selectivity; he thus concluded that the other half is causal. In the area of mental health, social psychologist Catherine Ross—summarizing her own research and that of other social scientists—wrote, "The positive effect of marriage on well-being is strong and consistent, and the selection of the psychologically healthy into marriage or the psychologically unhealthy out of marriage cannot explain the effect." Thus marriage itself can be assumed to have independent positive effects on its participants.

23 So, we must ask, what is it about marriage that causes these benefits? I think that four factors are key. First, the institution of marriage involves a long-term contract—"'til death do us part." This contract allow the partners to make choices that carry immediate costs but eventually bring benefits. The time horizon implied by marriage makes it sensible—a rational choice is at work here—for individuals to develop some skills and to neglect others because they count on their spouse to fill in where they are weak. The institution of marriage helps individuals honor this long-term contract by providing social support for the couple as a couple and by imposing social and economic costs on those who dissolve their union.

24 Second, marriage assumes a sharing of economic and social resources and what we can think of as co-insurance. Spouses act as a sort of small insurance pool against life's uncertainties, reducing their need to protect themselves—by themselves—from unexpected events.

25 Third, married couples benefit—as do cohabiting couples—from economies of scale.

26 Fourth, marriage connects people to other individuals, to their social groups (such as in-laws), and to other social institutions (such as churches and synagogues) which are themselves a source of benefits. These connections provide individuals with a sense of obligation to others, which gives life meaning beyond oneself.

27 Cohabitation has some but not all of the characteristics of marriage and so carries some but not all of the benefits. Cohabitation does not generally imply a lifetime commitment to stay together; a significant number of cohabiting couples disagree on the future of their relationship. Frances Goldscheider and Gail Kaufman believe that the shift to cohabitation from marriage signals "declining commitment within unions, of men and women to each other and to their relationship as an enduring unit, in exchange for more freedom, primarily for men." Perhaps as a result, many view cohabitation as an especially poor bargain for women.

28 The uncertainty that accompanies cohabitation makes both investment in the relationship and specialization with this partner much riskier than in marriage and so reduces them. Cohabitants are much less likely than married couples to pool financial resources and more likely to assume that each partner is responsible for supporting himself or herself financially. And whereas marriage connects individuals to other important social institutions, cohabitation seems to distance them from these institutions.

29   Of course, all observations concern only the average benefits of marriage. Clearly, some marriages produce substantially higher benefits for those involved. Some marriages produce no benefits and even cause harm to the men, women, and children involved. That fact needs to be recognized.

Reversing the Trend

30   Having stated this qualification, we must still ask, if the average marriage produces all of these benefits for individuals, why has it declined? Although this issue remains a subject of much research and speculation, a number of factors have been mentioned as contributing. For one, because of increases in women's employment, there is less specialization by spouses now than in the past; this reduces the benefits of marriage. Clearly, employed wives have less time and energy to focus on their husbands, and are less financially and emotionally dependent on marriage than wives who work only in the home. In addition, high divorce rates decrease people's certainty about the long-run stability of their marriage, and this may reduce their willingness to invest in it, which in turn increases the chance they divorce—a sort of self-fulfilling prophecy. Also, changes in divorce laws have shifted much of the financial burden for the breakup of the marriage to women, making investment within the marriage (such as supporting a husband in medical school) a riskier proposition for them.

31   Men, in turn, may find marriage and parenthood a less attractive option when they know that divorce is common, because they may face the loss of contact with their children if their marriage dissolves. Further, women's increased earnings and young men's declining financial well-being may have made women less dependent on men's financial support and made young men less able to provide it. Finally, public policies that support single mothers and changing attitudes toward sex outside of marriage, toward unmarried childbearing, and toward divorce have all been implicated in the decline in marriage. This brief list does not exhaust the possibilities, but merely mentions some of them.

32   So how can this trend be reversed? First, as evidence accumulates and is communicated to individuals, some people will change their behavior as a result. Some will do so simply because of their new understanding of the costs and benefits, to them, of the choices involved. In addition, we have seen that attitudes frequently change toward behaviors that have been shown to have negative consequences. The attitude change then raises the social cost of the newly stigmatized behavior.

33   In addition, though, we as a society can pull some policy levers to encourage or discourage behaviors. Public policies that include asset tests (Medicaid is a good example) act to exclude the married, as do AFDC programs in most states. The "marriage penalty" in the tax code is another example. These and other policies reinforce or undermine the institution of marriage. If, as I have argued, marriage produces individuals who drink less, smoke less, abuse substances less, live longer, earn more, are wealthier, and have children who do better, we need to give more thought and effort to supporting this valuable social institution.

Questions for Reading and Analysis

1. What is Waite's subject? What is her claim? Where does she state it?

2. Although marriage has declined, what has taken its place?

3. What groups are healthiest and live the longest? What three reasons does Waite list to explain these health facts?

4. In what ways can marriage increase wealth? Who, when married, loses in hourly wages?

5. What may be the causes of increased productivity for married men?

6. What are some effects of single-parent families on children?

7. How does the author defend her causal argument—that marriage itself is a cause of the financial, health, and contentment effects found in married people?

8. Why, if marriage has benefits, are fewer people getting married and more getting divorced?

9. How does the author help readers move through her longish essay?

10. What kind of evidence, primarily, does Waite provide?

Questions for Discussion and Response

1. Which statistic most surprises you? Why?

2. Do you think that the evidence Waite provides should encourage people to choose marriage over divorce, cohabitation, or the single life? If so, why? If not, why not?

3. What can be done to increase marriage benefits for women, the ones who have least benefited?

4. What can be done to change the movement away from marriage? What are Waite's suggestions? What are yours?

How to End the Abortion War

Roger Rosenblatt

A former senior writer at *Time* and then editor of *U.S. News and World Report*, Roger Rosenblatt (b. 1940) has continued his career in journalism as a regular contributor to magazines and newspapers. He is also the author of several books including *Life Itself: Abortion in the American Mind* (1992). The following article on abortion appeared in the January 19, 1992, issue of the *New York Times Magazine*.

1   The veins in his forehead bulged so prominently they might have been blue worms that had worked their way under the surface of his skin. His eyes bulged, too, capillaries zigzagging from the pupils in all direction. His face was pulled tight about the jaw, which thrust forward like a snowplow attachment on the grille of a truck. From the flattened O of his mouth, the word "murderer" erupted in a regular rhythm, the repetition of the r's giving the word the sound of an outboard motor that failed to catch.

2   She, for her part, paced up and down directly in front of him, saying nothing. Instead, she held high a cardboard sign on a stick, showing the cartoonish drawing of a

bloody coat hanger over the caption, "Never again." Like his, her face was taut with fury, her lips pressed together so tightly they folded under and vanished. Whenever she drew close to him, she would deliberately lower the sign and turn it toward him, so that he would be yelling his "murderer" at the picture of the coat hanger.

3   For nearly twenty years these two have been at each other with all the hatred they can unearth. Sometimes the man is a woman, sometimes the woman is a man. They are black, white, Hispanic, Asian; they make their homes in Missouri or New Jersey; they are teenagers and pharmacists and college professors; Catholic, Baptist, Jew. They have exploded at each other on the steps of the Capitol in Washington, in front of abortion clinics, hospitals, and politicians' homes, on village greens and the avenues of the cities. Their rage is tireless; at every decision of the United States Supreme Court or of the President or of the state legislatures, it rises like a missile seeking only the heat of its counterpart.

4   This is where America is these days on the matter of abortion, or where it seems to be. In fact, it is very hard to tell how the country really feels about abortion, because those feelings are almost always displayed in political arenas. Most ordinary people do not speak of abortion. Friends who gladly debate other volatile issues—political philosophy, war, race—shy away from the subject. It is too private, too personal, too bound up with one's faith or spiritual identity. Give abortion five seconds of thought, and it quickly spirals down in the mind to the most basic questions about human life, to the mysteries of birth and our relationship with our souls.

5   We simply will not talk about it. We will march in demonstrations, shout and carry placards, but we will not talk about it. In the Presidential election of 1992, we will cast votes for a national leader based in part on his or her position on abortion. Still, we will not talk about it.

6   The oddity in this unnatural silence is that most of us actually know what we feel about abortion. But because those feelings are mixed and complicated, we have decided that they are intractable. I believe the opposite is true: that we are more prepared than we realize to reach a common, reasonable understanding on this subject, and if we were to vent our mixed feelings and begin to make use of them, a solution would be at hand.

7   Seventy-three percent of Americans polled in 1990 were in favor of abortion rights. Seventy-seven percent polled also regard abortion as a kind of killing. (Forty-nine percent see abortion as outright murder, 28 percent solely as the taking of human life.) These figures represent the findings of the Harris and Gallup polls, respectively, and contain certain nuances of opinion within both attitudes. But the general conclusions are widely considered valid. In other words, most Americans are both for the choice of abortion as a principle and against abortion for themselves. One has to know nothing else to realize how conflicted a problem we have before and within us.

8   The fact that abortion entails conflict, however, does not mean that the country is bound to be locked in combat forever. In other contexts, living with conflict is not only normal to America, it is often the only way to function honestly. We are for both Federal assistance and states' autonomy; we are for both the First Amendment and normal standards of propriety; we are for both the rights of privacy and the needs of public health. Our most productive thinking usually contains an inner confession of mixed feelings. Our least productive thinking, a nebulous irritation resulting from a refusal to come to terms with disturbing and patently irreconcilable ideas.

9   Yet acknowledging and living with ambivalence is, in a way, what America was invented to do. To create a society in which abortion is permitted and its gravity appreciated is to create but another of the many useful frictions of a democratic society. Such a society does not devalue life by allowing abortion; it takes life with utmost seriousness and is, by the depth of its conflicts and by the richness of its difficulties, a reflection of life itself.

10   Why, then, are we stuck in political warfare on this issue? Why can we not make use of our ambivalence and move on?

11   The answer has to do with America's peculiar place in the history of abortion, and also with the country's special defining characteristics, both ancient and modern, with which abortion has collided. In the 4,000-year-old history extending from the Greeks and Romans through the Middle Ages and into the present, every civilization has taken abortion with utmost seriousness. Yet ours seems to be the only civilization to have engaged in an emotional and intellectual civil war over the issue.

12   There are several reasons for this. The more obvious include the general lack of consensus in the country since the mid-60's, which has promoted bitter divisions over many social issues—race, crime, war, and abortion, too. The sexual revolution of the 60's resulted in the heightened activity of people who declared themselves "pro-choice" *and* "pro-life"—misleading terms used here principally for convenience. The pro-life movement began in 1967, six years before *Roe v. Wade*. The women's movement, also revitalized during the 60's, gave an impetus for self-assertion to women on both sides of the abortion issue.

13   But there are less obvious reasons, central to America's special character, which have helped to make abortion an explosive issue in this country.

14   **Religiosity.** America is, and always has been, a religious country, even though it spreads its religiosity among many different religions. Perry Miller, the great historian of American religious thought, established that the New England colonists arrived with a ready-made religious mission, which they cultivated and sustained through all its manifestations, from charity to intolerance. The Virginia settlement, too, was energized by God's glory. Nothing changed in this attitude by the time the nation was invented. If anything, the creation of the United States of America made the desire to receive redemption in the New World more intense.

15   Yet individuals sought something in American religion that was different, more emotional than the religion in England. One member of the early congregation explained that the reason he made the long journey to America was "I thought I should find feelings." This personalized sense of religion, which has endured to the present, has an odd but telling relationship with the national attitude toward religion. Officially, America is an a-religious country: the separation of church and state is so rooted in the democracy it has become a cliché. Yet that same separation has created and intensified a hidden national feeling about faith and God, a sort of secret, undercurrent religion, which, perhaps because of its subterranean nature, is often more deeply felt and volatile than that of countries with official or state religions.

16   The Catholic Church seems more steadily impassioned about abortion in America than anywhere else, even in a country like Poland—so agitated, in fact, that it has entered into an unlikely, if not unholy, alliance with evangelical churches in the pro-life camp. In Catholic countries like Italy, France, and Ireland, religion is often so fluidly

mixed with social life that rules are bent more quietly, without our personal sort of moral upheaval.

17   Americans are moral worriers. We tend to treat every political dispute that arises as a test of our national soul. The smallest incident, like the burning of the flag, can bring our hidden religion to the surface. The largest and most complex moral problem, like abortion, can confound it for decades.

18   **Individualism.** Two basic and antithetical views of individualism have grown up with the country. Emerson, the evangelist of self-reliance and non-conformity, had a quasi-mystical sense of value of the individual self.[1] He described man as a self-sufficient microcosm: "The lightning which explodes and fashions planets, maker of planets and suns, is in him." Tocqueville had a more prosaic and practical view:[2] He worried about the tendency of Americans to withdraw into themselves at the expense of the public good, confusing self-assertion with self-absorption.

19   Abortion hits both of these views of the individual head on, of course; but both views are open to antipodal interpretations. The Emersonian celebration of the individual may be shared by the pro-choice advocate who sees in individualism one's right to privacy. It may be seen equally by a pro-life advocate as a justification for taking an individual stance—an antiliberal stance to boot—on a matter of conscience.

20   The idea of the independent individual may also be embraced by the pro-life position as the condition of life on which the unborn have a claim immediately after conception. Pro-life advocates see the pregnant woman as two individuals, each with an equal claim to the riches that American individualism offers.

21   Tocqueville's concern with individualism as selfishness is also available for adoption by both camps. The pro-life people claim that the pro-choice advocates are placing their individual rights above those of society, and one of the fundamental rights of American society is the right to life. Even the Supreme Court, when it passed *Roe v. Wade*, concluded that abortion "is not unqualified and must be considered against important state interests in regulation."

22   To those who believe in abortion rights, the "public good" consists of a society in which people, collectively, have the right to privacy and individual choice. Their vision of an unselfish, unself-centered America is one in which the collective sustains its strength by encouraging the independence of those who comprise it. Logically, both camps rail against the individual imposing his or her individual views on society at large, each feeling the same, if opposite, passion about both what society and the individual ought to be. Passion on this subject has led to rage.

23   **Optimism.** The American characteristic of optimism, like that of individualism, is affected by abortion in contradictory ways. People favoring the pro-life position see optimism exactly as they read individual rights: Every American, born or unborn, is entitled to look forward to a state of infinite hope and progress. The process of birth is itself an optimistic activity.

---

[1]Ralph Waldo Emerson (1803–1882) was the chief voice of the nineteenth century movement called transcendentalism.—Ed.

[2]Alexis de Tocqueville (1805–1859) was a French aristocrat and magistrate who toured the United States in 1833 and wrote *Democracy in America* (1835).—Ed.

24   Taking the opposite view, those favoring abortion rights interpret the ideas of hope and progress as a consequence of one's entitlement to free choice in all things, abortion definitely included. If the individual woman wishes to pursue her manifest destiny unencumbered by children she does not want, that is not only her business but her glory. The issue is national as well as personal. The pro-choice reasoning goes: The country may only reach its ideal goals if women, along with men, are allowed to achieve their highest potential as citizens, unburdened by limitations that are not of their own choosing.

25   Even the element of American "can-do" ingenuity applies. The invention of abortion, like other instruments of American optimism, supports both the pro-life and pro-choice stands. Hail the procedure for allowing women to realize full control over their invented selves. Or damn the procedure for destroying forever the possibility of a new life inventing itself. As with all else pertaining to this issue, one's moral position depends on the direction in which one is looking. Yet both directions are heaving with optimism, and both see life in America as the best of choices.

26   **Sexuality.** The connection of abortion with American attitudes toward sexuality is both economic and social. The American way with sex is directly related to the country's original desire to become a society of the middle class, and thus to cast off the extremes of luxury and poverty that characterized Europe and the Old World. The structure of English society, in particular, was something the new nation sought to avoid. Not for Puritan America was the rigid English class system, which not only fixed people into economically immobile slots but allowed and encouraged free wheeling sexual behavior at both the highest and lowest strata.

27   At the top of the English classes was a self-indulgent minority rich enough to ignore middle-class moral codes and idle enough to spend their time seducing servants. At the opposite end of the system, the poor also felt free to do whatever they wished with their bodies, since the world offered them so little. The masses of urban poor, created by the Industrial Revolution, had little or no hope of bettering their lot. Many of them wallowed in a kind of sexual Pandemonium, producing babies wantonly and routinely engaging in rape and incest. Between the two class extremes stood the staunch English middle class, with its hands on its hips, outraged at the behavior both above and below them, but powerless to insist on, much less enforce, bourgeois values.

28   This was not to be the case in America, where bourgeois values were to become the standards and the moral engine of the country. Puritanism, a mere aberrant religion to the English, who were able to get rid of it in 1660 after a brief eighteen years, was the force that dominated American social life for a century and a half. Since there has been a natural progression from Puritanism to Victorianism and from Victorianism to modern forms of fundamentalism in terms of social values, it may be said that the Puritans have really never loosened their headlock on American thinking. The Puritans offered a perfect context for America's desire to create a ruling middle class, which was to be known equally for infinite mobility (geographic, social, economic) and the severest forms of repression.

29   Abortion fits into such thinking more by what the issue implies than by what it is. In the 1800's and the early 1900's, Americans were able to live with abortion, even during periods of intensive national prudery, as long as the practice was considered the exception that proved the rule. The rule was that abortion was legally and morally discouraged. Indeed, most every modern civilization has adopted that attitude, which, put

simply, is an attitude of looking the other way in a difficult human situation, which often cannot and should not be avoided. For all its adamant middle-classness, it was not uncomfortable for Americans to look the other way either—at least until recently.

30   When abortion was no longer allowed to be a private, albeit dangerous, business, however, especially during the sexual revolution of the 60's, America's basic middle-classedness asserted itself loudly. Who was having all these abortions? The upper classes, who were behaving irresponsibly, and the lower orders, who had nothing to lose. Abortion, in other words, was a sign of careless sexuality and was thus an offense to the bourgeois dream.

31   The complaint was, and is, that abortion contradicts middle-class values, which dictate the rules of sexual conduct. Abortion, it is assumed, is the practice of the socially irresponsible, those who defy the solid norms that keep America intact. When *Roe v. Wade* was ruled upon, it sent the harshest message to the American middle class, including those who did not oppose abortion themselves but did oppose the disruption of conformity and stability. If they—certainly the middle-class majority—did not object to *Roe v. Wade* specifically, they did very much object to the atmosphere of lawlessness or unruliness that they felt the law encouraged. Thus the outcry; thus the warfare.

32   There may be one other reason for abortion's traumatic effect on the country in recent years. Since the end of the Second World War, American society, not unlike modern Western societies in general, has shifted intellectually from a humanistic to a social science culture; that is, from a culture used to dealing with contrarieties to one that demands definite, provable answers. The nature of social science is that it tends not only to identify, but to create issues that must be solved. Often these issues are the most significant to the country's future—civil rights, for example.

33   What social science thinking does not encourage is human sympathy. By that I do not mean the sentimental feeling that acknowledges another's pain or discomfort; I mean the intellectual sympathy that accepts another's views as both interesting and potentially valid, that deliberately goes to the heart of the thinking of the opposition and spends some time there. That sort of humanistic thinking may or may not be humane, but it does offer the opportunity to arrive at a humane understanding outside the realm and rules of politics. In a way, it is a literary sort of thinking, gone now from a post-literary age, a "reading" of events to determine layers of depth, complication, and confusion and to learn to live with them.

34   Everything that has happened in the abortion debate has been within the polarities that social science thinking creates. The quest to determine when life begins is a typical exercise of social science—the attempt to impose objective precision on a subjective area of speculation. Arguments over the mother's rights versus the rights of the unborn child are social science arguments, too. The social sciences are far more interested in rights than in how one arrives at what is right—that is, both their strength and weakness. Thus the abortion debate has been political from the start.

35   A good many pro-choice advocates, in fact, came to lament the political character of the abortion debate when it first began in the 60's. At that time, political thinking in America was largely and conventionally liberal. The liberals had the numbers; therefore, they felt that they could set the national agenda without taking into account the valid feelings or objections of the conservative opposition. When, in the Presidential election of 1980, it became glaringly apparent that the feelings of the conservative op-

position were not only valid but were politically ascendant, many liberals reconsidered the idea that abortion was purely a rights issue. They expressed appreciation of a more emotionally complicated attitude, one they realized that they shared themselves, however they might vote.

36   If the abortion debate had risen in a humanistic environment, it might never have achieved the definition and clarity of the *Roe v. Wade* decision, yet it might have moved toward a greater public consensus. One has to guess at such things through hindsight, of course. But in a world in which humanistic thought predominated, abortion might have been taken up more in its human terms and the debate might have focused more on such unscientific and apolitical components as human guilt, human choice and human mystery.

37   If we could find a way to retrieve this kind of conflicting thinking, and find a way to apply it to the country's needs, we might be on our way toward a common understanding on abortion, and perhaps toward a common good. Abortion requires us to think one way and another way simultaneously. Americans these days could make very good use of this bifurcated way of thinking.

38   This brings me back to the concern I voiced at the beginning: Americans are not speaking their true minds about abortion because their minds are in conflict. Yet living with conflict is normal in America, and our reluctance to do so openly in this matter, while understandable in an atmosphere of easy polarities, may help create a false image of our country in which we do not recognize ourselves. An American that declares abortion legal and says nothing more about it would be just as distorted as one that prohibited the practice. The ideal situation, in my view, would consist of a combination of laws, attitudes, and actions that would go toward satisfying both the rights of citizens and the doubts held by most of them.

39   Achieving this goal is, I believe, within reach. I know how odd that must sound when one considers the violent explosions that have occurred in places like Wichita as recently as August of last year, or when one sees the pro-life and pro-choice camps amassing ammunition for this year's Presidential campaign. But for the ordinary private citizen, the elements of a reasonably satisfying resolution are already in place. I return to the fact that the great majority of Americans both favor abortion rights and disapprove of abortion. Were that conflict of thought to be openly expressed, and were certain social remedies to come from it, we would not find a middle of the road on this issue—logically there is no middle of the road. But we might well establish a wider road, which would accommodate a broad range of beliefs and opinions and allow us to move on to more important social concerns.

40   What most Americans want to do with abortion is to permit but discourage it. Even those with the most pronounced political stands on the subject reveal this duality in the things they say: while making strong defenses of their positions, they nonetheless, if given time to work out their thoughts, allow for opposing views. I discovered this in a great many interviews over the past three years.

41   Pro-choice advocates are often surprised to hear themselves speak of the immorality of taking a life. Pro-life people are surprised to hear themselves defend individual rights, especially women's rights. And both sides might be surprised to learn how similar are their visions of a society that makes abortion less necessary through sex education, help for unwanted babies, programs to shore up disintegrating families and moral

values, and other forms of constructive community action. Such visions may appear Panglossian,[3] but they have been realized before, and the effort is itself salutary.

42   If one combines that sense of social responsibility with the advocacy of individual rights, the permit-but-discourage formula could work. By "discourage" I mean the implementation of social programs that help to create an atmosphere of discouragement. I do not mean ideas like parental consent or notification, already the law in some states, which, however well-intentioned, only whittle away at individual freedom. The "discourage" part is the easier to find agreement on, of course, but when one places the "permit" question in the realm of respect for private values, even that may become more palatable.

43   Already 73 percent of America finds abortion acceptable. Even more may find it so if they can tolerate living in a country in which they may exercise the individual right not to have an abortion themselves or to argue against others having one, yet still go along with the majority who want the practice continued. The key element for all is to create social conditions in which abortion will be increasingly unnecessary. It is right that we have the choice, but it would be better if we did not have to make it.

44   Were this balance of thought and attitude to be expressed publicly, it might serve some of the country's wider purposes as well, especially these days when there is so much anguish over how we have lost our national identity and character. The character we lost, it seems to me, was one that exalted the individual for what the individual did for the community. It honored and embodied both privacy and selflessness. A balanced attitude on abortion would also do both. It would make a splendid irony if this most painful and troublesome issue could be converted into a building block for a renewed national pride based on good will.

45   For that to happen, the country's leaders—Presidential candidates come to mind— have to express themselves as well. As for Congress, it hardly seems too much to expect our representatives to say something representative about the issue. Should *Roe v. Wade* be overturned, as may well happen, the country could be blown apart. To leave the matter to the states would lead to mayhem, a balkanization of what ought to be standard American rights. Congress used to pass laws, remember? I think it is time for Congress to make a law like *Roe v. Wade* that fully protects abortion rights, but legislates the kind of community help, like sex education, that would diminish the practice.

46   Taking a stand against abortion while allowing for its existence can turn out to be a progressive philosophy. It both speaks for moral seriousness and moves in the direction of ameliorating conditions of ignorance, poverty, the social self-destruction of fragmented families, and the loss of spiritual values in general. What started as a debate as to when life begins might lead to making life better.

47   The effort to reduce the necessity of abortion, then, is to choose life as wholeheartedly as it is to be "pro-life." By such an effort, one is choosing life for millions who do not want to be, who do not deserve to be, forever hobbled by an accident, a mistake or by miseducation. By such an effort, one is also choosing a different sort of life for the country as a whole—a more sympathetic life in which we acknowledge, privileged and unprivileged alike, that we have the same doubts and mysteries and hopes for one another.

---

[3]"Unrealistic" dreams, referring to the optimistic tutor to Candide, in Voltaire's novel *Candide*.—Ed.

⁴⁸   Earlier, I noted America's obsessive moral character, our tendency to treat every question that comes before us as a test of our national soul. The permit-but-discourage formula on abortion offers the chance to test our national soul by appealing to its basic egalitarian impulse. Were we once again to work actively toward creating a country where everyone had the same health care, the same sex education, the same opportunity for economic survival, the same sense of personal dignity and work, we would see both fewer abortions and a more respectable America.

Questions for Reading and Analysis

1. Consider Rosenblatt's introduction. What strategy does he use in the first three paragraphs? What makes paragraph 5 effective?

2. What is Rosenblatt's claim? Where does he state it?

3. What kind of argument is this? What does the author seek to accomplish on the abortion issue?

4. What are Americans' views on abortion? What do the polls reveal?

5. What is Rosenblatt's attitude toward ambivalence? Is it a mark of failure or a spur to productive thinking? Is it un-American? Or democratic?

6. Summarize the causes of America's ambivalence, as Rosenblatt sees it.

7. Explain America's contradictory attitudes toward religion.

8. How do American views of individualism affect the struggle over abortion? How does American optimism support contradictory views of abortion?

9. How do American attitudes toward class and sex affect attitudes toward abortion? Which group wants its moral code to be followed by everyone?

10. How has our "social science culture" shaped the debate over abortion?

11. What does Rosenblatt mean by a "humanistic environment"?

12. What larger good may come from dealing with our conflicting views on abortion? What kind of America does Rosenblatt want to see?

Questions for Discussion and Response

1. Rosenblatt suggests that ambivalence is not necessarily bad and that we should embrace our ambivalence over abortion. Is this a new idea for you? If so, does it make sense?

2. Pro-life advocates seem to be rejecting the "social science" approach by their slogan "It's a child, not a choice." Rosenblatt favors laws allowing for abortion. Does that make him a part of our "social science" culture? What evidence do you have in the essay that the author seems to be a humanistic or spiritual person?

3. In paragraph 39, Rosenblatt works with a metaphor to describe the stance on abortion he would like to see. How does he use the metaphor? Is it effective to express his idea?

4. Has Rosenblatt convinced you that a consensus is possible on abortion? If so, why? If not, has he convinced you that conciliation is a goal to strive for? Why or why not?

5. What has been your position on abortion? Has Rosenblatt altered your thinking in any way? If so, how? If not, why not?

CHAPTER 21

Global Issues: The Environment, Poverty, and the New Global Economy

The articles in this chapter examine several interconnected issues affecting all of us in the global community. One issue is, of course, global warming—a term referring to a series of climate changes in addition to higher average temperatures. Global warming is a problem, however, that cannot be addressed outside the context of Third World poverty and the gaps in energy use between rich and poor countries. Thus, global warming is not just a scientific topic but a topic that involves political and social issues.

We can add to the issues connected to global warming those stemming from the media's ineptness in presenting this issue clearly to citizens and the difficulties nonscientists have in understanding the language of scientists. S. George Philander, in the chapter's first article, seeks to help readers understand what scientists know and how they express their knowledge.

If global warming is a "global" problem, it may well need global solutions—but that in itself is a problem. Just how much of a problem it is has been underscored not only in the United States' reaction to the Kyoto accords but also in recent reactions to such global organizations as the World Bank and International Monetary Fund. Why are some people afraid of a global economy? Gregg Easterbrook helps us grasp some of these issues.

Reflecting on the following questions before you read will enrich your reading on this complex weave of issues:

1. What information do you already have on global warming? Is it, on reflection, enough information on which to base a position or understand various proposed solutions?

2. If you seek additional information, what kinds of information do you think would help you better understand the issues connected to global warming?

3. A global economy is here; the Internet has made this possible. What are your views on this subject? What problems can arise as a result of a global economy? What are the benefits?

4. What are your views on the relationship between humans and the environment? What are your views on the relationships among nations? Should nations cooperate in their use of natural resources and the preservation of the environment? If so, how can this best be accomplished? If not, what alternatives do you suggest?

Websites Relevant to This Chapter's Topic

United States Environmental Protection Agency

www.epa.gov

The EPA website provides current materials on the agency's programs and other resources.

World Wildlife Fund

www.panda.org/home.cfm

This active conservation organization provides much information on climate issues, animal conservation, and related issues.

World Bank

www.worldbank.org

Click on "Resources" to access a wealth of articles on various environmental, economic, and state-of-the-world issues.

Foundation for Research on Economics and the Environment

www.free-eco.org/links.html

The "Links" page of FREE's website lists think tanks, environmental organizations, and government offices.

The Uncertain Science of Global Warming

S. George Philander

S. George Philander (b. 1942) is a professor of geosciences at Princeton University and the author of many articles and books, including *El Niño, La Niña, and the Southern Oscillation* (1989) and *Is the Temperature Rising? The Uncertain Science of Global Warming* (1998), from which the following excerpt comes.

1   We are in a raft, gliding down a river, toward a waterfall. We have a map but are uncertain of our location and hence are unsure of the distance to the waterfall. Some of us are getting nervous and wish to land immediately; others insist that we can continue safely for several more hours. A few are enjoying the ride so much that they deny that there is any imminent danger although the map clearly shows a waterfall. A debate ensues but even though the accelerating currents make it increasingly difficult to land safely, we fail to agree on an appropriate time to leave the river. How do we avoid a disaster?

2   To decide on appropriate action we have to address two questions: How far is the waterfall, and when should we get out of the water? The first is a scientific question; the second is not. The first question, in principle, has a definite, unambiguous answer. The

second, which in effect is a political question, requires compromises. If we can distinguish clearly between the scientific and political aspects of the problem, we can focus on reaching a solution that is acceptable to all. Unfortunately, the distinction between science and politics can easily become blurred. This invariably happens when the scientific results have uncertainties.

3   Suppose that we have only approximate, not precise, estimates of the distance to the waterfall. Rather than leave it at that—rather than accept that we can do no better than predict that we will arrive at the waterfall in thirty minutes plus or minus ten minutes—some people will minimize the distance and insist that we will arrive in twenty minutes or less, while others will maximize the distance, stating confidently that we won't be there for forty minutes or more. Do these people disagree for scientific reasons? (Some may have more confidence in their instruments than others do.) Or do their different opinions simply reflect the difference between optimists and pessimists?

4   To cope with this problem, we usually start by addressing the uncertainties in the scientific results. After all, everyone knows that science, in principle, can provide precise answers. One of the first scientists to be acclaimed by the public for his accurate predictions was Isaac Newton:

> Nature and Nature's law lay hid in night
> God said, Let Newton be! and all was light.
> (*Alexander Pope, "Epistle XI. Intended for Sir Isaac Newton*
> *in Westminster Abbey")*

Since Newton's accomplishments in the seventeenth century, scientists have continued to impress the public with remarkably accurate predictions that have led to inventions that continue to transform our daily lives. If, today, the results concerning a certain scientific problem have uncertainties, then, surely, it is only a matter of time before scientists present us with more accurate results. It is therefore easy to agree on a postponement of difficult political decisions regarding certain environmental problems on the grounds that we will soon have more precise scientific information. This could prove disastrous should we suddenly find ourselves at the edge of the waterfall. We recently had such an experience.

5   The current fisheries crisis, which is most severe off the shores of New England and eastern Canada where many species of fish have practically disappeared, started a decade after scientists first warned that overfishing could cause a dangerous reduction in fish stock. The scientists sounded a timely alert, but poor judgment on the part of policymakers contributed to this disaster. That is not how policymakers view the matter. Some complain of the scientists' "penchant for speaking in terms of probabilities and confidence intervals" and propose that, in future, scientists make "more confident forecasts . . . to catch the attention of regulators." As is often the case in environmental problems, we arrived at an impasse because of the reluctance of scientists to give definitive answers and the unwillingness of policymakers to make difficult political decisions. United States Congressman George Brown, former chairman of the House Committee on Science, Space and Technology, wonders whether there is a conspiracy between these two groups, the scientists who are assured a continuation of funds to improve their predictions, and the politicians who avoid difficult decisions that can cost them their jobs.

6   The fisheries crisis exemplifies a type of environmental problem with which we have had ample experience, and which the biologist Garret Hardin describes as "a tragedy of the commons."

> Picture a pasture open to all. It is to be expected that each herdsman will try to keep as many cattle as possible on the commons. Such an arrangement may work reasonably satisfactorily for centuries because tribal wars, poaching, and disease keep the numbers of both men and beast well below the carrying capacity of the land. Finally, however, comes the day of reckoning, that is, the day when the long-desired goal of social stability becomes a reality. At this point, the inherent logic of the commons remorselessly generates tragedy.
>
> As a rational being, each herdsman seeks to maximize his gain. Explicitly or implicitly, more or less consciously, he asks, "What is the utility to me of adding one more animal to my herd?"

The benefit of one more animal goes entirely to the herdsman. When it is sold, he receives all the proceeds. The disadvantage, the additional overgrazing, is shared by all. It is clearly to the advantage of the herdsman to acquire another animal. The other herdsmen reason similarly. The result is ruin for all.

7   The creation of private ownership is one attempt to avoid a tragedy of the commons. The landowner, out of self-interest, will prevent the land from being ruined. His interests do not necessarily coincide with ours so that we place restrictions on some of his actions. For example, he has to observe regulations concerning the disposal of sewage and toxic wastes because the water below his land and the air above it, fluids that can move pollutants off his property, remain part of the commons.

8   Given that, in the past, we successfully avoided many tragedies of the commons, why did we fail to avoid a fisheries crisis? Part of the reason is the novelty of the phenomenon; a decline in fish stock on a global scale is without precedent (although we have decreased the whale population significantly). Whereas we readily accept regulations that minimize damage that might occur during disasters with which we have experience (e.g., building codes that maximize public safety during an earthquake), we often oppose regulations that amount to precautionary measures to mitigate potential environmental disasters for which there are no precedents. If such disasters should occur in relatively small regions, they will serve as painful lessons on the need for regulations. If, however, a potential disaster has a global scale, we cannot afford to learn our lesson in such an expensive manner. Finding ways to avoid global disasters is a matter of urgency because the rapid growth in our numbers, and in our technological prowess, is increasing the likelihood of such disasters.

9   The English curate Thomas Robert Malthus (1766–1834) anticipated some of the problems that are likely because of the steady rise in the human population. In 1798 he predicted that, because our numbers are increasing at a rate that far exceeds the rate at which arable land increases, we are heading for a "gigantic inevitable famine." His forecast proved wrong, at least in the case of Britain and other rich countries, because he failed to anticipate the extent to which scientific and technological advances would increase the productivity of the inhabitants of those countries. The

rising standards of living in the rich countries led to social changes that decreased the number of children born per family, thus stabilizing the populations. Presumably, the poor nations, by raising their standard of living, will in due course also halt the growth of their populations. Perhaps the present rapid rise in the world population is a temporary phenomenon, to be followed by a period of declining populations, whereafter the world population will stabilize at a relatively low number that our planet can accommodate comfortably. We all wish for such an end but, unless we are careful, the journey could prove very treacherous. We will face serious problems should the poor nations copy the current industrial and agricultural practices of the rich because, at present, the cost of a high standard of living is an enormous, adverse impact on the environment. The damage has been reversed, or at least mitigated in a few cases—certain rivers, once so polluted that they occasionally caught fire, are now clean and safe for fish—but other escalating environmental problems go essentially unattended. The fisheries crisis is one example. Another worrisome development is the rapid accumulation of greenhouse gases in the atmosphere. Rich countries may have limited the rate at which their populations grow, but they are increasing the rate at which they inject greenhouse gases into the atmosphere.

10   Toward the end of the nineteenth century, the Swedish chemist Svante August Arrhenius (1859–1927) alerted the world that our industrial activities, which are causing the increase in the atmospheric concentration of greenhouse gases, could result in global climatic changes. Nobody paid much attention to his predictions because of considerable uncertainties. For example, in the absence of instruments with which to monitor atmospheric carbon dioxide levels, many scientists assumed that oceanic absorption of that gas would prevent its accumulation in the atmosphere. During the past century, scientists have reduced the uncertainties significantly. There is now indisputable evidence that the atmospheric concentrations of several greenhouses gases, not only carbon dioxide, have indeed been increasing rapidly since the start of the Industrial Revolution. Mathematical models of Earth's climate now provide details of the global climate changes, including global warming, that we should expect. Furthermore, recent studies of past climates on Earth, which tell us about the response of this planet to perturbations, enable us to gauge the likely consequences of the perturbations that we are introducing. Empirical and theoretical evidence leave no doubt that the growth in the atmospheric concentration of greenhouse gases, if continued indefinitely, will cause global climatic changes. There is, however, considerable disagreement about the timing of those changes. Some experts paint alarming pictures of sea level that will soon rise to inundate New York, London, Tokyo, and other coastal cities; of pests and diseases that will spread into new territory; and of fertile farmlands that will soon become drought-stricken. Other experts assure us that our industrial and agricultural activities pose no immediate threat, that there is no likelihood of global warming in the foreseeable future. Do these contradictory statements reflect uncertainties in the scientific results, or are they expressions of ideological differences? Here we have another example of an impasse created by uncertainties in scientific results, and a reluctance to make difficult political decisions. The difficulty stems from our reluctance to accept that, although accurate predictions are, in principle, possible on the basis of the laws of physics, such forecasts

may be impossible in practice because scientists—especially those who study complex environmental problems—deal with idealization of reality. They too have to accept that

> Between the idea
> and the reality
> Between the motion
> and the act
> Falls the Shadow
>
> (*T. S. Eliot, "The Hollow Men"*)

11   During the century since Arrhenius first sounded an alert, scientists have decreased the uncertainties in his forecasts considerably and are likely to continue doing so. However, there will always be shadows cast by inevitable uncertainties. We therefore have to ask ourselves whether we can continue to defer action much longer, given that the problem we face is similar to that of the gardener in the following riddle.

A gardener finds that his pond has one lily pad on a certain day; two the next day; four the subsequent day and so on. After 100 days the pond is completely filled with lily pads. On what day was the pond half full?

Answer: Day 99

Suppose that the gardener, once he realizes what is happening, quickly enlarges the pond to twice its size. On what day will the new pond be completely filled?

Answer: Day 101

12   The riddle illustrates how any problem involving explosive growth requires action at a very early stage, long before there are clear indications of impending trouble. In the case of the debate about global warming, in which some people insist that we are close to day 1 while others are adamant that we are close to day 100, the riddle indicates that, far more important than a precise answer that brings the debate to an end, is recognition of the special nature of the problem, its geometric growth. With such problems, it is far wiser to act sooner rather than later. To defer action is to court disaster.

13   A major impediment to progress on novel environmental problems, such as global warming or the depletion of fish stock, is the unrealistic expectation of precise predictions endorsed unanimously by the scientific community. This expectation reflects ignorance of the trial-and-error methods by which scientists reduce uncertainties in their results. Scientists continually subject any proposed solution to tests and do not hesitate to modify (or even abandon) a solution should it prove inadequate. Sound scientific results that have logic and clarity as their hallmark are often achieved by making many missteps along a tortuous road. (The irony is similar to that of poets who labor arduously to produce poems that flow effortlessly.) In our attempts to cope with our environmental problems, we should adopt a similar approach of trial and error. Rather than implement comprehensive programs that decree a rigid course of action to reach grand, final solutions, we should promote adaptive programs whose evolution is determined by the results from those programs and by new scientific results that become available. It will then be easier to take action when there is no scientific consensus,

and it will be possible to correct mistakes at an early stage before scarce resources have been wasted. By adopting this approach, we are doing remarkably well in our efforts to minimize damage to Earth's protective ozone layer.

14   Because they recognize that the atmosphere is a commons whose protection is their responsibility, the nations of the world agreed in the Montreal Protocol of 1987 that each would limit its production of the chlorofluorocarbons (CFCs) that contribute to the depletion of the ozone layer. This was a remarkable decision because it was made before there was clear evidence that CFCs are harmful to the ozone layer; at the time, scientists had only warned that CFCs could pose a serious threat. The diplomats who negotiated the Montreal Protocol accepted the uncertainties in the scientific predictions and proceeded to take action. They wisely agreed on regulations that are subject to periodic reviews in order to accommodate new scientific results. The initial regulations called for a reduction in the production of CFCs. When the original predictions concerning the effect of CFCs on the atmosphere proved erroneous—scientists at first underestimated the harmful effects of CFCs—the regulations were made more stringent, and the nations decided to cease production of CFCs.

15   Progress in science depends on the continual testing of results and explanations. Such skepticism makes it highly unlikely that scientists will ever unanimously recommend a solution to a problem that is so complex that the results have inevitable uncertainties. For a specific problem, the available evidence at a certain time may favor one particular explanation—e.g., overfishing for the disappearance of fish—but because of uncertainties, other possibilities—such as poor sampling of the fish population—cannot be excluded. A continual refinement of measurement and theories reduces uncertainties causing the spectrum of scientific opinions to converge. As long as there is some uncertainty, however, a few dissenting voices will persist. These contrarians, although they are wrong most of the time, are valuable because they force a continual reexamination of scientific methods and results. On a few rare occasions, they are even right. A prominent example concerns the idea of continental drift. With the exception of a few dissenters, the geological community rejected this notion for many decades, but in the end the dissenters proved right. Today the majority of geologists accept that continents drift.

16   The evidence accumulated over the past 100 years—especially the rapid scientific progress over the past few years—has convinced most scientists that the current rapid increase in the atmospheric concentration of greenhouse gases will lead to global climatic changes. There are, of course, a few dissenters, who would probably be skeptical even if the scientific issues were of strictly academic interest and concerned another planet, Mars, for example. That the issues are not strictly of academic interest but also have political aspects complicates matters enormously and dramatically alters the role of the skeptics, who become the focus of considerable attention for reasons unrelated to the merits of their scientific arguments. By focusing attention on the small group of dissenters, those who wish a continual deferral of action create the false impression that there is little agreement in the scientific community. To appreciate what is happening, the public needs to become familiar with the methods and results of scientists, especially the reasons for inevitable uncertainties that preclude precise predictions with which everyone agrees.

17   Scientists can contribute to the mitigation of potential disasters even when they are unable to make precise predictions. Consider the case of earthquakes. Their time of

occurrence cannot be predicted, but it is possible to anticipate how Earth's surface will move should an earthquake occur and hence to build structures capable of surviving earthquakes. To ensure public safety, states enforce building codes that are in accord with the recommendations of earthquake engineers. The public, familiar with the disasters that earthquakes can cause, readily accepts those regulations. We need to recognize the need for regulations even in the case of environmental disasters for which there are no precedents. To avoid disasters such as the depletion of fish stock off the northeastern coast of the United States, we can demand of scientists more confident forecasts that "catch the attention of the regulators," but it would be wiser to accept that we have to act in spite of uncertainties, in spite of the inevitable shadow between the idea and the reality.

18   We cope successfully with some environmental problems but not with others. We sensibly agreed to limit the release of CFCs into the atmosphere, but we failed to act in time to avoid a fisheries crisis. We have yet to do something about the accumulation of greenhouse gases in the atmosphere. While we inject those gases into the atmosphere at an accelerating rate, we defer a decision on how soon to make a transition to environmentally sound technologies because of uncertainties in the scientific predictions and even bigger uncertainties about the cost of the transition. We are rushing toward dangerous rapids and possibly a waterfall but are reluctant to act because we do not know precisely how much time we have left before we are in serious trouble. In discussions about the appropriate time to leave the river, we should keep in mind that a step as drastic as leaving the river promptly and trekking across unknown terrain is but one option. It may be wiser to start by leaving the swift, accelerating part of the stream and moving where the flow is slow. Coping with uncertainties is not a novel challenge. All of us—businessmen, politicians, military strategists—routinely make decisions on the basis of uncertain information, usually after we have familiarized ourselves with the available facts. We who are privileged to live on this benign planet should at least attempt to understand it so that we can assess the likely consequences of our actions.

Questions for Reading and Analysis

1. Philander begins by putting us in a raft on a river. What is the point of his analogy? How does it mirror the issue of global warming? How does it show the interplay between science and politics?

2. What do we expect from scientists?

3. What does the author want us to learn from the current fisheries crisis?

4. What does Philander assert about the possibilities of global climate changes?

5. What is uncertain about global warming? How should we respond to the uncertainties? Why?

6. What kinds of evidence does the author provide to support his argument?

7. What is Philander's claim? What does he want us to think and to do as a result of reading his argument?

8. Philander is not writing for a scientific audience. How do you know that?

Questions for Discussion and Response

1. What is the most important new idea you learned from this essay? Why is it important?

2. Has Philander clarified your thinking about global climate change in any way? If so, how? If not, why not?

3. Evaluate Philander's strategies. Do his analogies and examples and quotations aid the development of his ideas and his argument? Why or why not?

A Global Green Deal

Mark Hertsgaard

Mark Hertsgaard is a freelance journalist who has published widely in newspapers and magazines. He also is the author of several books, including *On Bended Knee* (1988), *A Day in the Life* (1995) and *Earth Odyssey* (1998). His article appeared in *Time* magazine's special issue on the future (April/May 2000).

1   So what do we do? Everyone knows the planet is in bad shape, but most people are resigned to passivity. Changing course, they reason, would require economic sacrifice and provoke stiff resistance from corporations and consumers alike, so why bother? It's easier to ignore the gathering storm clouds and hope the problem magically takes care of itself.

2   Such fatalism is not only dangerous but mistaken. For much of the 1990s I traveled the world to write a book about our environmental predicament. I returned home sobered by the extent of the damage we are causing and by the speed at which it is occurring. But there is nothing inevitable about our self-destructive behavior. Not only could we dramatically reduce our burden on the air, water and other natural systems, we could make money doing so. If we're smart, we could make restoring the environment the biggest economic enterprise of our time, a huge source of jobs, profits and poverty alleviation.

3   What we need is a Global Green Deal: a program to renovate our civilization environmentally from top to bottom in rich and poor countries alike. Making use of both market incentives and government leadership, a 21st century Global Green Deal would do for environmental technologies what government and industry have recently done so well for computer and Internet technologies: launch their commercial takeoff.

4   Getting it done will take work, and before we begin we need to understand three facts about the reality facing us. First, we have no time to lose. While we've made progress in certain areas—air pollution is down in the U.S.—big environmental problems like climate change, water scarcity and species extinction are getting worse, and faster than ever. Thus we have to change our ways profoundly—and very soon.

5   Second, poverty is central to the problem. Four billion of the planet's 6 billion people face deprivation inconceivable to the wealthiest 1 billion. To paraphrase Thomas Jefferson, nothing is more certainly written in the book of fate than that the bottom two-thirds of humanity will strive to improve their lot. As they demand adequate heat

and food, not to mention cars and CD players, humanity's environmental footprint will grow. Our challenge is to accommodate this mass ascent from poverty without wrecking the natural systems that make life possible.

6   Third, some good news: we have in hand most of the technologies needed to chart a new course. We know how to use oil, wood, water and other resources much more efficiently than we do now. Increased efficiency—doing more with less—will enable us to use fewer resources and produce less pollution per capita, buying us the time to bring solar power, hydrogen fuel cells and other futuristic technologies on line.

7   Efficiency may not sound like a rallying cry for environmental revolution, but it packs a financial punch. As Joseph J. Romm reports in his book *Cool Companies*, Xerox, Compaq and 3M are among many firms that have recognized they can cut their greenhouse-gas emissions in half—and enjoy 50% and higher returns on investment—through improved efficiency, better lighting and insulation and smarter motors and building design. The rest of us (small businesses, homeowners, city governments, schools) can reap the same benefits.

8   Super-refrigerators use 87% less electricity than older, standard models while costing the same (assuming mass production) and performing better, as Paul Hawken and Amory and L. Hunter Lovins explain in their book *Natural Capitalism*. In Amsterdam the headquarters of ING Bank, one of Holland's largest banks, uses one-fifth as much energy per square meter as a nearby bank, even though the buildings cost the same to construct. The ING center boasts efficient windows and insulation and a design that enables solar energy to provide much of the building's needs, even in cloudy Northern Europe.

9   Examples like these lead even such mainstream voices as AT&T and Japan's energy planning agency, NEDO, to predict that environmental restoration could be a source of virtually limitless profit. The idea is to retrofit our farms, factories, shops, houses, offices and everything inside them. The economic activity generated would be enormous. Better yet, it would be labor intensive; investments in energy efficiency yield two to 10 times more jobs than investments in fossil fuel and nuclear power. In a world where 1 billion people lack gainful employment, creating jobs is essential to fighting the poverty that retards environmental progress.

10   But this transition will not happen by itself—too many entrenched interests stand in the way. Automakers often talk green but make only token efforts to develop green cars because gas-guzzling sport-utility vehicles are hugely profitable. But every year the U.S. government buys 56,000 new vehicles for official use from Detroit. Under the Global Green Deal, Washington would tell Detroit that from now on the cars have to be hybrid-electric or hydrogen-fuel-cell cars. Detroit might scream and holler, but if Washington stood firm, carmakers soon would be climbing the learning curve and offering the competitively priced green cars that consumers say they want.

11   We know such government pump-priming works; it's why so many of us have computers today. America's computer companies began learning to produce today's affordable systems during the 1960s while benefiting from subsidies and guaranteed markets under contracts with the Pentagon and the space program. And the cyberboom has fueled the biggest economic expansion in history.

12   The Global Green Deal must not be solely an American project, however. China and India, with their gigantic populations and ambitious development plans, could by

themselves doom everyone else to severe global warming. Already, China is the world's second largest producer of greenhouse gases (after the U.S.). But China would use 50% less coal if it simply installed today's energy-efficient technologies. Under the Global Green Deal, Europe, America and Japan would help China buy these technologies, not only because that would reduce global warming but also because it would create jobs and profits for workers and companies back home.

13   Governments would not have to spend more money, only shift existing subsidies away from environmentally dead-end technologies like coal and nuclear power. If even half the $500 billion to $900 billion in environmentally destructive subsidies now offered by the world's governments were redirected, the Global Green Deal would be off to a roaring start. Governments need to establish "rules of the road" so that market prices reflect the real social costs of clear-cut forests and other environmental abominations. Again, such a shift could be revenue neutral. Higher taxes on, say, coal burning would be offset by cuts in payroll and profits taxes, thus encouraging jobs and investment while discouraging pollution. A portion of the revenues should be set aside to assure a just transition for workers and companies now engaged in inherently antienvironmental activities like coal mining.

14   All this sounds easy enough on paper, but in the real world it is not so simple. Beneficiaries of the current system—be they U.S. corporate-welfare recipients, redundant German coal miners or cut-throat Asian logging interests—will resist. Which is why progress is unlikely absent a broader agenda of change, including real democracy: assuring the human rights of environmental activists and neutralizing the power of Big Money through campaign-finance reform.

15   The Global Green Deal is no silver bullet. It can, however, buy us time to make the more deep-seated changes—in our often excessive appetites, in our curious belief that humans are the center of the universe, in our sheer numbers—that will be necessary to repair our relationship with our environment.

16   None of this will happen without an aroused citizenry. But a Global Green Deal is in the common interest, and it is a slogan easily grasped by the media and the public. Moreover, it should appeal across political, class and national boundaries, for it would stimulate both jobs and business throughout the world in the name of a universal value: leaving our children a livable planet. The history of environmentalism is largely the story of ordinary people pushing for change while governments, corporations and other established interests reluctantly follow behind. It's time to repeat that history on behalf of a Global Green Deal.

Questions for Reading and Analysis

1. What is Hertsgaard's subject? What is his claim? Where does he state it?

2. Where does Hertsgaard get his label: a Global Green Deal?

3. To respond to our environmental problems, what three facts do we need to understand?

4. What are the advantages of increased efficiency in energy use?

5. What does the author suggest as a strategy for getting "green cars"?

6. How can America make the Green Deal global? Why should we want to help other countries?

7. Who will resist a Global Green Deal? What are the difficulties in creating a Global Green Deal? How can it be done?

Questions for Discussion and Response

1. What kinds of support does Hertsgaard provide for his claim? Is it effective?

2. Where does the author offer a conciliatory approach? Do you think that this strategy will make his proposals more acceptable to some who may be inclined to resist the idea initially? Explain your views.

3. What challenges does he anticipate, and how does he rebut them in his argument? Do you find his rebuttals successful?

4. Do you agree that we need a massive commitment to the environment? Does Hertsgaard have a good approach? Why or why not?

Why Mother Nature Should Love Cyberspace

Chris Taylor

Chris Taylor (b. 1973) read history at Merton College, Oxford, and holds a journalism degree from Columbia University. He is currently San Francisco bureau chief for *Time* magazine and published the following article in the *Time* special issue on the future (April/May 2000).

1   A massive environmental catastrophe is predicted, but help arrives in the form of new and utterly unexpected technology. America in the 21st century? No, London in the 19th. Some apocryphal Victorian, so the story goes, looked at the rate at which the number of horses on city streets was increasing and assured his peers that their capital would soon be knee-deep in horse manure. He got it wrong, largely because he failed to predict the imminent rise of the automobile. That brought its own problems, of course, but the point was that Victorians were blindsided by the future—which, as any would-be Cassandra soon learns, is seldom what it appears to be.

2   Think for a minute: Is there a technology right under our noses that will make many of our own environmental fears moot? Yes, there is. It's called the Internet. According to scores of studies, the dotcom revolution is already starting to have a profound impact on the way industry affects our world.

3   In the past two years alone, here's what has happened: more people are working from home; companies are using business-to-business (B2B) websites to coordinate their supply chain more efficiently; inventories are lower, meaning warehouses are emptier; and although the paperless office has failed to arrive, online habits are reducing paper needs by millions of tons. "We're still going to have to clean up the environment,"

says Joseph Romm of Washington's Center for Energy and Climate Solutions. "But the Internet is allowing a type of growth that uses energy and resources better."

4   You may scoff: Am I really going to save the planet by buying books on Barnesandnoble.com rather than Barnes & Noble at the mall? Actually, you just might. A book purchased online costs about one-sixteenth the energy of one bought in the store. For starters, it takes about 0.1 gal. (0.4 L) of fuel to ship an average 2.5-lb. (1.1-kg) book, whereas your average trip to the mall uses up 1 gal. (3.8 L) of gas. One minute spent driving, in general, uses the same amount of energy as 20 minutes' worth of time sitting at home with your computer.

5   Then there's all that waste from real-world stores, which need heating and lighting. Online retailers that employ nothing but warehouses have about eight times the number of sales per square foot of space used. According to the Organization for Economic Cooperation and Development, the Internet could make 12.5% of retail space superfluous. That would save around $5 billion worth of energy every year. For everything you buy with a point and a click, the planet thanks you.

6   The same goes for each newspaper, magazine, catalog and phone directory you read online. A study by the Boston Consulting Group says the Internet will reduce worldwide demand for paper about 2.7 million tons a year by 2003, and this is going to happen despite the fact that we're actually using more paper in our offices than ever. So where do the savings kick in? Well, think about all those letters to Grandma you would send by post if it weren't easier to e-mail her. Or all those catalogs Lands' End doesn't need to send because it's doing such a roaring trade online. Or newspapers. Worldwide, $27 billion in advertising will be siphoned away from your daily read and onto the Internet during the next five years, according to Forrester Research. That includes the 15% of all classified ads—cars, homes and lonely hearts—that are moving online. Your Sunday paper may never feel quite so weighty again. (Whether magazines like the one you're holding will shed a few grams remains to be seen.)

7   Consider the tremendous savings now that millions of us are able to work from home—or at least, dial into the office more than we drive there. After all, your refrigerator's always on; the heating is always on in the winter. You might as well be there, especially with lightning-fast broadband Internet connections. In the past three years there has been a 12% increase in the number of home-run businesses in the U.S. (not counting folks who quit their job to become full-time auction jockeys on eBay). As for the rest of us working stiffs, our firms may soon be grateful for the time we spend telecommuting. Some are already regulating electricity in their offices remotely, darkening unused areas and saving a ton of cash on energy bills.

8   The ease of e-commerce can also be a curse. If you demand overnight shipping on those books, it'll take six times the amount of fuel to get them to you as would normal delivery, thanks to jet-fuel costs. But environmental groups welcome the Net's energy efficiency. Says Ned Ford of the Sierra Club's energy committee: "Almost anybody who uses the Internet on a regular basis will feel the savings occurring." Given time, we might start to think of malls and offices as the 20th century version of horse manure—an unpleasant threat that, all of a sudden, got cleaned away.

Questions for Reading and Analysis

1. How does Taylor get the reader's attention in his opening paragraph? What is clever about his introduction?

2. What is Taylor's subject? What is his claim?

3. What is his primary support? In general, what kinds of evidence does he provide to support his claim?

4. This is a problem/solution type of argument. Does the author think that the solution he emphasizes will solve all of our environmental problems? What qualifiers does he offer?

Questions for Discussion and Response

1. What statistics in this essay are most surprising to you? Why?

2. What experiences have you had with the changes that Taylor catalogs? Do you shop online or work from home or e-mail your professor? Have you thought about how these actions may help the environment? Do you think that you should consider aiding the environment when you make choices about how to shop? Why or why not?

3. What other problems do we face that may help to make shopping malls obsolete?

4. Should we rely on new technologies to solve environmental problems? That is, stop worrying about the future and wait for the technological solution? Why or why not?

Who's Afraid of Globalization?

Gregg Easterbrook

A journalist and freelance writer, Gregg Easterbrook (b. 1953) is currently a senior editor at the *New Republic*. He is the author of *Beside Still Waters: Searching for Meaning in an Age of Doubt* (1998). His article on the global economy was published in *The Wall Street Journal* (April 14, 2000) at the time of major meetings of the World Bank, accompanied by protests staged outside meeting sites.

1   An awful lot is going on with this week's antiglobalization demonstrations in Washington, though no one is quite sure what. The protests thus mirror the nature of globalization itself: An awful lot is going on, but what?

2   At the deepest level, much of what inspires the foes of globalization is that world economic changes are occurring so fast that they can't keep up. They're not alone: Nobody understands globalization, including, events suggest, the International Monetary Fund or the World Bank. Frustrating though that fact may be, it might also be the proper way to proceed.

Fear of Change

3   Historically, it was conservatism that most feared economic change. Conservative writers of the late 19th century were aghast at the factories of England and New England. Soot was fouling the air, while the plants were drawing workers away from traditional agrarian communities and toward city centers. Conservatives feared that by separating workers from small-town life, the new industrial order would change women's roles, family structure, sexual mores and many other aspects of society. As recently as the 1950s writing of Russell Kirk, modern economics was seen by classical conservatives as a terrifying force, guaranteeing constant upheaval and change.

4   Today it is the left that fears the spread of economic change. And it is no coincidence that one of the complaints of the antiglobalization crowd is that modern economics is drawing developing world citizens away from traditional agrarian communities and toward city centers. The anti-World Trade Organization side may have some valid points. But first let's consider the new fear of globalization itself.

5   Antiglobilization sentiment stems in part from romanticized notions that the developing world would be better off if left untouched by the West. Only those who have lived favored lives in affluent nations could imagine this. Western contact with developing nations causes all kinds of problems, but as someone who has lived in the developing world (Pakistan), I can attest that roughly 99.9% of the earth's non-Western population yearns for the living standards, education and democracy of the West. Contact with the West may hardly be ideal—our culture, corporations and governments all have many faults. But interactions with the West are simply the developing world's best hope, and so must go forward.

6   Next, some fear of globalization stems from the realization that no one is in charge, particularly government—it's just happening! Lori Wallace, a leader of the anti-WTO movement, says in the current issue of *Foreign Policy* that she is just as worried about big government as about big business.

7   But this statement rings hollow. Surely her true objection is that most governments believe globalization should follow its present unplanned course. If there were multinational bureaucracies running the globalization show (instead of just granting license, as the WTO does), the left might feel very differently, since then it could lobby the agencies and attempt to dictate events. Instead, the show is running itself.

8   Yet having no one in charge is the nature of true, free economics—a sign of success (the ultimate decentralization), though not necessarily of calm nerves. And the sense that no one is in charge is sure to increase. There are six billion people in the world, and that sum is rising. Communication is getting easier and cheaper globally, and consumer demand is rising everywhere. The amalgamation of more people wanting more things and having more ideas more easily communicated creates a chaotic situation in which it's simply impossible for anyone to be sure what's going on, let alone predict what will happen next. We should make our peace with this, because global change—good change and bad—is here to stay, so long as political and economic freedom is sustained.

9   The changes wrought by globalization may be stressful and confusing, but so far, they are largely pro-people. Incomes and longevity are rising almost everywhere in the world, including for most of the world's poor; food production continues to rise faster

than population, staving off predicted Malthusian famines and saving the lives of billions (it's easy to take food for granted in the U.S., but in India, high-yield agriculture is the greatest benefit ever extended to the typical person); literacy rates and education levels are rising globally, with the biggest gains among the worst off; communications technology is eroding dictatorships and empowering typical people throughout the world, including, of course, those people opposing the WTO.

10   Suppose opponents of globalization managed to stop or severely restrict the chaotic, decentralized process of globalized economics and technology. The outcome would almost certainly be negative for everyone; it would be worst for the world's working class.

11   Circumstances for the majority of working people have improved in the U.S. in the seven years since the North American Free Trade Agreement, one of the first recent globalization experiments. Unemployment is near the postwar low, standards of living are rising and national growth is steady. (Recessions hit the working class much harder than the elites.) Consider that in the postwar era, those developing nations with WTO-style trade policies have achieved three times the economic growth of nations with restricted trade regimes.

12   Economic growth is no cure-all—it may bring pollution, inequity, overpaid chief executives, excessive materialism and other ills. But a simple glance at the globe tells you that, on balance, market economics and free trade maximize a nation's net well-being. And the national net well-being matters much more to the typical person than to elites, who can look after themselves.

13   In turn, if your complaint against international economics is inequitable results—such as CEOs making 420 times as much as hourly workers—handicapping world commerce will only result in driving the worker's share down. Extremes of inequality, a troubling problem of market economics, need to be addressed by some mechanism other than trade barriers.

14   Nevertheless the protesters in Washington are not without points that demand immediate hearing. They, including the AFL-CIO contingent, seem right to say that more labor protections should be included in trade accords—especially health and safety standards and living-wage minimums for workers in the developing world.

The U.S. Model

15   There is a shining, irrefutable argument that worker organizing and labor protection can go hand in hand with free-market prosperity, corporate profits and rising freedom and material standards for everyone. That argument is the 20th-century U.S. The need for unions may be declining here, but that is because during the period of U.S. industrial development, labor organizing moderated the excesses of the market and established the principle that every worker deserves a safe workplace and a living wage. Developing nations will benefit if they, too, evolve an ethic that considers everyone worthy of a decent life. As we offer our economics, culture, technology and standard of endless infuriating change to the rest of the world, we should offer our philosophy of labor protection, too.

Questions for Reading and Analysis

1. What is Easterbrook's subject? What is his claim? (Think carefully about how you word his main point.)

2. In the past, what group has feared economic changes? Currently, what group opposes change, including the changes brought by globalization?

3. What are two of the sources of antiglobalization? How does the author challenge these views?

4. What are some of the advantages of globalization?

5. If globalization were derailed, what would be the consequences? Who would suffer the most?

6. What are some legitimate concerns of protesters, in Easterbrook's view? How can we help address those problems?

Questions for Discussion and Response

1. Have you opposed—or known those who have opposed—such international trade agreements as NAFTA? If so, does Easterbrook answer any of your objections to these agreements for trade? Why or why not?

2. Evaluate Easterbrook's conciliatory approach at the end of his essay. Does his nod to legitimate concerns of the protestors strengthen his argument? Why or why not?

3. Why is it helpful to seek to analyze the causes for our fears of the future or of change? How can we benefit from an analysis such as Easterbrook's?

4. Do you agree with the author that, on balance, the global economy is good? Why or why not?

CHAPTER 22

Twenty-first Century Living: Where Are We Headed? Where Do We Want to Go?

This collection of five essays offers a mixed bag of impressions and concerns about contemporary life and the world we are creating for the new century. The works share a common interest in helping us see our world more clearly—seeing how we live or how we should be living or how others might see and comment on America's lifestyles. Some of the articles are positive, upbeat. Others are gloomier, raising questions about what we are doing to our sense of community. But you do not need, necessarily, to despair. Remember that many writers choose to respond to problems that need to be addressed. Presumably, if they write, they believe that intelligent people of goodwill can solve those problems. See what you can learn from both kinds of writers.

As you read in this chapter, consider some of the following questions:

1. What strategies for persuasion does each writer use? Are they effective?

2. What do the writers' views have in common? That is, do they see some of the same *kinds* of problems? What should we be most concerned about, according to these writers?

3. Which writer has given me the most to think about? Why? Are the ideas new ones for me? Startling in their presentation? About an issue I think is quite serious?

4. With which writer do I disagree the most? Why? Do I already have clear views on this topic? Do I disagree with the writer's attitude/tone/approach to the topic?

A Rude Awakening

Nancy Ann Jeffrey

A native New Yorker, Nancy Ann Jeffrey holds a degree in philosophy from Princeton University. She also studied at Oxford University on a Marshall scholarship. She is currently a reporter in the New York bureau of *The Wall Street Journal* covering health care issues.

1   Has America forgotten its manners? Barry Barnett is starting to think so. The health-benefits consultant was delivering a presentation to some new dot-com clients, when one of them suddenly cut him off and barked, "I don't care." So is famed restaurateur Danny Meyer, who watched with dismay recently as a customer interrupted a waitress to answer his cell phone—but grabbed her and told her to keep talking. And flight attendant Lori Vitto, who had to intervene when one passenger told another: "I hope you die."

2   It's "rush, rush, rush," says Ms. Vitto, a USAirways employee based in Washington. "People have no tolerance or compassion anymore."

3   Talk about a rude awakening. While impolite behavior has always been a fact of life, there is mounting evidence that incivility not only is on the rise but has become almost the norm in many parts of the culture. A recent University of North Carolina survey of 775 workers nationwide found that every single person had experienced some type of rude behavior on the job, including insults, curses, nasty e-mails and denigrating gossip. Restaurant reviewer Zagat Survey LLC found that gripes about service have tripled over the past five years. Meanwhile, air travel has practically become a combat zone, with customer-service complaints more than doubling last year alone, according to the U.S. Transportation Department.

4   Some see all this as the dark side of the New Economy. The Internet has bred a generation of brash young entrepreneurs that glorifies speed over decorum and innovation over tradition. High-tech gadgets, such as cellular phones, pagers and Palm Pilots, have also fostered antisocial tendencies, enabling people to isolate themselves even in public. So have sudden windfalls from the stock market, making some people think they can have whatever they want when they want it.

5   Some of these people "maybe forget where they came from," says events planner Robert Isabell, who has observed more of his clients demanding last-minute changes in arrangements long after it is feasible to make them. Hal Reiter, 50, president of Herbert Mines Associates, an executive-search firm in New York, adds that young dot-comers often end meetings by simply getting up and walking out of the room. "I've had guys get up without shaking hands, without saying goodbye, with none of the graciousness," he says.

6   But the rise in rudeness is by no means just a Silicon Valley phenomenon. The Ohio Farm Bureau recently warned farmers to keep their tractors off the road at rush hour because of an uptick in aggressive driving behavior. In Michigan, more than half the residents surveyed in a statewide poll last month said they curse daily. Even the South, though still associated with hospitality, "is very much like the rest of the country now," says Wyck Knox, chairman of Atlanta law firm Kilpatrick Stockton. Mr. Knox's particular pet peeve: people who scream into their cell phones in public places, oblivious to the sensibilities of those around them.

It's the Economy, Stupid

7 If the public is behaving badly these days, so are many of the workers who serve it. Thanks to an unemployment rate that last month hit a 30-year low, many employers are being forced to hire any staff they can find, with little regard for their people skills. A recent survey of small businesses shows that about one-third of such enterprises are having problems filling jobs, according to the National Federation of Independent Business in Washington. Says Jim Weidman, a spokesman for the federation: "A pulse is considered a plus in many cases."

8 That's about all New York lawyer Floyd Abrams found moving when he walked into a grocery store recently to buy a sandwich. The person in charge was sitting several feet away from the counter, eating his own sandwich. "He sort of looked at me like 'Who was I to interrupt his life?'" says Mr. Abrams, a prominent First Amendment specialist. He tried to buy a banana instead, but the employee at the cash register was reading a magazine and never even looked up. "It was as if I didn't exist," says Mr. Abrams, who finally gave up and walked out.

9 Some people politely defend rudeness. "I'm a proponent of rudeness that has a benefit," says Stephen Samuels, a consultant to Excite At Home Corp. and chairman of a start-up company in Westport, Conn., that develops content for television and the Internet. "I would rather be short and to the point and say 'let's get on with it' than caught up with excess politeness." Among the practices Mr. Samuels endorses: fast-blast e-mails with no cumbersome "pleases" or "thank yous," minimalist voice-mail messages, and cutting off people at meetings when they meander.

10 Others go so far as to disparage courtesy, labeling it not just inefficient but often insincere. "I think rudeness is better than dishonesty," says Harvard University's Alan Dershowitz, the law professor and criminal-defense lawyer. His gripe: people who come up to him and pay false compliments. "I know I'm very controversial, and I'd rather have people come over and say, 'I disagree with you,'" Mr. Dershowitz adds. "I don't like people who are a—-kissers."

Hit-and-Run Rudeness

11 Compounding the incivility at work and in service establishments, many people say they are encountering more hit-and-run rudeness from strangers—on the street, in the movie theater, at the grocery store. One key weapon: cellular phones and other high-tech gadgets, which many people use as a license to get lost in their wired world and ignore real human beings in their path. "They are in a trance," says Darlene Lutz, an art adviser who works with Madonna, among other clients. At Ms. Lutz's favorite local delicatessen recently, a man on a cell phone jumped ahead of her in line; when she objected, he stood his place and scolded her, "you took too long to decide."

12 Similarly, several weeks ago John M. Davis, an interior designer in New York, politely asked the man sitting behind him at the movies to stop talking during the film—but the man told him to "shut up" and kept talking. "It's become a continual thing in the movies," says Mr. Davis. "People think they are sitting in their living rooms."

13 To be sure, America has never exactly been world-renowned for politesse. After all, there are few more widely shared stereotypes in Europe than that of the rude American tourist, loudmouthed and quick to complain. But culture watchers say such behavior

tends to be particularly prevalent when the economy is strong—and this, of course, is the longest-running boom in U.S. history. The theme of the past decade, says Judith Martin, the syndicated columnist known as Miss Manners, might be "you shouldn't restrict anything you say on the grounds of consideration for other people."

14   Even outside the dot-com world, heightened competition and years of declining corporate loyalty seem to be undermining some age-old business practices. Some lawyers, for example, say they are seeing more instances of everything from not returning phone calls to lying in negotiations. People are "looking for a competitive edge or fearful of losing whatever status they think they have," says New York and Washington securities lawyer Harvey Pitt. He says the rudest incident he has encountered lately was when a supposed friend tried, unsuccessfully, to discourage a company from hiring him.

Road Outrage

15   But, no matter how prevalent rudeness gets, most people still find themselves stunned by it. Alison Ainsworth, a premed student at Bryn Mawr College in Pennsylvania, is still smarting from an encounter earlier this month with another driver. Driving a 15-foot rental truck down a narrow street, she realized she couldn't make it past a van coming from the opposite direction. She politely asked the driver of the van if he would back up, explaining that she was unfamiliar with the truck and that there were three cars behind her and no one behind him. Despite five minutes of further pleading, the man refused, insisting Ms. Ainsworth should be the one to move. At wit's end, she finally asked the drivers behind her to back up and then backed up herself. "I can understand road rage at rush hour, but this was a small street on a Saturday morning," she says. "I honestly don't understand it."

16   Fed up with such incidents, some people are fighting back, lecturing their children and employees about the importance of manners and even hiring etiquette consultants in some cases. Rosanne Thomas, an etiquette consultant in Boston who works with companies, says her business has increased tenfold during the past five years. Her mission: to polish the style of twenty- and thirtysomething employees who are technical whizzes but social disasters. "These young people know their jobs very well but they don't have the basics—how to introduce themselves, how to wield their forks and knives, how not to offend people," Ms. Thomas says.

Etiquette Training

17   Ellyn McColgan, president of the tax-exempt services division of Fidelity Investments in Boston, says she was horrified when she attended a buffet lunch a few years ago and watched young Fidelity employees rush to the front of the line to get their food first. At a cocktail party, the staffers ignored the clients they were supposed to schmooze. Table manners were also poor. "You would just watch people shovel food into their mouths," Ms. McColgan says. As a result, she called in Ms. Thomas, who has since trained several hundred Fidelity staffers in basic table manners and conversation skills.

18   But instilling better manners on a more widespread basis won't be easy. For one thing, politeness increasingly "is perceived as a weakness" in our society, says P.M. Forni, a professor and specialist in civility at Johns Hopkins University in Baltimore. For another thing, some forms of rudeness seem so inexplicable as to be almost unremediable.

19 That's certainly the feeling of Ms. Vitto, the USAirways flight attendant, who three months ago watched in shock as a fight nearly broke out, quite literally, over peanuts. A passenger, overhearing that pretzels rather than nuts would be served due to the allergy of a man sitting near him, started railing at the traveler at issue. "The guy went ballistic," says Ms. Vitto. "I was just blown away." She moved the allergic man to another seat.

Questions for Reading and Analysis

1. What is Jeffrey's subject? What is her claim? What type of argument is this?
2. How does Jeffrey open her essay? What is effective about her strategy?
3. What are some of the possible causes of the problem Jeffrey examines?
4. On what basis is rudeness defended by some people?
5. Where do we find incivility today in addition to the workplace and from service people?
6. How are some people dealing with today's rudeness? That is, what are some solutions to the problem? How confident is the author that these solutions will work?
7. What is Jeffrey's primary strategy for supporting her claim; that is, what *kind* of evidence does she provide?

Questions for Discussion and Response

1. Have you had experiences similar to those described by Jeffrey? If so, what were your reactions?
2. Do you talk on your cell phone in public places? Do you talk during movies? Do you get up and leave class when you feel like it? Do you consider any of these actions to be rude? Why or why not?
3. What should people do in response to rudeness? How should we handle the situations Jeffrey describes?
4. The author quotes Professor Forni as observing that "politeness increasingly 'is perceived as a weakness' in our society." Do you agree that politeness is a weakness? Why or why not? Do you agree with Forni that many Americans have this view?

"Numbed Down" in America

Mark Steinberg

A former associate deputy attorney general and director of the Office for National Security in the Department of Justice, Mark Steinberg (b. 1945) is a Los Angeles lawyer with a practice focused on intellectual property, antitrust, and general civil litigation. His article was published on June 17, 2000, in the *Washington Post*.

1   A college basketball coach who has amassed a phenomenal winning record on the basis of repeated intimidation and physical abuse of young players, officials and college administrators is told he can keep his job so long as he is not caught again doing what he should not have done even once.

2   The former members of a high school academic decathlon team who catapulted their school to glory, then shame, by cheating their way to victory in a national competition say that their biggest mistake was getting caught.

3   In an anonymous Internet posting in a chat room for law firm associates, a young lawyer muses about what to do if one is nearing but might not reach the billed-hour minimum required to qualify for an annual bonus: "I guess it would be easy enough to take on a pro bono case at year end and just pad your hours on that matter."

4   Another contributor to the same chat room, who identifies himself as a law student about to graduate, says: I "found out that all these years everyone—and I mean 80 percent of the class here at my law school—has been cheating. I'm a commuter student who works full-time so I've been a little out of it, but apparently students pay others to write papers for them, ask fellow students about exam questions before taking them (deliberately lying so they can take the same exam later), use cheat sheets etc."

5   These examples are points on a continuum, manifestations of another kind of crisis of values in America. This one is not about the morality or legality of abortion, the death penalty or birth control; it's about what conduct we should tolerate from those driven by the pursuit of success, whether on the basketball court, in academia or in business.

6   The question is worth discussing because the health of our social environment hinges on the answer. As more and more people come to see their jobs exclusively as vehicles for reaching the pot or medal of gold, our society in countless ways is becoming a less civil, less trustworthy, less pleasant place to be. We have begun to tolerate conduct that not so long ago we thought of—and responded to—as crude, immoral or just plain nasty.

7   The "numbing down" of our collective tolerance for mean, dishonest and abusive behavior is, in a way, a reflection of our own changing choices. Today there is an audience for gross violence, both real ("extreme" boxing) and simulated (professional wrestling). There is also an unparalleled reverence for wealth and those who produce it. Thus, in many of the major accounting, law and investment banking firms of America, the poorly kept secret is that there are "rainmakers"—people who produce disproportionate amounts of the firm's income—who can abuse and harass others without fear of reproach.

8   And finally—as Bobby Knight[1] can attest—today we are willing to pay an unnaturally high price for winning. That price goes well beyond the salary of someone like Knight, and even beyond our own diminished self-respect for continuing to fawn over him and others like him. The price we pay extends to something genuinely, unquestionably important: the values of those who see in these "winners" both the formula for achieving success and the rewards of it. Through abuse and bullying one can rise to the

---

[1]Knight, former basketball coach at Indiana University, was fired in the Summer of 2000—Ed.

top and, *mirabile dictu*, when one reaches the top, one can abuse and bully to one's heart's content.

9   That the ultimate price has been paid, yet again, is evident from the remark of one of the young people in Bobby Knight's charge. When asked how the debate over Knight's future might be brought to an end, a player said: "I'm pretty sure if we won a lot of games and won a national championship, it would cure all of this."

10   But if there is a cure for all of this, it will not be found in more of the same. Rather, it will come from close, candid examination of whether the values we say we hold are the values we practice. Are money and winning the exclusive measures of our success? Does achieving great victory justify a breach of ethics, civility or humanity? Should we countenance abuse and harassment by powerful people because they are powerful? Do we value ourselves more for whom we stand above than for what we have accomplished in our own estimation? Is loyalty to an institution—whether a team, a partnership or a corporation—an unfashionable and embarrassing relic of the past?

11   I grew up in a country in which I believed I knew how most of those who lived and worked around me would answer these questions. I like to think that I still do.

Questions for Reading and Analysis

1. What does Steinberg accomplish in his opening paragraphs? How does he use this material later in his essay?

2. What is the author's claim? Where does he state it?

3. Where does Steinberg's title come from? Why is "Numbed Down" in quotation marks?

4. What are the causes of our "numbed down" condition?

5. What solutions does Steinberg offer?

6. How would you describe the tone of this essay? Is the author angry? Bemused? Analytic? Sad? Something else?

Questions for Discussion and Response

1. Are you surprised by Steinberg's four opening examples? Why or why not?

2. Would you describe the four opening examples as revealing conduct that is "crude, immoral, or just plain nasty"? Why or why not?

3. Do you agree with the author that we have developed a tolerance for behavior that is presumably inconsistent with what we say we value? If you disagree, explain your position.

4. In his conclusion, the author asks many questions that he does not answer specifically. Do you understand how readers are supposed to answer the questions? Do you find this an effective conclusion? Why or why not?

The Idiocy of Urban Life

Henry Fairlie

Born in London and educated at Oxford, Henry Fairlie (1924–1990) began his career by writing for the *Observer* and the *London Times*. Moving to the United States, Fairlie contributed to both British and U.S. journals and wrote several books on American politics and culture, including *Republicans and Democrats in This Century* (1978) and *The Seven Deadly Sins Today* (1979). In "The Idiocy of Urban Life," published in the *New Republic* January 5/12, 1987, Fairlie, in an amusing but still serious manner, looks at life in the city and the suburbs.

1   Between about 3 a.m. and 6 a.m. the life of the city is civil. Occasionally the lone footsteps of someone walking to or from work echo along the sidewalk. All work that has to be done at those hours is useful—in bakeries, for example. Even the newspaper presses stop turning forests into lies. Now and then a car comes out of the silence and cruises easily through the blinking traffic lights. The natural inhabitants of the city come out from damp basements and cellars. With their pink ears and paws, sleek, well-groomed, their whiskers combed, rats are true city dwellers. Urban life, during the hours when they reign, is urbane.

2   These rats are social creatures, as you can tell if you look out on the city street during an insomniac night. But after 6 a.m., the two-legged, daytime creatures of the city begin to stir; and it is they, not the rats, who bring the rat race. You might think that human beings congregate in large cities because they are gregarious. The opposite is true. Urban life today is aggressively individualistic and atomized. Cities are not social places.

3   The lunacy of modern city life lies first in the fact that most city dwellers who can do so try to live outside the city boundaries. So the two-legged creatures have created suburbs, exurbs, and finally rururbs (rurbs to some). Disdaining rural life, they try to create simulations of it. No effort is spared to let city dwellers imagine they are living anywhere but in a city; patches of grass in the more modest suburbs, broader spreads in the richer ones further out; prim new trees planted along the streets; at the foot of the larger back yards, a pretense of bosky woodlands. Black & Decker thrives partly on this basic do-it-yourself rural impulse in urban life; and with the declining demand for the great brutes of farm tractors, John Deere has turned to the undignified business of making dinky toy tractors for the suburbanites to ride like Roman charioteers as they mow their lawns.

4   In the city itself gentrification means two tubs of geraniums outside the front door of a town house that has been prettified to look like a country cottage. The homes, restaurants, and even offices of city dwellers are planted thick with vegetation. Some executives have window boxes inside their high-rise offices; secretaries, among their other chores, must now be horticulturists. Commercials on television, aimed primarily at city dwellers, have more themes of the countryside than of urban life. Cars are never seen in a traffic jam, but whiz through bucolic scenery. Lovers are never in tenements, but drift through sylvan glades. Cigarettes come from Marlboro Country. Merrill Lynch is a bull. Coors is not manufactured in a computerized brewery, but taken from mountain streams.

5   The professional people buy second homes in the country as soon as they can afford them, and as early as possible on Friday head out of the city they have created. The

New York intellectuals and artists quaintly say they are "going to the country" for the weekend or summer, but in fact they have created a little Manhattan-by-the-Sea around the Hamptons, spreading over the Long Island potato fields whose earlier solitude was presumably the reason why they first went there. City dwellers take the city with them to the country, for they will not live without its pamperings. The main streets of America's small towns, which used to have hardware and dry-goods stores, are now strips of boutiques. Old-fashioned barbers become unisex hairdressing salons. The brown rats stay in the cities because of the filth the humans leave during the day. The rats clean it up at night. Soon the countryside will be just as nourishing to them, as the city dwellers take their filth with them.

6   The recent dispersal of the urban middle-class population is only the latest development in this now established lunatic pattern. People who work in Cleveland live as far out as lovely Geauga and Ashtabula counties in northeast Ohio, perhaps 30 or 50 miles away. A bank manager in Chardon, which used to be a gracious market town in Geauga, once explained to me how the city people who come to live there want about five acres of land. "But they want the five acres for themselves alone, and not for others who come to follow their example, though no one is going to supply the services—electricity, gas, sewerage, water—for a few people living on their five acres. So the place fills up, and soon they've rebuilt the urban life they said they were escaping. What is more, they don't like paying for those services, since the rich come out to escape the high city taxes." They also force up the price of land and old houses, so that real estate is put beyond the reach of farmers and others who must work there.

7   In the old industrial cities, people lived near their places of work. The mill hands lived around the cotton mill, and the mill owner lived close at hand, in the big house on the hill, looking down on the chimney stacks belching out the smoke that was the evidence they were producing and giving employment. The steelworkers and the steel magnate lived close to the steel mill. The German brewer Miller lived next to his brewery in Milwaukee. The city churches had congregations that were representative of both the resident population and the local working population. It wasn't so much that work gave meaning to life as that it created a community that extended into and enriched the residential community, and sustained a solidarity among the workers. It was the automakers, especially the ever revolutionary Henry Ford, who realized that their own product enabled them to build factories far from the dispersed homes of the workers, and not unconsciously they appreciated that a dispersed work force would be docile.

8   Work still gives meaning to rural life, the family, and churches. But in the city today work and home, family and church, are separated. What the office workers do for a living is not part of their home life. At the same time they maintain the pointless frenzy of their work hours in their hours off. They rush from the office to jog, to the gym or the YMCA pool, to work at their play with the same joylessness. In the suburbs there is only an artificial community life—look at the notice board of community activities in a new satellite town like Reston, outside Washington. They breathlessly exhort the resident to a variety of boring activities—amateur theatricals, earnest lectures by officers of the United Nations Association sing-songs—a Tupperware community culture as artificial as the "lake" in the supposed center of the town. These upright citizens of Reston were amazed one day when they found that their bored children were as hooked on drugs as those in any ghetto.

9   Even though the offices of today's businesses in the city are themselves moving out to the suburbs, this does not necessarily bring the workers back closer to their workplace. It merely means that to the rush-hour traffic into the city there is now added a rush-hour traffic out of the suburbs in the morning, and back around and across the city in the evening. As the farmer walks down to his farm in the morning, the city dweller is dressing for the first idiocy of his day, which he not only accepts but even seeks—the journey to work.

10   This takes two forms: solitary confinement in one's own car, or the discomfort of extreme overcrowding on public transport. Both produce angst. There are no more grim faces than those of the single drivers we pedestrians can glimpse at the stoplights during the rush hour. It is hard to know why they are so impatient in the morning to get to their useless and wearisome employments; but then in the evening, when one would have thought they would be relaxed, they are even more frenetic. Prisoners in boxes on wheels, they do not dare wonder why they do it. If they take to public transit, there may still be the ritual of the wife driving the breadwinner to the subway station, and meeting him in the evening. Life in the suburbs and exurbs has become a bondage to the hours of journeying.

11   The car, of course, is not a vehicle suitable to the city. The problems of traffic in the city, over which urban planners have wracked their brains for years, could be simply eliminated if private cars were banned, or if a swinging tax were levied on those who drive into the city alone. The dollar toll in New York should be raised to five dollars—each way. There should be a toll on all the bridges crossing the Potomac from Virginia, and at every point where the rush hour drivers cross the District line from Maryland. The urban dwellers in Virginia and Maryland make sure that their jurisdictions obstruct any legitimate way the District might force the suburban daytime users of the city to pay for its manifold services. But ten dollars a day to cross into Washington, in addition to parking fees, would soon cut down the urban idiocy of bringing a small room to work and parking it in precious space for eight hours.

12   On the bus or subway each morning and evening other urban dwellers endure the indignity of being crushed into unwelcome proximity with strangers whom they have no wish to communicate with except in terms of abuse, rancor, and sometimes violent hostility. The wonder is not that there is an occasional shooting on public transit, but that shootings are not daily occurrences. The crushing of people together on the subway can have unintended results. One of my memories is of being on a London tube at rush hour in my younger days, pressed against a young woman who was with her boyfriend. To my surprise, though not unwelcome, her hand slipped into mine. It squeezed. Mine squeezed back. Her expression when they got out at Leicester Square, and she found she'd been holding my hand, and even had begun pulling me off the train, has not been easy to forget in 35 years. But generally even eye contact on public transport is treated as an act of aggression or at least harassment.

13   This primary urban activity of getting to and from work has other curious features. As every Englishman visiting America for the first time remarks, the smell of deodorants on a crowded bus or subway in the morning is overpowering. Even the stale smell of the human body would be preferable. It must account for the glazed looks—perhaps all deodorants contain a gas introduced by the employers to numb the urban office workers to the fatuity of their labors.

¹⁴ But whether they have come by car or public transit, the urban office workers must continue their journey even after they have gotten to the city. They then must travel in one of the banks of elevators that often run the height of three city blocks or more. Once again they are herded into confined spaces. City people are so used to moving in herds that they even fight to cram themselves into the elevators, as they do into buses or subway cars, as if it mattered that they might get to their pointless occupations a minute later. The odd thing about the elevators themselves is that there are no fares for distances often longer than those between two bus stops. Office elevators are public transit, free to anyone who needs to use them—but there's no such thing as a free elevator ride, as the president will tell you. Banks of elevators occupy large areas of valuable city land on every floor. This and the cost of running and maintaining them is written into the rents paid by the employers. If the urban workers had not been reduced to a docile herd, they would demand that the employers who expect them to get to work subsidize all the public transport into the city, while leaving those who bring their rooms on wheels to pay for them themselves.

¹⁵ In the modern office building in the city there are windows that don't open. This is perhaps the most symbolic lunacy of all. Outdoors is something you can look at through glass but not touch or hear. These windows are a scandal because they endanger the lives of office workers in case of fire. But no less grievous, even on the fairest spring or fall day the workers cannot put their heads outside. The employers do not mind this, may have even conspired with the developers to dream up such an infliction, because the call of spring or fall would distract their employees. Thus it's not surprising that the urban worker has no knowledge of the seasons. He is aware simply that in some months there is air conditioning, and in others through the same vents comes fetid central heating. Even outside at home in their suburbs the city dwellers may know that sometimes it's hot, and sometimes cold, but no true sense of the rhythms of the seasons is to be had from a lawn in the back yard and a few spindly trees struggling to survive.

¹⁶ City dwellers can now eat the vegetables of their choice at almost any time of the year—always with the proviso that they will never taste a fresh vegetable, even though the best supermarkets have various ways to touch them up. Anyone who has not eaten peas picked that morning has never tasted a pea. The simple fact is that some frozen vegetables (frozen within hours of being picked) are fresher than the alleged fresh vegetables on the produce counter of the supermarkets. The suburbanite again struggles to simulate the blessings of rural life by maintaining a vegetable patch in the back yard. The main consequence of this melancholy pursuit comes in high summer, when office workers bring in their homegrown tomatoes to share with their colleagues, ill-colored, lump-faced objects with scars all over them, since they have not been staked correctly.

¹⁷ The city dweller reels from unreality to unreality through each day, always trying to recover the rural life that has been surrendered for the city lights. (City life, it is worth noticing, has produced almost no proverbs. How could it when proverbs—a rolling stone gathers no moss, and so on—are a distillation from a sane existence?) No city dweller, even in the suburbs, knows the wonder of a pitch-dark country lane at night. Nor does he naturally get any exercise from his work. When jogging and other childish pursuits began to exercise the unused bodies of city dwellers, two sensible doctors (a breed that has almost died with the general practitioner) said that city workers

could get their exercise better in more natural ways. They could begin by walking upstairs to their office floors instead of using the elevators.

18   Every European points out that Americans are the most round-shouldered people in the world. Few of them carry themselves with an upright stance, although a correct stance and gait is the first precondition of letting your lungs breathe naturally and deeply. Electric typewriters cut down the amount of physical exertion needed to hit the keys; the buttons on a word processor need even less effort, as you can tell from the posture of those who use them. They might as well be in armchairs. They rush out to jog or otherwise Fonda-ize their leisure to try to repair the damage done during the day.

19   Dieting is an urban obsession. Country dwellers eat what they please, and work it off in useful physical employments, and in the open air, cold or hot, rainy or sunny. Mailmen are the healthiest city workers. When was your mailman last ill for a day? If one reads the huge menus that formed a normal diet in the 19th century, you realize that even the city dwellers could dispatch these gargantuan repasts because they still shared many of the benefits of rural life. (Disraeli records a meal at the house of one lordly figure that was composed of nine meat or game entrées. The butler asked after the eighth, "Snipe or pheasant, my lord?") They rode horseback to work or to Parliament even in the coldest weather, and nothing jolts and enlivens the liver more than riding. Homes were cold in the winter, except in the immediate vicinity of the hearth or stove. Cold has a way of eating up excess fat. No wonder dieting is necessary in a cossetted life in which the body is forced to do no natural heavy work.

20   Everything in urban life is an effort either to simulate rural life or to compensate for its loss by artificial means. The greatest robbery from the country in recent years has of course been Levi's, which any self-respecting farmer or farm worker is almost ashamed to wear nowadays. It was when Saks Fifth Avenue began advocating designer jeans years ago that the ultimate urban parody of rural life was reached. The chic foods of the city have been called health foods, which would seem a tautology in the country. And insofar as there used to be entertainments in the city that enticed, these can now be enjoyed more than sufficiently on VCRs and stereos.

21   It is from this day-to-day existence of unreality, pretense, and idiocy that the city people, slumping along their streets even when scurrying, never looking up at their buildings, far less the sky, have the insolence to disdain and mock the useful and rewarding life of the country people who support them. Now go out and carry home a Douglas fir, call it a Christmas tree, and enjoy 12 days of contact with nature. Of course city dwellers don't know it once had roots.

Questions for Reading and Analysis

1. What elements of style in the opening paragraphs reveal Fairlie's purpose? What is his purpose? What is his claim?

2. What evidence does Fairlie provide that urban dwellers really want to live in the country?

3. How do city workers moving to the suburbs and rural communities affect those areas? What lifestyles do they seem to want to combine?

4. The patterns of living in the suburbs and working in the city have had, in Fairlie's view, what effect on family life? On recreation? What gives structure to their day?

5. To generalize from Fairlie's details, city life is lunacy because it creates what kind of world?

6. Analyze the author's style. By what techniques does he develop his satiric portrait of city life?

Questions for Discussion and Response

1. Does Fairlie make some sound observations? Does he overstate the case against city life? If so, in what ways? How would you challenge his views?

2. If Fairlie were a city manager, what changes would he impose on a community? On what grounds? Are these good ideas? Why or why not?

3. Do you live in a city, suburb, or rural area? Do you prefer your location, or would you rather move? If you are happy, why? If you want to move, why?

Are We Coming Apart or Together?

Pico Iyer

Educated at Oxford and Harvard Universities, Pico Iyer (b. 1957) is a freelance writer who frequently contributes to *Time* magazine. He is the author of several books, including *The Lady and the Monk: Four Seasons in Kyoto* (1991) and *The Global Soul: Jet Lag, Shopping Malls, and the Search for Home* (2000). This *Time* essay appeared on May 22, 2000.

1   It is a truth all but universally acknowledged that the more internationalism there is in the world, the more nationalism there will be: the more multinational companies, multicultural beings and planetary networks are crossing and transcending borders, the more other forces will, as if in response, fashion new divisions and aggravate old ones. Human nature abhors a vacuum, and it is only natural, when people find themselves in a desert, without boundaries, that they will try to assuage their vulnerability by settling into a community. Thus fewer and fewer wars take place these days across borders, and more and more take place within them.

2   Many Americans, rejoicing in an unprecedented period of economic success and celebrating the new horizons opened up by our latest technologies, are likely to embrace the future as a dashing (if unknown) stranger who's appeared at our door to whisk us into a strange new world. Those who travel, though, are more likely to see rising tribalism, widening divisions and all the fissures that propel ever more of the world into what looks like anarchy. Fully 97% of the population growth that will bring our numbers up to 9 billion by the year 2050 will take place in developing countries, where conditions are scarcely better than they were a hundred years ago. In many cases, in fact, history seems to be moving backward (in modern Zimbabwe, to take but one example, the average life expectancy has dwindled from 70 to 38 in recent years because of

AIDS). To travel today is to see a planet that looks more and more like a too typical downtown on a global scale: a small huddle of shiny high-rises reaching toward a multinational heaven, surrounded on every side by a wasteland of the poor, living in a state of almost biblical desperation.

3   When people speak of a "digital divide," they are, in effect, putting into 21st century technological terms what is an age-old cultural problem: that all the globalism in the world does not erase (and may in fact intensify) the differences between us. Corporate bodies stress connectedness, borderless economies, all the wired communities that make up our worldwide webs; those in Chechnya, Kosovo or Rwanda remind us of much older forces. And even as America exports its dotcom optimism around the world, many other countries export their primal animosities to America. Get in a cab near the Capitol, say, or the World Trade Center and ask the wrong question, and you are likely to hear a tirade against the Amhara or the Tigreans, Indians or Pakistanis. If all the world's a global village, that means that the ancestral divisions of every place can play out in every other. And the very use of that comforting word village tends to distract us from the fact that much of the world is coming to resemble a global city (with all the gang warfare, fragmentation and generalized estrangement that those centers of affluence promote). When the past century began, 13% of humans lived in cities; by the time it ended, roughly 50% did.

4   The hope, in the face of these counterclockwise movements, is that we can be bound by what unites us, which we have ever more occasion to see; that the stirring visions of Thomas Paine or Martin Luther King Jr. have more resonance than ever, now that an American can meet a Chinese counterpart—in Shanghai or San Francisco (or many places in between)—and see how much they have in common. What Emerson called the Over-soul reminds us that we are joined not only by our habits and our urges and our fears but also by our dreams and that best part of us that intuits an identity larger than you or I. Look up, wherever you are, and you can see what we have in common; look down—or inside—and you can see something universal. It is only when you look around that you note divisions.

5   The fresher and more particular hope of the moment is that as more and more of us cross borders, we can step out of, and beyond, the old categories. Every time a Palestinian man, say, marries a Singhalese woman (and such unions are growing more common by the day) and produces a half-Palestinian, half-Singhalese child (living in Paris or London, no doubt), an Israeli or a Tamil is deprived of a tribal enemy. Even the Palestinian or Singhalese grandparents may be eased out of longtime prejudices. Mongrelism—the human equivalent of World Music and "fusion culture"—is the brightest child of fragmentation.

6   Yet the danger we face is that of celebrating too soon a global unity that only covers much deeper divisions. Much of the world is linked, more than ever before, by common surfaces: people on every continent may be watching Michael Jordan advertising Nike shoes on CNN. But beneath the surface, inevitably, traditional differences remain. George Bernard Shaw declared generations ago that England and America were two countries divided by a common language. Now the world often resembles 200 countries divided by a common frame of cultural reference. The number of countries on the planet, in the 20th century, has more than tripled.

7 Beyond that, multinationals and machines tell us that we're all plugged into the same global circuit, without considering very much what takes place off-screen. China and India, to cite the two giants that comprise 1 in every 3 of the world's people, have recently begun to embrace the opportunities of the global marketplace and the conveniences of e-reality (and, of course, it is often engineers of Chinese and Indian origin who have made these new wonders possible). Yet for all that connectedness on an individual level, the Chinese government remains as reluctant as ever to play by the rules of the rest of the world, and Indian leaders make nuclear gestures as if Dr. Strangelove had just landed in Delhi. And as some of us are able to fly across continents for business or pleasure, others are propelled out of their homelands by poverty and necessity and war, in record numbers: the number of refugees in the world has gone up 1,000% since 1970.

8 It seems a safe bet, as we move toward the year 2025, that governments will become no more idealistic than they have ever been—they will always represent a community of interests. And corporations cannot afford to stress conscience or sacrifice before profit. It therefore falls to the individual, on her own initiative, to look beyond the divisions of her parents' time and find a common ground with strangers to apply the all-purpose adjective "global" to "identity" and "loyalty." Never before in history have so many people, whether in Manhattan or in Tuva, been surrounded by so much that is alien (in customs, languages, and neighborhoods). How we orient ourselves in the midst of all this foreignness and in the absence of the old certainties will determine how much our nations are disunited and how much we are bound by what Augustine called "things loved in common."

Questions for Reading and Analysis

1. What is Iyer's subject? What about our times does he want us to understand?

2. How have we come together? What is uniting the world?

3. How are we coming apart? What is meant by the "digital divide"? In what ways are there striking differences among us?

4. What does Iyer mean by "fusion culture"? As interracial and interethnic marriages unite us, what else is happening to create more barriers?

5. At what level are we likely to come together, if we manage to become more united by 2025?

Questions for Discussion and Response

1. Iyer includes a number of statistics. Which are the most surprising to you? Why?

2. Which of the ways that separate us do you consider most dangerous for global unity and world peace? Why?

3. Do you think that we should promote unity or promote the divisions represented by today's many new countries? Explain your position.

4. If you favor drawing the world together, how should we go about that? What can be done to promote global unity?

A Sense of Belonging

David Gergen

David Gergen is editor at large of *U.S. News and World Report* and a frequent voice on television political talk programs. He has been a political insider through many administrations, as revealed in his book *Eyewitness to Power: The Essence of Leadership, Nixon to Clinton* (2000). His *U.S. News* column appeared on December 6, 1999.

1   Back in the early 1980s, the Rev. Billy Graham paid a visit to Harvard and was greeted with a yawn. A few weeks ago, he returned to an entirely different atmosphere. Students camped out all night on Saturday so they could have a seat in Memorial Church when he preached on Sunday. His later appearance at the Kennedy School of Government drew a packed house, which turned into a religious revival as, one after another, young people proclaimed their faith in God.

2   There is something new in the air—and not just at Harvard. Across the land, Americans are hungering for something more than money and a new car. They are looking for answers that satisfy the soul and restore a sense of belonging to one another. We are a long way from there, but signs of cultural renewal are springing up all about us—and just in time.

3   In 1994, William J. Bennett issued the first *Index of Leading Cultural Indicators*, one of his many contributions to the common weal. In his report, he provided a boxcar of graphs and charts substantiating his main conclusion. "In many ways, the condition of America is not good," he wrote. "Over the past three decades we have experienced substantial social regression. . . . Unless these exploding social pathologies are reversed, they will lead to the decline and perhaps even to the fall of the American republic."

4   Bennett set forth five areas of social life that concerned him. Witness some of the changes in the years since:

5   **Crime.** The national crime rate has declined seven years in a row, and latest numbers are the lowest since 1985. Violent crime has followed a similar downward slope, dropping more than 6 percent in 1998. The Centers for Disease Control and Prevention reports that gun deaths dropped 21 percent between 1993 and 1997, while firearm-related injuries are down 41 percent.

6   **Family and children.** While there was a slight uptick in 1997, the divorce rate for married women is hovering at its lowest rate since 1974. Abortion, which steadily increased from 1983 through 1990, has been declining in the 1990s. Statistics show there were at least 208,000 fewer abortions per year toward the end of the decade than at the beginning.

7   **Education.** While SAT scores are up 16 points since the beginning of the decade, overall student performance has not yet shown serious improvement. But, as reported here earlier, the "standards" movement is now catching on and represents the most promising reform in 30 years. Linked with charter and choice, educational gains could come sooner than we think.

8   **Youth behavior.** Teenage pregnancy has dropped seven years in a row, and as the National Campaign to Prevent Teen Pregnancy moves ahead, it could conceivably cut rates in half in the next few years. Teen drug use is also down, and the Partnership for

a Drug-Free America reported last week that the number of teenagers who think refusal to use drugs is "really cool" is up to 40 percent.

9   **Popular culture and religion.** Charitable giving rose 16 percent from 1997 to 1998, the largest jump on record. We could be seeing the beginnings of a boom in philanthropy as donors create accounts at institutions like Fidelity and scan the AOL Web site to identify worthwhile charities. While membership in mainstream churches drifts downward, we are also seeing huge growth in large, new churches, many of them nondenominational. And conversation about God is returning to the dinner table, even as talk of sex seemingly diminishes.

10   Some say these trends simply reflect a better business climate. But the economy was bounding up in the 1960s and 1980s, too, and yet social indicators went south. More likely what we are seeing is an America that looked into the abyss and decided to change its mind.

11   No one should pop champagne corks yet. As Bennett warns in the introduction to his latest *Index*, "The nation we live in today is more violent and vulgar, coarse and cynical, rude and remorseless, deviant and depressed, than the one we once inhabited." We still have much to reverse and rebuild.

12   Nonetheless, these signs of cultural renewal should lift our sights as we head toward the holidays and a new century. Progress *is* possible. We still control our own destiny. One of our greatest strengths as a society is our resiliency—our capacity to snap back from bad times. Just in time, it seems, we're recovering our bearings.

Questions for Reading and Analysis

1. What is Gergen's subject? What is his claim? Where is it stated?

2. What were the five earmarks of social life that Bennett explored in 1994? Briefly state the changes Gergen finds at the end of 1999.

3. What challenge to his evidence does Gergen anticipate? How does he rebut the challenge?

4. What is the author's view of change and progress?

Questions for Discussion and Response

1. Which of Gergen's statistics most surprises you? Why?

2. What statistic surprises you the least—or not at all? Why?

3. Do you agree that we are "more violent and vulgar, coarse and cynical, rude and remorseless" than before? If you agree, do you see any reason to share Gergen's optimism? Why or why not?

4. Do you agree that we can chart our own destiny? If not, why not? If so, what do we need to do to create a new sense of belonging?

CHAPTER 23

Some Classic Arguments

This final chapter presents five of the many classic arguments worthy of your study and reflection. Your instructor may also recommend that you read Niccolò Machiavelli's *The Prince*, or George Orwell's "Politics and the English Language," or any of the *Federalist Papers*. All of these arguments illustrate excellent persuasive strategies. They also remind us that classics do not just influence their own times; they live on in our times both as models of good argument and as debates of enduring issues. As you read the essays here, observe how the authors use language, sentence patterns, metaphors, irony, and other strategies to powerfully drive home their claims.

A Modest Proposal

For Preventing the Children of Poor People in Ireland from Being a Burden to Their Parents or Country, and for Making Them Beneficial to the Public

Jonathan Swift

One of the most important 18th-century authors, Jonathan Swift (1667–1745) led several lives. Born in Dublin, he was ordained in the Anglican Church and spent many years as dean of St. Patrick's in Dublin. But Swift was also involved in the political and social life of London for some years, and throughout all parts of his career he kept busy writing, sometimes imaginative literature, sometimes political treatises. His most famous imaginative work is *Gulliver's Travels* (1726). Almost as well-known is the essay that follows, published in 1729. In "A Modest Proposal," as in all his satiric works, Swift's biting irony is present, but so also is his concern to improve humanity.

1   It is a melancholy object to those who walk through this great town[1] or travel in the country, whey they see the streets, the roads, and cabin doors crowded with beggars of the female sex, followed by three, four, or six children, all in rags, and importuning every passenger for an alms. These mothers, instead of being able to work for their honest livelihood, are forced to employ all their time in strolling to beg sustenance for their helpless infants, who, as they grow up, either turn thieves for want of work, or leave their dear native country to fight for the pretender[2] in Spain or sell themselves to the Barbados.

---

[1]   Dublin.—Ed.

[2]   James Stuart, claimant to the British throne lost by his father, James II, in 1688.—Ed.

2   I think it is agreed by all parties that this prodigious number of children in the arms, or on the backs, or at the heels of their mothers, and frequently of their fathers, is in the present deplorable state of the kingdom a very great additional grievance; and therefore, whoever could find out a fair, cheap, and easy method of making these children sound and useful members of the commonwealth would deserve so well of the public as to have his statue set up for a preserver of the nation.

3   But my intention is very far from being confined to provide only for the children of professed beggars; it is of a much greater extent, and shall take in the whole number of infants at a certain age who are born of parents in effect as little able to support them as those who demand our charity in the streets.

4   As to my own part, having turned my thoughts for many years upon this important subject, and maturely weighed the several schemes of other projectors,[3] I have always found them grossly mistaken in the computation. It is true a child just dropped from its dam may be supported by her milk for a solar year with little other nourishment; at most not above the value of two shillings, which the mother may certainly get, or the value in scraps, by her lawful occupation of begging; and, it is exactly at one year that I propose to provide for them in such a manner as instead of being a charge upon their parents or the parish, or wanting food and raiment for the rest of their lives, they shall on the contrary contribute to the feeding, and partly to the clothing, of many thousands.

5   There is likewise another great advantage in my scheme, that it will prevent those voluntary abortions, and that horrid practice of women murdering their bastard children, alas, too frequent among us, sacrificing the poor innocent babes, I doubt, more to avoid the expense than the shame, which would move tears and pity in the most savage and inhuman breast.

6   The number of souls in this kingdom being usually reckoned one million and a half, of these I calculate there may be about two hundred thousand couples whose wives are breeders; from which number I subtract thirty thousand couples who are able to maintain their own children, although I apprehend there cannot be so many, under the present distress of the kingdom; but this being granted, there will remain a hundred and seventy thousand breeders. I again subtract fifty thousand for those women who miscarry, or whose children die by accident or disease within the year. There only remain a hundred and twenty thousand children of poor parents annually born. The question therefore is, how this number shall be reared and provided for, which, as I have already said, under the present situation of affairs, is utterly impossible by all the methods hereto proposed. For we can neither employ them in handicraft or agriculture; we neither build houses (I mean in the country) nor cultivate land. They can very seldom pick up a livelihood by stealing until they arrive at six years old, except where they are of towardly parts[4]; although I confess they learn the rudiments much earlier, during which time they can, however, be properly looked upon only as probationers, as I have been informed by a principal gentleman in the country of Cavan, who protested to me that he never knew above one or two instances under the age of six, even in the part of the kingdom renowned for the quickest proficiency in that art.

---

3   Planners.—Ed.

4   Innate abilities.—Ed.

7   I am assured by our merchants that a boy or girl before twelve years old is no saleable commodity; and even when they come to this age they will not yield above three pounds, or three pounds and a half a crown at most, on the exchange; which cannot turn to account either to the parents or the kingdom, the charge of nutriment and rags having been at least four times that value.

8   I shall now therefore humbly propose my own thoughts, which I hope will not be liable to the least objection.

9   I have been assured by a very knowing American of my acquaintance in London that a young healthy child well nursed is at a year old a most delicious, nourishing, and wholesome food, whether stewed, roasted, baked, or boiled; and I make no doubt that it will equally serve in a fricassee or ragout.

10   I do therefore humbly offer it to public consideration that of the hundred and twenty-thousand children, already computed, twenty thousand may be reserved for breed, whereof only one fourth part to be males, which is more than we allow to sheep, black cattle, or swine; and my reason is that these children are seldom the fruits of marriage, a circumstance not much regarded by our savages, therefore one male will be sufficient to serve four females. That the remaining hundred thousand may at a year old be offered in sale to the persons of quality and fortune, through the kingdom, always advising the mother to let them suck plentifully in the last month, so as to render them plump and fat for the table. A child will make two dishes at an entertainment for friends; and when the family dines alone, the fore or hind quarter will make a reasonable dish, and seasoned with a little pepper or salt will be very good boiled on the fourth day, especially in winter.

11   I have reckoned upon a medium that a child just born will weigh twelve pounds, and in a solar year if tolerably nursed increaseth to twenty-eight pounds.

12   I grant this food will be somewhat dear, and therefore very proper for landlords, who, as they have already devoured most of the parents, seem to have the best title to the children.

13   Infant's flesh will be in season throughout the year, but more plentiful in March, and a little before and after. For we are told by a grave author, an eminent French physician,[5] that fish being a prolific diet, there are more children born in Roman Catholic countries about nine months after Lent than at any other season; therefore reckoning a year after Lent, the markets will be more gutted than usual, because the number of popish infants is at least three to one in this kingdom; and therefore it will have one other collateral advantage, by lessening the number of Papists among us.

14   I have already computed the charge of nursing a beggar's child (in which list I reckon all cottagers, laborers, and four-fifths of the farmers) to be about two shillings per annum, rags included; and I believe no gentleman would repine to give ten shillings for the carcass of a good fat child, which, as I have said, will make four dishes of excellent nutritive meat, when he hath only some particular friend or his own family to dine with him. Thus the squire will learn to be a good landlord, and grow popular among his tenants; the mother will have eight shillings net profit, and be fit for work until she produces another child.

---

5   Francois Rabelais.—Ed.

15   Those who are more thrifty (as I must confess the times require) may flay the carcass; the skin of which artificially dressed will make admirable gloves for ladies and summer boots for fine gentlemen.

16   As to our city of Dublin, shambles[6] may be appointed for this purpose, in the most convenient parts of it, and butchers we may be assured will not be wanting; although I rather recommend buying the children alive, and dressing them hot from the knife as we do roasting pigs.

17   A very worthy person, a true lover of his country, and whose virtues I highly esteem, was lately pleased in discoursing on this matter to offer a refinement upon my scheme. He said that many gentlemen of this kingdom, having of late destroyed their deer, he conceived that the want of venison might be well supplied by the bodies of young lads and maidens, not exceeding fourteen years of age nor under twelve, so great a number of both sexes in every county being now ready to starve for want of work and service; and these to be disposed of by their parents, if alive, or otherwise by their nearest relations. But with due deference to so excellent a friend and so deserving a patriot, I cannot be altogether in his sentiments. For as to the males, my American acquaintance assured me from frequent experience that their flesh was generally tough and lean, like that of our school-boys, by continual exercise, and their taste disagreeable; and to fatten them would not answer the charge. Then as to the females, it would, I think with humble submission, be a loss to the public, because they soon would become breeders themselves; and besides, it is not probable that some scrupulous people might be apt to censure such a practice (although indeed very unjustly) as a little bordering upon cruelty; which, I confess, hath always been with me the strongest objection against any project, how wellsoever intended.

18   But in order to justify my friend, he confessed that this expedient was put into his head by the famous Psalmanazar,[7] a native of the island Formosa who came from thence to London above twenty years ago, and in conversation told my friend that in his country when any young person happened to be put to death, the executioner sold the carcass to persons of quality as a prime dainty; and that in his time the body of a plump girl of fifteen, who was crucified for an attempt to poison the emperor, was sold to his Imperial Majesty's prime minister of state, and other great mandarins of the court, in joints from the gibbet, at four hundred crowns. Neither indeed can I deny that if the same use were made of several plump young girls in this town, who without one single groat to their fortunes cannot stir abroad without a chair, and appear at the playhouse and assemblies in foreign fineries which they never will pay for, the kingdom would not be the worse.

19   Some persons of a desponding spirit are in great concern about that vast number of poor people who are aged, diseased, or maimed, and I have been desired to employ my thoughts what course may be taken to ease the nation of so grievous an incumbrance. But I am not in the least pain upon that matter, because it is very well known that they are every day dying and rotting by cold and famine, and filth and vermin, as fast as can be reasonably expected. And as to the younger laborers, they are now in almost as hopeful a condition. They cannot get work, and consequently pine away for want of

---

6   Butcher shops.—Ed.

7   A known imposter who was French, not Formosan as he claimed.—Ed.

nourishment to a degree that if at any time they are accidentally hired to common labor, they have not strength to perform it; and thus the country and themselves are in a fair way of being soon delivered from the evils to come.

20   I have too long digressed, and therefore shall return to my subject. I think the advantages by the proposal which I have made are obvious and many, as well as of the highest importance.

21   For, first, as I have already observed, it would greatly lessen the number of Papists, with whom we are yearly overrun, being the principal breeders of the nation as well as our most dangerous enemies; and who stay at home on purpose with a design to deliver the kingdom to the pretender, hoping to take their advantage by the absence of so many good Protestants, who have chosen rather to leave their country than stay at home and pay tithes against their conscience to an idolatrous Episcopal curate.

22   Secondly, the poorer tenants will have something valuable of their own, which by law may be made liable to distress,[8] and help their landlord's rent; their corn and cattle being already seized, and money a thing unknown.

23   Thirdly, whereas the maintenance of a hundred thousand children, from two years old upwards, cannot be computed at less than ten shillings a piece per annum, the nation's stock will be thereby increased fifty thousand pounds per annum, besides the profit of a new dish introduced to the tables of all gentlemen of fortune in the kingdom who have any refinement in taste. And the money will circulate among ourselves, the goods being entirely of our own growth and manufacture.

24   Fourthly, the constant breeders, besides the gain of eight shillings sterling per annum by the sale of their children, will be rid of the charge of maintaining them after the first year.

25   Fifthly, this food would likewise bring great custom to taverns, where the vintners will certainly be so prudent as to procure the best receipts for dressing it to perfection, and consequently have their houses frequented by all the fine gentlemen, who justly value themselves upon their knowledge in good eating; and a skillful cook, who understands how to oblige his guests, will contrive to make it as expensive as they please.

26   Sixthly, this would be a great inducement to marriage, which all wise nations have either encouraged by rewards or enforced by laws and penalties. It would increase the care and tenderness of mothers towards their children, when they were sure of a settlement for life to the poor babes, provided in some sort by the public; to their annual profit instead of expense. We should soon see an honest emulation among the married women, which of them could bring the fattest child to the market. Men would become as fond of their wives during the time of their pregnancy as they are now of their mares in foal, their cows in calf, or sows when they are ready to farrow; nor offer to beat or kick them (as it is too frequent a practice) for fear of a miscarriage.

27   Many other advantages might be enumerated. For instance, the addition of some thousand carcasses in our exportation of barrelled beef, the propagation of swine's flesh, and improvement in the art of making good bacon, so much wanted among us by the great destruction of pigs, too frequent at our tables, which are no way comparable in taste or magnificence to a well-grown fat, yearling child, which roasted whole will make

---

8   Can be seized by lenders.—Ed.

a considerable figure at a lord mayor's feast or any other public entertainment. But this and many others I omit, being studious of brevity.

28   Supposing that one thousand families in this city would be constant customers for infants' flesh, besides others who might have it at merry meetings, particularly weddings and christenings, I compute that Dublin would take off annually about twenty thousand carcasses, and the rest of the kingdom (where probably they will be sold somewhat cheaper) the remaining eighty thousand.

29   I can think of no one objection that will possibly be raised against this proposal, unless it should be urged that the number of people will be thereby much lessened in the kingdom. This I freely own, and it was indeed one principal design in offering it to the world. I desire the reader will observe that I calculate my remedy for this one individual kingdom of Ireland and for no other that ever was, is, or I think ever can be upon earth. Therefore let no man talk to me of other expedients: of taxing our absentees at five shillings a pound: of using neither clothes nor household furniture except what is of our own growth and manufacture: of utterly rejecting the materials and instruments that promote foreign luxury: of curing the expensiveness or pride, vanity, idleness, and gaming in our women: of introducing a vein of parsimony, prudence and temperance: of learning to love our country, wherein we differ even from Laplanders and the inhabitants of Topinamboo[9]: of quitting our animosities and factions, nor act any longer like the Jews, who were murdering one another at the very moment their city was taken[10]: of being a little cautious not to sell our country and consciences for nothing: of teaching landlords to have at least one degree of mercy towards their tenants. Lastly, of putting a spirit of honesty, industry, and skill into our shopkeepers; who, if a resolution could now be taken to buy only our native goods, would immediately unite to cheat and exact upon us in the price, the measure, and the goodness, nor could ever yet be brought to make one fair proposal of just dealing, though often and earnestly invited to it.

30   Therefore I repeat, let no man talk to me of these and the like expedients, till he hath at least a glimpse of hope that there will ever be some hearty and sincere attempt to put them in practice.

31   But as to myself, having been wearied out for many years with offering vain, idle, visionary thoughts, and at length utterly despairing of success, I fortunately fell upon this proposal, which, as it is wholly new, so it hath something solid and real, of no expense and little trouble, full in our own power, and whereby we can incur no danger in disobliging England. For this kind of commodity will not bear exportation, the flesh being of too tender a consistence to admit a long continuance in salt, although perhaps I could name a country which would be glad to eat up our whole nation without it.

32   After all, I am not so violently bent upon my own opinion as to reject any offer proposed by wise men, which shall be found equally innocent, cheap, easy, and effectual. But before something of that kind shall be advanced in contradiction to my scheme, and offering a better, I desire the author, or authors, will be pleased maturely to consider two points. First, as things now stand, how they will be able to find food and

---

9   An area in Brazil.—Ed.

10   Some Jews were accused of helping the Romans and were executed during the Roman siege of Jerusalem in 70 A.D.—Ed.

raiment for a hundred thousand useless mouths and backs. And secondly, there being a round million of creatures in human figure throughout this kingdom, whose whole subsistence put into a common stock would leave them in debt two million of pounds sterling, adding those who are beggars by profession to the bulk of farmers, cottagers, and laborers, with their wives and children who are beggars, in effect; I desire those politicians who dislike my overture, and may perhaps be so bold to attempt an answer, that they will first ask the parents of these mortals whether they would not at this day think it a great happiness to have been sold for food at a year old in the manner I prescribe, and thereby have avoided such a perpetual scene of misfortunes as they have since gone through by the oppression of landlords, the impossibility of paying rent without money or trade, the want of common sustenance, with neither house nor clothes to cover them from the inclemencies of weather, and the most inevitable prospect of entailing the like or greater miseries upon their breed forever.

33   I profess, in the sincerity of my heart, that I have not the least personal interest in endeavoring to promote this necessary work, having no other motive than the public good of my country, by advancing our trade, providing for infants, relieving the poor, and giving some pleasure to the rich. I have no children by which I can propose to get a single penny, the youngest being nine years old, and my wife past childbearing.

Questions for Reading and Analysis

1. Swift was a minister, but he writes this essay as if he were in a different vocation. What voice do you hear or *persona* does he assume here? In what early paragraph does he reveal his persona? What are the traits of this persona?

2. How is the persona's argument organized? What is accomplished in paragraphs 1 through 7? In paragraphs 8 through 16? In paragraphs 17 through 19? In paragraphs 20 through 28? In paragraphs 29 through 33?

3. What specific advantages does the writer offer in defense of his proposal?

4. What specific passages and connotative words make us aware that this is a satirical piece using irony as its chief device?

5. After you recognize Swift's use of irony, what do you conclude to be his purpose in writing?

Questions for Discussion and Response

1. From reading this essay, what can you conclude about some of the problems in 18th-century Ireland and some of the English attitudes toward the Irish?

2. Can you find some passages in which Swift offers direct condemnation of existing conditions and attitudes?

3. What actual reforms would Swift like to see to improve life in Ireland?

4. What are some of the advantages of using irony? What does Swift gain by approaching his subject in this way? Are there any possible disadvantages in using irony? If so, what are they?

Civil Disobedience

Henry David Thoreau

Naturalist, essayist, poet, transcendentalist, Thoreau (1817–1862) was a man of wide interests. His two most famous works—*Walden* (1854) and the essay "Civil Disobedience" (delivered as a lecture in 1848 and published in 1849)—have influenced many readers who have shared his interest in a search for "higher laws."

1   I heartily accept the motto,—"That government is best which governs least;"[1] and I should like to see it acted up to more rapidly and systematically. Carried out, it finally amounts to this, which also I believe,—"That government is best which governs not at all;" and when men are prepared for it, that will be the kind of government which they will have. Government is at best but an expedient; but most governments are usually, and all governments are sometimes, inexpedient. The objections which have been brought against a standing army, and they are many and weighty, and deserve to prevail, may also at last be brought against a standing government. The standing army is only an arm of the standing government. The government itself, which is only the mode which the people have chosen to execute their will, is equally liable to be abused and perverted before the people can act through it. Witness the present Mexican war,[2] the work of comparatively a few individuals using the standing government as their tool; for, in the outset, the people would not have consented to this measure.

2   This American government,—what is it but a tradition, though a recent one, endeavoring to transmit itself unimpaired to posterity, but each instant losing some of its integrity? It has not the vitality and force of a single living man; for a single man can bend it to his will. It is a sort of wooden gun to the people themselves; and, if ever they should use it in earnest as a real one against each other, it will surely split. But it is not the less necessary for this; for the people must have some complicated machinery or other, and hear its din, to satisfy that idea of government which they have. Governments show thus how successfully men can be imposed on, even impose on themselves, for their own advantage. It is excellent, we must all allow; yet this government never of itself furthered any enterprise, but by the alacrity with which it got out of its way. *It* does not keep the country free. *It* does not settle the West. *It* does not educate. The character inherent in the American people has done all that has been accomplished; and it would have done somewhat more, if the government had not sometimes got in its way. For government is an expedient by which men would fain succeed in letting one another alone; and, as has been said, when it is most expedient, the governed are most let alone by it. Trade and commerce, if they were not made of India rubber, would never manage to bounce over the obstacles which legislators are continually putting in their way; and, if one were to judge these men wholly by the effects of their actions, and not partly by their intentions, they would deserve to be classed and punished with those mischievous persons who put obstructions on the railroads.

---

1   Motto of the monthly journal *United States Monthly Magazine and Democratic Review*.—Ed.

2   From 1846 to 1848.—Ed.

3   But, to speak practically and as a citizen, unlike those who call themselves no-government men, I ask for, not at once no government, but *at once* a better government. Let every man make known what kind of government would command his respect, and that will be one step toward obtaining it.

4   After all, the practical reason why, when the power is once in the hands of the people, a majority are permitted, and for a long period continue, to rule, is not because they are most likely to be in the right, nor because this seems fairest to the minority, but because they are physically the strongest. But a government in which the majority rule in all cases cannot be based on justice, even as far as men understand it. Can there not be a government in which majorities do not virtually decide right and wrong, but conscience?—in which majorities decide only those questions to which the rule of expediency is applicable? Must the citizen ever for a moment, or in the least degree, resign his conscience to the legislator? Why has every man a conscience, then? I think that we should be men first, and subjects afterward. It is not desirable to cultivate a respect for the law, so much as for the right. The only obligation which I have a right to assume, is to do at any time what I think right. It is truly enough said, that a corporation has no conscience; but a corporation of conscientious men is a corporation *with* a conscience. Law never made men a whit more just; and, by means of their respect for it, even the well-disposed are daily made the agents of injustice. A common and natural result of an undue respect for law is, that you may see a file of soldiers, colonel, captain, corporal, privates, powder-monkeys and all, marching in admirable order over hill and dale to the wars, against their wills, aye, against their common sense and consciences, which makes it very steep marching indeed, and produces a palpitation of the heart. They have no doubt that it is a damnable business in which they are concerned; they are all peaceably inclined. Now, what are they? Men at all? or small moveable forts and magazines, at the service of some unscrupulous man in power? Visit the Navy Yard, and behold a marine, such a man as an American government can make, or such as it can make a man with its black arts, a mere shadow and reminiscence of humanity, a man laid out alive and standing, and already, as one may say, buried under arms with funeral accompaniments, though it may be

"Not a drum was heard, nor a funeral note,
As his corse to the ramparts we hurried;
Not a soldier discharged his farewell shot
O'er the grave where our hero we buried."[3]

5   The mass of men serve the State thus, not as men mainly, but as machines, with their bodies. They are the standing army, and the militia, jailers, constables, *posse comitatus*, &c. In most cases there is no free exercise whatever of the judgment or of the moral sense; but they put themselves on a level with wood and earth and stones; and wooden men can perhaps be manufactured that will serve the purpose as well. Such command no more respect than men of straw, or a lump of dirt. They have the same sort of worth only as horses and dogs. Yet such as these even are commonly esteemed good citizens. Others, as most legislators, politicians, lawyers, ministers, and office-holders,

---

[3] By Charles Wolfe, 1791–1823.—Ed.

serve the State chiefly with their heads; and, as they rarely make any moral distinctions, they are as likely to serve the devil, without intending it, as God. A very few, as heroes, patriots, martyrs, reformers in the great sense, and *men*, serve the State with their consciences also, and so necessarily resist it for the most part; and they are commonly treated by it as enemies. A wise man will only be useful as a man, and will not submit to be "clay," and "stop a hole to keep the wind away,"[4] but leave that office to his dust at least:—

"I am too high-born to be propertied,
To be a secondary at control,
Or useful serving-man and instrument
To any sovereign state throughout the world."[5]

6   He who gives himself entirely to his fellow-men appears to them useless and selfish; but he who gives himself partially to them is pronounced a benefactor and philanthropist.

7   How does it become a man to behave toward this American government to-day? I answer that he cannot without disgrace be associated with it. I cannot for an instant recognize that political organization as *my* government which is the *slave's* government also.

8   All men recognize the right of revolution; that is, the right to refuse allegiance to and to resist the government, when its tyranny or its inefficiency are great and unendurable. But almost all say that such is not the case now. But such was the case, they think, in the Revolution of '75. If one were to tell me that this was a bad government because it taxed certain foreign commodities brought to its ports, it is most probable that I should not make an ado about it, for I can do without them: all machines have their friction; and possibly this does enough good to counterbalance the evil. At any rate, it is a great evil to make a stir about it. But when the friction comes to have its machine, and oppression and robbery are organized, I say, let us not have such a machine any longer. In other words, when a sixth of the population of a nation which has undertaken to be the refuge of liberty are slaves, and a whole country is unjustly overrun and conquered by a foreign army, and subjected to military law, I think that it is not too soon for honest men to rebel and revolutionize. What makes this duty the more urgent is the fact, that the country so overrun is not our own, but ours is the invading army.

9   Paley,[6] a common authority with many on moral questions, in his chapter on the "Duty of Submission to Civil Government," resolves all civil obligation into expediency; and he proceeds to say, "that so long as the interest of the whole society requires it, that is, so long as the established government cannot be resisted or changed without public inconveniency, it is the will of God that the established government be obeyed, and no longer."—"This principle being admitted, the justice of every particular case of resistance is reduced to a computation of the quantity of the danger and grievance on the one side, and of the probability and expense of redressing it on the other." Of this, he says, every man shall judge for himself. But Paley appears never to have contemplated those cases to which the rule of expediency does not apply, in which a people, as

---

4   Shakespeare, *Hamlet*, V.i. 236–37.—Ed.

5   Shakespeare, *King John*, V.i.i.79–82.—Ed.

6   British philosopher, William Paley.—Ed.

well as an individual, must do justice, cost what it may. If I have unjustly wrested a plank from a drowning man, I must restore it to him though I drown myself. This, according to Paley, would be inconvenient. But he that would save his life, in such a case, shall lose it. This people must cease to hold slaves, and to make war on Mexico, though it cost them their existence as a people.

10 In their practice, nations agree with Paley; but does any one think that Massachusetts does exactly what is right at the present crisis?

"A drab of state, a cloth-o'-silver slut,
To have her train borne up, and her soul trail in the dirt."[7]

Practically speaking, the opponents to a reform in Massachusetts are not a hundred thousand politicians at the South, but a hundred thousand merchants and farmers here, who are more interested in commerce and agriculture than they are in humanity, and are not prepared to do justice to the slave and to Mexico, *cost what it may*. I quarrel not with far-off foes, but with those who, near at home, co-operate with, and do the bidding of those far away, and without whom the latter would be harmless. We are accustomed to say, that the mass of men are unprepared; but improvement is slow, because the few are not materially wiser or better than the many. It is not so important that many should be as good as you, as that there be some absolute goodness somewhere; for that will leaven the whole lump. There are thousands who are *in opinion* opposed to slavery and to the war, who yet in effect do nothing to put an end to them; who, esteeming themselves children of Washington and Franklin, sit down with their hands in their pockets, and say that they know not what to do, and do nothing; who even postpone the question of freedom to the question of free-trade, and quietly read the prices-current along with the latest advices from Mexico, after dinner, and, it may be, fall asleep over them both. What is the price-current of an honest man and patriot to-day? They hesitate, and they regret, and sometimes they petition; but they do nothing in earnest and with effect. They will wait, well disposed, for others to remedy the evil, that they may no longer have it to regret. At most, they give only a cheap vote, and a feeble countenance and God-speed, to the right, as it goes by them. There are nine hundred and ninety-nine patrons of virtue to one virtuous man; but it is easier to deal with the real possessor of a thing than with the temporary guardian of it.

11 All voting is a sort of gaming, like chequers or backgammon, with a slight moral tinge to it, a playing with right and wrong, with moral questions; and betting naturally accompanies it. The character of the voters is not staked. I cast my vote, perchance, as I think right; but I am not vitally concerned that that right should prevail. I am willing to leave it to the majority. Its obligation, therefore, never exceeds that of expediency. Even voting *for the right* is *doing* nothing for it. It is only expressing to men feebly your desire that it should prevail. A wise man will not leave the right to the mercy of chance, nor wish it to prevail through the power of the majority. There is but little virtue in the action of masses of men. When the majority shall at length vote for the abolition of slavery, it will be because they are indifferent to slavery, or because there is but little

---

7 Tourneur, *The Revengers Tragadie*, IV.iv.—Ed.

slavery left to be abolished by their vote. *They* will then be the only slaves. Only *his* vote can hasten the abolition of slavery who asserts his own freedom by his vote.

12   I hear of a convention to be held at Baltimore, or elsewhere, for the selection of a candidate for the Presidency, made up chiefly of editors, and men who are politicians by profession; but I think, what is it to any independent, intelligent, and respectable man what decision they may come to, shall we not have the advantage of his wisdom and honesty, nevertheless? Can we not count upon some independent votes? Are there not many individuals in the country who do not attend conventions? But no: I find that the respectable man, so called, has immediately drifted from his position, and despairs of his country, when his country has more reason to despair of him. He forthwith adopts one of the candidates thus selected as the only *available* one, thus proving that he is himself *available* for any purposes of the demagogue. His vote is of no more worth than that of any unprincipled foreigner or hireling native, who may have been bought. Oh for a man who is a *man*, and, as my neighbor says, has a bone in his back which you cannot pass your hand through! Our statistics are at fault: the population has been returned too large. How many *men* are there to a square thousand miles in this country? Hardly one. Does not America offer any inducement for men to settle here? The American has dwindled into an Odd Fellow,—one who may be known by the development of his organ of gregariousness, and a manifest lack of intellect and cheerful self-reliance; whose first and chief concern, on coming into the world, is to see that the alms-houses are in good repair; and, before yet he has lawfully donned the virile garb, to collect a fund for the support of the widows and orphans that may be; who, in short, ventures to live only by the aid of the mutual insurance company, which has promised to bury him decently.

13   It is not a man's duty, as a matter of course, to devote himself to the eradication of any, even the most enormous wrong; he may still properly have other concerns to engage him; but it is his duty, at least, to wash his hands of it, and, if he gives it no thought longer, not to give it practically his support. If I devote myself to other pursuits and contemplations, I must first see, at least, that I do not pursue them sitting upon another man's shoulders. I must get off him first, that he may pursue his contemplations too. See what gross inconsistency is tolerated. I have heard some of my townsmen say, "I should like to have them order me out to help put down an insurrection of the slaves, or to march to Mexico,—see if I would go;" and yet these very men have each, directly by their allegiance, and so indirectly, at least, by their money, furnished a substitute. The soldier is applauded who refuses to serve in an unjust war by those who do not refuse to sustain the unjust government which makes the war; is applauded by those whose own act and authority he disregards and sets at nought; as if the State were penitent to that degree that it hired one to scourge it while it sinned, but not to that degree that it left off sinning for a moment. Thus, under the name of order and civil government, we are all made at last to pay homage to and support our own meanness. After the first blush of sin, comes its indifference; and from immoral it becomes, as it were, *un*moral, and not quite unnecessary to that life which we have made.

14   The broadest and most prevalent error requires the most disinterested virtue to sustain it. The slight reproach to which the virtue of patriotism is commonly liable, the noble are most likely to incur. Those who, while they disapprove of the character and measures of a government, yield to it their allegiance and support, are undoubtedly its most conscientious supporters, and so frequently the most serious obstacles to reform.

Some are petitioning the State to dissolve the Union, to disregard the requisitions of the President. Why do they not dissolve it themselves,—the union between themselves and the State,—and refuse to pay their quota into its treasury? Do not they stand in the same relation to the State, that the State does to the Union? And have not the same reasons prevented the State from resisting the Union, which have prevented them from resisting the State?

15   How can a man be satisfied to entertain an opinion merely, and enjoy *it?* Is there any enjoyment in it, if his opinion is that he is aggrieved? If you are cheated out of a single dollar by your neighbor, you do not rest satisfied with knowing that you are cheated, or with saying that you are cheated, or even with petitioning him to pay you your due; but you take effectual steps at once to obtain the full amount, and see that you are never cheated again. Action from principle,—the perception and the performance of right,—changes things and relations; it is essentially revolutionary, and does not consist wholly with any thing which was. It not only divides states and churches, it divides families; aye, it divides the *individual*, separating the diabolical in him from the divine.

16   Unjust laws exist: shall we be content to obey them, or shall we endeavor to amend them, and obey them until we have succeeded, or shall we transgress them at once? Men generally, under such a government as this, think that they ought to wait until they have persuaded the majority to alter them. They think that, if they should resist, the remedy would be worse than the evil. But it is the fault of the government itself that the remedy *is* worse than the evil. *It* makes it worse. Why is it not more apt to anticipate and provide for reform? Why does it not cherish its wise minority? Why does it cry and resist before it is hurt? Why does it not encourage its citizens to be on the alert to point out its faults, and *do* better than it would have them? Why does it always crucify Christ, and excommunicate Copernicus and Luther, and pronounce Washington and Franklin rebels?

17   One would think, that a deliberate and practical denial of its authority was the only offence never contemplated by government; else, why has it not assigned its definite, its suitable and proportionate penalty? If a man who has no property refuses but once to earn nine shillings for the State, he is put in prison for a period unlimited by any law that I know, and determined only by the discretion of those who placed him there; but if he should steal ninety times nine shillings from the State, he is soon permitted to go at large again.

18   If the injustice is part of the necessary friction of the machine of government, let it go, let it go: perchance it will wear smooth,—certainly the machine will wear out. If the injustice has a spring, or a pulley, or a rope, or a crank, exclusively for itself, then perhaps you may consider whether the remedy will not be worse than the evil; but if it is of such a nature that it requires you to be the agent of injustice to another, then, I say, break the law. Let your life be a counter friction to stop the machine. What I have to do is to see, at any rate, that I do not lend myself to the wrong which I condemn.

19   As for adopting the ways which the State has provided for remedying the evil, I know not of such ways. They take too much time, and a man's life will be gone. I have other affairs to attend to. I came into this world, not chiefly to make this a good place to live in, but to live in it, be it good or bad. A man has not every thing to do, but something; and because he cannot do *every thing*, it is not necessary that he should do *something* wrong. It is not my business to be petitioning the governor or the legislature any more than it is theirs to petition me; and, if they should not hear my petition, what

should I do then? But in this case the State has provided no way: its very Constitution is the evil. This may seem to be harsh and stubborn and unconciliatory; but it is to treat with the utmost kindness and consideration the only spirit that can appreciate or deserves it. So is all change for the better, like birth and death which convulse the body.

20   I do not hesitate to say, that those who call themselves abolitionists should at once effectually withdraw their support, both in person and property, from the government of Massachusetts, and not wait till they constitute a majority of one, before they suffer the right to prevail through them. I think that it is enough if they have God on their side, without waiting for that other one. Moreover, any man more right than his neighbors, constitutes a majority of one already.

21   I meet this American government, or its representative the State government, directly, and face to face, once a year, no more, in the person of its tax-gatherer; this is the only mode in which a man situated as I am necessarily meets it; and it then says distinctly, Recognize me; and the simplest, the most effectual, and, in the present posture of affairs, the indispensablest mode of treating with it on this head, of expressing your little satisfaction with and love for it, is to deny it then. My civil neighbor, the tax-gatherer, is the very man I have to deal with,—for it is, after all, with men and not with parchment that I quarrel,—and he has voluntarily chosen to be an agent of the government. How shall he ever know well what he is and does as an officer of the government, or as a man, until he is obliged to consider whether he shall treat me, his neighbor, for whom he has respect, as a neighbor and well-disposed man, or as a maniac and disturber of the peace, and see if he can get over this obstruction to his neighborliness without a ruder and more impetuous thought or speech corresponding with his action? I know this well, that if one thousand, if one hundred, if ten men whom I could name,— if ten *honest* men only,—aye, if *one* HONEST man, in this State of Massachusetts, *ceasing to hold slaves*, were actually to withdraw from this copartnership, and be locked up in the county jail therefor, it would be the abolition of slavery in America. For it matters not how small the beginning may seem to be: what is once well done is done for ever. But we love better to talk about it: that we say is our mission. Reform keeps many scores of newspapers in its service, but not one man. If my esteemed neighbor, the State's ambassador,[8] who will devote his days to the settlement of the question of human rights in the Council Chamber, instead of being threatened with the prisons of Carolina, were to sit down the prisoner of Massachusetts, that State which is so anxious to foist the sin of slavery upon her sister,—though at present she can discover only an act of inhospitality to be the ground of a quarrel with her,—the Legislature would not wholly waive the subject the following winter.

22   Under a government which imprisons any unjustly, the true place for a just man is also a prison. The proper place to-day, the only place which Massachusetts has provided for her freer and less desponding spirits, is in her prisons, to be put out and locked out of the State by her own act, as they have already put themselves out by their principles. It is there that the fugitive slave, and the Mexican prisoner on parole, and the Indian come to plead the wrongs of his race, should find them; on that separate, but more free and

---

8   Samuel Hoar (1778–1856) went from Concord to the South Carolina legislature to protest treatment of black seamen.

honorable ground, where the State places those who are not *with* her but *against* her,—the only house in a slave-state in which a free man can abide with honor. If any think that their influence would be lost there, and their voices no longer afflict the ear of the State, that they would not be as an enemy within its walls, they do not know by how much truth is stronger than error, nor how much more eloquently and effectively he can combat injustice who has experienced a little in his own person. Cast your whole vote, not a strip of paper merely, but your whole influence. A minority is powerless while it conforms to the majority; it is not even a minority then; but it is irresistible when it clogs by its whole weight. If the alternative is to keep all just men in prison, or give up war and slavery, the State will not hesitate which to choose. If a thousand men were not to pay their tax-bills this year, that would not be a violent and bloody measure, as it would be to pay them, and enable the State to commit violence and shed innocent blood. This is, in fact, the definition of a peaceable revolution, if any such is possible. If the tax-gatherer, or any other public officer, asks me, as one has done, "But what shall I do?" my answer is, "If you really wish to do any thing, resign your office." When the subject has refused allegiance, and the officer has resigned his office, then the revolution is accomplished. But even suppose blood should flow. Is there not a sort of blood shed when the conscience is wounded? Through this wound a man's real manhood and immortality flow out, and he bleeds to an everlasting death. I see this blood flowing now.

23   I have contemplated the imprisonment of the offender, rather than the seizure of his goods,—though both will serve the same purpose,—because they who assert the purest right, and consequently are most dangerous to a corrupt State, commonly have not spent much time in accumulating property. To such the State renders comparatively small service, and a slight tax is wont to appear exorbitant, particularly if they are obliged to earn it by special labor with their hands. If there were one who lived wholly without the use of money, the State itself would hesitate to demand it of him. But the rich man—not to make any invidious comparison—is always sold to the institution which makes him rich. Absolutely speaking, the more money, the less virtue; for money comes between a man and his objects, and obtains them for him; and it was certainly no great virtue to obtain it. It puts to rest many questions which he would otherwise be taxed to answer; while the only new question which it puts is the hard but superfluous one, how to spend it. Thus his moral ground is taken from under his feet. The opportunities of living are diminished in proportion as what are called the "means" are increased. The best thing a man can do for his culture when he is rich is to endeavour to carry out those schemes which he entertained when he was poor. Christ answered the Herodians according to their condition. "Show me the tribute-money," said he;—and one took a penny out of his pocket;—If you use money which has the image of Caesar on it, and which he has made current and valuable, that is, *if you are men of the State*, and gladly enjoy the advantages of Caesar's government, then pay him back some of his own when he demands it; "Render therefore to Caesar that which is Caesar's, and to God those things which are God's,"—leaving them no wiser than before as to which was which; for they did not wish to know.

24   When I converse with the freest of my neighbors, I perceive that, whatever they may say about the magnitude and seriousness of the question, and their regard for the public tranquility, the long and the short of the matter is, that they cannot spare the protection of the existing government, and they dread the consequences of disobedience to it to

their property and families. For my own part, I should not like to think that I ever rely on the protection of the State. But, if I deny the authority of the State when it presents its tax-bill, it will soon take and waste all my property, and so harass me and my children without end. This is hard. This makes it impossible for a man to live honestly and at the same time comfortably in outward respects. It will not be worth the while to accumulate property; that would be sure to go again. You must hire or squat somewhere, and raise but a small crop, and eat that soon. You must live within yourself, and depend upon yourself, always tucked up and ready for a start, and not have many affairs. A man may grow rich in Turkey even, if he will be in all respects a good subject of the Turkish government. Confucius said,—"If a State is governed by the principles of reason, poverty and misery are subjects of shame; if a State is not governed by the principles of reason, riches and honors are the subjects of shame." No: until I want the protection of Massachusetts to be extended to me in some distant southern port, where my liberty is endangered, or until I am bent solely on building up an estate at home by peaceful enterprise, I can afford to refuse allegiance to Massachusetts, and her right to my property and life. It costs me less in every sense to incur the penalty of disobedience to the State, than it would to obey. I should feel as if I were worth less in that case.

25   Some years ago, the State met me in behalf of the church, and commanded me to pay a certain sum toward the support of a clergyman whose preaching my father attended, but never I myself. "Pay it," it said, "or be locked up in the jail." I declined to pay. But, unfortunately, another man saw fit to pay it. I did not see why the schoolmaster should be taxed to support the priest, and not the priest the schoolmaster; for I was not the State's schoolmaster, but I supported myself by voluntary subscription. I did not see why the lyceum should not present its tax-bill, and have the State to back its demand, as well as the church. However, at the request of the selectmen, I condescended to make some such statement as this in writing:—"Know all men by these presents, that I, Henry Thoreau, do not wish to be regarded as a member of any incorporated society which I have not joined." This I gave to the town-clerk; and he has it. The State, having thus learned that I did not wish to be regarded as a member of that church, has never made a like demand on me since; though it said that it must adhere to its original presumption that time. If I had known how to name them, I should then have signed off in detail from all the societies which I never signed on to; but I did not know where to find a complete list.

26   I have paid no poll-tax for six years. I was put into a jail once on this account, for one night; and, as I stood considering the walls of solid stone, two or three feet thick, the door of wood and iron, a foot thick, and the iron grating which strained the light, I could not help being struck with the foolishness of that institution which treated me as if I were mere flesh and blood and bones, to be locked up. I wondered that it should have concluded at length that this was the best use it could put me to, and had never thought to avail itself of my services in some way. I saw that, if there was a wall of stone between me and my towns-men, there was a still more difficult one to climb or break through, before they could get to be as free as I was. I did not for a moment feel confined, and the walls seemed a great waste of stone and mortar. I felt as if I alone of all my townsmen had paid my tax. They plainly did not know how to treat me, but behaved like persons who are underbred. In every threat and in every compliment there was a blunder; for they thought that my chief desire was to stand the other side of that stone wall. I could

not but smile to see how industriously they locked the door on my meditations, which followed them out again without let or hinderance, and *they* were really all that was dangerous. As they could not reach me, they had resolved to punish my body; just as boys, if they cannot come at some person against whom they have a spite, will abuse his dog. I saw that the State was half-witted, that it was timid as a lone woman with her silver spoons, and that it did not know its friends from its foes, and I lost all my remaining respect for it, and pitied it.

27   Thus the State never intentionally confronts a man's sense, intellectual or moral, but only his body, his senses. It is not armed with superior wit or honesty, but with superior physical strength. I was not born to be forced. I will breathe after my own fashion. Let us see who is the strongest. What force has a multitude? They only can force me who obey a higher law than I. They force me to become like themselves. I do not hear of *men* being *forced* to live this way or that by masses of men. What sort of life were that to live? When I meet a government which says to me, "Your money or your life," why should I be in haste to give it my money? It may be in a great strait, and not know what to do: I cannot help that. It must help itself; do as I do. It is not worth the while to snivel about it. I am not responsible for the successful working of the machinery of society. I am not the son of the engineer. I perceive that, when an acorn and a chestnut fall side by side, the one does not remain inert to make way for the other, but both obey their own laws, and spring and grow and flourish as best they can, till one, perchance, overshadows and destroys the other. If a plant cannot live according to its nature, it dies; and so a man.

28   The night in prison was novel and interesting enough. The prisoners in their shirt-sleeves were enjoying a chat and the evening air in the door-way, when I entered. But the jailer said, "Come, boys, it is time to lock up;" and so they dispersed, and I heard the sound of their steps returning into the hollow apartments. My room-mate was introduced to me by the jailer, as "a first-rate fellow and a clever man." When the door was locked, he showed me where to hang my hat, and how he managed matters there. The rooms were whitewashed once a month; and this one, at least, was the whitest, most simply furnished, and probably the neatest apartment in the town. He naturally wanted to know where I came from, and what brought me there; and, when I had told him, I asked him in my turn how he came there, presuming him to be an honest man, of course; and, as the world goes, I believe he was. "Why," said he, "they accuse me of burning a barn; but I never did it." As near as I could discover, he had probably gone to bed in a barn when drunk, and smoked his pipe there; and so a barn was burnt. He had the reputation of being a clever man, had been there some three months waiting for his trial to come on, and would have to wait as much longer; but he was quite domesticated and contented, since he got his board for nothing, and thought that he was well treated.

29   He occupied one window, and I the other; and I saw, that if one stayed there long, his principal business would be to look out the window. I had soon read all the tracts that were left there, and examined where former prisoners had broken out, and where a grate had been sawed off, and heard the history of the various occupants of that room; for I found that even here there was a history and a gossip which never circulated beyond the walls of the jail. Probably this is the only house in the town where verses are composed, which are afterward printed in a circular form, but not published. I was shown quite a long list of verses which were composed by some young men who had been detected in an attempt to escape, who avenged themselves by singing them.

30   I pumped my fellow-prisoner as dry as I could, for fear I should never see him again; but at length he showed me which was my bed, and left me to blow out the lamp.

31   It was like travelling into a far country, such as I had never expected to behold, to lie there for one night. It seemed to me that I never had heard the town-clock strike before, nor the evening sounds of the village; for we slept with the windows open, which were inside the grating. It was to see my native village in the light of the middle ages, and our Concord was turned into a Rhine stream, and visions of knights and castles passed before me. They were the voices of old burghers that I heard in the streets. I was an involuntary spectator and auditor of whatever was done and said in the kitchen of the adjacent village-inn,—a wholly new and rare experience to me. It was a closer view of my native town. I was fairly inside of it. I never had seen its institutions before. This is one of its peculiar institutions; for it is a shire town. I began to comprehend what its inhabitants were about.

32   In the morning, our breakfasts were put through the hole in the door, in small oblong-square tin pans, made to fit, and holding a pint of chocolate, with brown bread, and an iron spoon. When they called for the vessels again, I was green enough to return what bread I had left; but my comrade seized it, and said that I should lay that up for lunch or dinner. Soon after, he was let out to work at haying in a neighboring field, whither he went every day, and would not be back till noon; so he bade me good-day, saying that he doubted if he should see me again.

33   When I came out of prison,—for some one[9] interfered, and paid the tax,—I did not perceive that great changes had taken place on the common, such as he observed who went in a youth, and emerged a tottering and gray-headed man; and yet a change had to my eyes come over the scene,—the town, and State, and country,—greater than any that mere time could effect. I saw yet more distinctly the State in which I lived. I saw to what extent the people among whom I lived could be trusted as good neighbors and friends; that their friendship was for summer weather only; that they did not greatly purpose to do right; that they were a distinct race from me by their prejudices and superstitions, as the Chinamen and Malays are; that, in their sacrifices to humanity, they ran no risks, not even to their property; that, after all, they were not so noble but they treated the thief as he had treated them, and hoped, by a certain outward observance and a few prayers, and by walking in a particular straight though useless path from time to time, to save their souls. This may be to judge my neighbors harshly; for I believe that most of them are not aware that they have such an institution as the jail in their village.

34   It was formerly the custom in our village, when a poor debtor came out of jail, for his acquaintances to salute him, looking through their fingers, which were crossed to represent the grating of a jail window, "How do ye do?" My neighbors did not thus salute me, but first looked at me, and then at one another, as if I had returned from a long journey. I was put into jail as I was going to the shoemaker's to get a shoe which was mended. When I was let out the next morning, I proceeded to finish my errand, and, having put on my mended shoe, joined a huckleberry party, who were impatient to put themselves under my conduct; and in half an hour,—for the horse was soon

---

9   Probably Maria Thoreau, his aunt.—Ed.

tackled,[10]—was in the midst of a huckleberry field, on one of our highest hills, two miles off; and then the State was nowhere to be seen.

35   This is the whole history of "My Prisons."[11]

36   I have never declined paying the highway tax, because I am as desirous of being a good neighbor as I am of being a bad subject; and, as for supporting schools, I am doing my part to educate my fellow-countrymen now. It is for no particular item in the tax-bill that I refuse to pay it. I simply wish to refuse allegiance to the State, to withdraw and stand aloof from it effectually. I do not care to trace the course of my dollar, if I could, till it buys a man, or a musket to shoot one with,—the dollar is innocent,—but I am concerned to trace the effects of my allegiance. In fact, I quietly declare war with the State, after my fashion, though I will still make what use and get what advantage of her I can, as is usual in such cases.

37   If others pay the tax which is demanded of me, from a sympathy with the State, they do but what they have already done in their own case, or rather they abet injustice to a greater extent than the State requires. If they pay the tax from a mistaken interest in the individual taxed, to save his property or prevent his going to jail, it is because they have not considered wisely how far they let their private feelings interfere with the public good.

38   This, then, is my position at present. But one cannot be too much on his guard in such a case, lest his action be biassed by obstinacy, or an undue regard for the opinions of men. Let him see that he does only what belongs to himself and to the hour.

39   I think sometimes, Why, this people mean well; they are only ignorant; they would do better if they knew how: why give your neighbors this pain to treat you as they are not inclined to? But I think, again, this is no reason why I should do as they do, or permit others to suffer much greater pain of a different kind. Again, I sometimes say to myself, When many millions of men, without heat, without ill-will, without personal feeling of any kind, demand of you a few shillings only, without the possibility, such is their constitution, of retracting or altering their present demand, and without the possibility, on your side, of appeal to any other millions, why expose yourself to this overwhelming brute force? You do not resist cold and hunger, the winds and the waves, thus obstinately; you quietly submit to a thousand similar necessities. You do not put your head into the fire. But just in proportion as I regard this as not wholly a brute force, but partly a human force, and consider that I have relations to those millions as to so many millions of men, and not of mere brute or inanimate things, I see that appeal is possible, first and instantaneously, from them to the Maker of them, and, secondly, from them to themselves. But, if I put my head deliberately into the fire, there is no appeal to fire or to the Maker of fire, and I have only myself to blame. If I could convince myself that I have any right to be satisfied with men as they are, and to treat them accordingly, and not according, in some respects, to my requisitions and expectations of what they and I ought to be, then, like a good Mussulman[12] and fatalist, I should endeavor to be satisfied with things as they are, and say it is the will of God. And, above all, there is this

---

10   Harnessed.—Ed.

11   Reference to memoirs of Italian patriot Silvio Pellico.—Ed.

12   A Moslem.—Ed.

difference between resisting this and a purely brute or natural force, that I can resist this with some effect; but I cannot expect, like Orpheus, to change the nature of the rocks and trees and beasts.

40   I do not wish to quarrel with any man or nation. I do not wish to split hairs, to make fine distinctions, or set myself up as better than my neighbors. I seek rather, I may say, even an excuse for conforming to the laws of the land. I am but too ready to conform to them. Indeed I have reason to suspect myself on this head; and each year, as the tax-gatherer comes round, I find myself disposed to review the acts and position of the general and state governments, and the spirit of the people, to discover a pretext for conformity. I believe that the State will soon be able to take all my work of this sort out of my hands, and then I shall be no better a patriot than my fellow-countrymen. Seen from a lower point of view, the Constitution, with all its faults, is very good; the law and the courts are very respectable; even this State and this American government are, in many respects, very admirable and rare things, to be thankful for, such as a great many have described them; but seen from a point of view a little higher, they are what I have described them; seen from a higher still, and the highest, who shall say what they are, or that they are worth looking at or thinking of at all?

41   However, the government does not concern me much, and I shall bestow the fewest possible thoughts on it. It is not many moments that I live under a government, even in this world. If a man is thought-free, fancy-free, imagination-free, that which *is not* never for a long time appearing *to be* to him, unwise rulers or reformers cannot fatally interrupt him.

42   I know that most men think differently from myself; but those whose lives are by profession devoted to the study of these or kindred subjects, content me as little as any. Statesmen and legislators, standing so completely within the institution, never distinctly and nakedly behold it. They speak of moving society, but have no resting-place without it. They may be men of a certain experience and discrimination, and have no doubt invented ingenious and even useful systems, for which we sincerely thank them; but all their wit and usefulness lie within certain not very wide limits. They are wont to forget that the world is not governed by policy and expediency. Webster never goes behind government, and so cannot speak with authority about it. His words are wisdom to those legislators who contemplate no essential reform in the existing government; but for thinkers, and those who legislate for all time, he never once glances at the subject. I know of those whose serene and wise speculations on this theme would soon reveal the limits of his mind's range and hospitality. Yet, compared with the cheap professions of most reformers, and the still cheaper wisdom and eloquence of politicians in general, his are almost the only sensible and valuable words, and we thank Heaven for him. Comparatively, he is always strong, original, and, above all, practical. Still his quality is not wisdom, but prudence. The lawyer's truth is not Truth, but consistency, or a consistent expediency. Truth is always in harmony with herself, and is not concerned chiefly to reveal the justice that may consist with wrong-doing. He well deserves to be called, as he has been called, the Defender of the Constitution. There are really no blows to be given by him but defensive ones. He is not a leader, but a follower. His leaders are the men of '87. "I have never made an effort," he says, "and never propose to make an effort; I have never countenanced an effort, and never mean to countenance

an effort, to disturb the arrangement as originally made, by which the various States came into the Union." Still thinking of the sanction which the Constitution gives to slavery, he says, "Because it was a part of the original compact,—let it stand." Notwithstanding his special acuteness and ability, he is unable to take a fact out of its merely political relations, and behold it as it lies absolutely to be disposed of by the intellect,—what, for instance, it behoves a man to do here in America to-day with regard to slavery, but ventures, or is driven, to make some such desperate answer as the following, while professing to speak absolutely, and as a private man,—from which what new and singular code of social duties might be inferred?—"The manner," says he, "in which the government of those States where slavery exists are to regulate it, is for their own consideration, under their responsibility to their constituents, to the general laws of propriety, humanity, and justice, and to God. Associations formed elsewhere, springing from a feeling of humanity, or any other cause, have nothing whatever to do with it. They have never received any encouragement from me, and they never will."[13]

43   They who know of no purer sources of truth, who have traced up its stream no higher, stand, and wisely stand, by the Bible and the Constitution, and drink at it there with reverence and humility; but they who behold where it comes trickling into this lake or that pool, gird up their loins once more, and continue their pilgrimage toward its fountain-head.

44   No man with a genius for legislation has appeared in America. They are rare in the history of the world. There are orators, politicians, and eloquent men, by the thousand; but the speaker has not yet opened his mouth to speak, who is capable of settling the much-vexed questions of the day. We love eloquence for its own sake, and not for any truth which it may utter, or any heroism it may inspire. Our legislators have not yet learned the comparative value of free-trade and of freedom, of union, and of rectitude, to a nation. They have no genius or talent for comparatively humble questions of taxation and finance, commerce and manufactures and agriculture. If we were left solely to the wordy wit of legislators in Congress for our guidance, uncorrected by the seasonable experience and the effectual complaints of the people, America would not long retain her rank among the nations. For eighteen hundred years, though perchance I have no right to say it, the New Testament, has been written; yet where is the legislator who has wisdom and practical talent enough to avail himself of the light which it sheds on the science of legislation?

45   The authority of government, even such as I am willing to submit to,—for I will cheerfully obey those who know and can do better than I, and in many things even those who neither know nor can do so well,—is still an impure one: to be strictly just, it must have the sanction and consent of the governed. It can have no pure right over my person and property but what I concede to it. The progress from an absolute to a limited monarchy, from a limited monarchy to a democracy, is a progress toward a true respect for the individual. Is a democracy, such as we know it, the last improvement

---

[13]Quotations are from a speech of Webster's in the Senate. Thoreau notes that these quotations were added for the printed version of the essay.—Ed.

possible in government? Is it not possible to take a step further towards recognizing and organizing the rights of man? There will never be a really free and enlightened State, until the State comes to recognize the individual as a higher and independent power, from which all its own power and authority are derived, and treats him accordingly. I please myself with imagining a State at last which can afford to be just to all men, and to treat the individual with respect as a neighbor; which even would not think it inconsistent with its own repose, if a few were to live aloof from it, not meddling with it, nor embraced by it, who fulfilled all the duties of neighbors and fellow-men. A State which bore this kind of fruit, and suffered it to drop off as fast as it ripened, would prepare the way for a still more perfect and glorious State, which also I have imagined, but not yet anywhere seen.

Questions for Reading and Analysis

1. Thoreau begins by expressing a desire for less government. After stating these views, Thoreau calls for what kind of government?

2. What, according to Thoreau, is everyone's obligation? What is not our obligation, with regard to the law or the government?

3. What does Thoreau want Americans of his time to think about their government? What are his two specific complaints about the government in 1848?

4. What should be our response to unjust laws?

5. When the government is unjust, where must the just person be found?

6. How did Thoreau feel about his night in jail?

7. Where does he offer a conciliatory passage? What common ground does he find?

8. In paragraph 42, Thoreau asserts that "The lawyer's truth is not Truth." What does he mean by this statement?

9. What is the central claim of Thoreau's argument?

Questions for Discussion and Response

1. What is one statement of Thoreau's that has most surprised or interested you? Why did you select that statement?

2. Do you agree with Thoreau that you must be responsible for your conscience, your morality, before being responsible to the government and the law? Why or why not?

3. Do you agree that unjust laws must be disobeyed as the vehicle for change? Why or why not?

4. Would you demonstrate against an unjust law, risking a night in prison for your cause? Why or why not?

Declaration of Sentiments

Elizabeth Cady Stanton

Elizabeth Cady Stanton (1815–1902) was one of the most important leaders of the women's rights movement. Educated at the Emma Willard Seminary in Troy, New York, Stanton studied law with her father before her marriage. An active reformer in the abolition and temperance movements, she later focused her attention on women's issues. At the Seneca Falls Convention in 1848 (the first women's rights convention), Stanton gave the opening speech and read her "Declaration of Sentiments." She founded and became president of the National Women's Suffrage Association in 1869. The "Declaration of Sentiments," patterned after the "Declaration of Independence," lists the grievances of women suffering under the tyranny of men.

1   When, in the course of human events, it becomes necessary for one portion of the family of man to assume among the people of the earth a position different from that which they have hitherto occupied, but one to which the laws of nature and of nature's God entitle them, a decent respect to the opinions of mankind requires that they should declare the causes that impel them to such a course.

2   We hold these truths to be self-evident: that all men and women are created equal; that they are endowed by their Creator with certain inalienable rights; that among these are life, liberty, and the pursuit of happiness; that to secure these rights governments are instituted, deriving their just powers from the consent of the governed. Whenever any form of government becomes destructive of these ends, it is the right of those who suffer from it to refuse allegiance to it, and to insist upon the institution of a new government, laying its foundation on such principles, and organizing its powers in such form, as to them shall seem most likely to effect their safety and happiness. Prudence, indeed, will dictate that governments long established should not be changed for light and transient causes; and accordingly all experience hath shown that mankind are more disposed to suffer, while evils are sufferable, than to right themselves by abolishing the forms to which they were accustomed. But when a long train of abuses and usurpations, pursuing invariably the same object evinces a design to reduce them under absolute despotism, it is their duty to throw off such government, and to provide new guards for their future security. Such has been the patient sufferance of the women under this government, and such is now the necessity which constrains them to demand the equal station to which they are entitled.

3   The history of mankind is a history of repeated injuries and usurpations on the part of man toward woman, having in direct object the establishment of an absolute tyranny over her. To prove this, let facts be submitted to a candid world.

4   He has never permitted her to exercise her inalienable right to the elective franchise.

5   He has compelled her to submit to laws, in the formation of which she had no voice.

6   He has withheld from her rights which are given to the most ignorant and degraded men—both natives and foreigners.

7   Having deprived her of this first right of a citizen, the elective franchise, thereby leaving her without representation in the halls of legislation, he has oppressed her on all sides.

8   He has made her, if married, in the eye of the law, civilly dead.

9   He has taken from her all right in property, even to the wages she earns.

10   He has made her, morally, an irresponsible being, as she can commit many crimes with impunity, provided they be done in the presence of her husband. In the covenant of marriage, she is compelled to promise obedience to her husband, he becoming, to all intents and purposes, her master—the law giving him power to deprive her of her liberty, and to administer chastisement.

11   He has so framed the laws of divorce, as to what shall be the proper causes, and in case of separation, to whom the guardianship of the children shall be given, as to be wholly regardless of the happiness of women—the law, in all cases, going upon a false supposition of the supremacy of man, and giving all power into his hands.

12   After depriving her of all rights as a married woman, if single, and the owner of property, he has taxed her to support a government which recognizes her only when her property can be made profitable to it.

13   He has monopolized nearly all the profitable employments, and from those she is permitted to follow, she receives but a scanty remuneration. He closes against her all the avenues to wealth and distinction which he considers most honorable to himself. As a teacher of theology, medicine, or law, she is not known.

14   He has denied her the facilities for obtaining a thorough education, all colleges being closed against her.

15   He allows her in Church, as well as State, but a subordinate position, claiming Apostolic authority for her exclusion from the ministry, and, with some exceptions, from any public participation in the affairs of the Church.

16   He has created a false public sentiment by giving to the world a different code of morals for men and women, by which moral delinquencies which exclude women from society, are not only tolerated, but deemed of little account in man.

17   He has usurped the prerogative of Jehovah himself, claiming it as his right to assign for her a sphere of action, when that belongs to her conscience and to her God.

18   He has endeavored, in every way that he could, to destroy her confidence in her own powers, to lessen her self-respect, and to make her willing to lead a dependent and abject life.

19   Now in view of this entire disfranchisement of one-half the people of this country, their social and religious degradation—in view of the unjust laws above mentioned, and because women do feel themselves aggrieved, oppressed, and fraudulently deprived of their most sacred rights, we insist that they have immediate admission to all the rights and privileges which belong to them as citizens of the United States.

20   In entering upon the great work before us, we anticipate no small amount of misconception, misrepresentation, and ridicule; but we shall use every instrumentality within our power to effect our object. We shall employ agents, circulate tracts, petition the State and National legislatures, and endeavor to enlist the pulpit and the press in our behalf. We hope this Convention will be followed by a series of Conventions embracing every part of the country.

Questions for Reading and Analysis

1. Summarize the ideas of paragraphs 1 and 2. Be sure to use your own words.
2. What is Stanton's claim? With what does she charge men?
3. What are the first three facts given by Stanton? Why are they presented first?
4. How have women been restricted by law if married or owning property? How have they been restricted in education and work? How have they been restricted psychologically?
5. What, according to Stanton, do women demand? How will they seek their goals?
6. Analyze the similarities and differences in Stanton's version and the original "Declaration." (See page 100.) What significant differences in wording and content do you find?
7. Do some research to find out when some of the specific grievances were eliminated. See how many you can put a date to.

Questions for Discussion and Response

1. Most—but not all—of Stanton's charges have been redressed, however slowly. Which continue to be legitimate complaints, either in whole or in part?
2. Do we need a new declaration of sentiments for women? If so, what specific charges would you list? If not, why not?
3. Do we need a declaration of sentiments for other groups—children, minorities, the elderly? If so, what specific charges should be listed? Select one group that you think needs a statement of grievances and prepare a declaration of sentiments for that group. If you do not think any group needs a declaration, explain why.

On Liberty

John Stuart Mill

John Stuart Mill (1806–1873) rose to be an important official in the East India Company and also made a permanent name for himself as one of our most influential philosophers. Mill reveals his breadth of knowledge and interests in the titles of some of his published works: *A System of Logic* (1843), *Principles of Political Economy* (1848), *Consideration on Representative Government* (1861), *The Subjection of Women* (1869), and *On Liberty* (1859), from which the following passages have been excerpted. In his essay *On Liberty* Mill examines the issue of what, if any, constraints should be placed on individual freedom. Mill, a believer in utilitarian philosophy, explores the issue in the context of individual freedom versus the social good, or the greatest good for the greatest number.

Introductory

1   The subject of this Essay is . . . Civil, or Social Liberty: the nature and limits of the power which can be legitimately exercised by society over the individual. A question

seldom stated, and hardly ever discussed, in general terms, but which profoundly influences the practical controversies of the age by its latent presence, and is likely soon to make itself recognized as the vital question of the future. It is so far from being new, that, in a certain sense, it has divided mankind, almost from the remotest ages, but in the stage of progress into which the more civilized portions of the species have now entered, it presents itself under new conditions, and requires a different and more fundamental treatment. . . .

2   In political and philosophical theories, as well as in persons, success discloses faults and infirmities which failure might have concealed from observation. The notion, that the people have no need to limit their power over themselves, might seem axiomatic, when popular government was a thing only dreamed about, or read of as having existed at some distant period of the past. Neither was that notion necessarily disturbed by such temporary aberrations as those of the French Revolution, the worst of which were the work of an usurping few, and which, in any case, belonged, not to the permanent working of popular institutions, but to a sudden and convulsive outbreak against monarchical and aristocratic despotism. In time, however, a democratic republic came to occupy a large portion of the earth's surface, and made itself felt as one of the most powerful members of the community of nations; and elective and responsible government became subject to the observations and criticisms which wait upon a great existing fact. It was now perceived that such phrases as "self-government," and "the power of the people over themselves," do not express the true state of the case. The "people" who exercise the power, are not always the same people with those over whom it is exercised, and the "self-government" spoken of, is not the government of each by himself, but of each by all the rest. The will of the people, moreover, practically means, the will of the most numerous or the most active *part* of the people; the majority, or those who succeed in making themselves accepted as the majority: the people, consequently, *may* desire to oppress a part of their number; and precautions are as much needed against this, as against any other abuse of power. The limitation, therefore, of the power of government over individuals, loses none of its importance when the holders of power are regularly accountable to the community, that is, to the strongest party therein. This view of things, recommending itself equally to the intelligence of thinkers and to the inclination of those important classes in European society to whose real or supposed interests democracy is adverse, has had no difficulty in establishing itself; and in political speculations "the tyranny of the majority" is now generally included among the evils against which society requires to be on its guard.

3   Like other tyrannies, the tyranny of the majority was at first, and is still vulgarly, held in dread, chiefly as operating through the acts of the public authorities. But reflecting persons perceived that when society is itself the tyrant—society collectively, over the separate individuals who compose it—its means of tyrannizing are not restricted to the acts which it may do by the hands of its political functionaries. Society can and does execute its own mandates: and if it issues wrong mandates instead of right, or any mandates at all in things with which it ought not to meddle, it practises a social tyranny more formidable than many kinds of political oppression, since, though not usually upheld by such extreme penalties, it leaves fewer means of escape, penetrating much more deeply into the details of life, and enslaving the soul itself. Protection, therefore, against the tyranny of the magistrate is not enough; there needs protection

also against the tyranny of the prevailing opinion and feeling; against the tendency of society to impose, by other means than civil penalties, its own ideas and practices as rules of conduct on those who dissent from them; to fetter the development, and, if possible, prevent the formation, of any individuality not in harmony with its ways, and compel all characters to fashion themselves upon the model of its own. There is a limit to the legitimate interference of collective opinion with individual independence; and to find that limit, and maintain it against encroachment, is as indispensable to a good condition of human affairs, as protection against political despotism.

4   But though this proposition is not likely to be contested in general terms, the practical question, where to place the limit—how to make the fitting adjustment between individual independence and social control—is a subject on which nearly everything remains to be done. All that makes existence valuable to any one, depends on the enforcement of restraints upon the actions of other people. Some rules of conduct, therefore, must be imposed, by law in the first place, and by opinion on many things which are not fit subjects for the operation of law. What these rules should be, is the principal question in human affairs; but if we except a few of the most obvious cases, it is one of those which least progress has been made in resolving. No two ages, and scarcely any two countries, have decided it alike; and the decision of one age or country is a wonder to another. Yet the people of any given age and country no more suspect any difficulty in it, than if it were a subject on which mankind had always been agreed. The rules which obtain among themselves appear to them self-evident and self-justifying. This all but universal illusion is one of the examples of the magical influence of custom, which is not only, as the proverb says, a second nature, but is continually mistaken for the first. The effect of custom, in preventing any misgiving respecting the rules of conduct which mankind impose on one another, is all the more complete because the subject is one on which it is not generally considered necessary that reasons should be given, either by one person to others, or by each to himself. People are accustomed to believe and have been encouraged in the belief by some who aspire to the character of philosophers, that their feelings, on subjects of this nature, are better than reasons, and render reasons unnecessary. The practical principle which guides them to their opinions on the regulation of human conduct, is the feeling in each person's mind that everybody should be required to act as he, and those with whom he sympathizes, would like them to act. No one, indeed, acknowledges to himself that his standard of judgment is his own liking; but an opinion on a point of conduct, not supported by reasons, can only count as one person's preference; and if the reasons, when given, are a mere appeal to a similar preference felt by other people, it is still only many people's liking instead of one. To an ordinary man, however, his own preference, thus supported, is not only a perfectly satisfactory reason, but the only one he generally has for any of his notions of morality, taste, or propriety, which are not expressly written in his religious creed; and his chief guide in the interpretation even of that. Men's opinions, accordingly, on what is laudable or blamable, are affected by all the multifarious causes which influence their wishes in regard to the conduct of others, and which are as numerous as those which determine their wishes on any other subject. Sometimes their reason—at other times their prejudices or superstitions: often their social affections, not seldom their anti-social ones, their envy or jealousy, their arrogance or contemptuousness: but most commonly, their desires or fears for themselves—their legitimate or illegitimate self-interest. Wherever

there is an ascendant class, a large portion of the morality of the country emanates from its class interests, and its feelings of class superiority. The morality between Spartans and Helots, between planters and negroes, between princes and subjects, between nobles and roturiers, between men and women, has been for the most part the creation of these class interests and feelings: and the sentiments thus generated, react in turn upon the moral feelings of the members of the ascendant class, in their relations among themselves. Where, on the other hand, a class, formerly ascendant, has lost its ascendency, or where its ascendency is unpopular, the prevailing moral sentiments frequently bear the impress of an impatient dislike of superiority. Another grand determining principle of the rules of conduct, both in act and forbearance which have been enforced by law or opinion, has been the servility of mankind towards the supposed preferences or aversions of their temporal masters, or of their gods. This servility though essentially selfish, is not hypocrisy; it gives rise to perfectly genuine sentiments of abhorrence; it made men burn magicians and heretics. Among so many baser influences, the general and obvious interests of society have of course had a share, and a large one, in the direction of the moral sentiments: less, however, as a matter of reason, and on their own account, than as a consequence of the sympathies and antipathies which grew out of them: and sympathies and antipathies which had little or nothing to do with the interests of society, have made themselves felt in the establishment of moralities with quite as great force. . . .

5   The object of this Essay is to assert one very simple principle, as entitled to govern absolutely the dealings of society with the individual in the way of compulsion and control, whether the means used be physical force in the form of legal penalties, or the moral coercion of public opinion. That principle is, that the sole end for which mankind are warranted, individually or collectively in interfering with the liberty of action of any of their number, is self-protection. That the only purpose for which power can be rightfully exercised over any member of a civilized community, against his will, is to prevent harm to others. His own good, either physical or moral, is not a sufficient warrant. He cannot rightfully be compelled to do or forbear because it will be better for him to do so, because it will make him happier, because, in the opinions of others, to do so would be wise, or even right. These are good reasons for remonstrating with him, or reasoning with him, or persuading him, or entreating him, but not for compelling him, or visiting him with any evil, in case he do otherwise. To justify that, the conduct from which it is desired to deter him must be calculated to produce evil to some one else. The only part of the conduct of any one, for which he is amenable to society, is that which concerns others. In the part which merely concerns himself, his independence is, of right, absolute. Over himself, over his own body and mind, the individual is sovereign.

6   It is, perhaps, hardly necessary to say that this doctrine is meant to apply only to human beings in the maturity of their faculties. We are not speaking of children, or of young persons below the age which the law may fix as that of manhood or womanhood. Those who are still in a state to require being taken care of by others, must be protected against their own actions as well as against external injury. . . .

7   It is proper to state that I forego any advantage which could be derived to my argument from the idea of abstract right as a thing independent of utility. I regard utility as the ultimate appeal on all ethical questions; but it must be utility in the largest sense,

grounded on the permanent interests of man as a progressive being. Those interests, I contend, authorize the subjection of individual spontaneity to external control, only in respect to those actions of each, which concern the interest of other people. If any one does an act hurtful to others, there is a *prima facie* case for punishing him, by law, or, where legal penalties are not safely applicable, by general disapprobation. There are also many positive acts for the benefit of others, which he may rightfully be compelled to perform; such as, to give evidence in a court of justice; to bear his fair share in the common defence, or in any other joint work necessary to the interest of the society of which he enjoys the protection; and to perform certain acts of individual beneficence, such as saving a fellow-creature's life, or interposing to protect the defenceless against ill-usage, things which whenever it is obviously a man's duty to do, he may rightfully be made responsible to society for not doing. A person may cause evil to others not only by his actions but by his inaction, and in neither case he is justly accountable to them for the injury. The latter case, it is true, requires a much more cautious exercise of compulsion than the former. To make any one answerable for doing evil to others, is the rule; to make him answerable for not preventing evil, is, comparatively speaking, the exception. Yet there are many cases clear enough and grave enough to justify that exception. In all things which regard the external relations of the individual, he is *de jure* amenable to those whose interests are concerned, and if need be, to society as their protector. There are often good reasons for not holding him to the responsibility; but these reasons must arise from the special expediencies of the case: either because it is a kind of case in which he is on the whole likely to act better, when left to his own discretion, than when controlled in any way in which society have it in their power to control him. . . .

8   There is a sphere of action in which society, as distinguished from the individual, has, if any, only an indirect interest; comprehending all that portion of a person's life and conduct which affects only himself, or, if it also affects others, only with their free, voluntary, and undeceived consent and participation. When I say only himself, I mean directly, and in the first instance: for whatever affects himself, may affect others *through* himself; and the objection which may be grounded on this contingency, will receive consideration in the sequel. This, then, is the appropriate region of human liberty. It comprises, first, the inward domain of consciousness; demanding liberty of conscience, in the most comprehensive sense; liberty of thought and feeling; absolute freedom of opinion and sentiment on all subjects, practical or speculative, scientific, moral, or theological. The liberty of expressing and publishing opinions may seem to fall under a different principle, since it belongs to that part of the conduct of an individual which concerns other people; but, being almost of as much importance as the liberty of thought itself, and resting in great part on the same reasons, is practically inseparable from it. Secondly, the principle requires liberty of tastes and pursuits; of framing the plan of our life to suit our own character; of doing as we like, subject to such consequences as may follow; without impediment from our fellow-creatures, so long as what we do does not harm them even though they should think our conduct foolish, perverse, or wrong. Thirdly, from this liberty of each individual, follows the liberty, within the same limits, of combination among individuals; freedom to unite, for any purpose not involving harm to others: the persons combining being supposed to be of full age, and not forced or deceived.

9   No society in which these liberties are not, on the whole, respected, is free, whatever may be its form of government; and none is completely free in which they do not exist absolute and unqualified. The only freedom which deserves the name, is that of pursuing our own good in our own way, so long as we do not attempt to deprive others of theirs, or impede their efforts to obtain it. Each is the proper guardian of his own health, whether bodily, or mental or spiritual. Mankind are greater gainers by suffering each other to live as seems good to themselves, than by compelling each to live as seems good to the rest. . . .

Of the Liberty of Thought and Discussion

10   The time, it is to be hoped, is gone by when any defense would be necessary of the "liberty of the press" as one of the securities against corrupt or tyrannical government. No argument, we may suppose, can now be needed against permitting a legislature or an executive, not identified in interest with the people, to prescribe opinions to them and determine what doctrines or what arguments they shall be allowed to hear. This aspect of the question, besides, has been so often and so triumphantly enforced by preceding writers that it need not be specially insisted on in this place. Though the law of England, on the subject of the press, is as servile to this day as it was in the time of the Tudors, there is little danger of its being actually put in force against political discussion except during some temporary panic when fear of insurrection drives ministers and judges from their propriety; and, speaking generally, it is not, in constitutional countries, to be apprehended that the government, whether completely responsible to the people or not, will often attempt to control the expression of opinion, except when in doing so it makes itself the organ of the general intolerance of the public. Let us suppose, therefore, that the government is entirely at one with the people, and never thinks of exerting any power of coercion unless in agreement with what it conceives to be their voice. But I deny the right of the people to exercise such coercion, either by themselves or by their government. The power itself is illegitimate. The best government has no more title to it than the worst. It is as noxious, or more noxious, when exerted in accordance with public opinion than when in opposition to it. If all mankind minus one were of one opinion, mankind would be no more justified in silencing that one person than he, if he had the power, would be justified in silencing mankind. Were an opinion a personal possession of no value except to the owner, if to be obstructed in the enjoyment of it were simply a private injury, it would make some difference whether the injury was inflicted only on a few persons or on many. But the peculiar evil of silencing the expression of an opinion is that it is robbing the human race, posterity as well as the existing generation—those who dissent from the opinion, still more than those who hold it. If the opinion is right, they are deprived of the opportunity of exchanging error for truth; if wrong, they lose, what is almost as great a benefit, the clearer perception and livelier impression of truth produced by its collision with error. . . .

11   We have now recognized the necessity to the mental well-being of mankind (on which all their other well-being depends) of freedom of opinion, and freedom of the expression of opinion, on four distinct grounds, which we will now briefly recapitulate:

¹² First, if any opinion is compelled to silence, that opinion may, for aught we can certainly know, be true. To deny this is to assume our own infallibility.

¹³ Secondly, though the silenced opinion be an error, it may, and very commonly does, contain a portion of truth; and since the general or prevailing opinion on any subject is rarely or never the whole truth, it is only by the collision of adverse opinions that the remainder of the truth has any chance of being supplied.

¹⁴ Thirdly, even if the received opinion be not only true, but the whole truth: unless it is suffered to be, and actually is, vigorously and earnestly contested, it will, by most of those who receive it, be held in the manner of a prejudice, with little comprehension or feeling of its rational grounds. And not only this, but, fourthly, the meaning of the doctrine itself will be in danger of being lost or enfeebled, and deprived of its vital effect on the character and conduct: the dogma becoming a mere formal profession, inefficacious for good, but cumbering the ground and preventing the growth of any real and heartfelt conviction from reason or personal experience.

Questions for Reading and Analysis

1. Explain the concept of "the tyranny of the majority." Under what kind of government is this potentially an issue?

2. In what two ways can the tyranny of the majority operate in society? Which may be the more formidable? Why?

3. In paragraph 3, Mill writes: "There is a limit to the legitimate interference of collective opinion with individual independence; and to find that limit . . . is as indispensable . . . as protection against political despotism." This statement establishes not one but two principles; what are they? What is asserted and what is implied in this statement?

4. Why, in Mill's view, are limits on individual behavior necessary in a society?

5. In what two ways does a society impose "rules of conduct" on citizens? How difficult do most people think it is? How do most people arrive at their views on these rules?

6. According to Mill, what is the one principle that should be the basis for deciding what constraints on individuals are appropriate? What is not a sufficient reason to restrict an individual?

7. What group is excluded from the principle referred to in question 6? Why?

8. What does Mill include in the "region of human liberty"? What should individuals be at liberty to do? Are freedom of thought and freedom of expression to be treated the same?

9. State the claim of Mill's argument.

10. What does freedom of the press provide a society?

11. Why should neither the government nor individuals repress opinion? Summarize Mill's four reasons for protecting freedom of expression of opinion.

Questions for Discussion and Reflection

1. Mill's examination of the bounds of individual liberty is necessarily abstract, since his goal is to establish a universal principle. Has he written clearly and persuasively, given his purpose? Why or why not?

2. Mill says that "a person may cause evil to others not only by his actions but by his inaction" and should be held accountable for both kinds of injuries. Apply this concept to a specific case: Should we have a "Good Samaritan" law that would require motorists to stop to aid a motorist in trouble? (Germany has such a law.) What would Mill say? Do you agree or disagree with Mill? Why?

3. Cigarette advertising is currently banned from television. Should all cigarette advertising be banned? What would Mill say? What do you say? Why?

4. What part of his argument would Mill use to justify prohibiting child pornography? Do you agree with him?

5. Should individuals be free to behave in ways that are "harmful" (in someone's view) to themselves, so long as they are not harming others? Or should a society seek to legislate on issues of personal morality or personal health? Defend your position.

6. Which one of Mill's reasons for not repressing freedom of expression is, in your view, the most persuasive? Why?

I Have a Dream

Martin Luther King, Jr.

Martin Luther King, Jr. (1929–1968), Baptist minister, civil rights leader dedicated to nonviolence, president of the Southern Christian Leadership Conference, Nobel Peace Prize winner in 1964, was assassinated in 1968. He was an important figure in the August 1963 poor people's march on Washington, where he delivered his speech from the steps of the Lincoln Memorial.

King's plea for equality, echoing the language and cadences of both the Bible and "The Gettysburg Address," has become a model of effective oratory.

1   Five score years ago, a great American, in whose symbolic shadow we stand, signed the Emancipation Proclamation. This momentous decree came as a great beacon light of hope to millions of Negro slaves who had been seared in the flames of withering injustice. It came as a joyous daybreak to end the long night of captivity.

2   But one hundred years later, we must face the tragic fact that the Negro is still not free. One hundred years later, the life of the Negro is still sadly crippled by the manacles of segregation and the chains of discrimination. One hundred years later, the Negro lives on a lonely island of poverty in the midst of a vast ocean of material prosperity. One hundred years later, the Negro is still languished in the corners of American society and finds himself an exile in his own land. So we have come here today to dramatize an appalling condition.

3   In a sense we have come to our nation's Capital to cash a check. When the architects of our republic wrote the magnificent words of the Constitution and the

Declaration of Independence, they were signing a promissory note to which every American was to fall heir. This note was a promise that all men would be guaranteed the unalienable rights of life, liberty, and the pursuit of happiness.

4   It is obvious today that America has defaulted on this promissory note insofar as her citizens of color are concerned. Instead of honoring this sacred obligation, America has given the Negro people a bad check which has come back marked "insufficient funds." But we refuse to believe that the bank of justice is bankrupt. We refuse to believe that there are insufficient funds in the great vaults of opportunity of this nation. So we have come to cash this check—a check that will give us upon demand the riches of freedom and the security of justice. We have also come to this hallowed spot to remind America of the fierce urgency of *now*. This is no time to engage in the luxury of cooling off or to take the tranquilizing drug of gradualism. *Now* is the time to make real the promises of Democracy. *Now* is the time to rise from the dark and desolate valley of segregation to the sunlit path of racial justice. *Now* is the time to open the doors of opportunity to all of God's children. *Now* is the time to lift our nation from the quicksands of racial injustice to the solid rock of brotherhood.

5   It would be fatal for the nation to overlook the urgency of the moment and to underestimate the determination of the Negro. This sweltering summer of the Negro's legitimate discontent will not pass until there is an invigorating autumn of freedom and equality. 1963 is not an end, but a beginning. Those who hope that the Negro needed to blow off steam and will now be content will have a rude awakening if the nation returns to business as usual. There will be neither rest nor tranquility in America until the Negro is granted his citizenship rights. The whirlwinds of revolt will continue to shake the foundations of our nation until the bright day of justice emerges.

6   But there is something that I must say to my people who stand on the warm threshold which leads into the palace of justice. In the process of gaining our right place we must not be guilty of wrongful deeds. Let us not seek to satisfy our thirst for freedom by drinking from the cup of bitterness and hatred. We must forever conduct our struggle on the high plane of dignity and discipline. We must not allow our creative protest to degenerate into physical violence. Again and again we must rise to the majestic heights of meeting physical force with soul force. The marvelous new militancy which has engulfed the Negro community must not lead us to a distrust of all white people, for many of our white brothers, as evidenced by their presence here today, have come to realize that their destiny is tied up with our destiny and their freedom is inextricably bound to our freedom. We cannot walk alone.

7   And as we walk, we must make the pledge that we shall march ahead. We cannot turn back. There are those who are asking the devotees of civil rights, "When will you be satisfied?" We can never be satisfied as long as the Negro is the victim of the unspeakable horrors of police brutality. We can never be satisfied as long as our bodies, heavy with the fatigue of travel, cannot gain lodging in the motels of the highways and the hotels of the cities. We cannot be satisfied as long as the Negro's basic mobility is from a smaller ghetto to a larger one. We can never be satisfied as long as a Negro in Mississippi cannot vote and a Negro in New York believes he has nothing for which to vote. No, no, we are not satisfied, and we will not be satisfied until justice rolls down like waters and righteousness like a mighty stream.

8   I am not unmindful that some of you have come here out of great trials and tribulations. Some of you have come fresh from narrow jail cells. Some of you have come

from areas where your quest for freedom left you battered by the storms of persecution and staggered by the winds of police brutality. You have been the veterans of creative suffering. Continue to work with the faith that unearned suffering is redemptive.

9   Go back to Mississippi, go back to Alabama, go back to South Carolina, go back to Georgia, go back to Louisiana, go back to the slums and ghettos of our northern cities, knowing that somehow this situation can and will be changed. Let us not wallow in the valley of despair.

10   I say to you today, my friends, that in spite of the difficulties and frustrations of the moment I still have a dream. It is a dream deeply rooted in the American dream.

11   I have a dream that one day this nation will rise up and live out the true meaning of its creed: "We hold these truths to be self-evident; that all men are created equal."

12   I have a dream that one day on the red hills of Georgia the sons of former slaves and the sons of former slaveowners will be able to sit down together at the table of brotherhood.

13   I have a dream that one day even the state of Mississippi, a desert state sweltering with the heat of injustice and oppression, will be transformed into an oasis of freedom and justice.

14   I have a dream that my four little children will one day live in a nation where they will not be judged by the color of their skin but by the content of their character.

15   I have a dream today.

16   I have a dream that one day the state of Alabama, whose governor's lips are presently dripping with the words of interposition and nullification, will be transformed into a situation where little black boys and black girls will be able to join hands with little white boys and white girls and walk together as sisters and brothers.

17   I have a dream today.

18   I have a dream that one day every valley shall be exalted, every hill and mountain shall be made low, the rough places will be made plain, and the crooked places will be made straight, and the glory of the Lord shall be revealed, and all flesh shall see it together.

19   This is our hope. This is the faith with which I return to the South. With this faith we will be able to hew out of the mountain of despair a stone of hope. With this faith we will be able to transform the jangling discords of our nation into a beautiful symphony of brotherhood. With this faith we will be able to work together, to pray together, to struggle together, to go to jail together, to stand up for freedom together, knowing that we will be free one day.

20   This will be the day when all of God's children will be able to sing with new meaning

My country, 'tis of thee,
Sweet land of liberty,
    Of thee I sing;
Land where my fathers died,
Land of the pilgrims' pride,
From every mountain-side
    Let freedom ring.

21   And if America is to be a great nation this must become true. So let freedom ring from the prodigious hilltops of New Hampshire. Let freedom ring from the mighty

mountains of New York. Let freedom ring from the heightening Alleghenies of Pennsylvania!

22   Let freedom ring from the snowcapped Rockies of Colorado!

23   Let freedom ring from the curvacious peaks of California!

24   But not only that; let freedom ring from Stone Mountain of Georgia!

25   Let freedom ring from Lookout Mountain of Tennessee!

26   Let freedom ring from every hill and molehill of Mississippi. From every mountainside, let freedom ring.

27   When we let freedom ring, when we let it ring from every village and every hamlet, from every state and every city, we will be able to speed up that day when all of God's children, black men and white men, Jews and Gentiles, Protestants and Catholics, will be able to join hands and sing in the words of the old Negro spiritual, "Free at last! thank God almighty, we are free at last!"

Questions for Reading and Analysis

1. King is directly addressing those participants in the poor people's march who have assembled at the Lincoln Memorial. What other audience did he have as well?

2. How does the language of the speech reflect King's vocation as a Christian minister? How does the language reflect his sense of his place in history?

3. What is the purpose, or what are the purposes, of the speech?

4. List all the elements of style discussed in Chapter 2 that King uses. What elements of style dominate?

5. What stylistic techniques do Lincoln and King share? What major device does Lincoln use that King does not use?

6. Explain each metaphor in paragraph 2.

Questions for Discussion and Response

1. List King's most vivid and powerful metaphors. Why do you find them effective?

2. Find one sentence that you find especially effective and explain why you think it is so effective. Is the effectiveness in part the way the sentence is structured?

3. If King were alive today, do you think he would want to see another march on Washington? If so, what would be the theme, or purpose, of the march? If not, why not?

4. Would King have supported the Million Man March? The rally of the Promise Keepers? Why or why not?

Understanding Literature

The same process of reading nonfiction critically can be used to understand literature—fiction, poetry, and drama. You still need to read what is on the page, looking up unfamiliar words and tracking down references you don't understand. You still need to examine the context, to think about who is writing to whom, under what circumstances, and in what literary format. And, to respond fully to the words, you need to analyze the writer's techniques for developing ideas and expressing attitudes.

Although it seems logical that the reading process should be much the same regardless of the work, not all readers of literature are willing to accept that logic. Some readers want a work of literature to mean whatever they think it means, but such an extreme personal response to reading overlooks what is basic to writing: the desire for communication between writer and reader. If you decide that a Robert Frost poem, for example, should mean whatever you are feeling when you read it, you might as well skip the reading of Frost and just commune with your feelings, or write your own poem to capture those feelings. Presumably, though, you read Frost to gain some new insight or new perspective from him, to see snow blanketing the landscape through Frost's eyes, to get beyond just your vision and be challenged to see something of human experience and emotion from a new vantage point.

Other readers of literature, wanting to understand each author they read, still hesitate over the concept of *literary analysis,* or at least over the word *analysis.* These readers complain that analysis will "tear the work apart" and "ruin it." If you are inclined to share this attitude, stop for a minute and think about the last sports event you watched. Do you remember thinking, "Davenport's going to serve wide and come in; she has to against Hingis." Or perhaps a friend explained: "North Carolina is so good at stalling to use up the clock; Duke will have to foul to get the ball and have a chance to tie the game." Both games are being analyzed! And that analysis makes each event more interesting, more fully experienced by those who understand at least some of the elements of tennis or basketball. Your own experience will tell you that most people who do not understand a sport do not enjoy watching the game. If compelled to watch, they usually do more eating than watching and often feel isolated from the group of cheering fans who keep up a running analysis of each play.

The analogy is clear. You, too, can be a fan of literature. You can enjoy reading and discussing your reading once you learn to use your active reading and analytic skills to open up a poem or story, and once you sharpen your knowledge of literary terms and concepts so that you can "speak the language" of literary criticism with the same confidence with which you discuss the merits of a safety blitz or a drop volley.

Getting the Facts: Active Reading, Summary, and Paraphrase

Armed with a commitment to read carefully and give the writer a chance to speak to you, begin with the following poem by Paul Dunbar. As you read, make marginal notes, circling a phrase you fancy, putting a question mark next to a difficult line, underscoring words you need to look up. Note, too, your emotional reactions as you read, but be patient. Difficult works may generate, on first reading, little emotion except frustration.

Promise

Paul Lawrence Dunbar

Born of former slave parents, Dunbar (1872–1906) was educated in Dayton, Ohio. After a first booklet of poems, *Oak and Ivy*, was printed in 1893, several friends helped Dunbar get a second collection, *Majors and Minors*, published in 1895. A copy was given to author and editor William Dean Howells, who reviewed the book favorably, increasing sales and Dunbar's reputation. This led to a national publisher issuing *Lyrics of Lowly Life* in 1896, the collection that secured Dunbar's fame.

I grew a rose within a garden fair,
And, tending it with more than loving care,
I thought how, with the glory of its bloom,
I should the darkness of my life illume;
And, watching, ever smiled to see the lusty bud   5
Drink freely in the summer sun to tinct its blood.

My rose began to open, and its hue
Was sweet to me as to it sun and dew;
I watched it taking on its ruddy flame
Until the day of perfect blooming came,   10
Then hasted I with smiles to find it blushing red—
Too late! Some thoughtless child had plucked my rose and fled!

"Promise" should not have been especially difficult to read, although you may have paused a moment over "illume" before connecting it to "illuminate," and you may have to check the dictionary for a definition of "tinct." Except for these possible snags, you should know what the poem says. Test yourself by listing all the facts of the poem. Pay attention to the poem's basic situation. Who is speaking? What is happening, or what thoughts is the speaker sharing? In this poem, the "I" is not further identified, so you will have to refer to him or her as the *speaker*. You should not call the speaker "Dunbar," however, because you do not know if Dunbar ever grew a rose. Just as fiction writers create characters in a story, so poets create "characters," speakers who may or may not be closely identified with themselves in experience or values.

In "Promise" the speaker is describing an event that has taken place. The speaker grew a rose, tended to it with care, and watched it begin to bloom; then, when the rose was in full bloom, some child picked the rose and took it away. The situation is fairly simple, isn't it? Too simple, unfortunately, for readers, determined to find hidden meanings, who decide that the speaker never grew a rose at all. But when anyone writes, "I grew a rose within a garden fair," it is wise to assume that the writer means just that. People do grow roses, most often in gardens, and then the gardens are made "fair" or beautiful by the flowers growing there. Read first for the facts: try not to jump too quickly to broad generalizations until you have had the chance to think about the details. Only then will you be prepared to experience the richness of meaning generated from the author's imaginative treatment of those facts.

As with nonfiction, one of the best ways to make certain you have understood a literary work is to write a summary or paraphrase. Since a summary condenses, you are most likely to write a summary of a story, novel, or play, whereas a paraphrase is usually reserved for poems or complex short passages. When you paraphrase a difficult poem, you are likely to end up with more words than in the original because your purpose is to turn cryptic lines into more ordinary sentences with normal word order. For example, Dunbar's "Then hasted I with smiles" can be paraphrased to read: "Then, full of smiles, I hurried."

When summarizing a literary work, remember to use your own words, draw no conclusions, giving only the facts, but focus your summary on the key events in the story. (Of course the selecting you do to write a summary represents preliminary analysis; you are making some choices about what is important in the work. The "steps" of observation, analysis, and interpretation do overlap.) Read the following short story by Langston Hughes and then write your own summary. Finally, compare yours to the summary that follows the story.

Early Autumn

Langston Hughes

Like many American writers, Langston Hughes (1902–1967) moved from the Middle West to New York City, lived and worked in France, and then returned to the United States to a career in writing. He was a journalist, fiction writer, and poet, the author of more than 60 books. Supporters helped him get a first book of poetry, *The Weary Blues*, published in 1926. The success of his novel *Not Without Laughter* (1930) secured his reputation and enabled him to become the first black American to support himself as a professional writer. Known as "the bard of Harlem," Hughes was an important public figure and voice for black writers. "Early Autumn" is reprinted from the collection *Something in Common* (1963).

When Bill was very young, they had been in love. Many nights they had spent walking, talking together. Then something not very important had come between them, and they didn't speak. Impulsively, she had married a man she thought she loved. Bill went away, bitter about women.

Yesterday, walking across Washington Square, she saw him for the first time in years.

"Bill Walker," she said.

He stopped. At first he did not recognize her, to him she looked so old.

"Mary! Where did you come from?"

Unconsciously, she lifted her face as though wanting a kiss, but he held out his hand. She took it.

"I live in New York now," she said.

"Oh"—smiling politely. Then a little frown came quickly between his eyes.

"Always wondered what happened to you, Bill."

"I'm a lawyer. Nice firm, way downtown."

"Married yet?"

"Sure. Two kids."

"Oh," she said.

A great many people went past them through the park. People they didn't know. It was late afternoon. Nearly sunset. Cold.

"And your husband?" he asked her.

"We have three children. I work in the bursar's office at Columbia."

"You're looking very . . ." (he wanted to say *old*) ". . . well," he said.

She understood. Under the trees in Washington Square, she found herself desperately reaching back into the past. She had been older than he then in Ohio. Now she was not young at all. Bill was still young.

"We live on Central Park West," she said. "Come and see us sometime."

"Sure," he replied. "You and your husband must have dinner with my family some night. Any night. Lucille and I'd love to have you."

The leaves fell slowly from the trees in the Square. Fell without wind. Autumn dusk. She felt a little sick.

"We'd love it," she answered.

"You ought to see my kids." He grinned.

Suddenly the lights came on up the whole length of Fifth Avenue, chains of misty brilliance in the blue air.

"There's my bus," she said.

He held out his hand. "Good-by."

"When . . ." she wanted to say, but the bus was ready to pull off. The lights on the avenue blurred, twinkled, blurred. And she was afraid to open her mouth as she entered the bus. Afraid it would be impossible to utter a word.

Suddenly she shrieked very loudly, "Good-by!" But the bus door had closed.

The bus started. People came between them outside, people crossing the street, people they didn't know. Space and people. She lost sight of Bill. Then she remembered she had forgotten to give him her address—or to ask him for his—or tell him that her youngest boy was named Bill, too.

SUMMARY OF "EARLY AUTUMN"

Langston Hughes's short story "Early Autumn" is about two people, Mary and Bill, who were in love once but broke up and did not speak to each other. Mary married someone else "impulsively" and does not see Bill again until one late afternoon, years later, in New York City's Washington Square. When Mary speaks, Bill does not at first recognize her. They discuss their jobs, their marriages, their children. When Mary invites Bill to visit, he says "Sure" and that she should have dinner with his family sometime. When Mary's bus arrives and she gets on, she has trouble speaking. She realizes that they have not set a date or exchanged addresses. She has also forgotten to tell him that her youngest son is named Bill.

Note that the summary is written in the present tense to recount the events that take place during the time of the story. Brevity is achieved by condensing several lines of dialogue into a statement such as "they discuss their jobs." Notice, too, that the summary is not the same as the original; the emotions of the characters, conveyed through what is said—and not said—are missing.

Now for a paraphrase. Read carefully the following sonnet by Shakespeare, looking up unfamiliar words and making notes. Remember to read to the end of a unit of thought, not just to the end of a line. Some sentences continue through several lines; if you pause before you reach punctuation, you will be confused. Write your own paraphrase, not looking ahead in the text, and then compare yours with the one that follows the poem.

Sonnet 116

William Shakespeare

Surely the best-known name in literature, William Shakespeare (1564–1616) is famous as both a dramatist and a poet. Rural Warwickshire and the market town of Stratford-on-Avon, where he grew up, showed him many of the character types who were to enliven his plays, as did the bustling life of a young actor in London. Apparently his sonnets were intended to be circulated only among his friends, but they were published nonetheless in 1609. His thirty-seven plays were first published together in 1623. Shakespeare's 154 sonnets vary, some focusing on separation and world-weariness, others on the endurance of love.

Let me not to the marriage of true minds
Admit impediments. Love is not love
Which alters when it alteration finds,
Or bends with the remover to remove.
O, no! it is an ever-fixed mark   5
That looks on tempests and is never shaken;
It is the star to every wand'ring bark,
Whose worth's unknown, although his height be taken.
Love's not Time's fool, though rosy lips and cheeks
Within his bending sickle's compass come;   10
Love alters not with his brief hours and weeks,
But bears it out even to the edge of doom.
    If this be error and upon me proved,
    I never writ, nor no man ever loved.

PARAPHRASE OF "SONNET 116"

I cannot accept barriers to the union of steadfast spirits. We cannot call love love if it changes because it discovers change or if it disappears during absence. On the contrary, love is a steady guide that, in spite of difficulties, remains unwavering. Love can define the inherent value in all who lack self-knowledge, though superficially they know who they are. Love does not lessen with time, though signs of physical beauty may fade. Love endures, changeless, eternally. If anyone can show me to be wrong in this position, I am no writer and no man can be said to have loved.

We have examined the facts of a literary work, what we can call the internal situation. But, as we noted in Chapter 2, there is also the external situation or context of any piece of writing. For many literary works, the context is not as essential to understanding as it is with nonfiction. You can read "Early Autumn," for instance, without knowing much about Langston Hughes, or the circumstances in which he wrote the story, although such information would enrich your reading experience. There is a body of information, however, that is very important, what we can call the external literary situation. Literary externals are those basic elements of a work that readers should take note of before they begin to read.

> ✔️   Remember: Active reading includes looking over a work first and predicting what will come next. Do not just start reading words without first understanding something about the work.

Let's review some of these essentials. First, don't make the mistake of calling every work a "story." When you read—and then later discuss—literature, make clear distinctions among stories, novels, plays, and poems. Poems can be further divided into narrative, dramatic, and lyric poems. A *narrative poem*, such as Homer's *The Iliad*, tells a story in verse. A *dramatic poem* records the speech of at least one character. A poem in which only one figure speaks—but clearly addresses words to someone who is present in a particular situation—is called a *dramatic monologue*. *Lyric poems*, Dunbar's "Promise," for example, may place the speaker in a situation or may express a thought or feeling with few if any situational details, but lyric poems have in common the convention that we as readers are listening in on someone's thoughts, not listening to words directed to a second, created figure. These distinctions make us aware of how the words of the poem are coming to us. Are we hearing a storyteller or someone speaking? Or, are we overhearing someone's thoughts?

Lyric poems can be further divided into many subcategories or types. Most instructors will expect you to be able to recognize some of these types. You should be able to distinguish between a poem in *free verse* (no prevailing metrical pattern) and one in *blank verse* (continuous unrhymed lines of iambic pentameter.) (Note: A metrical line will contain a particular number—pentameter is five—of one kind of metrical "foot." The iambic foot consists of one unstressed syllable followed by one stressed syllable.) You should also be able to tell if a poem is written in some type of *stanza* form (repeated units with the same number of lines, same metrical pattern, and same rhyme scheme), or if it is a *sonnet* (always 14 lines of iambic pentameter with one of two complex rhyme schemes labeled either English or Italian). You want to make it a habit to observe these external elements of any literary work before you read. Noting the type of work you are reading will give you a richer context for understanding that work. To sharpen your observation, complete the following exercise.

Exercise: Observing Literary Types and Using Literary Terms

1. After surveying this appendix, make a list of all the works of literature by primary type: short story, poem, play.

2. For each work on your list, add two additional pieces of information: whether the author is American or British, and in what century the work was written. Why should you be aware of the writer's dates and nationality as you read?

3. Further divide the poems into narrative, dramatic, or lyric, as appropriate.

4. List as many of the details of type or form as you can for each poem. For example, if the poem is written in stanzas, describe the stanza form used: the number of lines, the meter, the rhyme scheme. If the poem is a sonnet, determine the rhyme scheme. (Note: Rhyme scheme is indicated by using letters, assigning "a" to the first sound and using a new letter for each new sound. Thus, if two consecutive lines rhyme, the scheme is *aa, bb, cc, dd,* and so on.)

Seeing Connections: Analysis

Although we read first for the facts and an initial emotional response, we do not stop there, because as humans we seek meaning; we want to understand. Surely there is more to "Early Autumn" than the summary suggests; emotionally we know this to be true. As with nonfiction, one of the best places to start analysis is with a work's organization or structure. Lyric poems will be shaped by many of the same structures found in essays: chronological, spatial, general to particular, particular to general, a list of particulars with an unstated general point, and so forth. In "Promise," Dunbar gives one illustration, recounted chronologically, to make a point that is left unstated. "Sonnet 116" contains a list of characteristics of love underscored in the conclusion by the speaker's conviction that he is right.

ANALYSIS OF NARRATIVE STRUCTURE

In stories (and plays and narrative poems) we are given a series of events, in time sequence, involving one or more characters. In some stories episodes are only loosely connected but are unified around a central character (Mark Twain's *Adventures of Huckleberry Finn,* for example). Most stories present events that are at least to some extent related causally; that is, action A by the main character leads to event B, which requires action C by the main character. This kind of plot structure can be diagrammed, as in Figure 1.

Figure 1 introduces some terms and concepts useful in analyzing and discussing narratives. The story's *exposition* refers to the background details needed to get the story started, including the time and place of the story and relationships of the characters. In "Early Autumn" Hughes begins by telling us that the action will take place in lower Manhattan,

FIGURE 1   Plot Structure

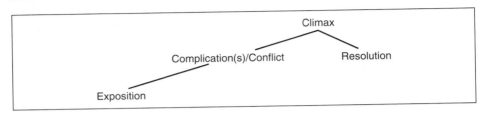

late in the afternoon, between a man and a woman who had once loved each other. The *complication* refers to an event; something happens to produce tension or conflict. In "Early Autumn" the meeting of Mary and Bill, after many years, could be an occasion for joy but seems to cause a complication instead. Mary expects to be kissed but Bill merely offers his hand; Bill smiles "politely" and then frowns. The meeting becomes a complication for both characters because it generates a *conflict* within each character. Bill's conflict seems the more manageable; he turns on his polite behavior to get through the unexpected encounter. Mary is more upset; seeing Bill makes her feel old, and she is hardly able to speak when she boards the bus. A key question arises: Why is Mary so upset?

Although some stories present one major complication leading to a climactic moment of decision or insight for the main character, many actually repeat the pattern, presenting several complications—each with an attempted resolution that generates yet another complication—until we reach the high point of tension, the *climax*. The climax then generates the story's *resolution* and ending. These terms are useful even though some stories end abruptly without having much resolution. An abbreviated resolution is part of the modern writer's view of reality, that life goes on, with problems remaining unresolved. The climax in "Early Autumn" comes when Mary boards her bus and then realizes that she will once again be separated from Bill. This story's climax is muted and merges quickly into the resolution of the last line. The ending offers little genuine resolution; our recognizing this fact helps us better understand the story.

ANALYSIS OF CHARACTER

An analysis of plot structure has shown that Mary is the more troubled character. You should recognize that Mary is not in conflict *with* Bill but rather is in conflict *over* him, or over her feelings for him, still strong in spite of years of a life without him. Note the close connection between complication (event) and conflict (what the characters are feeling). Fiction requires both plot and character, events and players in those events. In serious literature the greater emphasis is usually on character, on what we learn about human life through the interplay of character and incident.

As we shift attention from the plot of "Early Autumn" to the characters, it helps to consider how writers present character. Writers have several techniques for conveying character:

- Descriptive details (Bill's polite smile followed by a frown).
- Dramatic scenes. (Instead of telling us, they show us. Most of "Early Autumn" consists of dialogue between Mary and Bill.)

- Contrast among characters. (We have already observed that Mary and Bill react differently to their encounter.)
- Other elements in the work.

These are indirect, sometimes subtle techniques. Names can be significant, or characters can become associated with objects, or details of setting can become symbolic. Understanding character is always a challenge because we must infer from a few words, gestures, and actions. Looking at all of a writer's options for presenting character will keep us from overlooking important details.

ANALYSIS OF ELEMENTS OF STYLE AND TONE

Important elements in "Early Autumn" include the time of day and the title. How are they connected? What do they suggest about the characters? All the elements, discussed in Chapter 2, that shape a writer's style and create tone can be found in literary works as well and need to be considered as a part of your analysis. Hughes's title is actually a metaphor and, reinforced by the late-in-the-day meeting, suggests that this meeting comes too late for Mary to regain what she has lost—her youth and her youthful love. Shakespeare's "Sonnet 116" develops the speaker's ideas about love through a series of metaphors. The rose in Dunbar's "Promise," is not a metaphor, though, because it is not part of a comparison. Yet, as we read "Promise" we sense that the poem is about something more serious than the nurturing and stealing of one flower, no matter how beautiful. Again, this work's title gives us a clue that the rose stands for something more than itself; it is a symbol. Traditionally the red rose is a symbol of love. To tie the poem together, we will have to see how the title, the usual symbolic value of the rose, and the specifics of the poem connect.

Drawing Conclusions: Interpretation

We have studied the facts of several works and analyzed their structures and other key elements. To reach some conclusions from this information and shape it into an organized form is to offer an interpretation of the work. At this point, readers can be expected to disagree somewhat, but if we have all read carefully and applied our knowledge of literature, differences should, most of the time, be ones of focus or emphasis. Presumably no one is prepared to argue that "Promise" is about pink elephants or "Early Autumn" about the Queen of England, because neither work contains any facts to support those conclusions.

What conclusions can we reach about "Promise"? A beautiful flower has been nurtured into bloom by a speaker who expects it to brighten his or her life. The title lets us know that the rose represents great promise. Has a rival stolen the speaker's loved one, represented symbolically by the rose? A thoughtless child would not be an appropriate rival for an adult speaker, so in the context of this poem, the rose represents, more generally, something that the speaker cherishes in anticipation of the pleasure it will bring.

In "Early Autumn" the pain that Mary feels when she meets Bill in Washington Square comes from her awareness that she still loves Bill and that he is lost to her. Bill has gone on to a happy life in which she has no part. The lights blur because Mary's eyes are filled with tears as the conversation makes her aware that Bill has given her little thought over the years, whereas Mary, to keep some part of Bill in her life, has named her youngest son Bill. The details of the story, an analysis of plot and character conflict, and the story's metaphors support these conclusions.

Writing about Literature

When you are assigned a literary essay, you will usually be asked to write either an explication or an analysis. An *explication* presents a reading of a complex poem. It will combine paraphrase and explanation to clarify the poem's meaning. A *literary analysis* can take many forms. You may be asked to analyze one element in a work: character conflict, the use of setting, the tone of a poem. Or you could be asked to contrast two works. Usually an analytic assignment requires you to connect analysis to interpretation, for we analyze the parts to better understand the whole. If you are asked to examine the metaphors in a Shakespeare sonnet, for example, you will want to show how understanding the metaphors contributes to an understanding of the entire poem. In short, literary analysis is much the same as a style analysis of an essay, and thus the guidelines for writing about style discussed in Chapter 2 apply here as well.* Successful analyses are based on accurate reading, reflection on the work's emotional impact, and the use of details from the work to support conclusions.

Literary analyses can also incorporate material beyond the particular work. We can analyze a work in the light of biographical information or from a particular political ideology. Or, we can study the social-cultural context of the work, or relate it to a literary tradition. These are only a few of the many approaches to the study of literature, and they depend on the application of knowledge outside the work itself. For undergraduates, topics based on these approaches usually require research. The second student research essay in Section III (see pp. 275–79) is a literary analysis. Alan examines Faulkner's *Intruder in the Dust* as an initiation novel. He connects his analysis to works by Hawthorne and Arthur Miller. What is taken from his research is documented and helps develop and support his own conclusions about the story.

To practice close reading, analysis, and interpretation of literature, read the following works. Use the questions after each work to aid your analysis of and responses to the literature.

---

*Remember: The guidelines for referring to authors, titles, and direct quotations—presented in Chapter 1—also apply.

Sonnet 73

William Shakespeare

See p. 625 for information about Shakespeare.

That time of year thou mayst in me behold
When yellow leaves, or none, or few, do hang
Upon those boughs which shake against the cold,

Bare ruined choirs where late the sweet birds sang.
In me thou see'st the twilight of such day   5
As after sunset fadeth in the west,
Which by and by black night doth take away,
Death's second self, that seals up all in rest.
In me thou see'st the glowing of such fire
That on the ashes of his youth doth lie,   10
As the deathbed whereon it must expire,
Consumed with that which it was nourished by.
   This thou perceivest, which makes thy love more strong,
   To love that well which thou must leave ere long.

Questions for Analysis and Discussion

1. Paraphrase the poem.

2. Using letters to mark the pattern, determine the poem's rhyme scheme.

3. What structure, or grouping by lines, is suggested by the rhyme scheme? How does Shakespeare use this structure?

4. To what does the speaker compare himself in each quatrain (set of four lines)? What do the three comparisons have in common?

5. What is the emotional impact of each metaphor? Is the feeling more positive in some than in others? What does the poet gain by the order of the metaphors?

6. What attitude toward growing old does the speaker convey through the selection and ordering of the metaphors?

To His Coy Mistress

Andrew Marvell

One of the last poets of the English Renaissance, Andrew Marvell (1621–1678) graduated from Cambridge University, spent much of his young life as a tutor, and was elected to Parliament in 1659. He continued in public service until his death. Most of his best-loved lyric poems come from his years as a tutor. "To His Coy Mistress" was published in 1681.

Had we but world enough, and time,
This coyness, lady, were no crime.
We would sit down, and think which way
To walk, and pass our long love's day.
Thou by the Indian Ganges' side   5
Shouldst rubies find; I by the tide
Of Humber would complain. I would
Love you ten years before the Flood,
And you should, if you please, refuse
Till the conversion of the Jews.   10

My vegetable° love should grow   *slowly vegetative*
Vaster than empires, and more slow;
An hundred years should go to praise
Thine eyes, and on thy forehead gaze;
Two hundred to adore each breast,   15
But thirty thousand to the rest;
An age at least to every part,
And the last age should show your heart.
For, lady, you deserve this state,
Nor would I love at lower rate.   20
   But at my back I always hear
Time's wingèd chariot hurrying near;
And yonder all before us lie
Deserts of vast eternity.
Thy beauty shall no more be found,   25
Nor in thy marble vault shall sound
My echoing song; then worms shall try
That long preserved virginity,
And your quaint honor turn to dust,
And into ashes all my lust.   30
The grave's a fine and private place,
But none, I think, do there embrace.
   Now therefore, while the youthful hue
Sits on thy skin like morning dew,
And while thy willing soul transpires   35
At every pore with instant fires,
Now let us sport us while we may,
And now, like amorous birds of prey,
Rather at once our time devour
Than languish in his slow-chapped power.   40
Let us roll all our strength and all
Our sweetness up into one ball,
And tear our pleasures with rough strife
Thorough° the iron gates of life.   *through*   45
Thus, though we cannot make our sun
Stand still, yet we will make him run.

Questions for Analysis and Discussion

1. Describe the poem's external form.
2. How are the words coming to us? That is, is this a narrative, dramatic, or lyric poem?
3. Summarize the speaker's argument, using the structure *if, but, therefore*.

4. What figure of speech do we find throughout the first verse paragraph? What is its effect on the speaker's tone?

5. Find examples of irony and understatement in the second verse paragraph.

6. How does the tone shift in the second section?

7. Explain the personification in line 22.

8. Explain the metaphors in lines 30 and 45.

9. What is the paradox of the last two lines? How can it be explained?

10. What is the idea of this poem? What does the writer want us to reflect on?

The Man He Killed

Thomas Hardy

Born in a small village in Dorsetshire, Thomas Hardy (1840–1928) moved between London and Dorset until he finally settled permanently in Dorset in 1885. He is probably best known for such novels as *The Return of the Native* (1878) and *Tess of the d'Urbervilles* (1891), but he also wrote over nine hundred poems. His ashes are buried in Westminster Abbey with many of England's other great poets.

"Had he and I but met
  By some old ancient inn,
We should have sat us down to wet
  Right many a nipperkin!

"But ranged as infantry,   5
  And staring face to face,
I shot at him as he at me
  And killed him in his place.

"I shot him dead because—
  Because he was my foe,   10
Just so: my foe of course he was;
  That's clear enough; although

"He thought he'd 'list, perhaps,
  Off-hand like—just as I—
Was out of work—had sold his traps—   15
  No other reason why.

"Yes; quaint and curious war is!
  You shoot a fellow down
You'd treat if met where any bar is,
  Or help to half-a-crown."   20

Questions for Analysis and Discussion

1. How are the words of this poem coming to us? That is, is this a narrative, dramatic, or lyric poem? Who is speaking?
2. What has the speaker done?
3. How does the speaker feel about his experience?
4. What does Hardy want us to understand about war?
5. What primary strategy does Hardy use to convey his point?

Taxi

Amy Lowell

Educated at private schools and widely traveled, American Amy Lowell (1874–1925) was both a poet and a critic. Lowell frequently read her poetry and lectured on poetic techniques, defending her verse and that of other modern poets.

When I go away from you
The world beats dead
Like a slackened drum.
I call out for you against the jutted stars
And shout into the ridges of the wind.   5
Streets coming fast,
One after the other,
Wedge you away from me,
And the lamps of the city prick my eyes
So that I can no longer see your face.
Why should I leave you,
To wound myself upon the sharp edges of the night?   10

Questions for Analysis and Discussion

1. Classify the poem according to its external structure.
2. Is this a narrative, dramatic, or lyric poem?
3. Explain the simile in the opening three lines and the metaphor in the last line of the poem.
4. What is the poem's subject? What seems to be the situation in which we find the speaker?
5. How would you describe the tone of the poem? How do the details and the emotional impact of the metaphors help to create tone?
6. What is the poem's meaning or theme? In other words, what does the poet want us to understand from reading her poem?

The Story of an Hour

Kate Chopin

Now a highly acclaimed short-story writer, Kate Chopin (1851–1904) enjoyed a decade of publication and popularity from 1890 to 1900 and then critical condemnation followed by 60 years of neglect. Chopin began her writing career after her husband's death, having returned to her home in St. Louis with her six children. She saw two collections of her stories published—*Bayou Folk* in 1894 and *A Night in Acadie* in 1897—before losing her popularity with the publication of her short novel *The Awakening* in 1899, the story of a woman struggling to free herself from years of repression and subservience.

Knowing that Mrs. Mallard was afflicted with a heart trouble, great care was taken to break to her as gently as possible the news of her husband's death.

It was her sister Josephine who told her, in broken sentences; veiled hints that revealed in half concealing. Her husband's friend Richards was there, too, near her. It was he who had been in the newspaper office when intelligence of the railroad disaster was received, with Brently Mallard's name leading the list of "killed." He had only taken the time to assure himself of its truth by a second telegram, and had hastened to forestall any less careful, less tender friend in bearing the sad message.

She did not hear the story as many women have heard the same, with a paralyzed inability to accept its significance. She wept at once, with sudden, wild abandonment, in her sister's arms. When the storm of grief had spent itself she went away to her room alone. She would have no one follow her.

There stood, facing the open window, a comfortable, roomy armchair. Into this she sank, pressed down by a physical exhaustion that haunted her body and seemed to reach into her soul.

She could see in the open square before her house the tops of trees that were all aquiver with the new spring life. The delicious breath of rain was in the air. In the street below a peddler was crying his wares. The notes of a distant song which some one was singing reached her faintly, and countless sparrows were twittering in the eaves.

There were patches of blue sky showing here and there through the clouds that had met and piled one above the other in the west facing her window.

She sat with her head thrown back upon the cushion of the chair, quite motionless, except when a sob came up into her throat and shook her, as a child who has cried itself to sleep continues to sob in its dreams.

She was young, with a fair, calm face, whose lines bespoke repression and even a certain strength. But now there was a dull stare in her eyes, whose gaze was fixed away off yonder on one of those patches of blue sky. It was not a glance of reflection, but rather indicated a suspension of intelligent thought.

There was something coming to her and she was waiting for it, fearfully. What was it? She did not know; it was too subtle and elusive to name. But she felt it, creeping out of the sky, reaching toward her through the sounds, the scents, the color that filled the air.

Now her bosom rose and fell tumultuously. She was beginning to recognize this thing that was approaching to possess her, and she was striving to beat it back with her will—as powerless as her two white slender hands would have been.

When she abandoned herself a little whispered word escaped her slightly parted lips. She said it over and over under her breath: "free, free, free!" The vacant stare and the look of terror that had followed it went from her eyes. They stayed keen and bright. Her pulses beat fast, and the coursing blood warmed and relaxed every inch of her body.

She did not stop to ask if it were or were not a monstrous joy that held her. A clear and exalted perception enabled her to dismiss the suggestion as trivial.

She knew that she would weep again when she saw the kind, tender hands folded in death; the face that had never looked save with love upon her, fixed and gray and dead. But she saw beyond that bitter moment a long procession of years to come that would belong to her absolutely. And she opened and spread her arms out to them in welcome.

There would be no one to live for her during those coming years; she would live for herself. There would be no powerful will bending hers in that blind persistence with which men and women believe they have a right to impose a private will upon a fellow-creature. A kind intention or a cruel intention made the act seem no less a crime as she looked upon it in that brief moment of illumination.

And yet she had loved him—sometimes. Often she had not. What did it matter! What could love, the unsolved mystery, count for in face of this possession of self-assertion which she suddenly recognized as the strongest impulse of her being!

"Free! Body and soul free!" she kept whispering.

Josephine was kneeling before the closed door with her lips to the keyhole, imploring for admission. "Louise, open the door! I beg; open the door—you will make yourself ill. What are you doing, Louise? For heaven's sake open the door."

"Go away. I am not making myself ill." No; she was drinking in a very elixir of life through that open window.

Her fancy was running riot along those days ahead of her. Spring days, and summer days, and all sorts of days that would be her own. She breathed a quick prayer that life might be long. It was only yesterday she had thought with a shudder that life might be long.

She arose at length and opened the door to her sister's importunities. There was a feverish triumph in her eyes, and she carried herself unwittingly like a goddess of Victory. She clasped her sister's waist, and together they descended the stairs. Richards stood waiting for them at the bottom.

Someone was opening the front door with a latchkey. It was Brently Mallard who entered, a little travel-stained, composedly carrying his grip-sack and umbrella. He had been far from the scene of accident, and did not even know there had been one. He stood amazed at Josephine's piercing cry; at Richards' quick motion to screen him from the view of his wife.

But Richards was too late.

When the doctors came they said she had died of heart disease—of joy that kills.

Questions for Analysis and Discussion

1. Analyze the story's plot structure, using the terms presented in Figure 1 (p. 628).

2. What is Mrs. Mallard's conflict? Explain the opposing elements of her conflict as precisely as you can.

3. When Mrs. Mallard goes to her room, she gazes out the window. Consider the details of the scene; what do these details have in common? How do the details help us understand what Mrs. Mallard experiences?

4. Why is it inaccurate to say that Mrs. Mallard does not love her husband? Cite evidence from the story.

5. The author James Joyce has described a character's moment of insight or intuition as an "epiphany." What is Mrs. Mallard's epiphany?

6. Are we to agree with the doctor's explanation for Mrs. Mallard's death? What term is appropriate to describe the story's conclusion?

The Ones Who Walk Away from Omelas

Ursula K. Le Guin

A graduate of Radcliffe College and Columbia University, Ursula K. Le Guin (b. 1929) is the author of more than 20 novels and juvenile books, several volumes of poetry, and numerous stories and essays published in science fiction, scholarly, and popular journals. Her fiction stretches the categories of science fiction or fantasy and challenges a reader's moral understanding. First published in 1973, the following story, according to Le Guin, was inspired by a passage in William James's "The Moral Philosopher and the Moral Life" in which he asserts that we could not tolerate a situation in which the happiness of many people was purchased by the "lonely torment" of one "lost soul."

1 With a clamor of bells that set the swallows soaring, the Festival of Summer came to the city Omelas, bright-towered by the sea. The rigging of the boats in harbor sparkled with flags. In the streets between houses with red roofs and painted walls, between the old moss-grown gardens and under avenues of trees, past great parks and public buildings, processions moved. Some were decorous: old people in long stiff robes of mauve and gray, grave master workmen, quiet, merry women carrying their babies and chatting as they walked. In other streets the music beat faster, a shimmering of gong and tambourine, and the people went dancing, the procession was a dance. Children dodged in and out, their high calls rising like the swallows' crossing flights over the music and the singing. All the processions wound towards the north side of the city, where on the great water-meadow called the Green Fields boys and girls, naked in the bright air, with mudstained feet and ankles and long, lithe arms, exercised their restive horses before the race. The horses wore no gear at all but a halter without bit. Their manes were braided with streamers of silver, gold, and green. They flared their nostrils and pranced and boasted to one another; they were vastly excited, the horse being the only animal who has adopted our ceremonies as his own. Far off to the north and west the mountains stood up half circling

Omelas on her bay. The air of morning was so clear that the snow still crowning the Eighteen Peaks burned with white-gold fire across the miles of sunlit air, under the dark blue of the sky. There was just enough wind to make the banners that marked the race-course snap and flutter now and then. In the silence of the broad green meadows one could hear the music winding through the city streets, farther and nearer and ever approaching, a cheerful faint sweetness of the air that from time to time trembled and gathered together and broke out into the great joyous clanging of the bells.

2   Joyous! How is one to tell about joy? How describe the citizens of Omelas?

3   They were not simple folk, you see, though they were happy. But we do not say the words of cheer much any more. All smiles have become archaic. Given a description such as this one tends to make certain assumptions. Given a description such as this one tends to look next for the King, mounted on a splendid stallion and surrounded by his noble knights, or perhaps in a golden litter borne by great-muscled slaves. But there was no king. They did not use swords, or keep slaves. They were not barbarians. I do not know the rules and laws of their society, but I suspect that they were singularly few. As they did without monarchy and slavery, so they also got on without the stock exchange, the advertisement, the secret police, and the bomb. Yet I repeat that these were not simple folk, not dulcet shepherds, noble savages, bland utopians. They were not less complex than us. The trouble is that we have a bad habit, encouraged by pedants and sophisticates, of considering happiness as something rather stupid. Only pain is intellectual, only evil interesting. This is the treason of the artist: a refusal to admit the banality of evil and the terrible boredom of pain. If you can't lick 'em, join 'em. If it hurts, repeat it. But to praise despair is to condemn delight, to embrace violence is to lose hold of everything else. We have almost lost hold, we can no longer describe a happy man, nor make any celebration of joy. How can I tell you about the people of Omelas? They were not naïve and happy children—though their children were, in fact, happy. They were mature, intelligent, passionate adults whose lives were not wretched. O miracle! But I wish I could describe it better. I wish I could convince you. Omelas sounds in my words like a city in a fairy tale, long ago and far away, once upon a time. Perhaps it would be best if you imagined it as your own fancy bids, assuming it will rise to the occasion, for certainly I cannot suit you all. For instance, how about technology? I think that there would be no cars or helicopters in and above the streets; this follows from the fact that the people of Omelas are happy people. Happiness is based on a just discrimination of what is necessary, what is neither necessary nor destructive, and what is destructive. In the middle category, however—that of the unnecessary but undestructive, that of comfort, luxury, exuberance, etc.—they could perfectly well have central heating, subway trains, washing machines, and all kinds of marvelous devises not yet invented here, floating light-sources, fuelless power, a cure for the common cold. Or they could have none of that: it doesn't matter. As you like it. I incline to think that people from towns up and down the coast have been coming in to Omelas during the last days before the Festival on very fast trains and double-decked trams, and that the train station of Omelas is actually the handsomest building in town, though plainer than the magnificent Farmers' Market. But even granted trains, I fear that Omelas so far strikes some of you as goody-goody. Smiles, bells, parades, horses, bleh. If so, please add an orgy. If an orgy would help, don't hesitate. Let us not, however, have temples from which issue beautiful nude priests and priestesses already half in ecstasy and ready to copulate

with any man or woman, lover or stranger, who desires union with the deep godhead of the blood, although that was my first idea. But really it would be better not to have any temples in Omelas—at least, not manned temples. Religion yes, clergy no. Surely the beautiful nudes can just wander about, offering themselves like divine soufflés to the hunger of the needy and the rapture of the flesh. Let them join the processions. Let tambourines be struck above the copulations, and the glory of desire be proclaimed upon the gongs, and (a not unimportant point) let the offspring of these delightful rituals be beloved and looked after by all. One thing I know there is none of in Omelas is guilt. But what else should there be? I thought that first there were no drugs, but that is puritanical. For those who like it, the faint insistent sweetness of *drooz* may perfume the ways of the city, *drooz* which first brings a great lightness and brilliance to the mind and limbs, and then after some hours a dreamy languor, and wonderful visions at last of the very arcana and inmost secrets of the Universe, as well as exciting the pleasure of sex beyond all belief; and it is not habit-forming. For more modest tastes I think there ought to be beer. What else, what else belongs in the joyous city? The sense of victory, surely, the celebration of courage. But as we did without clergy, let us do without soldiers. The joy built upon successful slaughter is not the right kind of joy; it will not do; it is fearful and it is trivial. A boundless and generous contentment, a magnanimous triumph felt not against some outer enemy but in communion with the finest and fairest in the souls of all men everywhere and the splendor of the world's summer; this is what swells the hearts of the people of Omelas, and the victory they celebrate is that of life. I really don't think many of them need to take *drooz*.

4   Most of the processions have reached the Green Fields by now. A marvelous smell of cooking goes forth from the red and blue tents of the provisioners. The faces of small children are amiably sticky; in the benign grey beard of a man a couple of crumbs of rich pastry are entangled. The youths and girls have mounted their horses and are beginning to group around the starting line of the course. An old woman, small, fat, and laughing, is passing out flowers from a basket, and tall young men wear her flowers in their shining hair. A child of nine or ten sits at the edge of the crowd, alone, playing on a wooden flute. People pause to listen, and they smile, but they do not speak to him, for he never ceases playing and never sees them, his dark eyes wholly rapt in the sweet, thin magic of the tune.

5   He finishes, and slowly lowers his hands holding the wooden flute.

6   As if that little private silence were the signal, all at once a trumpet sounds from the pavilion near the starting line: imperious, melancholy, piercing. The horses rear on their slender legs, and some of them neigh in answer. Sober-faced, the young riders stroke the horses' necks and soothe them, whispering, "Quiet, quiet, there my beauty, my hope." They begin to form in rank along the starting line. The crowds along the racecourse are like a field of grass and flowers in the wind. The Festival of Summer has begun.

7   Do you believe? Do you accept the festival, the city, the joy? No? Then let me describe this one more thing.

8   In a basement under one of the beautiful public buildings of Omelas, or perhaps in the cellar of one of its spacious private homes, there is a room. It has one locked door, and no window. A little light seeps in dustily between cracks in the boards, secondhand from the cobwebbed window somewhere across the cellar. In one corner of the little

room a couple of mops, with stiff, clotted, foul-smelling heads, stand near a rusty bucket. The floor is dirt, a little damp to the touch, as cellar dirt usually is. The room is about three paces long and two wide: a mere broom closet or disused tool room. In the room a child is sitting. It could be a boy or a girl. It looks about six, but actually is nearly ten. It is feeble-minded. Perhaps it was born defective, or perhaps it has become imbecile through fear, malnutrition, and neglect. It picks its nose and occasionally fumbles vaguely with its toes or genitals, as it sits hunched in the corner farthest from the bucket and the two mops. It is afraid of the mops. It finds them horrible. It shuts its eyes, but it knows the mops are still standing there; and the door is locked; and nobody will come. The door is always locked; and nobody ever comes, except that sometimes—the child has no understanding of time or interval—sometimes the door rattles terribly and opens, and a person, or several people, are there. One of them may come in and kick the child to make it stand up. The others never come close, but peer in at it with fright-ened, disgusted eyes. The food bowl and the water jug are hastily filled, the door is locked, the eyes disappear. The people at the door never say anything, but the child, who has not always lived in the tool room, and can remember sunlight and its mother's voice, sometimes speaks. "I will be good," it says. "Please let me out. I will be good!" They never answer. The child used to scream for help at night, and cry a good deal, but now it only makes a kind of whining, "eh-haa-eh-haa," and it speaks less and less often. It is so thin there are no calves to its legs; its belly protrudes; it lives on a half-bowl of corn meal and grease a day. It is naked. Its buttocks and thighs are a mass of festered sores, as it sits in its own excrement continually.

9   They all know it is there, all the people of Omelas. Some of them have come to see it, others are content merely to know it is there. They all know that it has to be there. Some of them understand why, and some do not, but they all understand that their hap-piness, the beauty of their city, the tenderness of their friendships, the health of their children, the wisdom of their scholars, the skill of their makers, even the abundance of their harvest and the kindly weathers of their skies, depend wholly upon this child's abominable misery.

10   This is usually explained to children when they are between eight and twelve, whenever they seem capable of understanding; and most of those who come to see the child are young people, though often enough an adult comes, or comes back, to see the child. No matter how well the matter has been explained to them, these young specta-tors are always shocked and sickened at the sight. They feel disgust, which they had thought themselves superior to. They feel anger, outrage, impotence, despite all the ex-planations. They would like to do something for the child. But there is nothing they can do. If the child were brought up into the sunlight out of that vile place, if it were cleaned and fed and comforted, that would be a good thing, indeed; but if it were done, in that day and hour all the prosperity and beauty and delight of Omelas would wither and be destroyed. Those are the terms. To exchange all the goodness and grace of every life in Omelas for that single, small improvement: to throw away the happiness of thou-sands for the chance of the happiness of one: that would be to let guilt within the walls indeed.

11   The terms are strict and absolute; there may not even be a kind word spoken to the child.

^{12} Often the young people go home in tears, or in a tearless rage, when they have seen the child and faced this terrible paradox. They may brood over it for weeks or years. But as time goes on they begin to realize that even if the child could be released, it would not get much good of its freedom: a little vague pleasure of warmth and food, no doubt, but little more. It is too degraded and imbecile to know any real joy. It has been afraid too long ever to be free of fear. Its habits are too uncouth for it to respond to humane treatment. Indeed, after so long it would probably be wretched without walls about it to protect it, and darkness for its eyes, and its own excrement to sit in. Their tears at the bitter injustice dry when they begin to perceive the terrible justice of reality, and to accept it. Yet it is their tears and anger, the trying of their generosity and the acceptance of their helplessness, which are perhaps the true source of the splendor of their lives. Theirs is no vapid, irresponsible happiness. They know that they, like the child, are not free. They know compassion. It is the existence of the child, and their knowledge of its existence, that makes possible the mobility of their architecture, the poignancy of their music, the profundity of their science. It is because of the child that they are so gentle with children. They know that if the wretched one were not there snivelling in the dark, the other one, the flute-player, could make no joyful music as the young riders line up in their beauty for the race in the sunlight of the first morning of summer.

^{13} Now do you believe in them? Are they not more credible? But there is one more thing to tell, and this is quite incredible.

^{14} At times one of the adolescent girls or boys who go to see the child, does not go home to weep or rage, does not, in fact, go home at all. Sometimes also a man or woman much older falls silent for a day or two, and then leaves home. These people go out into the street, and walk down the street alone. They keep walking, and walk straight out of the city of Omelas, through the beautiful gates. They keep walking across the farmlands of Omelas. Each one goes alone, youth or girl, man or woman. Night falls; the traveler must pass down village streets, between the houses with yellow-lit windows, and on out into the darkness of the fields. Each alone, they go west or north, towards the mountains. They go on. They leave Omelas, they walk ahead into the darkness, and they do not come back. The place they go towards is a place even less imaginable to most of us than the city of happiness. I cannot describe it at all. It is possible that it does not exist. But they seem to know where they are going, the ones who walk away from Omelas.

Questions for Analysis and Discussion

1. What is the general impression you get of the city of Omelas from the opening paragraph? To what senses does the author appeal?

2. Describe the people of Omelas. Are they happy? Do they have technology? Guilt? Religion? Soldiers? Drugs?

3. What shocking detail emerges about Omelas? On what does this ideal community thrive?

4. How do the children and teens respond to the locked-up child at first? How do they reconcile themselves to the situation? What do some residents do?

5. Can you understand the reason most residents accept the situation? Can you understand those who walk away? With which group do you most identify? Why?

6. On what does Le Guin want us to reflect? How would you state the story's theme?

Trifles

Susan Glaspell

Born in Iowa, Susan Glaspell (1882?–1948) attended Drake University and then began her writing career as a reporter with the *Des Moines Daily News.* She also started writing and selling short stories; her first collection, *Lifted Masks,* was published in 1912. She completed several novels before moving to Provincetown with her husband, who started the Provincetown Players in 1915. Glaspell wrote seven short plays and four long plays for this group, including *Trifles* (1916). The well-known "Jury of Her Peers" (1917) is a short-story version of the play *Trifles.* Glaspell must have recognized that the plot of *Trifles* was a gem worth working with in more than one literary form.

Characters

George Henderson, County Attorney

Henry Peters, Sheriff

Lewis Hale, A Neighboring Farmer

Mrs. Peters

Mrs. Hale

SCENE: *The kitchen in the now abandoned farmhouse of* JOHN WRIGHT, *a gloomy kitchen, and left without having been put in order—unwashed pans under the sink, a loaf of bread outside the bread-box, a dish-towel on the table—other signs of incompleted work. At the rear the outer door opens and the* SHERIFF *comes in followed by the* COUNTY ATTORNEY *and* HALE. *The* SHERIFF *and* HALE *are men in middle life; the* COUNTY ATTORNEY *is a young man; all are much bundled up and go at once to the stove. They are followed by the two women—the* SHERIFF's *wife first; she is a slight wiry woman, a thin nervous face.* MRS. HALE *is larger and would ordinarily be called more comfortable looking, but she is disturbed now and looks fearfully about as she enters. The women have come in slowly, and stand close together near the door.*

COUNTY ATTORNEY

[*Rubbing his hands.*] This feels good. Come up to the fire, ladies.

MRS. PETERS

[*After taking a step forward.*] I'm not—cold.

SHERIFF

[*Unbuttoning his overcoat and stepping away from the stove as if to mark the beginning of official business.*] Now, Mr. Hale, before we move things about, you explain to Mr. Henderson just what you saw when you came here yesterday morning.

COUNTY ATTORNEY
By the way, has anything been moved? Are things just as you left them yesterday?

SHERIFF
[*Looking about.*] It's just the same. When it dropped below zero last night I thought I'd better send Frank out this morning to make a fire for us—no use getting pneumonia with a big case on, but I told him not to touch anything except the stove—and you know Frank.

COUNTY ATTORNEY
Somebody should have been left here yesterday.

SHERIFF
Oh—yesterday. When I had to send Frank to Morris Center for that man who went crazy—I want you to know I had my hands full yesterday. I knew you could get back from Omaha by today and as long as I went over everything here myself—

COUNTY ATTORNEY
Well, Mr. Hale, tell just what happened when you came here yesterday morning.

HALE
Harry and I had started to town with a load of potatoes. We came along the road from my place and as I got here I said, "I'm going to see if I can't get John Wright to go in with me on a party telephone." I spoke to Wright about it once before and he put me off, saying folks talked too much anyway, and all he asked was peace and quiet—I guess you know about how much he talked himself; but I thought maybe if I went to the house and talked about it before his wife, though I said to Harry that I didn't know as what his wife wanted made much difference to John—

COUNTY ATTORNEY
Let's talk about that later, Mr. Hale. I do want to talk about that, but tell now just what happened when you got to the house.

HALE
I didn't hear or see anything; I knocked at the door, and still it was all quiet inside. I knew they must be up, it was past eight o'clock. So I knocked again, and I thought I heard somebody say, "Come in." I wasn't sure, I'm not sure yet, but I opened the door— this door [*indicating the door by which the two women are still standing*] and there in that rocker—[*pointing to it*] sat Mrs. Wright.
[*They all look at the rocker.*]

COUNTY ATTORNEY
What—was she doing?

HALE

She was rockin' back and forth. She had her apron in her hand and was kind of—pleating it.

COUNTY ATTORNEY

And how did she—look?

HALE

Well, she looked queer.

COUNTY ATTORNEY

How do you mean—queer?

HALE

Well, as if she didn't know what she was going to do next. And kind of done up.

COUNTY ATTORNEY

How did she seem to feel about your coming?

HALE

Why, I don't think she minded—one way or other. She didn't pay much attention. I said, "How do, Mrs. Wright, it's cold, ain't it?" And she said, "Is it?"—and went on kind of pleating at her apron. Well, I was surprised; she didn't ask me to come up to the stove, or to set down, but just sat there, not even looking at me, so I said, "I want to see John." And then she—laughed. I guess you would call it a laugh. I thought of Harry and the team outside, so I said a little sharp: "Can't I see John?" "No," she says, kind o' dull like. "Ain't he home?" says I. "Yes," says she, "he's home." "Then why can't I see him?" I asked her, out of patience. " 'Cause he's dead," says she. "*Dead?*" says I. She just nodded her head, not getting a bit excited, but rockin' back and forth. "Why—where is he?" says I, not knowing what to say. She just pointed upstairs—like that [*himself pointing to the room above*]. I got up, with the idea of going up there. I walked from there to here—then I says, "Why, what did he die of?" "He died of a rope around his neck," says she, and just went on pleatin' at her apron. Well, I went out and called Harry. I thought I might—need help. We went upstairs and there he was lyin'—

COUNTY ATTORNEY

I think I'd rather have you go into that upstairs, where you can point it all out. Just go on now with the rest of the story.

HALE

Well, my first thought was to get that rope off. It looked . . . [*Stops, his face twitches*] . . . but Harry, he went up to him, and he said, "No, he's dead all right, and we'd better not touch anything." So we went back downstairs. She was still sitting that same way. "Has anybody been notified?" said Harry. He said it business-like—and she stopped pleatin' of her apron. "I don't know," she says. "You don't *know?*" says Harry. "No," says she. "Weren't you sleepin' in the bed with him?" says Harry. "Yes," says she, "but I was on the inside." "Somebody slipped a rope round his neck and strangled him and you didn't wake up?" says Harry. "I didn't wake up," she said after him. We must'a looked as if we didn't see how that could be, for after a minute she said, "I sleep sound." Harry was going to ask her more questions but I said maybe we ought to let her tell her story first to the coroner, or the sheriff, so Harry went fast as he could to Rivers' place, where there's a telephone.

COUNTY ATTORNEY

And what did Mrs. Wright do when she knew that you had gone for the coroner?

HALE

She moved from that chair to this one over here [*Pointing to a small chair in the corner*] and just sat there with her hands held together and looking down. I got a feeling that I ought to make some conversation, so I said I had come in to see if John wanted to put in a telephone, and at that she started to laugh, and then she stopped and looked at me—scared. [*The* County Attorney, *who has had his notebook out, makes a note.*] I dunno, maybe it wasn't scared. I wouldn't like to say it was. Soon Harry got back, and then Dr. Lloyd came, and you, Mr. Peters, and so I guess that's all I know that you don't.

COUNTY ATTORNEY

[*Looking around.*] I guess we'll go upstairs first—and then out to the barn and around there. [*To the* Sheriff.] You're convinced that there was nothing important here—nothing that would point to any motive.

SHERIFF

Nothing here but kitchen things.
[*The* County Attorney, *after again looking around the kitchen, opens the door of a cupboard closet. He gets up on a chair and looks on a shelf. Pulls his hand away, sticky.*]

COUNTY ATTORNEY

Here's a nice mess.
[*The women draw nearer.*]

MRS. PETERS

[*To the other woman.*] Oh, her fruit; it did freeze. [*To the* Lawyer.] She worried about that when it turned so cold. She said the fire'd go out and her jars would break.

SHERIFF

Well, can you beat the woman! Held for murder and worryin' about her preserves.

COUNTY ATTORNEY

I guess before we're through she may have something more serious than preserves to worry about.

HALE

Well, women are used to worrying over trifles.
[*The two women move a little closer together.*]

COUNTY ATTORNEY

[*With the gallantry of a young politician.*] And yet, for all their worries, what would we do without the ladies? [*The women do not unbend. He goes to the sink, takes a dipperful of water from the pail and pouring it into a basin, washes his hands. Starts to wipe them on the roller-towel, turns it for a cleaner place.*] Dirty towels! [*Kicks his foot against the pans under the sink.*] Not much of a housekeeper, would you say, ladies?

MRS. HALE

[*Stiffly.*] There's a great deal of work to be done on a farm.

COUNTY ATTORNEY

To be sure. And yet [*with a little bow to her*] I know there are some Dickson County farmhouses which do not have such roller towels.
[*He gives it a pull to expose its full length again.*]

MRS. HALE

Those towels get dirty awful quick. Men's hands aren't always as clean as they might be.

COUNTY ATTORNEY

Ah, loyal to your sex, I see. But you and Mrs. Wright were neighbors. I suppose you were friends, too.

MRS. HALE

[*Shaking her head.*] I've not seen much of her of late years. I've not been in this house—it's more than a year.

COUNTY ATTORNEY

And why was that? You didn't like her?

MRS. HALE

I liked her all well enough. Farmers' wives have their hands full, Mr. Henderson. And then—

COUNTY ATTORNEY

Yes—?

MRS. HALE

[*Looking about.*] It never seemed a very cheerful place.

COUNTY ATTORNEY

No—it's not cheerful. I shouldn't say she had the homemaking instinct.

MRS. HALE

Well, I don't know as Wright had, either.

COUNTY ATTORNEY

You mean that they didn't get on very well?

MRS. HALE

No, I don't mean anything. But I don't think a place'd be any cheerfuller for John Wright's being in it.

COUNTY ATTORNEY

I'd like to talk more of that a little later. I want to get the lay of things upstairs now. [*He goes to the left, where three steps lead to a stair door.*]

SHERIFF

I suppose anything Mrs. Peters does'll be all right. She was to take in some clothes for her, you know, and a few little things. We left in such a hurry yesterday.

COUNTY ATTORNEY

Yes, but I would like to see what you take, Mrs. Peters, and keep an eye out for anything that might be of use to us.

MRS. PETERS

Yes, Mr. Henderson.
[*The women listen to the men's steps on the stairs, then look about the kitchen.*]

MRS. HALE

I'd hate to have men coming into my kitchen, snooping around and criticizing.
[*She arranges the pans under the sink which the* Lawyer *had shoved out of place.*]

MRS. PETERS

Of course it's no more than their duty.

MRS. HALE

Duty's all right, but I guess that deputy sheriff that came out to make the fire might have got a little of this on. [*Gives the roller towel a pull.*] Wish I'd thought of that sooner. Seems mean to talk about her for not having things slicked up when she had to come away in such a hurry.

MRS. PETERS

[*Who has gone to a small table in the left corner of the room, and lifted one end of a towel that covers a pan.*] She had bread set.
[*Stands still.*]

MRS. HALE

[*Eyes fixed on a loaf of bread beside the breadbox, which is on a low shelf at the other side of the room. Moves slowly toward it.*] She was going to put this in there. [*Picks up loaf, then abruptly drops it. In a manner of returning to familiar things.*] It's a shame about her fruit. I wonder if it's all gone. [*Gets up on the chair and looks.*] I think there's some here that's all right, Mrs. Peters. Yes—here; [*holding it toward the window*] this is cherries, too. [*Looking again.*] I declare I believe that's the only one. [*Gets down, bottle in her hand. Goes to the sink and wipes it off on the outside.*] She'll feel awful bad after all her hard work in the hot weather. I remember the afternoon I put up my cherries last summer.

[*She puts the bottle on the big kitchen table, center of the room. With a sigh, is about to sit down in the rocking-chair. Before she is seated realizes what chair it is; with a slow look at it, steps back. The chair which she has touched rocks back and forth.*]

MRS. PETERS

Well, I must get those things from the front room closet. [*She goes to the door at the right, but after looking into the other room, steps back.*] You coming with me, Mrs. Hale? You could help me carry them.

[*They go in the other room; reappear, Mrs. Peters carrying a dress and skirt, Mrs. Hale following with a pair of shoes.*]

MRS. PETERS

My, it's cold in there.
[*She puts the clothes on the big table, and hurries to the stove.*]

MRS. HALE

[*Examining the skirt.*] Wright was close. I think maybe that's why she kept so much to herself. She didn't even belong to the Ladies Aid. I suppose she felt she couldn't do her part, and then you don't enjoy things when you feel shabby. She used to wear pretty clothes and be lively, when she was Minnie Foster, one of the town girls singing in the choir. But that—oh, that was thirty years ago. This all you was to take in?

MRS. PETERS

She said she wanted an apron. Funny thing to want, for there isn't much to get you dirty in jail, goodness knows. But I suppose just to make her feel more natural. She said they was in the top drawer in this cupboard. Yes, here. And then her little shawl that always hung behind the door. [*Opens stair door and looks.*] Yes, here it is.
[*Quickly shuts door leading upstairs.*]

MRS. HALE

[*Abruptly moving toward her.*] Mrs. Peters?

MRS. PETERS

Yes, Mrs. Hale?

MRS. HALE

Do you think she did it?

MRS. PETERS

[*In a frightened voice.*] Oh, I don't know.

MRS. HALE

Well, I don't think she did. Asking for an apron and her little shawl. Worrying about her fruit.

MRS. PETERS

[*Starts to speak, glances up, where footsteps are heard in the room above. In a low voice.*] Mr. Peters says it looks bad for her. Mr. Henderson is awful sarcastic in a speech and he'll make fun of her sayin' she didn't wake up.

MRS. HALE

Well, I guess John Wright didn't wake when they was slipping that rope under his neck.

MRS. PETERS

No, it's strange. It must have been done awful crafty and still. They say it was such a—funny way to kill a man, rigging it all up like that.

MRS. HALE

That's just what Mr. Hale said. There was a gun in the house. He says that's what he can't understand.

MRS. PETERS

Mr. Henderson said coming out that what was needed for the case was a motive; something to show anger, or—sudden feeling.

MRS. HALE

[*Who is standing by the table.*] Well, I don't see any signs of anger around here. [*She puts her hand on the dish towel which lies on the table, stands looking down at table, one half of which is clean, the other half messy.*] It's wiped to here. [*Makes a move as if to finish work, then turns and looks at loaf of bread outside the breadbox. Drops towel. In that voice of coming-back to familiar things.*] Wonder how they are finding things upstairs. I hope she had it a little more red-up up there. You know, it seems kind of *sneaking.* Locking her up in town and then coming out here and trying to get her own house to turn against her!

MRS. PETERS

But Mrs. Hale, the law is the law.

MRS. HALE

I s'pose 'tis. [*Unbuttoning her coat.*] Better loosen up your things, Mrs. Peters. You won't feel them when you go out.

[Mrs. Peters *takes off her fur tippet, goes to hang it on hook at back of room, stands looking at the under part of the small corner table.*]

MRS. PETERS

She was piecing a quilt.

[*She brings the large sewing basket and they look at the bright pieces.*]

MRS. HALE

It's log cabin pattern. Pretty, isn't it? I wonder if she was goin' to quilt it or just knot it? [*Footsteps have been heard coming down the stairs. The* Sheriff *enters followed by* Hale *and the* City Attorney.]

SHERIFF

They wonder if she was going to quilt it or just knot it!
[*The men laugh, the women look abashed.*]

COUNTY ATTORNEY

[*Rubbing his hands over the stove.*] Frank's fire didn't do much up there, did it? Well, let's go out to the barn and get that cleared up.
[*The men go outside.*]

MRS. HALE

[*Resentfully.*] I don't know as there's anything so strange, our takin' up our time with little things while we're waiting for them to get the evidence. [*She sits down at the big table smoothing out a block with decision.*] I don't see as it's anything to laugh about.

MRS. PETERS

[*Apologetically.*] Of course they've got awful important things on their minds. [*Pulls up a chair and joins* Mrs. Hale *at the table.*]

MRS. HALE

[*Examining another block.*] Mrs. Peters, look at this one. Here, this is the one she was working on, and look at the sewing! All the rest of it has been so nice and even. And look at this! It's all over the place! Why, it looks as if she didn't know what she was about!
[*After she has said this they look at each other, then start to glance back at the door. After an instant* Mrs. Hale *has pulled at a knot and ripped the sewing.*]

MRS. PETERS

Oh, what are you doing, Mrs. Hale?

MRS. HALE

[*Mildly.*] Just pulling out a stitch or two that's not sewed very good. [*Threading a needle.*] Bad sewing always made me fidgety.

MRS. PETERS

[*Nervously.*] I don't think we ought to touch things.

MRS. HALE

I'll just finish up this end. [*Suddenly stopping and leaning forward.*] Mrs. Peters?

MRS. PETERS

Yes, Mrs. Hale?

MRS. HALE

What do you suppose she was so nervous about?

MRS. PETERS

Oh—I don't know. I don't know as she was nervous. I sometimes sew awful queer when I'm just tired. [Mrs. Hale *starts to say something, looks at* Mrs. Peters, *then goes on sewing.*] Well I must get these things wrapped up. They may be through sooner than we think. [*Putting apron and other things together.*] I wonder where I can find a piece of paper, and string.

MRS. HALE

In that cupboard, maybe.

MRS. PETERS

[*Looking in cupboard.*] Why, here's a bird-cage. [*Holds it up.*] Did she have a bird, Mrs. Hale?

MRS. HALE

Why, I don't know whether she did or not—I've not been here for so long. There was a man around last year selling canaries cheap, but I don't know as she took one; maybe she did. She used to sing real pretty herself.

MRS. PETERS

[*Glancing around.*] Seems funny to think of a bird here. But she must have had one, or why would she have a cage? I wonder what happened to it.

MRS. HALE

I s'pose maybe the cat got it.

MRS. PETERS

No, she didn't have a cat. She's got that feeling some people have about cats—being afraid of them. My cat got in her room and she was real upset and asked me to take it out.

MRS. HALE

My sister Bessie was like that. Queer, ain't it?

MRS. PETERS

[*Examining the cage.*] Why, look at this door. It's broke. One hinge is pulled apart.

MRS. HALE

[*Looking too.*] Looks as if someone must have been rough with it.

MRS. PETERS

Why, yes.
[*She brings the cage forward and puts it on the table.*]

MRS. HALE

I wish if they're going to find any evidence they'd be about it. I don't like this place.

MRS. PETERS

But I'm awful glad you came with me, Mrs. Hale. It would be lonesome for me sitting here alone.

MRS. HALE

It would, wouldn't it? [*Dropping her sewing.*] But I tell you what I do wish, Mrs. Peters. I wish I had come over sometimes when *she* was here. I—[*looking around the room*]—wish I had.

MRS. PETERS

But of course you were awful busy, Mrs. Hale—your house and your children.

MRS. HALE

I could've come. I stayed away because it weren't cheerful—and that's why I ought to have come. I—I've never liked this place. Maybe because it's down in a hollow and you don't see the road. I dunno what it is, but it's a lonesome place and always was. I wish I had come over to see Minnie Foster sometimes. I can see now—
[*Shakes her head.*]

MRS. PETERS

Well, you mustn't reproach yourself, Mrs. Hale. Somehow we just don't see how it is with other folks until—something comes up.

MRS. HALE

Not having children makes less work—but it makes a quiet house, and Wright out to work all day, and no company when he did come in. Did you know John Wright, Mrs. Peters?

MRS. PETERS

Not to know him; I've seen him in town. They say he was a good man.

MRS. HALE

Yes—good; he didn't drink, and kept his word as well as most, I guess, and paid his debts. But he was a hard man, Mrs. Peters. Just to pass the time of day with him—[*Shivers.*] Like a raw wind that gets to the bone. [*Pauses, her eye falling on the cage.*] I should think she would'a wanted a bird. But what do you suppose went with it?

MRS. PETERS

I don't know, unless it got sick and died.
[*She reaches over and swings the broken door, swings it again, both women watch it.*]

MRS. HALE

You weren't raised round here, were you? [Mrs. Peters *shakes her head*.] You didn't know—her?

MRS. PETERS

Not till they brought her yesterday.

MRS. HALE

She—come to think of it, she was kind of like a bird herself—real sweet and pretty, but kind of timid and—fluttery. How—she—did—change. [*Silence; then as if struck by a happy thought and relieved to get back to everyday things.*] Tell you what, Mrs. Peters, why don't you take the quilt in with you? It might take up her mind.

MRS. PETERS

Why, I think that's a real nice idea, Mrs. Hale. There couldn't possibly be any objection to it, could there? Now, just what would I take? I wonder if her patches are in here—and her things.
[*They look in the sewing basket.*]

MRS. HALE

Here's some red. I expect this has got sewing things in it. [*Brings out a fancy box.*] What a pretty box. Looks like something somebody would give you. Maybe her scissors are in here. [*Opens box. Suddenly puts her hand to her nose.*] Why—[Mrs. Peters *bends nearer, then turns her face away*.] There's something wrapped up in this piece of silk.

MRS. PETERS

Why, this isn't her scissors.

MRS. HALE

[*Lifting the silk.*] Oh, Mrs. Peters—it's—
[Mrs. Peters *bends closer.*]

MRS. PETERS

It's the bird.

MRS. HALE

[*Jumping up.*] But, Mrs. Peters—look at it! Its neck! Look at its neck! It's all—other side *to.*

MRS. PETERS

Somebody—wrung—its—neck.
[*Their eyes meet. A look of growing comprehension, or horror. Steps are heard outside. Mrs. Hale slips box under quilt pieces, and sinks into her chair. Enter Sheriff and County Attorney. Mrs. Peters rises.*]

COUNTY ATTORNEY

[*As one turning from serious things to little pleasantries.*] Well ladies, have you decided whether she was going to quilt it or knot it?

MRS. PETERS

We think she was going to—knot it.

COUNTY ATTORNEY

Well, that's interesting, I'm sure. [*Seeing the bird-cage.*] Has the bird flown?

MRS. HALE

[*Putting more quilt pieces over the box.*] We think the—cat got it.

COUNTY ATTORNEY

[*Preoccupied.*] Is there a cat?
[Mrs. Hale *glances in a quick covert way at* Mrs. Peters.]

MRS. PETERS

Well, not *now*. They're superstitious, you know. They leave.

COUNTY ATTORNEY

[*To* SHERIFF PETERS, *continuing an interrupted conversation.*] No sign at all of anyone having come from the outside. Their own rope. Now let's go up again and go over it piece by piece. [*They start upstairs.*] It would have to have been someone who knew just the—
[MRS. PETERS *sits down. The two women sit there not looking at one another, but as if peering into something and at the same time holding back. When they talk now it is in the manner of feeling their way over strange ground, as if afraid of what they are saying, but as if they can not help saying it.*]

MRS. HALE

She liked the bird. She was going to bury it in that pretty box.

MRS. PETERS

[*In a whisper.*] When I was a girl—my kitten—there was a boy took a hatchet, and before my eyes—and before I could get there—[*Covers her face an instant.*] If they hadn't held me back I would have—[*Catches herself, looks upstairs where steps are heard, falters weakly*]—hurt him.

MRS. HALE

[*With a slow look around her.*] I wonder how it would seem never to have had any children around. [*Pause.*] No, Wright wouldn't like the bird—a thing that sang. She used to sing. He killed that, too.

MRS. PETERS

[*Moving uneasily.*] We don't know who killed the bird.

MRS. HALE

I knew John Wright.

MRS. PETERS

It was an awful thing was done in this house that night, Mrs. Hale. Killing a man while he slept, slipping a rope around his neck that choked the life out of him.

MRS. HALE

His neck. Choked the life out of him.
[*Her hand goes out and rests on the bird-cage.*]

MRS. PETERS

We don't know who killed him. We don't *know*.

MRS. HALE

[*Her own feeling not interrupted.*] If there'd been years and years of nothing, then a bird to sing to you, it would be awful—still, after the bird was still.

MRS. PETERS

[*Something within her speaking.*] I know what stillness is. When we homesteaded in Dakota, and my first baby died—after he was two years old, and me with no other then—

MRS. HALE

[*Moving.*] How soon do you suppose they'll be through, looking for the evidence?

MRS. PETERS

I know what stillness is. [*Pulling herself back.*] The law has got to punish crime, Mrs. Hale.

MRS. HALE

[*Not as if answering that.*] I wish you'd seen Minnie Foster when she wore a white dress with blue ribbons and stood up there in the choir and sang. [*A look around the room.*] Oh, I *wish* I'd come over here once in a while! That was a crime! That was a crime! Who's going to punish that?

MRS. PETERS

[*Looking upstairs.*] We mustn't—take on.

MRS. HALE

I might have known she needed help! I know how things can be—for women. I tell you, it's queer, Mrs. Peters. We live close together and we live far apart. We all go through the same things—it's all just a different kind of the same thing. [*Brushes her eyes, noticing the bottle of fruit, reaches out for it.*] If I was you I wouldn't tell her her fruit was gone. Tell her it *ain't*. Tell her it's all right. Take this in to prove it to her. She—she may never know whether it was broke or not.

MRS. PETERS

[*Takes the bottle, looks about for something to wrap it in; takes petticoat from the clothes brought from the other room, very nervously begins winding this around the bottle. In a false*] *voice.*] My, it's a good thing the men couldn't hear us. Wouldn't they just laugh! Getting all stirred up over a little thing like a—dead canary. As if that could have anything to do with—with—wouldn't they *laugh!*

[*The men are heard coming down stairs.*]

Mrs. Hale

[*Under her breath.*] Maybe they would—maybe they wouldn't.

County Attorney

No, Peters, it's all perfectly clear except a reason for doing it. But you know juries when it comes to women. If there was some definite thing. Something to show—some-thing to make a story about—a thing that would connect up with this strange way of doing it—

[*The women's eyes meet for an instant. Enter Hale from outer door.*]

Hale

Well, I've got the team around. Pretty cold out there.

County Attorney

I'm going to stay here awhile by myself. [*To the* Sheriff.] You can send Frank out for me, can't you? I want to go over everything. I'm not satisfied that we can't do better.

Sheriff

Do you want to see what Mrs. Peters is going to take in?

[*The* Lawyer *goes to the table, picks up the apron, laughs.*]

County Attorney

Oh, I guess they're not very dangerous things the ladies have picked out. [*Moves a few things about, disturbing the quilt pieces which cover the box. Steps back.*] No, Mrs. Peters doesn't need supervising. For that matter, a sheriff's wife is married to the law. Ever think of it that way, Mrs. Peters?

Mrs. Peters

Not—just that way.

Sheriff

[*Chuckling.*] Married to the law. [*Moves toward the other room.*] I just want you to come in here a minute, George. We ought to take a look at these windows.

County Attorney

[*Scoffingly.*] Oh, windows!

Sheriff

We'll be right out, Mr. Hale.

[Hale *goes outside. The* Sheriff *follows the* County Attorney *into the other room. Then* Mrs. Hale *rises, hands tight together, looking intensely at* Mrs. Peters, *whose eyes make a slow turn, finally meeting* MRS. HALE's. *A moment* MRS. HALE *holds her, then her own eyes point the way to where the box is concealed. Suddenly* MRS. PETERS *throws back quilt pieces and tries to put the box in the bag she is wearing. It is too big. She opens box, starts to take bird out, cannot touch it, goes to pieces, stands there helpless. Sound of a knob turning in the other room.* Mrs. Hale *snatches the box and puts it in the pocket of her big coat. Enter* COUNTY ATTORNEY *and* SHERIFF.]

COUNTY ATTORNEY

[*Facetiously.*] Well, Henry, at least we found out that she was not going to quilt it. She was going to—what is it you call it, ladies?

MRS. HALE

[*Her hand against her pocket.*] We call it—knot it, Mr. Henderson.

Questions for Analysis and Discussion

1. Explain the situation as the play begins.

2. Examine the dialogue of the men. What attitudes about themselves—their work, their abilities, their importance—are revealed? What is their collective opinion of women?

3. When Mrs. Hale and Mrs. Peters discover the dead bird, what do they begin to understand?

4. What other "trifles" in the kitchen provide additional evidence as to what has happened?

5. What trifles can be seen as symbols? What do they reveal about Mrs. Wright's life and character?

6. What is the play about primarily? Is it a murder mystery? Does it speak for feminist values? Is it about not seeing—not really knowing others? In a few sentences, state what you consider to be the play's dominant theme. Then list the evidence you would use to support your conclusion.

7. Is there any sense in which one could argue that Mrs. Wright had a right to kill her husband? If you were a lawyer, how would you plan her defense? If you were on the jury, what sentence would you recommend?

Writing Assignments

1. In a short essay, give an explication of either Amy Lowell's "Taxi" or Thomas Hardy's "The Man He Killed." You will need to explain both what the poem says and what it means—or what it accomplishes.

2. Analyze William Shakespeare's selection and ordering or metaphors in "Sonnet 73." What attitude toward death is developed through that selection and arrangement?

3. Analyze Mrs. Mallard's conflict, and decision about that conflict, as the basis for your understanding of the dominant theme in "The Story of an Hour."

4. You are Mrs. Wright's attorney (see *Trifles*, p. 642). Write your closing argument in her defense, explaining why only a light sentence is warranted for Mrs. Wright. Select details from the play to support your assertions about Mrs. Wright's character and motivation.

5. In an essay explain what you think are the most important ideas about community in Ursula K. Le Guin's "The Ones Who Walk Away from Omelas."

Methvin, Eugene H. "The Death Penalty is Fairer Than Ever." *The Wall Street Journal*, May 10, 2000. Reprinted from The Wall Street Journal © 2000 Dow Jones & Company, Inc. All Rights Reserved.

Morin, Richard. "Paradise Lost." *The Washington Post*, July 9, 2000. Reprinted by permission of the author.

Mundy, Lisa. "The Dissension of Species." *The Washington Post*, October 5, 1997. Copyright © 1997, The Washington Post. Reprinted by permission.

Myers, Michele Tolela. "Cyber U: What's Missing." *The Washington Post*, March 21, 2000. Reprinted by permission.

Nivola, Pietro. "Pumps and Pocketbooks." *The Washington Post*, April 24, 2000. Reprinted by permission of the author.

O'Connell, Sean. "Dinosaur." Review by Sean O'Connell from MSN Entertainment. Reprinted by permission of the author.

Philander, S. George. From *Is the Temperature Rising?* Copyright © 1998 by Princeton University Press. Reprinted by permission of Princeton University Press.

Politt, Katha. "Affirmative Action for Men?" *The Nation*, December 27, 1999. Reprinted by permission.

Quindlen, Anna. "The Problem of the Color Line." *Newsweek*, March 13, 2000. Reprinted by permission of International Creative Management, Inc. Copyright © 2000 by Anna Quindlen.

Raspberry, William. "The Real Pregnancy Problem." *The Washington Post*, October 1, 1999. Copyright © 1999, The Washington Post Writers Group. Reprinted with permission.

Ravitch, Diane. "Put Teachers to the Test." *The Washington Post*, February 25, 1998. Reprinted by permission.

Reader's Guide to Periodical Literature. Excerpts from *Reader's Guide to Periodical Literature*, 1975. Reprinted by permission of the H.W. Wilson Company.

Rodriguez, Gregory and Ronald Takaki. "California's Big Squeeze." *The Nation*, October 5, 1998. Reprinted by permission.

Rosenblatt, Roger. "How to End the Abortion War." *The New York Times*, January 19, 1992. Copyright © 1992 by the New York Times Co. Reprinted by permission.

Sadker, David. "Gender Games." *The Washington Post*, July 31, 2000. Reprinted by permission.

Samuelson, Robert J. "Century of Freedom." *Newsweek*, December 22, 1999. Copyright © 1999 *Newsweek*. Reprinted with permission.

Schiffren, Lisa. "Gay Marriage, an Oxymoron." *The New York Times*, March 1, 1987. Copyright © 1987 by The New York Times Co. Reprinted by permission.

Schrage, Michael. "E-Mail or E-Sting? Your Boss Knows, But He's Not Telling." *Fortune*, March 20, 2000. Copyright © 2000 Time Inc. Reprinted by permission.

Silko, Leslie Marmon. "The Border-Patrol State." Copyright © 1994 by Leslie Marmon Silko. First published in *The Nation*; reprinted with the permission of The Wylie Agency.

Singer, Peter. Copyright © 1995 by Peter Singer. From *Rethinking Life and Death: The Collapse of Our Traditional Values* by Peter Singer. Reprinted by permission of St. Martin's Press, LLC.

Singer, Peter A., and Mark Siegler. "Euthanasia—A Critique." *New England Journal of Medicine*, June 20, 1990. Copyright © 1990 Massachusetts Medical Society. All rights reserved.

Sowell, Thomas. "The Dumbing Down of Education Is Becoming an International Trend." *Insight*, January 24, 2000. Reprinted with permission of *Insight*. Copyright 2000 News World Communications, Inc. All rights reserved.